AMERICAN
Voices

AMERICAN
Voices

A THEMATIC/RHETORICAL READER

WARREN ROSENBERG
Wabash College

HAROLD SCHECHTER
Queens College

JONNA GORMELY SEMEIKS
C. W. Post College

1817

HARPER & ROW, PUBLISHERS
NEW YORK
Cambridge, Philadelphia, San Francisco, Washington,
London, Mexico City, São Paulo, Singapore, Sydney

Sponsoring Editor: Lucy Rosendahl
Project Editor: Ellen Meek Tweedy
Text Design: Graphnick Design
Cover Design: Delgado Design
Production Manager: Jeanie Berke
Production Assistant: Beth Ackerman
Compositor: ComCom Division of Haddon Craftsmen, Inc.
Printer and Binder: R.R. Donnelly & Sons Company
Cover Printer: Lehigh Press

For permission to use copyrighted materials,
grateful acknowledgment is made to
copyright holders listed on pages 489-493.

Library of Congress Cataloging-in-Publication Data

American voices.

1. College readers.   2. English language—Rhetoric.
I. Rosenberg, Warren.   II. Schechter, Harold.
III. Semeiks, Jonna Gormely.
PE1417.A43   1987   808'.0427   87-15057
ISBN 0-06-045763-5

89 90 9 8 7 6 5 4

For Julia
and
for Bruce Santher

Contents

Chapter Two
People and Places ★ Description
55

Chapter Three
The Consumer Society ★ Example
103

Chapter Four
Men and Women ★ Comparison and Contrast
147

Chapter Five
Working and Playing ★ Cause and Effect
205

Chapter Six
Science and Technology ★ Process Analysis
249

Chapter Seven
Popular Art ★ *Classification*
293

Chapter Eight
Language ★ *Definition*
345

Chapter Nine
Controversies ★ *Argument and Persuasion*
395

Appendix
★
455

Preface

Our aim in creating *American Voices: A Thematic/Rhetorical Reader* was to put together a collection of stimulating contemporary writing by both professionals and students in a format that would make the book as useful as possible in the composition class. The resulting anthology is, we believe, a reader with an usually attractive combination of features.

ORGANIZATION

The book is divided into nine chapters, each dealing with a significant aspect of life in contemporary America: Growing Up, People and Places, The Consumer Society, Men and Women, Working and Playing, Science and Technology, Popular Art, Language, and Controversies. By focusing on matters of immediate and personal concern to most students, our book is designed to stimulate their thinking, generate spirited classroom discussion, and, most important of all, engage their interest as writers. Moreover, the thematic unity of the book—as opposed to the rather random mix of topics found in so many essay collections—should give the average composition course an added degree of coherence.

At the same time, our approach is in no way limiting. Within the larger thematic framework, we have included a broad range of important and provocative topics. This, along with the generous number of selections, will insure great flexibility and freedom of choice for instructors. To provide even more variety, we have included eighteen short stories and poems, which, like the essays, are organized by theme.

Perhaps the most practical feature of our anthology, however, is its dual organization: the selections are grouped not only according to theme but also according to rhetorical category, beginning with relatively simple types of writing (narration, description), progressing to more complex expository forms (example, comparison and contrast, cause and effect, process analysis, classification, definition), and ending with argument and persuasion. Thus within a given chapter, all of the selections treat a single topic and at the same time exemplify a single rhetorical mode. This approach has the advantage of bringing each of these modes into particularly sharp focus for student writers, who can see how it is repeated (and adapted) in a number of different essays dealing with a common subject.

SELECTIONS

Given the thematic focus of our book—life in contemporary America—we have sought to include representative pieces by many of the nation's best, and often most popular, practicing essayists, writers whose work is prized by composition instructors and students alike. Some of the essays we reprint will also be well-known to instructors, since our sense is that many teachers prefer an anthology that contains a certain number of pieces of proven and durable appeal. For the most part, however, we have tried to compile an original collection of first-rate works, ones that have never appeared in a college textbook before. The essays by students, of course, are being published for the first time and we offer this work in the hope that it will inspire and help the readers of this book to create writing of their own that is clear, compelling, and perceptive. Finally, as a glance at the Contents will confirm, we have kept in mind the importance of anthologizing work by women and minority writers.

In general, our selections are brief enough so that, within the space of a single lesson, an assigned essay can be reviewed or even reread, thoroughly analyzed and discussed, and used as the basis for an in-class writing exercise. Within each chapter, the essays are arranged in ascending order of difficulty (though none of the essays is beyond the reach of the average freshman). The chapters conclude with a student essay, a short story, and a poem. Apart from their inherent pleasures, the stories and poems can be put to various uses in a composition class. And, while the essays we reprint are, of course, far clearer and more effective illustrations of the different rhetorical modes, we have made an effort to find fiction and verse which also fit in with our dual organization.

APPARATUS

Our intention has been to provide teaching aids that composition instructors will find useful but not restrictive or overly intrusive. Every chapter begins with an introduction on the composition process that explains, in straightforward, detailed, and practical terms, precisely what the rhetorical method consists of and how it is used. Within the nine main chapters, each selection is preceded by a biographical and bibliographical headnote and followed by questions—on content, diction, style, tone, vocabulary, and organization—and by suggestions for writing, which supply more than enough exercises and assignments for a semester (indeed for a full year).

Finally, to add to our book's versatility and appeal, we have appended a group of somewhat longer and more challenging pieces by seven of America's most important contemporary essayists.

For their review of the manuscript we thank Robert DiYanni, Pace University; Kim Flachmann, California State College, Bakersfield; Donald Gray, Indiana University; Audrey J. Roth, Miami-Dade Community College; Martha Saunders, West Georgia College; Patrick Scott, University of South Carolina; and Robert E. Yarber, San Diego Mesa College.

For their invaluable assistance, we would like to thank Steve Watkins and Julia Rosenberg, who, despite her own demanding work, gave unstintingly of her time and intelligence.

Warren Rosenberg
Harold Schechter
Jonna Gormely Semeiks

CHAPTER *One*

GROWING UP
Narration

You hurry into the dorm after lunch to pick up some books for your next class. Four students, one laughing so hard she is clutching another for support, surround a figure whose back is turned to you. You move closer and hear the sound of a familiar voice recounting last night's play opening. You were at the play and you haven't time to stop, but you can't resist joining the circle to hear Sarah, the female lead, describe it: the costume that wouldn't zip after the steak and fries dinner with her boyfriend; the director's opening-night hysteria; the missed cues; the lengthy, overly passionate kiss of the male lead at the end and the curtain that failed to drop and release her from it. A half-hour passes and, already ten minutes late for your biology class, you run upstairs, grab your books, and sprint toward the science building.

If you've been snagged often enough by a sad or funny story to recognize yourself in this anecdote, or if it interested you enough to make you want to read further, the strategy of opening with a story has worked. A narrative—any story of an event, either true or fictitious—has an almost magical appeal for people. The phrase "once upon a time" is enough to make any child's eyes widen with anticipation. The addiction many of us have to mystery novels, a favorite soap opera, or any film that tells a story proves we do not outgrow that excitement. The moment we sense a story is coming, during a professor's lecture, for example, or during dinner with relatives, we begin to pay attention. Whatever the cause of this universal fascination with narratives, writers, whether they are professionals or students, can use them in a variety of ways: to grab the reader's attention and compel him or her to continue reading; to illustrate an idea or prove a point; to make an abstract statement more concrete (and thus more comprehensible); to make a generalization more specific; to transform a dry and theoretical discussion into something interesting and memorable.

Most college students (journalism majors are an obvious exception) will not write lengthy stories that stand alone. Instead, their stories will be brief, will be part of another piece of writing, and thus will serve one of the above purposes. But because crafting a good narrative, like creating a good description, develops skills that are invaluable for more conventional kinds of college writing, very often composition instructors will ask all students to write a narrative early in the semester. Although a student may choose to invent an entire story, or to tell, because it is particularly interesting, someone else's story—a friend's or parent's, for example—many students get started more easily and produce more if they write about what they know best: their own lives. Sometimes students would rather not write about events they think are too personal for the classroom. But since the instructor almost always leaves the choice of a particular subject up to the writer, students who feel acutely that one subject is inappropriate or upsetting can choose another. Try not to avoid all disturbing subjects, however. The emotional power generated by recreating a conflict-filled event can lead to a more effective essay, and sometimes to unexpected self-revelations. For example, Maxine Hong Kingston's harrowing description of an afternoon when she tormented a classmate, "doing the worst thing I had yet done to another person," is a powerful piece of writing. And the reader can tell that Kingston, as an adult retelling the incident, has, perhaps for the first time, understood why she did what she did.

Let us say your teacher assigns a paper asking you to tell the story of an event in your childhood you wish you could forget, but can't. The length of the essay is left up to you, and you are given no other guidelines. First, you need to remember one event, or several among which you can choose. If nothing immediately comes to mind, you can *brainstorm,* make free associative lists of names and places from your childhood, until the "right" one emerges. (See Elizabeth Bishop's "Primer Class," in which she tells us that seeing any column of numbers immediately returns her to kindergarten.) A related activity is *free-writing.* With the assignment, or a key word like "childhood" in mind, write for ten minutes without stopping. Try to get down your thoughts as quickly as they come to you, without being concerned about perfect spelling, grammar, complete sentences, paragraph divisions, or any of the other things you labor over later on in the writing process. After ten minutes, reread what you have written, looking for a usable event. (You may have to try free-writing several times.) If you are still hopelessly trapped in the present, you might look through old photograph albums, call a sibling or parent or friend to reminisce, or read any of the essays in this chapter, which all concern growing up.

Now, assume you have found a good subject for your essay. Because you are going to tell a story about yourself, a decision about *point of view* (the perspective from which a narrative is told) is easy. You are the narrator, and so you will use the first person singular pronoun (''I'') when recounting your tale. (If you were writing about someone else's life, you might or might not want to be part of the story. And if you were writing fiction, your options expand still more.) The question of where to start your story is more difficult—should you begin with the event itself? Earlier? Later? What details do you want to include? What does your audience need to know? What is it likely to *want* to know? Choosing the right amount of detail is as important as choosing the right kind. Finally, what point are you trying to make with your story? (These same questions apply, by the way, whether your narrative is fiction or nonfiction and whether it is ''your'' story or your brother's.)

One of the key decisions, then, that a writer has to make is how far back in the story to start. Although we all started by being born, you will probably want to begin at a point closer to the event you will be narrating. Most of the writers in this chapter first establish a *context* of relevant background information. If the reader knows about the setting (time and place), and the important people in the narrative, he or she is more likely to be affected by the event itself. Delaying the event also tends to build suspense, an important component of successful narratives.

Russell Baker in ''Selling the Post,'' for instance, wants to tell the story of the unpleasant period in his childhood when his mother forced him to sell magazines. Baker does not begin narrating the specific incident until paragraph ten (''Buddy,'' she said one day, ''I want you to come home right after school this afternoon. Somebody's coming and I want you to meet him.'') This is the first *scene* of the essay (the action is *dramatized* through description and dialogue). To lead up to this point, Baker introduces his mother, sister Doris, and the time period, ''fifty years ago.'' The geographical setting comes a bit later (''we lived in Belleville, New Jersey''), when the information is most useful to the reader. This background information is given in *summary* form (it is related, that is, and not dramatized), with brief anecdotes inserted to add vividness. In addition to scenes and summary, a narrative often contains *analysis,* reflections by the narrator on the meaning and significance of the story. Baker's narrative is broken up by passages that explain childhood incidents from his adult perspective. An example is the paragraph beginning ''My mother and I fought this battle almost as long as I can remember'' (p.16).

Baker, like most of the writers in this chapter, tells the details of his story in *chronological* order, according to how the narrative actually unfolded in time. Another common technique is the *flashback.* Having begun a story at some point after the central event occurs, a writer using a flashback then goes back in time to narrate the incident itself. This technique involves the reader by connecting the past to the present. You might study Alice Walker's essay reprinted in the appendix for an example of a writer who employs both chronolog-ical ordering and flashbacks. The choice of how to arrange the incidents in your narrative should be based on what point you are trying to make and what mood you are trying to evoke.

Traditionally, stories have been structured to assure audience involvement. The ancient Greeks believed that the ideal narrative should begin with *rising action*—with the stage set with characters and the plot becoming increasingly complicated—move toward a *climax,* in which all story elements converge in a sequence of significant action, and conclude with *falling action* or resolution, when the effects of the climax on the characters are presented. This pyramidal structure has worked for thousands of years; as you study the fiction and nonfic-tion narratives in this chapter and think of your favorite stories, you will discover how, with certain variations, they almost always conform to this pattern.

Another way to involve readers in your personal narrative is to make them experience the event almost as you did. In the same way that an odor can flood the mind with sense memories—pictures, sounds, tastes—you can use language to set off a string of associations in your reader. In the following paragraph, Eudora Welty recreates her experience of going to bed on a train as a child:

> The swaying porter would be making ready our berths for the night, pulling the shade down just so, drawing the green fishnet hammock across the window so the clothes you took off could ride along beside you, turning down the tight-made bed, standing up the two snowy pillows as high as they were wide, switching on the eye of the reading lamp, starting the tiny electric fan—you suddenly saw its blades turn into gauze and heard its insect murmur; and drawing across it all the pair of thick green theaterlike curtains—billowing, smelling of cigar smoke—between which you would crawl or dive headfirst to button them together with yourself inside, to be seen no more that night. (*One Writer's Beginnings,* p. 74)

Notice Welty's use of *imagery,* words that evoke the senses. We can see the "swaying" porter, the "green fishnet hammock," the blades turning like "gauze"; hear the "insect murmur" of the fan; smell the cigar smoke in the curtains. Imagery, precisely observed detail ("pillows as high as they were wide"), and participles like "drawing," "turning," "standing," "switching," and "billowing" in place of past tense verbs give the passage immediacy. A moment almost half a century old seems to come to life on the page. In writing your own personal narratives, try to recreate the incident in your mind, choosing the language that will come closest to evoking the scene for the reader.

In describing the event and its setting, do not forget the people who were part of the story. Vividly presented characters make narratives memorable, either because these characters are special in some way (*Reader's Digest* pub-lishes an article each month called "The Most Unforgettable Character I've Met") or because they create *conflict.* Thus Captain Ahab, the protagonist of Herman Melville's *Moby Dick,* is unforgettable, in part because the author describes his bizarre appearance in great detail (a wooden leg, a huge scar extending from his eyes to his legs). This includes presenting Ahab's unique way of talking: "The path to my fixed purpose is laid with iron rails, whereon my soul is grooved to run." As you will see in the essays reprinted here, recreating the way a character talks is the most effective way to bring him or her to life. (You might use Toni Cade Bambara's story "The Lesson," a first-person narrative, as a model of realistically rendered speech.) But Ahab is also memorable because he seems to be in conflict with everyone and everything—and conflict, whether between two characters, between a character and his or her surroundings, or even within a character (between his desires and his conscience, for example), is often essential to an engaging narrative. The tension created by this central conflict makes a story difficult to put down. You can use character conflict as a useful device for finding a subject for your own narrative. Try writing a protest letter to someone in your recent or even distant past—your second-grade teacher, Aunt Myrtle, your Little League coach. (It isn't necessary to mail the letter.) You will be surprised at how much forgotten detail about the person and the events surrounding your relationship will emerge.

Narratives that relate interesting stories with just the right amount and kind of detail, that are structured in the most appropriate and compelling way, that establish character and conflict, will undoubtedly capture reader interest. But how many times, after hearing, reading, or watching a good story, have you said, "Well, that was fun, but what's the point?" Childhood fables and tales and our early schooling have trained us to seek the *moral,* or message, in stories. For narratives that you write in composition class, the instructor will very likely ask you to be sure your narrative makes a point, either *explicitly,* spelled out in a one-sentence statement called a *thesis,* or *implicitly,* woven into the fabric of the story to be discovered by the reader. In Bambara's story, for example, the lesson referred to in the title seems to be explicitly revealed in a thesis statement near the end, but as we listen to the narrator we sense that there are other implicit lessons being suggested. Certain important themes, for there can be more than one "message" or meaning in a story, are presented by writers indirectly; we must draw them out of the story ourselves. (And indeed part of our pleasure in reading stories comes from our figuring out what they mean.) However the point of a story is presented, readers should feel that everything in the narrative—plot, character, background details—contributes; we should not feel a moral is tacked on. Nor should we feel that an enjoyable and complex experience is reduced to a one-sentence cliché.

Sometimes you will not see the point of a story you are writing until you complete a first draft. In that case, you can revise the narrative by adding, cutting, or emphasizing details or characters so that subsequent versions more efficiently deliver your meaning.

During your college career, you will be reading and writing narratives in classes other than composition. Even though it is unlikely, as we said earlier, that an entire paper will be a narrative, you will include narratives in debates, research papers, and essay exams. For example, on a history essay exam you may be asked to trace the Puritan experience in America. You will have to decide when and where in the Puritan story to begin (with the landing in America? with the persecution in Europe?), how much detail to include, given the limits on your time, and where to stop. You might include mini-character sketches along the way—Anne Bradstreet, Cotton Mather. And you may want to unify the essay with a thesis: "The Puritans did not come to America like so many others merely to escape oppression; they came to establish a model society in the wilderness." Narratives are used in other courses like philosophy, as illustrations for problems in ethics and logic; in psychology, sociology, and anthropology as case studies; and even in mathematics and the sciences, as problems ("If two boats, one weighing ten tons and the other fifty, set out for the same destination with a tail wind of ten knots, which will arrive first?").

A student in a course on the 1960s recently wrote a research paper on Bob Dylan using narrative, among other rhetorical modes. His working thesis was that Dylan, through his life and music, helped define his times. With the thesis in mind, the student had to decide how much of Dylan's life to include, in what order to present the information, and which events to emphasize. He also had to choose which anecdotes, among the many about the singer, to relate. He decided to focus most closely on the early sixties, when Dylan first came on the music scene, relegating his early life to a page of summary in the paper's second paragraph. The writer included a lengthy anecdote on Dylan's name change (from Robert Zimmerman), because he felt the renaming symbolized the "be whoever you want to be" character of the times. Although this student used several other writing modes—definition to talk about Dylan's move from folk music to folk-rock, analysis to study his song lyrics, and argument to give evidence from experts on Dylan's importance—effective narrative techniques helped him structure the whole.

Narrative in college writing is more than entertaining ornament. It is a useful strategy for engaging reader interest, discovering your own ideas, delivering a message, and giving shape to reality.

Elizabeth Bishop
PRIMER CLASS
★ ★ ★

Known primarily as a poet, Elizabeth Bishop did not begin writing her prose memoirs of childhood, from which "Primer Class" is taken, until late in life. One reason she waited so long was that her early years were troubled by death and separation. Her father died in 1911, the year of her birth, and that same year, her mother became insane. Raised by her maternal grandparents in Nova Scotia, she was separated from them when she was sent, at the age of 7, to live with wealthier relatives in her birthplace, Worcester, Massachusetts. Not until after she was 40 and had moved to Brazil did Bishop find herself secure enough to write about her childhood. Another impetus was the act of translating the childhood diary of a Brazilian girl, a book Bishop felt "kept the girl's childhood for us, as fresh as paint."

The same can be said of Bishop's "Primer Class," reprinted from the posthumously published Collected Prose *(1984). In this narrative, her poet's eye and sensibility fix on the smallest details, which at first seem to have no importance in themselves. Joining Bishop in looking back, however, readers are likely to see glimpses of their own childhoods and of their first, sometimes harrowing, days in school.*

―――――

Every time I see long columns of numbers, handwritten in a certain way, a strange sensation or shudder, partly aesthetic, partly painful, goes through my diaphragm. It is like seeing the dorsal fin of a large fish suddenly cut through the surface of the water—not a frightening fish like a shark, more like a sailfish. The numbers have to be only up to but under a hundred, rather large and clumsily written, and the columns squeezed together, with long vertical lines between them, drawn by hand, long and crooked. They are usually in pencil, these numbers that affect me so, but I've seen them in blue crayon or blurred ink, and they produce the same effect. One morning our newspaper delivery man, an old Italian named Tony, whom I'd seen over and over again, threw back the pages of his limp, black, oilcloth-covered account book to my page, and there, up and down, at right angles to the pages' blue lines, he had kept track of my newspapers in pencil, in columns of ones and ones, twos and threes. My diaphragm contracted and froze. Or Faustina, the old black lottery-ticket seller, and *her* limp school notebook with a penciled-off half-inch column waveringly drawn for each customer. Or my glimpse of a barkeeper's apparently homemade, home-stitched pad, as he consulted long thin numbers referring to heaven knows what (how many drinks each of his customers had had?), and then put the pad away again, under the bar.

The real name of this sensation is memory. It is a memory I do not even have to try to remember, or reconstruct; it is always right there, clear and complete. The mysterious numbers, the columns, that impressed me so much—a mystery I never solved when I went to Primer Class in Nova Scotia!

Primer Class was a sort of Canadian equivalent of kindergarten; it was the year you went to school before you went to "First Grade." But we didn't sit about sociably and build things, or crayon, or play, or quarrel. We sat one behind the other in a line of small, bolted-down desks and chairs, in the same room with grades one, two, three, and four. We were at the left, facing the teacher, and I think there were seven or eight of us. We were taught reading and writing and arithmetic, or enough of them to prepare us for the "First Grade"; also, how to behave in school. This meant to sit up straight, not to scrape your feet on the floor, never to whisper, to raise your hand when you had to go out, and to stand up when you were asked a question. We used slates; only the real grades could buy scribblers, beautiful, fat writing pads, with colored pictures of horses and kittens on the covers, and pale tan paper with blue lines. They could also go up front to sharpen their pencils into the wastebasket.

I was five. My grandmother had already taught me to write on a slate my name and my family's names and the names of the dog and the two cats. Earlier she had taught me my letters, and at first I could not get past the letter *g,* which for some time I felt was far enough to go. *My* alphabet made a satisfying short song, and I didn't want to spoil it. Then a visitor called on my grandmother and asked me if I knew my letters. I said I did and, accenting the rhythm, gave him my version. He teased me so about stopping at *g* that I was finally convinced one must go on with the other nineteen letters. Once past *g,* it was plain sailing. By the time school started, I could read almost all my primer, printed in both handwriting and type, and I loved every word. First, as a frontispiece, it had the flag in full color, with "One Flag, One King, One Crown" under it. I colored in the black-and-white illustrations that looked old-fashioned, even to me, using mostly red and green crayons. On the end pages I had tried to copy the round cancellation marks from old envelopes: "Brooklyn, N.Y. Sept. 1914," "Halifax, Aug. 1916," and so on, but they had not turned out well, a set of lopsided crumbling wheels.

The summer before school began was the summer of numbers, chiefly number eight. I learned their shapes from the kitchen calendar and the clock in the sitting room, though I couldn't yet tell time. Four and five were hard enough, but I think I was in love with eight. One began writing it just to the right of the top, and drew an S downwards. This wasn't too difficult, but the hardest part was to hit the bottom line (ruled on the slate by my grandmother) and come up again, against the grain, that is, against the desire of one's painfully cramped fingers, and at the same time not make it a straight line, but a sort of upside down and backwards S, and all this in *curves.* Eights also made the worst noise on the slate. My grandmother would send me outside to practice, sitting on the back steps. The skreeking was slow and awful.

The slate pencils came two for a penny, with thin white paper, diagonally striped in pale blue or red, glued around them except for an inch left bare at one end. I loved the slate and the pencils almost as much as the primer. What I liked best about the slate was washing it off at the kitchen sink, or in the watering trough, and then watching it dry. It dried like clouds, and then the very last wet streak would grow tinier and tinier, and thinner and thinner; then suddenly it was gone and the slate was pale gray again and dry, dry, dry.

I had an aunt, Mary, eleven or twelve years older than me, who was in the last, or next-to-last, year of the same school. She was very pretty. She wore white middy blouses with red or blue silk ties, and her brown hair in a braid down her back. In the mornings I always got up earlier than Aunt Mary and ate my porridge at the kitchen table, wishing that she would hurry and get up too. We ate porridge from bowls, with a cup of cream at the side. You took a spoonful of porridge, dipped it into the cream, then ate it; this was to keep the porridge hot. We also had cups of tea, with cream and sugar; mine was called "cambric tea." All during breakfast I listened for the school bell, and wished my aunt would hurry up; she rarely appeared before the bell started ringing, over on the other side of the river that divided the village in two. Then she would arrive in the kitchen braiding her hair, and say, "That's just the *first* bell!" while I was dying to be out the door and off. But first I had to pat Betsy, our little dog, and then kiss Grandmother goodbye. (My grandfather would have been up and out for hours already.)

My grandmother had a glass eye, blue, almost like her other one, and this made her especially vulnerable and precious to me. My father was dead and my mother was away in a sanatorium. Until I was teased out of it, I used to ask Grandmother, when I said goodbye, to promise me not to die before I came home. A year earlier I had privately asked other relatives if they thought my grandmother could go to heaven with a glass eye. (Years later I found out that one of my aunts had asked the same question when she'd been my age.) Betsy was also included in this deep but intermittent concern with the hereafter; I was told that of course she'd go to heaven, she was such a good little dog, and not to worry. Wasn't our minister awfully fond of her, and hadn't she even surprised us by trotting right into church one summer Sunday, when the doors were open?

Although I don't remember having been told it was a serious offense, I was very afraid of being late, so most mornings I left Mary at her breakfast and ran out the back door, around the house, past the blacksmith's shop, and was well across the iron bridge before she caught up with me. Sometimes I had almost reached the school when the second bell, the one that meant to come in immediately from the schoolyard, would be clanging away in the cupola. The school was high, bare and white-clapboarded, dark-red-roofed, and the four-sided cupola had white louvers. Two white outhouses were set farther back, but visible, on either side. I carried my slate, a rag to wash it with, and a small medicine bottle filled with water. Everyone was supposed to bring a bottle of water and a clean rag; spitting on the slates and wiping them off with the hand was a crime. Only the bad boys did it, and if she caught them the teacher hit them on the top of the head with her pointer. I don't imagine that wet slate, by itself, had a smell; perhaps slate pencils do; sour, wet rags do, of course, and perhaps that is what I remember. Miss Morash would pick one up at arm's length and order the owner to take it outside at once, saying *Phaaagh,* or something like that.

That was our teacher's name, Georgie Morash. To me she seemed very tall and stout, straight up and down, with a white starched shirtwaist, a dark straight skirt, and a tight, wide belt that she often pushed down, in front, with both hands. Everything, back and front, looked smooth and hard; maybe it was corsets. But close to, what I mostly remember about Miss Morash, and mostly looked at, were her very white shoes, Oxford shoes, surprisingly white, white like flour, and large, with neatly tied white laces. On my first day at school my Aunt Mary had taken me into the room for the lower grades and presented me to Miss Morash. She bent way over, spoke to me kindly, even patted my head and, although told to look up, I could not take my eyes from those silent, independent-looking, powdery-white shoes.

Miss Morash almost always carried her pointer. As she walked up and down the aisles, looking over shoulders at the scribblers or slates, rapping heads, or occasionally boxing an ear, she talked steadily, in a loud, clear voice. This voice had a certain fame in the village. At dinner my grandfather would quote what he said he had heard Miss Morash saying to us (or even to me) as he drove by that morning, even though the schoolhouse was set well back from the road. Sometimes when my grandmother would tell me to stop shouting, or to speak more softly, she would add, "That Georgie!" I don't remember anything Miss Morash ever said. Once when the Primer Class was gathered in a semicircle before one of the blackboards, while she showed us (sweepingly) how to write the capital *C,* and I was considering, rather, the blue sky beyond the windows, I too received a painful rap on the head with the pointer.

There was another little girl in the Primer Class, besides me, and one awful day she wet her pants, right in the front seat, and was sent home. There were two little Micmac Indian boys, Jimmy and Johnny Crow, who had dark little faces and shiny black hair and eyes, just alike. They both wore shirts of blue cotton, some days patterned with little white sprigs, on others with little white anchors. I couldn't take my eyes off these shirts or the boys' dark bare feet. Almost everyone went barefoot to school, but I had to wear brown sandals with buckles, against my will. When I went home the first day and was asked who was in Primer Class with me, I replied, "Manure MacLaughlin," as his name had sounded to me. I was familiar with manure—there was a great pile of it beside the barn—but of course his real name was Muir, and everyone laughed. Muir wore a navy-blue cap, with a red-and-yellow maple leaf embroidered above the visor.

There was a poor boy, named Roustain, the dirtiest and raggediest of us all, who was really too big for Primer Class and had to walk a long way to school, when he came at all. I heard thrilling stories about him and his brother, how their father whipped them all the time, *horsewhipped* them. We were still horse-and-buggy-minded (though there were a few automobiles in the village), and one of the darkest, most sinister symbols in our imaginations was the horsewhip. It *looked* sinister: long, black, flexible at a point after the handle, sometimes even with lead in it, tasseled. It made a swish *whissh*ing sound and sometimes figured in nightmares. There was even a song about the Roustains:

I'm a Roustain from the mountain,
I'm a Roustain, don't you see,
I'm a Roustain from the mountain,
You can smell the fir on me.

Not only did their father whip them, but their mother didn't take care of them at all. There were no real beds in their house and no food, except for a big barrel of molasses, which often swarmed with flies. They'd dip pieces of bread in the molasses, when they had bread, and that was all they had for dinner.

The schoolroom windows, those autumn days, seemed very high and bright. On one window ledge, on the Primer Class side, there were beans sprouting up in jars of water. Their presence in school puzzled me, since at home I'd already grown "horse bean" to an amazing height and size in my own garden (eighteen inches square), as well as some radishes and small, crooked carrots. Beyond, above the sprouting beans, the big autumn clouds went grandly by, silver and dazzling in the deep blue. I would keep turning my head to follow them, until Miss Morash came along and gave it a small push back in the right direction. I loved to hear the other grades read aloud, unless they hesitated too much on words or phrases you could guess ahead. Their stories were better, and longer, than those in my primer. I already knew by heart "The Gingerbread Boy" and "Henny Penny," in my primer, and had turned against them. I was much more interested when the third grade read about Bruce watching the spider spin his web. Every morning school began with the Lord's Prayer, sitting down, then we stood up and sang "O maple leaf, our emblem dear." Then sometimes—and not very well, because it was so much harder—we sang "God save our gracious king," but usually stopped with the first verse.

Only the third and fourth grades studied geography. On their side of the room, over the blackboard, were two rolled-up maps, one of Canada and one of the whole world. When they had a geography lesson, Miss Morash pulled down one or both of these maps, like window shades. They were on cloth, very limp, with a shiny surface, and in pale colors—tan, pink, yellow, and green—surrounded by the blue that was the ocean. The light coming in from their windows, falling on the glazed, crackly surface, made it hard for me to see them properly from where I sat. On the world map, all of Canada was pink; on the Canadian, the provinces were different colors. I was so taken with the pull-down maps that I wanted to snap them up, and pull them down again, and touch all the countries and provinces with my own hands. Only dimly did I hear the pupils' recitations of capital cities and islands and bays. But I got the general impression that Canada was the same size as the world, which somehow or other fitted into it, or the other way around, and that in the world and Canada the sun was always shining and everything was dry and glittering. At the same time, I knew perfectly well that this was not true.

One morning Aunt Mary was even later than usual at breakfast, and for some reason I decided to wait for her to finish her porridge. Before we got to the bridge the second bell—the bell that really meant it—started ringing. I was terrified because up to this time I had never actually been late, so I began to run as fast as I possibly could. I could hear my aunt behind, laughing at me. Because her legs were longer than mine, she caught up to me, rushed into the schoolyard and up the steps ahead of me. I ran into the classroom and threw myself, howling, against Miss Morash's upright form. The class had their hands folded on the desks, heads bowed, and had reached "Thy kingdom come." I clutched the teacher's long, stiff skirt and sobbed. Behind me, my awful aunt was still *laughing*. Miss Morash stopped everyone in mid-prayer, and propelled us all three out into the cloakroom, holding me tightly by the shoulder. There, surrounded by all the japanned hooks, which held only two or three caps, we were private, though loud giggles and whispering reached us from the schoolroom. First Miss Morash in stern tones told Mary she was *very* late for the class she attended overhead, and ordered her to go upstairs at once. Then she tried to calm me. She said in a very kindly way, not at all in her usual penetrating voice, that being only a few minutes late wasn't really worth tears, that everything was quite all right, and I must go into the classroom now and join in the usual morning songs. She wiped off my face with a folded white handkerchief she kept tucked in her belt, patted my head, and even kissed me two or three times. I was overcome by all this, almost to the point of crying all over again, but keeping my eyes fixed firmly on her two large, impersonal, flour-white shoes, I managed not to give way. I had to face my snickering classmates, and I found I could. And that was that, although I was cross with Aunt Mary for a long time because it was all her fault.

For me this was the most dramatic incident of Primer Class, and I was never late again. My initial experiences of formal education were on the whole pleasurable. Reading and writing caused me no suffering. I found the first easier, but the second was enjoyable—I mean *artistically* enjoyable—and I came to admire my own handwriting in pencil, when I got to that stage, perhaps as a youthful Chinese student might admire his own brushstrokes. It was wonderful to see that the letters each had different expressions, and that the same letter had different expressions at different times. Sometimes the two capitals of my name looked miserable, slumped down and sulky, but at others they turned fat and cheerful, almost with roses in their cheeks. I also had the "First Grade" to look forward to, as well as geography, the maps, and longer and much better stories. The one subject that baffled me was arithmetic. I knew all the numbers of course, and liked to write them—I finally mastered the eight—but when I watched the older grades at arithmetic class, in front of the blackboard with their columns of figures, it was utterly incomprehensible. Those mysterious numbers!

QUESTIONS

1. How do Bishop's first two paragraphs set up her narrative?

2. How would you describe the overall organizational principle of the essay? Look at each paragraph to see how it relates to those surrounding it.

3. Select examples of imagery in the essay. To which of the senses do they appeal? How are images connected to memory?

4. How does Bishop manage to recreate in her narrative the feeling of being 5 years old again?

5. Bishop does not describe "the most dramatic incident of Primer Class" until the next-to-the-last paragraph. Why does she wait so long? Is this an effective or ineffective strategy? Explain.

SUGGESTIONS FOR WRITING

1. Write a letter to a grammar school classmate reminding him or her of an upsetting incident you both experienced. (You might use some of the techniques suggested in the introduction to this chapter to awaken your memory.)

2. Tell the story of your first time doing anything you are now familiar with (a job, driving, going out on a date). Imagine you are writing for a reader who may not have done the activity yet. Make the reader feel the unfamiliarity of the activity and your trepidation about doing it.

Russell Baker
SELLING THE POST
★ ★ ★

"I'm basically a guy with a yearning for the past," Russell Baker told an interviewer in 1972, "a time when things were better. . . . It's probably a sign of the hardening of the mental arteries, this yearning for boyhood, the kind of thing I dislike when I hear it from other people." In Growing Up *(1982), the autobiography of his childhood (for which he won a second Pulitzer Prize), Baker indulges his desire to relive and reshape his past. As the following chapter from this book illustrates, Baker is a skillful, graceful writer, a piercing observer of daily life, and a first-class humorist, in the tradition of Mark Twain and James Thurber. In all of these ways he has been pleasing readers in weekly newspaper columns since 1962, and has become for many the conscience of America, a sane voice in the chaos of modern American life.*

Born in Virginia in 1925, Baker grew up during the Depression with his mother and younger sister. His father had died of diabetes at the age of 33, and a younger sister had been given to more well-to-do relatives during these difficult times. "Selling the Post," Chapter Two of Baker's autobiography, tells the story of how he decided to become a writer.

I began working in journalism when I was eight years old. It was my mother's idea. She wanted me to "make something" of myself and, after a levelheaded appraisal of my strengths, decided I had better start young if I was to have any chance of keeping up with the competition.

The flaw in my character which she had already spotted was lack of "gumption." My idea of a perfect afternoon was lying in front of the radio rereading my favorite Big Little Book, *Dick Tracy Meets Stooge Viller.* My mother despised inactivity. Seeing me having a good time in repose, she was powerless to hide her disgust. "You've got no more gumption than a bump on a log," she said. "Get out in the kitchen and help Doris do those dirty dishes."

My sister Doris, though two years younger than I, had enough gumption for a dozen people. She positively enjoyed washing dishes, making beds, and cleaning the house. When she was only seven she could carry a piece of short-weighted cheese back to the A&P, threaten the manager with legal action, and come back triumphantly with the full quarter-pound we'd paid for and a few ounces extra thrown in for forgiveness. Doris could have made something of herself if she hadn't been a girl. Because of this defect, however, the best she could hope for was a career as a nurse or schoolteacher, the only work that capable females were considered up to in those days.

This must have saddened my mother, this twist of fate that had allocated all the gumption to the daughter and left her with a son who was content with Dick Tracy and Stooge Viller. If disappointed, though, she wasted no energy on self-pity. She would make me make something of myself whether I wanted to or not. "The Lord helps those who help themselves," she said. That was the way her mind worked.

She was realistic about the difficulty. Having sized up the material the Lord had given her to mold, she didn't overestimate what she could do with it. She didn't insist that I grow up to be President of the United States.

Fifty years ago parents still asked boys if they wanted to grow up to be President, and asked it not jokingly but seriously. Many parents who were hardly more than paupers still believed their sons could do it. Abraham Lincoln had done it. We were only sixty-five years from Lincoln. Many a grandfather who walked among us could remember Lincoln's time. Men of grandfatherly age were the worst for asking if you wanted to grow up to be President. A surprising number of little boys said yes and meant it.

I was asked many times myself. No, I would say, I didn't want to grow up to be President. My mother was present during one of these interrogations. An elderly uncle, having posed the usual question and exposed my lack of interest in the Presidency, asked, "Well, what *do* you want to be when you grow up?"

I loved to pick through trash piles and collect empty bottles, tin cans with pretty labels, and discarded magazines. The most desirable job on earth sprang instantly to mind. "I want to be a garbage man," I said.

My uncle smiled, but my mother had seen the first distressing evidence of a bump budding on a log. "Have a little gumption, Russell," she said. Her calling me Russell was a signal of unhappiness. When she approved of me I was always "Buddy."

When I turned eight years old she decided that the job of starting me on the road toward making something of myself could no longer be safely delayed. "Buddy," she said one day, "I want you to come home right after school this afternoon. Somebody's coming and I want you to meet him."

When I burst in that afternoon she was in conference in the parlor with an executive of the Curtis Publishing Company. She introduced me. He bent low from the waist and shook my hand. Was it true as my mother had told him, he asked, that I longed for the opportunity to conquer the world of business?

My mother replied that I was blessed with a rare determination to make something of myself.

"That's right," I whispered.

"But have you got the grit, the character, the never-say-quit spirit it takes to succeed in business?"

My mother said I certainly did.

"That's right," I said.

He eyed me silently for a long pause, as though weighing whether I could be trusted to keep his confidence, then spoke man-to-man. Before taking a crucial step, he said, he wanted to advise me that working for the Curtis Publishing Company placed enormous responsibility on a young man. It was one of the great companies of America. Perhaps the greatest publishing house in the world. I had heard, no doubt, of the *Saturday Evening Post?*

Heard of it? My mother said that everyone in our house had heard of the *Saturday Post* and that I, in fact, read it with religious devotion.

Then doubtless, he said, we were also familiar with those two monthly pillars of the magazine world, the *Ladies Home Journal* and the *Country Gentleman.*

Indeed we were familiar with them, said my mother.

Representing the *Saturday Evening Post* was one of the weightiest honors that could be bestowed in the world of business, he said. He was personally proud of being a part of that great corporation.

My mother said he had every right to be.

Again he studied me as though debating whether I was worthy of a knighthood. Finally: "Are you trustworthy?"

My mother said I was the soul of honesty.

"That's right," I said.

The caller smiled for the first time. He told me I was a lucky young man. He admired my spunk. Too many young men thought life was all play. Those young men would not go far in this world. Only a young man willing to work and save and keep his face washed and his hair neatly combed could hope to come out on top in a world such as ours. Did I truly and sincerely believe that I was such a young man?

"He certainly does," said my mother.

"That's right," I said.

He said he had been so impressed by what he had seen of me that he was going to make me a representative of the Curtis Publishing Company. On the following Tuesday, he said, thirty freshly printed copies of the *Saturday Evening Post* would be delivered at our door. I would place these magazines, still damp with the ink of the presses, in a handsome canvas bag, sling it over my shoulder, and set forth through the streets to bring the best in journalism, fiction, and cartoons to the American public.

He had brought the canvas bag with him. He presented it with reverence fit for a chasuble. He showed me how to drape the sling over my left shoulder and across the chest so that the pouch lay easily accessible to my right hand, allowing the best in journalism, fiction, and cartoons to be swiftly extracted and sold to a citizenry whose happiness and security depended upon us soldiers of the free press.

The following Tuesday I raced home from school, put the canvas bag over my shoulder, dumped the magazines in, and, tilting to the left to balance their weight on my right hip, embarked on the highway of journalism.

We lived in Belleville, New Jersey, a commuter town at the northern fringe of Newark. It was 1932, the bleakest year of the Depression. My father had died two years before, leaving us with a few pieces of Sears, Roebuck furniture and not much else, and my mother had taken Doris and me to live with one of her younger brothers. This was my Uncle Allen. Uncle Allen had made something of himself by 1932. As salesman for a soft-drink bottler in Newark, he had an income of $30 a week; wore pearl-gray spats, detachable collars, and a three-piece suit; was happily married; and took in threadbare relatives.

With my load of magazines I headed toward Belleville Avenue. That's where the people were. There were two filling stations at the intersection with Union Avenue, as well as an A&P, a fruit stand, a bakery, a barber shop, Zuccarelli's drugstore, and a diner shaped like a railroad car. For several hours I made myself highly visible, shifting position now and then from corner to corner, from shop window to shop window, to make sure everyone could see the heavy black lettering on the canvas bag that said THE SATURDAY EVENING POST. When the angle of the light indicated it was suppertime, I walked back to the house.

"How many did you sell, Buddy?" my mother asked.

"None."

"Where did you go?"

"The corner of Belleville and Union Avenues."

"What did you do?"

"Stood on the corner waiting for somebody to buy a *Saturday Evening Post.*"

"You just stood there?"

"Didn't sell a single one."

"For God's sake, Russell!"

Uncle Allen intervened. "I've been thinking about it for some time," he said, "and I've about decided to take the *Post* regularly. Put me down as a regular customer." I handed him a magazine and he paid me a nickel. It was the first nickel I earned.

Afterwards my mother instructed me in salesmanship. I would have to ring doorbells, address adults with charming self-confidence, and break down resistance with a sales talk pointing out that no one, no matter how poor, could afford to be without the *Saturday Evening Post* in the home.

I told my mother I'd changed my mind about wanting to succeed in the magazine business.

"If you think I'm going to raise a good-for-nothing," she replied, "you've got another think coming." She told me to hit the streets with the canvas bag and start ringing doorbells the instant school was out next day. When I objected that I didn't feel any aptitude for salesmanship, she asked how I'd like to lend her my leather belt so she could whack some sense into me. I bowed to superior will and entered journalism with a heavy heart.

My mother and I had fought this battle almost as long as I could remember. It probably started even before memory began, when I was a country child in northern Virginia and my mother, dissatisfied with my father's plain workman's life, determined that I would not grow up like him and his people, with calluses on their hands, overalls on their backs, and fourth-grade educations in their heads. She had fancier ideas of life's possibilities. Introducing me to the *Saturday Evening Post,* she was trying to wean me as early as possible from my father's world where men left with their lunch pails at sunup, worked with their hands until the grime ate into the pores, and died with a few sticks of mail-order furniture as their legacy. In my mother's vision of the better life there were desks and white collars, well-pressed suits, evenings of reading and lively talk, and perhaps—if a man were very, very lucky and hit the jackpot, really made something important of himself—perhaps there might be a fantastic salary of $5,000 a year to support a big house and a Buick with a rumble seat and a vacation in Atlantic City.

And so I set forth with my sack of magazines. I was afraid of the dogs that snarled behind the doors of potential buyers. I was timid about ringing the doorbells of strangers, relieved when no one came to the door, and scared when someone did. Despite my mother's instructions, I could not deliver an engaging sales pitch. When a door opened I simply asked, "Want to buy a *Saturday Evening Post*?" In Belleville few persons did. It was a town of 30,000 people, and most weeks I rang a fair majority of its doorbells. But I rarely sold my thirty copies. Some weeks I canvassed the entire town for six days and still had four or five unsold magazines on Monday evening; then I dreaded the coming of Tuesday morning, when a batch of thirty fresh *Saturday Evening Post*s was due at the front door.

"Better get out there and sell the rest of those magazines tonight," my mother would say.

I usually posted myself then at a busy intersection where a traffic light controlled commuter flow from Newark. When the light turned red I stood on the curb and shouted my sales pitch at the motorists.

"Want to buy a *Saturday Evening Post*?"

One rainy night when car windows were sealed against me I came back soaked and with not a single sale to report. My mother beckoned to Doris.

"Go back down there with Buddy and show him how to sell these magazines," she said.

Brimming with zest, Doris, who was then seven years old, returned with me to the corner. She took a magazine from the bag, and when the light turned red she strode to the nearest car and banged her small fist against the closed window. The driver, probably startled at what he took to be a midget assaulting his car, lowered the window to stare, and Doris thrust a *Saturday Evening Post* at him.

"You need this magazine," she piped, "and it only costs a nickel."

Her salesmanship was irresistible. Before the light changed half a dozen times she disposed of the entire batch. I didn't feel humiliated. To the contrary. I was so happy I decided to give her a treat. Leading her to the vegetable store on Belleville Avenue, I bought three apples, which cost a nickel, and gave her one.

"You shouldn't waste money," she said.

"Eat your apple." I bit into mine.

"You shouldn't eat before supper," she said. "It'll spoil your appetite."

Back at the house that evening, she dutifully reported me for wasting a nickel. Instead of a scolding, I was rewarded with a pat on the back for having the good sense to buy fruit instead of candy. My mother reached into her bottomless supply of maxims and told Doris, "An apple a day keeps the doctor away."

By the time I was ten I had learned all my mother's maxims by heart. Asking to stay up past normal bedtime, I knew that a refusal would be explained with, "Early to bed and early to rise, makes a man healthy, wealthy, and wise." If I whimpered about having to get up early in the morning, I could depend on her to say, "The early bird gets the worm."

The one I most despised was, "If at first you don't succeed, try, try again." This was the battle cry with which she constantly sent me back into the hopeless struggle whenever I moaned that I had rung every doorbell in town and knew there wasn't a single potential buyer left in Belleville that week. After listening to my explanation, she handed me the canvas bag and said, "If at first you don't succeed . . ."

Three years in that job, which I would gladly have quit after the first day except for her insistence, produced at least one valuable result. My mother finally concluded that I would never make something of myself by pursuing a life in business and started considering careers that demanded less competitive zeal.

One evening when I was eleven I brought home a short "composition" on my summer vacation which the teacher had graded with an A. Reading it with her own schoolteacher's eye, my mother agreed that it was top-drawer seventh grade prose and complimented me. Nothing more was said about it immediately, but a new idea had taken life in her mind. Halfway through supper she suddenly interrupted the conversation.

"Buddy," she said, "maybe you could be a writer."

I clasped the idea to my heart. I had never met a writer, had shown no previous urge to write, and hadn't a notion how to become a writer, but I loved stories and thought that making up stories must surely be almost as much fun as reading them. Best of all, though, and what really gladdened my heart, was the ease of the writer's life. Writers did not have to trudge through the town peddling from canvas bags, defending themselves against angry dogs, being rejected by surly strangers. Writers did not have to ring doorbells. So far as I could make out, what writers did couldn't even be classified as work.

I was enchanted. Writers didn't have to have any gumption at all. I did not dare tell anybody for fear of being laughed at in the schoolyard, but secretly I decided that what I'd like to be when I grew up was a writer.

QUESTIONS

1. How important is setting (time and place) to Baker's story?

2. How does Baker get across his feelings of dread at having to sell the magazines? (Does the narrative remind you of any similar experiences you have had?)

3. Baker's sister, Doris, makes a brief but important appearance in the story. What role does she play?

4. How would you characterize the tone of Baker's essay? Is the tone consistent with the point and purpose of "Selling the Post"? Explain.

SUGGESTIONS FOR WRITING

1. Tell the story of an embarrassing experience you had, but tell it humorously. (Writing something others will find amusing is not an easy task; you might study the techniques of the following humorists included in this anthology: Woody Allen, Andy Rooney, Roy Blount, Jr., and Art Buchwald.)

2. Turn Baker's story into a script for a TV situation comedy. Use only dialogue, with occasional stage directions. Introduce the characters, background, conflict, and resolution, employing a bare minimum of exposition. For models, use the dialogue in the Baker, Bambara, and Kingston pieces, and your own knowledge of TV shows.

Harry Crews
THE SCALDING
★ ★ ★

Place is critically important to the writing of Harry Crews. His autobiography, from which "The Scalding" is taken, is subtitled "the biography of a place." Born in rural Georgia, Crews is a new participant in a tradition of Southern writers, including Thomas Wolfe, William Faulkner, and Robert Penn Warren, who seek to capture the essential atmosphere of their region. They emphasize precisely observed, realistic detail, including the recreation of local dialect, but introduce a romantic element as well.

After being discharged from the Marines in 1956, Crews enrolled at the University of Florida to study writing. He received his degree, taking a break to wander through the United States and Mexico on a motorcycle, and since then he has published twelve books. A cursory reading of Crews might create the impression that he is a kind of primitive artist simply telling things the way they happened. A closer study of his style, however, suggests a writer with a sophisticated command of his medium.

As winter grew deeper and we waited for hog-killing time, at home the center was not holding. Whether it was because the crops were in and not much work was to be done or whether it was because of my having just spent so long a time crippled in the bed, daddy had grown progressively crazier, more violent. He was gone from home for longer and longer periods of time, and during those brief intervals when he was home, the crashing noise of breaking things was everywhere about us. Daddy had also taken to picking up the shotgun and screaming threats while he waved it about, but at that time he had not as yet fired it.

While that was going on, it occurred to me for the first time that being alive was like being awake in a nightmare.

I remember saying aloud to myself: "Scary as a nightmare. Jest like being awake in a nightmare."

Never once did I ever think that my life was not just like everybody else's, that my fears and uncertainties were not universal. For which I can only thank God. Thinking so could only have made it more bearable.

My sleepwalking had become worse now that I could get out of bed on my unsure legs. I woke up sometimes in the middle of the night in the dirt lane by the house or sometimes sitting in my room in a corner chewing on something. It didn't matter much what: the sleeve of my gown or the side of my hand or even one time the laces of a shoe. And when I would wake up, it was always in terror, habitually remembering now what Auntie had said about the birds spitting in my mouth. No, more than *remembering* what she had said. Rather, seeing what she had said, the image of a bird burned clearly on the backs of my eyelids, its beak hooked like the nose of a Byzantine Christ, shooting spit thick as phlegm on a solid line into my open and willing mouth. With such dreams turning in my head it came time for us to all help kill and butcher hogs. Daddy was laid up somewhere drunk; we had not seen him in four days. So he did not go with us to Uncle Alton's to help with the slaughter. Farm families swapped labor at hog-killing time just as they swapped labor to put in tobacco or pick cotton. Early one morning our tenant farmers, mama, my brother, and I walked the half mile to Uncle Alton's place to help put a year's worth of meat in the smokehouse. Later his family would come and help us do the same thing.

Before it was over, everything on the hog would have been used. The lights (lungs) and liver—together called haslet—would be made into a fresh stew by first pouring and pouring again fresh water through the slit throat—the exposed throat called a goozle—to clean the lights out good. Then the fat would be trimmed off and put with the fat trimmed from the guts to cook crisp into cracklins to mix with cornbread or else put in a wash pot to make soap.

The guts would be washed and then turned and washed again. Many times. After the guts had been covered with salt overnight, they were used as casings for sausage made from shoulder meat, tenderloin, and—if times were hard—any kind of scrap that was not entirely fat.

The eyes would be removed from the head, then the end of the snout cut off, and the whole thing boiled until the teeth could be picked out. Whatever meat was left, cheeks, ears, and so on, would be picked off, crushed with herbs and spices and packed tightly into muslin cloth for hog's headcheese.

The fat from the liver, lungs, guts, or wherever was cooked until it was as crisp as it would get and then packed into tin syrup buckets to be ground up later for cracklin cornbread. Even the feet were removed, and after the outer layer of split hooves was taken off, the whole thing was boiled and pickled in vinegar and peppers. If later in the year the cracklins started to get rank, they would be thrown into a cast-iron wash pot with fried meat's grease, any meat for that matter that might have gone bad in the smokehouse, and some potash and lye and cooked into soap, always made on the full of the moon so it wouldn't shrink. I remember one time mama out in the backyard making soap when a chicken for some reason tried to fly over the wash pot but didn't make it. The chicken dropped flapping and squawking into the boiling fat and lye. Mama, who was stirring the mixture with an old ax handle, never missed a beat. She just stirred the chicken right on down to the bottom. Any kind of meat was good for making soap.

By the time we got to Uncle Alton's the dirt floor of the smokehouse had been covered with green pine tops. After the pork stayed overnight in tubs of salt, it would be laid on the green pine straw all night, sometimes for two nights, to get all the water out of it. Then it was taken up and packed again in salt for three or four days. When it was taken out of the salt for the last time, it was dipped in plain hot water or else in a solution of crushed hot peppers and syrup or wild honey. Then it was hung over a deep pile of smoldering hickory spread across the entire floor of the smokehouse. The hickory was watched very carefully to keep any sort of blaze from flaring up. Day and night until it was over, light gray smoked boiled continuously from under the eaves and around the door where the meat was being cured. It was the sweetest smoke a man was ever to smell.

It was a bright cold day in February 1941, so cold the ground was still frozen at ten o'clock in the morning. The air was full of the steaming smell of excrement and the oily, flatulent odor of intestines and the heavy sweetness of blood—in every way a perfect day to slaughter animals. I watched the hogs called to the feeding trough just as they were every morning except this morning it was to receive the ax instead of slop.

A little slop *was* poured into their long communal trough, enough to make them stand still while Uncle Alton or his boy Theron went quietly among them with the ax, using the flat end like a sledgehammer (shells were expensive enough to make a gun out of the question). He would approach the hog from the rear while it slopped at the trough, and then he would straddle it, one leg on each side, patiently waiting for the hog to raise its snout from the slop to take a breath, showing as it did the wide bristled bone between its ears to the ax.

It never took but one blow, delivered expertly and with consummate skill, and the hog was dead. He then moved with his hammer to the next hog and straddled it. None of the hogs ever seemed to mind that their companions were dropping dead all around them but continued in a single-minded passion to eat. They didn't even mind when another of my cousins (this could be a boy of only eight or nine because it took neither strength nor skill) came right behind the hammer and drew a long razor-boned butcher knife across the throat of the fallen hog. Blood spurted with the still-beating heart, and a live hog would sometimes turn to one that was lying beside it at the trough and stick its snout into the spurting blood and drink a bit just seconds before it had its own head crushed.

It was a time of great joy and celebration for the children. We played games and ran (I gimping along pretty well by then) and screamed and brought wood to the boiler and thought of that night, when we would have fresh fried pork and stew made from lungs and liver and heart in an enormous pot that covered half the stove.

The air was charged with the smell of fat being rendered in tubs in the backyard and the sharp squeals of the pigs at the troughs, squeals from pure piggishness at the slop, never from pain. Animals were killed but seldom hurt. Farmers took tremendous precautions about pain at slaughter. It is, whether or not they ever admit it when they talk, a ritual. As brutal as they sometimes are with farm animals and with themselves, no farmer would ever eat an animal he had willingly made suffer.

The heel strings were cut on each of the hog's hind legs, and a stick, called a gambreling stick, or a gallus, was inserted into the cut behind the tendon and the hog dragged to the huge cast-iron boiler, which sat in a depression dug into the ground so the hog could be slipped in and pulled out easily. The fire snapped and roared in the depression under the boiler. The fire had to be tended carefully because the water could never quite come to a boil. If the hog was dipped in boiling water, the hair would set and become impossible to take off. The ideal temperature was water you could rapidly draw your finger through three times in succession without being blistered.

Unlike cows, which are skinned, a hog is scraped. After the hog is pulled from the water, a blunt knife is drawn over the animal, and if the water has not been too hot, the hair slips off smooth as butter, leaving a white, naked, utterly beautiful pig.

To the great glee of the watching children, when the hog is slipped into the water, it defecates. The children squeal and clap their hands and make their delightfully obscene children's jokes as they watch it all.

On that morning, mama was around in the back by the smokehouse where some hogs, already scalded and scraped, were hanging in the air from their heel strings being disemboweled. Along with the other ladies she was washing out the guts, turning them inside out, cleaning them good so they could later be stuffed with ground and seasoned sausage meat.

Out in front of the house where the boiler was, I was playing pop-the-whip as best I could with my brother and several of my cousins. Pop-the-whip is a game in which everyone holds hands and runs fast and then the leader of the line turns sharply. Because he is turning through a tighter arc than the other children, the line acts as a whip with each child farther down the line having to travel through a greater space and consequently having to go faster in order to keep up. The last child in the line literally gets *popped* loose and sent flying from his playmates.

I was popped loose and sent flying into the steaming boiler of water beside a scalded, floating hog.

I remember everything about it as clearly as I remember anything that ever happened to me, except the screaming. Curiously, I cannot remember the screaming. They say I screamed all the way to town, but I cannot remember it.

What I remember is John C. Pace, a black man whose daddy was also named John C. Pace, reached right into the scalding water and pulled me out and set me on my feet and stood back to look at me. I did not fall but stood looking at John and seeing in his face that I was dead.

The children's faces, including my brothers, showed I was dead, too. And I knew it must be so because I knew where I had fallen and I felt no pain—not in that moment—and I knew with the bone-chilling certainty most people are spared that, yes, death does come and mine had just touched me.

John C. Pace ran screaming and the other children ran screaming and left me standing there by the boiler, my hair and skin and clothes steaming in the bright cold February air.

In memory I stand there alone with the knowledge of death upon me, watching steam rising from my hands and clothes while everybody runs and, after everybody has gone, standing there for minutes while nobody comes.

That is only memory. It may have been but seconds before my mama and Uncle Alton came to me. Mama tells me she heard me scream and started running toward the boiler, knowing already what had happened. She has also told me that she could not bring herself to try to do anything with that smoking ghostlike thing standing by the boiler. But she did. They all did. They did what they could.

But in that interminable time between John pulling me out and my mother arriving in front of me, I remember first the pain. It didn't begin as bad pain, but rather like maybe sandspurs under my clothes.

I reached over and touched my right hand with my left, and the whole thing came off like a wet glove. I mean, the skin on the top of the wrist and the back of my hand, along with the fingernails, all just turned loose and slid on down to the ground. I could see my fingernails lying in the little puddle my flesh made on the ground in front of me.

Then hands were on me, taking off my clothes, and the pain turned into something words cannot touch, or at least my words cannot touch. There is no way for me to talk about it because when my shirt was taken off, my back came off with it. When my overalls were pulled down, my cooked and glowing skin came down.

I still had not fallen, and I stood there participating in my own butchering. When they got the clothes off me, they did the worst thing they could have done; they wrapped me in a sheet. They did it out of panic and terror and ignorance and love.

That day there happened to be a car at the farm. I can't remember who it belonged to, but I was taken into the backseat into my mama's lap—God love the lady, out of her head, pressing her boiled son to her breast—and we started for Alma, a distance of about sixteen miles. The only thing that I can remember about the trip was that I started telling mama that I did not want to die. I started saying it and never stopped.

The car we piled into was incredibly slow. An old car and very, very slow, and every once in a while Uncle Alton, who was like a daddy to me, would jump out of the car and run alongside it and helplessly scream for it to go faster and then he would jump on the running board until he couldn't stand it any longer and then he would jump off again.

But like bad beginnings everywhere, they sometimes end well. When I got to Dr. Sharp's office in Alma and he finally managed to get me out of the sticking sheet, he found that I was scalded over two-thirds of my body but that my head had not gone under the water (he said that would have killed me), and for some strange reason I have never understood, the burns were not deep. He said I would probably even outgrow the scars, which I have. Until I was about fifteen years old, the scars were puckered and discolored on my back and right arm and legs. But now their outlines are barely visible.

The only hospital at the time was thirty miles away, and Dr. Sharp said I'd do just as well at home if they built a frame over the bed to keep the covers off me and also kept a light burning over me twenty-four hours a day. (He knew as well as we did that I couldn't go to a hospital anyway, since the only thing Dr. Sharp ever got for taking care of me was satisfaction for a job well done, if he got that. Over the years, I was his most demanding and persistent charity, which he never mentioned to me or mama. Perhaps that is why in an age when it is fashionable to distrust and hate doctors, I love them.)

So they took me back home and put a buggy frame over my bed to make it resemble, when the sheet was on it, a covered wagon, and ran a line in from the Rural Electrification Administration so I could have the drying light hanging just over me. The pain was not nearly so bad now that I had for the first time in my life the miracle of electricity close enough to touch. The pain was bad enough, though, but relieved to some extent by some medicine Dr. Sharp gave us to spray out of a bottle onto the burns by pumping a black rubber ball. When it dried, it raised to form a protective, cooling scab. But it was bad to crack. The bed was always full of black crumbs, which Auntie worked continually at. When they brought me home, Auntie, without anybody saying a word to her, came back up the road to take care of me.

The same day Hollis Toomey came, too. He walked into the house without knocking or speaking to anyone. Nobody had sent for him. But whenever anybody in the county was burned, he showed up as if by magic, because he could talk the fire out of you. He did not call himself a faith healer, never spoke of God, didn't even go to church, although his family did. His was a gift that was real, and everybody in the county knew it was real. For reasons which he never gave, because he was the most reticent of men and never took money or anything else for what he did, he was drawn to a bad burn the way iron filings are drawn to a magnet, never even saying, "You're welcome," to those who thanked him. He was as sure of his powers and as implacable as God.

When he arrived, the light had not yet been brought into the house, and the buggy frame was not yet over my bed and I was lying in unsayable pain. His farm was not far from ours, and it was unlike any other in the county. Birds' nests made from gourds, shaped like crooked-necked squash with a hole cut in one side with the seeds taken out, hung everywhere from the forest of old and arching oak trees about his house. Undulating flocks of white pigeons flew in and out of his hayloft. He had a blacksmith shed, black as smut and always hot from the open hearth where he made among other things iron rims for wagon wheels. He could hand-craft a true-shooting gun, including the barrel which was not smooth-bore but had calibrated riflings. He owned two oxen, heavier than mules, whose harness, including the double yoke, he had made himself. His boys were never allowed to take care of them. He watered them and fed them and pulled them now and again to stumps or trees. But he also had the only Belgian draft horse in the county. The horse was so monstrously heavy that you could hitch him to two spans of good mules—four of them—and he would walk off with them as though they were goats. So the oxen were really useless. It just pleased him to keep them.

He favored very clean women and very dirty men. He thought it was the natural order of things. One of the few things I ever heard him say, and he said it looking off toward the far horizon, speaking to nobody: "A man's got the *right* to stink."

His wife always wore her hair tightly bunned at the back of her head under a stiffly starched white bonnet. Her dresses were nearly to her ankles, and they always looked and smelled as if they had just come off the clothesline after a long day in the sun.

Hollis always smelled like his pockets were full of ripe chicken guts, and his overalls were as stiff as metal. He didn't wear a beard; he wore a stubble. The stubble was coal black despite the fact he was over sixty, and it always seemed to be the same length, the length where you've got to shave or start telling everybody you're growing a beard. Hollis Toomey did neither.

When I saw him in the door, it was as though a soothing balm had touched me. This was Hollis Toomey, who was from my county, whose boys I knew, who didn't talk to God about your hurt. He didn't even talk to *you;* he talked to the *fire.* A mosquito couldn't fly through a door he was standing in he was so wide and high, and more, he was obviously indestructible. He ran on his own time, went where he needed to go. Nobody ever thought of doing anything for him, helping him. If he wanted something, he made it. If he couldn't make it, he took it. Hollis Toomey was not a kind man.

My daddy had finally come home, red-eyed and full of puke. He was at the foot of the bed, but he didn't say a word while Hollis sat beside me.

Hollis Toomey's voice was low like the quiet rasping of a file on metal. I couldn't hear most of what he had to say, but that was all right because I stopped burning before he ever started talking. He talked to the fire like an old and respected adversary, but one he had beaten consistently and had come to beat again. I don't remember him once looking at my face while he explained: "Fire, this boy is mine. This bed is mine. This room is mine. It ain't nothing here that's yours. It's a lot that is, but it ain't nothing here that is."

At some point while he talked he put his hands on me, one of them spread out big as a frying pan, and I was already as cool as spring water. But I had known I would be from the moment I had seen him standing in the door. Before it was over, he cursed the fire, calling it all kinds of sonofabitch, but the words neither surprised nor shocked me. The tone of his voice made me know that he was locked in a real and terrible conflict with the fire. His hands flexed and hurt my stomach, but it was nothing compared to the pain that had been on me before he came.

I had almost dozed off when he suddenly got up and walked out of the room.

My daddy called, "Thank you," in a weak, alcohol-spattered voice. Hollis Toomey did not answer.

When they finally got the buggy frame up, it was not as terrible as I at first thought it was going to be. I was, of course, by then used to the bed and that was no problem and the buggy frame gave a new dimension, a new feeling to the sickbed. With the frame arching over me it was a time for fantasy and magic because I lived in a sort of playhouse, a kingdom that was all mine.

At least I pretended it was a kingdom, pretended it in self-defense. I did not want to be there, but there was no help for it, so I might as well pretend it was a kingdom as anything else. And like every child who owns anything, I ruled it like a tyrant. There was something very special and beautiful about being the youngest member of a family and being badly hurt.

Since it pleased me to do so, I spent a lot of time with the Sears, Roebuck catalogue, started writing and nearly finished a detective novel, although at that time I had never seen a novel, detective or otherwise. I printed it out with a soft-lead pencil on lined paper, and it was about a boy who, for his protection, carried not a pistol but firecrackers. He solved crimes and gave things to poor people and doctors. The boy was also absolutely fearless.

I was given a great deal of ginger ale to drink because the doctor or mama or somebody thought that where burns were concerned, it had miraculous therapeutic value. This ginger ale was the store-bought kind, too, not some homemade concoction but wonderfully fizzy and capped in real bottles. Since Hoyet and I almost never saw anything from the store, I drank as much of it as they brought me, and they brought me a lot. I never learned to like it but could never get over my fascination with the bubbles that rose in the bottle under the yellow light hanging from the buggy frame.

But I was tired of being alone in bed, and since I was going into my second major hurt back to back, I decided I might as well assert myself.

Old Black Bill had sired several kids the previous spring, and one of them was himself black and a male, so I named him Old Black Bill, too, and he grew up with me under the buggy frame. No animal is allowed in a farmhouse in Bacon County, at least to my knowledge. Dogs stay in the yard. Cats usually live in the barn catching rats, and goats, well, goats only get in the house if they have first been butchered for the table.

But I had been scalded and I was special. And I knew even then that an advantage unused becomes no advantage at all. So I insisted Old Black Bill's kid be brought to my bed. I was only about three weeks into my recovery, and I thought that a goat would be good company.

They brought him in, and I fed him bits of hay and shelled corn under the buggy frame. We had long conversations. Or rather, I had long monologues and he, patiently chewing, listened.

The two tall windows at the foot of my bed opened onto a forty-acre field. Through the long winter days Old Black Bill and I watched it being prepared to grow another crop. First the cornstalks were cut by a machine with revolving blades, pulled by a single mule. Then two mules were hitched to a big rake, so big a man could ride on it. When all the stalks were piled and burned, the land had to be broken, completely turned under, the single hardest job on a farm for the farmer and his mules.

Every morning, when the light came up enough for me to see into the field, Willalee's daddy, Will, would already be out there behind a span of mules walking at remarkable speed, breaking the hard, clayish earth more than a foot deep. Sometimes daddy was out there plowing, too. Most of the time he was not.

Willalee's daddy would mark off an enormous square, fifteen acres or better, then follow that square around and around, always taking about a fourteen-inch bite with the turnplow so that when he went once around on each of the four sides of the square, the land still to be broken would have been reduced by fourteen inches on a side.

A man breaking land would easily walk thirty miles or more every day, day in and day out, until the entire farm was turned under. Even though the mules were given more corn and more hay than they were used to, they still lost weight. Every night when they were brought to the barn, they had high stiff ridges of salt outlining where their collars and backbands and trace chains and even their bridles had been.

With only my head out from under the buggy frame, continually dried and scabbed by the burning light, I watched the plows drag on through the long blowing days, Willalee's daddy moving dim as a ghost in the sickly half-light of the winter sun. Then after the longest, hardest time, the turnplow was taken out of the field, and the row marker brought in to lay off the lines in the soft earth where the corn would finally begin to show in the springtime. The row marker was made out of a trunk of a tree, sometimes a young oak, more often a pine, made by boring holes thirty-six inches apart and inserting a straight section of limb into each of the holes. Two holes were bored into the top of the log for handles and two holes in the front of the log for the shaves, between which the mule was hitched to drag the whole rig across the turned-under field, marking off four rows at a time.

Some farmers always had crops that grew in rows straight as a plumb line. Others didn't seem to care about it much, one way or the other. It was not unusual for a farmer bumping along in a wagon behind a steaming mule in the heat of summer to comment on how the rows were marked off on each farm he passed.

"Sumbitch, he musta been drunk when he laid them off."

"I bet he has to git drunk again ever time he plows that mess."

"I guess he figgers as much'll grow in a crooked row as a straight one."

For reasons I never knew, perhaps it was nothing more complicated than pride of workmanship, farmers always associated crooked rows with sorry people. So much of farming was beyond a man's control, but at least he could have whatever nature allowed to grow laid off in straight rows. And the feeling was that a man who didn't care enough to keep his rows from being crooked couldn't be much of a man.

In all the years in Bacon County, I never saw any rows straighter than the ones Willalee's daddy put down. He would take some point of reference at the other end of the field, say, a tree or a post, and then keep his eye on it as the mule dragged the row marker over the freshly broken ground, laying down those first critical rows. If the first four rows were straight, the rest of the field would be laid off straight, because the outside marker would always run in the last row laid down.

It didn't hurt to have a good mule. As was true of so many other things done on the farm, it was much easier if the abiding genius of a good mule was brought to bear on the job. There were mules in Bacon County that a blind man could have laid off straight rows behind. Such mules knew only one way to work: the right way. To whatever work they were asked to do, they brought a lovely exactitude, whether it was walking off rows, snaking logs, sledding tobacco without a driver, or any of the other unaccountable jobs that came their way during a crop year.

After the field was marked in a pattern of rows, Willalee's daddy came in with the middlebuster, a plow with a wing on both sides that opens up the row to receive first the fertilizer and then the seed. When all the rows had been plowed into shallow trenches, Will appeared in the field early one morning with a two-horse wagon full of guano, universally called *gyou-anner.* It was a commercial fertilizer sold in 200-pound bags, and Will had loaded the wagon before daylight by himself and brought it at sunup into the field where he unloaded one bag every three rows across the middle of the field.

Shortly after he left with the wagon, he came back with the guano strower and Willalee Bookatee. Willalee had a tin bucket with him. He plodded sleepily behind his daddy, the bucket banging at his knees. The guano strower was a kind of square wooden box that got smaller at the bottom, where there was a metal shaft shaped like a corkscrew and over which the guano had to fall as it poured into the trench opened by the middlebuster. The corkscrew shaft broke up any lumps in the fertilizer and made sure it kept flowing. Two little tongue-shaped metal plows at the back of the guano strower were set so that one ran on each side of the furrow. They covered up the thin stream of fertilizer the instant after it was laid down.

Willalee was out there to fill up the guano strower for his daddy, a bad, boring job and one reserved exclusively for small boys. Willalee would open one of the bags, fill the strower, and his daddy would head for the end of the row. As soon as he was gone, Willalee would go back to the sack, and since he could not pick up anything that heavy, he would have to dip the bucket full with his hands. Then he had nothing to do but shift from foot to foot, the fertilizer burning his arms and hands and before long his eyes, and wait for his daddy to come back down the row. When he did, Willalee would fill up the strower and the whole thing would be to do over again.

QUESTIONS

1. As we point out in the headnote, the subtitle of Crews's book from which this excerpt is taken is "the biography of a place." What details help to

establish setting, and what does this careful evocation of rural Georgia add to the story?

2. Crews seems to take a long time to get to the central event in the narrative, the scalding. Is this a flaw in the story's construction or an effective strategy? Explain.

3. The concluding third of the story, which speaks about Crews's being set up in bed, the plowing of the field, and the pet kid, seems anticlimactic after the horror of the scalding. Why does Crews conclude the narrative this way?

4. Is there a point to this story? What might it be?

5. At one point Crews writes, "the pain turned into something words cannot touch." But he does manage to use words that make the reader cringe. Carefully study the scalding scene and analyze exactly how Crews achieves this effect.

6. Crews draws an extremely realistic picture of farm life. Underline the concrete details and the farm terms he employs. Also, take note of the metaphors and similes he uses by circling them. How do they reflect farm life as well?

7. Crews is particularly skilled at depicting physical movement. Choose any paragraph that describes an action (hog slaughtering, the scalding, plowing) and analyze the verbs and adverbs Crews uses. Do they account for the cinematic quality of the essay?

SUGGESTIONS FOR WRITING

1. Write a narrative focusing on a time you or someone you know was in an accident or suffered some physical injury. Set up the situation as dramatically as possible, inventing details if you like, and then try to recreate exactly how you felt. Use "The Scalding" as a model.

2. Many of us have experienced days, weeks, or even months of inactivity while ill or recuperating from an illness. Write about such a period in your life. Describe the mixture of pleasure and unpleasantness such an experience usually entails. What discoveries and observations did you make while unable to participate in normal activities? Did you get a new perspective on the world?

Maxine Hong Kingston
THE QUIET GIRL
★ ★ ★

Kingston was born in 1940 in Stockton, California, the oldest child of Chinese immigrant parents. Her father, who had been a scholar in China, became part owner of a laundry, and her mother, trained in medicine and midwifery, worked along with her husband. The father responded to his diminishment in status with frequent bouts of depression, but Kingston's mother struggled to keep China a part of the family's American life. To that end she "talked story," telling endless tales of China, all with a particular moral or practical purpose. Kingston's desire to become a writer was fueled by these stories and by the difficulty of trying to live in two cultures at once.

In her first book, The Woman Warrior: Memoirs of a Girlhood Among Ghosts *(1976), from which "The Quiet Girl" is taken, Kingston mixes autobiography, fiction, and myth in an attempt to explain her childhood to the reader and to herself. As she said in a recent interview, "Some of the things that happen to us in life seem to have no meaning, but when you write them down you find the meanings for them: or, as you translate life into words, you force a meaning. Meaning is intrinsic in words and stories."*

Most of us eventually found some voice, however faltering. We invented an American-feminine speaking personality, except for that one girl who could not speak up even in Chinese school.

She was a year older than I and was in my class for twelve years. During all those years she read aloud but would not talk. Her older sister was usually beside her; their parents kept the older daughter back to protect the younger one. They were six and seven years old when they began school. Although I had flunked kindergarten, I was the same age as most other students in our class; my parents had probably lied about my age, so I had had a head start and came out even. My younger sister was in the class below me; we were normal ages and normally separated. The parents of the quiet girl, on the other hand, protected both daughters. When it sprinkled, they kept them home from school. The girls did not work for a living the way we did. But in other ways we were the same.

We were similar in sports. We held the bat on our shoulders until we walked to first base. (You got a strike only when you actually struck at the ball.) Sometimes the pitcher wouldn't bother to throw to us. "Automatic walk," the other children would call, sending us on our way. By fourth or fifth grade, though, some of us would try to hit the ball. "Easy out," the other kids would say. I hit the ball a couple of times. Baseball was nice in that there was a definite spot to run to after hitting the ball. Basketball confused me because when I caught the ball I didn't know whom to throw it to. "Me. Me," the kids would be yelling. "Over here." Suddenly it would occur to me I hadn't memorized which ghosts were on my team and which were on the other. When the kids said, "Automatic walk," the girl who was quieter than I kneeled with one end of the bat in each hand and placed it carefully on the plate. Then she dusted her hands as she walked to first base, where she rubbed her hands softly, fingers spread. She always got tagged out before second base. She would whisper-read but not talk. Her whisper was as soft as if she had no muscles. She seemed to be breathing from a distance. I heard no anger or tension.

I joined in at lunchtime when the other students, the Chinese too, talked about whether or not she was mute, although obviously she was not if she could read aloud. People told how *they* had tried *their* best to be friendly. *They* said hello, but if she refused to answer, well, they didn't see why they had to say hello anymore. She had no friends of her own but followed her sister everywhere, although people and she herself probably thought I was her friend. I also followed her sister about, who was fairly normal. She was almost two years older and read more than anyone else.

I hated the younger sister, the quiet one. I hated her when she was the last chosen for her team and I, the last chosen for my team. I hated her for her China doll hair cut. I hated her at music time for the wheezes that came out of her plastic flute.

One afternoon in the sixth grade (that year I was arrogant with talk, not knowing there were going to be high school dances and college seminars to set me back), I and my little sister and the quiet girl and her big sister stayed late after school for some reason. The cement was cooling, and the tetherball poles made shadows across the gravel. The hooks at the rope ends were clinking against the poles. We shouldn't have been so late; there was laundry work to do and Chinese school to get to by 5:00. The last time we had stayed late, my mother had phoned the police and told them we had been kidnapped by bandits. The radio stations broadcast our descriptions. I had to get home before she did that again. But sometimes if you loitered long enough in the schoolyard, the other children would have gone home and you could play with the equipment before the office took it away. We were chasing one another through the playground and in and out of the basement, where the playroom and lavatory were. During air raid drills (it was during the Korean War, which you knew about because every day the front page of the newspaper printed a map of Korea with the top part red and going up and down like a window shade), we curled up in this basement. Now everyone was gone. The playroom was army green and had nothing in it but a long trough with drinking spigots in rows. Pipes across the ceiling led to the drinking fountains and to the toilets in the next room. When someone flushed you could hear the water and other matter, which the children named, running inside the big pipe above the drinking spigots. There was one playroom for girls next to the girls' lavatory and one playroom for boys next to the boys' lavatory. The stalls were open and the toilets had no lids, by which we knew that ghosts have no sense of shame or privacy.

Inside the playroom the lightbulbs in cages had already been turned off. Daylight came in x-patterns through the caging at the windows. I looked out and, seeing no one in the schoolyard, ran outside to climb the fire escape upside down, hanging on to the metal stairs with fingers and toes.

I did a flip off the fire escape and ran across the schoolyard. The day was a great eye, and it was not paying much attention to me now. I could disappear with the sun; I could turn quickly sideways and slip into a different world. It seemed I could run faster at this time, and by evening I would be able to fly. As the afternoon wore on we could run into the forbidden places—the boys' big yard, the boys' playroom. We could go into the boys' lavatory and look at the urinals. The only time during school hours I had crossed the boys' yard was when a flatbed truck with a giant thing covered with canvas and tied down with ropes had parked across the street. The children had told one another that it was a gorilla in captivity; we couldn't decide whether the sign said "Trail of the Gorilla" or "Trial of the Gorilla." The thing was as big as a house. The teachers couldn't stop us from hysterically rushing to the fence and clinging to the wire mesh. Now I ran across the boys' yard clear to the Cyclone fence and thought about the hair that I had seen sticking out of the canvas. It was going to be summer soon, so you could feel that freedom coming on too.

I ran back into the girls' yard, and there was the quiet sister all by herself. I ran past her, and she followed me into the girls' lavatory. My footsteps rang hard against cement and tile because of the taps I had nailed into my shoes. Her footsteps were soft, padding after me. There was no one in the lavatory but the two of us. I ran all around the rows of twenty-five open stalls to make sure of that. No sisters. I think we must have been playing hide-and-go-seek. She was not good at hiding by herself and usually followed her sister; they'd hide in the same place. They must have gotten separated. In this growing twilight, a child could hide and never be found.

I stopped abruptly in front of the sinks, and she came running toward me before she could stop herself, so that she almost collided with me. I walked closer. She backed away, puzzlement, then alarm in her eyes.

"You're going to talk," I said, my voice steady and normal, as it is when talking to the familiar, the weak, and the small. "I am going to make you talk, you sissy-girl." She stopped backing away and stood fixed.

I looked into her face so I could hate it close up. She wore black bangs, and her cheeks were pink and white. She was baby-soft. I thought that I could put my thumb on her nose and push it bonelessly in, indent her face. I could poke dimples into her cheeks. I could work her face around like dough. She stood still, and I did not want to look at her face anymore; I hated fragility. I walked around her, looked her up and down the way the Mexican and Negro girls did when they fought, so tough. I hated her weak neck, the way it did not support her head but let it droop; her head would fall backward. I stared at the curve of her nape. I wished I was able to see what my own neck looked like from the back and sides. I hoped it did not look like hers; I wanted a stout neck. I grew my hair long to hide it in case it was a flower-stem neck. I walked around to the front of her to hate her face some more.

I reached up and took the fatty part of her cheek, not dough, but meat, between my thumb and finger. This close, and I saw no pores. "Talk," I said. "Are you going to talk?" Her skin was fleshy, like squid out of which the glassy blades of bones had been pulled. I wanted tough skin, hard brown skin. I had callused my hands; I had scratched dirt to blacken the nails, which I cut straight across to make stubby fingers. I gave her face a squeeze. "Talk." When I let go, the pink rushed back into my white thumbprint on her skin. I walked around to her side. "Talk!" I shouted into the side of her head. Her straight hair hung, the same all these years, no ringlets or braids or permanents. I squeezed her other cheek. "Are you? Huh? Are you going to talk?" She tried to shake her head, but I had hold of her face. She had no muscles to jerk away. Her skin seemed to stretch. I let go in horror. What if it came away in my hand? "No, huh?" I said, rubbing the touch of her off my fingers. "Say 'No,' then," I said. I gave her another pinch and a twist. "Say 'No.'" She shook her head, her straight hair turning with her head, not swinging side to side like the pretty girls'. She was so neat. Her neatness bothered me. I hated the way she folded the wax paper from her lunch; she did not wad her brown paper bag and her school papers. I hated her clothes—the blue pastel cardigan, the white blouse with the collar that lay flat over the cardigan, the homemade flat, cotton skirt she wore when everybody else was wearing flared skirts. I hated pastels; I would wear black always. I squeezed again, harder, even though her cheek had a weak rubbery feeling I did not like. I squeezed one cheek, then the other, back and forth until the tears ran out of her eyes as if I had pulled them out. "Stop crying," I said, but although she habitually followed me around, she did not obey. Her eyes dripped; her nose dripped. She wiped her eyes with her papery fingers. The skin on her hands and arms seemed powdery-dry, like tracing paper, onion paper. I hated her fingers. I could snap them like breadsticks. I pushed her hands down. "Say 'Hi,'" I said. "'Hi'. Like that. Say your name. Go ahead. Say it. Or are you stupid? You're so stupid, you don't know your own name, is that it? When I say, 'What's your name?' you just blurt it out, O.K.? What's your name?" Last year the whole class had laughed at a boy who couldn't fill out a form because he didn't know his father's name. The teacher sighed, exasperated and was very sarcastic, "Don't you notice things? What does your mother call him?" she said. The class laughed at how dumb he was not to notice things. "She calls him father of me," he said. Even we laughed although we knew that his mother did not call his father by name, and a son does not know his father's name. We laughed and were relieved that our parents had had the foresight to tell us some names we could give the teachers. "If you're not stupid," I said to the quiet girl, "what's you name?" She shook her head, and some hair caught in the tears; wet black hair stuck to the side of the pink and white face. I reached up (she was taller than I) and took a strand of hair. I pulled it. "Well, then, let's honk your hair," I said. "Honk. Honk." Then I pulled the other side—"ho-o-n-nk"—a long pull; "ho-o-n-n-nk"—a longer pull. I could see her little white ears, like white cutworms curled underneath the hair. "Talk!" I yelled into each cutworm.

I looked right at her. "I know you talk," I said. "I've heard you." Her eyebrows flew up. Something in those black eyes was startled, and I pursued it. "I was walking past your house when you didn't know I was there. I heard you yell in English and in Chinese. You weren't just talking. You were shouting. I heard you shout. You were saying, 'Where are you?' Say that again. Go ahead, just the way you did at home." I yanked harder on the hair, but steadily, not jerking. I did not want to pull it out. "Go ahead. Say, 'Where are you?' Say it loud enough for your sister to come. Call her. Make her come help you. Call her name. I'll stop if she comes. So call. Go ahead."

She shook her head, her mouth curved down, crying. I could see her tiny white teeth, baby teeth. I wanted to grow big strong yellow teeth. "You do have a tongue," I said. "So use it." I pulled the hair at her temples, pulled the tears out of her eyes. "Say, 'Ow' " I said. "Just 'Ow.' Say, 'Let go.' Go ahead. Say it. I'll honk you again if you don't say, 'Let me alone.' Say, 'Leave me alone,' and I'll let you go. I will. I'll let go if you say it. You can stop this anytime you want to, you know. All you have to do is tell me to stop. Just say, 'Stop.' You're just asking for it, aren't you? You're just asking for another honk. Well then, I'll have to give you another honk. Say, 'Stop.' " But she didn't. I had to pull again and again.

Sounds did come out of her mouth, sobs, chokes, noises that were almost words. Snot ran out of her nose. She tried to wipe it on her hands, but there was too much of it. She used her sleeve. "You're disgusting," I told her. "Look at you, snot streaming down your nose, and you won't say a word to stop it. You're such a nothing." I moved behind her and pulled the hair growing out of her weak neck. I let go. I stood silent for a long time. Then I screamed, "Talk!" I would scare the words out of her. If she had had little bound feet, the toes twisted under the balls, I would have jumped up and landed on them—crunch!—stomped on them with my iron shoes. She cried hard, sobbing aloud. "Cry, 'Mama,' " I said. "Come on. Cry, 'Mama.' Say, 'Stop it.' "

I put my finger on her pointed chin. "I don't like you. I don't like the weak little toots you make on your flute. Wheeze. Wheeze. I don't like the way you don't swing at the ball. I don't like the way you're the last one chosen. I don't like the way you can't make a fist for tetherball. Why don't you make a fist? Come on. Get tough. Come on. Throw fists." I pushed at her long hands; they swung limply at her sides. Her fingers were so long, I thought maybe they had an extra joint. They couldn't possibly make fists like other people's. "Make a fist," I said. "Come on. Just fold those fingers up; fingers on the inside, thumbs on the outside. Say something. Honk me back. You're so tall, and you let me pick on you.

"Would you like a hanky? I can't get you one with embroidery on it or crocheting along the edges, but I'll get you some toilet paper if you tell me to. Go ahead. Ask me. I'll get it for you if you ask." She did not stop crying. "Why don't you scream, 'Help'?" I suggested. "Say, 'Help.' Go ahead." She cried on. "O.K. O.K. Don't talk. Just scream, and I'll let you go. Won't that feel good? Go ahead. Like this." I screamed not too loudly. My voice hit the tile and rang it as if I had thrown a rock at it. The stalls opened wider and the toilets wider and darker. Shadows leaned at angles I had not seen before. I was very late. Maybe a janitor had locked me in with this girl for the night. Her black eyes blinked and stared, blinked and stared. I felt dizzy from hunger. We had been in this lavatory together forever. My mother would call the police again if I didn't bring my sister home soon. "I'll let you go if you say just one word," I said. "You can even say 'a' or 'the,' and I'll let you go. Come on. Please." She didn't shake her head anymore, only cried steadily, so much water coming out of her. I could see the two duct holes where the tears welled out. Quarts of tears but no words. I grabbed her by the shoulder. I could feel bones. The light was coming in queerly through the frosted glass with the chicken wire embedded in it. Her crying was like an animal's—a seal's—and it echoed around the basement. "Do you want to stay here all night?" I asked. "Your mother is wondering what happened to her baby. You wouldn't want to have her mad at you. You'd better say something." I shook her shoulder. I pulled her hair again. I squeezed her face. "Come on! Talk! Talk! Talk!" She didn't seem to feel it anymore when I pulled her hair. "There's nobody here but you and me. This isn't a classroom or a playground or a crowd. I'm just one person. You can talk in front of one person. Don't make me pull harder and harder until you talk." But her hair seemed to stretch; she did not say a word. "I'm going to pull harder. Don't make me pull anymore, or your hair will come out and you're going to be bald. Do you want to be bald? You don't want to be bald, do you?"

Far away, coming from the edge of town, I heard whistles blow. The cannery was changing shifts, letting out the afternoon people, and still we were here at school. It was a sad sound—work done. The air was lonelier after the sound died.

"Why won't you talk?" I started to cry. What if I couldn't stop, and everyone would want to know what happened? "Now look what you've done," I scolded. "You're going to pay for this. I want to know why. And you're going to tell me why. You don't see I'm trying to help you out, do you? Do you want to be like this, dumb (do you know what dumb means?), your whole life? Don't you ever want to be a cheerleader? Or a pompon girl? What are you going to do for a living? Yeah, you're going to have to work because you can't be a housewife. Somebody has to marry you before you can be a housewife. And you, you are a plant. Do you know that? That's all you are if you don't talk. If you don't talk, you can't have a personality. You'll have no personality and no hair. You've got to let people know you have a personality and a brain. You think somebody is going to take care of you all your stupid life? You think you'll always have your big sister? You think somebody's going to marry you, is that it? Well, you're not the type that gets dates, let alone gets married. Nobody's going to notice you. And you have to talk for interviews, speak right up in front of the boss. Don't you know that? You're so dumb. Why do I waste my time on you?" Sniffling and snorting, I couldn't stop crying and talking at the same time. I kept wiping my nose on my arm, my sweater lost somewhere (probably not worn because my mother said to wear a sweater). It seemed as if I had spent my life in that basement, doing the worst thing I had yet done to another person. "I'm doing this for your own good," I said. "Don't you dare tell anyone I've been bad to you. Talk. Please talk."

I was getting dizzy from the air I was gulping. Her sobs and my sobs were bouncing wildly off the tile, sometimes together, sometimes alternating. "I don't understand why you won't say just one word," I cried, clenching my teeth. My knees were shaking, and I hung on to her hair to stand up. Another time I'd stayed too late, I had had to walk around two Negro kids who were bonking each other's head on the concrete. I went back later to see if the concrete had cracks in it. "Look. I'll give you something if you talk. I'll give you my pencil box. I'll buy you some candy. O.K.? What do you want? Tell me. Just say it, and I'll give it to you. Just say, 'yes,' or, 'O.K.,' or, 'Baby Ruth.' " But she didn't want anything.

I had stopped pinching her cheek because I did not like the feel of her skin. I would go crazy if it came away in my hands. "I skinned her," I would have to confess.

Suddenly I heard footsteps hurrying through the basement, and her sister ran into the lavatory calling her name. "Oh, there you are," I said. "We've been waiting for you. I was only trying to teach her to talk. She wouldn't cooperate, though." Her sister went into one of the stalls and got handfuls of toilet paper and wiped her off. Then we found my sister, and we walked home together. "Your family really ought to force her to speak," I advised all the way home. "You mustn't pamper her."

The world is sometimes just, and I spent the next eighteen months sick in bed with a mysterious illness. There was no pain and no symptoms, though the middle line in my left palm broke in two. Instead of starting junior high school, I lived like the Victorian recluses I read about. I had a rented hospital bed in the living room, where I watched soap operas on TV, and my family cranked me up and down. I saw no one but my family, who took good care of me. I could have no visitors, no other relatives, no villagers. My bed was against the west window, and I watched the seasons change the peach tree. I had a bell to ring for help. I used a bedpan. It was the best year and a half of my life. Nothing happened.

But one day my mother, the doctor, said, "You're ready to get up today. It's time to get up and go to school." I walked about outside to get my legs working, leaning on a staff I cut from the peach tree. The sky and trees, the sun were immense—no longer framed by a window, no longer grayed with a fly screen. I sat down on the sidewalk in amazement—the night, the stars. But at school I had to figure out again how to talk. I met again the poor girl I had tormented. She had not changed. She wore the same clothes, hair cut, and manner as when we were in elementary school, no make-up on the pink and white face, while the other Asian girls were starting to tape their eyelids. She continued to be able to read aloud. But there was hardly any reading aloud anymore, less and less as we got into high school.

I was wrong about nobody taking care of her. Her sister became a clerk-typist and stayed unmarried. They lived with their mother and father. She did not have to leave the house except to go to the movies. She was supported. She was protected by her family, as they would normally have done in China if they could have afforded it, not sent off to school with strangers, ghosts, boys.

QUESTIONS

1. How does the anecdote of the softball game illustrate Kingston's feelings about the girl?

2. Kingston often digresses to make parenthetical comments and supply back-

ground information. How helpful is this to the reader's appreciation of the central event, her humiliation of the girl?

3. Kingston calls this "the worst thing I had yet done to another person." What has she learned from the experience? What are we supposed to take away from the story?

4. How does Kingston use language to evoke elementary school? Refer to specific imagery and concrete details, and compare her observations to your own memories.

SUGGESTIONS FOR WRITING

1. Dredge up the worst thing you have done to another person and tell the story as honestly as possible. Include in the narrative, implicitly or explicitly, what you have learned from recreating the incident.

2. Design a narrative around a conflict between two contrasting characters. You can use a first-person voice, as Kingston has, or a third-person narrator. Remember to have the essay lead to some resolution and point.

3. Most of us have had an exceptionally close friendship with another person come to an end, for any one of a number of reasons, and some of us can remember an equally intense enmity for another person that also ceased. Write a narrative depicting a relationship like either of these and try to account for its ending.

Susan Allen Toth
CHRISTMAS VACATION
★ ★ ★

Born in Ames, Iowa, in 1940, Toth's major published works have been autobiographical. In Blooming: A Small Town Girlhood *(1981), she wrote an acclaimed memoir of growing up in a post-World War II American small town.* Ivy Days: Making My Way Out East *(1984), from which the following narrative is excerpted, recounts her life as she moves beyond the confines of Ames to the much different geographical, intellectual, and social territory of Smith College in Massachusetts. Toth, now a Professor of English at Macalaster College, is particularly skilled at recreating the often contradictory and rapidly changing feelings of youth: bewilderment, self-assurance, insecurity, fear, intense pleasure. "Christmas Vacation" describes an experience that is familiar to all of us and asks a universal question: "Can we ever really go home again?"*

When the morning of Christmas vacation arrived, with its promise of a noon dismissal, our whole house was in an uproar. Suitcases were piled in the downstairs hall, boots and books jumbled in heaps, coats stacked on living-room chairs for quick get-aways. Taxis, booked weeks in advance, would be waiting outside Seelye Hall for the girls who had tight travel connections. Luckily, I had arranged to share a cab, snatching an offered space from a girl in my History class. A whir of excitement, rare in Lawrence House, filled the halls, as we tacitly abandoned any pretense at Quiet Hours and slammed doors, yelled farewells, laughed and jostled each other down the stairs with our suitcases.

Right after breakfast, those of us who were traveling any distance gathered in the dining room to make our bag lunches. The cooks put out a large glass bowl of peanut butter, another of tuna-fish-and-mayonnaise, and a third of egg salad, next to an institutional-sized loaf of slightly stale white bread. In an even larger bowl were oranges, bananas, and a few shiny red apples. The apples looked so appealing they went fast, as I learned when I quickly snatched the last two. Imagining two impoverished days on trains, I slathered half a dozen sandwiches together. I tried not to remind myself I didn't like either egg salad or mayonnaise. For four years, vacation after vacation, Christmas and Easter and summer, the fare on the dining-room table never changed. Peanut butter, tuna fish, egg salad. Telling myself it was free, I always packed twice as much as I could eat. After only a few hours on a warm, crowded train, the egg salad got soggy, the tuna fish smelled funny, the bananas turned brown, and most of all, the sweetish apples were soft and mealy. The smell of apple permeated everything. Even when I tried tinfoil or plastic bags, the apples seemed to tinge every other bit of food. Even today when I think of trains, I still smell the slightly sickening, cidery aroma of softening apples. Yet, seeing those bright red apples in the bowl, year after year, I could never resist them. They signified something about health, vacation, and freedom.

That first Christmas vacation I was too excited to eat right away. When I finally passed the hurdle of changing trains in Springfield, walked down the tunnel to the right track, and found my seat on the New York Central's New England States, I settled back with a great sigh of relief for the overnight trip to Chicago. I watched the changing scenery in a daze of relaxation and happiness. No longer did I need to crane my neck and watch like a tourist for new sights. I had been this way before. The country didn't exactly look familiar, perhaps because I'd passed much of it before during the night, but I didn't care. I didn't need to study the landscape. At one end was Northampton. At the other end was home.

Though I had of course packed my textbooks, I left them in my bag. Somehow Smith seemed to disappear as soon as we left the station in Springfield. I was blissfully alone, able to measure out the miles by watching, daydreaming and dozing between cities. Consulting my timetable, I checked each stop, numbering them like beads, moving them onto another side of an abacus I'd invented. That was Syracuse, Syracuse is gone, no more Syracuse. Now Buffalo, Buffalo in two hours, after Buffalo I'll try to sleep. All that will be left then is Cleveland; after Cleveland, Chicago; and then I'm practically home.

When the hours grew long, I read. Every vacation I packed special paperback books for my train trips, buying them weeks in advance and savoring their possibilities as they lay, untouched, on my shelf. I only chose books I couldn't justify reading otherwise, books that I'd never find in Freshman English or Creative Writing or Introduction to the Novel. One year it was Agatha Christie, another *The Silver Chalice,* once—as a senior—*Love without Fear.* As if my own emotional state weren't pitched high enough, I plunged deep into those feverish worlds, vibrating to passions that drifted on as endlessly as the miles, pausing now and then to look out the window and muse about romance, sex, mystery. To keep myself company during meals, I continued to read. Through rape, regret, and salvation, I munched absentmindedly on stale sandwiches, trying to forget the smell of apples. Underneath it all, I always heard the comforting sound of the wheels, carrying me home.

When I reached Chicago, everything speeded up. As soon as I'd left the New York Central, I was back in country that I knew. The few Smith girls I'd recognized on the New England States got off by Chicago, heading to unknown destinations. I went alone to the LaSalle Street Station to catch the Chicago and Northwestern.

Before long we crossed the Mississippi into Iowa. Crawling through the Chicago suburbs, then Rock Island-Moline-Davenport, the train was stuck in urban grime, a harsh industrial landscape that didn't look so different from Cleveland or Buffalo. The Midwest hadn't had much snow that Christmas, and everything seemed grayish-brown and dirty. Looking out the window, I didn't think I had much to celebrate. But soon the wheels of the train sounded more encouraging, as they hurried faster and faster, covering ground with exuberant speed. Now the towns disappeared, and mostly I saw fields, farms, and the gentle curve of an infinite horizon. Smoke and soot evaporated, and the world looked clean again.

I no longer tried to read. During the last hour of the trip, I pulled my wool cap tightly over my ears, buttoned my coat, and stood outside the cars on a swaying metal platform. After two days in stale coaches, the fresh air, cold and crisp, felt wonderful. Below my feet, the deafening sound of metal on metal told me what was happening was real. I blinked and stared, my eyes watering with cold and excitement. Right there, so close I could almost touch them, were silos and fences and snow-sprinkled stubble, grazing black cattle and old-fashioned corncribs and rows of Butler storage bins. I was practically home.

Most of all, I breathed in lungfuls of space, taking huge breaths as if I'd come from a dark submarine into a world of bright skies. In later years, when I sometimes traveled on night trains, I sensed a loneliness about that Midwestern space, as I watched the separate lights of distant farms flutter and disappear in the darkness. But even then, with a sadness I could not explain, I was glad the land stretched so far. Out there, in the country where I belonged, was all the room I felt I would ever need.

Soon we were passing through towns whose basketball teams I had booed, whose cheerleaders I might recognize, whose Presbyterian youth fellowships had attended our synod conferences. I even welcomed the swinging signposts at the tiny stations we whipped past, because they bore names I recognized: Mechanicsville, Belle Plaine, Tama, State Center. As our train meandered through the center of larger towns, I saw people on the streets who looked like people in Ames, doing their shopping, driving their cars, or standing at corners. Most of them didn't notice us, and I was aware how removed they were from the excitement I felt. Of course, they couldn't know I was going home. I was glad to see the store signs, Sears, Super Valu, Our Own Hardware; I liked the new developments with their tract ramblers dotting the edges of town; I wanted to wave at an old brick school that looked just like Louise Crawford Elementary, back in Ames.

It was late afternoon when the train slowed for its arrival in Ames. Hugging myself and stamping my feet, I leaned as far over the platform as I dared to catch my first glimpse of the station. Suddenly I saw them: a huddled group, my best friend, Peggy O'Reilly and five or six others, with my mother standing just to the side. They began waving and screaming as soon as they saw me, and I waved and screamed back. Then the train stopped, I was in the midst of hugs and laughter, registering startled impressions of different haircuts and new winter coats, talking with everyone at once. My mother cleared her throat. "Don't I get a hug too?" she said with a smile. Unlike my friends, she had not run or pushed, so they had reached me first. I felt an awful pang. How long I had anticipated the moment when I would first see her! But she was smiling, and I put my guilt aside.

That moment at the train station, when I plunged into the welcoming circle of my old friends, was the highlight of my Christmas vacation. Happy as I was to pull into our driveway, plop my bags down in my old room, and sink into my chair at the kitchen table, I was somehow more relieved than ecstatic. I wasn't sure why I felt faintly let down. Everything was just as I'd remembered, though perhaps a little more cluttered, just a bit smaller. I noticed a worn spot on the rug and a heap of Mother's magazines on my bookcase. So much had happened to me, so much had changed, I thought, and yet I wasn't sure how I could even begin to explain. I made an effort, told a few stories about Smith that sounded flat out of context, and realized sometime that first evening that I probably couldn't find the words—or the time—to describe what it was like for me out East.

Though I told my mother what I thought she might want to hear, I had less success with my friends. We found we were not nearly as interested in listening to each other as when we'd promised in our letters, "I'll tell you all about it when I see you." When my old friend Christy described the giant papier-mâché panda the Pi Phis had built for Northwestern's Homecoming, my mind began to wander. As I tried to evoke our exciting bicycle trip on Mountain Day, Christy interrupted, politely, with a bit of news about the Northwestern marching band. Though Peggy O'Reilly and I shared details about our college roommates, I think both of us felt surprisingly estranged. After only a few months, our new worlds had swallowed us up.

But we had little time for introspection. Every hour the phone rang, till Mother sighed in exasperation, as if I were thirteen again. People dropped in all through the day, family friends, neighbors, younger friends still in high school. At night the old gang gathered for party after party, mostly informal get-togethers in someone's living room or in the booths of the Rainbow Cafe or at round tables in the Oak Grill. A few of my former boyfriends called for private dates, a movie or ice-skating or just "going out." Somewhere in the midst of all the commotion was Christmas, a short lull, with the usual stockings, turkey dinner, and visiting relatives. On the night of the Christmas Formal, an annual high-school event, three or four of us decided, for a lark, to visit the Great Hall of the Iowa State Union, where it was always held. Once we'd gone to the Christmas Dance as eager participants, nervous, anticipating the night for weeks. Now, dressed in ordinary coats and boots, we shuffled outside the door for a few minutes, watching the new sophomores, juniors, and seniors whirling and dipping inside in their tulles and tuxedos. A few kids recognized us and waved, but we didn't try to go into the hall. Feeling subdued, and old, we left the Union and headed downtown to see if we could spot anyone coming out of the Sportsman's Lounge.

After Christmas, I began to feel scared. The days had gone so quickly. In less than a week, I would have to go down to the train station again, to leave Ames once more and return to Smith. I had done almost none of my backlogged work for midyear exams. My mother said she'd hardly seen me. I had promised Bob we'd go out once more, and Peggy said we still needed to have a good long talk. As I looked ahead to January, I could not imagine surviving the rigors of five three-hour exams. I had never taken any essay test longer than an hour. I was sure I wouldn't know enough to fill all that time and all those bluebooks. I was three weeks behind in Ancient History, four chapters in Geology. I didn't know the French subjunctive, and I'd been conning my way through class discussions about Henry James. What would happen to me?

One night I broke down in front of my mother and cried. I didn't want to go back, I said. She listened sympathetically, her face creased with concern. "Well, I didn't dream you felt this way," she finally said. "You don't have to stay there, you know. Perhaps you should come home and go to Iowa State, or transfer somewhere else at the end of the year." Those did not seem to me like possible solutions. I knew I had to go back. I tried to recover; I didn't want Mother to worry. "No, of course it's not really that bad," I said. "It's a great school. I know that. I wouldn't think of not going back."

Getting on the train on that cold January morning was one of the hardest things I have ever done. Most of my friends had already left, and only my mother, sister, and Peggy came down to the station to see me off. Mother had packed a special lunch bag, with brownies, home-made bread, and an apple she said wouldn't smell. As I hugged my mother good-bye, I wished I had spent more time at home with her. I promised Peggy I would write soon. I knew she hated going back to the convent, and I felt bad for her too. When the train pulled out, I stood on the outside platform, waving, tears welling up, with that recognizable rock in my stomach, until the station had faded from sight. Inside the coach I cried for a while, blowing hard into a handful of Kleenex, hoping no one would notice. I didn't think I could ever be more miserable.

But within a few hours, I began to feel better. I was an old hand at train travel now, and I knew where we were going. After a while I opened my Ancient History book to begin some cramming. It was going to be a long, dull trip, and I might as well make some use of it. I could look forward to Mother's lunch, and maybe tonight I'd eat in the dining car with some money she'd given me. At least I was going to get the exams over with.

When the taxi stopped in front of Lawrence House two days later, I was astonished to find that I felt excited. I hurried up the stairs. When I checked my box, I found some mail waiting. A new calendar had been posted, listing the upcoming foreign films, chapel talks, and lectures. The wooden floors in Lawrence, waxed in our absence, gleamed as bright as they had in September. A fresh linen napkin was rolled in my napkin box. Someone's *New York Times* had been tossed on a chair. I grabbed it, realizing I hadn't seen one for two weeks. On the landing, I studied the week's menus, written in Mrs. Stevens' elegant script, and was pleased to see two of my favorites coming soon, cherry crisp and sticky buns. Upstairs in my hall I saw a sheet of paper tacked to the door of my room. Sophie had written a poem to welcome me back. "I'm here already, so come see me right away," she had penciled on the bottom.

As I read Sophie's poem, I grinned at her funny verses. She had decorated the note with little stick figures. I was so glad she was already here. I dumped my bags in my room, glancing at the furniture to see that nothing had changed. Then I dashed across the hall to see if Sophie and I could go together to Friendly's Ice Cream Parlor for supper. I wanted to have a Big Beef, rare ground sirloin dripping with juice on soppy buttered toast. We didn't have anything quite like that in Ames. Although I didn't want to admit it to Sophie, who knew how homesick I'd been all fall, I was oddly relieved to be back in Lawrence. This, I guessed, was where I belonged now. Somehow, I felt I had come home.

QUESTIONS

1. Why does Toth decide to emphasize certain incidents and give minimal space to others? Support your response. (For example, the Christmas celebration is described in only one sentence, while the food she will take on the trip gets a paragraph of description.)

2. What contrasts are drawn between the East and the Midwest?

3. Why is the trip a disappointment and what does Toth realize as a result?

4. The second paragraph of the essay is intensely descriptive. Analyze Toth's use of imagery there. What significance does her emphasis on food have in this paragraph and elsewhere?

5. How does Toth use concrete details almost as a strategy of organization to measure the progress of her journey? Give plenty of examples.

6. How does Toth organize her narrative? Point out the key transitional words and phrases. To what extent does the story conform to the classical pattern of rising action, climax, and resolution? (See the introduction to this chapter.)

SUGGESTIONS FOR WRITING

1. Tell the story of a time when you were anticipating something that eventually turned out to be a disappointment. Try to use Toth's structure as a model.

2. Through her story Toth illustrates how going away to college represents a turning point in our lives. Write a narrative that dramatizes a similar turning point in your life.

STUDENT ESSAY

Jim Vermeulen
SEEING GRANDMA
★ ★ ★

Jim Vermeulen came to writing relatively late in life and by a decidedly unconventional route. Born in Queens, New York, in 1946, Vermeulen entered the New York City Police Department in 1964 after graduating from high school. He served on the force for the next twenty years, ultimately attaining the rank of Detective Sergeant, assigned to the Borough of Brooklyn.

In 1983, Vermeulen decided to return to school and entered the Adult College Education program at Queens College, the City University of New York. In July, 1985, he suffered a heart attack, retired from the Police Department, and became a full-time student at Queens. It wasn't until the fall semester of 1986 that he began writing seriously, producing short pieces of fiction based on his experiences with the NYPD. Vermeulen is currently completing his college degree with the intention of establishing a new career as a teacher and writer.

"What does she look like, Daddy?"

I don't remember what he said and I'm not sure I even heard his description. What I saw was a beautiful silver-haired woman with creamy skin and an understanding, patient smile. Though we had never met, I instinctively knew certain things about her. She was addicted to kissing and hugging small children. When she wasn't hugging and kissing, she was baking cookies in her kitchen. And, no matter how close it was to dinner, my grandmother would sneak me a cookie with a wink and a smile. She would know that cookies were more important than a dinner.

I was only six when I took the subway ride through New York City to 145th Street and Broadway, an upper-middle-class neighborhood in those days, my mind filled with anticipation and joy at finally seeing my father's mother. She had just returned from Belgium with a man my father called Uncle Louie. The train hurled along, causing my body to ricochet from the window frame to my father's side and back again until my shoulder ached. "Daddy, are you sure we're going the right way?" I yelled to overcome the roar of the speeding cars. "Yes," he said, patting my knee. He told me stirring tales of his childhood and of his travels between New York and Europe while I looked at the walls of the dirty train and the posters advertising cigarettes and chewing gum. From a poster behind the slow-spining ceiling fan, a young, pretty Miss Subway smiled down at us.

My father was a huge man with broad shoulders and big hands. His real hair color could only be seen when his crew cut grew out; the rest of the time he seemed to have grey hair. He always wore a jacket and tie when he travelled and that day he wore a blue jacket and red tie. There was always a special scent to my father, a comforting smell that is difficult to describe except to say that it was a smell that stays in your mind for your whole life, like the feel of your first baseball glove or the comfort that comes from your bed after a long trip. After a while, he lifted me off the heated cane seat and onto his lap. Through the dirty window, we watched a black tunnel swallow us up. His strong arms held me close. I shut my eyes and saw myself standing at the railing of a large ocean liner, waving to the crowd on the pier. Balloons floated up into the cloudless blue sky. I was sailing to Europe, as my father had when he was a boy. My grandmother stood proudly beside me, her hand clasping my shoulder.

"Jim, wake up. We're here." My father shook me. I leaped off his legs, still groggy from sleep, and looked for the silver-haired woman.

"This is only the station," he laughed. "We still have to walk two blocks to her apartment. On the way we'll stop and get a cake. You can pick it out."

The tall, silver-haired woman leaned over the counter and smiled at me. Behind her stood the rows of freshly baked breads: long thin Italian, fat rye, black breads, brown breads and breads whose dough looked knotted together. Below them were baskets of different size rolls, seeded and unseeded, hard and soft.

"Well, little fella, what would you like?" she said in a deep German accent.

"A cake,—it's for my grandma!" I yelled up over the counter.

"Well, then, you must pick a very special one." The woman looked at my father and smiled.

I leaned both of my hands on the long glass display case and looked at the assortment of beautifully decorated cakes and pies. On the top shelf the apple, cherry and blueberry pies stood next to each other. I inched slowly from one end to the other, dragging my nose along the glass, past the white coconut cake, the lemon chiffon and into the area of the chocolate icing. My eyes grew wider as I saw the large dark chocolate cake among the mochas. It was decorated with pink and yellow flowers. "That one," I pointed.

The woman took the cake out of the case and lowered it carefully into a large white box. She tied the box with a string which she broke with her hand. Then she pulled out a tray and called me to come around the corner.

"Any boy who's going to see his grandma deserves a nice cookie," she said, presenting the long tray covered with yellow star-shaped cookies. Centered in the middle of each cookie was a bright red cherry. I took one. "Take another," the woman winked, "for later. Put it in your pocket."

"Thank you," I said, ready to explode. Leaving the store I thought, if this woman is so nice, imagine how wonderful my own grandmother will be! I pulled at my father's hand, trying to make him go faster. Laughing, he picked up the pace.

The enormous old grey building with the tall and narrow windows stood in front of us. The stone at the entrance was shaped like leaves and flowers. The doors were a dark wood with a dozen window panes. Two large brass handles shone in the sunlight. We entered.

"What floor, please?" the elevator man asked.

"I'm going to visit my grandmother," I almost shouted. "She lives on the sixth floor and she's waiting for me."

"Well, we better get going then," the man smiled at my father.

I sat on the corner stool with a boost from the uniformed man. He looked like a general. It was the most beautiful elevator I had ever seen. Gleaming brown wood and mirrors surrounded my father and me. At last the bell to the elevator sounded and before the door opened, I was already running.

"Here's 6C, Daddy," I yelled. I stood on my toes and stretched my arm as far as it would go. My fingertip pressed the bell to the apartment. I also knocked on the door. I can still remember the sound of the footsteps coming. The door sprang open and there stood a tall, silver-haired woman dressed in a gray flowered blouse and black skirt. She wore heavy black shoes. She smiled at my father. Taking the bakery box and placing it on a small table near the door, she kissed him on the cheek.

"Mom, this is my son," he said proudly, pushing me in front of him, hands on my shoulders. "Jim, say hello to your grandmother."

After all the anticipation and excitement, I suddenly became very shy and lowered my head and eyes. But it didn't matter. I knew she would pick me up and hug me and cover my face with kisses and then lead me into the kitchen and to the home-made cookies.

"Hello, Jim," she said, patting me on the head. "Pete, I wanted to talk to you. It's very important." My father followed her into the apartment. His shoulders slumped. Then she stopped and looked at me, still standing at the entrance, near the white box. "Jim, here's a dime. Go to the corner and get yourself a soda or something." My father didn't say anything.

The elevator man opened the door and I walked to the front of the building and sat on the stoop. I reached into my pocket and felt the small cookie with the cherry in the middle. I took it out. I thought of the bakery woman with the silver hair and pressed the cookie to my lips. I began to cry.

QUESTIONS

1. Vermeulen skillfully creates the voice and perspective of a 6-year-old child in this narration. Point to specific phrases, details, and incidents that make it clear you are seeing the world through the eyes of a small boy.

2. Why does Vermeulen include the anecdotes about the woman in the bakery and the elevator man? What do these anecdotes contribute to the narrative?

3. Were you surprised by the way the story ended? Why or why not?

4. Look at the details Vermeulen gives you about his father and his grand-mother. What generalizations do they allow you to make about the character of each? From the details you get about the boy, can you generalize about his character?

5. What is the meaning or the theme of this narration? Does Vermeulen give you enough information to decide? Would the story be more or less moving and memorable if he had told you the meaning explicitly?

SUGGESTIONS FOR WRITING

1. Write a story about something or someone you idealized or romanticized when you were a child, but subsequently came to see in a more realistic light. Tell the story from the point of view of a child. Then tell the same story again, this time from the point of view of a young adult, remembering the experience and commenting on your disillusionment.

2. Write a narration about an incident—or several brief incidents—that expresses or reveals the nature of your relationship with a grandmother, grand-father, or another older relative.

Toni Cade Bambara
THE LESSON
★ ★ ★

One of America's leading black feminist writers, Toni Cade Bambara was born in New York City. She received her B.A. from Queens College, then studied theater in Florence, mime in Paris, and dance and film back in New York. She has worked as an investigator for the New York Depart-ment of Welfare, as a recreation director in the psychiatry department of Metropolitan Hospital, as an English teacher in a college program for underprepared freshmen, as director of a preschool program, and most recently as a college professor. These varied experiences have no doubt shaped Bambara's writing: close observation, realistic depictions of com-mon people and their manner of speaking, and commitment to social equality all characterize her work. She is particularly known for her portrayals of "black women at the edge of a new awareness . . . who create their own choices about the kinds of women they will be," according to Mary Helen Washington in her review of Bambara's The Sea Birds Are Still Alive, *a 1977 collection of stories. Her most recent novel is* The Salt Eaters *(1980).*

Sylvia, the narrator of "The Lesson," which was first published in Gorilla, My Love *(1972), is, to use Washington's phrase, "at the edge of awareness." Although the story is fictional, the reader senses that Sylvia is the kind of smart, tough product of the city streets who might be a younger version of the author herself.*

———

Back in the days when everyone was old and stupid or young and foolish and me and Sugar were the only ones just right, this lady moved on our block with nappy hair and proper speech and no makeup. And quite naturally we laughed at her, laughed the way we did at the junk man who went about his business like he was some big-time president and his sorry-ass horse his secretary. And we kinda hated her too, hated the way we did the winos who cluttered up our parks and pissed on our handball walls and stank up our hallways and stairs so you couldn't halfway play hide-and-seek without a goddamn gas mask. Miss Moore was her name. The only woman on the block with no first name. And she was black as hell, cept for her feet, which were fish-white and spooky. And she was always planning these boring-ass things for us to do, us being my cousin, mostly, who lived on the block cause we all moved North the same time and to the same apartment then spread out gradual to breathe. And our parents would yank our heads into some kinda shape and crisp up our clothes so we'd be presentable for travel with Miss Moore, who always looked like she was going to church, though she never did. Which is just one of things the grown-ups talked about when they talked behind her back like a dog. But when she came calling with some sachet she'd sewed up or some gingerbread she'd made or some book, why then they'd all be too embarrassed to turn her down and we'd get handed over all spruced up. She'd been to college and said it was only right that she should take responsibility for the young ones' education, and she not even related by marriage or blood. So they'd go for it. Specially Aunt Gretchen. She was the main gofer in the family. You got some old dumb shit foolishness you want somebody to go for, you send for Aunt Gretchen. She been screwed into the go-along for so long, it's a blood-deep natural thing with her. Which is how she got saddled with me and Sugar and Junior in the first place while our mothers were in a la-de-da apartment up the block having a good ole time.

So this one day Miss Moore rounds us all up at the mailbox and it's puredee hot and she's knockin herself out about arithmetic. And school suppose to let up in summer I heard, but she don't never let up. And the starch in my pinafore scratching the shit outta me and I'm really hating this nappy-head bitch and her goddamn college degree. I'd much rather go to the pool or to the show where it's cool. So me and Sugar leaning on the mailbox being surly, which is a Miss Moore word. And Flyboy checking out what everybody brought for lunch. And Fat Butt already wasting his peanut-butter-and-jelly sandwich like the pig he is. And Junebug punchin on Q.T.'s arm for potato chips. And Rosie Giraffe shifting from one hip to the other waiting for somebody to step on her foot or ask her if she from Georgia so she can kick ass, preferably Mercedes'. And Miss Moore asking us do we know what money is, like we a bunch of retards. I mean real money, she say, like it's only poker chips or monopoly papers we lay on the grocer. So right away I'm tired of this and say so. And would much rather snatch Sugar and go to the Sunset and terrorize the West Indian kids and take their hair ribbons and their money too. And Miss Moore files that remark away for next week's lesson on brotherhood, I can tell. And finally I say we oughta get to the subway cause it's cooler and besides we might meet some cute boys. Sugar done swiped her mama's lipstick, so we ready.

So we heading down the street and she's boring us silly about what things cost and what our parents make and how much goes for rent and how money ain't divided up right in this country. And then she gets to the part about we all poor and live in the slums, which I don't feature. And I'm ready to speak on that, but she steps out in the street and hails two cabs just like that. Then she hustles half the crew in with her and hands me a five-dollar bill and tells me to calculate 10 percent tip for the driver. And we're off. Me and Sugar and Junebug and Flyboy hangin out the window and hollering to everybody, putting lipstick on each other cause Flyboy a faggot anyway, and making farts with our sweaty armpits. But I'm mostly trying to figure how to spend this money. But they all fascinated with the meter ticking and Junebug starts laying bets as to how much it'll read when Flyboy can't hold his breath no more. Then Sugar lays bets as to how much it'll be when we get there. So I'm stuck. Don't nobody want to go for my plan, which is to jump out at the next light and run off to the first bar-b-que we can find. Then the driver tells us to get the hell out cause we there already. And the meter reads eighty-five cents. And I'm stalling to figure out the tip and Sugar say give him a dime. And I decide he don't need it bad as I do, so later for him. But then he tries to take off with Junebug foot still in the door so we talk about his mama something ferocious. Then we check out that we on Fifth Avenue and everybody dressed up in stockings. One lady in a fur coat, hot as it is. White folks crazy.

"This is the place," Miss Moore say, presenting it to us in the voice she uses at the museum. "Let's look in the windows before we go in."

"Can we steal?" Sugar asks very serious like she's getting the ground rules squared away before she plays. "I beg your pardon," say Miss Moore, and we fall out. So she leads us around the windows of the toy store and me and Sugar screamin, "This is mine, that's mine, I gotta have that, that was made for me, I was born for that," till Big Butt drowns us out.

"Hey, I'm going to buy that there."

"That there? You don't even know what it is, stupid."

"I do so," he say punchin on Rosie Giraffe. "It's a microscope."

"Whatcha gonna do with a microscope, fool?"

"Look at things."

"Like what, Ronald?" ask Miss Moore. And Big Butt ain't got the first notion. So here go Miss Moore gabbing about the thousands of bacteria in a drop of water and the somethinorother in a speck of blood and the million and one living things in the air around us is invisible to the naked eye. And what she say that for? Junebug go to town on that "naked" and we rolling. Then Miss Moore ask what it cost. So we all jam into the window smudgin it up and the price tag say $300. So then she ask how long'd take for Big Butt and Junebug to save up their allowances. "Too long," I say. "Yeh," adds Sugar, "outgrown it by that time." And Miss Moore say no, you never outgrow learning instruments. "Why, even medical students and interns and," blah, blah, blah. And we ready to choke Big Butt for bringing it up in the first damn place.

"This here costs four hundred eighty dollars," say Rosie Giraffe. So we pile up all over her to see what she pointin out. My eyes tell me it's a chunk of glass cracked with something heavy, and different-color inks dripped into the splits, then the whole thing put into a oven or something. But for $480 it don't make sense.

"That's a paperweight made of semi-precious stones fused together under tremendous pressure," she explains slowly, with her hands doing the mining and all the factory work.

"So what's a paperweight?" asks Rosie Giraffe.

"To weigh paper with, dumbbell," say Flyboy, the wise man from the East.

"Not exactly," say Miss Moore, which is what she say when you warm or way off too. "It's to weigh paper down so it won't scatter and make your desk untidy." So right away me and Sugar curtsy to each other and then to Mercedes who is more the tidy type.

"We don't keep paper on top of the desk in my class," say Junebug, figuring Miss Moore crazy or lyin one.

"At home, then," she say. "Don't you have a calendar and a pencil case and a blotter and a letter-opener on your desk at home where you do your homework?" And she know damn well what our homes look like cause she nosys around in them every chance she gets.

"I don't even have a desk," say Junebug. "Do we?"

"No. And I don't get no homework neither," say Big Butt.

"And I don't even have a home," say Flyboy like he do at school to keep the white folks off his back and sorry for him. Send this poor kid to camp posters, is his specialty.

"I do," says Mercedes. "I have a box of stationery on my desk and a picture of my cat. My godmother bought the stationery and the desk. There's a big rose on each sheet and the envelopes smell like roses."

"Who wants to know about your smelly-ass stationery," say Rosie Giraffe fore I can get my two cents in.

"It's important to have a work area all your own so that . . ."

"Will you look at this sailboat, please," say Flyboy, cuttin her off and pointin to the thing like it was his. So once again we tumble all over each other to gaze at this magnificent thing in the toy store which is just big enough to maybe sail two kittens across the pond if you strap them to the posts tight. We all start reciting the price tag like we in assembly. "Handcrafted sailboat of fiberglass at one thousand one hundred ninety-five dollars."

"Unbelievable," I hear myself say and am really stunned. I read it again for myself just in case the group recitation put me in a trance. Same thing. For some reason this pisses me off. We look at Miss Moore and she lookin at us, waiting for I dunno what.

"Who'd pay all that when you can buy a sailboat set for a quarter at Pop's, a tube of glue for a dime, and a ball of string for eight cents? It must have a motor and a whole lot else besides," I say. "My sailboat cost me about fifty cents."

"But will it take water?" say Mercedes with her smart ass.

"Took mine to Alley Pond Park once," say Flyboy. "String broke, Lost it. Pity."

"Sailed mine in Central Park and it keeled over and sank. Had to ask my father for another dollar."

"And you got the strap," laugh Big Butt. "The jerk didn't even have a string on it. My old man wailed on his behind."

Little Q.T. was staring hard at the sailboat and you could see he wanted it bad. But he too little and somebody'd just take it from him. So what the hell. "This boat for kids, Miss Moore?"

"Parents silly to buy something like that just to get all broke up," say Rosie Giraffe.

"That much money it should last forever," I figure.

"My father'd buy it for me if I wanted it."

"Your father, my ass," say Rosie Giraffe getting a chance to finally push Mercedes.

"Must be rich people shop here," say Q.T.

"You are a very bright boy," say Flyboy. "What was your first clue?" And he rap him on the head with the back of his knuckles, since Q.T. the only one he could get away with. Though Q.T. liable to come up behind you years later and get his licks in when you half expect it.

"What I want to know is," I says to Miss Moore though I never talk to her, I wouldn't give the bitch that satisfaction, "is how much a real boat costs? I figure a thousand'd get you a yacht any day."

"Why don't you check that out," she says, "and report back to the group?" Which really pains my ass. If you gonna mess up a perfectly good swim day least you could do is have some answers. "Let's go in," she say like she got something up her sleeve. Only she don't lead the way. So me and Sugar turn the corner to where the entrance is, but when we get there I kinda hang back. Not that I'm scared, what's there to be afraid of, just a toy store. But I feel funny, shame. But what I got to be shamed about? Got as much right to go in as anybody. But somehow I can't seem to get hold of the door, so I step away for Sugar to lead. But she hangs back too. And I look at her and she looks at me and this is ridiculous. I mean, damn, I have never ever been shy about doing nothing or going nowhere. But then Mercedes steps up and then Rosie Giraffe and Big Butt crowd in behind and shove, and next thing we all stuffed into the doorway with only Mercedes squeezing past us, smoothing out her jumper and walking right down the aisle. Then the rest of us tumble in like a glued-together jigsaw done all wrong. And people lookin at us. And it's like the time me and Sugar crashed into the Catholic church on a dare. But once we got in there and everything so hushed and holy and the candles and the bow-in and the handkerchiefs on all the drooping heads, I just couldn't go through with the plan. Which was for me to run up to the altar and do a tap dance while Sugar played the nose flute and messed around in the holy water. And Sugar kept givin me the elbow. Then later teased me so bad I tied her up in the shower and turned it on and locked her in. And she'd be there till this day if Aunt Gretchen hadn't finally figured I was lying about the boarder takin a shower.

Same thing in the store. We all walkin on tiptoe and hardly touchin the games and puzzles and things. And I watched Miss Moore who is steady watchin us like she waiting for a sign. Like Mama Drewery watches the sky and sniffs the air and takes note of just how much slant is in the bird formation. Then me and Sugar bump smack into each other, so busy gazing at the toys, 'specially the sailboat. But we don't laugh and go into our fat-lady bump-stomach routine. We just stare at that price tag. Then Sugar run a finger over the whole boat. And I'm jealous and want to hit her. Maybe not her, but I sure want to punch somebody in the mouth.

"Watcha bring us here for, Miss Moore?"

"You sound angry, Sylvia. Are you mad about something?" Givin me one of them grins like she tellin a grown-up joke that never turns out to be funny. And she's lookin very closely at me like maybe she plannin to do my portrait from memory. I'm mad, but I won't give her that satisfaction. So I slouch around the store bein very bored and say, "Let's go."

Me and Sugar at the back of the train watchin the tracks whizzing by large then small then gettin gobbled up in the dark. I'm thinkin about this tricky toy I saw in the store. A clown that somersaults on a bar then does chin-ups just cause you yank lightly at his leg. Cost $35. I could see me askin my mother for a $35 birthday clown. "You wanna who that costs what?" she'd say, cocking her head to the side to get a better view of the hole in my head. Thirty-five dollars could buy new bunk beds for Junior and Gretchen's boy. Thirty-five dollars and the whole household could go visit Granddaddy Nelson in the country. Thirty-five dollars would pay for the rent and the piano bill too. Who are these people that spend that much for performing clowns and $1,000 for toy sailboats? What kinda work they do and how they live and how come we ain't in on it? Where we are is who we are, Miss Moore always pointin out. But it don't necessarily have to be that way, she always adds then waits for somebody to say that poor people have to wake up and demand their share of the pie and don't none of us know what kind of pie she talkin about in the first damn place. But she ain't so smart cause I still got her four dollars from the taxi and she sure ain't gettin it. Messin up my day with this shit. Sugar nudges me in my pocket and winks.

Miss Moore lines us up in front of the mailbox where we started from, seem like years ago, and I got a headache for thinkin so hard. And we lean all over each other so we can hold up under the draggy-ass lecture she always finishes us off with at the end before we thank her for borin us to tears. But she just looks at us like she readin tea leaves. Finally she say, "Well, what did you think of F.A.O. Schwartz?"

Rosie Giraffe mumbles, "White folks crazy."

"I'd like to go there again when I get my birthday money," says Mercedes, and we shove her out the pack so she has to lean on the mailbox by herself.

"I'd like a shower. Tiring day," say Flyboy.

Then Sugar surprises me by sayin, "You know, Miss Moore, I don't think all of us here put together eat in a year what that sailboat costs." And Miss Moore lights up like somebody goosed her. "And?" she say, urging Sugar on. Only I'm standin on her foot so she don't continue.

"Imagine for a minute what kind of society it is in which some people can spend on a toy what it would cost to feed a family of six or seven. What do you think?"

"I think," say Sugar pushing me off her feet like she never done before, cause I whip her ass in a minute, "that this is not much of a democracy if you ask me. Equal chance to pursue happiness means an equal crack at the dough, don't it?" Miss Moore is besides herself and I am disgusted with Sugar's treachery. So I stand on her foot one more time to see if she'll shove me. She shuts up, and Miss Moore looks at me, sorrowfully I'm thinkin. And somethin weird is goin on, I can feel it in my chest.

"Anybody else learn anything today?" lookin dead at me. I walk away and Sugar has to run to catch up and don't even seem to notice when I shrug her arm off my shoulder.

"Well, we got four dollars anyway," she says.

"Uh hunh."

"We could go to Hascombs and get half a chocolate layer and then go to the Sunset and still have plenty money for potato chips and ice-cream sodas."

"Uh hunh."

"Race you to Hascombs," she say.

We start down the block and she gets ahead which is O.K. by me cause I'm goin to the West End and then over to the Drive to think this day through. She can run if she want to and even run faster. But ain't nobody gonna beat me at nuthin.

QUESTIONS

1. What do we learn about the narrator from the first line of the story? How does Bambara manage to convey a separation between the older Sylvia who narrates the story and the younger Sylvia who acts in it?

2. Trace the changes in Sylvia (the narrator) throughout the story. Are there any changes that she may not be aware of but that we as readers are? Explain.

3. What is "the lesson" the title refers to? Is it stated explicitly or implicitly?

SUGGESTIONS FOR WRITING

1. Retell "The Lesson" from Miss Moore's point of view. (Keep the first-person perspective.)

2. Once the children have left F.A.O. Schwartz (a very expensive children's toy store on Fifth Avenue in New York City), Sugar maintains that America "is not much of a democracy." After rereading her speech and listing some of the events and facts that have led her to make it, write an essay in which you attack or defend her opinion.

Gary Gildner
FIRST PRACTICE

★ ★ ★

Born in the Midwest in 1938, Gary Gildner is a poet whose primary concern is with the past and the role it plays in the creation of our present selves. In books like Digging for Indians *(1971),* Nails *(1975),* Letters from Vicksburg *(1976), and* The Runner *(1978), he weaves childhood narrative, historical events, and social commentary into striking acts of poetic self-definition. "Clarity, setting, story, engagement, promise, conflict, music (gathering sound), mystery, resolution"—these are Gildner's own words for what he most values in his poetry.*

"First Practice," the title work from his first collection of poems, published in 1969, clearly embodies Gildner's list of important elements. In it he goes behind the straightforward narrative of a commonplace boyhood event to question some strongly held American values.

After the doctor checked to see
we weren't ruptured,
the man with the short cigar took us
under the grade school,
where we went in case of attack
or storm, and said

he was Clifford Hill, he was
a man who believed dogs
ate dogs, he had once killed
for his country, and if
there were any girls present
for them to leave now.
                              No one
left. OK, he said, he said I take
that to mean you are hungry

men who hate to lose as much
as I do. OK. Then
he made two lines of us
facing each other,
and across the way, he said,
is the man you hate most
in the world,
and if we are to win
that title I want to see how.
But I don't want to see
any marks when you're dressed,
he said. He said, *Now.*

QUESTIONS

1. How would you describe the narrator after reading the first two stanzas? What do we know about him? How does the poet establish the character of Clifford Hill?

2. Why does the narrator repeat "he said" so often? Are other words repeated in the poem? Which ones, and to what effect?

3. Because this poem is *free verse,* and thus has no regular meter or line length, the poet is clearly free to end lines where he wishes. How do Gildner's choices help or hinder the poem's narrative?

4. What do you think Gildner is trying to say through the story he tells in "First Practice"?

SUGGESTION FOR WRITING

Rewrite "First Practice" as a narrative written in prose. Then write a paragraph describing what changes you made and explaining why you had to make them.

CHAPTER Two

PEOPLE AND PLACES
Description

Apart from the exercises your composition teacher is likely to assign, it is doubtful that you will ever be called upon to write a piece of pure description. Descriptive writing—which is, in effect, a way of painting a picture with words—rarely stands alone. Rather, it is almost always used as a device to strengthen or support one of the other types of prose found in this book. Narrative writers are particularly dependent upon description to bring their stories to life, to make the people and places involved seem real to the reader. Expository essays—which might compare two objects, explain a process, or attempt to prove a point—also rely heavily on description. Indeed, virtually every selection in this anthology makes use, to one extent or another, of description. Alison Lurie's provocative analysis of the symbolic ''language'' of clothing styles (Chapter Three) and Richard Selzer's moving depiction of the final days of a terminally ill cancer patient (Chapter Six) are only two examples.

It's no exaggeration, therefore, to say that description is not merely useful but frequently *integral* to most other forms of nonfiction writing: argument, persuasion, comparison and contrast, classification, process analysis. Perhaps an even more important reason for studying and practicing description is that, in learning how to write it, you will be mastering those essential skills that are the basis of all good prose. These include the ability to: (1) make exact and faithful observations of the world around you, as well as of your own responses to that world; (2) find the most precise and effective ways of putting those observations into words; and (3) select and organize specific, supporting details to strengthen your essay, to make what you are saying as clear, convincing, and interesting as possible to your audience.

Descriptive writing can be divided into two broad categories: *objective* (or purely factual) and *subjective* (or personal). The one you choose will depend on the kind of paper you are asked to write. If, for example, you are writing a report on personal computers—comparing the features of the IBM-PC to those of the Apple MacIntosh—your approach will be largely objective. The purpose of this type of description is to convey information, not emotion, to set down, with the precision and detachment of a research scientist, the unadorned facts about the object you are describing, without including your personal impressions, interpretations, or feelings. Scientific and technical subjects, in fact, often call for objective description. For example, if you were writing a paper on the *carcharoden carcharis,* or great white shark, for a biology class, you might describe it as an extremely aggressive, predatory fish, ranging in length from sixteen to thirty feet and distinguished by a white underbelly, a crescent-shaped dorsal fin, and large, black eyes with no visible pupils.

By contrast, here is Peter Matthiessen's powerful *subjective* description of his first face-to-face encounter with a great white, from his book *Blue Meridian* (which served as the inspiration for Peter Benchley's *Jaws*):

> The first shark had vivid scars about the head and an oval scar under the dorsal, and in the molten water of late afternoon it was a creature very different from the one seen from the surface. . . . From snout to keel, the underside was a deathly white, all but the black undertips of the broad pectorals. The shark passed slowly, first the slack jaw with the triangular splayed teeth, then the dark eye, impenetrable and empty as the eye of God, next the gill slits like knife slashes in paper, then the pale slab of the flank, aflow with silver ripplings of light, and finally the thick, short twitch of its hard tail. Its aspect was less savage than implacable, a silent thing of merciless serenity.

What makes this passage so effective is that Matthiessen manages to give us not simply a description of the shark's physical characteristics but a vivid impression of its awesome, ominous, totally inhuman nature. Matthiessen, in short, wants to do more than show us a great white; he wants to give us the shivers, to make us feel what it is like to be floating within arm's length of such a monster. The difference between the detached, scientific description of the shark and Matthiessen's intense, impressionistic one is somewhat like the difference between listening to a local weather report on TV ("showers today, with temperatures in the low forties") and being out in the icy rain.

Of course, descriptions that consist exclusively of either factual information or personal impressions are extreme cases; while they may lean more heavily on one approach or the other, most pieces of descriptive writing rely on a combination of both. Take a look, for example, at the selection by William Least Heat Moon, who skillfully blends facts ("the Oil City Bar was north of the railroad tracks near the spot where the Great Northern accidentally founded Shelby in 1891 by dumping off an old box car") with his own individual perceptions and responses ("to one side was a small room lighted only by the blue neon flicker of a beer sign—the kind of light you could go mad in"). It is also important to remember that, no matter what type of description you write, the qualities that will make it effective are always the same.

First, your language must be as precise and expressive as possible. Imagine how unsatisfactory Matthiessen's description of the great white shark would be if he had simply written, "I was floating underwater when a big, scary-looking shark swam by." This is the vague and overly general style of description we tend to use in casual conversation—for instance, when we tell a friend that we saw the new Clint Eastwood movie on Saturday night and it was really exciting. By comparison, reading a good piece of description is much closer to the experience of actually watching a movie, with a picture presented to us that is so vivid and richly detailed that it almost seems real. Your job as a writer is to use language to produce this kind of picture—to conjure up, with your words, the living image of the thing you are describing.

Let's take a closer look at Matthiessen's paragraph to see how carefully he selects his words to create such an image. Like all good writers, Matthiessen uses modifiers very sparingly. Describing the appearance of the water from his vantage point below the surface, Matthiessen manages, with just a single, well-chosen adjective ("the *molten* water") to give the reader a powerful, almost physical sense of the ocean: dense, burning beneath the fierce, tropical sun—an alien, even slightly hellish place. Inexperienced writers (and even many mediocre professionals) are prone to simply pile on adjectives and adverbs, a technique that makes writing flabby and dull. (In one of his stories, the well-known horror writer H. P. Lovecraft, a notorious practitioner of overblown prose, describes a monster this way: "It lumbered slobberingly into sight and gropingly squeezed its gelatinous green immensity through the black doorway into the tainted outside air of that poison city of madness." If good descriptive writing is clear and concrete, this sentence is the verbal equivalent of a large mud puddle.) Adjectives and adverbs are fine in moderation and, in fact, are often indispensable. But you should keep in mind that other parts of speech, particularly forceful, expressive verbs, can bring an otherwise flat descriptive passage to life. To say, for example (as Matthiessen does elsewhere in his book), that a rubber dinghy "sploshed up and down" in the waves is much more graphic than to say it moved up and down.

Another sign of Matthiessen's skill as a writer is his sensitivity to the *connotations*—the emotional implications—of his words. Instead of using the neutral term "nostrils," he speaks of the shark's "snout," a word which, because we tend to associate it with pigs and similar creatures, suggests the swinishness, the ugly and indiscriminate appetite, of the fish. Similarly, by referring to the shark's "slack jaw," Matthiessen suggests certain repugnant qualities—mindlessness, brutishness—that are not implied by other phrases (open mouth, for example) that denote the same meaning.

When Matthiessen describes the shark's gills by saying they looked "like knife slashes in paper," he is making use of an extremely important descriptive device known as a *simile*. Similes, which are one of the main forms of *figurative language*, allow writers to draw a clear picture of something unfamiliar (in this case, an anatomical feature of a great white shark) by comparing it to something easy to visualize (slashes in paper). A related, and equally useful, figure of speech is the *metaphor*. The difference between a metaphor and a simile is that, whereas the latter makes an explicit comparison introduced by "like" or "as," the analogy drawn by a metaphor is implied. For instance, when we write that "the shark was a silver torpedo, headed straight for our boat," we are being metaphorical. We don't literally mean that the shark was a deadly underwater missile armed with explosives, but we are suggesting a similarity between the two objects. In a simile, we would state the comparison directly: "The shark headed straight for our boat like a silver torpedo" (or "as swiftly as a torpedo").

We use similes and metaphors all the time in our everyday speech, when we say, for example, that the laundry smelled "fresh as a daisy" or that the ground was covered with "a blanket of snow." The trouble with these and similar figures of speech is that, while they were undoubtedly very striking and even poetic when they were first invented, they have been used so often that they have become clichés—dead words instead of living images. Since the purpose of writing a description is to present a fresh and vivid picture to the reader, there is no point in using figurative language unless you can invest it with some imagination and originality. Keep in mind, too, that for a metaphor or simile to serve its purpose, the two things you are comparing must share more than superficial similarities. Matthiessen's analogy works because the image of the knife slashes conveys something of the violent and dangerous nature of the shark. Other objects resemble gill slits, but clearly it would have been far less effective to write that the shark's gills looked like slats on a Venetian blind or the slotted hot-air vent on an electric blow-dryer.

Writing a good description, then, involves choosing individual nouns, verbs, and modifiers, as well as similes and metaphors, with great care. It also involves paying close attention to your choice of *detail*. Carefully selected detail can replace lifeless generalization or it can buttress the kind of generalization your description requires. While it is important to have a wealth of specific details to choose from, and particularly those concrete details that appeal to *all* the senses—not only sight, but also touch, taste, hearing, and smell—keep in mind that a description is not a long list of components, or a catalogue in which you dutifully record every feature you can think of. The main or dominant impression you are trying to produce should determine your choice of detail. If, for example, your composition teacher were to ask for a written description of your dorm room or your bedroom at home, and you wanted to convey an impression of how nicely decorated it is, you would focus on certain details: your rock posters, handwoven Navajo wall-hanging, framed photographs of family and friends, and so on. Another person with a very different impression of your room (one of your parents, for instance) would undoubtedly emphasize other details, such as the pile of unwashed underwear heaped in a corner or the empty Big Mac containers scattered under your bed.

Of course, as a preliminary step, before you actually begin composing your essay, you may simply want to write down as many details as you can. (Later you can choose which to use.) Many professional writers keep journals in which they record random observations of the world around them, which serve as the raw material for their finished work. Here is an excerpt from the journals of Henry David Thoreau, in which he lists the various sights and sounds he encountered during a country walk:

> Standing on the bridge over the Mill Brook on the Turnpike, there being but little ice on the south side, I see several small waterbugs swimming about, as in the spring.
>
> I see the terminal shield fern very fresh, as an evergreen, at Saw Mill Brook . . . .
>
> I go up the brook, walking on it most of the way, surprised that it will bear me. How it falls from rock to rock, as down a flight of stairs, all through that rocky wood, from the swamp which is its source to the Everett farm. . . .
>
> Returning through Britton's field, I notice the stumps of chestnuts cut a dozen years ago. This tree grows rapidly, and one layer seems not to adhere very firmly to another. . . .
>
> Looking toward the wood in the horizon, it is seen to be very hazy.
>
> At Ditch Pond, I hear what I suppose to be a fox barking, an exceedingly husky, hoarse, and ragged note, prolonged perhaps by the echo, like a feeble puppy or even a child endeavoring to scream, but choked with fear. . . .

If, like Thoreau, you are writing about a subject you have access to, then describing it will require close and careful observation. On the other hand, if you are writing about something or someone far away or in your past—a childhood friend's house, for instance, whose basement always gave you the creeps—you will have to conjure it up in your memory as completely as possible. Before you put a single word on paper, shut your eyes and place yourself in the setting you wish to describe. Walk all around the basement; look closely at its ceiling, its walls, its contents; touch them; inhale the atmosphere of the room.

Once you have decided on the dominant impression you want to produce and have picked out the specific details that will forcefully convey this impression to the reader, your final task is to organize your description in a way that is both internally coherent and consistent with your purpose. Describing the shark, for example, Peter Matthiessen begins with its snout and then moves along its body as it slowly glides past his observation cage. This kind of *spacial* organization would also make sense in your description of the basement. You might begin with the rickety wooden stairs leading down into the basement, then move clockwise around the dark room, or start with the cobwebby ceiling and then proceed down the walls to the damp and dirty floor. Other common patterns include moving from the smallest details to the largest, the least important to the most important, the more ordinary to the most unusual. However you choose to arrange the details of your description, the key is to pick a pattern that the reader won't have any trouble following and then stick to it. In this way, you will be accomplishing the main goal of descriptive writing, which is to impose a logical order on an assortment of sensory details: to create a clear and well-shaped picture that will not merely allow, but will compel, readers to share your perceptions and feelings.

Martin Filler
GRACELAND
★ ★ ★

Elvis Presley is one of those pop entertainers whose lives take on the dimensions of myth. His evolution from a 1950s rock idol—the sneering incarnation of teen rebellion—to a grotesquely fat Las Vegas showman, dead of a drug overdose at age 42, is a story that seems powerfully suggestive, a lurid morality tale about fame, fortune, and the spiritual corruption of the American artist.

To speak about the spiritual in relation to a man once known as "Elvis the Pelvis" might seem wildly inappropriate. But Elvis was—and remains—"The King" to millions of worshipful followers, who regard him with quasi-religious awe, fill their homes with iconic images of their idol (in the form of assorted Presley "collectibles"), and make regular pilgrimages to their own pop Mecca, Elvis's garish dream-mansion, Graceland.

Though the following two selections in this chapter both emphasize the extravagantly tacky decor of Graceland, the reader comes away from each with a somewhat different impression. This is because the writers themselves have different attitudes and intentions. The first piece, by architecture and design critic Martin Filler, is by far the more detached. A widely published writer, whose essays have appeared in scores of publications (among them Art in America, Design Quarterly, Vogue, *and* The Wall Street Journal*), Filler is interested in Graceland as an "American Shrine"—a place which reflects not only Presley's tastes but those of the society that produced (and deified) him.*

This selection is an excerpt from a lengthy article on Graceland that appeared in the March 1984 issue of House & Garden *magazine, where Filler has worked as editor since 1979.*

_____

The interior design of Graceland might best be described as American Roadside Regal. To the right of the foyer are the living room and the music room; to the left, the dining room. All are decorated in the showy-genteel manner that predominates throughout the parlor rooms at Graceland: gilt furniture, silky fabrics, elaborately draped curtains and portieres, crystal chandeliers, pale wall-to-wall carpeting, marble and mirror paneling, and on almost every wall a gold-framed family portrait, often a photograph painted over in oils. Though much has been made by Albert Goldman of the tackiness of these rooms, in truth they are not much different from those of many other Tennessee tyro tycoons circa 1957.

Much less typical are the rooms of the house designed for Elvis's own amusement rather than for receiving relatives and friends in the time-honored Southern tradition. Here we see his imagination run wild. As at Versailles, the nerve center at Graceland was the bedroom of the King. The bed chamber, which is not open to the public and which the Presley family has declined to have photographed, is decorated in high swinging-bachelor style. The room is centered by Elvis's nine-by-nine-foot bed with its black vinyl headboard, afloat on a sea of red wall-to-wall carpeting. The walls are covered in fake black suede, which also screens the windows to create the cocoonlike atmosphere that Presley craved. The bed is flanked by easels bearing portraits of two of the most important people in Elvis Presley's life: his mother and Jesus Christ.

Then there is the TV Room in the basement, with its mirrored ceiling, its wrap-around mirrored soda fountain, its supergraphic mural with Elvis's trade-mark lightning-bolt logo, and three television sets in a row (an idea he got from LBJ, who liked to keep an eye on all three networks at once). Across the hall is the pool room, tented in some 750 yards of patchwork-printed fabric, with a stained-glass lamp hanging over the table where he played his preferred billiard game, eightball.

But the most jaw-dropping of all is the Jungle Room, Elvis's favorite room at Graceland. Decorated in a style that might be termed Early Goona-Goona, or perhaps Tahitian Provincial, the forty-foot-long den is fitted out with a staggering suite of massive pieces (from Donald's Furniture in Memphis) that combine ferociously carved animal forms with fake-fur upholstery. Here the star of *Blue Hawaii* would ensconce himself with the good old boys of his enormous entourage and watch Kung-Fu films on the projection-TV screen, which was set up in front of the built-in waterfall wall (complete with colored-light effects).

When that recreation palled, they could take themselves out to the small, windowless, concrete gymnasium building that Elvis had built directly behind the house in 1975—complete with racquetball courts, sauna, and whirlpool baths—where Presley, a confirmed night owl, would often play with his pals until sunup. Another favorite diversion was his slot-car race track, which was kept for many years in the one-story structure erected just to the south of the main house in 1965. In time, however, Elvis's vast collection of memorabilia had expanded to such an extent that the large shed was converted into the Trophy Room, the most compelling part of Graceland.

There is something at once poignant and repellent about the Trophy Room (which is actually a series of gallerylike spaces), and it is here that the myth of Elvis Presley seems most convincing and most real. Elvis was a compulsive keeper of the bits and pieces of his life; significant and trivial, worthless and rare, hucksterish and human, they are juxtaposed in this place with irresistible effect. Here is his mama and daddy's marriage certificate; his seventh-grade achievement test (80 in phys. ed., 79 in dictation, 61 in literature—no testing in music); the portraits of the artist as a young Adonis. Then one passes through the Hall of Gold, an astounding corridor lined with the singer's 163 Gold and Platinum records and albums, including his very first, for "Don't Be Cruel."

Finally, one comes to the largest room, which holds the oddest of the artifacts: headless effigies wearing the black brocade tuxedo and the white wedding dress in which Elvis and Priscilla were married; an array of the fake-jewel-encrusted jumpsuits he was given to performing in late in his career; a wall full of his favorite firearms and the narcotics-agent badges that the drug-dependent Presley obsessively collected; his motorcycle and a number of guitars; his suitcases, still packed, from the concert tour he was to have begun the day after he died; his favorite books—on the Kennedy assassination and the occult; his eleven-carat diamond ring and his heavy gold pendant with the Hebrew word for "life."

After a half-hour of rapt voyeurism in this gallery, one is relieved to step outside and survey the grounds of Graceland, which conform to the American suburban type as much as the house itself does. The large "front yard" is handsomely landscaped but, of course, is never used, while the much smaller backyard seems cramped and cluttered; the contrast between the two makes the porticoed exterior seem much like a Hollywood false-front. But before the visitor departs, there is still what for most people is the emotional high point of the pilgrimage to Graceland: Meditation Garden, the final resting place of the departed King.

Two days after his death Elvis was buried in nearby Forest Hill Cemetery, but within six weeks the combination of staggering crowds and a corpse-kidnap threat led to the decision to reinter Presley (and his beloved mother) in the more secure setting of Graceland. Now, like Richard Wagner and Andrew Jackson, he lies in death just a few feet from the house in which he lived. The name "Meditation Garden" suggests a tranquil retreat but in fact is more like Forest Lawn than the contemplative spaces of Japan. Just past the kidney-shaped swimming pool is a brick and white-columned peristyle, inset with four stained-glass windows. A circular fountain is at the center, and directly before it is an unlit eternal flame, at the head of the bronze marker bearing the name ELVIS AARON PRESLEY. On any given day it is surrounded by floral offerings, though their quantity predictably swells around the anniversaries of his birth and death. Several forms are recurring favorites—guitars, hound dogs, and that Southern classic, the broken, bleeding heart.

Yet it is the words, not the flowers, that stick in the mind. Cast in bronze on the tombstone is Vernon Presley's lengthy but touching epitaph to his son, and around it are the handwritten tributes left by fans, which are soon made illegible by the rain. They speak of Elvis as the most devoted see him, not as a mere popular personality, but as *divus loci*—the god of the place. Pinned to a little wooden cross not long ago were these lines: "From the womb of your loving mother/ To the hearts of your loving fans/ To the arms of our Saviour Jesus/ With whom you do now stand."

QUESTIONS

1. What specific details does Filler use to support his statement that, in the rooms "designed for Elvis's own amusement," we see "his imagination run wild"?

2. What impression of Elvis—his tastes, pastimes, personality—do you get from this description of his house? How does Filler seem to feel about Elvis? About Graceland? How do the details Filler includes in his description reflect his judgment of Graceland?

3. Filler concludes his article by writing, "What makes Elvis such a potent legend is the way in which his saga commingles so much of the schizoid American experience: ambition and luck, materialism and piety, generosity and greed, humility and hubris are all present in larger-than-life proportions." How many of those elements are evident—made manifest—in the very way Elvis's house is decorated?

4. Throughout most of his article, Filler remains detached and objective in his appraisal of Graceland. Are there any places where that objectivity breaks down?

5. How would you characterize the tone of the paragraph describing Graceland's "Jungle Room"? How do you account for that tone? What picture is evoked by Filler's description of the style as "Early Goona-Goona"?

6. Filler's typical paragraph begins with a topic sentence that gives the overall impression of the room he is describing and then gives specific details that support the impression. Point to some paragraphs that are organized this way. Do you find this approach effective? Why or why not?

7. What effect does Filler create by quoting the lines from the "handwritten tribute" pinned to a small wooden cross at Elvis's grave? Why do you think he includes these lines?

SUGGESTION FOR WRITING

Pick your favorite (or least favorite) celebrity—rock singer, movie or TV star, media personality. Then imagine what his or her house looks like on the inside and write an essay describing this place as though you were taking the reader on a guided tour. Try to use details that capture the essence of the celebrity's personality.

Albert Goldman
GRACELAND
★ ★ ★

A former Columbia University English professor and pop music critic for Life *magazine, Albert Goldman is the author of a number of books, including* Freakshow: The Rocksoulbluesjazzsickjewblackhumorsexpoppsych Gig and Other Scenes from the Counterculture *(1971);* Ladies and Gentleman—Lenny Bruce!! *(1974); and* Grass Roots: Marijuana in America Today *(1979). None of these books, however, created as much of a stir—or sold nearly as many copies—as his controversial 1981 bestseller,* Elvis. *This exhaustively detailed biography is continuously (some would say morbidly) fascinating, partly because of the shocking revelations it contains, but even more, perhaps, because of the intensity of Goldman's dislike for the singer. It's hard to think of another biographer who has such profound and undisguised contempt for his subject. The Presley that emerges from the pages of Goldman's book is little more than an ignorant hillbilly with a wide range of character disorders—a pathological mama's boy with an addictive personality, aberrant appetites, and a modicum of talent.*

The following excerpt is taken from the book's first chapter, "The King's Palace, the King's Pleasure."

Though the holidays are long past, Graceland looks still like a picture on a Christmas card. The classic colonial façade, with its towering white columns and pilasters, is aglow with jewel lights, rose, amethyst and emerald. The templelike pediment is outlined in pale blue fire. This same eerie electric aura runs like St. Elmo's fire along the eaves, zigzags up and down the gables and shimmies down the drainpipes to the ground. Here it pales beside the brilliance of a rank of Christmas trees that have been transformed into cones of ruby, topaz, carnelian and aquamarine incandescence.

Prominently displayed on the front lawn is an elaborate crèche. The stable is a full-scale adobe house strewn with straw. Life-sized are the figures of Joseph and Mary, the kneeling shepherds and Magi, the lambs and ewes, as well as the winged annunciatory angel hovering over the roof beam. Real, too, is the cradle in which the infant Jesus sleeps.

When you step through the ten-foot oak door and enter the house, you stop and stare in amazement. Having just come from the contemplation of the tenderest scene in the Holy Bible, imagine the shock of finding yourself in a *whorehouse*! Yet there is no other way to describe the drawing room of Graceland except to say that it appears to have been lifted from some turn-of-the-century bordello down in the French Quarter of New Orleans. Lulu White or the Countess Willie Piazza might have contrived this plushy parlor for the entertainment of Gyp the

Blood. The room is a gaudy mélange of red velour and gilded tassels, Louis XV furniture and porcelain bric-a-brac, all informed by the kind of taste that delights in a ceramic temple d'amour housing a miniature Venus de Milo with an electrically simulated waterfall cascading over her naked shoulders.

Looking a little closer, you realize that the old madams of the French Quarter would have been horrified at the quality of the hangings and furniture at Graceland. They decorated their sporting houses with magnificent pieces crafted in Europe, upholstered them in the finest reps and damasks, laid costly Persian carpets on their floors and hung imposing oil paintings on their walls. Though it cost a lot of money to fill up Graceland with the things that appealed to Elvis Presley, nothing in the house is worth a dime.

Take that fake fireplace that blocks with its companion bookcases (filled with phony leather bindings) the two big windows that should offer a commanding view of the front lawn. This hokey facsimile looks like it was bought at the auction of some bankrupt road company of *East Lynne.* Or consider the Louis Quinze furniture strewn about the parlor. Every piece is elaborately carved and gilded, escutcheoned and cabrioleted; but it's not only fake (Louis XV's upholsterers didn't go in for sectional sofas), it's that dreadful fake antique that Italian gangsters dote on: garish, preposterous, uncomfortable and cheating wherever it can, as in the substitution of velour for velvet. Or look at the real fireplace of white marble that stands against the back wall of the room, obviously innocent of use. It, too, has been flanked not with bookcases but with a great spread of smoked-glass mirror threaded with gold seams. The whole ensemble is crowned with an electric clock inside a three-foot sunburst that looks like someone took an ostrich egg and smashed it against the glass.

The entrance to the adjoining music room is flanked by two tall, broad windows adorned with painted peacocks. Marvelously campy as are these bits of stained glass, they can't hold a candle to the bizarre chamber they frame. In this mad room, King Elvis's obsession with royal red reaches an intensity that makes you gag. Not so much a room as a crimson cocoon, every inch of it is swathed in red satin drapes, portieres, valences and braided ropes. As weird as anything in Edgar Allan Poe, the effect is that of stepping into the auricle of an immense heart. At the center of this king-sized valentine is the crowning touch: a concert grand piano that appears to have been dipped in liquid gold.

The entrance to the next room is blocked by a tall folding screen covered with mirrored glass. Screens and other masking devices abound at Graceland because Gladys and Vernon, Elvis's parents, imbued him with the old hillbilly superstition: Never close up windows or doors. Through this folding looking glass lies one of Elvis's favorite spots, the trophy room. A pop archeologist would find the excavation of this site a satisfying occupation. No part of Graceland was subject to more visions and revisions.

Originally, this room was a patio adjoining the dressing rooms for the outdoor pool. On hot Nilotic nights, Elvis and the Guys (known to the media as the "Memphis Mafia") would sit here cutting the ripe red hearts out of iced watermelons and vying to see who could eat the most. As they consumed this sweet satisfying pap, they would spit the pits out on the ground as Sweetpea, Gladys's Pomeranian, pranced about in the black hail.

In the late sixties, Elvis decided to build a forty-foot room over the patio to house his slot car racecourse. On a huge raised platform, a figure-eight track was laid out, in whose grooves could be fitted expensive scale-model replicas of Ferraris, Maseratis, Lotuses and Porsches. By means of an electric drive system, you could race these little cars around the tracks and up and down inclines at great speeds, which Elvis sought constantly to increase by means of continual improvements in the cars' motors. Manipulating the pistol-grip controls, you could make the cars skid, spin out and crash. It was a grand if costly game, and the Guys enjoyed it enormously.

Like all of Elvis's toys, the slot cars soon lost their charm. One day the track was banished to the attic, where it was stored alongside cartons of old teddy bears, discarded guitars and gilt lamps from the house on Audubon Avenue. Elvis never allowed anything to be cast out of Graceland except human beings. Once an object, no matter how trivial, came into his possession, it remained with him for the rest of his life.

Commencing in the Royal Period, the slot car room became the trophy room. Elvis pushed back the end wall twenty feet to make a chamber fit for a pharaoh's tomb. Then he filled it with gold. He ranked his fifty-three gold records along one wall, like patents of nobility. Against the opposite wall, he piled up, like the offerings before a shrine, a great heap of gold loving cups, gold statuettes and gold tablets. The effect is less that of a trophy case than of the display case of a trophy manufacturer.

The showcase effect is even more pronounced in the center of the room, which is occupied by a set of old-fashioned department store counters, under whose glass tops or stuffed inside storage drawers and cupboards lie an immense profusion of plaques, medals, certificates and scrapbooks received from professional organizations, charities and fan clubs. Like any true sovereign, King Elvis never forgets that all his wealth and power are derived from his subjects. No matter what they offer him, whether it be a huge stuffed animal or a little crocheted doily, he not only keeps the gift but puts it on display.

The oddest feature of the trophy room is the soda fountain that stands in one corner, one of two at Graceland, the other one being downstairs in the poolroom. Soda fountains and jukeboxes are symbolic objects for fifties rock heroes, no more to be wondered at than the old binnacle in the den of a steamship captain or the pair of crossed sabers on the wall of a retired general. What is disconcerting about this domestic altar is its formica meanness. Yet it would be out of character for Elvis to own a handsome old green marble counter with mottled glass lamps and quaint seltzer pulls because Elvis detests everything antique with the heartfelt disgust of a real forward-looking American of his generation. Like so many of his kind, he gloats over the spectacle of the wrecking ball bashing down the walls of historic Memphis. In fact, he likes to get into the driver's seat of a bulldozer and smash down old buildings himself. As he says: "When I wuz growin' up in Tupelo, I lived with enough fuckin' antiques to do me for a lifetime." That is why everything about the King must be spanking new, from his Louis XV furniture to his late model Seeburg jukebox—so drab compared to a dazzling peacock Wurlitzer.

On the left-hand side of the entrance hall is the dining room. In the center of the crimson carpet is a large quadrangle of black marble tiles on which is set the table: an eight-foot oval of mirrored glass on an ebonized and fluted wooden pedestal. Round the table in great state stand ten tall, ladder-backed Louis XIV chairs with tufted velour seats. They appear to have been drawn up for King Elvis and the Nine Worthies. (When Elvis dines with the Guys, he often jokes about Jesus breaking bread with his disciples. They respond by singing the old hymn, "What a Friend We Have in Jesus," substituting "Elvis" for "Jesus.") Above the table hangs a brass Louis XIV chandelier with two tiers of scrolled candlearms fitted with glass lusters. At each corner of the room, like bumpers on a game board, are tall diagonal bric-a-brac cabinets or chrome-plated étagères crammed with statuettes, vases, jars, boxes, plaques, goblets, ewers, compotes, porringers, shells, cloches, etc., *viz:*

ceramic statuette of a grey poodle

ceramic statuette of a nude girl with perched bird

pair of Portuguese glazed pottery drug jars

five specimens of butterflies in plastic cases

artificial floral bouquet under a glass cloche

two glass bowls with bouquet of black and white feathers

model of 1932 antique radio

ceramic statuette of a trumpeting elephant

Wherever Elvis goes in his travels, he indulges his middle-aged woman's passion for knickknacks, curios and chatzkahs. A domestic appraiser once remarked that Elvis appeared to have furnished Graceland largely from roadside stands.

A familiar feature of a number of the world's greatest palaces is a room decorated in an exotic style, inspired, perhaps, by the culture of one of the ruler's most remote or colorful provinces. Graceland possesses such a room; indeed, of all the public rooms in the mansion, it is the King's favorite. The den is an addition to the original building, created by enlarging and enclosing a back porch that ran along the entire rear wall. The room looks like Elvis scooped up the setting for one of his Hawaiian movies and brought it home inside a sixty-foot walnut hope chest. You reach the den by going through the kitchen, which is all white formica, walnut paneling and Kitchen-Aid stainless steel, with a couple of oddly feminine touches, like the calico carpeting and the hanging lampshades painted with fruits and vegetables. Entering the den, the first thing that strikes you is a towering statue of the god Tiki, confronting the visitor with outstretched arms holding an empty bowl. Obviously not an ashtray nor an hors d'oeuvre tray nor a place to drop your calling card, this empty basin is a puzzler. In any case, the statue serves to proclaim the room's provenance.

The style of the den could be characterized as Polynesian Primitive or Ugh! The decorator divided its sixty-foot length with another of those hinged screens that one finds all over Graceland. This one is composed of huge panels of stressed, stained pine perforated in long spermatozoid scrolls cut in the wood with a chain saw. On the side of the screen opposite that dominated by the figure of Tiki is a seating area focused upon an early-model Advent video projector.

Here, as Elvis watches his favorite football teams or boxing matches with the Guys, he enjoys the full flavor of the Polynesian Primitive. The huge sofa and the pair of oversized armchairs are carved out of the same dark coarse pine as the room divider and upholstered with thick, dark artificial fur. As the chairs have huge pawlike armrests, the impression created by this curious suite is rather like the Three Bears watching TV. This animalistic sofa is also Elvis's favorite downstairs dining spot. Like so many boy-men, he dislikes the formality of table service. Whenever possible, he has his meals served to him here on the cocktail table, a huge slab of boldly grained wood cut out of the crotch of a cypress tree and surfaced with what appears to be about a quarter-inch layer of lustrous polyurethane.

The most impressive feature of the den is the wall behind the TV, which is straight out of the lobby of a Waikiki Beach resort hotel. Constructed of layers of rough-cut fieldstone, it has been arranged artfully like a natural cataract and equipped with pipes and a pumping system so that a constant stream of soothing water flows down over the jutting rocks, catching as it falls the colors cast by the lamps concealed in the ceiling. What more perfect object of contemplation could be imagined for a man who is perpetually stoned?

The King's bedchamber is the most bizarre room in the hillbilly palace. The walls are padded and tufted with button-studded strips of black artificial suede. The crimson carpet covers not only the floor but rises at the foot of the bed like a red wave, atop which rides an enormous color TV set. Confronting the bed are two big windows that overlook the front lawn. Sealed with the same black upholstery that covers the walls, they are crowned with gold valences and hung with floor-length crimson drapes, producing a somberly surrealistic image, like a painting by Magritte. The space between the windows is filled with a mirror, which reflects the bed.

What a bed! An immense slab, nine by nine, a double king size, it has a mortuary headboard of black quilted Naugahide, with a built-in plastic back angle and retractable armrests of speckled metal, like the skeletons of those padded "husbands" beloved of suburban matrons. To one side is an easel supporting a large photograph of Elvis's mother; on the other a sepia-toned portrait of Jesus Christ. Back in the corners of the room crouch big round seats covered with white fake fur like enormous bunnies.

As in a funeral parlor, the light in this inner sanctum is always dim, supplied by cove lamps that illuminate the ceiling but produce below only a murky subaqueous gloaming. The air is chilled, the temperature being driven down during the hot Memphis summer by powerful refrigeration units that groan night and day to keep the King from sweating. The odor of the room is sometimes fetid, the stink of a Bowery flophouse full of dirty old men incontinent of their urine and feces. The most grotesque object in this Cave of Morphia, this black and crimson womb, this padded cell, is the King.

QUESTIONS

1. What similarities and differences do you notice between Goldman's description of Graceland and Filler's? How do you account for the differences?

2. It is clear from this short selection (and throughout the book) that Goldman despises not only Elvis but the culture he represents. What is that culture, and where is Goldman's dislike of it made clear?

3. Look at the third paragraph, in which Goldman compares the inside of Graceland to a bordello. Notice how the author selects a single, specific object to epitomize the "kind of taste" that informs the whole room (indeed, the whole mansion). What is that object, and why is it such an effective choice? What kind of taste does it bespeak?

4. Throughout this selection, Goldman uses figurative language very skillfully. Point to several striking similes and explain what makes them effective.

5. Goldman's tone is a mixture of horrified incredulity and utter contempt. How, precisely, is that attitude conveyed in his choice of words and images? Point to specific examples.

6. What effect does Goldman create by simply listing—without comment—a handful of the "knickknacks" found in Elvis's dining room? What impression of Graceland (and its owner) is Goldman attempting to convey? How successful is he at conveying it?

7. Point to some of the phrases Goldman uses to characterize Elvis. What picture of "The King" emerges from this short selection?

8. Goldman sums up the essence of Graceland by calling it a "hillbilly palace." What exactly does he mean by that phrase? How does his choice of imagery and language throughout this selection reinforce that characterization?

SUGGESTION FOR WRITING

Pick a place you know (a restaurant, public building, movie theater, an acquaintance's house) that is decorated in a style you regard as utterly garish or vulgar—in short, as the epitome of tastelessness. Then write an essay in which you try to convey the tacky spirit of the place. Be as detailed as possible.

Eudora Welty
RODNEY'S LANDING

★ ★ ★

One of America's most eminent writers of fiction, Eudora Welty has lived most of her life in Jackson, Mississippi, the place of her birth. Because the bulk of her fiction is set in the South, it is often labeled "regionalist" writing. Her best work, however, transcends that rather narrow definition. In classic stories like "Death of a Traveling Salesman," "Why I Live at the P.O.," "A Worn Path," and "First Love," she deals with such universal themes as the transience of life, the mysterious forces that separate people (or bind them together), the indomitable strength of the human spirit, and the redemptive power of love. Her work has earned her numerous honors (including the William Dean Howells Medal of the American Academy of Arts and Letters, the National Medal for Literature, The National Institute of Arts and Letters Gold Medal for the Novel, and the Presidential Medal of Freedom), as well as a wide and appreciative readership.

Though Welty is best known for her short stories, she has also written several novels (among them the Pulitzer Prize-winning The Optimist's Daughter *and* The Ponder Heart, *which was turned into a successful Broadway play); a best-selling autobiography,* One Writer's Beginnings *(1984); and numerous essays, reviews, and critical articles. The following excerpt is from her essay, "Notes on River Country," collected in her 1978 volume* The Eye of the Story.

Today Rodney's Landing wears the cloak of vegetation which has caught up this whole land for the third time, or the fourth, or the hundredth. There is something Gothic about the vines, in their structure in the trees—there are arches, flying buttresses, towers of vines, with trumpet flowers swinging in them for bells and staining their walls. And there is something of a warmer grandeur in their very abundance—stairways and terraces and whole hanging gardens of green and flowering vines, with a Babylonian babel of hundreds of creature voices that make up the silence of Rodney's Landing. Here are nests for birds and thrones for owls and trapezes for snakes, every kind of bower in the world. From earliest spring there is something, when garlands of yellow jasmine swing from tree to tree, in the woods aglow with dogwood and redbud, when the green is only a floating veil in the hills.

And the vines make an endless flourish in summer and fall. There are wild vines of the grape family, with their lilac and turquoise fruits and their green, pink and white leaves. Muscadine vines along the stream banks grow a hundred feet high, mixing their dull, musky, delicious grapes among the bronze grapes of the scuppernong. All creepers with trumpets and panicles of scarlet and yellow cling to the treetops. On shady stream banks hang lady's eardrops, fruits and flowers dangling pale jade. The passionflower puts its tendrils where it can, its strange flowers of lilac rays with their little white towers shining out, or its fruit, the maypop, hanging. Wild wistaria hangs its flowers like flower-grapes above reach, and the sweetness of clematis, the virgin's-bower which grows in Rodney, and of honeysuckle, must fill even the highest air. There is a vine that grows to great heights, with heart-shaped leaves as big and soft as summer hats, overlapping and shading everything to deepest jungle blue-green.

Ferns are the hidden floor of the forest, and they grow, too, in the trees, their roots in the deep of mossy branches.

All over the hills the beautiful white Cherokee rose trails its glossy dark-green leaves and its delicate luminous-white flowers. Foliage and flowers alike have a quality of light and dark as well as color in Southern sun, and sometimes a seeming motion like dancing due to the flicker of heat, and are luminous or opaque according to the time of day or the density of summer air. In early morning or in the light of evening they become translucent and ethereal, but at noon they blaze or darken opaquely, and, the same flower may seem sultry or delicate in its being all according to when you see it.

It is not hard to follow one of the leapings of old John Law's mind, then, and remember how he displayed diamonds in the shop windows in France—during the organization of his Compagnie d'Occident—saying that they were produced in the cups of the wildflowers along the lower Mississippi. And the closer they grew to the river, the more nearly that might be true.

Deep in the swamps the water hyacinths make solid floors you could walk on over still black water, the Southern blue flag stands thick and sweet in the marsh. Lady's-tresses, greenish-white little orchids with spiral flowers and stems twisted like curls and braids, grow there, and so do nodding lady's-tresses. Water lilies float, and spider lilies rise up like little coral monsters.

The woods on the bluffs are the hardwood trees—dark and berried and flowered. The magnolia is the spectacular one with its heavy cups—they look as heavy as silver—weighing upon its aromatic, elliptical, black-green leaves, or when it bears its dense pink cones. I remember an old botany book, written long ago in England, reporting the magnolia by hearsay, as having blossoms "so large as to be distinctly visible a mile or more—seen in the mass, we presume." But I tested the visibility power of the magnolia, and the single flower can be seen for several miles on a clear day. One magnolia cousin, the cucumber tree, has long sleevelike leaves and pale-green flowers which smell strange and cooler than the grandiflora flower. Set here and there in this country will be a mimosa tree, with its smell in the rain like a cool melon cut, its puffs of pale flowers settled in its sensitive leaves.

Perhaps the live oaks are the most wonderful trees in this land. Their great girth and their great spread give far more feeling of history than any house or ruin left by man. Vast, very dark, proportioned as beautifully as a church, they stand majestically in the wild or line old sites, old academy grounds. The live oaks under which Aaron Burr was tried at Washington, Mississippi, in this section, must have been old and impressive then, to have been chosen for such a drama. Spanish moss invariably hangs from the live oak branches, moving with the wind and swaying its long beards, darkening the forests; it is an aerial plant and strangely enough is really a pineapple, and consists of very, very tiny leaves and flowers, springy and dustily fragrant to the touch; no child who has ever "dressed up" in it can forget the sweet dust of its smell. It would be hard to think of things that happened here without the presence of these live oaks, so old, so expansive, so wonderful, that they might be sentient beings. W. H. Hudson, in his autobiography, *Far Away and Long Ago,* tells of an old man who felt reverentially toward the ancient trees of his great country house, so that each night he walked around his park to visit them one by one, and rest his hand on its bark to bid it goodnight, for he believed in their knowing spirits.

Now and then comes a report that an ivory-billed woodpecker is seen here. Audubon in his diary says the Indians began the slaughter of this bird long before Columbus discovered America, for the Southern Indians would trade them to the Canadian Indians—four buckskins for an ivory bill. Audubon studied the woodpecker here when he was in the Natchez country, where it lived in the deepest mossy swamps along the windings of the river, and he called it "the greatest of all our American woodpeckers and probably the finest in the world." The advance of agriculture rather than slaughter has really driven it to death, for it will not live except in a wild country.

This woodpecker used to cross the river "in deep undulations." Its notes were "clear, loud, and rather plaintive . . . heard at a considerable distance . . . and resemble the false high note of a clarinet." "Pait, pait, pait," Audubon translates it into his Frenchlike sound. It made its nest in a hole dug with the ivory bill in a tree inclined in just a certain way—usually a black cherry. The holes went sometimes three feet deep, and some people thought they went spirally. The bird ate the grapes of the swampland. Audubon says it would hang by its claws like a titmouse on a grapevine and devour grapes by the bunch—which sounds curiously as though it knew it would be extinct before very long. This woodpecker also would destroy any dead tree it saw standing—chipping it away "to an extent of twenty or thirty feet in a few hours, leaping downward with its body . . . tossing its head to the right and left, or leaning it against the bark to ascertain the precise spot where the grubs were concealed, and immediately renewing its blows with fresh vigor, all the while sounding its loud notes, as if highly delighted." The males had beautiful crimson crests, the females were "always the most clamorous and the least shy." When caught, the birds would fight bitterly, and "utter a mournful and very piteous cry." All vanished now from the earth—the piteous cry and all; unless where Rodney's swamps are wild enough still, perhaps it is true, the last of the ivory-billed woodpeckers still exist in the world, in this safe spot, inaccessible to man.

QUESTIONS

1. The preceding excerpt appears toward the end of a lyrical essay in which Welty evokes a vivid sense of "a small section of old Mississippi River country and its little chain of lost towns between Vicksburg and Natchez." What is the dominant impression of the countryside surrounding Rodney's Landing that Welty creates in this selection? Describe the landscape in your own words.

2. Why does Welty call the live oaks "the most wonderful trees in this land"? Why does she refer to the anecdote from W. H. Hudson's autobiography?

3. If this essay has a central theme it is that, in spite of "commerce and the way of rivers and roads"—in short, regardless of the inevitable changes wrought by time—nature itself endures. Welty's intention is to evoke the unchanging "sense of place" in this small area of the South. How does her description of the natural world serve to reinforce this theme?

4. Why does Welty devote so much space to describing the ivory-billed woodpecker? How does it relate to the theme of change and permanence?

5. Look up the term "Gothic." Why does Welty use it to describe the vines in Rodney's Landing?

6. Welty uses a great deal of very precise language in this selection. She takes care to call the foliage and flowers around Rodney's Landing by their exact name. Look up any names you aren't familiar with (e.g., muscadine vines, scuppernong, maypop, clematis). Why does Welty name the vegetation so precisely?

7. Is it possible for readers to visualize the landscape Welty describes even if they are not familiar with the names of all the flowers and plants? Why or why not? What makes Welty's use of such flower names as lady's eardrops, passionflower, and virgin's-bower so effective?

8. Clearly one of Welty's intentions in this selection is to evoke a rich sense of the natural abundance, the wonderful lushness, of the landscape around Rodney's Landing. How does her choice of words and images help her achieve this aim?

SUGGESTION FOR WRITING

Welty, who was born and has lived most of her life in Mississippi, clearly has a deep emotional connection to the countryside she describes in this selection. Pick a place that you feel similarly attached to—your hometown, the place your grandparents live (or lived), a favorite vacation spot from your childhood—and describe it in a way that will give the reader a sense, not only of its physical characteristics, but also of what it means to you.

William Least Heat Moon
OIL CITY BAR
★ ★ ★

The story of how Blue Highways *came to be written is almost as interesting as the book itself. In the spring of 1978, William Trogdon—a college English instructor of part-Osage Indian ancestry—was laid off from his job at a small school in Columbia, Missouri. Several months earlier, his marriage of ten years had fallen apart. With his life in ruins, he decided on a quintessentially American solution: to hit the road. He embarked on a 14,000-mile journey through the back roads of America, hoping to find, among other things, himself.*

Trogdon had no preplanned itinerary. He followed his impulses, searching for obscure, out-of-the-way places with eccentric names: Dime Box, Texas; Scratch Ankle, Alabama; Whynot, Mississippi; Remote, Oregon. At first, he intended to do nothing more than keep a personal record—on film and on paper—of his journey and the people he met during it. But by the time he returned to Columbia, he had to decided to shape his experiences into a book. The manuscript went through eight drafts and took four years to complete.

When Blue Highways *was finally published in 1982 under Trogdon's Indian name, William Least Heat Moon, it became an immediate critical and commercial success. A nationwide best-seller, it was hailed as one of the best travel memoirs ever written about our country—a book which (in the words of novelist Jim Harrison) describes "with true heat and pungency... an America that scarcely anybody knows about, an America that we have been led to believe no longer exists."*

What does the traveler do at night in a strange town when he wants conversation? In the United States, there's usually a single choice: a tavern.

The Oil City Bar was north of the railroad tracks near the spot where the Great Northern accidentally founded Shelby in 1891 by dumping off an old boxcar. From it the town grew, and the antecedents still showed.

One of the authors of the Montana Federal Writers' Project describes Shelby in the 1890s as

> the sort of town that producers of western movies have ever since been trying to reproduce in papier-mâché. . . . The town playboys were featured in the *Police Gazette* after holding up an opera troupe passing through on a railroad train. . . . The men shot out the engine headlight, the car windows, and the red signal lights, and forced the conductor to execute a clog dance.

I was out looking around to see how the old Wild West was doing when I came across the Oil City Bar. Although the night had turned cold and gusty, only the screendoor was closed; the wooden one stood open so men in down vests wouldn't overheat. A shattered pool cue lay in the corner, and to one side was a small room lighted only by the blue neon flicker of a beer sign—the kind of light you could go mad in. Left of the ten-point buck trophy and above the gallon jars of pickled pig's feet and hard-boiled eggs hung a big lithograph of a well-formed woman, shotgun in hand. She was duck hunting. Other than her rubber boots, she wore not a stitch.

A man, somewhat taller than the barstool and dressed in yellow from shoulders to cowboy boots, drank with assembly-line regularity. He leered wobbly-eyed at the huntress, tried to speak, but blew a bubble instead.

I blame what was about to happen to him on the traditional design of the American bar: a straight counter facing a mirrored wall, which forces the customer to stare at himself or put a crick in his neck looking at someone else. The English build their bars in circles or horseshoes or right angles—anything to get another face in your line of sight. Their bars, as a result, are more sociable. For the American, he stares into his own face, or at bottles of golden liquors, or at whatever hangs above the bar; conversation declines and drinking increases. If the picture above the bar is a nude, as is common in old Western bars, you have an iconography for creating unfulfilled desire: the reality of a man's own six o'clock face below the dream of perfect flesh.

I turned away from the huntress to watch a pool game. There was a loud *flump* beside me. Knees to his chest, the man in yellow lay dead drunk on the floor. He looked like a cheese curl. His friend said, "Chuckie's one good little drinker."

A woman of sharp face, pretty ten years ago, kept watching me. She had managed to pack her hips into what she hoped was a pair of mean jeans; a cigarette was never out of her mouth, and, after every deep draw, her exhalations were smokeless. She was trying for trouble, but I minded my own business. More or less. The man with her, Lonnie, walked up to me. He looked as if he were made out of whipcord. "Like that lady?" he said.

"What lady is that?"

"One you been staring at."

"Without my glasses, I can't distinguish a man from a woman." That was a lie.

"The lady said you were distinguishing her pretty good."

Well, boys, there you have it. Some fading face trying to make herself the center of men's anger, proving she could still push men to their limits.

"Couldn't recognize her from here if I did know her."

He pressed up close. Trouble coming. "Don't tell *me,*" he said. "Happens all the time. She thinks men stare at her."

"Look. No offense, but I've no interest in the woman."

"I can see it, and she can see it, and that's the trouble. But let's talk."

It was an act he had been coerced into. He was faking it. He called for two beers and set one in front of me. "Take it," he said. "When I sit down, I'm going to tell her you apologized for staring but you just thought she was one hell of a fox. Don't make a liar out of me."

He walked off. That was the silliest row I never got into.

I went to the restroom. When I came out, Lonnie was standing at the bar and the woman had gone to sit with three other women. She didn't buy it, I thought. DRIFTER BLOWN AWAY IN BAR.

"Trouble?" I said.

"Forget it. She works with those broads. Casterating bitches every one."

There was a commotion that got loud and moved outside to the windy street.

Two men from Mountain Bell, the phone company, were going to fight. They came at each other, locked outstretched arms and pushed, circling slowly as if turned by the prairie wind. They tired and revolved slower, but neither let go or fell down. A police car drove up and honked. The fighters went to the squadcar, both leaning on the window to listen. After a while, they slumped off in opposite directions, and that was the end of it.

Lonnie and I watched from the bar. After it was over, he said, "Jack Dempsey had a real fight here."

"A fight in this very bar?"

"Not a bar fight—heavyweight boxing. Shelby built a grandstand for it. Forty thousand seats. Seven thousand people showed up. Town almost went bust."

The woman came over to Lonnie and said, "Let's go." She was mad. I left soon after, walking out into the streets of the new Wild West.

QUESTIONS

1. Why does Least Heat Moon begin with the excerpt from the Montana Federal Writers' Project history of Shelby?

2. What kind of place is the Oil City Bar? How would you describe its atmosphere? What details are particularly effective in evoking a sense of the place?

3. Describe Lonnie in your own words. How does Least Heat Moon manage to create such a vivid character in such a brief piece of writing?

4. Discuss the fight between the two men from Mountain Bell. What is notable about it? What effect does Least Heat Moon's description of it have on the reader?

5. Least Heat Moon's tone is often dry and tinged with irony. Point to some places in this selection that exemplify this tone. In what sense is the entire incident at the Oil City Bar ironic?

6. One of the best things about this selection (and, in fact, the book as a whole) is Least Heat Moon's skillful use of dialogue. What makes the dialogue here—particularly Lonnie's exchanges with Least Heat Moon—so effective?

7. After Lonnie first approaches him, Least Heat Moon writes, "Well, boys, there you have it. . . ." Whom is Least Heat Moon addressing here? Does this sentence fit in with the rest of the piece? Does it contribute anything to the selection? If so, what?

SUGGESTIONS FOR WRITING

1. Lonnie's date seems to be a natural troublemaker. If you know anyone like her—man or woman—write an essay describing that person.

2. Lonnie and the woman he is with seem, in many ways, to be a mismatched

couple. She is (in his words) a "casterating bitch," whereas Lonnie, in spite of his show of cowboy toughness, seems to be a reasonable and easygoing person. Write an essay in which you describe any couple you know—or any pair of friends—whose personalities seem diametrically opposed to one another.

Jennifer Allen
STRANGER IN A STRANGE LAND
★ ★ ★

Born into a "magazine family" (her father is a vice president of Reader's Digest*), freelancer Jennifer Allen was still a teenager when her first article was published in* Seventeen. *She served as a* Mademoiselle *guest editor while a student at Yale and after graduation worked at a number of magazines. Her articles have appeared in various publications (including* Life *and* The New York Times*), and for several years she contributed a regular column, "Private Lives," to* New York *magazine. Recently, Allen has turned to writing fiction and is currently at work on a novel.*

The following essay—one of Allen's "Private Lives" pieces for New York—*originally appeared in November 1982.*

Anyone could tell she has grown up in the city. Suburban children do not, at eighteen, look five or six years older than they are, do not walk with her loose, diffident assurance, elegant as a cat. Their eyes are not this cool and discriminating; they do not have her sure sense of style. She is tall and wears orchid or lime or striped stockings—her legs should win a prize—and pointy bootlets that stop at the ankle and fluffy little miniskirts from Norma Kamali. On top are giant men's sweaters and pearl chokers she buys at thrift shops on Amsterdam Avenue.

The only tipoff that she is still a teenager is her voice, which is singsongy, like a bird's chirp. She also speaks very quickly, slurring one word into the next, so that when she talks to people who are older than she is—something she tries to avoid whenever possible—she is often forced to repeat herself several times while they smile and strain to understand her. Otherwise, she is a study in sophistication. She grew up in the city; she is not easy to shock. Her father lives with his girl friend. Her mother is in the movie business and gets her passes to screenings. She has had a book dedicated to her, has met Robert Evans and Shelley Duvall, has had her hair sculpted at Kenneth's (badly, she says). She likes her Sunday breakfasts from Zabar's and knows the selection at Dumas by heart. In many ways she is all grown up already: She has been traversing the city by herself for years, doesn't wobble in spike heels, doesn't paint her face with makeup like a teenager but wears just the right amount.

She is miserable, of course. Her style, experience, and miniskirts are all for naught, useless, going to waste. Some fluky twist of fate has landed her at the wrong college. Not that she wasn't resigned to going to college in the first place. On the contrary, she understood and accepted the concept of higher education: yet another way station society has for you to hang out in until it will accept you as an adult, a stopping place in which to eat Cap'n Crunch and talk about sex while you wait for adulthood. Adulthood: that state of grace wherein it is possible to eat dinner out every night, meet people for drinks at midnight if you want, and afford the clothes at Charivari.

High school was like that, a place to wait. She grasped this early on, would not get suckered into being a good sport, having school spirit, Making the Most of It. In vain, anxious guidance counselors implored her to partake in extracurricular activities; instead, she devoted her afternoons to eating pizza and sunning herself on the sidewalk in front of the school. To fulfill the gym requirement, she took jogging because all you had to do to pass was walk around the reservoir twice a week. In her last year, she would not even go to parties or to Trader Vic's with her old set of school friends, but took up with a college art student who wore holey old clothes and had a very cool, choppy haircut. She never showed up to have her picture taken for the yearbook, would have happily skipped the graduation ceremony if she had had any say in the matter.

But she was not prepared for college to be as rude as high school. Never mind how she ended up at this particular place—a friend of a friend had a sister who went here and liked it, something like that—but it is in the middle of nowhere, eight hours from New York by car, a tiny school surrounded by cabbage patches, apple orchards, and boarded-up drive-in movie theaters as far as the eye can see. The kids are from places like Buffalo and Utica and Troy, reminisce about their high-school proms, and dress in brand-new Top-Siders and Fair Isle sweaters and turtlenecks with little frogs printed on them. The girls have brought their yearbooks and stuffed animals to college with them, wear too much makeup, send greeting cards to their boyfriends that say "The best thing that ever happened to me . . . is you," and probably think Fiorucci is a kind of pasta. The boys look twelve years old, like REO Speedwagon, deck their dorm walls with college banners, and have never been to a Bowie concert or the midnight show of *Eraserhead.*

All these kids believe that college is a huge deal, a once-in-a-lifetime opportunity to meet new people and be independent and live in the world. Molly has seen so much of the world already—exhibitionists in the park, the Peppermint Lounge, bums cakey with dirt sleeping on the sidewalk, Broadway shows. As if to make it absolutely clear that she is hardly anticipating four years of enriching experiences but will just be passing through, she got ready for college in three hours flat, dismissing the school's helpful advice to pack an iron, laundry bag, hangers, wastepaper basket—items she rarely if ever has any use for—and stuffing all of her clothes into five battered cardboard boxes. That—plus some Elvis Costello tapes, a typewriter, and two pencils—was it.

On the drive to school, her father gives several careful speeches on such subjects as how to open a checking account and the importance of eating three meals a day. Molly talks about being psyched for Thanksgiving vacation, when she will come into the city and see friends, and wonders whether she will actually be expected to meet the girl who wrote her the incredibly dorky letter over the summer saying that she was Molly's Big Sister.

As the hours pass and the landscape thins out to a shopping mall here and there, an occasional diner, sagging old barns, Molly's fluttery voice is heard no more. She was sure her father had exaggerated when he said the school was eight hours from the city, but the trip is taking forever, and there are even road signs for Canada. Gloom hangs heavy in the car. Finally, her father turns off the highway and drives down the main street of the college town, the kind of town Molly has seen only in movies like *The Last Picture Show.* She stares at the dreary dress shoppes, Hair Palaces, hardware stores, J. C. Penney—not one campy card shop, not one antique-clothes boutique. Molly is silent and looks stalwart, like a mourner at a funeral who is trying not to crumple. Look at the lake, says her father, pointing to a sparkly expanse of blue to the left of town. Molly says she is really psyched for Thanksgiving vacation and is going to make friends with someone who has a car.

When she gets to her dorm room, she finds that her roommate has come and gone but made her presence known. Her side of the room is already a snug warren of domesticity: checked bedspread with matching bolster pillows to make it look like a couch, plants hanging from ornamental wooden plaques, posters with love poems and sunsets on them, a stack of mellow rock records, and, on the shelves above her desk, a stash of snack food—Ritz crackers, peanut butter, Cup-a-Soups—and lifetime supplies of Q-Tips cotton swabs, multiple vitamins, and tampons. Molly groans and checks out the closet: a dozen belts made of grosgrain ribbon, many sweaters, and, on a *shoe tree,* the hated Top-Siders. Molly cannot believe it. "Oh, God," she says finally, "we have the same down jacket." Twelve minutes later, when Molly is finished unpacking her boxes, her side of the room looks like a jail cell. Molly looks at the empty shelves above her desk. "I should have brought a dictionary," she says, and tries to smile. It is difficult to say good-bye to her, like leaving someone stranded on a desert island.

She doesn't come to the city on weekends, because she has no way of getting here, but she calls home a lot, speaking in a faint, thin voice, like a sick person. Civilization, she says, does not exist here. By this she means that the pizza in town is soggy, that the one movie theater is showing a film she saw on an airplane a year ago, and that no one knows what a bagel is. At school, cider-and-doughnut parties, blow-dryers, and dorm meetings abound. No one drinks anything but 50-cents-a-glass beer; no one knows that the only real drinks are ones with at least three ingredients, one of which must be Kahlúa. *All My Children* is some small comfort, and—her father is delighted, but careful not to let on to her how proud it makes him—she is studying. Molly actually frets about her papers, wrestles with Martin Buber and Virginia Woolf, is bothered by B's. She talks about acing final exams and getting extra credit in Psych by volunteering for an experiment— academic strategizing that has never been heard from her before.

Still, she wants to transfer. To a school near a city. In the meantime, she wants a car. Could she have her father's car, which is just languishing and getting rusty in a city garage? No, she can't, she is told, and her voice gets even wispier.

By Parents' Weekend, when her father visits her, Molly has found one friend to be miserable with, a big, blond, sturdy girl named Anna. Anna, who is from Stockholm, also detests cider and doughnuts and dorm meetings. She has taught Molly to say "hello" and "s——" in Swedish; together they have combed the only thrift shop in town and have bought pillbox hats with veils that they put on to laugh at each other. While the other girls talk giddily of boys, of upcoming dates, Molly and Anna, both badly burned by love over the summer, discuss the futility of love, the fickleness of men, knowing as two 30-year-olds.

They know one boy at school, and the only reason they cultivate him is that he has a car. Not that there is anywhere to go around here except Friendly's, but eventually maybe she and Anna can borrow the car and take off for Boston or New York or even Syracuse. Syracuse will at least have first-run movies and bars that aren't crawling with kids from school. It really sucks that she and Anna don't have their own car—Molly's father's car, for example, Molly tells her father several times during the weekend—but she guesses this boy's car is better than nothing at all. Molly's father pretends to be deaf and asks if she has enough blankets and money.

Molly is sipping a White Russian and bringing up this subject again over dinner with her father and Anna at the only fancy restaurant in the area when a miracle happens. It is too good to be true: Her father announces that something has come up, that he has to fly back to the city tomorrow and—calm down, Molly, he says—leave the car with her for a few weeks, until Thanksgiving. Molly's face is luminous with joy. She and Anna embrace at the table, knocking over a dish of rolls, then leave their shrimp cocktails to bolt to the ladies' room and discuss their blissfully good fortune. As they make their way across the restaurant, which is packed with parents and the kids Molly and Anna have no use for, you can hear their voices, tweeting and trilling at each other.

QUESTIONS

1. Describe Molly in your own words. How would you characterize her personality? Does anything about her behavior suggest that she is not quite as mature as she likes to believe?

2. How is the other side of Molly's dorm room—the half inhabited by her roommate—described? Judging from the details we are given, what sort of person does the roommate seem to be?

3. How would you describe Allen's tone in this essay? Is it satiric? Disapproving? Objective? How does she seem to feel about Molly?

4. In describing Molly, Allen relies almost entirely on details relating to style,

possessions, and glamorous names. We are told how Molly dresses, what restaurants she enjoys going to, which celebrities she has met. In what sense is this descriptive method appropriate, given Allen's subject? How does it create a vivid sense of Molly's personality (without ever explicitly describing that personality)?

5.   From time to time, Allen uses language that is meant to evoke Molly's own style of speech. Point to some words and phrases that give us a sense of Molly's own voice and tone.

6.   Look at the last sentence of the essay. Why does Allen use the words "tweeting" and "trilling" to describe the sound of Molly's and Anna's voices?

SUGGESTIONS FOR WRITING

1.   Describe the room of someone you know well (roommate, best friend, sibling). Be selective and precise. Choose specific, concrete details that will convey a vivid sense of your subject's personality.

2.   Describe someone you know whom you consider a "phony"—someone stuck-up, pretentious, or excessively vain. Don't generalize about this individual's personality. Use specific details (of dress, behavior, speech) that will make this person come alive for the reader.

Edward Hoagland
TWO CLOWNS
★ ★ ★ ★

All essayists, Edward Hoagland has written, can be divided into two types: those who "prefer subject matter they can rejoice in" and those who like to write about things "they deplore and wish to savage with ironies." As the following selection makes clear (and as he himself acknowledges), Hoagland falls into the first category. His essays, writes critic Christopher Lehmann-Haupt, are "the rejoicings of an enthusiast, the outpourings of a boyish lover of circuses and bear tracks, tugboats and girlie shows, rodeos and rural solitude."

As a writer—not only of essays but also of novels and short stories— Hoagland has wide-ranging interests. He is at once a lover of the wilderness, well known for his passionate, precisely observed descriptions of nature, and a die-hard New Yorker, who writes with equal gusto about the urban scene. As a young man, Hoagland worked for a period with a traveling circus, an experience that formed the basis of his first published book, the 1956 novel Cat Man. *His intimate knowledge of and appreciation for circus performing are evident in the following piece, "Two*

Clowns," which originally appeared as part of a 1971 Life *magazine*
article on the 101st annual tour of "The Greatest Show on Earth," the
Ringling Brothers, Barnum & Bailey Circus.

———

Clowning is the one profession in the circus which has no limits on what can be
done, and where youth and physique don't count for much. A man may start late
in it or may operate in the realm of hallucination if he wants. Usually clowns take
a role which is close to the earth—a plowman-pieman-tinker type, a barefoot
sprite whose sex is uncertain because he's infantile. They're overly tall or small
or in some way out of it—innocent and light of heart, yet stuck with some
disfigurement which is an extension of what the rest of us are supposed to want:
a nose with "character," for instance, or tously hair and a fair skin. But these
possibilities ample for the average rather passive though contentious fellow who
makes clowning his career, are trivial detail in the persona of the few great clowns.
After apprenticing in paleface as a simpleton for a few years, with a thick, giddy,
up-arching, imprinted smile, such men will gradually start to draw a more scored
and complicated personality with the greasepaint, developing a darker role.

Otto Griebling,* who is the best American clown, wears a rag heap that has
grown so shapeless as to seem mountainous. His nose, instead of bulbous, is bent
and decomposing in a face the color of a frying pan. His resentful stare, eaten up
with grievances, is as calculating as a monkey's. He plays a bum whose universe
has been so mutilated and circumscribed that all he knows is that he's free to sit
where he is sitting or walk where he is going to walk, and any impulse we may
feel to try and cheer him up is itself cause for outrage, not worth even a bitter
laugh. He hasn't lost so much that he isn't afraid of further blows, but as he
shuffles along with a notebook, compiling a blacklist, marking people in the
audience down, all his grudges blaze in his face. Like a sore-footed janitor (he's
seventy-four), he climbs into the crowd to put the heat on selected guests—begins
perversely dusting their chairs, falling in love at close quarters, gazing at some
squirming miss with his whole soul, leaning closer still, until, inexplicably furious,
he slaps her with his cleaning cloth—she may try kissing him but it won't work.
Now that in actual life his vocal cords have been removed, Griebling has inaugu-
rated a "broadcast," too. Wearing a headset and a microphone, he follows the
rest of the clowns, whispering a commentary on their fate, on each mishap. His
role is madder, more paranoid and ruined, than Emmett Kelly's famous tramp
was; less lachrymose, it fits the times. With faded baggage tickets pinned to his
cloak, he tries to powder his scorched face, looks for old enemies in the crowd.
Obviously long past attempting to cope, he simply wants revenge; yet he's so
small-time that instead of being fearful we laugh at him.

Added to Griebling's troubles is the same seething irritant that seems to
bother all clowns. Nobody likes these ovations which are bestowed on the man

———

*Otto Griebling died in New York City, April 19, 1972.

in the center ring. Suddenly he loses patience, grabs three tin plates, clacks them together and insists that the audience hail *him*. He juggles perfunctorily, since what he's interested in is not the juggling but the applause, and signals with his hands for a real crescendo. Setting two sides of the arena against each other, he works them up almost to the level the trapeze troupe achieved. But he isn't a bit satisfied. It never quite reaches the imagined pitch. Besides, it is too late for consolation now—too much of his life already has gone by!

Pio Nock is the Swiss master clown. He's old enough to have a daughter who romps on the single trapeze, dangling her yellow hair, wriggling from side to side, looking like butterfat in the strong lights. Nock confronted big cats and the flying trapeze when he was young and now is a high-wire clown, although he does some conventional clowning as well. He plays a sort of country cousin, a man floundering past the prime of life with nothing to show for it except his scars, not even an ironic viewpoint or the pleasure of vindictiveness. Where Griebling stands in baffled fury, past tears or shouting, torn between petulance and outraged astonishment, Nock is a man who doesn't look for root causes, doesn't even suspect that he has enemies or that the odds might be stacked against him. From every misfortune he simply goes on trying to learn. And for this characterization he doesn't rely much on greasepaint or costumes; instead, he makes queer hollow hoots, like the sounds in a birdhouse. As a trademark they have the advantage over costumes that the kids also can imitate them. They troop out of the auditorium parroting him.

Whenever Nock's country bumpkin gets slapped around, he's always willing to forgive the prankster if only the fellow will teach him how to do that particular trick so that Nock will never be slapped around quite the same way again. Of course, during the show we discover that there are more pranks on the earth than Nock will ever become proof against. We learn that life has limited its gifts to him to these few satisfactions—after the fact. After all, if the world appears upside down it must only be because he is standing on his head. Punishment follows each blunder; yet when he sees a nice girl—his daughter—up on the high wire, he decides that he wants to make an endeavor at that also. At first the ringmaster stops him, but escaping the ringmaster's grasp, he climbs a rope ladder and in pantomime is instructed by her in the rudiments of wire-walking, cheeping eagerly at every lesson learned. The next thing he knows, he is out on the wire, terrified, alone, all the tips forgotten, whistling if he can. Whistling in the dark, a man in a jam, he teeters, steps on his own feet, gaining experience by trial and error, keeping his courage up with those strange hoots, which seem to epitomize how absurdly fragile life is, how often we see a tragedy in the making, as well as its end. The band plays music representing the wry look we wear while watching a stranger's funeral procession pass.

Nock stumbles on the wire and slips to his knees; wobbling, he looks downward, giving an unforgettable peep of fear. He's a short man with long legs and one of those wedgelike noses that even without makeup poke out starkly. His hoot is really like a sigh distilled—the sigh that draws on one's own resources as being the only source from which to draw. A man in the wrong place, again he jerks and nearly falls, giving his peep of mortality, and casts all his hopes just on the process of being methodical, doing what he's been taught as if by rote, which is what most of us do when we are in over our heads. But now he discovers he's learning! His obtuseness has shielded him from the danger a little, and suddenly he finds that he is getting the knack. He lets out a tombstone-chiseler's hoot. Now comes the moment when he can enjoy himself after having learned a particular dodge.

Pio Nock and Otto Griebling are great stars, and the image they leave in my head is so accessible that I don't miss them after the circus moves on. In the case of those performers who do mere heroics the memory does not survive as vividly.

QUESTIONS

1. According to Hoagland, the comic personalities of great clowns like Otto Streibling and Pio Nock gradually become "dark" and "complicated." Locate and discuss the details—of dress, gesture, and action—that Hoagland provides to illustrate these terms.

2. How does Hoagland manage to portray these two men, not as professional buffoons, but as serious actors, performing roles of depth and complexity? How does Hoagland's vocabulary, his choice of words, contribute to the seriousness of the piece?

3. Define the following words, referring to a dictionary if necessary: bulbous, circumscribed, blacklist, lachrymose, perfunctorily, ironic, petulance, rudiments, wry, obtuseness.

4. Go through this essay carefully, underlining Hoagland's metaphors and similes. Is Hoagland's use of figurative language effective? Explain.

5. Hoagland describes both clowns in detail. Which parts of his description seem most vivid to you? Why? Having read through the essay, which details do you recall most clearly?

6. One of the interesting things about this essay—whose subject is a pair of professional funnymen—is its tone. How would you describe Hoagland's tone? Is it at all humorous? Is it appropriate to the subject? Is it effective? Why or why not?

SUGGESTIONS FOR WRITING

1. Describe your favorite comedian as vividly as you can. You might choose a stand-up comic like Joan Rivers, a comic actor like Bill Murray, or anyone you know who is especially funny. Make sure to use details that will give the reader a sharp sense of this person's appearance, personality, and comedic style.

2. Write a description of a circus, carnival, or amusement park. Use details that will capture the atmosphere of the place—its sights, sounds, and smells.

Edward Abbey
DOWN THERE IN THE ROCKS
★ ★ ★

Although an Easterner by birth, Edward Abbey is closely identified, as a writer, with the American Southwest. In his novels and essays, he speaks as an impassioned defender of the wilderness, celebrating its grandeur and heaping contempt on those who exploit, pollute, and vandalize it, from greedy land developers to rapacious strip miners to mindlessly destructive tourists.

Abbey is no armchair naturalist, waxing sentimental about the beauties of a world he only visits during summer vacations. Having worked as a park ranger and fire lookout from 1956–71, he is on intimate terms with the natural world and claims a closer spiritual kinship with the American Indian than with the average citizen of our contemporary, high-tech society (in an official biography, he identifies his religion as Piute). He is a man, in the words of critic John Leonard, "who wants to go up a mountain or into the desert alone" and "he does not want to be followed by cement trucks, mobile homes, cabin cruisers, helicopters and souvenir stands."

Abbey's books include Desert Solitaire *(1968),* Black Sun *(1971),* The Monkey Wrench Gang *(1975),* The Journey Home *(1977),* The Hidden Canyon *(1978), and* Abbey's Road *(1979), from which the following essay is taken.*

———

We're driving these two little boats down Lake Powell in Utah, Clair Quist and his girl friend Pamela Davis in one, me and Mark Davis in the other. Mark, Pam, and Clair are professional river guides, boatmen, characters, honest folk. They work for an outfit called Moki-Mac (or Murky Muck) Expeditions out of Green River, Utah. Work for it? Hell, Clair and his two brothers own the damn thing. Whatever it is. What it is, is one of the three or four best river-running outfits in the West.

Nobody's working today. This is a holiday outing for the four of us. Our goal is Escalante Canyon and its arboreal system of branch canyons. We're going by way of the so-called lake because we plan to explore a few side canyons, the mouths of which are now under water. Starting at Bullfrog Marina, our course takes us south-southwest past old familiar landmarks. Halls Creek Canyon, the south end of the Waterpocket Fold, the Rincon, the mouth of Long Canyon. Around that next bend will be the opening to the Escalante.

Bright blue above, the golden sun at high noon. On either side the red walls of what once had been—and will again be—Glen Canyon. No use fretting about it anymore. We throw our orange peels overboard to feed the fish. These hatchery fish will eat anything. Clair and Mark amuse themselves by steering as close as they can, without quite ramming them, to the buoys marking the channel. There's nothing much else to do out here on this smooth expanse of flat and stagnant water. Pam reads a book; I stare at the cliffs, and at the domes, plateaus, and mountains beyond, remembering what I sometimes wish I could forget: Glen Canyon as it was, the wild river, the beaches, the secret passages and hidden cathedrals of stone, the wilderness alive and sweet and charged with mystery, miracle, magic.

No use fretting. I throw my torn beer can into the lake, where it sinks and disappears. We clear the corner and plane up-canyon into the broad Escalante. Sheer, slick vertical walls of Navajo sandstone rising on either side, one wall in blue shadow, the other in radiant light. But nothing lives along those stone barriers; all that was living and beautiful lies many fathoms below, drowned in dead water and buried under slime. No matter. Forget it.

Cabin cruisers roar past; we wallow across their wakes. A houseboat like a floating boxcar comes toward us, passes. The people on board stare, then wave tentatively, unsure whether or not we, in our little open boats, deserve the dignity of recognition. That doesn't matter either. We wave back.

A few miles up the canyon we go ashore in a cove without a name. Others have been here before, as the human dung and toilet paper, the tinfoil, plastic plates, abandoned underwear, rusty fishhooks, tangled lines, discarded socks, empty Coors cans, and broken glass clearly attest. But on the shores of Lake Powell, Jewel of the Colorado and National Recreational Slum, you have no choice. All possible campsites look like this one. There is no lower form of life known to zoological science than the motorboat fisherman, the speedboat sight-seer.

We have stopped here because we want to climb an old stockman's trail that leads to the rim from this vicinity. We tie the boats to a rock, load our packs, and ascend the humps of bare slickrock toward the skyline 800 feet above. Halfway up we find traces of the long-abandoned trail—wide, shallow steps chiseled in the sandstone, sufficient to enable a horse to climb or descend.

Over the rim, out of sight of the lake and its traffic, we make camp for the night. In the morning we march north and west over a petrified sea of stone waves, across sandy flats studded with juniper, yucca, single-leaf ash, scrubby Gambel oak, and up monolithic ridges that seem to lead right into the sky. Far beyond are the salmon pink walls of upper Stevens Canyon, the Circle Cliffs, and the incomprehensible stone forms, pale rose and mystical, of the great monocline known as Waterpocket Fold. We'll never get there; this is merely a reconnoiter, a scouting trip, and we're not even sure we want to get there. Perhaps a few places are best left unexplored, seen from a distance but never entered, never walked upon. Let them be, for now.

At some point out there, among a circle of sandstone mammaries hundreds of feet high, we find a deep groove in the endless rock. Down in the groove stands a single cottonwood tree, alive and golden with its October leaves. Alone in all these square miles of desolate grandeur, this dry Elysium, it is the tree of life. We find a way down to it, and sure enough, as we had hoped, we discover a series of deep potholes, some of them half-filled with sand, but others with water. Old rainwater, but clear and cool and heartening. We fill our jugs and bottles and camp nearby for a couple of days.

Campfire of juniper and scrub oak. The smell of coffee, the incense of burning wood. Vast, lurid sunsets flare across the sky, east as well as west, portending storm and winter, but we don't care. Showers of meteors streak across the field of the stars, trailing languid flames. An old, worn moon goes down as the rising sun comes out. In the chill mornings we make a breakfast and track off again in another direction. What direction? Any direction.

One afternoon we sit by a pool on the lip of stone that overhangs the head of one of the Escalante's many side canyons. The drop-off must be 1,000 feet straight down. Down . . . and . . . down and . . . down, your mind falls to the green pool in a sandy basin far below. Perennial springs flow there, under this overhanging spout we lie upon; we can see the glaze and glitter of a stream snaking through jungles of willow, box elder, redbud, and Frémont poplar toward the Escalante River somewhere beyond, hidden in its profound meanders.

We see a natural stone arch below, under the west wall, and balanced rocks, free-standing pillars, pinnacles, alcoves, grottos, half-dome amphitheaters. The pathways of many deer curve with the contours of the talus slopes. A redtail hawk rides the air, soaring *beneath* us. Ravens clack and croak and flap around, quarreling over nothing. Over anything. Over nothing.

In the shallow pond at our side are hundreds of tadpole shrimp, the grotesque, helmet-headed *Apus longicaudatus,* swimming back and forth, pursuing one another, the large capturing and devouring the small. They look like tiny horseshoe crabs—or like miniature trilobites from the earliest seas of all, come back to haunt us with the memory of the earth's long, strange, splendid, and meaningless history. The spiral of time. The circle of life. The vanity of death. The black hole of space.

The hot radiance of the sun, pouring on our prone bodies, suffusing our flesh, melting our bones, lulls us toward sleep. Over the desert and the canyons, down there in the rocks, a huge vibration of light and stillness and solitude shapes itself into the form of hovering wings spread out across the sky from the world's rim to the world's end. Not God—the term seems insufficient—but something unnameable, and more beautiful, and far greater, and more terrible.

My friends and I touch one another, smiling, and roll a few boulders into the canyon, only for fun, meaning no harm. We listen, and when the bedrock stops trembling, and after the last far-off echoes of our thunder die away, we shoulder our packs and start the long tramp back to where we came from, wherever that was. It makes no difference. Willing or not, ready or not, we'll get there.

Behind us, back at the canyon's head, the sun blazes down on the shallow pool. The hooded grope things swim writhing through the water. One thousand feet beneath, the spring continues to flow and the little stream to snake its shining way through canyon jungle toward the hidden river. The hawk soars, the ravens quarrel. And no man sees. And no woman hears. No one is there. Everything is there.

QUESTIONS

1. Abbey creates a vivid contrast between Lake Powell itself and the places in the canyons where he and his friends camp out. They are two radically different worlds. How do they differ from each other?

2. Look closely at the language Abbey uses to describe the sights on Lake Powell. How are his feelings of bitterness and disgust conveyed in his choice of words and images? What is the effect of his saying several times early in his essay "No use fretting" and "no matter"?

3. How would you describe Abbey's attitude toward the wilderness and how is that attitude conveyed in language? How would you characterize his tone when he writes about the wilderness? What, if anything, does he discover— feel himself in touch with—"down there in the rocks"?

4. *Onomatopoeia* refers to the use of words whose sounds suggest their meanings (crash, slam, hiss, crunch, etc.). Where, in Abbey's description of the creatures he observes in the wilderness, does he make use of onomatopoeic language?

5. A less precise observer than Abbey, camping in an area as seemingly desolate as the wilderness surrounding Lake Powell, might simply see endless stretches of red-brown rock. How does Abbey use specific, concrete details to create a vivid picture of landscape that, far from being barren, is "charged with mystery, miracle, magic"? How does Abbey create an impression of his desert area as a place of endless, almost miraculous, variety?

SUGGESTIONS FOR WRITING

1. Describe a place you know that has been defaced, destroyed, or simply allowed to deteriorate. It doesn't have to be a wilderness area ruined by thoughtless vacationers. It might be anything—a vandalized playground, an old-time movie palace razed to make way for a parking lot, a dilapidated but once-beautiful house, etc.

2. Most people have their own refuge or retreat—a place where they can go to "get away from it all." It might be a faraway vacation spot or a quiet corner of the local library. Describe your own special place, using details that will give readers a clear sense of its meaning in your life.

STUDENT ESSAY

Mary Whatley
HOW DO YOU SAY "ELF" IN FRENCH?
★ ★ ★

Like her well-traveled father, the subject of this affectionate reminiscence, Mary Whatley has spent a good deal of time on the move. Born and reared in Chicago, she resettled in Fort Lauderdale, Florida, at the age of 10, after her parents divorced. She spent alternate years with her father and mother and, she writes, "managed to go to three high schools in four years, living in Wiesbaden, West Germany, and Alameda, California, as well as Fort Lauderdale."

In 1967, she entered Merritt College in Oakland, California, to study fine arts but left before receiving her degree. Over the next dozen years, she lived in a variety of cities—Berkeley, San Francisco, Chicago, New York, Brattleboro—supporting herself in a variety of ways: as a ballet teacher, bookkeeper, dental assistant, waitress, and stage manager.

Following her marriage in 1980, she returned to New York City and resumed her college education in 1984. At present, she lives with her husband and daughter in Connecticut, where (besides pursuing her bachelor's degree at Charter Oaks College) she "manages a commercial art studio, devotes time and energy to rehabilitating the Whatley house, and tries to get to an aerobics class as regularly as possible."

———

Back in the mid-60's Dad was in his early 40's. My best friend, Jill, swore that he looked exactly like Jack Lemmon. I could see the resemblance, too. His face, especially the eyes, and coloring were very similar. He was boyish, mischievous and handsome, all at the same time. His thick, medium-brown hair was worn in a longish crew cut, and his clothes were Ivy League. Jill had a crush on my dad and I had a crush on hers: he was just like David Niven. While Colonel M. was extremely dashing and sophisticated (he wore a little moustache and drove a Porsche and hung around kids as little as possible), my father was quite relaxed, loved being around the five of us kids, and had a special fondness for teasing young girls. If my chubby, pre-teen stepsister had not been in the kitchen for an hour or so, Dad would loudly announce, "I think that chocolate cake is about gone!" Within a minute, Debbie would casually approach the kitchen door, not wanting to appear interested, because she'd fallen for this trick too many times before, but needing to know for sure. We'd all ignore her until she'd finally break down and ask, "Where's the cake?" We'd answer with howls of laughter. He hasn't pulled this gag in years, but I think it would still work.

Dad was a salesman for an Illinois company, Pines, which made specialized machinery for bending steel tubing. At that time his company made the biggest and most advanced equipment of this sort. It was needed by virtually every automobile and aircraft company in the world, as well as by other types of manufacturers. The volume of Pines' business in Europe finally warranted having someone over there permanently. Although Dad's education was in architectural engineering, a Dale Carnegie course and training on Pines benders readied him to sell to the European market. Recently divorced from my mother, my dad left the Chicago area, where he had lived all his life, and bravely moved to West Germany, with his new wife and her three young children. Eventually my brother, Mike, and I joined them. Neither Dad nor his wife, Flo, spoke German, so the business of renting an apartment was a major ordeal. It took a year and a half just to get the telephone installed. Shopping for food was a daily adventure, since there was no refrigerator.

Dad was interested in other languages, cultures, and foods. He had confidence in his product, and the economy was favorable for business. All of these things helped make him successful representing his company, and his life opened up in a way he'd never dreamed possible. He enjoyed his work and the weekly travelling and made friends all over Europe. He travelled weekdays and came home to Wiesbaden on weekends with wonderful stories. He described to us how drab and depressing Moscow was, but how beautiful its subway stations were. One was festooned with crystal chandeliers, another covered with murals, and another patterned in brilliant mosaics. Another time he returned home quite excited because at Opel he had driven a new prototype for a car they would call the GT.

Dad had lots of amusing stories to tell about his travels. He especially enjoyed his trips to France and meeting with his buddy, Simon, who was originally from Russia. One afternoon they pulled into a gas station that sold Elf gasoline. The attendants were dressed in green jerkins and tights, pointed ankle-high boots, and green peaked caps. My dad asked Simon, "How do you say elf in French?" Simon said, "What's an elf?" Dad explained, "Little, mythical characters that live in the woods and make toys and dress like these guys." "Oh, I don't know! We'll have to ask Serge when we get back to the office." Now, most of the people my dad knew over there, including Simon and Serge, spoke several languages. When they got back to the factory, Simon asked Serge, "How do we say elf in French?" Serge looked stunned! "Why, Simon, you speak German! *Onze,* of course!" Dad and Simon burst out laughing. You see, *elf* in German means eleven. Eleven in French is *onze.* (Elf in French is *lutin.*) This is the sort of joke Dad loved. Perhaps because of his exposure to so many different tongues, the stories he would tell us often had to do with language. Another time, on a trip to Sweden, my father was walking back to his hotel after a late dinner. Two bums approached him from out of the dark, and one spoke to him. Dad said, "I don't speak Swedish." The man then said, "Oh, excuse me, Sir, I didn't realize. Could you possibly spare a few kronor so my friend and I can buy a cup of coffee?" While my father was getting the coins out of his pocket, he complimented the man on his English. "Really, Sir, my German is much better," was the response.

But not all of Dad's experiences were funny. The last night of a three-day stay in Warsaw, he and his dealer, Lutz, met a man in the hotel bar, who claimed he was from Sioux City, Iowa, and was currently living in Switzerland. Dad thought his American accent was slightly odd, but when he invited them across the street to the disco at the Bristol Hotel, they went. He took the drink order to the bar and returned with drinks. My father took one sip of his screwdriver and instantly felt that his arms and legs were paralyzed. Two chairs seemed to appear out of nowhere and this "American from Sioux City" pushed him into one, sat in the other, and started questioning him about his business in Poland and his American company. After a while the man seemed satisfied with Dad's answers, and Lutz helped Dad back to his hotel where he became ill. He went to bed and they left the next day.

Whenever Dad returned to the States during those years, he'd get a visit from a man from our government. He'd give Dad his card and say, "That, of course, is not my real name. Call me anytime you think I should know something." He'd then ask my father about the machines he sold in Iron Curtain countries, and what they were going to be used for. He wanted to know the size of factories and shipyards and so on. He always wanted Dad to go more often to these places and see more plants, but Dad only did what his business required him to do. He loved espionage novels, but he didn't want to be a spy himself.

Spring break of 1965, Dad, Mike, and I took the train to Paris. By that time we had all gotten used to life in a small German city. But when I saw how Dad maneuvered around Paris, I was enormously impressed. He put us up at the Hotel de l'Opera, a small, classic place with a cage elevator. He took us to The Louvre, Galleries Lafayette, and best of all, to Simon's house for dinner. Simon also went with us to the Palace at Versailles, and he and Dad got to chatting with a gardener who let us into a walled garden, where supposedly no Americans had been since President and Mrs. Kennedy.

By 1970, with the beginning of the recession, sales had slackened off, so Dad was promoted back to Illinois. He and Flo arrived home with a house full of German antiques and crystal, cases of wine they'd grown to love, and hundreds of wonderful memories. Many of these memories had to do with the kindness and warmth of the Germans, the Swiss, the French, the Swedish—whoever. He was in Portugal, for instance, when Kennedy was shot. The people in his hotel—the waiters and busboys, desk clerks and chambermaids—were crying when he came in that afternoon. A Norwegian couple approached him and said, "We're so sorry. Your President has been killed."

Dad often says that the European's attitudes towards Americans were softer in those days; I'm sure they were. But that's not the only reason my father had such a splendid time those seven years abroad or was treated so well by nearly all the Europeans he met. He had a genuine interest in history and the old cities and landmarks. George K. in England offered to take him and an associate to see an old Norman close. Dad said, "Great!" But the other American's response was "What? An old pile of stones?" That didn't surprise me. I often heard my American high school friends in Germany complain that the stores, the ice cream or whatever, "are not like in the States." But my attitude was the same as Dad's. "You can't get bread and cheese like this at home," he would say.

QUESTIONS

1. Whatley begins her essay by announcing that her father "looked exactly like Jack Lemmon." Why would she choose to begin this way? What effect does this information have on the reader?

2. Describe Whatley's attitude toward her father. What details in her description help you define her attitude?

3. Whatley recounts a number of anecdotes about her father in order to portray his character. Look at several of those anecdotes and describe what character traits they illustrate.

4. Notice that almost all of Whatley's memories have to do with her father's European experiences. Can you think of reasons why the writer has chosen to restrict her reminiscences of her father to this specific seven-year period?

SUGGESTIONS FOR WRITING

1. Record, in as much detail as you can, three or four anecdotes from your mother's or father's life. These can be stories that were told to you or incidents you witnessed or participated in. What do these anecdotes tell you about your parent? What character traits do they suggest? After you've answered these questions, write a description of your mother or father, using the anecdotes to illustrate salient points about her or him.

2. Describe a family vacation or trip, concentrating on the behavior of family members and on the ways in which the things you saw and experienced affected each of you.

Joyce Carol Oates
STALKING

★ ★ ★

A powerful and prolific writer, Joyce Carol Oates has produced a steady flow of novels, short stories, poems, plays, and critical essays since 1963, when her publishing career began with the appearance of her first short story collection, By the North Gate. *She started writing fiction while still in elementary school, and her first novel—about a dope addict's efforts to rehabilitate himself—was submitted to a publisher when Oates was only 15 years old. (The book was considered too depressing for young readers and turned down.)*

Oates's novels and stories are full of violence, perversion, and madness. As a result, some critics have condemned her work as excessively lurid. Another common complaint about Oates's fiction is that there is simply too much of it. Her output has been so daunting that, as biographer

Michael Joslin points out, some critics have urged her to stop publishing for a while. Oates, however, shows no sign of slowing down. Although sprawling at times, Oates's fiction is marked by brilliant social observation and great imaginative power. Discussing her art in an interview, Oates describes her overriding aim as an "obvious yet perhaps audacious feat: I would like to create the psychological and emotional equivalent of an experience so completely and in such exhaustive detail that anyone who reads it sympathetically will have experienced *that event in his mind (which is where we live anyway)."*

Oates's many books include: A Garden of Earthly Delights *(1967);* Expensive People *(1968);* them *(1969);* Wonderland *(1972);* Do With Me What You Will *(1973); and* Bellefleur *(1980). "Stalking" is from her 1972 collection of stories,* Marriages and Infidelities.

The Invisible Adversary is fleeing across a field.

Gretchen, walking slowly, deliberately, watches with her keen unblinking eyes the figure of the Invisible Adversary some distance ahead. The Adversary has run boldly in front of all that traffic—on long spiky legs brisk as colts' legs—and jumped up onto a curb of new concrete, and now is running across a vacant field. The Adversary glances over his shoulder at Gretchen.

Bastard, Gretchen thinks.

Saturday afternoon. November. A cold gritty day. Gretchen is out stalking. She has hours for her game. Hours. She is dressed for the hunt, her solid legs crammed into old blue jeans, her big, square, strong feet jammed into white leather boots that cost her mother forty dollars not long ago, but are now scuffed and filthy with mud. Hopeless to get them clean again, Gretchen doesn't give a damn. She is wearing a dark green corduroy jacket that is worn out at the elbows and the rear, with a zipper that can be zipped swiftly up or down, attached to a fringed leather strip. On her head nothing, though it is windy today.

She has hours ahead.

Cars and trucks and buses from the city and enormous interstate trucks hauling automobiles pass by on the highway; Gretchen waits until the way is nearly clear, then starts out. A single car is approaching. *Slow down, you bastard,* Gretchen thinks; and like magic he does.

Following the footprints of the Invisible Adversary. There is no sidewalk here yet, so she might as well cut right across the field. A gigantic sign announces the site of the new Pace & Fischbach Building, an office building of fifteen floors to be completed the following year. The land around here is all dug up and muddy; she can see the Adversary's footsteps leading right past the gouged-up area . . . and there he is, smirking back at her, pretending panic.

I'll get you. Don't worry, Gretchen thinks carefully.

Because the Adversary is so light-footed and invisible, Gretchen doesn't make any effort to be that way. She plods along as she does at school, passing from classroom to classroom, unhurried and not even sullen, just unhurried. She knows she is very visible. She is thirteen years old and weighs one hundred and thirty-five pounds. She's only five feet three—stocky, muscular, squat in the torso and shoulders, with good strong legs and thighs. She could be good at gym, if she bothered; instead, she just stands around, her face empty, her arms crossed and her shoulders a little slumped. If forced, she takes part in the games of volleyball and basketball, but she runs heavily, without spirit, and sometimes bumps into other girls, hurting them. *Out of my way,* she thinks; at such times her face shows no expression.

And now? . . . The Adversary is peeking out at her from around the corner of a gas station. Something flickers in her brain. *I see you,* she thinks, with quiet excitement. The Adversary ducks back out of sight. Gretchen heads in his direction, plodding through a jumbled, bulldozed field of mud and thistles and debris that is mainly rocks and chunks of glass. The gas station is brand new and not yet opened for business. It is all white tile, white concrete, perfect plate-glass windows with white-washed X's on them, a large driveway and eight gasoline pumps, all proudly erect and ready for business. But the gas station has not opened since Gretchen and her family moved here—about six months ago. Something must have gone wrong. Gretchen fixes her eyes on the corner where the Adversary was last seen. He can't escape.

One wall of the gas station's white tile has been smeared with something like tar. Dreamy, snakelike, thick twistings of black. Black tar. Several windows have been broken. Gretchen stands in the empty driveway, her hands jammed into her pockets. Traffic is moving slowly over here. A barricade has been set up that directs traffic out onto the shoulder of the highway, on a narrow, bumpy, muddy lane that loops out and back again onto the pavement. Cars move slowly, carefully. Their bottoms scrape against the road. The detour signs are great rectangular things, bright yellow with black zigzag lines. SLOW. DETOUR. In the two center lanes of the highway are bulldozers not being used today, and gigantic concrete pipes to be used for storm sewers. Eight pipes. They are really enormous; Gretchen's eyes crinkle with awe, just to see them.

She remembers the Adversary.

There he is—headed for the shopping plaza. *He won't get away in the crowds,* Gretchen promises herself. She follows. Now she is approaching an area that is more completed, though there are still no sidewalks and some of the buildings are brand-new and yet unoccupied, vacant. She jumps over a concrete ditch that is stained with rust-colored water and heads up a slight incline to the service drive of the Federal Savings Bank. The drive-in tellers' windows are all dark today, behind their green-tinted glass. The whole bank is dark, closed. Is this the bank her parents go to now? It takes Gretchen a minute to recognize it.

Now a steady line of traffic, a single lane, turns onto the service drive that leads to the shopping plaza. BUCKINGHAM MALL. 101 STORES. Gretchen notices a few kids her own age, boys or girls, trudging in jeans and jackets ahead of her, through the mud. They might be classmates of hers. Her attention is captured again by the Invisible Adversary, who has run all the way up to the Mall and is hanging around the entrance of the Cunningham Drug Store, teasing her.

You'll be sorry for that, you bastard, Gretchen thinks with a smile.

Automobiles pass her slowly. The parking lot for the Mall is enormous, many acres. A city of cars on a Saturday afternoon. Gretchen sees a car that might be her mother's, but she isn't sure. Cars are parked slanted here, in lanes marked LOT K, LANE 15; LOT K, LANE 16. The signs are spheres, bubbles, perched up on long slender poles. At night they are illuminated.

Ten or twelve older kids are hanging around the drugstore entrance. One of them is sitting on top of a mailbox, rocking it back and forth. Gretchen pushes past them—they are kidding around, trying to block people—and inside the store her eye darts rapidly up and down the aisles, looking for the Invisible Adversary.

Hiding here? Hiding?

She strolls along, cunning and patient. At the cosmetics counter a girl is showing an older woman some liquid make-up. She smears a small oval onto the back of the woman's hand, rubs it in gently. "That's Peach Pride," the girl says. She has shimmering blond hair and eyes that are penciled to show a permanent exclamatory interest. She does not notice Gretchen, who lets one hand drift idly over a display of marked-down lipsticks, each for only $1.59.

Gretchen slips the tube of lipstick into her pocket. Neatly. Nimbly. Ignoring the Invisible Adversary, who is shaking a finger at her, she drifts over to the newsstand, looks at the magazine covers without reading them, and edges over to another display. Packages in a cardboard barrel, out in the aisle. Big bargains. Gretchen doesn't even glance in the barrel to see what is being offered . . . she just slips one of the packages in her pocket. No trouble.

She leaves by the other door, the side exit. A small smile tugs at her mouth.

The Adversary is trotting ahead of her. The Mall is divided into geometric areas, each colored differently; the Adversary leaves the blue pavement and is now on the green. Gretchen follows. She notices the Adversary going into a Franklin Joseph store.

Gretchen enters the store, sniffs in the perfumy, overheated smell, sees nothing that interests her on the counters or at the dress racks, and so walks right to the back of the store, to the Ladies Room. No one inside. She takes the tube of lipstick out of her pocket, opens it, examines the lipstick. It has a tart, sweet smell. A very light pink: *Spring Blossom.* Gretchen goes to the mirror and smears the lipstick onto it, at first lightly, then coarsely; part of the lipstick breaks and falls into a hair-littered sink. Gretchen goes into one of the toilet stalls and tosses the tube into the toilet bowl. She takes handfuls of toilet paper and crumbles them into a ball and throws them into the toilet. Remembering the package from the drugstore, she takes it out of her pocket—just toothpaste. She throws it, cardboard package and all, into the toilet bowl, then, her mind glimmering with an idea, she goes to the apparatus that holds the towel—a single cloth towel on a roll—and tugs at it until it comes loose, then pulls it out hand over hand, patiently, until the entire towel is out. She scoops it up and carries it to the toilet. She pushes it in and flushes the toilet.

The stuff doesn't go down, so she tries again. This time it goes part-way down before it gets stuck.

Gretchen leaves the rest room and strolls unhurried through the store. The Adversary is waiting for her outside—peeking through the window—wagging a finger at her. *Don't you wag no finger at me,* she thinks, with a small tight smile. Outside, she follows him at a distance. Loud music is blaring around her head. It is rock music, piped out onto the colored squares and rectangles of the Mall, blown everywhere by the November wind, but Gretchen hardly hears it.

Some boys are fooling around in front of the record store. One of them bumps into Gretchen and they all laugh as she is pushed against a trash can. "Watch it, babe!" the boy sings out. Her leg hurts. Gretchen doesn't look at them but, with a cold, swift anger, her face averted, she knocks the trash can over onto the sidewalk. Junk falls out. The can rolls. Some women shoppers scurry to get out of the way and the boys laugh.

Gretchen walks away without looking back.

She wanders through Sampson Furniture, which has two entrances. In one door and out the other, as always; it is a ritual with her. Again she notices the sofa that is like the sofa in their family room at home—covered with black and white fur, real goatskin. All over the store there are sofas, chairs, tables, beds. A jumble of furnishings. People stroll around them, in and out of little displays, displays meant to be living rooms, dining rooms, bedrooms, family rooms. . . . It makes Gretchen's eyes squint to see so many displays: like seeing the inside of a hundred houses. She slows down, almost comes to a stop. Gazing at a living-room display on a raised platform. Only after a moment does she remember why she is here—whom she is following—and she turns to see the Adversary beckoning to her.

She follows him outside again. He goes into Dodi's Boutique and, with her head lowered so that her eyes seem to move to the bottom of her eyebrows, pressing up against her forehead, Gretchen follows him. *You'll regret this,* she thinks. Dodi's Boutique is decorated in silver and black. Metallic strips hang down from a dark ceiling, quivering. Salesgirls dressed in pants suits stand around with nothing to do except giggle with one another and nod their heads in time to the music amplified throughout the store. It is music from a local radio station. Gretchen wanders over to the dress rack, for the hell of it. Size 14. "The time is now 2:35," a radio announcer says cheerfully. "The weather is 32 degrees with a chance of showers and possible sleet tonight. You're listening to WCKK, Radio Wonderful. . . ." Gretchen selects several dresses and a salesgirl shows her to a dressing room.

"Need any help?" the girl asks. She has long swinging hair and a high-shouldered, indifferent, bright manner.

"No," Gretchen mutters.

Alone, Gretchen takes off her jacket. She is wearing a navy blue sweater. She zips one of the dresses open and it falls off the flimsy plastic hanger before she can catch it. She steps on it, smearing mud onto the white wool. *The hell with it.* She lets it lie there and holds up another dress, gazing at herself in the mirror.

She has untidy, curly hair that looks like a wig set loosely on her head. Light brown curls spill out everywhere, bouncy, a little frizzy, a cascade, a tumbling of curls. Her eyes are deep set, her eyebrows heavy and dark. She has a stern, staring look, like an adult man. Her nose is perfectly formed, neat and noble. Her upper lip is long, as if it were stretched to close with difficulty over the front teeth. She wears no make-up, her lips are perfectly colorless, pale, a little chapped, and they are usually held tight, pursed tightly shut. She has a firm, rounded chin. Her facial structure is strong, pensive, its features stern and symmetrical as a statue's, blank, neutral, withdrawn. Her face is attractive. But there is a blunt, neutral, sexless stillness to it, as if she were detached from it and somewhere else, uninterested.

She holds the dress up to her body, smooths it down over her breasts, staring.

After a moment she hangs the dress up again, and runs down the zipper so roughly that it breaks. The other dress she doesn't bother with. She leaves the dressing room, putting on her jacket.

At the front of the store the salesgirl glances at her . . . "—Didn't fit?—" "No," says Gretchen.

She wanders around for a while, in and out of Carmichael's, the Mall's big famous store, where she catches sight of her mother on an escalator going up. Her mother doesn't notice her. She pauses by a display of "winter homes." Her family owns a home like this, in the Upper Peninsula, except theirs is larger. This one comes complete for only $5330: PACKAGE ERECTED ON YOUR LOT—YEAR-ROUND HOME FIBER GLASS INSULATION—BEAUTIFUL ROUGH-SAWN VERTICAL B. C. CEDAR SIDING WITH DEEP SIMULATED SHADOW LINES FOR A RUGGED EXTERIOR.

Only 3:15. For the hell of it, Gretchen goes into the Big Boy restaurant and orders a ground-round hamburger with French fries. Also a Coke. She sits at the crowded counter and eats slowly, her jaws grinding slowly, as she glances at her reflection in the mirror directly in front of her—her mop of hair moving almost imperceptibly with the grinding of her jaws—and occasionally she sees the Adversary waiting outside, coyly. *You'll get yours,* she thinks.

She leaves the Big Boy and wanders out into the parking lot, eating from a bag of potato chips. She wipes her greasy hands on her thighs. The afternoon has turned dark and cold. Shivering a little, she scans the maze of cars for the Adversary—yes, there he is—and starts after him. He runs ahead of her. He runs through the parking lot, waits teasingly at the edge of a field, and as she approaches he runs across the field, trotting along with a noisy crowd of four or five loose dogs that don't seem to notice him.

Gretchen follows him through that field, trudging in the mud, and through another muddy field, her eyes fixed on him. Now he is at the highway—hesitating there—now he is about to run across in front of traffic—now, now—now he darts out—

Now! He is struck by a car! His body knocked backward, spinning backward. Ah, now, *now how does it feel?* Gretchen asks.

He picks himself up. Gets to his feet. Is he bleeding? Yes, bleeding! He stumbles across the highway to the other side, where there is a sidewalk. Gretchen follows him as soon as the traffic lets up. He is staggering now, like a drunken man. *How does it feel? Do you like it now?*

The Adversary staggers along the sidewalk. He turns onto a side street, beneath an archway. *Piney Woods.* He is leading Gretchen into the Piney Woods subdivision. Here the homes are quite large, on artificial hills that show them to good advantage. Most of the homes are white colonials with attached garages. There are no sidewalks here, so the Adversary has to walk in the street, limping like an old man, and Gretchen follows him in the street, with her eyes fixed on him.

Are you happy now? Does it hurt? Does it?

She giggles at the way he walks. He looks like a drunken man. He glances back at her, white-faced, and turns up a flagstone walk . . . goes right up to a big white colonial house. . . .

Gretchen follows him inside. She inspects the simulated brick of the foyer: yes, there are blood spots. He is dripping blood. Entranced, she follows the splashes of blood into the hall, to the stairs . . . forgets her own boots, which are muddy . . . but she doesn't feel like going back to wipe her feet. The hell with it.

Nobody seems to be home. Her mother is probably still shopping, her father is out of town for the weekend. The house empty. Gretchen goes into the kitchen, opens the refrigerator, takes out a Coke, and wanders to the rear of the house, to the family room. It is two steps down from the rest of the house. She takes off her jacket and tosses it somewhere. Turns on the television set. Sits on the goatskin sofa and stares at the screen: a return of a Shotgun Steve show, which she has already seen.

If the Adversary comes crawling behind her, groaning in pain, weeping, she won't even bother to glance at him.

QUESTIONS

1. Describe the setting of this story. What are the main characteristics of the community Gretchen inhabits? What aspects of modern society does Oates seem to be commenting on in this story?

2. Why does Oates include the detail about Gretchen's white boots near the beginning of the story? What does this detail tell you about Gretchen—and her relationship to her mother?

3. In Gretchen, Oates creates a portrait of a young girl who, though subject to disturbing fantasies and violent impulses, seems strikingly impassive, devoid of emotion. How does Oates's *prose style*—the structure and rhythm of her sentences—serve to reinforce this characterization? How does it contribute to our sense of Gretchen's mental state?

4. Who is the Invisible Adversary? In what way are the few descriptive details Oates supplies—the reference to the Adversary's "long, spiky legs," for example—significant? What is the nature of Gretchen's "game"?

5. When Gretchen first arrives at the mall, she sees a car that "might be her mother's, but she isn't sure." Later, she "catches sight of her mother on an

escalator, going up." But "her mother doesn't recognize her." Why are these details in the story? How do they shed light on Gretchen's behavior—and on the story's central theme? What *is* its central theme?

6.   What is the *dominant impression* of the modern, suburban world that Oates creates in this story and what are some of the recurring descriptive details she uses to create it?

SUGGESTIONS FOR WRITING

1.   Gretchen's Invisible Adversary is the product of her loneliness, as well as of the psychological disturbance brought about (Oates suggests) by both the conditions of modern life and the girl's own family situation. It is not unusual, however, for young children to have invisible or imaginary *friends*. If you remember having an imaginary playmate as a child, write an essay describing this figure. Alternatively, write an essay describing your favorite childhood doll or toy.

2.   Though Gretchen's behavior is extreme, there are, unfortunately, many children with lives just as empty, loveless, and unhappy as hers. If you know someone like Gretchen—a young boy or girl who is lonely, aimless, cut off from friends and family—write an essay describing him or her.

Philip Booth
HARD COUNTRY
★ ★ ★

Booth is one of our most accomplished poets. A New Englander by birth, he portrays his native landscape—and particularly the Maine seacoast—in taut, spare language that powerfully evokes the starkness of the setting. "Mr. Booth's style," says reviewer Alan Cheuse, "reticent though it is, can be very beautiful." Another critic, Daniel Jaffe, compares Booth's work to "pieces of granite, solid and full of undiminished fascination." His poems "seem cut from the earth or netted from the sea," Jaffe writes. "They share in depths and mysteries."

Booth's books include The Islanders *(1961),* Weathers and Edges *(1966), and* Available Light *(1976). "Hard Country" is from his 1970 collection,* Margins.

In hard
country each white
house, separated
by granite outcrop
from each white

house, pitches
its roofline
against the hard sky.
Hand-split
shakes, fillet
and face plank, clap-
board, flashing
and lintel: every
fit part over-
laps from the ridge
board on down, wind
tight and water
tight, down
to the sideyard back
door, shut against
eavesdrop.

Nobody
takes storm windows
off: each blank
pane, framed by
its own sharp
moulding, looks out
without shutters at
juniper, granite,
and hackmatack.
Granite takes
nothing for granted,
hackmatack's spiney;
junipers mind their
ledged roots. Save
for a day when its back
door opens on lilac,
there isn't a house
in this country
that sleeps or
wakes.

In hard
country Orion,
come summer, hunts
late; but belts its
prime stars all
winter when sun
is short: each white

house, separated
by granite outcrop
from each white
house, pitches
its private roof
against horizon
and season; each white
clapboard, wind
tight and water
tight, juts
against weather
its own four inches
of shadow and
light.

QUESTIONS

1. Where does this poem seem to be set? How do you know?

2. How would you characterize the landscape Booth portrays here? How does the language of the poem—the words Booth chooses, the way his lines are broken up—help evoke a sense of the physical setting? What physical details and images does Booth use to create a sense of the *hardness* of hard country?

3. What are the houses in hard country like? Why does Booth describe them but not their inhabitants? Why are there no human beings in this poem?

4. How would you characterize Booth's tone? Given his subject, what makes this tone so appropriate?

SUGGESTION FOR WRITING

Describe a place that you consider bleak, forbidding, or otherwise unappealing. It doesn't have to be a natural locale. Your subject might be a desolate city street, a depressing stretch of highway, or a run-down section of town. Or you might, in fact, describe a natural landscape—one that (in contrast to the sunny, idyllic stereotype found on picture postcards and in travel brochures) seems harsh and inhospitable.

CHAPTER *Three*

THE CONSUMER SOCIETY
Example

Exemplification—the use of specific examples to support or clarify a point we are trying to make—is a very basic rhetorical strategy, something we rely on all the time in our everyday speech. If you were talking to a friend about the high cost of dining in restaurants, for example, you would probably, in the most natural way, cite a few examples drawn from your own recent experience: paying $6 for a hamburger at a downtown steakhouse, ordering a croissant and a cup of coffee at a sidewalk cafe and getting a bill for $4.95, and so on. Alternatively, you might offer a single, striking instance that vividly illustrated your point, such as the time you and a date went to a posh French restaurant and ended up spending over a hundred dollars for something called *choucroute garnie à l'asacienne,* which turned out to be a fancy version of hot dogs and sauerkraut. By the same token, if an acquaintance were to tell you that you were basically a decent human being but that you occasionally did things that hurt people, you would undoubtedly ask him or her to be more specific. "Like what?" you might say in such a situation. "Give me some examples." In short, as listeners and readers we expect to hear general statements backed up by specific examples; as speakers and writers, we communicate most effectively when we provide them.

If you have ever had a friend say, "I know *exactly* what you mean" and then proceed to misconstrue your every word, you know how easy it is to be misunderstood. Using examples is the best way to get your ideas across clearly and accurately. Presented with a vague, overly general statement, people naturally tend to supply examples of their own. If a novelist were to describe her main character as simply a "handsome man," different readers would inevitably imagine different examples of that extremely general type. One person might picture a character who looked like Clint Eastwood; another might envision Bruce Springsteen. Your job as a writer, however, is to make readers see things *your* way. And exemplification will help minimize the possibility that you will be misinterpreted.

Examples, however, can do more than clarify an idea. They can also help convince readers of its validity. Participants in political debates constantly use examples to prove their own worth and their opponents' incompetence. The challenger cites specific instances when she voted to support education, national defense, and Social Security. The incumbent counters by noting that, under his administration, unemployment dropped to the lowest level in a decade—an impressive illustration of the economic gains made during his term in office. An unsupported claim ("I am against tax increases") is obviously much less persuasive than one which can be bolstered by a few hard facts ("In 1979 I sponsored the bill that reduced the state sales tax by 50 percent"). Even if you agree with a writer's position to begin with, a bare-boned assertion takes on added weight and power when it is fleshed out with specific examples.

The use of examples also makes your prose more interesting. You should try to find ones that are striking or imaginative or unusual in some way. After all, there is little point in attempting to enliven a flat generalization with dull supporting illustrations. One of the reasons Nora Ephron's witty essay on the twenty-fourth annual Pillsbury Bake-Off works as well as it does is that the examples she cites—concoctions like Lorraine Wallman's "Cheesy Crescent Twist-Ups" and Sharon Schubert's "Wiki Wiki Coffee Cake"—not only say a good deal about the state of middle-American cuisine but also sound so funny.

Ephron's essay demonstrates another important point: namely, that for your examples to be effective they must also be representative. Though a Wiki Wiki Coffee Cake may be a rare and even unique form of pastry which few people have ever had the privilege to taste, it is typical of the kind of cooking that goes on at a Pillsbury Bake-Off. It perfectly illustrates the qualities Ephron finds everywhere at the affair: the snack-food sensibility, the cuteness, the "frenzied creativity." Just as good descriptive writing relies on carefully selected, sensory details—ones that contribute to a single, dominant impression—expository essays require you to find those examples that are most pertinent to and supportive of your main idea. By citing instances of rampant malfunctioning which anyone can relate to, Marvin Harris makes it hard to disagree with his assessment that our lives are filled with "things that don't fit, things that don't last, things that don't work":

Vacuum cleaners have plastic handles that wobble and break; their cords come loose from the switch; their motors burn out. Tug hard on your shoelaces when they're a month old and they'll come apart. Or the little plastic tips come off and you can't pass the frayed ends through the holes. Go to the medicine chest for a bandaid. "Tear off end, pull string down," it says. But the string slips to the side and comes out.

The number of supporting examples you use depends, for the most part, on the kind of point you are trying to make. Defining the quality he calls "the right stuff"—that "amalgam of stamina, guts, fast neural synapses, and old fashioned hell raising" which all self-respecting test pilots aspire to—Tom Wolfe requires only a single, noteworthy example to illustrate one of its main features, the premium placed on absolute "cool" and the contempt for anyone who fails to display it:

> Combat had its own infinite series of tests, and one of the greatest sins was "chattering" or "jabbering" on the radio. The combat frequency was to be kept clear of all but strategically essential messages, and all unenlightening comments were regarded as evidence of funk, of the wrong stuff. A Navy pilot (in legend, at any rate) began shouting, "I've got a MiG at zero! A MiG at zero!"—meaning that it had maneuvered in behind him and was locked in on his tail. An irritated voice cut in and said, "Shut up and die like an aviator."

Newspaper writers who specialize in "human interest" stories often rely on one *extended example* to drive home a point. These journalists know that to make readers truly grasp the plight of the unemployed, a whole pageful of statistics is not nearly so effective as the example of one out-of-work coal miner who can't afford to buy a Christmas present for his 5-year-old daughter. At other times, however, a writer dealing with a broad subject—a large-scale trend, for instance—might feel it necessary to cite a range of brief examples. To prove his point about America's runaway quality crisis, Marvin Harris mentions a whole array of instances, from small annoyances (shoddy vacuum cleaners and defective shoelaces) to major catastrophes, such as the collapse of the aerial walkways in Kansas City's Hyatt Regency Hotel, which killed over a hundred people. In the end, there is no hard-and-fast rule to determine the number of examples you should use. The right number is as many as it takes for you to explain, clarify, or prove your thesis.

Professional writers like Harris get their examples from various places. Some are clearly drawn from firsthand experience. Others are the product of research (e.g., Harris's citation of the recall statistics for 1979 Ford Mustangs). Once again, the decisive factor—the one that will determine not only the number but the source of your examples—is the kind of essay you are writing. A twenty-page research paper on the solar heating industry will obviously require you to spend some time gathering facts in the library.

In general, however, the typical composition paper you will be writing for class can be supported with personal examples. Don't underestimate the extent of your knowledge; once you start looking at a topic—even one relating to a large social issue—in light of your own experiences, you will be surprised at how many good examples you can come up with. If you are writing about the conflicting demands of work and motherhood on today's married women, think of people you know (an older sister, perhaps, or an aunt) who are juggling a career and child-raising. What do these examples tell you? What generalizations can you draw from them? If you are assigned a paper on the present state of the economy, start by taking a close look at your own situation. Are you and your family better off now than you were a few years ago? You are bound to come up with concrete illustrations—the new Volvo your parents just bought or, conversely, the fact that your family was unable to afford a summer vacation for the first time in your memory—that will support your point of view.

When it comes to arranging your examples into a coherent organization, the most straightforward method is to move from the general to the specific. A basic way to organize an individual paragraph is to begin with a topic sentence that states the main idea, then follow it with several short, concrete examples (or, alternatively, a single somewhat more detailed one). Keep in mind, however, that exemplification can also serve as the organizing strategy for an entire essay. In such cases, the thesis statement appears in a separate introductory paragraph, while each of the succeeding paragraphs develops one major supporting example. Here is a sample outline for an exemplification essay on the topic of contemporary movies:

Paragraph I.   Introduction. Thesis: For all their advanced technology and flashy effects, contemporary movies are often nothing more than updated versions of old-fashioned children's stories.

Paragraph II.   First Example: *Star Wars* is a science fiction version of *The Wizard of Oz.*
- A.   Its orphan hero, Luke Skywalker, lives on an isolated farm with his aunt and uncle.
- B.   He dreams of faraway places and high adventure.
- C.   He travels to exotic lands, where he meets, among other companions, a talking robot who is like a futuristic "Tin Woodman" and a creature called Chewbacca who bears more than a passing resemblance to the Cowardly Lion.
- D.   He learns that the key to his happiness is inside himself.

Paragraph III.   Second Example: *E.T.* is a high-tech retelling of *Peter Pan.*
- A.   E.T. comes from a faraway "Never Land."
- B.   He is being hunted by a scientific "Captain Hook," distinguished by an ominous metal key ring instead of a steel hook.

C. He takes his young friend, Elliot, for a late-night spin across the sky.

D. The movie celebrates the wonder of childhood and views adulthood as a fallen state.

Paragraph IV. Third Example: *Carrie* is "Cinderella," reconceived as a Brian DePalma/Stephen King nightmare.

A. Carrie is persecuted by her evil mother.

B. She manages to attend the senior prom in the company of a teenage "Prince Charming" and becomes "queen of the ball."

C. At midnight, however, the evening takes a serious turn for the worse.

Paragraph V. Conclusion: Restatement of Thesis.

Whether you use it to give structure to a single paragraph or an entire essay, this kind of thesis-support organization, in which you state your main idea and then illustrate it with solid, lively examples, is one of the most valuable and versatile rhetorical strategies you can master.

Andrew A. Rooney
WRAPPINGS

Since joining CBS-TV's top-rated "60 Minutes" news program in 1978, Andy Rooney has become tremendously popular as a droll and down-to-earth commentator, a "homespun Homer" (in the words of Newsweek *writer Elizabeth Peer) "whose celebrations of the commonplace and jeremiads against the degenerating twentieth century are cheered" by millions of Americans. Well before achieving his current celebrity status, however, Rooney had a long and impressive career as a writer. "It makes me mad," he told one interviewer, "when people come up to me and don't know I lived before 1979."*

Born in Albany, New York, in 1919, Rooney was a reporter for the G.I. newspaper Stars and Stripes *during World War II. He coauthored two books on military subjects while in the army. After being discharged, he launched a career as a freelance magazine writer. Dissatisfied with his income, Rooney began writing for television, supplying material to various performers, from Arthur Godfrey to Victor Borge.*

Since 1959, Rooney has been affiliated primarily with CBS-TV, where he has written, produced, and narrated a series of award-winning programs on American life. His greatest success, however, came when he began to deliver his short, wry commentaries on "60 Minutes." By now,

Rooney has become something of an American institution. Besides his weekly TV appearance, he provides a syndicated column to over 250 newspapers, and his recent books—collections of his TV and newspaper essays—have been enormous best-sellers.
 The following piece is taken from And More By Andy Rooney.

———

Depending on what mood I'm in, I find it either irritating, funny or civilized when I think about how we protect protective coverings in this country.

When I come home from the grocery store and start to unpack, I am always unfavorably impressed with the layers of protective or decorative wrappings we cover our food with.

There is hardly anything we buy that doesn't come in at least two wrappings, and then several of them are assembled by the cashier at the checkout counter and put into a small bag. Then several of the small bags are grouped together and put into a big bag. If you have several big bags with small bags in them, they give you a cardboard box to put the-packages-in-the-little-bags-in-the-big-bags in.

A lot of things we buy wouldn't really need any protective wrapping at all. The skin of an orange protects an orange pretty well for most of its natural life, but we aren't satisfied with what nature has given it. We wrap ten of them in plastic or put them in a net bag, and we put the plastic bag in a paper bag. The orange inside the skin, inside the plastic which is in a paper bag, must wonder where it is.

A box of cookies or crackers often has waxed paper next to the cookies, a cardboard box holding the cookies and then waxed paper and a decorative wrapping around the cardboard box. What seems to be called for here is some stiff, decorative waxed paper.

We have always wrapped our cars in an incredible number of protective layers. We put fenders over the wheels to protect ourselves from flying dirt. Then we put bumpers front and back to protect the fenders. We proceed from there to put chrome on the bumpers to protect them from rust, and we undercoat the fenders to protect *them* from the dirt they're protecting us from.

We paint the car to protect the metal, wax the paint to protect that and then we build a two-car garage to protect the whole thing. If it was a child, it would be spoiled.

I'm laughing, but I'm a protector of things myself. I use wood preserver before I paint lumber, and when I buy a raincoat I always spray it with Scotchgard or some other silicone water resister. Over the years, I'll bet I've spent more on Scotchgard than I have on raincoats.

A good book is designed with a hard cover to protect its contents. The hard cover is protected from dirt and abuse by a dust jacket. A lot of people who are very careful with books cover the dust jacket with a plastic cover of its own.

A relative of ours bought a new couch recently because she liked the fabric it was covered with. She liked it so much she didn't want it to get dirty, so she bought a slipcover to put over it and she laid little oblong pieces of cloth over the arms where the wear is heaviest to protect the slipcover. She called them antimacassars.

We may never again see the fabric she's protecting.

QUESTIONS

1. This essay consists of little more than a series of examples, illustrating Rooney's main point. What are these examples? Are they effective? Why or why not?

2. Describe, as precisely as you can, the quality of the *voice* that speaks through this essay. How important is that voice to the success of this piece—and to Rooney's appeal in general?

3. Beginning writers are often advised to avoid repetitious language. In his third paragraph, however, Rooney deliberately violates this elementary rule, repeating the word "bag" seven times in three sentences. Why? What effect does he achieve by using repetition this way? Can you find any other places in this essay where Rooney uses the same technique?

4. The cover of Rooney's best-selling book, *And More By Andy Rooney,* hails the author as "America's Everyman." How does Rooney manage, through his language, to make himself seem like a spokesman for the whole country— a person who (in the words of Walter Cronkite) articulates "all the frustrations with modern life that the rest of us Everymen suffer with silence or mumbled oaths"?

SUGGESTIONS FOR WRITING

1. In the preface to *And More By Andy Rooney,* Rooney writes, "It is my opinion that prejudice saves us all a great deal of time. I have a great many well-founded prejudices, and I have no intention of giving up any of them except for very good reasons. I don't like turnips and I don't like liver. Call it prejudice if you wish, but I have no intention of ever trying either again just to make sure I don't like them. I *am* sure." Write a humorous essay in which you describe your own prejudices. Try, if possible, to capture Rooney's tone.

2. Pick one of the following statements (all taken from Rooney's essay, "Rules of Life") and write an essay in which you either agree or take issue with it, supporting your position with examples drawn from your own observations and experiences:

   "The best things in life are not free, they're expensive."

   "Not everyone has a right to his own opinion."

   "Happiness depends more on how life strikes you than on what happens."

"Enthusiasm on the job gets you further than education or brains."

"Money is not the root of all evil."

"Every so often you ought to do something dangerous. It doesn't have to be physical."

"Not many of us are able to change our lives on purpose; we are all permanent victims of the way we are, but we should proceed as though this were not true."

Michael Korda
SYMBOLS OF SUCCESS
★ ★ ★

Born in London in 1933, Michael Korda received his B.A. at Oxford in 1956 and, soon afterwards, emigrated to the United States. After working briefly as a script reader for CBS-TV, he moved to the publishing house of Simon & Schuster, where he rapidly advanced from editorial assistant to his present position as Editor-in-Chief and Corporate Vice President.

In addition to his successful career as an editor, Korda is a prolific and talented author, who has published best-selling books in several genres. He has written several extremely popular how-to books: Male Chauvinism! How It Works *(1973),* Power! How to Get It, How to Use It! *(1975), and* Success! *(1977). His 1979 memoir,* Charmed Lives: A Family Romance—*which focuses on his uncle, Alexander Korda, a legendary figure in the British motion picture industry—was both a critical and commercial success. More recently, Korda has turned to writing fiction, producing two best-selling novels,* Worldly Goods *(1982) and* Queenie *(1985).*

The following selection is excerpted from Success!

The world is so full of success symbols that it is hard to know which ones, if any, are worth owning. It is possible to spend as much as $1,000 for a Vuitton attaché case. Hunting World in New York sells attaché cases in exotic leathers for prices that go as high as $5,000. Presumably there are people who buy them, or they wouldn't be made.

Status as a Private Joke

There are two different kinds of success symbols. The first consists of those things we want because they seem to symbolize or reward our success to ourselves. The second consists of the status objects that announce to other people that we have succeeded. A $5,000 attaché case is in the first category, since it hardly looks different from a $200 attaché case, and its value is known only to the person who is carrying it or the person who paid for it. The pleasure here is simply in *knowing* that your brief case is worth the price of a new car, even though it appears to any uninformed stranger like just another well-made piece of leather goods.

Certain success symbols have a built-in totemic factor. The Cartier "tank watch" for men may be bought at Cartier's for $750 (plus $350 for the hinged gold buckle on the leather strap). Exact copies of it, gold-plated and with presumably inferior mechanisms, may be purchased at any department store for $100 or less, and even bear the Cartier name. In this case, the pleasure lies in the owner's quiet satisfaction that only he knows whether he paid over $1,000 or less than a hundred, as well as the feeling that other people must surely realize that a successful man would never wear an imitation of the real thing. I once sat at a meeting and realized that every person present seemed to be wearing the identical "tank watch," including myself, but I would have been reluctant to ask which people were wearing the genuine article. Note: *the status of an object does not depend on the fact that it can't be copied.* Quite the contrary: Cartier sold more of their watches after the copies began to appear in the marketplace.

A great many people like to surround themselves with just this kind of status symbol. It is something in the nature of a private joke, like having your initials hand-embroidered on your undershorts. Even though the success symbols that most people covet are generally for attracting the attention of others rather than for some obscure private pleasure, sometimes the two can be combined. Ownership of a Rolls-Royce (the new Camargue version can be yours for about $90,000) can obviously be a source of personal satisfaction *and* a public symbol.

Once you're a major success—that is to say, making more than $100,000 a year, and with every likelihood of continuing to do so in the future, you may feel inclined to gratify your individual taste and whim in choosing those symbols of success that please you the most. This is one of the major rewards of becoming a success in the first place. You always wanted a Porsche Targa 911E in dark-chocolate-colored lacquer, hand rubbed to a high gloss? Nothing prevents you from ordering one, once you have the $20,000. You want an office furnished with eighteenth-century English antiques, sporting prints and Bokhara carpets? As a success, this is your privilege. You aspire to own a triplex overlooking Central Park? Just the apartment you have in mind is available. Success frees you to make a reality of your fantasies. Some people can stand this, others can't—they find what was desirable as a fantasy becomes uninteresting when they can actually own it. On the whole, most people make the adjustment.

Over the years, it has always interested me to observe what happens to authors who make a huge movie or paperback sale, and find themselves suddenly rich. In each case, there is some fantasy object that they have always desired, and can now afford. The ones who go right out and buy it—whether it's a red Ferrari Dino, a pair of Tiffany Schlumberger cuff links, a pair of matched Purdy shotguns, a diamond ring from Harry Winston—survive and manage to handle their new found wealth quite well. The ones who don't go out and make the vital, initial splurge frequently end up either losing all their money or going to pieces as a result.

Like these authors, you probably have a fantasy object, the one stupid, useless and totally desirable thing you have always wanted to buy and knew you never would. When you become a real success, you should be liberated to the point where you can bring yourself to purchase it. It's important to enjoy the pleasures that success affords you. If you don't, you're likely to find yourself halted in mid-career and unable to move further on.

Essential and Nonessential Status Symbols for Your Success Identity

On the way up, the problem is a little bit different. You cannot afford to indulge your fantasies. *Yet there are many symbols which can give you the aura of success in other people's eyes,* thus speeding up the process of establishing your success identity.

CARS

In the old days, people worried a great deal about what kind of car they should own. A junior executive might drive a Chevrolet, for example, but would hesitate to buy an Oldsmobile or a Buick, on the grounds that his relative status within the corporate hierarchy would not entitle him to drive a car that was "out of his league." On the other hand, once he was promoted, he would feel obliged to "trade up" to a more expensive car. This kind of thing is much less true of American society than it used to be. The interest in ecology and the risk of a new energy crisis, combined with the popularity of foreign cars, have made the car *a very unreliable status object,* except at the highest level. Nowadays, a man may be making $75,000 a year and drive a VW Dasher. One of the most successful men I know drives to work on a Honda motorcycle, and Chester Davis, who used to be Howard Hughes' personal attorney, drives himself in a small foreign compact (though it has a phone with four lines and a hold button on the front seat). No, very few people are likely to care what you drive on the way up.

BRIEF CASES

A good brief case is essential. Here is something that needn't cost a fortune, but definitely establishes your status in the business world. I have seen men come to work in the morning carrying A&P shopping bags or canvas barrack bags. This is a mistake. A good, solid brief case, either in black or brown leather, makes it clear that you are serious enough about your prospects to have invested $200 or so in one. My personal opinion is that a brief case that opens at the top, has accordion sides to allow for expansion, two solid handles and a brass lock is best at the under-$50,000-a-year level. Above that level, an attaché case is more appropriate, providing it's not too bulky. At the very top it is best to carry a slim leather portfolio or nothing.

Whatever you choose, this is not a place to skimp. Your brief case goes everywhere you do, and is a highly visible symbol of your status and success potential. Do *not* buy:

★   Aluminum attaché cases with plastic handles (Halliburton Zero). However practical they seem, the effect is to make you look like a photographer carrying his equipment or a man on his way to the local pistol range.

★   Fiberglass attaché cases.

If you can't afford leather, then vinyl will have to do. In fact, some of the vinyls don't look bad at all when they're new. Unlike leather, however, they do not improve with age, and become scuffed and faded, instead of settling down into a well-worn gloss. My advice, though, is that it's worth spending the money for a solid leather brief case right at the beginning. Well looked after, with a little saddle soap, it will help you up every step of the ladder to success, until you reach the final rungs when you can do without one altogether.

Never let your brief case be checked through as baggage on an airflight. It will emerge tattered, shabby and covered with stickers that are impossible to remove. Keep it with you, and even if you don't have any important papers to put in it, you can at least load it with all the things you would otherwise have to carry in your pockets.

LIGHTING A CIGARETTE

If you smoke, a cigarette lighter is a very useful status symbol. Here again, you can spend several thousand dollars for a Dupont, Cartier, or Dunhill lighter, but this is hardly necessary. *The best status symbol in the world is an elderly Zippo that looks and works as if it's come through the wars.* If you have to buy a new one, age it before using by scraping it back and forth in gravel and sand, then banging it a bit with a sharp rock.

The latest item in this area is a Braun electronic gas lighter, which looks like a solid rectangle of black steel. Everyone who owns one says that there are only three people in the United States who have similar lighters, a sure sign of a reliable, growing status object.

Many people carry prestige matchbooks in their pockets for show. (It is always amusing to see their expression when you make them tear off a match and light it for your cigarette.) In Washington, the matchbooks that bear the legend "Air Force One" are a very good status object. In New York, I once knew a young man on Wall Street who went to the trouble of having several hundred personalized matchbooks made up on which he had elegantly imprinted the name "David Rockefeller." He was always delighted to give you a book of matches or light your cigarette and attributes a great deal of his early success to the aura his matchbooks gave him. Even today, he has a reputation as a man with powerful friends. "It was," he said, "the best twenty dollars I ever spent."

On the whole, it's tacky to carry matches from "21," Lutèce, Scandia, Le Bistro or the Pump Room, if you haven't eaten there. The result is more likely to be a close auditing of your expense account than any immediate gain in status.

QUESTIONS

1. Korda relies heavily on specific examples to support and illustrate his general statements. Do you think his examples are effective? Why or why not?

2. Korda never pretends to be offering anything but serious, straightforward advice in this piece. When *Success!* was first published, however, some reviewers saw it as satirical, a clever parody of our cultural preoccupation with materialism and "making it." Is there anything in Korda's language and the kinds of examples he uses that makes it possible to judge his intentions? Discuss.

3. If you think that this excerpt is not satirical, how do you feel about Korda's unabashed glorification of status symbols? Do you find it admirable or objectionable? Explain.

SUGGESTIONS FOR WRITING

1. Korda defines "success" strictly in terms of money, power, and possessions. Do you agree with this view? Write an essay in which you define, as specifically as possible, your own idea of success.

2. According to Korda, "Success frees you to make a reality of your fantasies." Write an essay describing the fantasy or fantasies you would "make real" if you could afford anything you wanted.

3. Korda clearly believes in the saying, "If you've got it, flaunt it." Write an essay in which you explain why you either agree or disagree with this philosophy.

Marvin Harris
WHY NOTHING WORKS
★ ★ ★

One of our country's most prominent (and provocative) anthropologists, Marvin Harris has taught at Columbia University since 1952 and is the author of a number of highly influential works, including The Rise of Anthropological Theory *(1968) and the popular undergraduate text,* Culture, People, Nature: An Introduction to General Anthropology. *In recent years, Harris has published several lively studies of human cultural behavior which have attracted a wide readership and generated a fair amount of controversy. His most widely known books are* Cows, Pigs, Wars, and Witches: The Riddles of Culture *(1974) and* Cannibals and Kings: The Origins of Cultures *(1977).*

The following excerpt is taken from Harris's 1981 book, America Now: The Anthropology of a Changing Culture. *In defining the subject of his study, Harris doesn't mince words; the very first paragraph of the book gets straight to the point: "This book is about cults, crimes, shoddy goods, and the shrinking dollar. It's about porno parlors, and sex shops, and men kissing in the streets. It's about daughters shacking up, women on the rampage, marriages postponed, divorces on the rise, and no one having kids. It's about old ladies getting mugged and raped, people shoved in front of trains, and shoot-outs at the gas pumps. And letters that take weeks to get delivered, waiters who throw the food at you, rude sales help, and computers that bill you for things you never bought. It's about broken benches, waterless fountains. . . . It's about shoelaces that break in a week, bulbs that keep burning out, pens that won't write, cars that rust. . . . It's about a lot of other things that are new and strange in America today."*

Is America "dying of a broken part"? When bolts supporting Hartford's Civic Center snapped, the entire steel-and-concrete roof plunged into the ten-thousand-seat auditorium. Luckily, the spectators had left a few hours earlier and no one was hurt. But one hundred and eleven people died when two aerial walkways in Kansas City's new Hyatt Regency Hotel crashed to the lobby floor. At Three Mile Island a relief valve got stuck in the open position and brought the nuclear core to the brink of a meltdown. A few months later a forty-five-cent circuit board in the military computer alert system signaled that the Soviet Union had just launched a missile attack. And in New York City, Los Angeles, Houston, Atlanta, and other cities, twenty-five hundred brand-new Grumman buses costing $130,000 each developed cracks and sagging rear ends as soon as they hit their first pothole and had to be removed from service. Commenting on the flaws in the vehicle's design, Alan Kiepper, general manager of the Atlanta Transit Authority, quipped: "This was a horse, designed by a committee, which came out a dromedary."

In the aborted operation intended to rescue the American hostages from Teheran, three of the mission's eight helicopters broke down in the Iranian Desert. A crack in the sixteen-foot tail rotor blade disabled one, a broken fitting on a hydraulic pipe disabled another, and a malfunctioning gyroscope finished off the third. Apprised of what had gone wrong on the rescue mission, the owner of a household appliance repair shop in Brooklyn told reporter Michael Daly: "What do you expect? The United States can't even produce a good toaster anymore." The shop owner, Norma Treadwell, added, "Now nothing works."

America has become a land plagued by loose wires, missing screws, things that don't fit, things that don't last, things that don't work. Push the handle on the pop-up toaster and it won't stay down. Or it stays down and burns the toast. Newer models, says Treadwell, have short-lived thermostats instead of durable timers. Faulty thermostats also plague hair dryers and coffeemakers. Electric fans used to work forever; now the plastic blades develop cracks and have to be replaced. Vacuum cleaners have plastic handles that wobble and break; their cords come loose from the switch; their motors burn out. Tug hard on your shoelaces when they're a month old and they'll come apart. Or the little plastic tips come off and you can't pass the frayed ends through the holes. Go to the medicine chest for a bandaid. "Tear off end, pull string down," it says. But the string slips to the side and comes out. On the same principle, there is the packing bag for books. "Pull tab down." But the tab breaks off sending a shower of dirty fluff over the floor.

Louis Harris conducted a poll in 1979 in which 57 percent of the respondents said they were "deeply worried" about the poor quality of the products they were buying. Seventy-seven percent expressed the feeling that "manufacturers don't care about me." Based on a separate sampling of national opinion, *U.S. News & World Report* concluded "dissatisfaction runs wider and deeper than many experts suspected." Of the people responding to the pollsters' questions, 59 percent said they had returned one or more unsatisfactory products to the place of purchase during the preceding twelve months. A year later the figure had risen to 70 percent. According to a study published in the *Harvard Business Review,* 20 percent of all product purchases on the average lead to some form of dissatisfaction (other than price) among the purchasers.

Autos are high on the list of products that cause problems for their owners. About 30 percent of respondents reported they were dissatisfied or had a nonprice complaint about their cars. More than half of all complaints about auto repairs come from owners of vehicles still under new car warranties.

With the passage of federal highway safety and environmental protection legislation, huge recalls of vehicles with actually or potentially hazardous defects throw some light on the magnitude of the quality problems plaguing the U.S. auto industry. In 1979 for example, the Ford Motor Company recalled 16,000 of its 1979 Mustangs and Capris for defective power steering; 3,400 of its 1979 Mustangs for unsafe engine fans; 77,700 of its vans for defective front brake hoses; 400,000 Capris for front seat backs that could collapse and gear shift levers that could come apart; 70,000 of its light trucks for defects in wheel assemblies; and 390,000 of its 1969–1973 full-sized Fords, Mercurys, Meteors, and Lincoln Continentals for possible defects in the steering system. Meanwhile General Motors was recalling 172,000 of its 1977 and 1978 Monzas, Sunbirds, and Starfires for steering problems; 430,000 of its 1978 Pontiacs for defective pollution control devices; 372,000 of its 1977 and 1978 Cadillacs for possibly defective accelerator pedals; 19,500 cars of various models equipped with defective cruise control switches; 13,000 subcompacts for carburetor fuel-feed hose defects; 1,800,000 of its 1978 intermediate-sized cars and pickup trucks for defective front wheel-bearing assemblies; 41,500 Cadillac Sevilles equipped with electronic fuel injection engines that could cause fires; 1,300,000 full-size cars for front seat belts that can come loose under stress; and 16,000 of its 1979 light trucks for defective bolts in the steering arms.

But safety recall statistics alone will never properly memorialize the overall product-quality disaster embodied in America's aging fleet of gas-guzzling cars. Beyond being dangerous, they were massively inconvenient and unreliable. Fresh from the factory, windows and trunks leaked, bodies rattled, radiators boiled over, tires went flat. They were too heavy to be steered without power steering or to be stopped without power brakes. Their doors were too big to open next to other parked cars. Their curved side windows lacked once standard small triangular deflectors that in times gone by had served to cross-ventilate the front seat. Without these deflectors there was no way to get the airstream to enter the passenger compartment even while traveling at high speed with windows completely rolled down. "Fresh air" ducts merely supplied the passengers with air raised to engine temperature. Without air conditioning, many models became unusable even on relatively cool days. Because the interior dimensions had grown so huge, the driver could no longer reach across to close or open the window on the passenger side. This called for electric windows with motors housed inside the doors. The constant opening and slamming of the driver's door loosened the electric connections and the driver's window soon functioned intermittently. To pay tolls the driver then had to open the door and get out. When it rained, the driver got soaked, for while the car's shape kept out cooling breezes, its outward flaring body actually placed the top of the driver's head in a vertical line that was several inches beyond the roof. Windshield wipers were tucked into recessed compartments which collected leaves and trash and which froze solid after the first snowstorm. The thin wires sandwiched inside the windshield which replaced external antennas rendered the radio useless except for the closest and most powerful stations. Because the windshield had grown so huge, there was no place to put the rearview mirror. Gluing it to the windshield was a brilliant if temporary solution which ended when the surprised owner would open the door one morning and find the mirror staring at the roof from the middle of the front seat.

The U.S. auto industry serves as a convenient example of America's product-quality problems because so much of the public's economic well-being and safety depends on automobile-related jobs and on passenger car transportation. But quality disasters similar to that of the gas guzzlers characterize many different kinds of goods recently made in the U.S.A., even though their impact may be less dramatic. Hi fi records, for example. According to record store owners interviewed for the *Wall Street Journal,* the defect rate in major releases runs as high as 20 percent. Warped discs which cause needles to skip, scratchiness, pops, ticks, and other noises are the most frequent source of complaint.

What caused such an outpouring of defective and shoddy products? The problem cannot be that the United States literally doesn't know how to make a good toaster anymore. A nation capable of putting a whole computer on a thumbnailsize wafer and of sending astronauts to the moon and space probes to Saturn must surely possess the technical knowhow necessary for making a reliable toaster.

According to a law attributed to the savant known only as Murphy, "if anything can go wrong, it will." Corollaries to Murphy's Law suggest themselves as clues to the shoddy goods problem: If anything can break down, it will; if anything can fall apart, it will; if anything can stop running, it will. While Murphy's Law can never be wholly defeated, its effects can usually be postponed. Much of human existence consists of efforts aimed at making sure that things don't go wrong, fall apart, break down, or stop running until a decent interval has elapsed after their manufacture. Forestalling Murphy's Law as applied to products demands intelligence, skill, and commitment. If these human inputs are assisted by special quality-control instruments, machines, and scientific sampling procedures, so much the better. But gadgets and sampling alone will never do the trick since these items are also subject to Murphy's Law. Quality-control instruments need maintenance; gauges go out of order; X rays and laser beams need adjustments. No matter how advanced the technology, quality demands intelligent, motivated human thought and action.

Some reflection about the material culture of prehistoric and preindustrial peoples may help to show what I mean. A single visit to a museum which displays artifacts used by simple preindustrial societies is sufficient to dispel the notion that quality is dependent on technology. Artifacts may be of simple, even primitive design, and yet be built to serve their intended purpose in a reliable manner during a lifetime of use. We acknowledge this when we honor the label "handmade" and pay extra for the jewelry, sweaters, and handbags turned out by the dwindling breeds of modern-day craftspeople.

What is the source of quality that one finds, let us say, in a Pomo Indian basket so tightly woven that it was used to hold boiling water and never leaked a drop, or in an Eskimo skin boat with its matchless combination of lightness, strength, and seaworthiness? Was it merely the fact that these items were handmade? I don't think so. In unskilled or uncaring hands a handmade basket or boat can fall apart as quickly as baskets or boats made by machines. I rather think that the reason we honor the label "handmade" is because it evokes not a technological relationship between producer and product but a social relationship between producer and consumer. Throughout prehistory it was the fact that producers and consumers were either one and the same individuals or close kin that guaranteed the highest degree of reliability and durability in manufactured items. Men made their own spears, bows and arrows, and projectile points; women wove their own baskets and carrying nets, fashioned their own clothing from animal skins, bark, or fiber. Later, as technology advanced and material culture grew more complex, different members of the band or village adopted craft specialties such as pottery-making, basket-weaving, or canoe-building. Although many items were obtained through barter and trade, the connection between producer and consumer still remained intimate, permanent, and caring.

A man is not likely to fashion a spear for himself whose point will fall off in midflight; nor is a woman who weaves her own basket likely to make it out of rotted straw. Similarly, if one is sewing a parka for a husband who is about to go hunting for the family with the temperature at sixty below, all stitches will be perfect. And when the men who make boats are the uncles and fathers of those who sail them, they will be as seaworthy as the state of the art permits.

In contrast, it is very hard for people to care about strangers or about products to be used by strangers. In our era of industrial mass production and mass marketing, quality is a constant problem because the intimate sentimental and personal bonds which once made us responsible to each other and to our products have withered away and been replaced by money relationships. Not only are the producers and consumers strangers but the women and men involved in various stages of production and distribution—management, the worker on the factory floor, the office help, the salespeople—are also strangers to each other. In larger companies there may be hundreds of thousands of people all working on the same product who can never meet face-to-face or learn one another's names. The larger the company and the more complex its division of labor, the greater the sum of uncaring relationships and hence the greater the effect of Murphy's Law. Growth adds layer on layer of executives, foremen, engineers, production workers, and sales specialists to the payroll. Since each new employee contributes a diminished share to the overall production process, alienation from the company and its product are likely to increase along with the neglect or even purposeful sabotage of quality standards.

My basic contention is that after World War II, quality problems reached crisis proportions as a result of the unprecedented increase in the size and complexity of U.S. manufacturing corporations and hence in the quantity of alienated and uncaring workers and managers. This is not to say that only large corporations have quality problems; small companies can also produce shoddy goods but in a free enterprise system they are not likely to remain in business very long. Not only do giant corporations tend to produce alienated workers, managers, and shoddy goods on a giant scale but they tend to stay in business.

QUESTIONS

1. What point does Harris make by comparing American goods to artifacts produced by prehistoric and preindustrial cultures? What is it, according to Harris, that "guaranteed the highest degree of durability and reliability" in the handmade products of pretechnological societies? What is Harris's "basic contention" about the causes of the widespread quality problem in American manufactured goods? Does this contention make sense to you? Why or why not?

2. Can you think of examples of technology that work well and consistently? Name them. What would be the effect if these examples were incorporated in Harris's essay?

3. Harris's typical paragraph consists of a thesis statement followed by specific, supporting examples. Point to a few paragraphs organized this way. What makes this organizational strategy effective? How else does Harris use exemplification to strengthen his argument in this selection?

4. How does Harris combine objective data with personal, firsthand experience to bolster his argument? Does this combination work? Why or why not?

5. How does Harris manage to convey, through his language and the kinds of examples he uses, a sense of anger and frustration at our country's runaway quality problem?

SUGGESTIONS FOR WRITING

1.   Write an essay describing a bad experience you've had with a faulty product.

2.   Write an essay in which—using examples drawn from your own experience—
     you support Harris's contention that American consumer goods are increas-
     ingly shoddy. (Alternatively, write an essay disagreeing with this point of
     view.)

Alison Lurie
FASHION AND STATUS
★ ★ ★

*A professor of English at Cornell University, Alison Lurie is the author of
a number of highly praised novels, including* Love and Friendship *(1962),*
The War Between the Tates *(1974), and* Foreign Affairs *(winner of the
1985 Pulitzer Prize for Fiction). A writer of great style and wit, she has
also published several children's stories and is a frequent contributor of
essays to the* New York Review of Books.

   In her provocative and entertaining study, The Language of Clothes
*(1981), from which the following selection is taken, Lurie looks at the
various meanings that are expressed through the "sign system" of clothing.
As she explains at the start of the book, "For thousands of years human
beings have communicated with one another first in the language of
clothes. Long before I am near enough to talk to you on the street, in a
meeting, or at a party, you announce your sex, age and class to me through
what you are wearing—and very possibly give me important information
(or misinformation) as to your occupation, origin, personality, opinions,
tastes, sexual desires, and current mood. I may not be able to put what
I observe into words, but I register the information unconsciously; and you
simultaneously do the same for me. By the time we meet and converse, we
have already spoken to each other in an older and more universal tongue."*

Man from the earliest times has worn clothes to overcome his feelings of inferiority and to achieve a conviction of his superiority to the rest of creation, including
members of his own family and tribe, and to win admiration and to assure himself
that he "belongs."   —Lawrence Langner

Clothing designed to show the social position of its wearer has a long history. Just
as the oldest languages are full of elaborate titles and forms of address, so for
thousands of years certain modes have indicated high or royal rank. Many
societies passed decrees known as *sumptuary laws* to prescribe or forbid the
wearing of specific styles by specific classes of persons. In ancient Egypt only
those in high position could wear sandals; the Greeks and Romans controlled the
type, color and number of garments worn and the sorts of embroidery with which

they could be trimmed. During the Middle Ages almost every aspect of dress was regulated at some place or time—though not always with much success. The common features of all sumptuary laws—like that of edicts against the use of certain words—seem to be that they are difficult to enforce for very long.

Laws about what could be worn by whom continued to be passed in Europe until about 1700. But as class barriers weakened and wealth could be more easily and rapidly converted into gentility, the system by which color and shape indicated social status began to break down. What came to designate high rank instead was the evident cost of a costume: rich materials, superfluous trimmings and difficult-to-care-for styles; or, as Thorstein Veblen later put it, Conspicuous Consumption, Conspicuous Waste and Conspicuous Leisure. As a result, it was assumed that the people you met would be dressed as lavishly as their income permitted. In Fielding's *Tom Jones,* for instance, everyone judges strangers by their clothing and treats them accordingly; this is presented as natural. It is a world in which rank is very exactly indicated by costume, from the rags of Molly the gamekeeper's daughter to Sophia Western's riding habit "which was so very richly laced" that "Partridge and the post-boy instantly started from their chairs, and my landlady fell to her curtsies, and her ladyships, with great eagerness." The elaborate wigs characteristic of this period conferred status partly because they were both expensive to buy and expensive to maintain.

By the early eighteenth century the social advantages of conspicuous dress were such that even those who could not afford it often spent their money on finery. This development was naturally deplored by supporters of the status quo. In Colonial America the Massachusetts General Court declared its "utter detestation and dislike, that men or women of mean condition, should take upon them the garb of Gentlemen, by wearing Gold or Silver lace, or Buttons, or Points at their knees, or to walk in great Boots; or Women of the same rank to wear Silk or Tiffiny hoods, or Scarfes . . ." What "men or women of mean condition"— farmers or artisans—were supposed to wear were coarse linen or wool, leather aprons, deerskin jackets, flannel petticoats and the like.

To dress above one's station was considered not only foolishly extravagant, but deliberately deceptive. In 1878 an American etiquette book complained,

> It is . . . unfortunately the fact that, in the United States, but too much attention is paid to dress by those who have neither the excuse of ample means nor of social claims. . . . We Americans are lavish, generous, and ostentatious. The wives of our wealthy men are glorious in garb as are princesses and queens. They have a right so to be. But when those who can ill afford to wear alpaca persist in arraying themselves in silk . . . the matter is a sad one.

Contemporary Status: Fine Feathers and Tattered Souls

Today simple ostentation in dress, like gold or silver lace, is less common than it used to be; but clothes are as much a sign of status as ever. The wives of our wealthy men are no longer praised for being glorious in garb; indeed, they constantly declare in interviews that they choose their clothes for ease, comfort, convenience and practicality. But, as Tom Wolfe has remarked, these comfortable, practical clothes always turn out to have been bought very recently from the most expensive shops; moreover, they always follow the current rules of Conspicuous Consumption, Waste and Leisure.

At the same time, as high-status clothes have become superficially less gorgeous they have increasingly tended to take on an aura of moral virtue. A 1924 guide to good manners clearly suggests this:

> An honest heart may beat beneath the ragged coat, a brilliant intellect may rise above the bright checked suit and the yellow tie, the man in the shabby suit may be a famous writer, the girl in the untidy blouse may be an artist of great promise, but as a general rule, the chances are against it and such people are dull, flat, stale, and unprofitable both to themselves and to other people.

The implication is that an ill-dressed person is also probably dishonest, stupid and without talent. Today this idea is so well established that one of our foremost historians of costume, Anne Hollander, has refused to admit that true virtue can shine through ugly or ragged clothes, as in the tale of Cinderella:

> In real life . . . rags obviously cannot be "seen through" to something lovely underneath because they themselves express and also create a tattered condition of soul. The habit of fine clothes, however, can actually produce a true personal grace.

In a society that believes this, it is no wonder that many of those who can ill afford to wear alpaca—or its modern equivalent, polyester—are doing their best to array themselves in silk. Popular writers no longer complain that those of modest means wear clothes above their rank; instead they explain how best to do so: how to, as the title of one such book puts it, *Dress for Success*. At the moment there are so many such guidebooks it may seem surprising that their advice is not followed by more people. However, as my friend the lady executive remarks, "wardrobe engineering won't do much for you if your work is lousy . . . or if you're one of an army of aspirants in impeccable skirted suits all competing for the same spot. As with investment advice, once everyone agrees that it's the thing to do, it's time to look for value somewhere else."

There are other problems with dressing to advance your status professionally. First and most obviously, it is very expensive. The young executive who buys a high-priced suit instead of a stereo system or a week's vacation in Portugal or the Caribbean is giving up certain present pleasure for possible future success in a society that regards hedonistic self-fulfillment as a right. Second, there are one's colleagues to consider. For many people, agreeable working conditions and well-disposed birds are worth more than a possible promotion in the bush. The clerk who dresses like his boss is apt to be regarded by other clerks as a cold fish or an ass-kisser; the secretary in her severe skirted suit is seen as snotty and pretentious: Who does she think she is, in that getup? Moreover, somebody who is distrusted and disliked by his or her equals is very unlikely ever to become their superior. It is also a rare boss who wants to have employees who dress exactly as he or she does—especially since they are usually younger and may already have the edge in appearance. Fortunately for the manufacturers, however, there are more ways than one of advertising high status. Today, "simple," "easy-care" and "active" may be the bywords of fashion copy; but fashionable luxury, waste and inconvenience continue to flourish in new forms.

Conspicuous Addition: Eating and Layering

The most primitive form of Conspicuous Consumption is simply to consume so much food that one becomes conspicuous by one's bulk, a walking proof of having dined often and well. Fatness, frequently a sign of high status in primitive tribes, has also been admired in more civilized societies. In late nineteenth-century Europe and America it was common among well-to-do men, who often, as Robert Brain has remarked, "were as proud of their girth as a Bangwa chief, the big belly being a sign of imposing male power. It was a culture trait among German men, for whom fatness reflected wealth and status." The late-Victorian woman, too, was often as handsomely solid and well-upholstered as her furniture.

In general, the fashionable size seems to vary according to real or imagined scarcity of food. When a large proportion of the population is known to be actually going hungry, it is chic to be well-padded and to dine lavishly. When (as in England and America in the 1960s) there seems to be at least enough starchy food to go around, it becomes chic to be thin, thus demonstrating that one is existing on an expensive protein diet rather than on proletarian bread, potatoes, franks and beans. Today, when food prices are rising astronomically and the facts of world hunger have come to the attention even of café society, it is again no longer necessary to be very thin in order to be chic.

Another simple and time-honored way of consuming conspicuously is to wear more clothes than other people do. "More" of course is relative: when most people went naked, the mere wearing of garments conferred prestige. In ancient Egypt, for instance, slaves and servants often wore nothing, or at most a brief loincloth; aristocrats put on clothes not out of modesty or for warmth, but to indicate rank. Even in colder climates and more Puritanical societies it has generally been true that the more clothes someone has on, the higher his or her status. This principle can be observed in medieval and Renaissance art, where peasants wear relatively few garments, while kings and queens (including the King and Queen of Heaven) are burdened with layers of gowns and robes and mantles, even in indoor scenes. The recent fashion for "layered" clothes may be related, as is sometimes claimed, to the energy shortage; it is also a fine way of displaying a large wardrobe.

In any contemporary gathering, no matter what its occasion, the well-to-do can be observed to have on more clothes. The men are more likely to wear vests; the women are more apt to wear panty hose, superfluous scarves and useless little wraps. Even in hot weather the difference is plain. At an outdoor restaurant on a summer day the customers who have more money and have had it longer will be the ones in jackets and/or long-sleeved shirts and dresses. If it gets frightfully hot they may roll up their sleeves, but in such a way that there is no doubt about their actual length. On the beach, though the rich may splash into the waves in suits as skimpy as anyone else's, the moment they emerge they will make a dash for the conspicuous raw-silk beach kimono, terry swim dress or linen shirt that matches their bathing suit and restores the status quo.

Conspicuous Labeling

Not long ago, expensive materials could be identified on sight, and fashionable men and women recognized Savile Row tailoring or a Paris designer dress at a glance. In the twentieth century, however, synthetics began to counterfeit wool, silk, linen, leather, fur, gold and precious stones more and more successfully. At the same time, manufacturing processes became more efficient, so that a new and fashionable style could be copied in a few months and sold at a fraction of its original price. Meanwhile, the economic ability to consume conspicuously had been extended to millions of people who were ignorant of the subtleties of dress, who could not tell wool from Orlon or Schiaparelli from Sears Roebuck. As a result there was a world crisis in Conspicuous Consumption. For a while it seemed as if it might actually become impossible for most of us to distinguish the very rich from the moderately rich or the merely well-off by looking at what they were wearing.

This awful possibility was averted by a bold and ingenious move. It was realized that a high-status garment need not be recognizably of better quality or more difficult to produce than other garments; it need only be recognizably more expensive. What was necessary was somehow to incorporate the price of each garment into the design. This was accomplished very simply: by moving the maker's name from its former modest inward retirement to a place of outward prominence. Ordinary shoes, shirts, dresses, pants and scarves were clearly and indelibly marked with the names, monograms or insignia of their manufacturers. The names or trademarks were then exhaustively publicized—a sort of saturation bombing technique was used—so that they might become household words and serve as an instant guide to the price of the clothes they adorned. These prices were very high, not because the clothes were made of superior materials or constructed more carefully, but because advertising budgets were so immense.

When this system was first tried, certain critics scoffed, averring that nobody in their right mind would pay sixty dollars for a pair of jeans labeled Gloria Vanderbilt when a more or less identical pair labeled Montgomery Ward could be purchased for twelve. Others claimed that consumers who wanted a monogram on their shirts and bags would want it to be their own monogram and not that of some industrialist they had never met. As everyone now knows, they were wrong. Indeed, it soon became apparent that even obviously inferior merchandise, if clearly labeled and known to be extravagantly priced, would be enthusiastically purchased. There was, for instance, a great boom in the sale of very ugly brown plastic handbags, which, because they were boldly stamped with the letters "LV," were known to cost far more than similar but less ugly brown leather handbags. Cotton T-shirts that faded or shrank out of shape after a few washings but had the word Dior printed on them were preferred to better-behaved but anonymous T-shirts. Those who wore them said (or were claimed in advertisements to say) that they felt "secure." After all, even if the shirt was blotchy and tight, everyone knew it had cost a lot of money, and if it got too bad you could always buy another of the same kind. Thus Conspicuous Consumption, as it so often does, merged into Veblen's second type of sartorial status.

QUESTIONS

1. What does Lurie mean when she observes that "as high-status clothes have become superficially less gorgeous they have increasingly tended to take on an aura of moral virtue"?

2. Examine the organization of this excerpt from *The Language of Clothes.* How are historical examples incorporated in it? Why does Lurie include this historical material?

3. As a novelist and essayist, Lurie is known for her irony and humor. Where, in this selection, is her tone unmistakably ironic?

4. Part of what makes Lurie's discussion so clear and easy to follow is her skillful use of transitions both within and between paragraphs. Read over the essay, underlining all the transitional words and phrases you find.

5. Throughout this selection, Lurie supports her generalizations not only with specific examples but also with quotes from a wide range of sources. Look closely at the way in which Lurie integrates this material into her sentences and paragraphs. What makes her use of these quotes so effective?

SUGGESTIONS FOR WRITING

1. Do you think that young people in our society put too much emphasis on personal appearance, that they are overly concerned with how they— and other people—look? Write a paper in which you set forth your point of view.

2. According to Lurie, it is "no longer necessary to be very thin in order to be chic." Using examples drawn from your own experiences and observations, write an essay that either supports or takes issue with this assertion.

3. It is clear that Lurie does not think much of designer jeans and other such "high-status" garments. Do you share her low opinion of these clothes or disagree with it? Explain.

Nora Ephron
BAKING OFF
★ ★ ★

Nora Ephron first achieved fame as a journalist, a wry, witty observer of the contemporary cultural scene. Her articles have appeared in a wide range of magazines, from The New Yorker *to* Rolling Stone, *and have been collected in several critically acclaimed books:* Wallflower at the Orgy *(1970),* Crazy Salad *(1975), and* Scribble, Scribble *(1978).*

In the past few years, Ephron has turned—with great success—to other forms of writing. Her first novel, Heartburn *(1983), a thinly disguised, comical account of her marriage to Watergate journalist Carl Bernstein, was a national best-seller. The daughter of two Hollywood scriptwriters, Ephron has also begun writing for the movies. Her screenplay for the hit film* Silkwood *(cowritten with Alice Arlen) received an Academy Award nomination in 1983.*

The following selection is from Crazy Salad.

Roxanne Frisbie brought her own pan to the twenty-fourth annual Pillsbury Bake-Off. "I feel like a nut," she said. "It's just a plain old dumb pan, but everything I do is in that crazy pan." As it happens, Mrs. Frisbie had no cause whatsoever to feel like a nut: it seemed that at least half the 100 finalists in the Bake-It-Easy Bake-Off had brought something with them—their own sausages, their own pie pans, their own apples. Edna Buckley, who was fresh from representing New York State at the National Chicken Cooking Contest, where her recipe for fried chicken in a batter of beer, cheese, and crushed pretzels had gone down to defeat, brought with her a lucky handkerchief, a lucky horseshoe, a lucky dime for her shoe, a potholder with the Pillsbury Poppin' Fresh Doughboy on it, an Our Blessed Lady pin, and all of her jewelry, including a silver charm also in the shape of the doughboy. Mrs. Frisbie and Mrs. Buckley and the other finalists came to the Bake-Off to bake off for $65,000 in cash prizes; in Mrs. Frisbie's case, this meant making something she created herself and named Butterscotch Crescent Rolls—and which Pillsbury promptly, and to Mrs. Frisbie's dismay, renamed Sweet 'N Creamy Crescent Crisps. Almost all the recipes in the finals were renamed by Pillsbury using a lot of crispy snicky snacky words. An exception to this was Sharon Schubert's Wiki Wiki Coffee Cake, a name which ought to have been snicky snacky enough; but Pillsbury, in a moment of restraint, renamed it One-Step Tropical Fruit Cake. As it turned out, Mrs. Schubert ended up winning $5,000 for her cake, which made everybody pretty mad, even the contestants who had been saying for days that they did not care who won, that winning meant nothing and was quite beside the point; the fact was that Sharon Schubert was a previous Bake-Off winner, having won $10,000 three years before for her Crescent Apple Snacks, and in addition had walked off with a trip to

Puerto Vallarta in the course of this year's festivities. Most of the contestants felt she had won a little more than was really fair. But I'm getting ahead of the story.

The Pillsbury Company has been holding Bake-Offs since 1948, when Eleanor Roosevelt, for reasons that are not clear, came to give the first one her blessing. This year's took place from Saturday, February 24, through Tuesday, February 27, at the Beverly Hilton Hotel in Beverly Hills. One hundred contestants—97 of them women, 2 twelve-year-old boys, and 1 male graduate student— were winnowed down from a field of almost 100,000 entrants to compete for prizes in five categories: flour, frosting mix, crescent main dish, crescent dessert, and hot-roll mix. They were all brought, or flown, to Los Angeles for the Bake-Off itself, which took place on Monday, and a round of activities that included a tour of Universal Studios, a mini-version of television's *Let's Make A Deal* with Monty Hall himself, and a trip to Disneyland. The event is also attended by some 100 food editors, who turn it from a mere contest into the incredible publicity stunt Pillsbury intends it to be, and spend much of their time talking to each other about sixty-five new ways to use tuna fish and listening to various speakers lecture on the consumer movement and food and the appliance business. General Electric is co-sponsor of the event and donates a stove to each finalist, as well as the stoves for the Bake-Off; this year, it promoted a little Bake-Off of its own for the microwave oven, an appliance we were repeatedly told was the biggest improvement in cooking since the invention of the Willoughby System. Every one of the food editors seemed to know what the Willoughby System was, just as everyone seemed to know what Bundt pans were. "You will all be happy to hear," we were told at one point, "that only one of the finalists this year used a Bundt pan." The food editors burst into laughter at that point; I am not sure why. One Miss Alex Allard of San Antonio, Texas, had already won the microwave contest and $5,000, and she spent most of the Bake-Off turning out one Honey Drizzle Cake after another in the microwave ovens that ringed the Grand Ballroom of the Beverly Hilton Hotel. I never did taste the Honey Drizzle Cake, largely because I suspected—and this was weeks before the *Consumers Union* article on the subject—that microwave ovens were dangerous and probably caused peculiar diseases. If God had wanted us to make bacon in four minutes, He would have made bacon that cooked in four minutes.

"The Bake-Off is America," a General Electric executive announced just minutes before it began. "It's family. It's real people doing real things." Yes. The Pillsbury Bake-Off is an America that exists less and less, but exists nonetheless. It is women who still live on farms, who have six and seven children, who enter county fairs and sponsor 4-H Clubs. It is Grace Ferguson of Palm Springs, Florida, who entered the Bake-Off seventeen years in a row before reaching the finals this year, and who cooks at night and prays at the same time. It is Carol Hamilton, who once won a trip on a Greyhound bus to Hollywood for being the most popular girl in Youngstown, Ohio. There was a lot of talk at the Bake-Off about how the Bake-It-Easy theme had attracted a new breed of contestants this year, younger contestants—housewives, yes, but housewives who used whole-wheat flour and Granola and sour cream and similar supposedly hip ingredients in their recipes and were therefore somewhat more sophisticated, or urban, or something-of-the-sort than your usual Bake-Off contestant. There were a few of these—two, to be exact: Barbara Goldstein of New York City and Bonnie Brooks of Salisbury, Maryland, who actually visited the Los Angeles County Art Museum during a free afternoon. But there was also Suzie Sisson of Palatine, Illinois, twenty-five years old and the only Bundt-pan person in the finals, and her sentiments about life were the same as those that Bake-Off finalists presumably have had for years. "These are the beautiful people," she said, looking around the ballroom as she waited for her Bundt cake to come out of the oven. "They're not the little tiny rich people. They're nice and happy and religious types and family-oriented. Everyone talks about women's lib, which is ridiculous. If you're nice to your husband, he'll be nice to you. Your family is your job. They come first."

I was seven years old when the Pillsbury Bake-Off began, and as I grew up reading the advertisements for it in the women's magazines that were lying around the house, it always seemed to me that going to a Bake-Off would be the closest thing to a childhood fantasy of mine, which was to be locked overnight in a bakery. In reality, going to a Bake-Off *is* like being locked overnight in a bakery—a very bad bakery. I almost became sick right there on Range 95 after my sixth carbohydrate-packed sample—which happened, by coincidence, to be a taste of the aforementioned Mrs. Frisbie's aforementioned Sweet 'N Creamy Crescent Crisps.

But what is interesting about the Bake-Off—what is even significant about the event—is that it is, for the American housewife, what the Miss America contest used to represent to teen-agers. The pinnacle of a certain kind of achievement. The best in the field. To win the Pillsbury Bake-Off, even to be merely a finalist in it, is to be a great housewife. And a creative housewife. "Cooking is very creative." I must have heard that line thirty times as I interviewed the finalists. I don't happen to think that cooking is very creative—what interests me about it is, on the contrary, its utter mindlessness and mathematical certainty. "Cooking is very relaxing"—that's my bromide. On the other hand, I have to admit that some of the recipes that were concocted for the Bake-Off, amazing combinations of frosting mix and marshmallows and peanut butter and brown sugar and chocolate, were practically awe-inspiring. And cooking, it is quite clear, is only a small part of the apparently frenzied creativity that flourishes in these women's homes. I spent quite a bit of time at the Bake-Off chatting with Laura Aspis of Shaker Heights, Ohio, a seven-time Bake-Off finalist and duplicate-bridge player, and after we had discussed her high-protein macaroons made with coconut-almond frosting mix and Granola, I noticed that Mrs. Aspis was wearing green nail polish. On the theory that no one who wears green nail polish wants it to go unremarked upon, I remarked upon it.

"That's not green nail polish," Mrs. Aspis said. "It's platinum nail polish that I mix with green food coloring."

"Oh," I said.

"And the thing of it is," she went on, "when it chips, it doesn't matter."

"Why is that?" I asked.

"Because it stains your nails permanently," Mrs. Aspis said.

"You mean your nails are permanently green?"

"Well, not exactly," said Mrs. Aspis. "You see, last week they were blue, and the week before I made purple, so now my nails are a combination of all three. It looks like I'm in the last throes of something."

On Sunday afternoon, most of the finalists chose to spend their free time sitting around the hotel and socializing. Two of them—Marjorie Johnson of Robbinsdale, Minnesota, and Mary Finnegan of Minneota, Minnesota—were seated at a little round table just off the Hilton ballroom talking about a number of things, including Tupperware. Both of them love Tupperware.

"When I built my new house," Mrs. Johnson said, "I had so much Tupperware I had to build a cupboard just for it." Mrs. Johnson is a very tiny, fortyish mother of three, and she and her dentist husband have just moved into a fifteen-room house she cannot seem to stop talking about. "We have this first-floor kitchen, harvest gold and blue, and it's almost finished. Now I have a second kitchen on my walk-out level and that's going to be harvest gold and blue, too. Do you know about the new wax Congoleum? I think that's what I put in—either that or Shinyl Vinyl. I haven't had to wash my floors in three months. The house isn't done yet because of the Bake-Off. My husband says if I'd spent as much time on it as I did on the Bake-Off, we'd be finished. I sent in sixteen recipes—it took me nearly a year to do it."

"That's nothing," said Mrs. Finnegan. "It took me twenty years before I cracked it. I'm a contest nut. I'm a thirty-times winner in the *Better Homes & Gardens* contest. I won a thousand dollars from Fleischmann's Yeast. I won Jell-O this year, I'm getting a hundred and twenty-five dollars' worth of Revere cookware for that. The Knox Gelatine contest. I've won seven blenders and a quintisserie. It does four things—fries, bakes, roasts, there's a griddle. I sold the darn thing before I even used it."

"Don't tell me," said Mrs. Johnson. "Did you enter the Crystal Sugar Name the Lake Home contest?"

"Did I enter?" said Mrs. Finnegan. "Wait till you see this." She took a pen and wrote her submission on a napkin and held it up for Mrs. Johnson. The napkin read "Our Entry Hall." "I should have won that one," said Mrs. Finnegan. "I did win the Crystal Sugar Name the Dessert contest. I called it 'Signtation Squares.' I think I got a blender on that one."

"Okay," said Mrs. Johnson. "They've got a contest now, Crystal Sugar Name a Sauce. It has pineapple in it."

"I don't think I won that," said Mrs. Finnegan, "but I'll show you what I sent in." She held up the napkin and this time what she had written made sense. "Hawaiian More Chant," it said.

"Oh, you're clever," said Mrs. Johnson.

"They have three more contests so I haven't given up," said Mrs. Finnegan.

On Monday morning at exactly 9 A.M., the one hundred finalists marched four abreast into the Hilton ballroom, led by Philip Pillsbury, former chairman of the board of the company. The band played "Nothin' Says Lovin' Like Somethin' from the Oven," and when it finished, Pillsbury announced: "Now you one hundred winners can go to your ranges."

Chaos. Shrieking. Frenzy. Furious activity. Cracking eggs. Chopping onions. Melting butter. Mixing, beating, blending. The band perking along with such carefully selected tunes as "If I Knew You Were Coming I'd Have Baked a Cake." Contestants running to the refrigerators for more supplies. Floor assistants rushing dirty dishes off to unseen dishwashers. All two hundred members of the working press, plus television's Bob Barker, interviewing any finalist they could get to drop a spoon. At 9:34 A.M., Mrs. Lorraine Walmann submitted her Cheesy Crescent Twist-Ups to the judges and became the first finalist to finish. At 10 A.M., all the stoves were on, the television lights were blasting, the temperature in the ballroom was up to the mid-nineties, and Mrs. Marjorie Johnson, in the course of giving an interview about her house to the Minneapolis *Star,* had forgotten whether she had put one cup of sugar or two into her Crispy Apple Bake. "You know, we're building this new house," she was saying. "When I go back, I have to buy living-room furniture." By 11 A.M., Mae Wilkinson had burned her skillet corn bread and was at work on a second. Laura Aspis had lost her potholder. Barbara Bellhorn was distraught because she was not used to California apples. Alex Allard was turning out yet another Honey Drizzle Cake. Dough and flour were all over the floor. Mary Finnegan was fussing because the crumbs on her Lemon Cream Bars were too coarse. Marjorie Johnson was in the midst of yet another interview on her house. "Well, let me tell you," she was saying, "the shelves in the kitchen are built low. . . ." One by one, the contestants, who were each given seven hours and four tries to produce two perfect samples of their recipes, began to finish up and deliver one tray to the judges and one tray to the photographer. There were samples everywhere, try this, try that, but after six tries, climaxed by Mrs. Frisbie's creation, I stopped sampling. The over-kill was unbearable: none of the recipes seemed to contain one cup of sugar when two would do, or a delicate cheese when Kraft American would do, or an actual minced onion when instant minced onions would do. It was snack time. It was convenience-food time. It was less-work-for-Mother time. All I could think about was a steak.

By 3 P.M., there were only two contestants left—Mrs. Johnson, whose dessert took only five minutes to make but whose interviews took considerably longer, and Bonnie Brooks, whose third sour-cream-and-banana cake was still in the oven. Mrs. Brooks brought her cake in last, at 3:27 P.M., and as she did, the packing began. The skillets went into brown cartons, the measuring spoons into barrels, the stoves were dismantled. The Bake-Off itself was over—and all that remained was the trip to Disneyland, and the breakfast at the Brown Derby . . . and the prizes.

And so it is Tuesday morning, and the judges have reached a decision, and any second now, Bob Barker is going to announce the five winners over national television. All the contestants are wearing their best dresses and smiling, trying to smile anyway, good sports all, and now Bob Barker is announcing the winners. Bonnie Brooks and her cake and Albina Flieller and her Quick Pecan Pie win

$25,000 each. Sharon Schubert and two others win $5,000. And suddenly the show is over and it is time to go home, and the ninety-five people who did not win the twenty-fourth annual Pillsbury Bake-Off are plucking the orchids from the centerpieces, signing each other's programs, and grumbling. They are grumbling about Sharon Schubert. And for a moment, as I hear the grumbling everywhere—"It really isn't fair." . . . "After all, she won the trip to Mexico"—I think that perhaps I am wrong about these women: perhaps they are capable of anger after all, or jealousy, or competitiveness, or something I think of as a human trait I can relate to. But the grumbling stops after a few minutes, and I find myself listening to Marjorie Johnson. "I'm so glad I didn't win the grand prize," she is saying, "because if you win that, you don't get to come back to the next Bake-Off. I'm gonna start now on my recipes for next year. I'm gonna think of something really good." She stopped for a moment. "You know," she said, "it's going to be very difficult to get back to normal living."

QUESTIONS

1. Why does Ephron include the anecdote about Laura Aspis, the housewife with the green nail polish? What does Ephron's remark about "the apparently frenzied creativity that flourishes in these women's homes" suggest about the life of the typical American housewife?

2. How would you define Ephron's attitude towards the women who participate in this contest? How does she manage to convey this attitude, and where do her feelings come through most strongly? What makes these women seem so alien to her? Judging from this essay, what kind of person does Ephron herself seem to be? Do you find her more—or less—attractive than the women she is writing about? Explain.

3. Which magazine would be a more appropriate place for this article—*Good Housekeeping* or *Ms.*? Explain.

4. Why did the Pillsbury officials rename Mrs. Frisbie's recipe "Sweet 'N Creamy Crescent Crisps"? Why is this a more "snicky snacky" name than "Butterscotch Crescent Rolls"? What does Ephron *mean* by "snicky snacky"? How is the phrase suggestive of her own feelings about the contest?

5. How does Ephron use exemplification throughout this essay to bring it to life and convey her own attitudes—toward the Bake-Off, the contestants, and the larger cultural issues the essay touches on? Which of her examples are most effective? What *makes* them effective?

6. Look at the paragraph beginning "Chaos. Shrieking. Frenzy." How do the sentences in this paragraph evoke a sense of "furious activity"?

7. Why does Ephron switch to the present tense in the final paragraph? Why does she say she may have been wrong about the women in the Bake-Off, and why does she conclude by quoting one of the participants?

SUGGESTIONS FOR WRITING

1. For many of the women at the Pillsbury Bake-Off, entering contests is clearly
    a hobby they pursue with great passion. Write an essay describing any group
    of ardent hobbyists you are familiar with (coin collectors, "Star Trek" fans,
    opera buffs, sports enthusiasts, etc.). Provide enough specific examples to give
    readers a clear sense of the particular personality types that the hobby seems
    to attract.

2. If you have ever entered a contest, write an essay describing the experience.

3. It is clear that Ephron regards the Bake-Off as a quintessentially American
    phenomenon. Write an essay in which you describe a similar event, pageant,
    or spectacle (e.g., the Academy Awards, the Miss America contest, the Super
    Bowl) and explain what makes it so uniquely American.

Phyllis Rose
SHOPPING AND OTHER SPIRITUAL ADVENTURES IN AMERICA TODAY

★ ★ ★

*The following selection originally appeared in the "Hers" column, a
weekly feature of* The New York Times. *Although newspapers have always run pieces specifically aimed at their female readers (traditionally,
on such topics as sewing, cooking, shopping, child rearing, and advice to
the lovelorn), the "Hers" column is different. It is meant to serve as a
forum for the contemporary woman, a place where each guest contributor
can relate—and meditate on—a personal experience that she believes is
meaningful for her sex in general.*

*Phyllis Rose, the author of this lively, thought-provoking piece, is a
professor of English at Wesleyan University. Her books include* Parallel
Lives: Five Victorian Marriages *(1983) and* Woman of Letters: A Life
of Virginia Woolf, *which was nominated for a 1978 National Book Award.
She is currently at work on a biography of Josephine Baker, the famous
nightclub singer of the 1920s.*

Last year a new Waldbaum's Food Mart opened in the shopping mall on Route
66. It belongs to the new generation of superdupermarkets open 24 hours that
have computerized checkout. I went to see the place as soon as it opened and I
was impressed. There was trail mix in Lucite bins. There was freshly made pasta.
There were coffee beans, 4 kinds of tahini, 10 kinds of herb teas, raw shrimp in
shells and cooked shelled shrimp, fresh-squeezed orange juice. Every sophistication known to the big city, even goat's cheese covered with ash, was now available
in Middletown, Conn. People raced from the warehouse aisle to the bagel bin to

the coffee beans to the fresh fish market, exclaiming at all the new things. Many of us felt elevated, graced, complimented by the presence of this food palace in our town.

This is the wonderful egalitarianism of American business. Was it Andy Warhol who said that the nice thing about Coke is, no can is any better or worse than any other? Some people may find it dull to cross the country and find the same chain stores with the same merchandise from coast to coast, but it means that my town is as good as yours, my shopping mall as important as yours, equally filled with wonders.

Imagine what people ate during the winter as little as 75 years ago. They ate food that was local, long-lasting and dull, like acorn squash, turnips and cabbage. Walk into an American supermarket in February and the world lies before you: grapes, melons, artichokes, fennel, lettuce, peppers, pistachios, dates, even strawberries, to say nothing of ice cream. Have you ever considered what a triumph of civilization it is to be able to buy a pound of chicken livers? If you lived on a farm and had to kill a chicken when you wanted to eat one, you wouldn't ever accumulate a pound of chicken livers.

Another wonder of Middletown is Caldor, the discount department store. Here is man's plenty: tennis racquets, pantyhose, luggage, glassware, records, toothpaste, Timex watches, Cadbury's chocolate, corn poppers, hair dryers, warm-up suits, car wax, light bulbs, television sets. All good quality at low prices with exchanges cheerfully made on defective goods. There are worse rules to live by. I feel good about America whenever I walk into this store, which is almost every midwinter Sunday afternoon, when life elsewhere has closed down. I go to Caldor the way English people go to pubs: out of sociability. To get away from my house. To widen my horizons. For culture's sake. Caldor provides me too with a welcome sense of seasonal change. When the first outdoor grills and lawn furniture appear there, it's as exciting a sign of spring as the first crocus or robin.

Someone told me about a Soviet emigré who practices English by declaiming, at random, sentences that catch his fancy. One of his favorites is, "Fifty percent off all items today only." Refugees from Communist countries appreciate our supermarkets and discount department stores for the wonders they are. An Eastern European scientist visiting Middletown wept when she first saw the meat counter at Waldbaum's. On the other hand, before her year in America was up, her pleasure turned sour. She wanted everything she saw. Her approach to consumer goods was insufficiently abstract, too materialistic. We Americans are beyond a simple, possessive materialism. We're used to abundance and the possibility of possessing things. The things, and the possibility of possessing them, will still be there next week, next year. So today we can walk the aisles calmly.

It is a misunderstanding of the American retail store to think we go there necessarily to buy. Some of us shop. There's a difference. Shopping has many purposes, the least interesting of which is to acquire new articles. We shop to cheer ourselves up. We shop to practice decision-making. We shop to be useful and productive members of our class and society. We shop to remind ourselves how much is available to us. We shop to remind ourselves how much is to be striven for. We shop to assert our superiority to the material objects that spread themselves before us.

Shopping's function as a form of therapy is widely appreciated. You don't really need, let's say, another sweater. You need the feeling of power that comes with buying or not buying it. You need the feeling that someone wants something you have—even if it's just your money. To get the benefit of shopping, you needn't actually purchase the sweater, any more than you have to marry every man you flirt with. In fact, window-shopping, like flirting, can be more rewarding, the same high without the distressing commitment, the material encumbrance. The purest form of shopping is provided by garage sales. A connoisseur goes out with no goal in mind, open to whatever may come his or her way, secure that it will cost very little. Minimum expense, maximum experience. Perfect shopping.

I try to think of the opposite, a kind of shopping in which the object is all-important, the pleasure of shopping at a minimum. For example, the purchase of blue jeans. I buy new blue jeans as seldom as possible because the experience is so humiliating. For every pair that looks good on me, 15 look grotesque. But even shopping for blue jeans at Bob's Surplus on Main Street—no frills, bare-bones shopping—is an event in the life of the spirit. Once again I have to come to terms with the fact that I will never look good in Levi's. Much as I want to be mainstream, I never will be.

In fact, I'm doubly an oddball, neither Misses nor Junior, but Misses Petite. I look in the mirror, I acknowledge the disparity between myself and the ideal, I resign myself to making the best of it: I will buy the Lee's Misses Petite. Shopping is a time of reflection, assessment, spiritual self-discipline.

It is appropriate, I think, that Bob's Surplus has a communal dressing room. I used to shop only in places where I could count on a private dressing room with a mirror inside. My impulse then was to hide my weaknesses. Now I believe in sharing them. There are other women in the dressing room at Bob's Surplus trying on blue jeans who look as bad as I do. We take comfort from one another. Sometimes a woman will ask me which of two items looks better. I always give a definite answer. It's the least I can do. I figure we are all in this together, and I emerge from the dressing room not only with a new pair of jeans but with a renewed sense of belonging to a human community.

When a Solzhenitsyn rants about American materialism, I have to look at my digital Timex and check what year this is. Materialism? Like conformism, a hot moral issue of the 50's, but not now. How to spread the goods, maybe. Whether the goods are the Good, no. Solzhenitsyn, like the visiting scientist who wept at the beauty of Waldbaum's meat counter but came to covet everything she saw, takes American materialism too materialistically. He doesn't see its spiritual side. Caldor, Waldbaum's, Bob's Surplus—these, perhaps, are our cathedrals.

QUESTIONS

1. In her opening description of the goods available at the new Waldbaum's supermarket, Rose chooses her examples very carefully. What sense of the

store is she trying to convey through these examples? Why doesn't she mention any of the other, more typical items that are undoubtedly available at the store—things like canned tuna, laundry detergent, and Hamburger Helper?

2. Look at the paragraph that begins, "It's a misunderstanding of the American retail store to think we go there necessarily to buy." The last five sentences of this paragraph have an identical structure. As a rule, writers do their best to make their prose interesting by varying the structure of their sentences. Why does Rose ignore this rule? What effect does she achieve through this deliberate repetition? Are there any other places in this essay where Rose violates certain rules of structure and style for rhetorical effect?

3. How do you feel about the final sentence of this essay? What makes it so striking—such a powerful way to end the piece?

4. What makes this essay so unconventional and provocative—so refreshingly different from the standard attacks on "American materialism" and compulsive consumption? How does this essay fulfill the goal of all truly first-rate writing—to make us look at important issues in a new light?

SUGGESTIONS FOR WRITING

1. Write an essay in which you explain, as specifically as you can, why you do—or don't—like to shop.

2. Write a description of your favorite supermarket, department store, or shopping mall. Try to evoke its atmosphere as vividly as possible.

3. Do you agree with Rose's belief that there is a "spiritual side" to American consumerism and that our department stores and supermarkets "are our cathedrals"? Write an essay in which you support or refute Rose's point of view.

STUDENT ESSAY

Richard Allen Cabe
CONFESSIONS OF A CONSUMER JUNKIE
★ ★ ★

Richard Allen Cabe—a self-described "squandermaniac"—developed his keen appreciation for reckless expenditure during his childhood in Southern California. As an undergraduate at UCLA, Cabe put his aptitude for buying and spending to constructive use by majoring in economics. In addition to conspicuous consumption, Cabe's hobbies include skiing, scuba

diving, racquetball, and car racing. By his own admission, he wrote the
following essay "for the money."

————————

A very long time ago—I think when I was eight, the year my parents started
giving me a measly quarter for an allowance—a strange phenomenon started to
occur with some regularity. I began to spend more than I earned. As a kid, this
just meant that I had to keep promising my older sister I'd be her slave for a week
if she'd give me *her* quarter. As I grew older and greedier, though (and my sister
wiser), the solutions weren't so easily come by. My dad didn't think mowing the
lawn was worth the thirty bucks I needed for some sneakers I'd been eyeing. (In
fact, he didn't think I needed the sneakers, either.)

So, what with all those goods calling out to me from store windows and my
lack of sufficient cash, I soon found myself in debt. I hear you say, "What's the
big deal? Everybody is. Even the *government!*" Fine, I reply, but I didn't have
a Treasury Department in my garage to print up new currency. Issuing my own
municipal bonds wasn't very well received among my friends and family either.
My "Send me to Hawaii, and I promise I'll pay you back in 30 years" bond went
over about as well as soggy cereal at the breakfast table. It's never seemed fair
that the city of Detroit can issue a bond for a new garbage dump (they need
another one there?), and people will climb over each other to get a piece of
that.

Obviously, drastic action had to be taken. I got together with my buddy,
Aaron, not because I thought that he could help (he never helps), but because
something drastic usually happens when we take action. Aaron, visibly struggling
to decipher the pencil smudges in my checkbook and on frayed I.O.U.'s, pored
over the facts of my indebtedness again and again. "Too few dollars chasing too
many goods," he muttered. Aaron is an economics major, but I didn't need an
economist to tell me this. "Your personal disposable income, expressed as a
percentage of your net salary," he went on, "is remarkably low." Simply put, I
needed more money.

After we'd debated and rejected a life of crime, he suggested the next best
thing: a credit card. Better yet, a whole wallet full of them! Why, I could have
carte blanche in all of the most desirable spots in Los Angeles: the fanciest
department stores, the costliest restaurants, even (not that I frequent such places,
of course) the greasiest mud wrestling joints. I reveled in the thought of an
astronomical credit limit based on no apparent merit—democratic capitalism at
its finest! And who wouldn't revel? Most of have experienced the exhilaration of
getting a credit card in the mail. It's like someone sending you $1,500 just for
being a good guy! Forget the 20% interest payment each month, we'll worry
about that later!

Luckily, later caught up with me sooner. Trying to sleep that night, I envi-
sioned all the toys that I would accumulate. Blissful for a while, the fantasy
soured when I saw that they were all trailing price tags, brutal reminders of the

enormous debt that I would be swimming in. Yes, the vigilant forces that governed my financially woeful world would rear their ugly heads, laugh and spit bounced check notices at me, sneering, "Old boy, you're right back where you started."

After hours of deliberating the next day, Aaron and I began to realize that the only way to check my propensity to consume involved a degree of responsibility on my part, distasteful as it seemed. I drew up a budget and purchased a ledger, determined to record my every monetary move, my every fiscal flinch. My economist "friend" patiently explained the rules of this new and depressing game. All of my transactions must be entered in the ledger, even $150 bar tabs. (How was I to know that seconds after I'd shouted, to impress my date, "Beers for everyone, my treat!" an Australian rugby team would overrun the nearly deserted bar?)

Well, I was determined to make this new system work. And it *did* work—for several days even. I dutifully entered every purchase into the ledger, no matter how trivial. "9/22 laundry 75¢," I'd write. "9/23 gas $10." "9/24 food $12.23." "9/25 beer $46.75."

The problems started after about a week. There are some things that one buys that one doesn't want the world to read about, even though I was the only one who read the ledger. For example, athlete's foot powder (it was for a friend, I assure you) was denoted by a picture of a foot with an X through it. I symbolized the bar tab for the rugby team by drawing a kangaroo having its head bashed with a hammer. Some other entries weren't embarrassing at all, except for how frequently they were listed. Beer is a glorious beverage to be sure, dear readers, but its appearance every fourth line was the downfall of the ledger as a solution to my excessive consumerism. Surely, I reasoned, the only way to minimize the recurrence of the beer entries was to BUY MORE OF OTHER THINGS!! From that point on, the pages seemed to fly by. Soon after, the ledger was abandoned because of severe writer's cramp.

I have come to terms with my fate: I am truly a consumer junkie. Keeping up with the Joneses, rampant deficit spending, polo shirts with this year's hottest emblem on them, German-engineered cars, state-of-the-art stereo systems so complex I can't figure out what all the buttons are for: these are my lot in life. They say that admitting your problem to yourself and others is half the battle in reforming. My confession (which cost me a lot less than most of the items in my ledger) provides me with great consolation—I might someday be cured!

But not, I hope, too soon.

QUESTIONS

1. What is Cabe's real attitude toward consumerism? How can you tell?

2. Characterize the tone of this essay. What details help Cabe to achieve that tone?

3. Whom is Cabe satirizing in "Confessions of a Consumer Junkie"? Discuss.

4. Name some of the examples Cabe uses in his essay. Which, in your opinion, are most memorable or effective? Why? If you were the writer, would you have added more examples? If so, why and where?

SUGGESTIONS FOR WRITING

1. Recently, some journalists and cultural critics have asserted that America is increasingly preoccupied with material possessions, dominated by materialistic values. In an essay, take issue or agree with this assertion, using examples to support your point of view.

2. Cabe's essay is satirical, of course, but it also frankly celebrates material possessions and pursuits. Many people might think, in fact, that his penultimate paragraph gives the readers glimpses of "the good life." What do you think? Write an essay defining the good life.

John Updike
STILL OF SOME USE
★ ★ ★

Born and raised in a small farming town in southeastern Pennsylvania, John Updike was writing short stories by the time he was 8, though his earliest ambition was to be a cartoonist. He majored in English at Harvard, where he contributed to and later edited the Harvard Lampoon. *Soon after he graduated his short story, "Friends from Philadelphia," was published by* The New Yorker, *and Updike has been closely associated with the magazine ever since. In the mid-fifties, he spent two years on its staff, and most of his short fiction—as well as poetry, essays, and book reviews—continues to appear first in its pages.*

Ever since the publication of his first novel, The Poorhouse Fair, *in 1959, Updike's work has been treated respectfully by critics, many of whom have nevertheless complained that he is all style and no substance, an artist of great technical virtuosity but with little to say. Recently, however, he has come to be widely recognized as one of America's most important writers. While his fiction treats diverse subjects, he is best known as a sensitive and lyrical chronicler of the lives of middle- and working-class men and women. In his best-known books—*Couples *(1968) and his three novels about Harry "Rabbit" Angstrom,* Rabbit Run *(1960),* Rabbit Redux *(1971), and* Rabbit is Rich *(1981)—Updike reveals, with grace, sympathy, and insight, the spiritual and sexual yearnings of ordinary people trapped in the sterile, secular world of late twentieth-century America.*

"Still of Some Use" originally appeared in the October 6, 1980 issue of The New Yorker.

—————

When Foster helped his ex-wife clean out the attic of the house where they had once lived and which she was now selling, they came across dozens of forgotten, broken games. Parcheesi, Monopoly, Lotto; games aping the strategies of the stock market, of crime detection, of real-estate speculation, of international diplomacy and war; games with spinners, dice, lettered tiles, cardboard spacemen, and plastic battleships; games bought in five-and-tens and department stores feverish and musical with Christmas expectations; games enjoyed on the afternoon of a birthday and for a few afternoons thereafter and then allowed, shy of one or two pieces, to drift into closets and toward the attic. Yet, discovered in their bright flat boxes between trunks of outgrown clothes and defunct appliances, the games presented a forceful semblance of value: the springs of their miniature launchers still reacted, the logic of their instructions would still generate suspense, given a chance. "What shall we do with all these games?" Foster shouted, in a kind of agony, to his scattered family as they moved up and down the attic stairs.

"Trash 'em," his younger son, a strapping nineteen, urged.

"Would the Goodwill want them?" asked his ex-wife, still wife enough to think that all of his questions deserved answers. "You used to be able to give things like that to orphanages. But they don't call them orphanages anymore, do they?"

"They call them normal American homes," Foster said.

His older son, now twenty-two, with a cinnamon-colored beard, offered, "They wouldn't work anyhow; they all have something missing. That's how they got to the attic."

"Well, why didn't we throw them away at the time?" Foster asked, and had to answer himself. Cowardice, the answer was. Inertia. Clinging to the past.

His sons, with a shadow of old obedience, came and looked over his shoulder at the sad wealth of abandoned playthings, silently groping with him for the particular happy day connected to this and that pattern of coded squares and colored arrows. Their lives had touched these tokens and counters once; excitement had flowed along the paths of these stylized landscapes. But the day was gone, and scarcely a memory remained.

"Toss 'em," the younger decreed, in his manly voice. For these days of cleaning out, the boy had borrowed a pickup truck from a friend and parked it on the lawn beneath the attic window, so the smaller items of discard could be tossed directly into it. The bigger items were lugged down the stairs and through the front hall and out; already the truck was loaded with old mattresses, broken clock-radios, obsolete skis and boots. It was a game of sorts to hit the truck bed with objects dropped from the height of the house. Foster flipped game after game at the target two stories below. When the boxes hit, they exploded, throwing a spray of dice, tokens, counters, and cards into the air and across the lawn. A box called Mousetrap, its lid showing laughing children gathered around a Rube

Goldberg device, drifted sideways, struck one side wall of the truck, and spilled its plastic components into a flower bed. As a set of something called Drag Race! floated gently as a snowflake before coming to rest, much diminished, on a stained mattress, Foster saw in the depth of downward space the cause of his melancholy: he had not played enough with these games. Now no one wanted to play.

Had he and his wife avoided divorce, of course, these boxes would have continued to gather dust in an undisturbed attic, their sorrow unexposed. The toys of his own childhood still rested in his mother's attic. At his last visit, he had wound the spring of a tin Donald Duck that had responded with an angry clack of its bill and a few stiff strokes on its drum. A tin shield with concentric grooves for marbles still waited in a bushel basket with his alphabet blocks and lead airplanes—waited for his childhood to return.

His ex-wife paused where he squatted at the attic window and asked him, "What's the matter?"

"Nothing. These games weren't used much."

"I know. It happens fast. You better stop now; it's making you too sad."

Behind him, his family had cleaned out the attic; the slant-ceilinged rooms stood empty, with drooping insulation. "How can you bear it?" he asked her, of the emptiness.

"Oh, it's fun, once you get into it. Off with the old, on with the new. The new people seem nice. They have little children."

He looked at her and wondered if she was being brave or truly hard-hearted. The attic trembled slightly. "That's Ted," she said.

She had acquired a boyfriend, a big athletic banker fleeing from domestic embarrassments in a neighboring town. When Ted slammed the kitchen door two stories below, the glass shade of a kerosene lamp that, though long unused, Foster hadn't had the heart to throw out of the window vibrated in its copper clips, emitting a thin note like a trapped wasp's song. Time to go. Foster's dusty knees creaked when he stood. His ex-wife's eager steps raced ahead of him down through the emptied house. He followed, carrying the lamp, and set it finally on the bare top of a bookcase he had once built, on the first-floor landing. He remembered screwing the top board, a prize piece of knot-free pine, into place from underneath, so not a nailhead marred its smoothness.

After all the vacant rooms and halls, the kitchen seemed indecently full of heat and life. "Dad, want a beer?" the red-bearded son asked. "Ted brought some." The back of the boy's hand, holding forth the dewy can, blazed with fine ginger hairs. His girlfriend, wearing gypsy earrings and a "No Nukes" sweatshirt, leaned against the disconnected stove, her hair in a bandanna and a black smirch becomingly placed on one temple. From the kind way she smiled at Foster, he felt this party was making room for him.

"No, I better go."

Ted shook Foster's hand, as he always did. He had a thin pink skin and silver hair whose fluffy waves seemed mechanically induced. Foster could look him in the eye no longer than he could gaze at the sun. He wondered how such a radiant brute had got into such a tame line of work. Ted had not helped with the attic today because he had been off in his old town, visiting his teen-age twins. "I hear you did a splendid job today," he announced.

"They did," Foster said. "I wasn't much use. I just sat there stunned. All those things I had forgotten buying."

"Some were presents," his son reminded him. He passed the can his father had snubbed to his mother, who took it and tore up the tab with that defiant-sounding *pssff.* She had never liked beer, yet tipped the can to her mouth.

"Give me one sip," Foster begged, and took the can from her and drank a long swallow. When he opened his eyes, Ted's big hand was cupped under Mrs. Foster's chin while his thumb rubbed away a smudge of dirt along her jaw which Foster had not noticed. This protective gesture made her face look small, pouty, frail, and somehow parched. Ted, Foster noticed now, was dressed with a certain comical perfection in a banker's Saturday outfit—softened bluejeans, crisp tennis sneakers, lumberjack shirt with cuffs folded back. The youthful outfit accented his age, his hypertensive flush. Foster saw them suddenly as a touching, aging couple, and this perception seemed permission to go.

He handed back the can.

"Thanks for your help," his former wife said.

"Yes, we do thank you," Ted said.

"Talk to Tommy," she unexpectedly added. She was still sending out trip wires to slow his departures. "This is harder on him than he shows."

Ted looked at his watch, a fat, black-faced thing he could swim underwater with. "I said to him coming in, 'Don't dawdle till the dump closes.'"

"He loafed all day," his brother complained, "mooning over old stuff, and now he's going to screw up getting to the dump."

"He's very sensi-tive," the visiting gypsy said, with a strange chiming brightness, as if repeating something she had heard.

Outside, the boy was picking up litter that had fallen wide of the truck. Foster helped him. In the grass there were dozens of tokens and dice. Some were engraved with curious little faces—Olive Oyl, Snuffy Smith, Dagwood—and others with hieroglyphs—numbers, diamonds, spades, hexagons—whose code was lost. He held out a handful for Tommy to see. "Can you remember what these were for?"

"Comic-Strip Lotto," the boy said without hesitation. "And a game called Gambling Fools there was a kind of slot machine for." The light of old chances and payoffs flickered in his eyes as he gazed down at the rubble in his father's hand. Though Foster was taller, the boy was broader in the shoulders, and growing. "Want to ride with me to the dump?" Tommy asked.

"I would, but I better go." He, too, had a new life to lead. By being on this forsaken property at all, Foster was in a sense on the wrong square, if not *en prise.* Once, he had begun to teach this boy chess, but in the sadness of watching him lose—the little bowed head frowning above his trapped king—the lessons had stopped.

Foster tossed the tokens into the truck; they rattled to rest on the metal. "This depress you?" he asked his son.

"Naa." The boy amended, "Kind of."

"You'll feel great," Foster promised him, "coming back with a clean truck. I used to love it at the dump, all that old happiness heaped up, and the seagulls."

"It's changed since you left. They have all these new rules. The lady there yelled at me last time, for putting stuff in the wrong place."

"She did?"

"Yeah. It was scary." Seeing his father waver, he added, "It'll only take twenty minutes." Though broad of build, Tommy had beardless cheeks and, between thickening eyebrows, a trace of that rounded, faintly baffled blankness babies have, that wrinkles before they cry.

"O.K.," Foster said, greatly lightened. "I'll protect you."

QUESTIONS

1. Look at the description of the "forgotten, broken games" in the opening paragraph. Why does Updike describe them in such great detail? How does he manage, through the power of his descriptive language, to invest these simple, even trivial, objects with so much meaning and melancholy? How does he use children's playthings as symbols in this story? What are they symbolic of?

2. How is the metaphor of game playing used throughout this story? In what sense are the characters playing a game?

3. Explain the story's title. How does it relate to the final scene between Foster and Ted and, specifically, to the last line of the story? Why does Foster feel "greatly lightened" at the very end?

4. In a *Time* magazine cover story on Updike, Paul Gray characterizes the "famous, or infamous, Updike style" as "tiny things described at great length." Judging from this story, do you feel that this is a valid summation of Updike's style? Why or why not?

SUGGESTIONS FOR WRITING

1. When Foster, depressed by the emptiness of his former house, asks his wife, "How can you bear it?" she breezily answers, "Oh, it's fun, once you get used to it. Off with the old, on with the new." Do you agree with Foster's ex-wife that the past is easily disposed of and that it is always possible to start life anew? Or do you believe that things are more complex—that it is not easy to free yourself of the past, of memories, and of strong personal ties? Write an essay explaining your viewpoint, basing your discussion on examples drawn from your own life experiences.

2. Most of us have some place in our homes—an attic, basement, closet, garage,

etc.—that we use as a storeroom for unused objects. Write a detailed description of your family's storage place and its contents. Be as specific and concrete as you can.

3. Write a description of your favorite childhood plaything. Try to convey your feelings about this object (game, toy, doll, etc.) in your description.

4. Some people are almost obsessive accumulators—they have trouble throwing anything away (broken appliances, worn-out clothing, old magazines). Other people seem unattached to their possessions and have no trouble getting rid of them. Write a description of anyone you know who falls into either of these categories.

Howard Nemerov
BOOM!

Howard Nemerov was born in New York City in 1920, the son of a wealthy department store owner (Nemerov's sister was the famed photographer, Diane Arbus). After graduating from Harvard in 1941, he enlisted in the Royal Canadian Air Force and served as a combat pilot during the Second World War. Since the late 1940s, he has been a teacher at various universities and has long been recognized as one of America's foremost poets.

Nemerov's poetry is known for its combination of ironic humor and pessimism—its "dark joking," in the words of one commentator. Nemerov himself acknowledges the accuracy of this description. Speaking of the way his work has been received by critics, Nemerov has written, "The charge typically raised . . . has been that my poems are jokes, even bad jokes. I incline to agree, insisting however that they are bad jokes, and even terrible jokes, emerging from the nature of things as well as from my propensity for coming at things a touch subversively and from the blind side, or the dark side, the side everyone concerned with 'values' would just as soon forget."

The following poem, taken from Nemerov's Collected Poems *(1977), displays the poet's biting wit and satirical brilliance. Nemerov's other books include,* The Image and the Law *(1947),* Guide to the Ruins *(1950),* The Salt Garden *(1955),* The Winter Lightning *(1968),* Gnomes and Occasions *(1973),* The Western Approaches *(1975), and* Inside the Onion *(1984).*

SEES BOOM IN RELIGION, TOO

Atlantic City, June 23, 1957 (AP).—*President Eisenhower's pastor said tonight that Americans are living in a period of "unprecedented religious activity" caused partially by paid vacations, the eight-hour day and modern conveniences.*

"These fruits of material progress," said the Rev. Edward L. R. Elson of the National Presbyterian Church, Washington, "have provided the leisure, the energy, and the means for a level of human and spiritual values never before reached."

Here at the Vespasian-Carlton, it's just one
religious activity after another; the sky
is constantly being crossed by cruciform
airplanes, in which nobody disbelieves
for a second, and the tide, the tide
of spiritual progress and prosperity
miraculously keeps rising, to a level
never before attained. The churches are full,
the beaches are full, and the filling-stations
are full, God's great ocean is full
of paid vacationers praying an eight-hour day
to the human and spiritual values, the fruits,
the leisure, the energy, and the means, Lord,
the means for the level, the unprecedented level,
and the modern conveniences, which also are full.
Never before, O Lord, have the prayers and praises
from belfry and phonebooth, from ballpark and barbecue
the sacrifices, so endlessly ascended.

It was not thus when Job in Palestine
sat in the dust and cried, cried bitterly;
when Damien kissed the lepers on their wounds
it was not thus; it was not thus
when Francis worked a fourteen-hour day
strictly for the birds; when Dante took
a week's vacation without pay and it rained
part of the time, O Lord, it was not thus.

But now the gears mesh and the tires burn
and the ice chatters in the shaker and the priest
in the pulpit, and Thy Name, O Lord,
is kept before the public, while the fruits
ripen and religion booms and the level rises
and every modern convenience runneth over,
that it may never be with us as it hath been
with Athens and Karnak and Nagasaki,
nor Thy sun for one instant refrain from shining
on the rainbow Buick by the breezeway
or the Chris Craft with the uplift life raft;
that we may continue to be the just folks we are,

plain people with ordinary superliners and
disposable diaperliners, people of the stop'n'shop
'n'pray as you go, of hotel, motel, boatel,
the humble pilgrims of no deposit no return
and please adjust thy clothing, who will give to Thee,
if Thee will keep us going, our annual
Miss Universe, for Thy Name's Sake, Amen.

QUESTIONS

1. What is the relationship between the newspaper item at the start of the poem and the poem itself?

2. At the start of the poem, the speaker declares that "Here at the Vespasian-Carlton, it's just one/religious activity after another." How many religious activities does he go on to describe? What does the description of the "cruciform airplanes" crossing the sky have to do with "religious activity"?

3. This poem takes the form of a prayer of thanksgiving. What exactly is the speaker being thankful for? What is the connection, for example, between the full churches, full beaches, and full filling stations?

4. Explain the joke in the line, "it was not thus when Francis worked a fourteen hour day/strictly for the birds." Explain the references to Athens, Karnak, and Nagasaki. Why does Nemerov mention them? What do his allusions to Job, Damien, and Dante add to the poem?

5. Discuss Nemerov's use of irony in this poem. How does the language of the poem—the *way* the speaker talks—contribute to the irony? Who does the speaker seem to be?

6. What makes Nemerov's use of the verb "chatters" so effective in the second line of stanza three?

SUGGESTION FOR WRITING

Do you believe that our society places too much importance on material values and not enough on spiritual ones? Which do you think are more important for personal happiness? Write an essay explaining your point of view.

CHAPTER *Four*

MEN AND WOMEN
Comparison and Contrast

Comparison as a mode of thinking and as a way to organize writing is, next to narration and description, the most natural to employ. Small children must compare objects to learn about the world and their relationship to it: "Am I bigger than Bobby?" "Which will make a better castle—wet sand or dry sand?" "Isn't a butterfly like a bird?" As adults, we use comparison and contrast constantly in our daily lives, for almost every decision we make to do something means deciding not to do something else at the same time. When it comes to writing a comparison/contrast essay, we not only have to look closely at the two (or more) subjects we are considering, we have to decide why we are looking at them and how best to organize our discussion.

Often, as in an essay exam, the instructor will suggest a specific topic for comparison ("Compare your attitudes toward an important subject—sex, work, money—to those of your parents." "What are the main differences between high school and college?"). If you select your own topic, remember to choose subjects that have a number of aspects in common. If you were to compare two fast-food restaurants—McDonald's and Wendy's, for example—you would immediately have several categories to use as a basis for comparison: quality of food, variety, price, service, and atmosphere. Within each of these categories the writer's personal experiences will provide the details for comparison. Don't choose two subjects that have only one or two apparent similarities, or you will rapidly run out of things to say. You might decide, for instance, to compare a fast-food restaurant to a bank, since both often have "drive-thru" facilities; after making that connection, however, you are unlikely to find many points of comparison. In choosing your own topic, you should also consider the length of the assignment and the extent of your own knowledge. You will not have enough space to compare Soviet and Chinese communism fully in a 500-word essay. Finally, ask yourself if your knowledge of *both* the subjects you want to compare is roughly the same. If not, either do some research or choose two other subjects you do know with an equal degree of thoroughness.

After selecting a topic (or being assigned one), you need to decide what your purpose is in writing the essay. An essay without a clearly stated purpose will leave the reader continually asking "Why?" as he or she reads. Simply listing a string of similarities or differences will not sustain the reader's interest very long. You will find, however, that a purpose usually comes to mind along with the subject. The fast-food restaurant comparison will obviously lead to a choice of the better one of the two. This is, in fact, one of the common purposes of the comparison and contrast mode: to evaluate two things and judge between them. This purpose will put a premium on contrasting (showing the differences between) rather than on comparing (showing similarities).

Another purpose of the comparison/contrast essay is to explain to the reader something unfamiliar in light of something well known. Movie reviewers, for example, frequently turn to this technique when they are writing about the sequel to a hit movie. The reader who has not yet seen *Beverly Hills Cop II, Superman III,* or *Rocky IV* can nevertheless get a clear impression of the movie by hearing how it compares to its predecessors. A final purpose of the comparison/contrast essay is to get to know both subjects in greater detail than if you were writing about only one. In such cases, it is not necessary to express a preference for either of the things you are comparing.

To crystalize your thinking and guide you in writing, it is important to state your main idea in one sentence, sometimes called a tentative thesis. It is tentative because you may modify it as you explore your subject further. Sample thesis statements might be:

1. "Although McDonald's and Wendy's are similar in a number of ways, there are good reasons to prefer Wendy's." (Making a choice)

2. "Growing up on a U.S. military base in Europe is radically different from growing up in any American city or suburb." (Exploring the unfamiliar through the familiar)

3. "It doesn't matter which you choose: large universities and small colleges both have a great deal to offer." (Examining both subjects in detail)

Notice that each statement takes a particular, narrowly expressed stand. This will help focus your essay.

Once you have a subject, purpose, and a tentative thesis, you need to decide on an organizational plan. This is particularly important in a comparison and contrast essay because comparisons can flow so spontaneously that you may think your paper has an effective organization when, in fact, it doesn't. The two main options for organization are:

1. *Parallel Order,* in which you discuss the *subjects* one at a time. For example, you would first discuss all the important points relating to McDonald's—location, atmosphere, service, food—and then go on to discuss the same points in relation to Wendy's.

2. *Point-by-Point Order.* Here, you take up the *points* one at a time, so that, in comparing the two restaurants, you would first discuss the location of McDonald's in comparison to that of Wendy's, then compare their atmospheres, and so on.

The Parallel Order method is generally desirable for shorter essays, because it allows the reader to absorb everything about one subject before moving on to the next. If you have a great deal of material to present, however, there is the danger that the reader will have forgotten the first subject (without the frequent use of reminders) by the time he or she has progressed halfway through the second. The Point-by-Point Order method avoids that problem, though you do run the risk of sounding as though you are simply making a list. Careful development, especially the use both of detailed examples and effective transitions ("on the other hand," "in contrast"), should help you avoid that trap.

Let's use the thesis "Although McDonald's and Wendy's are similar in a number of ways, there are good reasons to prefer Wendy's" to see what an outline of each of the organizational patterns would look like:

Parallel Order

Paragraph I. Introduction (Why you are writing this essay, perhaps illustrated with an anecdote. Conclude the paragraph with your thesis statement.)

Paragraph II. McDonald's
A. Location (convenience, accessibility)
B. Atmosphere (design, comfort of seating, cleanliness, noise)
C. Service (speed, courtesy)
D. Food (variety, taste, price)

Paragraph III. Wendy's
A. Location
B. Atmosphere }
C. Service   } (Same elements compared)
D. Food

Paragraph IV. Conclusion (Summary of results and explanation of why you arrived at your thesis.)

Point-by-Point Order

Paragraph I. Introduction (Same as above)

Paragraph II. Location
    A. McDonald's
    B. Wendy's

Paragraph III. Atmosphere
    A. McDonald's
    B. Wendy's

Paragraph IV. Service
    A. McDonald's
    B. Wendy's

Paragraph V. Food
    A. McDonald's
    B. Wendy's

Paragraph VI. Conclusion (Same as in Parallel Order)

The number of paragraphs you devote to any one aspect should be determined by the amount of information you have. In the Point-by-Point Order paper, you might want to combine location and atmosphere into one paragraph and devote separate paragraphs to service and food because you have more to say about these. On the other hand, in the Parallel Order essay, you might divide the long paragraph on McDonald's into two smaller ones—the first on location and atmosphere, the second on service and food (you would then do the same for the paragraph on Wendy's)—simply because large blocks of uninterrupted prose tend to tire the reader.

Notice also that the categories are presented in a particular order. Location and atmosphere go first because they are similar in both chains. In fact, McDonald's may have more conveniently located restaurants, so you would concede its superiority to Wendy's on that point. But in service and in the most important category—food—you may feel that Wendy's wins because of its courteous help, superior salad bar, spicier chili, and juicier hamburgers. These points, then, would come in the more emphatic final position, before your conclusion, and would mirror the thesis statement, which acknowledges initial similarities but ultimately indicates a preference for Wendy's. This structure could be reversed if your thesis was, "Although Wendy's has better food, there is very little difference between it and McDonald's." Emphasize those points that support the thesis and organize your essay accordingly.

As you will see when you study the writing collected in this chapter, professional writers do not mechanically follow any prescribed organizational pattern. All of the selections, including the short story and the poem that conclude this chapter, use comparison and contrast, but subject and method are so subtly blended that it will take close reading on your part to analyze each author's strategy. To help you do this, study the following paragraph taken from an article on the women's movement by Vivian Gornick:

> The rallying cry of the black civil rights movement had always been ''Give us back our manhood!'' What exactly does that mean? Where is black manhood? How has it been taken from blacks? And how can it be retrieved? The answer lies in one word: responsibility; blacks have been deprived of the privilege of assuming responsibility, therefore, they have been deprived of manhood. Women have been deprived of exactly the same thing and in every real sense have thus been deprived of womanhood. We have never been prepared to assume responsibility; we have never been prepared to make demands upon ourselves; we have never been taught to expect the development of what is best in ourselves because no one has ever expected anything of us—or for us. Because no one has ever had any intention of turning over any serious work to us. Both we and the blacks lost the ballgame before we ever got up to play. In order to live you've got to have nerve, and we were stripped of our nerve before we began. Black is ugly and female is inferior. These are the primary lessons of our experience, and in these ways both blacks and women have been kept, not as functioning nationals, but rather as operating objects; oh, to be sure, blacks are despised objects, and women protected objects, but a human being who remains as a child throughout his or her adult life is an object, not a mature specimen, and the definition of a child is: one without responsibility.

Note how Gornick begins using the Parallel Order method by talking about ''black manhood'' in the first six sentences. Then, in the next three sentences she discusses only ''womanhood,'' using the phrase ''exactly the same thing'' as a transition. In the last four sentences of the paragraph, Gornick shifts to the Point-by-Point Order method, comparing and contrasting blacks and women in each sentence. The paragraph culminates in a long topic sentence which asserts that both blacks and women have been treated like children in American society. Her repeated use of ''both'' and ''we'' further cements the comparison structurally and thematically. Once you have mastered the basic organizational patterns of the comparison and contrast essay, try to combine them, as Gornick has done, to produce a more flexible and interesting composition.

Time *Magazine*
MALE AND FEMALE: DIFFERENCES BETWEEN THEM
★ ★ ★

The impact of the women's movement on every aspect of American life has been profound. In May 1972—acknowledging the "epic change" feminism had begun to effect "in the way we see each other, not only sexually, *but historically, sociologically, psychologically, and in the deeper, almost inaccessible closets of daily habit"—*Time *magazine devoted an entire issue to the subject. Besides its cover story, "The New Woman: Where She Is and Where She's Going," each of the magazine's regular departments (Art, Books, Business, Education, Law, Medicine, Religion, Science, etc.) focused on feminist issues.*

The following essay, which appeared as part of the Behavior section, was written by Contributing Editor Virginia Adams.

"The Book of Genesis had it wrong. In the beginning God created Eve," says Johns Hopkins Medical Psychologist John Money. What he means is that the basic tendency of the human fetus is to develop as a female. If the genes order the gonads to become testicles and put out the male hormone androgen, the embryo will turn into a boy; otherwise it becomes a girl: "You have to add something to get a male," Money notes. "Nature's first intention is to create a female."

Nature may prefer women, but virtually every culture has been partial to men. That contradiction raises an increasingly pertinent question (as well as the hackles of militant feminists): Are women immutably different from men? Women's Liberationists believe that any differences—other than anatomical—are a result of conditioning by society. The opposing view is that all of the differences are fixed in the genes. To scientists, however, the nature-nurture controversy is oversimplified. To them, what human beings are results from a complex interaction between both forces. Says Oxford Biologist Christopher Ounsted: "It is a false dichotomy to say that this difference is acquired and that one genetic. To try and differentiate is like asking a penny whether it is really a heads penny or a tails penny." As Berkeley Psychologist Frank Beach suggests, "Predispositions may be genetic; complex behavior patterns are probably not."

The idea that genetic predispositions exist is based on three kinds of evidence. First, there are the "cultural universals" cited by Margaret Mead. Almost everywhere, the mother is the principal caretaker of the child, and male dominance and aggression are the rule. Some anthropologists believe there has been an occasional female-dominated society; others insist that none have existed.

Sex Typing

Then there is the fact that among most ground-dwelling primates, males are dominant and have as a major function the protection of females and offspring. Some research suggests that this is true even when the young are raised apart from adults, which seems to mean that they do not learn their roles from their society.

Finally, behavioral sex differences show up long before any baby could possibly perceive subtle differences between his parents or know which parent he is expected to imitate. "A useful strategy," says Harvard Psychologist Jerome

Kagan, "is to assume that the earlier a particular difference appears, the more likely it is to be influenced by biological factors."

Physical differences appear even before birth. The heart of the female fetus often beats faster, and girls develop more rapidly. "Physiologically," says Sociologist Barbette Blackington, "women are better-made animals." Males do have more strength and endurance—though that hardly matters in a technological society.

Recent research hints that there may even be sex differences in the brain. According to some experimenters, the presence of the male hormone testosterone in the fetus may "masculinize" the brain, organizing the fetal nerve centers in characteristic ways. This possible "sex typing" of the central nervous system before birth may make men and women respond differently to incoming stimuli, Sociologist John Gagnon believes.

In fact, newborn girls do show different responses in some situations. They react more strongly to the removal of a blanket and more quickly to touch and pain. Moreover, experiments demonstrate that twelve-week-old girls gaze longer at photographs of faces than at geometric figures. Boys show no preference then, though eventually they pay more attention to figures. Kagan acknowledges the effect of environment, but he has found that it exerts a greater influence on girls than on boys. The female infants who experienced the most "face-to-face interaction" with their mothers were more attentive to faces than girls whose mothers did not exchange looks with them so much. Among boys, there was no consistent relationship.

Internal Organs

As some psychologists see it, this very early female attention to the human face suggests that women may have a greater and even partly innate sensitivity to other human beings. Perhaps this explains why girls seem to get more satisfaction from relationships with people.

Even after infancy, the sexes show differential interests that do not seem to grow solely out of experience. Psychoanalyst Erik Erikson has found that boys and girls aged ten to twelve use space differently when asked to construct a scene with toys. Girls often build a low wall, sometimes with an elaborate doorway, surrounding a quiet interior scene. Boys are likely to construct towers, façades with cannons, and lively exterior scenes. Erikson acknowledges that cultural influences are at work, but he is convinced that they do not fully explain the nature of children's play. The differences, he says, "seem to parallel the morphology [shape and form] of genital differentiation itself: in the male, an external organ, erectible and intrusive; internal organs in the female, with vestibular access, leading to statically expectant ova."

In aptitude as well as in interest, sex differences become apparent early in life. Though girls are generally less adept than boys at mathematical and spatial reasoning, they learn to count sooner and to talk earlier and better. Some scientists think this female verbal superiority may be caused by sex-linked differences in the brain. Others believe it may exist because, as observation proves, mothers talk to infant girls more than to baby boys. But does the mother's talking cause the child to do likewise, or could it be the other way round? Psychologist Michael Lewis suggests the possibility that girls are talked to more because, for biological reasons, they respond more than boys to words and thus stimulate their mothers to keep talking.

Evidence that parental behavior does affect speech comes from tests made by Kagan among poor Guatemalan children. There, boys are more highly valued than girls, are talked to more and become more verbal. In the U.S., Psychiatrist David Levy has found that boys who are atypically good with words and inept with figures have been overprotected by their mothers. Psychologist Elizabeth Bing has observed that girls who excel at math and spatial problems have often been left to work alone by their mothers, while highly verbal girls have mothers who offer frequent suggestions, praise and criticism.

While girls outdo boys verbally, they often lag behind in solving analytical problems, those that require attention to detail. Girls seem to think "globally," responding to situations as a whole instead of abstracting single elements. In the "rod and frame test," for instance, a subject sits in a dark room before a luminous rod inside a slightly tilted frame, and is asked to move the rod to an upright position. Boys can separate the rod visually from the frame and make it stand straight; girls, misled by the tipped frame, usually adjust the rod not to the true vertical but to a position parallel with the sides of the frame.

In another experiment, children are asked to group related pictures. Boys again pay attention to details, perhaps putting together pictures that show people with an arm raised; girls make functional groups of, for example, a doctor, a nurse and a wheelchair.

In all such differences, environmental influence is suggested by the fact that children who think analytically most often prove to have mothers who have encouraged initiative and exploration, while youngsters who think globally have generally been tied to their mother's apron strings. In Western society, of course, it is usually boys who are urged toward adventure. Herein, perhaps—there is no proof—lies an explanation for the apparent male capacity to think analytically.

In IQ tests, males and females score pretty much alike. Since this is true, why do women seem less creative? Many social scientists are convinced that the reasons are cultural. Women, they say, learn early in life that female accomplishment brings few rewards. In some cases, women cannot be creative because they are discriminated against. In other instances, a woman's creativity may well be blunted by fear of nonconformity, failure or even success itself. Unlike men, Kagan says, women are trained to have strong anxiety about being wrong.

To many psychoanalysts, however, the explanation lies in the fact that women possess the greatest creative power of all: bringing new life into being; thus they need not compensate by producing works of art. Men, it is theorized, are driven to make up for what seem to them a deficiency. That they feel keenly, though unconsciously, their inability to bear children is shown in dreams reported on the analyst's couch, in the behavior of small boys who play with dolls and walk around with their stomachs thrust forward in imitation of their pregnant mothers and in primitive rites and ancient myths. According to these myths, presumably conceived by males, Adam delivered Eve from his rib cage, Zeus gave birth to Athena out of his head, and when Semele was burned to death, Zeus seized Dionysus from her womb and sewed him up in his thigh until the infant had developed.

There are personality differences between the sexes too. Although no trait is confined to one sex—there are women who exceed the male average even in supposedly masculine characteristics—some distinctions turn up remarkably early. At New York University, for example, researchers have found that a female infant stops sucking a bottle and looks up when someone comes into the room; a male pays no attention to the visitor.

Another Kagan experiment shows that girls of twelve months who become frightened in a strange room drift toward their mothers, while boys look for something interesting to do. At four months, twice as many girls as boys cry when frightened in a strange laboratory. What is more, Kagan says, similar differences can be seen in monkeys and baboons, which "forces us to consider the possibility that some of the psychological differences between men and women may not be the product of experience alone but of subtle biological differences."

Female Passivity

Many researchers have found greater dependence and docility in very young girls, greater autonomy and activity in boys. When a barrier is set up to separate youngsters from their mothers, boys try to knock it down; girls cry helplessly. There is little doubt that maternal encouragement—or discouragement—of such behavior plays a major role in determining adult personality. For example, a mother often stimulates male autonomy by throwing a toy far away from her young son, thus tacitly suggesting to him that he leave her to get it.

Animal studies suggest that there may be a biological factor in maternal behavior; mothers of rhesus monkeys punish their male babies earlier and more often than their female offspring; they also touch their female babies more often and act more protective toward them.

As for the controversial question of female "passivity," Psychoanalyst Helen Deutsch believes that the concept has been misunderstood. "There is no contradiction between being feminine and working. The ego can be active in both men and women," she says. It is only in love and in sex that passivity is particularly appropriate for women. As she sees it, passivity is no more than a kind of openness and warmth; it does not mean "inactivity, emptiness or immobility."

Another controversy rages over the effect of hormones. Militant women, who discount hormonal influence, disagree violently with scientific researchers, who almost unanimously agree that hormones help determine how people feel and act. So far, there have been few studies of male hormones, but scientists think they may eventually discover hormonal cycles in men that produce cyclic changes in mood and behavior. As for females, studies have indicated that 49% of female medical and surgical hospital admissions, most psychiatric hospital admissions and 62% of violent crimes among women prisoners occur on premenstrual and menstrual days. At Worcester State Hospital in Massachusetts, Psychologists Donald and Inge Broverman have found that estrogen sharpens sensory perception. They believe that this heightened sensitivity may lead more women than men to shy away from situations of stress.

Fierce Bulls

One trait thought to be affected by hormones is aggressiveness. In all cultures, investigators report, male infants tend to play more aggressively than females. While scientists think a genetic factor may be involved, they also observe that society fosters the difference by permitting male aggression and encouraging female adaptability. Some suggest that females may be as aggressive as men—but with words instead of deeds.

The definitive research on hormones and aggression is still to be done. However, it has been established that the female hormone estrogen inhibits aggression in both animal and human males. It has also been proved that the male hormone androgen influences aggression in animals. For example, castration produces tractable steers rather than fierce bulls.

The influence of androgen begins even before birth. Administered to pregnant primates, the hormone makes newborn females play more aggressively than ordinary females. Moreover, such masculinized animals are usually aggressive as long as they live, even if they are never again exposed to androgen.

According to some experts, this long-lasting effect of hormones administered or secreted before birth may help explain why boys are more aggressive than girls even during their early years when both sexes appear to produce equal amounts of male and female hormones. Other observers have suggested that the spurt in male-hormone production at puberty could be one of the causes of delinquency in adolescent boys, but there is no proof that this is so.

Will there some day be a "unisex" society with no differences between men and women, except anatomical ones? It seems unlikely. Anatomy, parturition and gender, observes Psychologist Joseph Adelson, cannot be wished away "in a spasm of the distended will, as though the will, in pursuit of total human possibility, can amplify itself to overcome the given." Or, as Psychoanalyst Therese Benedek sees it, "biology precedes personality."

"Nature has been the oppressor," observes Michael Lewis. Women's role as caretaker "was the evolutionary result of their biological role in birth and feeding." The baby bottle has freed women from some of the tasks of that role, but, says University of Michigan Psychologist Judith Bardwick, "the major responsibility for child rearing is the woman's, even in the Soviet Union, the Israeli kibbutz, Scandinavia and mainland China." Furthermore, though mothering skills are mostly learned, it is a fact that if animals are raised in isolation and then put in a room with the young of the species, it is the females who go to the infants and take care of them.

"Perhaps the known biological differences can be totally overcome, and society can approach a state in which a person's sex is of no consequence for any significant activity except childbearing," admits Jerome Kagan. "But we must ask if such a society will be satisfying to its members." As he see it, "complementarity" is what makes relationships stable and pleasurable.

Psychoanalyst Martin Symonds agrees. "The basic reason why unisex must fail is that in the sexual act itself, the man has to be assertive, if tenderly, and the woman has to be receptive. What gives trouble is when men see assertiveness as aggression and women see receptiveness as submission." Unisex, he sums up, would be "a disaster," because children need roles to identify with and rebel against. "You can't identify with a blur. A unisex world would be a frictionless environment in which nobody would be able to grow up."

The crucial point is that a difference is not a deficiency. As Biologist Ounsted puts it, "We are all human beings and in this sense equal. We are not, however, the same." In the opinion of John Money, "You can play fair only if you recognize and respect authentic differences."

Though scientists disagree about the precise nature and causes of these differences, there is no argument about two points: society plays a tremendous part in shaping the differences, and most women are capable of doing whatever they want. Only in the top ranges of ability, says Kagan, are innate differences significant; for typical men and women, "the biological differences are totally irrelevant." Psychiatrist Donald Lunde agrees. "There is no evidence," he asserts, "that men are any more or less qualified by biological sex differences alone to perform the tasks generally reserved for them in today's societies."

QUESTIONS

1. Why does the author begin the essay with a quote? Is this an effective strategy? Explain.

2. The paragraphs in this essay tend to be organized in a very straightforward way. Typically, they consist of a clear transition and a strong topic sentence, followed by specific supporting details—facts, quotes, etc. Find at least five paragraphs in the article that exemplify this model and, for each one, point out its various parts: transition, central idea, supporting material.

3. Which organizational plan—parallel order or point-by-point order—does Adams use in comparing the sexes? Does she use it consistently? By what means does she keep the comparison from becoming repetitive or mechanical?

4. Throughout the essay Adams poses various questions. Point to some of them. Do you think she relies too heavily on this technique? What are its advantages? Disadvantages?

5. Do you think that—given the author's exclusive concentration on the *differences* between men and women—any conclusions can be drawn about her

feminist (or antifeminist) leanings? Is there any evidence in the essay that she *values* the differences between the sexes?

SUGGESTIONS FOR WRITING

1. Being as specific as possible, write an essay in which you describe the major differences you have observed between men and women (apart from the obvious biological ones). Alternatively, write a comparison essay in which you discuss the important ways men and women are the *same*.

2. Write an essay in which you compare male and female heroes in recent movies or on television. Do you see any evidence in films or on TV that America is becoming a more "unisex" society?

John Glusman
RIGHTEOUSNESS
★ ★ ★

John Glusman is editor-in-chief of Washington Square Press at Simon & Schuster. A former member of the faculty of the New School for Social Research, his essays, articles, and reviews have appeared in numerous newspapers, magazines, and journals, including the Christian Science Monitor, The Progressive, GEO, *and* Dissent.

"Righteousness," originally published in a special issue of Ms. *magazine devoted to men's views, uses comparison/contrast, among other modes, to expose a character trait the author believes hinders meaningful dialogue between the sexes.*

The hottest board game since Scrabble, Trivial Pursuit is little more than an extended trivia test: Who sang "Johnny Angel"? What's the favorite food of dragonflies? Where would you be if you whiled away your time playing a didjeridoo in Wagga Wagga? After playing it once, I was soon hooked, angry at myself when I couldn't answer the obvious, and foolishly proud when I did. And I soon realized that Trivial Pursuit feeds on a compulsion: the compulsion to prove oneself right.

"Why do you always have to be so right," I can hear my wife saying in exasperation, "even when you're wrong?" "I can't help it," I'd reply, seeking the biological way out. "It must be in my genes." After all, I come from a family of doctors, and doctors are particularly prone to righteousness, perhaps because their patients always expect them to be right.

I remember my grandmother used to introduce my father to her friends as if she had found the key to immortality. "This is my son," she'd beam, "the doctor." In her eyes he could do no wrong, and as children we felt similarly. At an early age, a premium was placed upon learning and the importance of the cold, demonstrable fact. There was little room for ambiguity: one was right or wrong, simple as that. On one occasion I was severely reprimanded for prescribing two aspirin, plenty of liquids, and plenty of rest to someone describing the symptoms of a common cold. "How do you know it's just a cold?" I was challenged. "You're not a doctor." My father later reminded me that I was the only layperson in the family, which made me feel about as good as a guinea pig in a Skinner box without the consolation of a pellet. As if to compensate for my lack of expertise, I sometimes mistook righteousness for truth.

Now at first it seems that most people want to be right, they want that pellet in Skinner's box, be it a parental nod of approval, an A on an exam, or a bonus to their salary. But on reflection, it appears that the compulsion to prove oneself right is a predominantly male phenomenon, and the righteous are unable to distinguish good from evil, right from wrong. Of course there *is* such a thing as female righteousness, and although both are expressions of discontent, their initial aims may be quite different. Male righteousness is an assertion of power, of independence, a way of showing both men and women who's on top. It's a response to a perceived, not necessarily a real, threat, a means of establishing a safe distance for fear of contact, a shying away from intimacy and the concomitant risk of pain. Male righteousness, in other words, is a defensive response.

Female righteousness can be defensive too, the "Back off, Bud; I don't want to know you" response that men dismiss as bitchiness. But when it says, "I don't care what you think. You can't hurt me," it is being used offensively. For hurt has already entered the picture. Female righteousness, then, instead of anticipating pain, may already be an expression of it—growing out of an unfulfilled yearning for closeness. It is an indirect way of reaching out to reestablish contact, instead of preventing it.

I remember one young woman, the daughter of a very successful businessman, who was herself the image of success—bright, attractive, aggressive, and particularly skilled in the art of talking back. We had always enjoyed a lively repartee, and an intellectually stimulating relationship, until she finally told me how hurt she had been by some of the things I had said. I had always admired her forthrightness and ability to stand up to others, but it became evident that she had suffered far more from our verbal jousts than she ever let on. She just wouldn't give in, and maintained her defense so well that I had continued to thrust and parry. When I finally realized what had happened—and it took a falling out for her real feelings to emerge—it was too late. There was no way of undoing the damage that had been done. And here we were both in the wrong; I, for underestimating her sensitivity and overestimating her strength, and she, for her inability to admit her real feelings for fear of hurting her image, in the process of which she was hurt herself.

For talking back is one thing; talking *to* another person something else. Talking back can, in fact, be the bridge to an open dialogue. But it is a shaky one, because it is bound to meet with resistance, whereas a simple question, such as "Why do you say that?" "What's wrong?" or, more to the point, "What do you want?" can stop the righteous male dead in his tracks. (After all, righteousness is an expression of need.) By denying the righteous male the response he expects— acquiescence or indignation—you have changed his perspective. He can no longer talk *down;* he must talk *to.* His monologue has been turned into a dialogue.

QUESTIONS

1. What does Glusman see as the sources of men's obsession with being right? Does he base his generalizations too heavily on personal experience, or do you find his reasoning persuasive? Discuss.

2. How does Glusman distinguish female righteousness from male? Does he support his claims adequately? Explain.

3. What thesis emerges in the final paragraph? What does Glusman want to happen to the righteous male?

4. How does Glusman use word play in his title? Why does he begin his essay with the anecdote about the game Trivial Pursuit?

5. Explain the reference to Skinner's Box. What does Glusman's use of the image suggest about the audience he is writing for?

6. Which paragraphs of Glusman's essay use comparison and contrast? What other modes does he employ? How are these paragraphs organized, and which words and phrases function as transitions in Glusman's discussion?

SUGGESTIONS FOR WRITING

1. Think of another quality like "Righteousness," and discuss its presence in males and females, noting and analyzing any variations that you see. Some possibilities are "Competitiveness," "Strength," "Sexiness," and "Ambitiousness."

2. Glusman isolates a character trait in himself, as well as in other men, that he doesn't like. Think of a character trait you possess and would like to change. Write an essay comparing the person you are now with the person you would like to be—without the unwanted trait, that is.

Phyllis Schlafly
UNDERSTANDING THE DIFFERENCE
★ ★ ★

Although Phyllis Schlafly has labeled herself "the sweetheart of the silent majority," her life and ideology often seem at odds. Born in 1924 to a well-to-do St. Louis family, Schlafly nonetheless "worked nights, forty-eight hours a week, in an ammunition plant, test-firing machine guns, to put herself through college," according to biographer Carol Felsenthal. After graduating from Washington University in 1944, Schlafly earned an M.A. from Radcliffe College in 1945. At the age of 52 she earned a law degree because a legislator had criticized her for testifying on a particular issue without one. A prolific author, an active Republican Party worker, leader of the anti-ERA movement, and spokesperson for numerous other conservative causes, Schlafly nonetheless asserts that a woman's place is in the home.

In "Understanding the Difference," reprinted from her book The Power of the Positive Woman *(1977), Schlafly insists that men tend to be more logical and abstract than women, who are likely to be emotional, personal, and mystical. Yet her own skills as a polemicist and political organizer are formidable, and her arguments as presented in the following excerpt played an important role in the failure of the Equal Rights Amendment to gain legislative approval.*

———

The first requirement for the acquisition of power by the Positive Woman is to understand the differences between men and women. Your outlook on life, your faith, your behavior, your potential for fulfillment, all are determined by the parameters of your original premise. The Positive Woman starts with the assumption that the world is her oyster. She rejoices in the creative capability within her body and the power potential of her mind and spirit. She understands that men and women are different, and that those very differences provide the key to her success as a person and fulfillment as a woman.

The women's liberationist, on the other hand, is imprisoned by her own negative view of herself and of her place in the world around her. This view of women was most succinctly expressed in an advertisement designed by the principal women's liberationist organization, the National Organization for Women (NOW), and run in many magazines and newspapers and as spot announcements on many television stations. The advertisement showed a darling curlyheaded girl with the caption: "This healthy, normal baby has a handicap. She was born female."

This is the self-articulated, dog-in-the-manger, chip-on-the-shoulder, fundamental dogma of the women's liberation movement. Someone—it is not clear who, perhaps God, perhaps the "Establishment," perhaps a conspiracy of male chauvinist pigs—dealt women a foul blow by making them female. It becomes necessary, therefore, for women to agitate and demonstrate and hurl demands on society in order to wrest from an oppressive male-dominated social structure the status that has been wrongfully denied to women through the centuries.

By its very nature, therefore, the women's liberation movement precipitates a series of conflict situations—in the legislatures, in the courts, in the schools, in industry—with man targeted as the enemy. Confrontation replaces cooperation as the watchword of all relationships. Women and men become adversaries instead of partners.

The second dogma of the women's liberationists is that, of all the injustices perpetrated upon women through the centuries, the most oppressive is the cruel fact that women have babies and men do not. Within the confines of the women's liberationist ideology, therefore, the abolition of this overriding inequality of women becomes the primary goal. This goal must be achieved at any and all costs—to the woman herself, to the baby, to the family, and to society. Women must be made equal to men in their ability *not* to become pregnant and *not* to be expected to care for babies they may bring into the world.

This is why women's liberationists are compulsively involved in the drive to make abortion and child-care centers for all women, regardless of religion or income, both socially acceptable and government-financed. Former congress-woman Bella Abzug has defined the goal: "to enforce the constitutional right of females to terminate pregnancies that they do not wish to continue."

If man is targeted as the enemy, and the ultimate goal of women's liberation is independence from men and the avoidance of pregnancy and its consequences, then lesbianism is logically the highest form in the ritual of women's liberation. Many, such as Kate Millett, come to this conclusion, although many others do not.

The Positive Woman will never travel that dead-end road. It is self-evident to the Positive Woman that the female body with its baby-producing organs was not designed by a conspiracy of men but by the Divine Architect of the human race. Those who think it is unfair that women have babies, whereas men cannot, will have to take up their complaint with God because no other power is capable of changing that fundamental fact. On some college campuses, I have been assured that other methods of reproduction will be developed. But most of us must deal with the real world rather than with the imagination of dreamers.

Another feature of the woman's natural role is the obvious fact that women can breast-feed babies and men cannot. This functional role was not imposed by conspiratorial males seeking to burden women with confining chores but must be recognized as part of the plan of the Divine Architect for the survival of the human race through the centuries and in the countries that know no pasteurization of milk or sterilization of bottles.

The Positive Woman looks upon her femaleness and her fertility as part of her purpose, her potential, and her power. She rejoices that she has a capability for creativity that men can never have.

The third basic dogma of the women's liberation movement is that there is no difference between male and female except the sex organs, and that all those physical, cognitive, and emotional differences you *think* are there, are merely the result of centuries of restraints imposed by a male-dominated society and sex-stereotyped schooling. The role imposed on women is, by definition, inferior, according to the women's liberationists.

The Positive Woman knows that, while there are some physical competitions in which women are better (and can command more money) than men, including those that put a premium on grace and beauty, such as figure skating, the superior physical strength of males over females in competitions of strength, speed, and short-term endurance is beyond rational dispute.

In the Olympic Games, women not only cannot win any medals in competition with men, the gulf between them is so great that they cannot even qualify for the contests with men. No amount of training from infancy can enable women to throw the discus as far as men, or to match men in push-ups or in lifting weights. In track and field events, individual male records surpass those of women by 10 to 20 percent.

Female swimmers today are beating Johnny Weissmuller's records, but today's male swimmers are better still. Chris Evert can never win a tennis match against Jimmy Connors. If we removed lady's tees from golf courses, women would be out of the game. Putting women in football or wrestling matches can only be an exercise in laughs.

The Olympic Games, whose rules require strict verification to ascertain that no male enters a female contest and, with his masculine advantage, unfairly captures a woman's medal, formerly insisted on a visual inspection of the contestants' bodies. Science, however, has discovered that men and women are so innately different physically that their maleness/femaleness can be conclusively established by means of a simple skin test of fully clothed persons.

If there is *anyone* who should oppose enforced sex-equality, it is the women athletes. Babe Didrikson, who played and defeated some of the great male athletes of her time, is unique in the history of sports.

If sex equality were enforced in professional sports, it would mean that men could enter the women's tournaments and win most of the money. Bobby Riggs has already threatened: "I think that men fifty-five years and over should be allowed to play women's tournaments—like the Virginia Slims. Everybody ought to know there's no sex after fifty-five anyway."

The Positive Woman remembers the essential validity of the old prayer: "Lord, give me the strength to change what I can change, the serenity to accept what I cannot change, and the wisdom to discern the difference." The women's liberationists are expending their time and energies erecting a make-believe world in which they hypothesize that *if* schooling were gender-free, and *if* the same money were spent on male and female sports programs, and *if* women were permitted to compete on equal terms, *then* they would prove themselves to be physically equal. Meanwhile, the Positive Woman has put the ineradicable physical differences into her mental computer, programmed her plan of action, and is already on the way to personal achievement.

Thus, while some militant women spend their time demanding more money for professional sports, ice skater Janet Lynn, a truly Positive Woman, quietly signed the most profitable financial contract in the history of women's athletics. It was not the strident demands of the women's liberationists that brought high prizes to women's tennis, but the discovery by sports promoters that beautiful female legs gracefully moving around the court made women's tennis a highly marketable television production to delight male audiences. . . .

Despite the claims of the women's liberation movement, there are countless physical differences between men and women. The female body is 50 to 60 percent water, the male 60 to 70 percent water, which explains why males can dilute alcohol better than women and delay its effect. The average woman is about 25 percent fatty tissue, while the male is 15 percent, making women more buoyant in water and able to swim with less effort. Males have a tendency to color blindness. Only 5 percent of persons who get gout are female. Boys are born bigger. Women live longer in most countries of the world, not only in the United States where we have a hard-driving competitive pace. Women excel in manual dexterity, verbal skills, and memory recall.

Arianna Stassinopoulos in her book *The Female Woman* has done a good job of spelling out the many specific physical differences that are so innate and so all-pervasive that "even if Women's Lib was given a hundred, a thousand, ten thousand years in which to eradicate *all* the differences between the sexes, it would still be an impossible undertaking. . . ."

Does the physical advantage of men doom women to a life of servility and subservience? The Positive Woman knows that she has a complementary advantage which is at least as great—and, in the hands of a skillful woman, far greater. The Divine Architect who gave men a superior strength to lift weights also gave women a different kind of superior strength.

The women's liberationists and their dupes who try to tell each other that the sexual drive of men and women is really the same, and that it is only societal restraints that inhibit women from an equal desire, an equal enjoyment, and an equal freedom from the consequences, are doomed to frustration forever. It just isn't so, and pretending cannot make it so. The differences are not a woman's weakness but her strength. . . .

The differences between men and women are also emotional and psychological. Without woman's innate material instinct, the human race would have died out centuries ago. There is nothing so helpless in all earthly life as the newborn infant. It will die within hours if not cared for. Even in the most primitive, uneducated societies, women have always cared for their newborn babies. They didn't need any schooling to teach them how. They didn't need any welfare workers to tell them it is their social obligation. Even in societies to whom such concepts as "ought," "social responsibility," and "compassion for the helpless" were unknown, mothers cared for their new babies.

Why? Because caring for a baby serves the natural maternal need of a woman. Although not nearly so total as the baby's need, the woman's need is nonetheless real.

The overriding psychological need of a woman is to love something alive. A baby fulfills this need in the lives of most women. If a baby is not available to fill that need, women search for a baby-substitute. This is the reason why women have traditionally gone into teaching and nursing careers. They are doing what comes naturally to the female psyche. The schoolchild or the patient of any age provides an outlet for a woman to express her natural maternal need.

This maternal need in women is the reason why mothers whose children have grown up and flown from the nest are sometimes cut loose from their psychological moorings. The maternal need in women can show itself in love for grandchildren, nieces, nephews, or even neighbors' children. The maternal need in some women has even manifested itself in an extraordinary affection lavished on a dog, a cat, or a parakeet.

This is not to say that every woman must have a baby in order to be fulfilled. But it is to say that fulfillment for most women involves expressing their natural maternal urge by loving and caring for someone.

The women's liberation movement complains that traditional stereotyped roles assume that women are "passive" and that men are "aggressive." The anomaly is that a woman's most fundamental emotional need is not passive at all, but active. A woman naturally seeks to love affirmatively and to show that love in an active way by caring for the object of her affections.

The Positive Woman finds somebody on whom she can lavish her maternal love so that it doesn't well up inside her and cause psychological frustrations. Surely no woman is so isolated by geography or insulated by spirit that she cannot find someone worthy of her maternal love. All persons, men and women, gain by sharing something of themselves with their fellow humans, but women profit most of all because it is part of their very nature.

One of the strangest quirks of women's liberationists is their complaint that societal restraints prevent men from crying in public or showing their emotions, but permit women to do so, and that therefore we should "liberate" men to enable them, too, to cry in public. The public display of fear, sorrow, anger, and irritation reveals a lack of self-discipline that should be avoided by the Positive Woman just as much as by the Positive Man. Maternal love, however, is not a weakness but a manifestation of strength and service, and it should be nurtured by the Positive Woman.

Most women's organizations, recognizing the preference of most women to avoid hard-driving competition, handle the matter of succession of officers by the device of a nominating committee. This eliminates the unpleasantness and the tension of a competitive confrontation every year or two. Many women's organizations customarily use a prayer attributed to Mary, Queen of Scots, which is an excellent analysis by a woman of women's faults:

> Keep us, O God, from pettiness; let us be large in thought, in word, in deed. Let us be done with fault-finding and leave off self-seeking. . . . Grant that we may realize it is the little things that create differences, that in the big things of life we are at one. . . .

Finally, women are different from men in dealing with the fundamentals of life itself. Men are philosophers, women are practical, and 'twas ever thus. Men may philosophize about how life began and where we are heading; women are concerned about feeding the kids today. No woman would ever, as Karl Marx did, spend years reading political philosophy in the British Museum while her child starved to death. Women don't take naturally to a search for the intangible and the abstract. The Positive Woman knows who she is and where she is going, and she will reach her goal because the longest journey starts with a very practical first step.

Amaury de Riencourt, in his book *Sex and Power in History,* shows that a successful society depends on a delicate balancing of different male and female factors, and that the women's liberation movement, which promotes unisexual values and androgyny, contains within it "a social and cultural death wish and the end of the civilization that endorses it."

One of the few scholarly works dealing with woman's role, *Sex and Power in History* synthesizes research from a variety of disciplines—sociology, biology, history, anthropology, religion, philosophy, and psychology. De Riencourt traces distinguishable types of women in different periods in history, from prehistoric to modern times. The "liberated" Roman matron, who is most similar to the present-day feminist, helped bring about the fall of Rome through her unnatural emulation of masculine qualities, which resulted in a large-scale breakdown of the family and ultimately of the empire.

De Riencourt examines the fundamental, inherent differences between men and women. He argues that man is the more aggressive, rational, mentally creative, analytical-minded sex because of his early biological role as hunter and provider. Woman, on the other hand, represents stability, flexibility, reliance on intuition, and harmony with nature, stemming from her procreative function.

Where man is discursive, logical, abstract, or philosophical, woman tends to be emotional, personal, practical, or mystical. Each set of qualities is vital and complements the other. Among the many differences explained in de Riencourt's book are the following:

> Women tend more toward conformity than men—which is why they often excel in such disciplines as spelling and punctuation where there is only one correct answer, determined by social authority. Higher intellectual activities, however, require a mental independence and power of abstraction that they usually lack, not to mention a certain form of aggressive boldness of the imagination which can only exist in a sex that is basically aggressive for biological reasons. . . .

De Riencourt provides impressive refutation of two of the basic errors of the women's liberation movement: (1) that there are no emotional or cognitive differences between the sexes, and (2) that women should strive to be like men.

A more colloquial way of expressing the de Riencourt conclusion that men are more analytical and women more personal and practical is in the different answers that one is likely to get to the question, "Where did you get that steak?" A man will reply, "At the corner market," or wherever he bought it. A woman will usually answer, "Why? What's the matter with it?"

An effort to eliminate the differences by social engineering or legislative or constitutional tinkering cannot succeed, which is fortunate, but social relationships and spiritual values can be ruptured in the attempt. Thus the role reversals being forced upon high school students, under which guidance counselors urge reluctant girls to take "shop" and boys to take "home economics," further confuse a generation already unsure about its identity. They are as wrong as efforts to make a left-handed child right-handed.

QUESTIONS

1. How well does Schlafly support each of her assertions? Which are her strongest arguments? Her weakest? Is Schlafly's presentation of the feminist position fair? Why or why not?

2. How, other than by using logic, does Schlafly attempt to persuade her readers? (Look for appeals to emotion, faith, tradition, and so on.) How effective are these persuasive techniques?

3. How does Schlafly's word choice serve to discredit her opponent's position and enhance her own? Give examples.

4. What transitional devices does Schlafly use in the opening sentences of each paragraph to make her argument flow?

5. Identify Schlafly's purposes in writing this essay. Then, after examining the organization of "Understanding the Difference," discuss how that organization reflects her purposes.

SUGGESTIONS FOR WRITING

1. Schlafly insists that the differences between men and women are "natural" or innate, while other observers see these differences as culturally determined. Write an essay defending *one* of these positions.

2. As an interesting alternative, write the same essay from the viewpoint of someone of the opposite sex.

Susan Brownmiller
EMOTION

Veteran journalist and founder of Women Against Pornography, Susan Brownmiller came to national prominence in 1975 with the publication of Against Our Will: Men, Women, and Rape. *That book, called by one reviewer "a landmark work in the literature of awareness," became a best-seller and catapulted Brownmiller to the cover of* Time *as one of its twelve women of the year. In her recent book,* Femininity *(1984), the Brooklyn-born, Cornell-educated writer defines "femininity" ("a nostalgic tradition of imposed limitations") and argues that it is currently, and unfortunately, making a comeback among women after a period of rela-*

*tive rejection. Brownmiller uses a combination of personal experiences,
extensive reading, and observation to support her book-length definition.
After analyzing the physical manifestations of femininity (body, hair,
clothes, voice, movement), she moves on to discuss emotional manifestations, which are more difficult to explain because they are "impossible to
quantify."*

*Although she concentrates on women in "Emotion," an excerpt from
her 1984 book, Brownmiller still uses comparison and contrast because
male emotions and patterns of behavior are included. By the end of the
selection, in fact, we realize that femininity cannot be defined in isolation
from masculinity; each exists only because the other does.*

———

A 1970 landmark study, known in the field as *Broverman and Broverman,* reported that "Cries very easily" was rated by a group of professional psychologists
as a highly feminine trait. "Very emotional," "Very excitable in a minor crisis"
and "Feelings easily hurt" were additional characteristics on the feminity scale.
So were "Very easily influenced," "Very subjective," "Unable to separate feelings
from ideas," "Very illogical" and "Very sneaky." As might be expected, masculinity was defined by opposing, sturdier values: "Very direct," "Very logical,"
"Can make decisions easily," "Never cries." The importance of *Broverman and
Broverman* was not in nailing down a set of popular assumptions and conventional perceptions—masculine-feminine scales were well established in the literature of psychology as a means of ascertaining normality and social adjustment—
but in the authors' observation that stereotypic femininity was a grossly negative
assessment of the female sex and, furthermore, that many so-called feminine traits
ran counter to clinical descriptions of maturity and mental health.

Emotional femininity is a tough nut to crack, impossible to quantify yet hard
to ignore. As the task of conforming to a specified physical design is a gender
mission that few women care to resist, conforming to a prepackaged emotional
design is another imperative task of gender. To satisfy a societal need for sexual
clarification, and to justify second-class status, an emblematic constellation of
inner traits, as well as their outward manifestations, has been put forward historically by some of the world's great thinkers as proof of the "different" feminine
nature.

"Woman," wrote Aristotle, "is more compassionate than man, more easily
moved to tears. At the same time, she is more jealous, more querulous, more apt
to scold and to strike. She is, furthermore, more prone to despondency and less
hopeful than man, more void of shame or self-respect, more false of speech, more
deceptive and of more retentive memory. She is also more wakeful, more shrinking, more difficult to rouse to action, and she requires a smaller amount of
nutriment."

Addressing a suffrage convention in 1855, Ralph Waldo Emerson had kind-
lier words on the nature of woman, explicating the nineteenth-century view that
her difference was one of superior virtue. "Women," he extolled, "are the civ-

ilizers of mankind. What is civilization? I answer, the power of good women. . . . The starry crown of woman is in the power of her affection and sentiment, and the infinite enlargements to which they lead." (In less elevated language, the Emersonian view was perhaps what President Reagan had in mind when he cheerfully stated, "Why, if it wasn't for women, we men would still be walking around in skin suits carrying clubs.")

A clarification is in order. Are women believed to possess a wider or deeper emotional range, a greater sensitivity, say, to the beauties of nature or to the infinite complexities of feeling? Any male poet, artist, actor, marine biologist or backpacker would strenuously object. Rather, it is commonly agreed that women are tossed and buffeted on the high seas of emotion, while men have the tough mental fiber, the intellectual muscle, to stay in control. As for the civilizing influence, surely something more is meant than sophistication, culture and taste, using the correct fork or not belching after dinner. The idealization of emotional femininity, as women prefer to see themselves affirmed, is more exquisitely romantic: a finer temperament in a more fragile vessel, a gentler nature ruled by a twin need to love and to be protected: one who appreciates—without urgency to create—good art, music, literature and other public expressions of the private soul; a flame-bearer of spiritual values by whose shining example the men of the world are inspired to redemption and to accomplish great things.

Two thousand years ago *Dominus flevit,* Jesus wept as he beheld Jerusalem. "Men ceased weeping," proposed Simone de Beauvoir, "when it became unfashionable." Now it is Mary, *Mater Dolorosa,* who weeps with compassion for mankind. In mystical visions, in the reliquaries of obscure churches and miraculous shrines, the figure of the Virgin, the world's most feminine woman, has been seen to shed tears. There are still extant cultures in which men are positively lachrymose (and kissy-kissy) with no seeming detriment to their masculine image, but the Anglo-Saxon tradition, in particular, requires keeping a stiff upper lip. Weeping, keening women shrouded in black are an established fixture in mourning rites in many nations. Inconsolable grief is a feminine role, at least in its unquiet representations. In what has become a stock photograph in the national news magazines, women weep for the multitudes when national tragedy (a terrorist bombing, an air crash, an assassination) strikes.

The catharsis of tears is encouraged in women—"There, there, now, let it all out"—while a man may be told to get a grip on himself, or to gulp down a double Scotch. Having "a good cry" in order to feel better afterward is not usually recommended as a means of raising the spirits of men, for the cathartic relief of succumbing to tears would be tempered by the uncomfortable knowledge that the loss of control was hardly manly. In the 1972 New Hampshire Presidential primary, Senator Edmund Muskie, then the Democratic front-runner, committed political suicide when he publicly cried during a campaign speech. Muskie had been talking about some harsh press comments directed at his wife when the tears filled his eyes. In retrospect it was his watershed moment: Could a man who became tearful when the going got rough in a political campaign be expected to face the Russians? To a nation that had delighted in the hatless, overcoatless macho posturing of John F. Kennedy, the military successes of General Ike and the irascible outbursts of "Give 'em hell" Harry Truman, the answer was No. Media accounts of Muskie's all-too-human tears were merciless. In the summer of 1983 the obvious and unshakable grief displayed by Israeli prime minister Menachem Begin after the death of his wife was seized upon by the Israeli and American press as evidence that a tough old warrior had lost his grip. Sharing this perception of his own emotional state, perhaps, Begin shortly afterward resigned.

Expressions of anger and rage are not a disqualifying factor in the masculine disposition. Anger in men is often understood, or excused, as reasonable or just. Anger in men may even be cast in a heroic mold—a righteous response to an insult against honor that will preclude a manly, aggressive act. Because competitive acts of personal assertion, not to mention acts of outright physical aggression, are known to flow from angry feelings, anger becomes the most unfeminine emotion a woman can show.

Anger in a woman isn't "nice." A woman who seethes with anger is "unattractive." An angry woman is hard, mean and nasty; she is unreliably, unprettily out of control. Her face contorts into unpleasant lines: the jaw juts, the eyes are narrowed, the teeth are bared. Anger is a violent snarl and a hostile threat, a declaration of war. The endless forbearance demanded of women, described as the feminine virtue of patience, prohibits an angry response. Picture a charming old-fashioned scene: The mistress of the house bends low over her needlework, cross-stitching her sampler: "Patience is a virtue, possess it if you can/Seldom seen in women, never seen in man." Does the needle jab through the cloth in uncommon fury? Does she prick her thumb in frustration?

Festering without a permissible release, women's undissolved anger has been known to seep out in petty, mean-spirited ways—fits of jealousy, fantasies of retaliation, unholy plots of revenge. Perhaps, after all, it is safer to cry. "Woman's aptitude for facile tears," wrote Beauvoir, "comes largely from the fact that her life is built upon a foundation of impotent revolt."*

Beauvoir hedged her bet, for her next words were these: "It is also doubtless true that physiologically she has less nervous control than a man." Is this "doubtless true," or is it more to the point, as Beauvoir continues, that "her education has taught her to let herself go more readily"?

Infants and children cry out of fear, frustration, discomfort, hunger, anxiety at separation from a parent, and rage. Surveying all available studies of crying newborns and little children, psychologists Eleanor Maccoby and Carol Jacklin found no appreciable sexual difference. If teenage girls and adult women are known to cry more than men—and there is no reason to question the popular wisdom in this regard—should the endocrine changes of adolescence be held to account? What of those weepy "blue days" of premenstrual tension that genuinely afflict so many women? What about mid-life depression, known in some circles

---

*"Facile" is the English translator's match for the French *facile,* more correctly rendered as "easy." Beauvoir did not mean to ascribe a stereotype superficiality to women in her remark.

as "the feminine malady"? Are these conditions, as some men propose, a sign of "raging hormonal imbalance" that incapacitates the cool, logical functioning of the human brain? Or does feminine depression result, as psychiatrist Willard Gaylin suggests, when confidence in one's coping mechanism is lost?

Belief in a biological basis for the instability of female emotions has a notorious history in the development of medical science. Hippocrates the physician held that hysteria was caused by a wandering uterus that remained unfulfilled. Discovery in the seventeenth century that the thyroid gland was larger in women inspired that proposition that the thyroid's function was to give added grace to the feminine neck, but other beliefs maintained that the gland served to flush impurities from the blood before it reached the brain. A larger thyroid "was necessary to guard the female system from the influence of the more numerous causes of irritation and vexation" to which the sex was unfortunately disposed. Nineteenth-century doctors averred that womb-related disorders were the cause of such female complaints as "nervous prostration." For those without money to seek out a physician's care, Lydia E. Pinkham's Vegetable Compound and other patent medicines were available to give relief. In the 1940s and '50s, prefrontal lobotomy was briefly and tragically in vogue for a variety of psychiatric disorders, particularly among women, since the surgical procedure had a flattening effect on raging emotions. Nowadays Valium appears to suffice.

Beginning in earnest in the 1960s, one line of research has attempted to isolate premenstrual tension as a contributing cause of accidents, suicide, admittance to mental hospitals and the commission of violent crimes. Mood swings, irritability and minor emotional upsets probably do lead to more "acting out" by females at a cyclical time in the month, but what does this prove beyond the increasingly accepted fact that the endocrine system has a critical influence on the human emotional threshold? Suicide, violent crime and dangerous psychiatric disorders are statistically four to nine times more prevalent in men. Should we theorize, then, that "raging hormonal imbalance" is a chronic, year-round condition in males? A disqualifying factor? By any method of calculation and for whatever reason—hormonal effects, the social inhibitions of femininity, the social pleasure of the masculine role, or all of these—the female gender is indisputably less prone to irrational, antisocial behavior. The price of inhibited anger and a nonviolent temperament may well be a bucketful of tears.

Like the emotion of anger, exulting in personal victory is a harshly unfeminine response. Of course, good winners of either sex are supposed to display some degree of sportsmanlike humility, but the merest hint of gloating triumph—"Me, me, me, I did it!"—is completely at odds with the modesty and deference expected of women and girls. Arm raised in a winner's salute, the ritualized climax of a prizefight, wrestling match or tennis championship, is unladylike, to say the least. The powerful feeling that victory engenders, the satisfaction of climbing to the top of the heap or clinching a deal, remains an inappropriate emotion. More appropriate to femininity are the predictable tears of the new Miss America as she accepts her crown and scepter. Trembling lip and brimming eyes suggest a Cinderella who has stumbled upon good fortune through unbelievable, undeserved luck. At her moment of victory the winner of America's favorite pageant appears overcome, rather than superior in any way. A Miss America who raised her scepter high like a trophy would not be in keeping with the feminine ideal.

The maidenly blush, that staple of the nineteenth-century lady's novel, was an excellent indicator of innocent virginal shyness in contrast to the worldliness and sophistication of men. In an age when a variety of remarks, largely sexual, were considered uncouth and not for the ears of virtuous women, the feminine blush was an expected response. On the other side of the ballroom, men never blushed, at least not in romantic fiction, since presumably they were knowledgeable and sexually practiced. Lowered eyes, heightened color, breathlessness and occasional swooning were further proofs of a fragile and innocent feminine nature that required protection in the rough, indelicate masculine world. (In the bestselling Harlequin and Silhouette books devoured by romance addicts who need the quick fix, the maidenly blush is alive and well.)

In a new age of relative sexual freedom, or permissiveness, at any rate, squeals and moans replace the blush and the downcast eye. Screaming bobbysoxers who fainted in the aisle at the Paramount Theater when a skinny young Frank Sinatra crooned his love ballads during the 1940s (reportedly, the first wave of fainting girls was staged by promoters) presaged the whimpering orgasmic ecstasy at rock concerts in huge arenas today. By contrast, young men in the audience automatically rise to their feet and whistle and shout when the band starts to play, but they seldom appear overcome.

Most emphatically, feminine emotion has gotten louder. The ribald squeal of the stereotypic serving wench in Elizabethan times, a supposed indicator of loose, easy ways, seem to have lost its lower-class stigma. One byproduct of our media-obsessed society, in which privacy is considered a quaint and rather old-fashioned human need, has been the reproduction of the unmistakable sounds of female orgasm on a record (Donna Summer's "Love to Love You Baby," among other hits). More than commercialization of sex is operative here. Would the sounds of male orgasm suffice for a recording, and would they be unmistakable? Although I have seen no studies on this interesting sex difference, I believe it can be said that most women do vocalize more loudly and uncontrollably than men in the throes of sexual passion. Is this response physiological, compensatory or merely symptomatic of the feminine mission to display one's feelings (and the corresponding masculine mission to keep their feelings under control)?

Feminine emotion specializes in sentimentality, empathy and admissions of vulnerability—three characteristics that most men try to avoid. Linking these traits to female anatomy became an article of faith in the Freudian school. Erik Erikson, for one, spoke of an "inner space" (he meant the womb) that yearns for fulfillment through maternal love. Helene Deutsch, the grande dame of Freudian feminine psychology, spoke of psychic acceptance of hurt and pain; menstrual cramps, defloration and the agonies of childbirth called for a masochistic nature she believed was innate.

Love of babies, any baby and all babies, not only one's own, is a celebrated and anticipated feminine emotion, and a woman who fails to ooh and ahh at the snapshot of a baby or cuddle a proffered infant in her arms is instantly suspect. Evidence of a maternal nature, of a certain innate competence when handling a baby or at least some indication of maternal longing, becomes a requirement of gender. Women with no particular feeling for babies are extremely reluctant to admit their private truth, for the entire weight of woman's place in the biological division of labor, not to mention the glorification of motherhood as woman's greatest and only truly satisfactory role, has kept alive the belief that all women yearn to fulfill their biological destiny out of a deep emotional need. That a sizable number of mothers have no genuine aptitude for the job is verified by the records of hospitals, family courts and social agencies where cases of battery and neglect are duly entered—and perhaps also by the characteristic upper-class custom of leaving the little ones to the care of the nanny. But despite this evidence that day-to-day motherhood is not a suitable or a stimulating occupation for all, the myth persists that a woman who prefers to remain childless must be heartless or selfish or less than complete.

Books have been written on maternal guilt and its exploitation, on the endemic feeling that whatever a mother does, her loving care may be inadequate or wrong, with consequences that can damage a child for life. Trends in child care (bottle feeding, demand feeding, not picking up the crying baby, delaying the toilet training or giving up an outside job to devote one's entire time to the family) illuminate the fear of maternal inadequacy as well as the variability or "expert" opinion in each generation. Advertising copywriters successfully manipulate this feminine fear when they pitch their clients' products. A certain cereal, one particular brand of packaged white bread, must be bought for the breakfast table or else you have failed to love your child sufficiently and denied him the chance to "build a strong body twelve ways." Until the gay liberation movement began to speak for itself, it was a commonplace of psychiatric wisdom that a mother had it within her power to destroy her son's heterosexual adjustment by failing to cut his baby curls, keep him away from dance class or encourage his interest in sports.

A requirement of femininity is that a woman devote her life to love—to mother love, to romantic love, to religious love, to amorphous, undifferentiated caring. The territory of the heart is admittedly a province that is open to all, but women alone are expected to make an obsessional career of its exploration, to find whatever adventure, power, fulfillment or tragedy that life has to offer within its bounds. There is no question that a woman is apt to feel most feminine, most confident of her interior gender makeup, when she is reliably within some stage of love—even the girlish crush or the stage of unrequited love or a broken heart. Men have suffered for love, and men have accomplished great feats in the name of love, but what man has ever felt at the top of his masculine form when he is lovesick or suffering from heartache?

Gloria Steinem once observed that the heart is a sex-distinctive symbol of feminine vulnerability in the marketing of fashion. Heart-shaped rings and heart-shaped gold pendants and heart-shaped frames on red plastic sunglasses announce an addiction to love that is beyond the pale of appropriate design for masculine ornamentation. (A man does not wear his heart on his sleeve.) The same observation applies a little less stringently to flowers.

Rare is the famous girl singer, whatever her age, of popular music (blues, country, Top Forty, disco or rock) who is not chiefly identified with some expression of love, usually its downside. Torchy bittersweet ballads and sad, suffering laments mixed with vows of eternal fidelity to the rotten bastard who done her wrong communicate the feminine message of love at any cost. Almost unique to the female singer, I think, is the poignant anthem of battered survival, from Fanny Brice's "My Man" to Gloria Gaynor's "I Will Survive," that does not quite shut the door on further emotional abuse if her man should return.

But the point is not emotional abuse (except in extreme, aberrant cases); the point is feeling. Women are instructed from childhood to be keepers of the heart, keepers of the sentimental memory. In diaries, packets of old love letters and family albums, in slender books of poetry in which a flower is pressed, a woman's emotional history is preserved. Remembrance of things past—the birthday, the anniversary, the death—is a feminine province. In the social division of labor, the wife is charged with maintaining the emotional connection, even with the husband's side of the family. Her thoughtful task is to make the long-distance call, select the present and write the thank-you note (chores that secretaries are asked to do by their bosses). Men are busy; they move forward. A woman looks back. It is significant that in the Biblical parable it was Lot's wife who looked back for one last precious glimpse of their city, their home, their past (and was turned into a pillar of salt).

Love confirms the feminine psyche. A celebrated difference between men and women (either women's weakness or women's strength, depending on one's values) is the obstinate reluctance, the emotional inability of women to separate sex from love. Understandably. Love makes the world go round, and women are supposed to get dizzy—to rise, to fall, to feel alive in every pore, to be undone. In place of a suitable attachment, an unlikely or inaccessible one may have to do. But more important, sex for a woman, even in an age of accessible contraception, has reproductive consequences that render the act a serious affair. Casual sex can have a most uncasual resolution. If a young girl thinks of love and marriage while a boy thinks of getting laid, her emotional commitment is rooted not only in her different upbringing but in her reproductive biology as well. Love, then, can become an alibi for thoughtless behavior, as it may also become an identity, or a distraction, à la Emma Bovary or Anna Karenina, from the frustrations of a limited life.*

---

*The overwhelming influence of feminine love is frequently offered as a mitigating explanation by women who do unfeminine things. Elizabeth Bentley, the "Red Spy Queen" of the cold war Fifties, attributed her illegal activities to her passion for the Russian master spy Jacob Golos. Judith Coplon's defense for stealing Government documents was love for another Russian, Valentin Gubichev. More recently, Jean Harris haplessly failed to convince a jury that her love for "Scarsdale diet" Doctor Herman Tarnower was so great that she could not possibly have intended to kill him.

Christian houses of worship, especially in poor neighborhoods, are filled disproportionately by women. This phenomenon may not be entirely attributable to the historic role of the Catholic and Protestant religions in encouraging the public devotions of women (which Judaism and Islam did not), or because women have more time for prayer, or because in the Western world they are believed to be more religious by nature. Another contributing factor may be that the central article of Christian faith, "Jesus loves you," has particular appeal for the gender that defines itself through loving emotions.

Women's special interest in the field of compassion is catered to and promoted. Hollywood "weepies," otherwise known as four-handkerchief movies, were big-studio productions that were tailored to bring in female box-office receipts. Columns of advice to the lovelorn, such as the redoubtable "Dear Dorothy Dix" and the current "Dear Abby," were by tradition a woman's slot on daily newspapers, along with the coverage of society births and weddings, in the days when females were as rare in a newsroom as they were in a coal mine. In the heyday of the competitive tabloids, sob-sister journalism, that newsroom term for a human-interest story told with heart-wrenching pathos (usually by a tough male reporter who had the formula down pat), was held in contempt by those on the paper who covered the "hard stuff" of politics, crime and war. (Nathanael West's famous antihero labored under the byline of Miss Lonelyhearts.) Despite its obvious audience appeal, "soft stuff" was, and is, on the lower rungs of journalism—trivial, weak and unmanly.

In Government circles during the Vietnam war, it was considered a sign of emotional softness, of lily-livered liberals and nervous nellies, to suggest that Napalmed babies, fire-bombed villages and defoliated crops were reason enough to pull out American forces. The peace movement, went the charge, was composed of cowards and fuzzy thinkers. Suspicion of an unmanly lack of hard practical logic always haunts those men who espouse peace and nonviolence, but women, the weaker sex, are permitted a certain amount of emotional leeway. Feminine logic, after all, is reputedly governed by the heartstrings. Compassion and sentiment are the basis for its notorious "subjectivity" compared to the "objectivity" of men who use themselves as the objective standard.

As long as the social division of labor ordains that women should bear the chief emotional burden of caring for human life from the cradle to the grave while men may demonstrate their dimorphic difference through competitive acts of physical aggression, emblematic compassion and fear of violence are compelling reasons for an aversion to war and other environmental hazards. When law and custom deny the full range of public expression and economic opportunity that men claim for themselves, a woman must place much of her hopes, her dreams, her feminine identity and her social importance in the private sphere of personal relations, in the connective tissue of marriage, family, friendship and love. In a world out of balance, where men are taught to value toughness and linear vision as masculine traits that enable them to think strategically from conquest to conquest, from campaign to campaign without looking back, without getting sidetracked by vulnerable feelings, there is, and will be, an emotional difference between the sexes, a gender gap that may even appear on a Gallup poll.

If a true shape could emerge from the shadows of historic oppression, would the gender-specific experience of being female still suggest a range of perceptions and values that differ appreciably from those of men? It would be premature to offer an answer. Does a particular emotion ultimately resist separation from its historic deployment in the sexual balance of power? In the way of observation, this much can be said: The entwining of anatomy, history and culture presents such a persuasive emotional argument for a "different nature" that even the best aspects of femininity collaborate in its perpetuation.

QUESTIONS

1. How does Brownmiller define emotional femininity in paragraphs two through six? Which generalizations about women do you accept? Reject? Explain.

2. List the characteristics, found in the rest of the essay, that fill out Brownmiller's definition. What is the male counterpart of each of these characteristics?

3. Throughout the essay, Brownmiller makes many generalizations, such as: "Anger in a woman isn't nice" and "The catharsis of tears is encouraged in women—'there, there, now, let it all out'—while a man may be told to get a grip on himself, or to gulp down a double scotch." Does she adequately support such generalizations? Does she have to? Explain.

4. What does Brownmiller mean in the next to last paragraph when she calls this "a world out of balance"? How does she make her thesis explicit here?

5. Brownmiller's diction frequently alternates between the formal and the colloquial or clichéd ("lachrymose," then "kissy-kissy"; or "inhibited anger" and "bucketful of tears"). Find more examples. What is the effect of this stylistic strategy? What is Brownmiller's purpose in using it?

6. Characterize the essay's tone, and defend your characterization.

7. Transitions between paragraphs in the essay are sometimes abrupt. Find examples, and decide whether this is a conscious strategy. If so, what might Brownmiller's purpose be in employing it?

SUGGESTIONS FOR WRITING

1. Although Brownmiller compares feminine and masculine emotion and behavior, she concentrates on women, and draws most of her illustrations from female experience. Rewrite the essay emphasizing behavior and emotions typically associated with the male sex. You need not restrict yourself to Brownmiller's thesis.

2. Write a letter to a member of the opposite sex comparing or contrasting your experience as a male or female to Brownmiller's gender stereotypes. Your purpose might range from defending yourself, to defending your sex, to corroborating Brownmiller's observations.

Carol Gilligan
IMAGES OF RELATIONSHIPS
★ ★ ★

Ms. *magazine's Woman of the Year for 1984, Carol Gilligan is an associate professor at the Harvard Graduate School of Education. According to Linsy Van Gelder in a* Ms. *article from that issue entitled "Carol Gilligan: Leader For a Different Kind of Future," Gilligan's work on the psychology of female sensibility will not only open "possibilities for new understanding between the genders . . . but has implications for a rather different kind of future—one in which humanity takes its cues not from Big Brother, but from sisters, mothers, and daughters."*

Gilligan's book, In a Different Voice *(1982), has had a profound effect on scholars, both male and female. As the following excerpt reveals, Gilligan's work exposes the male biases in scholarship and has in the process begun to change the questions academic disciplines ask, and even their language. When reading "Images of Relationships," stop after the moral dilemma is presented to jot down your own decision about it, as well as your explanation of your decision. Later you can compare your response to the children's.*

In 1914, with his essay "On Narcissism," Freud swallows his distaste at the thought of "abandoning observation for barren theoretical controversy" and extends his map of the psychological domain. Tracing the development of the capacity to love, which he equates with maturity and psychic health, he locates its origins in the contrast between love for the mother and love for the self. But in thus dividing the world of love into narcissism and "object" relationships, he finds that while men's development becomes clearer, women's becomes increasingly opaque. The problem arises because the contrast between mother and self yields two different images of relationships. Relying on the imagery of men's lives in charting the course of human growth, Freud is unable to trace in women the development of relationships, morality, or a clear sense of self. This difficulty in fitting the logic of his theory to women's experience leads him in the end to set women apart, marking their relationships, like their sexual life, as "a 'dark continent' for psychology" (1926, p. 212).

Thus the problem of interpretation that shadows the understanding of women's development arises from the differences observed in their experience of relationships. To Freud, though living surrounded by women and otherwise seeing so much and so well, women's relationships seemed increasingly mysterious, difficult to discern, and hard to describe. While this mystery indicates how theory can blind observation, it also suggests that development in women is masked by a particular conception of human relationships. Since the imagery of relationships shapes the narrative of human development, the inclusion of women, by changing that imagery, implies a change in the entire account.

The shift in imagery that creates the problem in interpreting women's development is elucidated by the moral judgments of two eleven-year-old children, a boy and a girl, who see, in the same dilemma, two very different moral problems. While current theory brightly illuminates the line and the logic of the boy's thought, it casts scant light on that of the girl. The choice of a girl whose moral judgments elude existing categories of developmental assessment is meant to highlight the issue of interpretation rather than to exemplify sex differences per se. Adding a new line of interpretation, based on the imagery of the girl's thought, makes it possible not only to see development where previously development was not discerned but also to consider differences in the understanding of relationships without scaling these differences from better to worse.

The two children were in the same sixth-grade class at school and were participants in the rights and responsibilities study, designed to explore different conceptions of morality and self. The sample selected for this study was chosen to focus the variables of gender and age while maximizing developmental potential by holding constant, at a high level, the factors of intelligence, education, and social class that have been associated with moral development, at least as measured by existing scales. The two children in question, Amy and Jake, were both bright and articulate and, at least in their eleven-year-old aspirations, resisted easy categories of sex-role stereotyping, since Amy aspired to become a scientist while Jake preferred English to math. Yet their moral judgments seem initially to confirm familiar notions about differences between the sexes, suggesting that the edge girls have on moral development during the early school years gives way at puberty with the ascendance of formal logical thought in boys.

The dilemma that these eleven-year-olds were asked to resolve was one in the series devised by Kohlberg to measure moral development in adolescence by presenting a conflict between moral norms and exploring the logic of its resolution. In this particular dilemma, a man named Heinz considers whether or not to steal a drug which he cannot afford to buy in order to save the life of his wife. In the standard format of Kohlberg's interviewing procedure, the description of the dilemma itself—Heinz's predicament, the wife's disease, the druggist's refusal to lower his price—is followed by the question, "Should Heinz steal the drug?" The reasons for and against stealing are then explored through a series of questions that vary and extend the parameters of the dilemma in a way designed to reveal the underlying structure of moral thought.

Jake, at eleven, is clear from the outset that Heinz should steal the drug. Constructing the dilemma, as Kohlberg did, as a conflict between the values of property and life, he discerns the logical priority of life and uses that logic to justify his choice:

For one thing, a human life is worth more than money, and if the druggist only makes $1,000, he is still going to live, but if Heinz doesn't steal the drug, his wife is going to die. *(Why is life worth more than money?)* Because the druggist can get a thousand dollars later from rich people with cancer, but Heinz can't get his wife again. *(Why not?)* Because people are all different and so you couldn't get Heinz's wife again.

Asked whether Heinz should steal the drug if he does not love his wife, Jake replies that he should, saying that not only is there "a difference between hating and killing," but also, if Heinz were caught, "the judge would probably think it was the right thing to do." Asked about the fact that, in stealing, Heinz would be breaking the law, he says that "the laws have mistakes, and you can't go writing up a law for everything that you can imagine."

Thus, while taking the law into account and recognizing its function in maintaiing social order (the judge, Jake says, "should give Heinz the lightest possible sentence"), he also sees the law as man-made and therefore subject to error and change. Yet his judgment that Heinz should steal the drug, like his view of the law as having mistakes, rests on the assumption of agreement, a societal consensus around moral values that allows one to know and expect others to recognize what is "the right thing to do."

Fascinated by the power of logic, this eleven-year-old boy locates truth in math, which, he says, is "the only thing that is totally logical." Considering the moral dilemma to be "sort of like a math problem with humans," he sets it up as an equation and proceeds to work out the solution. Since his solution is rationally derived, he assumes that anyone following reason would arrive at the same conclusion and thus that a judge would also consider stealing to be the right thing for Heinz to do. Yet he is also aware of the limits of logic. Asked whether there is a right answer to moral problems, Jake replies that "there can only be right and wrong in judgment," since the parameters of action are variable and complex. Illustrating how actions undertaken with the best of intentions can eventuate in the most disastrous of consequences, he says, "like if you give an old lady your seat on the trolley, if you are in a trolley crash and that seat goes through the window, it might be that reason that the old lady dies."

Theories of developmental psychology illuminate well the position of this child, standing at the juncture of childhood and adolescence, at what Piaget describes as the pinnacle of childhood intelligence, and beginning through thought to discover a wider universe of possibility. The moment of preadolescence is caught by the conjunction of formal operational thought with a description of self still anchored in the factual parameters of his childhood world—his age, his town, his father's occupation, the substance of his likes, dislikes, and beliefs. Yet as his self-description radiates the self-confidence of a child who has arrived, in Erikson's terms, at a favorable balance of industry over inferiority—competent, sure of himself, and knowing well the rules of the game—so his emergent capacity for formal thought, his ability to think about thinking and to reason things out in a logical way, frees him from dependence on authority and allows him to find solutions to problems by himself.

This emergent autonomy follows the trajectory that Kohlberg's six stages of moral development trace, a three-level progression from an egocentric understanding of fairness based on individual need (stages one and two), to a conception of fairness anchored in the shared conventions of societal agreement (stages three and four), and finally to a principled understanding of fairness that rests on the free-standing logic of equality and reciprocity (stages five and six). While this boy's judgments at eleven are scored as conventional on Kohlberg's scale, a mixture of stages three and four, his ability to bring deductive logic to bear on the solution of moral dilemmas, to differentiate morality from law, and to see how laws can be considered to have mistakes points toward the principled conception of justice that Kohlberg equates with moral maturity.

In contrast, Amy's response to the dilemma conveys a very different impression, an image of development stunted by a failure of logic, an inability to think for herself. Asked if Heinz should steal the drug, she replies in a way that seems evasive and unsure:

> Well, I don't think so. I think there might be other ways besides stealing it, like if he could borrow the money or make a loan or something, but he really shouldn't steal the drug—but his wife shouldn't die either.

Asked why he should not steal the drug, she considers neither property nor law but rather the effect that theft could have on the relationship between Heinz and his wife:

> If he stole the drug, he might save his wife then, but if he did, he might have to go to jail, and then his wife might get sicker again, and he couldn't get more of the drug, and it might not be good. So, they should really just talk it out and find some other way to make the money.

Seeing in the dilemma not a math problem with humans but a narrative of relationships that extends over time, Amy envisions the wife's continuing need for her husband and the husband's continuing concern for his wife and seeks to respond to the druggist's need in a way that would sustain rather than sever connection. Just as she ties the wife's survival to the preservation of relationships, so she considers the value of the wife's life in a context of relationships, saying that it would be wrong to let her die because, "if she died, it hurts a lot of people and it hurts her." Since Amy's moral judgment is grounded in the belief that, "if somebody has something that would keep somebody alive, then it's not right not to give it to them," she considers the problem in the dilemma to arise not from the druggist's assertion of rights but from his failure of response.

As the interviewer proceeds with the series of questions that follow from Kohlberg's construction of the dilemma, Amy's answers remain essentially unchanged, the various probes serving neither to elucidate nor to modify her initial response. Whether or not Heinz loves his wife, he still shouldn't steal or let her die; if it were a stranger dying instead, Amy says that "if the stranger didn't have anybody near or anyone she knew," then Heinz should try to save her life, but he should not steal the drug. But as the interviewer conveys through the repetition of questions that the answers she gave were not heard or not right, Amy's confidence begins to diminish, and her replies become more constrained and unsure. Asked again why Heinz should not steal the drug, she simply repeats, "Because it's not right." Asked again to explain why, she states again that theft would not be a good solution, adding lamely, "if he took it, he might not know how to give it to his wife, and so his wife might still die." Failing to see the dilemma as a self-contained problem in moral logic, she does not discern the internal structure of its resolution; as she constructs the problem differently herself, Kohlberg's conception completely evades her.

Instead, seeing a world comprised of relationships rather than of people standing alone, a world that coheres through human connection rather than through systems of rules, she finds the puzzle in the dilemma to lie in the failure of the druggist to respond to the wife. Saying that "it is not right for someone to die when their life could be saved," she assumes that if the druggist were to see the consequences of his refusal to lower his price, he would realize that "he should just give it to the wife and then have the husband pay back the money later." Thus she considers the solution to the dilemma to lie in making the wife's condition more salient to the druggist or, that failing, in appealing to others who are in a position to help.

Just as Jake is confident the judge would agree that stealing is the right thing for Heinz to do, so Amy is confident that, "if Heinz and the druggist had talked it out long enough, they could reach something besides stealing." As he considers the law to "have mistakes," so she sees this drama as a mistake, believing that "the world should just share things more and then people wouldn't have to steal." Both children thus recognize the need for agreement but see it as mediated in different ways—he impersonally through systems of logic and law, she personally through communication in relationship. Just as he relies on the conventions of logic to deduce the solution to this dilemma, assuming these conventions to be shared, so she relies on a process of communication, assuming connection and believing that her voice will be heard. Yet while his assumptions about agreement are confirmed by the convergence in logic between his answers and the questions posed, her assumptions are belied by the failure of communication, the interviewer's inability to understand her response.

Although the frustration of the interview with Amy is apparent in the repetition of questions and its ultimate circularity, the problem of interpretation is focused by the assessment of her response. When considered in the light of Kohlberg's definition of the stages and sequence of moral development, her moral judgments appear to be a full stage lower in maturity than those of the boy. Scored as a mixture of stages two and three, her responses seem to reveal a feeling of powerlessness in the world, an inability to think systematically about the concepts of morality or law, a reluctance to challenge authority or to examine the logic of received moral truths, a failure even to conceive of acting directly to save a life or to consider that such action, if taken, could possibly have an effect. As her reliance on relationships seems to reveal a continuing dependence and vulnerability, so her belief in communication as the mode through which to resolve moral dilemmas appears naive and cognitively immature.

Yet Amy's description of herself conveys a markedly different impression. Once again, the hallmarks of the preadolescent child depict a child secure in her sense of herself, confident in the substance of her beliefs, and sure of her ability to do something of value in the world. Describing herself at eleven as "growing and changing," she says that she "sees some things differently now, just because I know myself really well now, and I know a lot more about the world." Yet the world she knows is a different world from that refracted by Kohlberg's construction of Heinz's dilemma. Her world is a world of relationships and psychological truths where an awareness of the connection between people gives rise to a recognition of responsibility for one another, a perception of the need for response. Seen in this light, her understanding of morality as arising from the recognition of relationship, her belief in communication as the mode of conflict resolution, and her conviction that the solution to the dilemma will follow from its compelling representation seem far from naive or cognitively immature. Instead, Amy's judgments contain the insights central to an ethic of care, just as Jake's judgments reflect the logic of the justice approach. Her incipient awareness of the "method of truth," the central tenet of nonviolent conflict resolution, and her belief in the restorative activity of care, lead her to see the actors in the dilemma arrayed not as opponents in a contest of rights but as members of a network of relationships on whose continuation they all depend. Consequently her solution to the dilemma lies in activating the network by communication, securing the inclusion of the wife by strengthening rather than severing connections.

But the different logic of Amy's response calls attention to the interpretation of the interview itself. Conceived as an interrogation, it appears instead as a dialogue, which takes on moral dimensions of its own, pertaining to the interviewer's uses of power and to the manifestations of respect. With this shift in the conception of the interview, it immediately becomes clear that the interviewer's problem in understanding Amy's response stems from the fact that Amy is answering a different question from the one the interviewer thought had been posed. Amy is considering not *whether* Heinz should act in this situation (*"should* Heinz steal the drug?"*) but rather *how* Heinz should act in response to his awareness of his wife's need ("Should Heinz *steal* the drug?"). The interviewer takes the mode of action for granted, presuming it to be a matter of fact; Amy assumes the necessity for action and considers what form it should take. In the interviewer's failure to imagine a response not dreamt of in Kohlberg's moral philosophy lies the failure to hear Amy's question and to see the logic in her response, to discern that what appears, from one perspective, to be an evasion of the dilemma signifies in other terms a recognition of the problem and a search for a more adequate solution.

Thus in Heinz's dilemma these two children see two very different moral problems—Jake a conflict between life and property that can be resolved by logical deduction, Amy a fracture of human relationship that must be mended with its own thread. Asking different questions that arise from different conceptions of the moral domain, the children arrive at answers that fundamentally diverge, and the arrangement of these answers as successive stages on a scale of increasing moral maturity calibrated by the logic of the boy's response misses the different truth revealed in the judgment of the girl. To the question, "What does he see that she does not?" Kohlberg's theory provides a ready response, manifest in the scoring of Jake's judgments a full stage higher than Amy's in moral maturity; to the question, "What does she see that he does not?" Kohlberg's theory has nothing to say. Since most of her responses fall through the sieve of Kohlberg's scoring system, her responses appear from his perspective to lie outside the moral domain.

Yet just as Jake reveals a sophisticated understanding of the logic of justification, so Amy is equally sophisticated in her understanding of the nature of choice. Recognizing that "if both the roads went in totally separate ways, if you pick one, you'll never know what would happen if you went the other way," she explains that "that's the chance you have to take, and like I said, it's just really a guess." To illustrate her point "in a simple way," she describes her choice to spend the summer at camp:

> I will never know what would have happened if I had stayed here, and if something goes wrong at camp, I'll never know if I stayed here if it would have been better. There's really no way around it because there's no way you can do both at once, so you've got to decide, but you'll never know.

In this way, these two eleven-year-old children, both highly intelligent and perceptive about life, though in different ways, display different modes of moral understanding, different ways of thinking about conflict and choice. In resolving Heinz's dilemma, Jake relies on theft to avoid confrontation and turns to the law to mediate the dispute. Transposing a hierarchy of power into a hierarchy of values, he defuses a potentially explosive conflict between people by casting it as an impersonal conflict of claims. In this way, he abstracts the moral problem from the interpersonal situation, finding in the logic of fairness an objective way to decide who will win the dispute. But this hierarchical ordering, with its imagery of winning and losing and the potential for violence which it contains, gives way in Amy's construction of the dilemma to a network of connection, a web of relationships that is sustained by a process of communication. With this shift, the moral problem changes from one of unfair domination, the imposition of property over life, to one of unnecessary exclusion, the failure of the druggist to respond to the wife.

QUESTIONS

1. Gilligan introduces her discussion by citing Freud's theory of male and female development. What is her strategy here? In what way is her introduction connected to the rest of her essay? What makes her introduction difficult to understand? Are its ideas—and its phrase "the imagery of relationships"— clearer by the time you finish the essay? Discuss.

2. Choose two paragraphs in the essay, underline concrete words and circle abstract ones, and determine how many of each type there are. What conclusions about Gilligan's style can you draw from analyzing abstract and concrete language in the essay?

3. Why does Gilligan use the children's exact words instead of a paraphrase of them?

4. Is there a difference in the language Gilligan uses initially and then later on to describe Jake's response? Is there a difference in her description of Amy's? Find examples of words and phrases that substantiate such a shift, and explain why Gilligan uses this strategy.

5. Write an outline of the essay that will make Gilligan's use of comparison and contrast stand out.

SUGGESTIONS FOR WRITING

1. Adopting the role of psychologist, devise and execute an experiment similar to Gilligan's among your classmates or friends. Think of a moral dilemma appropriate to your ages and interview one or more males and females. (The use of a tape recorder will simplify your task.) Then write an essay reporting and analyzing the results; distribute the report to the class and discuss it.

2. Write a response to Gilligan which either supports her conclusions or disputes them, based on a personal experience you have had. Compare and contrast your thoughts and actions to those Gilligan would expect of someone of your sex.

Edmund White
SEXUAL CULTURE
★ ★ ★

A powerfully articulate defender and expositor of homosexual culture, Edmund White is a novelist, playwright, and the author of several nonfiction guides to gay life in America. His novels Forgetting Elena *(1973) and* Nocturnes for the King of Naples *(1978) won praise both for the "poetic brilliance" of their prose and for their insightful portrayal of complex human relationships. Perhaps his best known—and most controversial—*

book, however, is States of Desire *(1980), a first-person account of White's travels through the gay communities of Boston, San Francisco, New York, and other major American cities. White is also the author of* The Joy of Gay Sex *(1977, cowritten with Charles Silverstein),* A Boy's Own Story *(1982), and, most recently,* Caracole *(1985).*

"Sexual Culture" was first published in the December 1983 issue of the magazine Vanity Fair.

───────

"Do gay men have friends—I mean," she said, "are they friends with each other?" Since the woman asking was a New Yorker, the owner of one of the city's simplest and priciest restaurants, someone who's known gays all her life, I found the question honest, shocking, and revealing of a narrow but bottomless abyss between us.

Of course New York is a city of total, even absolute strangers rubbing shoulders: the Hasidim in their yellow school bus being conveyed back to Brooklyn from the jewelry district, beards and black hats glimpsed through mud-splattered windows in a sun-dimmed daguerreotype; the junkie pushing the baby carriage and telling his wife, the prostitute, as he points to his tattooed biceps, "I haven't partied in this vein for years"; Moonies doing calisthenics at midnight in their Eighth Avenue center high above empty Thirty-fourth Street . . . But this alienation wasn't religious or ethnic. The woman and I spoke the same language, knew the same people; we both considered Marcella Hazan fun but no substitute for Simone Beck. How odd that she, as lower-upper-middle-class as I, shouldn't know whether gay men befriended one another.

It was then that I saw how mysterious gay culture is—not homosexuality, which is merely an erotic tropism, but modern American gay culture, which is a special way of laughing, spending money, ordering priorities, encoding everything from song lyrics to mirror-shiny military shoes. None of the usual modes for a subculture will do, for gay men are brought up by heterosexuals to be straight, they seek other men through what feels very much like a compulsion though they enter the ghetto by choice, yet once they make that choice it reshapes their lives, even their bodies, certainly their wardrobes. Many gay men live among straights as Marranos, those Spanish Jews who pretended during the Inquisition to convert to Christianity but continued to observe the old rites in cellars, when alone, in the greatest secrecy. Gays aren't *like* blacks or Jews since they often *are* black or Jewish, and their affectional preference isn't a color or a religion though it has spawned a culture not unlike an ethnic minority's. Few Jews have Christian siblings, but most gays have straight brothers and sisters or at least straight parents. Many American Jews have been raised to feel they belong to the Chosen People, at once superior and inferior to gentiles, but every gay discovers his sexual nature with a combination of pain and relief, regret at being excluded from the tribe but elation at discovering the solution to the puzzle.

Gays aren't a nationality. They aren't Chicanos or Italo-Americans or Irish-Americans, but they do constitute one of the most potent political forces in big cities such as New York, Philadelphia, Washington (where gays and blacks elected Marion Barry mayor), Houston, Los Angeles, and San Francisco (where gays are so numerous they've splintered into countless factions, including the lesbian S/M group Samois and the Sisters of Perpetual Indulgence, a group of drag nuns, one of whose members ran in a cowl and wimple as a candidate in the last citywide election). Not ethnic but a minority, not a polis but political, not a nationality but possessed of a costume, customs, and a patois, not a class but an economic force (not only as a market for records, films, vacations, and clothes but also as an army of worker ants who, for better or worse, have gentrified the center cities, thereby creating a better tomorrow for single young white heterosexual professionals).

Imagine a religion one enters against one's parents' will—and against one's own. Imagine a race one joins at sixteen or sixty without changing one's hue or hair texture (unless at the tanning or beauty salon). Imagine a sterile nation without descendants but with a long, misty regress of ancestors, without an articulated self-definition but with a venerable history. Imagine an exclusive club that includes a P.R. (Puerto Rican) boy of sixteen wearing ankle-high black-and-white Converse basketball shoes and a petrol green shirt sawed off to reveal a Praxitelean stomach—and also includes a P.R. (Public Relations) WASP executive of forty in his Prince of Wales plaids and Cole-Haan tasseled loafers.

If one is gay, one is always in a crucial relationship to gayness as such, a defining category that is so full it is nearly empty (Renaud Camus writes: "Homosexuality is always elsewhere because it is everywhere"). No straight man stands in rapt contemplation of his straightness unless he's an ass. To be sure, heterosexuals may wonder over the significance of their homosexual fantasies, though even that morbid exercise is less popular now than formerly; as Barbara Ehrenreich acutely observes in her new study of the heterosexual male revolt, *The Hearts of Men,* the emergence of gay liberation ended the period in which everyone suspected everyone else of being "latently" homosexual. Now there are open homosexuals, and heterosexual men are exempt from the automatic suspicion of deviance.

No homosexual can take his homosexuality for granted. He must sound it, palpate it, auscultate it as though it were the dead limb of a tree or the living but tricky limb of a body; for that reason all homosexuals are "gay philosophers" in that they must invent themselves. At a certain point one undergoes a violent conversion into a new state, the unknown, which one then sets about knowing as one will. Surely everyone experiences his or her life as an artifact, as molten glass being twirled and pinched into a shape to cool, or as a novel at once capacious and suspenseful, but no one is more a *Homo faber* (in the sense of both "fabricator" and "fabulist") than a homo. It would be vain, of course, to suggest that this creativity is praiseworthy, an ambition rather than a response.

Sometimes I try to imagine how straights—not fundamentalist know-nothings, not rural innocents, not Freudian bigots, but educated urban heterosexuals—look at gay men (do they even see lesbians?). When they see gay men, what do they see? A mustache, a pumped-up body in black jeans and a tank top, an eye-catching tattoo (braided rope around the biceps)? And what do they think ("they," in this case, *hypocrite lecteur,* being *you*)? Do you see something at once ludicrous and mildly enviable in the still youthful but overexercised body of this forty-year-old clone with the aggressive stare and soft voice? If you're a woman, do you find so much preening over appearance in a grown man . . . well, if not offensive, at least unappetizing; energy better spent on a career, on a family—on you? If you're a man, does it incense you that this jerk is out of harness, too loose, too free, has so lightly made a mockery of manhood? Once, on a radio call-in show a cop called in to tell me he had to admire the old-style queens back when it was rough being queer but that now, jeez, these guys swapping spit wit' a goil one week, wit' a guy the next, they're too lazy, they just don't know the fine art of being a man, it's all just too easy.

Your sentiments, perhaps?

Do you see gays as menacing satyrs, sex fiends around whom it's dangerous to drop your soap, *and* as feeble sissies, frail wood nymphs locked within massive trunks and limbs? Or, more positively if just as narrowly, are you a sybaritic het who greets the sight of gays with cries of glee, convinced you've stumbled on liberty hall, where sexual license of every sort—including your sort—is bound to reign? In fact, such sybarites often do regard gay men as comrades in arms, fellow libertines, and fellow victims in a country phobic to pleasure.

Or do gays just irk you? Do you regard them as a tinselly distraction in your peripheral vision? As errant, obstinate atoms that can't be drawn into any of the usual social molecules, men who if they insist on their gayness won't really do at any of the solemnities, from dinner parties to debutante balls, all of which depend on strict gender dimorphism for a rational seating plan? Since any proper gathering requires the threat of adultery for excitement and the prospect of marriage as a justification, of what earthly use are gays? Even the few fearless straight guys who've invaded my gay gym drift toward one another, not out of soap-dropping panic but because otherwise their dirty jokes fall on deaf or prettily blushing ears and their taunting, butt-slapping mix of rivalry and camaraderie provokes a weird hostility or a still weirder thrill.

And how do gays look at straights? In Andrew Holleran's superb new novel, *Nights in Aruba,* the narrator wonders "what it would be like to be the head of a family, as if with that all my problems would drop away, when in fact they would have merely been replaced by another set. I would not have worried about the size of my penis, the restrictions of age, the difficulty of finding love; I would have worried about mortgages, tuition, my youngest daughter's asthma, my competition at Shearson Loeb Rhoades." What makes this speculation so charac-teristically gay is that it is so focused on the family man, for if the nineteenth-century tart required, even invented the convent-bred virgin to contemplate, in the same way the homosexual man today must insult and revere, mock and envy this purely imaginary bourgeois paterfamilias, a creature extinct except in gay fantasies. Meanwhile, of course, the family man devotes his time to scream therapy and tai chi, ticking off Personals in the *Village Voice* and wriggling out of visits from his kids, two punked-out teens who live in a feminist compound with his divorced wife, now a lesbian potter of great sensitivity and verve if low energy.

So much for how the two sexes (straight and gay) regard each other. If the camera were to pull back and frame both worlds in the lens, how would the two systems compare?

The most obvious difference is that whereas heterosexuality does include two sexes, since homosexuality does not it must improvise a new polarity moment by moment. Such a polarity seems necessary to sexual desire, at least as it is constructed in our culture. No wonder that some gay men search out the most extreme opposites (someone of a distant race, a remote language, another class or age); no wonder that even that convinced heterosexual Flaubert was finally able to unbend with a boy prostitute in Egypt, an exotic who provided him with all the difference desire might demand. Other gay men seek out their twins—so that the beloved, I suppose, can stand in for oneself as one bows down to this false god and plays in turn his father, teacher, son, godfather, or god. Still others institutionalize the polarity in that next-best thing to heterosexuality: sadomasochism, the only vice that anthologizes all family and romantic relationships.

Because every gay man loves men, he comes to learn at first hand how to soothe the savage breast of the male ego. No matter how passive or girlish or shy the new beau might be in the boudoir, he will become the autocrat of the dinner table. Women's magazines are always planning articles on gay men and straight women; I'd say what they have most in common, aside from a few shared sexual techniques, is a body of folk wisdom about that hardhead, that bully, that maddeningly self-involved creature, the human male. As studies have surprisingly shown, men talk more than women, interrupt them more often, and determine the topics of conversation and object to women's assertions with more authority and frequency. When two gay men get together, especially after the first romantic urge to oblige the other wanes, a struggle for conversational dominance ensues, a conflict only symptomatic of larger arguments over every issue from where to live to how and whom to entertain.

To be sure, in this way the gay couple resembles the straight duo that includes an assertive, liberated woman. But while most of the young straight liberated women I know, at least, may protect their real long-range interests (career, mode of life, emotional needs) with vigilance, they're still willing to accommodate *him* in little social ways essential to harmony.

One benign side of straight life is that women conceive of men as "characters," as full-bodied, multifaceted beings who are first social, second familial, third amorous or amicable, and only finally physical. I'm trying politely to say that women are lousy judges of male beauty; they're easily taken in by such superficial traits as loyalty, dependability, charm, a sense of humor. Women don't, or at least didn't, judge men as so much beefcake. But men, both straight and gay, start with looks, the most obvious currency of value, worth, price. Let's say that women see men as characters in a long family novel in which the men are introduced complete with phrenology, genealogy, and one annoying and two endearing traits, whereas men see their partners (whether male or female) as cars, makes to be instantly spotted, appraised, envied, made. A woman wants to be envied for her husband's goodness, his character, whereas a man wants to be envied for his wife's beauty, rarity, status—her drivability. Straight life combines the warmth and *Gemütlichkeit* of the nineteenth-century bourgeois (the woman) with the steely corporate ethos of the twentieth-century functionary (the man). If gay male life, freed of this dialectic, has become supremely efficient (the trapdoor beside the bed) and only momentarily intimate (a whole life cycle compressed into the one-night stand), then the gain is dubious, albeit an extreme expression of one trend in our cultural economy.

But of course most morality, that is, popular morality—not real morals, which are unaffected by consensus, but mores, which are a form of fashion—is nothing but a species of nostalgia, a cover-up for pleasurable and profitable but not yet admissible innovations. If so many people condemn promiscuity, they do so at least partly because there is no available rhetoric that could condone, much less glamorize, impermanence in love. Nevertheless, it strikes me that homosexuals, masters of improvisation fully at home with the arbitrary and equipped with an internal compass that orients them instantly to any social novelty, are perhaps the most sensitive indicators of the future.

The birthrate declines, the divorce rate climbs, and popular culture (movies, television, song lyrics, advertising, fashions, journalism) is so completely and irrevocably secularized that the so-called religious revival is of no more lasting importance than the fad for Kabuki in a transistorized Japan—a temporary throwback, a slight brake on the wheel. In such a world the rate of change is so rapid that children, once they are in school, can learn little from their parents but must assimilate new forms of behavior from their peers and new information from specialized instructors. As a result, parental authority declines, and the demarcations between the generations become ever more formidable. Nor do the parents regret their loss of control, since they're devoting all their energy to cultivating the inner self in the wholesale transition of our society from an ethic of self-sacrifice to one of self-indulgence, the so-called aristocraticization of middle-class life that has dominated the peaceful parts of this century in the industrialized West.

In the contemporary world the nineteenth-century experiment of companionate marriage, never very workable, has collapsed utterly. The exact nature of the collapse isn't very clear yet because of our distracting, probably irrelevant habit of psychologizing every crisis (thus the endless speculations in the lowbrow press on the Irresponsible Male and the Defeminized Female or the paradoxical and cruelly impracticable advice to women readers to "go for it all—family, career, marriage, romance, *and* the reveries of solitude"). We treat the failure of marriage as though it were the failure of individuals to achieve it—a decline in grit or maturity or commitment or stamina rather than the unraveling of a poorly tied knot. Bourgeois marriage was meant to concentrate friendship, romance, and sex into an institution at once familial and economic. Only the most intense surveillance could keep such a bulky, ill-assorted load from bursting at the seams. Once the hedonism of the '60s relaxed that tension, people began to admit that friendship tranquilizes sexual desires (when mates become siblings, the incest taboo sets in) and that romance is by its very nature evanescent though indefinitely renewable given an endless supply of fresh partners. Neither sexual nor romantic attraction, so capricious, so passionate, so unstable, could ever serve as the basis for an enduring relationship, which can be balanced only on the plinth of esteem, that easy, undramatic, intimate kind of love one would say resembled family love if families were more loving.

It is this love that so many gay couples know about, aim for, and sometimes even express. If all goes well, two gay men will meet through sex, become lovers, weather the storms of jealousy and the diminution of lust, develop shared interests (a hobby, a business, a house, a circle), and end up with a long-term, probably sexless camaraderie that is not as disinterested as friendship or as seismic as passion or as charged with contradiction as fraternity. Younger gay couples feel that this sort of relationship, when it happens to them, is incomplete, a compromise, and they break up in order to find total fulfillment (i.e., tireless passion) elsewhere. But older gay couples stay together, cultivate their mild, reasonable love, and defend it against the ever-present danger of the sexual allure exercised by a newcomer. For the weak point of such marriages is the eternally recurring fantasy, first in one partner and then the other, of "total fulfillment." Needless to say, such couples can wreak havoc on the newcomer who fails to grasp that Bob and Fred are not just roommates. They may have separate bedrooms and regular extracurricular sex partners or even beaux, but Bob monitors Fred's infatuations with an eye attuned to nuance, and at a certain point will intervene to banish a potential rival.

I think most straight people would find these arrangements more scandalous than the infamous sexual high jinks of gays. Because these arrangements have no name, no mythology, no public or private acknowledgment, they're almost invisible even to the participants. Thus if you asked Bob in a survey what he wanted, he might say he wanted a "real" lover. He might also say Fred was "just a roommate, my best friend, we used to be lovers." So much for explicit analysis, but over the years Bob has cannily steered his affair with Fred between the Scylla of excessive fidelity (which is finally so dull no two imaginative gay men could endure it) and the Charybdis of excessive tolerance (which could leave both men feeling so neglected they'd seek love elsewhere for sure).

There are, of course, countless variants to this pattern. The men live together or they don't. If they don't, they can maintain the civilized fiction of romance for years. They plan dates, honeymoons, take turns sleeping over at each other's house, and avoid conflicts about domestic details. They keep their extracurricular sex lives separate, they agree not to snoop—or they have three-ways. Or one of the pair has an active sex life and the other has abandoned the erotic arena.

Are gay men friends with each other? the woman asked me.

The question may assume that gays are only sexual, and that a man eternally on the prowl can never pause for mere affection—that a gay Don Juan is lonely.

Or perhaps the question reveals a confusion about a society of one gender. Since a straight woman has other women for friends and men for lovers, my questioner might have wondered how the same sex could serve in both capacities.

The first supposition—that gay men are only sexual—is an ancient prejudice, and like all prejudices mostly untrue but in one sense occasionally accurate. If politically conscious homosexuals prefer the word *gay* to *homosexual,* they do so because they want to make the world regard attraction to members of the same gender as an affectional preference as well as a sexual orientation.

For instance, there are some gay men who prefer the feel of women's bodies to men's, who are even more comfortable sexually with women, but whose emotions crave contact with other men. Gay men have unfinished emotional business with other men—scary, promising, troubling, absorbing business—whereas their sentiments toward women (at least women not in their family) are much simpler, more stable, less fraught. Affection, passionate affection, is never simple; it is built out of equal parts of yearning, fear, and appetite. For that reason the friendship of one gay man fiercely drawn to another is as tense as any heterosexual passion, whereas a sexless, more disinterested gay friendship is as relaxed, as good-tempered as a friendship, say, between two straight men.

Gay men, then, do divide other gays into two camps—those who are potential partners (lovers) and those who are not (friends). But where gay life is more ambiguous than the world at large (and possibly for that reason more baffling to outsiders) is that the members of the two camps, lovers and friends, are always switching places or hovering somewhere in the margin between. It is these unconfessed feelings that have always intrigued me the most as a novelist—the unspoken love between two gay men, say, who pretend they are just friends, cruising buddies, merely filling in until Mr. Right comes along (mercifully, he never does).

In one sense, the public's prejudice about a gay obsession with sex is valid. The right to have sex, even to look for it, has been so stringently denied to gays for so many centuries that the drive toward sexual freedom remains a bright, throbbing banner in the fierce winds whipping over the ghetto. Laws against sex have always created the biggest problems for homosexuals; they helped to define the very category of homosexuality. For that reason, the gay community, despite its invention of a culture no more eroticized than any other, still cannot give up its origin in sexual desire and its suppression.

But what about the "excessive" promiscuity of gay men, the infamous quickies, a phenomenon only temporarily held in check by the AIDS crisis? Don't the quickies prove that gay men are essentially bizarre, fundamentally lacking in judgment—*oversexed*? Of course, gay men behave as all men would were they free of the strictures of female tastes, needs, prohibitions, and expectations. There is nothing in gay male life that cannot be attributed either to its minority status or to its all-male population. All men want quick, uncomplicated sexual adventure (as well as sustained romantic passion); in a world of all men, that desire is granted.

The very universality of sexual opportunity within the modern gay ghetto has, paradoxically, increased the importance of friendship. In a society not based on the measured denial or canalization of sexual desire, there is more energy left over for friendship. Relationships are less loaded in gay life (hence the celebrated gay irony, a levity equivalent to seeing through conventions). In so many ways gays are still prisoners of the dominant society, but in this one regard gays are freer than their jailers: because gay relationships are not disciplined by religious, legal, economic, and political ceremonies but only by the dictates of conscience and the impulses of the heart, they don't stand for anything larger. They aren't symbols but realities, not laws but entities sufficient unto themselves, not consequential but ecstatic.

QUESTIONS

1. Who is the audience—the "you"—White is addressing in his essay?

2. Discuss White's rhetorical strategy in the second section of "Sexual Culture," where he imagines how heterosexuals regard homosexuals and vice versa. How does he use the gay view of "straights" to make a point about the "straight" view of gays? What is White's point?

3. What are the central differences between the "two systems," gay and straight?

4. What is the "benign side of straight life" White discusses? Why is it benign? Why is this side missing from gay male life?

5. Describe the pattern for gay relationships that White outlines in this essay. In what important ways does this pattern resemble—and differ from—heterosexual relationships?

6. Judging from the tone of this piece, how would you characterize White's attitude toward gay life? Toward straight men? Toward straight women? Toward traditional, heterosexual marriage?

7. Point to places where White deliberately uses parallel sentence structure and the repetition of particular phrases for a striking rhetorical effect.

8. White's prose is challenging—but it is a pleasure to read. What are the special characteristics of his prose style?

SUGGESTIONS FOR WRITING

1. Homosexuality is clearly an issue about which most people have strong feelings. Write an essay in which you describe, as honestly as you can, your opinion of gay life.

2. One distinction White draws between straight men and women is the emphasis each puts on good looks. According to White, "Women don't, or at least didn't, judge men as so much beefcake. But men . . . start with looks." Do

you agree with this contention? Write an essay in which you support or refute it by drawing on your own feelings, experiences, and observations of
others.

3. According to White, "Neither sexual nor romantic attraction . . . could ever
    serve as the basis for an enduring relationship." Write an essay that either
    defends or takes issue with this assertion.

STUDENT ESSAY

Coleen Cardillo
MEN WILL BE BOYS: A WOMAN'S PERSPECTIVE

★ ★ ★

*Coleen Cardillo was born in Taiwan, came to the United States as a child,
and grew up in Mount Vernon, New York. Her interest in writing developed during her student days at Pace University, where she eventually
became editor-in-chief of the college literary magazine.*

*Cardillo later transferred to the C.W. Post campus of Long Island
University. There, she majored in business management and marketing
and was elected to the Delta Mu Delta and Omicron Delta Kappa honor
societies. The following essay—a provocative meditation on the differences
between the sexes—was written during her senior year at Post.*

*A resident of Long Island, Cardillo describes herself as an enthusiastic
competitive runner, who frequently participates in regional road races and
contributes occasional articles to* Islandwide Runner *magazine.*

Reflecting on "the opposite sex"—on those characteristics that make men, if not
antithetical to, then at least distinctly different from, women—I think of the
smallest things, the amusing things, first. Men sing in the shower, for instance,
while I have yet to hear a woman do this. Men are ashamed of worrying about
the size or shape of their bodies, whereas women like to show that they do. Men
usually carry their money folded in half, the bills in no particular order, but
women generally keep their bills unfolded, with the bigger denominations at the
back. Men hate to carry pennies around in their pockets and often store them in
a jar or a drawer until they have amassed so many that wrapping them in paper
holders and taking them to the bank becomes, they insist, an impossible task, at
which point they start filling a new jar. Women keep pennies in their change
purses and somehow manage to get rid of them as legal tender during the course
of the day. Men stride out bare-headed in the coldest weather, while most women
wear a hat or a scarf on their heads. Yet we go nearly bare-legged on subfreezing

days, with nothing on our feet but sheer stockings and thin-soled shoes that expose our toes.

And so on. My list is by no means comprehensive—everyone could surely construct his or her own—nor graven in stone. It simply illustrates that at some level the sexes remain, happily, incomprehensible to each other.

But what are the larger differences, those that, far from amusing us, often fuel conflicts and misunderstanding between the sexes? Let me begin by saying that one of the most important characteristics I have noted about men, based on purely personal observation and a certain amount of introspection, is that they are "group-beings." Men work in groups, fight in groups, join groups, form groups and obey group demands. They may aspire to lead the group, they may be in competition with other groups, they may quit one group for another, but the opinion of the group is what matters most to men. They crave group approval. Their lives are bound up in constant hierarchical struggles in which what matters most is the opinion of their fellow men. For men, self-esteem is to be found in the group. A woman, on the other hand, is more likely to find self-esteem in the way she lives, in what she does, in the totality of her life. Because her self-esteem originates within herself, and not in a group, she tends always to underestimate the extent to which men are subject to peer pressure. To understand this is to understand why certain myths are important to men. They have a built-in capacity for romantic fantasy that enables those of them who hated the army to look back on their military service a decade or two later with nostalgia or to talk about the company they work for as if they were an integral part of it, even when it's on the verge of firing them. That's because they need to belong.

Another difference I've noted is that men have romantic illusions about sex to a far greater degree than women. (Women have romantic illusions about *men*. It has been said that "Mr. Right is never dead in the minds of most women.") Women are far more pragmatic when it comes to sex. There are several good reasons for this. In the first place, women are the objects of pornography, not generally consumers of it. But more important, women live on intimate terms with their sexuality and its physical consequences. They are the ones who get pregnant, have abortions, menstruate and take Pap tests at regular intervals. No man has quite the same intimate connection to his sexual apparatus, or for that matter, the same fears. Young women are coping with menstruation at an age when boys are still living in a pornographic fantasy world, and the result is that men remain, by comparison with women, curiously innocent. To men, sex is something they do, not something they live with. It is something external to them, as opposed to the something internal it is to women.

A related difference is that, as men grow older, they tend to turn back toward their childhoods. Men re-create in adult life a kind of after-the-fact childhood. If they can afford to, they buy sports cars, boats, motorcycles, snowmobiles, gadgets and expensive toys that substitute for the ones they had—or were deprived of—as children. All men want to relive or recover their boyhood, for the truth is that men do not, at heart, want to grow up. In fact, they fight growing up until the day they die. Women, however, seem to operate under a different set of rules. Girls want to grow up, to assume the status of adults, to trade in their dolls for babies, or at least for the other things of real life. The doll, remember, is simply a child's symbolic substitute for a baby, while a boy's toys are mostly items of fantasy and adventure, unrelated to anything that will be central to him in adult life.

It's perhaps hard for women to understand that once men reach a certain age, they try desperately to recapture the elements of their childhood—whether it's a matter of surrounding themselves with possessions, taking up hobbies or playing sports with the guys—at exactly the moment when women are most interested in the real world. I was struck by this on a visit to Florida, where I noticed that many retired couples had switched roles. The men were out playing on the golf courses, at the racetracks or on the docks of the local marina, while most of the women had taken whatever part-time jobs they could find because they wanted "to be involved in things." The women, in short, wanted to work, earn a salary, "keep busy," while the husbands wanted to return to the games of boyhood.

The great institutions of our world are, in large measure, magnifications of those games and the rules they were played by. Hence, the importance to men of "team spirit," of competition, even where competition may be wasteful and harmful to the common good; of loyalty that all too often involves turning a blind eye to injustice, corruption and stupidity; of the childish violence and cruelty that war represents. Yet one cannot take away from men their achievements. After all, they have created the technology that has placed humanity in control of its environment.

If I had to name, then, the one thing that best defines the difference between men and women, it would be that men remain, throughout their lives, boys playing games. Perhaps because it was always left to women to create stability, perhaps because women have to bear the consequences of sexuality in the form of motherhood, perhaps because coming of age for women is an initiation into solitary pain and responsibility rather than into adventure and group membership, women are, I think, less often victims of fantasy than men, more alert to and pragmatic about the consequences of things, and more capable, in general, of maturity.

QUESTIONS

1. As the name of the writer, the title of the essay, and one line in the first paragraph make clear, "Men Will Be Boys" was written by a young woman. Are there other things in the essay that allow you to tell its writer is female? Discuss.

2. Note that Cardillo begins her essay by pointing out the "amusing" differences between men and women and ends by discussing the "serious differences." What effect does this organization of her material have on you? What effect would reversing the order have?

3. What, according to Cardillo, are the sex-linked traits found in men? What are the consequences of these traits? Do you agree or disagree with Cardillo?

4. Discuss Cardillo's use of concrete detail in paragraphs 1, 4, and 5. What is the function of these details? How different would the essay be without them?

5. From the evidence of the essay, analyze Cardillo's attitude toward men. She is careful to say that her remarks are based on "purely personal observation." Do your own observations of men and women bear hers out? Discuss.

SUGGESTIONS FOR WRITING

1. Interview separately your mother and your father (or any other older male or female relative), asking them what they think the chief differences are between men and women. It might be helpful to draw up a list of questions first, such as "How different are the friendships men and women have with members of the same sex?" "How different is their behavior with children?" "What differences do you see once a couple retires?" and so on. Then write a comparison and contrast essay based on the results of your interviews.

2. Follow the procedure presented in suggestion #1. But before you write your essay, interview a male and female peer about the differences they see between young women and men of your age. (You may have to modify the questions you ask of both groups of interviewees.) Then compare and contrast the opinions of older men and women with those of your contemporaries. Draw conclusions from your data. Are there fewer differences between men and women now than there were a generation or two ago? More? Identify the changes your interviews turn up.

Bruce Jay Friedman
LIVING TOGETHER

★ ★ ★

A writer often identified with that brand of mordant comedy known as "black humor," Bruce Jay Friedman began his writing career as a columnist for his high school newspaper. After serving in the armed forces, he went to work for a publisher of men's action magazines, eventually becoming editor of Man, Man's World, *and* Male. *During this time, his stories began to appear in such places as* The New Yorker, Playboy, Esquire, *and the* Saturday Evening Post.

Friedman's first novel, Stern *(1962), won more rave reviews than readers, but his next book,* A Mother's Kisses *(1964)—about a 17-year-old boy's neurotic relationship with his pathologically possessive mother—became a best-seller.*

In addition to his fiction (including the novels The Dick *and* About

Harry Towns, *as well as two short story collections), Friedman has had two plays produced and has sold several books and screenplays to Hollywood. Among them are* The Lonely Guy's Guide to Life *(1979), which was made into a movie starring Steve Martin, and* Doctor Detroit, *a Dan Ackroyd vehicle that grew out of a short story originally published in* Esquire *The following selection was also published in* Esquire.

Shot down twice in marriage, loser after a multitude of affairs, Pellegrino, in his forties, was about to pack it in romantically, when a fresh and delightful young woman suddenly bobbed up before him at a party like an apple in a barrel. Her eyes were wide, her movements graceful. She spoke with an ingratiating chuckle. Pellegrino's date was a good-natured blonde who had been raised in trailer courts and with whom he had come, characteristically, to a dead end. She could not have cared less—but the new woman was courteous and discreet, telling him only that she worked as an executive on the eighth floor of a well-known department store. When she wandered off to stand at the edge of the party, Pellegrino was far from smitten, but full of questions. She wore a tweed jacket, tailored slacks, was somewhat older than the women he was used to. Was she too "responsible" for him? He had a charge card at her department store and enjoyed wandering throughout the men's clothing section. What if he simply showed up on the eighth floor? Would she dismiss him with a cynical laugh? He caught another glimpse of her and grappled with the most important question of all—did she have enough tush? A harsh, nonhumanistic concern for some, perhaps, but not for Pellegrino.

To be on the safe side, he made no effort to see her, shopping at a department store he wasn't that crazy about. Still, the idea of her nagged at him, that chuckle, the question of her body. Once in a while, he summoned her forth for a brief, slimhipped fantasy in the night.

A year later, fate poked him in the ribs—he met her again at a reunion for people with strong Sixties concerns. He failed to recognize her: her hair was swept back, her great eyes tipsy over the rim of a cocktail glass. Was she a little faded around the edges? The hostess introduced them with great expectations. Pellegrino was correct, then swiftly went about his business—yet another blonde, a little overweight but at least a folk singer.

But she stubbornly kept after him—he remembered virtually swatting her away—until she yanked at his lapels and said, "Don't you even remember me? Katherine? The wedding reception?" The instant she identified herself, he realized he had been in love with her for a year, although he was, of course, careful not to tell her this. After a quick, forlorn look at the folk singer, he said he had thought about her a lot. What an amazing stroke of luck to run into her again. She said she had gone to Scotland to read books in solitude and had thought about him often, too. What a waste, they both agreed. He apologized for not recognizing her. But was it really his fault? "You've rearranged your hair," he said. Instantly, she reached back and let it fall, if not tumble—moving closer to the woman he remembered, though far from on the nose. He wanted to leave with her. Suddenly he realized that they had been talking across a wounded veteran in a wheelchair, her friend. He knew what that chuckle of hers was—compassion. To his everlasting shame, he made only reflexive small talk with the veteran, then yanked her away. In his defense, he could only tell himself (1) he was afraid of people in wheelchairs and (2) such was his love.

They tumbled through the streets to a restaurant he knew. Beneath the marquee she raised a horrified hand to her mouth and said, "Here!" Never in all the time he was to know her did she explain her resistance to the innocuous eating place. They took a table in the rear. For an hour or so he reveled in that sweet chuckle, his only possible disappointment in her being perhaps one reference too many to cartoons she had enjoyed in *The New Yorker.* As far as he knew, they were alone, bathed in a private light. Later, he found out the owner had observed them and told a cherished waiter: "Pellegrino is with a woman."

At midnight, on their way to an undecided destination, they kissed in the street, or rather, tried out each other's mouths with a happy result.

"It's probably not a good idea to go home together, is it?" she pleaded. Though he had arguments on hand to buttress both sides of the question, he more or less agreed.

"But half an hour after I see you again . . ." she trailed off. He tucked the promise away, as if in a wallet. They kissed again; this time he reached around through silk and was amazed he had ever questioned the excellence of her tush.

He could not honestly testify that he was counting the days until their next date, but when he saw her, he fell in love again, this time with her apartment, a floor-through in Murray Hill with sallow light and luxuriously worn furniture, the pieces confidently spaced apart—a serious person's home. (*Monastic* was the word that lingered.) Amazingly, they both owned copies of a best-selling poster. His was framed. In a masterstroke of carelessness, she had affixed hers to the wall with a thumbtack.

Breathlessly, she sparkled on. She came from a family of nurses. Twin brothers lived in China. Her favorite books? Ones written by retired members of the diplomatic corps. He sat in silence. From time to time, he glanced at his watch. Then he said: "Time's up."

"Oh my God, I didn't," she said.

"You did."

Dutifully, responsibly, she marched off to her loft bed, Pellegrino behind her, almost in step. The bed had no guardrail. One bad dream meant curtains for the sleeper. They made love, failing, by some margin, to enter paradise. But when he saw her dressing in the sallow light beneath the staircase, his knees became weak; he flew at her silhouette.

And so they began to not quite live together. Three days on, four days off. She raced to get him concert tickets, artfully arranged his chair so that he was suddenly and painlessly watching BBC productions. They slept together at his place while her cats starved. Other nights, he packed her off, clinging to his need to see strangers whom he no longer enjoyed.

"Oh, please," she said to him one day, "let's live together."

"I'd do it," he said, "but I want it to come from me, spontaneously." The next night it did. Finally, seamlessly, after ten years of profitless fencing, Pellegrino shared his life with another person. He waited for a heavy beam to fall across his shoulders. Slowly, cautiously, he stood erect.

She took up perhaps a bit too much drawer space. But she charmed his friends and cooked healthy, weightless concoctions, making subtle use of garlic. Tirelessly she made beds. She helped him with his work. Pellegrino, a writer of movie trailers, was stuck one day, unable to break through on a low-budget film—the theme, adolescent turmoil in Eastern Europe. He mentioned it in bed. The next morning he found her huddled in a chair; she'd stayed up all night, thinking he wanted her to come up with an entire trailer on her own. He hugged her, told her that wasn't it at all. Within minutes, she gave him a fresh angle of vision. By tacit agreement, they called it encouragement, though she did much more.

To a friend, he said, "She's made every moment of my life a delight."

They traveled. He took her to his favorite hotels. She approached them cautiously; then, to his slight irritation, she seized them up as if they were her own discoveries. To duck room service, they bought their own groceries. He sent her on ahead with bundles so that his entrance to the lobby could be formal. She made up songs with Pellegrino as the central character, spinning wild lyrics in the air; miraculously, when all seemed lost, she reined them in, got them to rhyme. She told him he was beautiful, that women took secret looks at him. "That's ridiculous," he said. But how could he help loving it when she said these things?

At night, with his nose pressed against the wool of her freshly laundered nightgown, he forgot for the moment about death.

But then things took a turn. The trailer business dried up, a casualty in a complex strike. At first Pellegrino felt unaffected, even amused. He had never been on strike before. Here was a chance to try out the sensation. He had planned to write a play on just such an occasion. He pounced on his typewriter. No play came. On a whim, they changed apartments, having been charmed by high ceilings and a rococo detail or two. They quickly saw it was a mistake—too long, too thin, a sliver of a space held out over raging midtown traffic as if by a hand. Pellegrino's daughter came to visit, fresh from art school, carrying prize-winning sketches and disapproval. Trying to please the child, she wound up serving undercooked hams. The three of them sat in silence at neighborhood restaurants, then returned to the small flat. Seeking privacy, they circled one another in cold geometric patterns. When the daughter left, Pellegrino pawed at the dirt while the strike took its grim toll.

To break up his afternoons, he took to watching foreign films at local art houses. One day, he gashed his wrist in the men's room of a culture complex. He thought of suing but lacked the energy. Holding a paper towel to the wound, he went upstairs to the movie house. There, while his blood pumped, he watched two hours of French irony.

He went back to the apartment to stare at his love. Oblivious to the screaming traffic, she sat beneath the louvered windows, sampling lightweight British mysteries. A tumbler of cognac, meant to be concealed, peeped out from behind a lamp base. She'd left her job to help Pellegrino, nursing him when he had no illness. Recently there had been talk of an advanced degree in international relations. It remained talk. She had taken on weight. He'd squinted his eyes to block out an extra chin. No longer could it be finessed. In the refrigerator, tins of gourmet macaroni came and went. Was it time to bring in the word *fat*?

He walked into the bedroom, actually a space created by a room divider, and wondered how he had reached this state, a serious fellow, age forty-five in view, with no book-lined study. He looked at her side of the bed. When they first began to live together, she'd hollered out defiant antiwar cries in her sleep, left over from old Sixties rallies. He'd found this charming. Now she did great, silent, heaving rolls, an ocean liner during a stormy crossing. His choice was to lie on the floor or roll with her.

He walked back to the living room. She looked at him, as she always did, happy, expectant. In truth, she'd stayed away from stronger books for just such occasions; the mysteries could be interrupted at no great price. He told her he didn't have this in mind at all. The two of them crammed together in a skinny apartment. And he certainly hadn't known about the drinking. Did she think he wanted to team up with a juicer? (How he'd longed to use that word.) And it was high time they talked about the fat stuff. He wasn't talking about a few pounds, which he had to concede he had put on himself. He was talking full-out fat. Did the phrase El Grosserino mean anything to her? Was that part of their arrangement, that she would pork up for him? And what about the fabled women he was supposed to be allowed to see but somehow didn't. It's true, it's true, she'd said go right ahead, just don't fall in love. Well, that was some condition. They had talked about a child. Forget that, please. That's all he needed, a new family in a shitty apartment with a porked-up juicer.

She listened to all of this with a quizzical smile, as if somehow she had wandered into the wrong theater to see an odd play but was too generous or polite to leave. It was only when he said that he hated every single second of his life that the color ran out of her face. "All right then, go," she said. "Or *I'll* go." With lightning speed, as if sprung from a trap, she flashed across the room and lunged for a battered suitcase.

"No, no," he said, panicked, blocking her path, "never." With all his might, he hugged her to him, arms encircling her thick waist, which he was now convinced could be trimmed down after two or three weeks of intensive exercise.

"I wouldn't blow this for anything in the world."

QUESTIONS

1. Compare and contrast Pellegrino and his lover. Why do you think that—as the opening words of the story inform us—Pellegrino has been so unsuccessful at marriage and romance?

2. Why are we never told the name of Pellegrino's lover? What effect does this omission have on our understanding of and response to the story?

3. The second time Pellegrino runs into the woman, he suddenly realizes that "he had been in love with her for a year." How deeply in love does Pellegrino seem to be? What details does Friedman include in his story to indicate that this may be just another doomed relationship?

4. How would you describe the predominant tone of this story? Does it seem amused? Cynical? Sympathetic? Detached? How does Friedman seem to feel about his characters?

5. Friedman is one of our most celebrated writers of "black humor," a kind of literature characterized by what critic Donald Hall calls "a combination of despair and laughter." Does this definition seem applicable to "Living Together"? Can you point out any specific instances of humor—"black" or otherwise?

6. Does the dialogue in this story seem realistic to you? Why or why not?

7. Compare the way Pellegrino's love looks to him at the end of the story to the way she is described at the beginning. How do you account for this change? (Pay particular attention to the language he uses in referring to her at the end.)

SUGGESTIONS FOR WRITING

1. Have you ever had a close and loving relationship with someone that has gone sour—become so strained and unpleasant that you have been forced to break it up? If so, write a personal experience essay in which you compare the untroubled beginnings of the relationship to its later, difficult stages.

2. "Living Together" is, in many ways, a uniquely contemporary love story. Write an essay in which you compare Friedman's tale to the sort of idealized, boy-meets-girl romance portrayed in countless Hollywood movies and popular novels of the "Harlequin Romance" variety.

Adrienne Rich
LIVING IN SIN
★ ★ ★

Widely regarded as one of America's finest poets, Adrienne Rich began writing poetry which was conventional in theme and mode but which has, over the years, become radicalized. Her first volume, A Change of World *(1951), won the Yale Series of Younger Poets Award. In that collection, she introduced two themes that would dominate her work: time and the condition of women. The poems of her next period, of which "Living in*

Sin" (1955) is an example, are characterized by a growing anger over woman's dependence on man. When women are confined to a world whose parameters are housework, "time is male," she once wrote. Rich's work in the sixties and seventies, both in form and content, tries to burst those boundaries:

> *I'd rather*
> *taste blood, yours or mine, flowing*
> *from a sudden slash, than cut all day*
> *with blunt scissors on dotted lines*
> *like the teacher told.*

Her most recent poetry is openly hostile to male values. Rich came to feminism, she explains, because she felt "endangered, psychically and physically, by this society, and because we have come to an edge of history when men—in so far as they are embodiments of the patriarchal idea— have become dangerous to children and other living things, themselves included."

She had thought the studio would keep itself;
No dust upon the furniture of love.
Half heresy, to wish the taps less vocal,
The panes relieved of grime. A plate of pears,
A piano with a Persian shawl, a cat
Stalking the picturesque amusing mouse
Had been her vision when he pleaded "Come."
Not that at five each separate stair would writhe
Under the milkman's tramp; that morning light
So coldly would delineate the scraps
Of last night's cheese and blank sepulchral bottles;
That on the kitchen shelf among the saucers
A pair of beetle-eyes would fix her own—
Envoy from some black village in the mouldings . . .
Meanwhile her night's companion, with a yawn
Sounded a dozen notes upon the keyboard,
Declared it out of tune, inspected whistling
A twelve hours' beard, went out for cigarettes;
While she, contending with a woman's demons,
Pulled back the sheets and made the bed and found
A fallen towel to dust the table-top,
And wondered how it was a man could wake
From night to day and take the day for granted.
By evening she was back in love again,
Though not so wholly but throughout the night

She woke sometimes to feel the daylight coming
Like a relentless milkman up the stairs.

QUESTIONS

1. In lines 9–10 and in the final two lines, Rich mentions the milkman. What does the milkman symbolize in this poem? What makes this symbol effective? What connection might the symbol have to the repeated mention of night and day in the poem?

2. What differences between men and women is Rich pointing out in her poem?

3. How does the mood of the first seven lines of the poem differ from that of the remaining lines? What sounds and words suggest a shift?

4. How does Rich use the studio apartment as a metaphor for the lover's relationship?

5. What examples of figurative language—especially metaphor and personification—can you find in the poem?

6. Explain the significance of the poem's title. Can you find any other instances of religious language in the poem?

SUGGESTION FOR WRITING

"Translate" Rich's poem into prose. Then write an essay comparing prose and poetry as modes of expression, using her poem and your translation as the main examples.

CHAPTER *Five*

WORKING AND PLAYING
Cause and Effect

A student is called in to see her adviser, who wants to know why she has received A's in chemistry and math, but D's in English and history. After a moment's reflection the student explains, "I always do better in courses that I like." In this example of cause-and-effect reasoning, the student isolates one cause to account for what is probably a more complicated situation. (This is *oversimplification.*) Actually, her liking chemistry and math may be an *effect* of her doing well in those courses, and not a *cause* at all. She may do well because she has a greater aptitude for sciences than for the humanities, she may have had better preparation for those courses, or she may have better teachers (or teachers she likes better) in math and chemistry this semester. There may even be other factors she has not considered, like the time of day the courses are given. Perhaps math and chemistry are given in the morning, when the student is alert, and English and history in the afternoon, when she is tired and preoccupied with afterschool activities. The answer to the adviser's question is probably some combination of reasons, not just the one the student quickly came up with.

As this anecdote reveals, cause-and-effect reasoning attempts to answer the question "Why?", and is therefore used not only in many forms of writing but in almost every kind of human interaction. We are constantly trying to find out why something occurs, or why someone did or did not do something. All parents are familiar with those childhood years when their sons and daughters preface every question with "Why?" Most of us carry this curiosity about causality into adulthood, and hunger to read all we can about the motives behind events. Books and articles on such subjects as why Hitler came to power, why Bruce Springsteen is so popular, what causes cancer, and why Reagan won the presidential election are avidly read.

In the following excerpt from Oscar Handlin's *The Uprooted,* a Pulitzer Prize-winning study of American immigration, the author uses cause and effect to explain why the Irish emigrated to America:

> Westward from Ireland went four and a half million. On that crowded island a remorselessly rising population, avaricious absentee landlords, and English policy that discouraged the growth of industry early stimulated emigration. Until 1846 this had been largely a movement of younger sons, of ambitious farmers and artisans. In that year rot destroyed the potato crop and left the cotters without the means of subsistence. Half a million died and three million more lived on only with the aid of charity. No thought then of paying rent, of holding on to the land; the evicted saw their huts pulled down and with bitter gratitude accepted from calculating poor-law officials the price of passage away from home. For decades after, till the end of the nineteenth century and beyond, these peasants continued to leave, some victims of later agricultural disasters, some sent for by relatives already across, some simply unable to continue a way of life already thoroughly disrupted.

In this summary paragraph, Handlin concisely presents the causes of Irish emigration to America. Earlier in the book he had discussed each cause—rising population, greedy landlords, suppression of industry, the potato famine—in greater detail, employing a significant amount of research. A college paper will obviously not demand the extensive research needed for a book, but for cause-and-effect papers you will often have to do some research. Few of us know enough about complex historical, political, scientific, and cultural events to write informed answers to such questions as "Why did the Irish emigrate to America?" "Why did Reagan defeat Carter so overwhelmingly?" "Why can't we find a cure for AIDS?" or "Why did the novel become so popular in the nineteenth century?".

The "Whys" of a causal relationship, however, are only half of the equation. Through cause and effect we can also analyze the effects any phenomenon might have in the past, present, or future. "What effect did the establishment of Israel have on the surrounding area?" "What effect did the discovery of the telescope have on astronomy?" and "What might be the effects of a new divorce law on children?" are just three out of an infinite number of questions we can ask about effects. As the following section from Toni Morrison's novel *The Bluest Eye* illustrates, cause-and-effect analysis is not restricted to informative essays, or even to nonfiction. In this passage the narrator describes the effects an attractive, wealthy new female student has on her school:

> She enchanted the entire school. When teachers called on her, they smiled encouragingly. Black boys didn't trip her in the halls; white boys didn't stone her, white girls didn't suck their teeth when she was assigned to be their work partners; black girls stepped aside when she wanted to use the sink in the girls' toilet, and their eyes genuflected under sliding lids. She never had to search for anybody to eat with in the cafeteria—they flocked to the table of her choice, where she opened fastidious lunches, shaming our jelly-stained bread with egg-salad sandwiches cut into four dainty squares, pink-frosted cupcakes, stalks of celery and carrots, proud, dark apples. She even bought and liked white milk.
> Frieda and I were bemused, irritated, and fascinated by her.

Here Morrison proves her topic sentence, that the new girl "enchanted the entire school," by showing the specific effects she had on teachers and students.

Clearly cause and effect can be used in various forms of writing depending on your purpose. Handlin wanted to explain and inform, so he used cause and effect to structure his information. He uses the language of historical writing—dates, statistics, events—although he also employs adjectives and images not usually found in such writing ("avaricious," "bitter gratitude"). Morrison's purposes are to entertain and, in this instance, establish an atmosphere. She combines narration and description, yet structures her paragraph as a series of effects. Her language borders on the poetic ("eyes genuflected," "fastidious lunches," "proud, dark apples"), appropriate for fiction. Similarly, the essays collected in this chapter show how flexible cause and effect can be, for they vary widely in form (short story, poem, personal reminiscence) and purpose (to entertain, to inform, to argue).

Whatever your purpose may be in using cause and effect, there are certain guidelines you must keep in mind. First, limit your thesis (if it is the type of writing that requires a thesis) to what you can realistically prove. A thesis like "The twenty year decline in SAT scores is directly attributable to the upheaval in the sixties" is dramatic and controversial, but how can it be proven? Because the decline began in 1970, the time sequence certainly suggests causality, but it would be difficult to think of a method for testing the exact relationship, which is the aim of cause-and-effect reasoning. The kind of cause-and-effect essay in which the writer attempts to prove future effects is particularly likely to have a thesis that claims more than the writer can prove. We can see the attraction (and abuse) of such essays if we glance at the titles of articles in both popular and serious magazines: "Killer Bees Will Overrun the Southwest," "Feminism Will Destroy the Family as We Know It," "The Coming Nuclear Winter." When writers try to predict the effect of something, they obviously open themselves to being proven wrong. Essays like these must, by definition, limit their claims.

Alvin Toffler, who specializes in this form of cause and effect *(Future Shock,*

The Third Wave), is usually very careful in his predictions. When trying to assess the effect of the word processor on the future employment of secretaries, Toffler stops short of saying that the secretary will be automated out of existence, even though his argument seems to be leading in that direction. After citing contradictory evidence on the issue, he concludes in *The Third Wave:* "It is clear that the level of employment is not merely a reflection of technological advance. It does not simply rise and fall as we automate or fail to do so. Employment is the net result of many converging policies." Thus Toffler does not make a claim for what he cannot prove.

A second guideline you should follow in writing cause-and-effect essays is to distinguish between what are known as *immediate* (or sufficient) causes and *remote* (or contributing) causes. If you were assigned to write an essay on "Why I Came to College," one immediate cause might be parental pressure, while a remote cause would be the prevailing attitude in the fifties that linked college with success. The *chain* of causes begins with the concern about money and having a profession that your parents learned as children growing up in the 1950s, and ends with them pressuring you to attend college in the 1980s. A second immediate cause might be your strong desire to become a surgeon which resulted from two remote causes—the influence of your cousin Susan, a successful neurosurgeon, and the positive impression a seventh grade biology class made on you. A diagram of these chains of causes and effects would look like this:

REMOTE CAUSES	IMMEDIATE CAUSES	EFFECT
1950s attitudes ------------ >	Parental pressure	⎫ Decision to go to college
Aunt Susan, neurosurgeon, 7th grade biology ----- >	Desire to be a surgeon	⎭

If you were to write this paper and substitute a remote for an immediate cause, you would confuse your reader, who would have to figure out how attitudes in the 1950s, 30 years before, led to your decision to go to college. You need to trace the entire sequence of events to be clear and complete when using remote cause or only write about immediate causes.

As a final guideline, you should be aware of two errors in logic frequently made by users of cause-and-effect reasoning: seeing one event as the cause of another simply because it precedes it (*"post hoc, ergo propter hoc"* meaning after this, therefore because of this); and seeing one event as the cause of another because it is frequently associated with it (mistaking a correlation for a cause). We have already seen an example of the first fallacy in the thesis on the sixties causing the decline in SAT scores. The fact that an event we wish to explain followed a likely causal event does not, in itself, prove any connection. The link, if it exists, must be proven. A recent University of Michigan study on academic habits and success in school provides an example of the second error, confusing correlation with cause. The study found that the amount of time students spent studying had very little correlation with the grades they received. The best indicators of grades were how often students came to class, and whether or not they sat in the first three rows. These rather surprising findings, however, should not lead you to reduce your study time or fight for a seat in the second row. The findings merely suggest a statistical correlation; people who sit in the first three rows or always attend class are more *likely* to succeed in college. There is no guarantee. Perhaps the best students tend to sit in the front. It does not then follow that sitting in the front will necessarily make *you* a better student, unless the study pinpoints certain specific reasons why sitting in the front can directly lead to earning higher grades. Stephen J. Gould's essay "Losing the Edge," in this chapter, provides an example of how statistics can be used to establish causes. In Marie Winn's attack on *Mad* magazine as a destroyer of youth, also found in this chapter, she comes close to committing the correlation fallacy, yet she seems to garner enough internal evidence to avoid this pitfall.

Keeping these guidelines in mind, how should you begin to write a cause-and-effect essay? Let us imagine that your composition instructor asks you to write an essay on the causes of some contemporary phenomenon. You consider a number of possibilities gleaned from free-writing, brainstorming, midnight talks with fellow students—rock videos, a black vice-presidential candidacy, an increase in the number of foreign students on American campuses, growing campus protests over South Africa. These all seem like good topics, but while you are trying to decide among them you read an article in the newspaper: "VCR's and Microwave Ovens Leading Sellers." Although you do not own a microwave, your parents have recently bought a videocassette recorder, and the experience is fresh in your mind. You realize that you were the last of all of your friends to have one and begin to wonder why these machines are so popular. You jot down some of your own reasons: freedom over what you watch, a way to indulge your love of films any time you want to, the ability to cut out commercials (which you hate), and the chance to record your favorite tennis players, see them in slow motion, and practice your strokes.

Listing the reasons your parents purchased a VCR is a critical first step, which could be helpful in writing a personal paper. In themselves, though, they do not explain why VCR's have become so popular for the general public, and the assignment asks for an explanation of that. The personal reasons do suggest some general ones:

1. All people would like to have greater control over what they watch, and when they watch it.

2. Most people would prefer to cut commercials out of the programs they watch, and the VCR can do this.

3. It is certainly more economical and convenient to watch a film on your TV for a minimal rental fee than to drive to a theater, park, and pay $5 or more per person.

4.   It is especially useful for parents of small children, because programs can be selected and played when it is convenient.

5.   They are fun to use.

6.   They have various educational uses.

7.   Everyone else seems to have one.

When all of these reasons are combined with the recent dramatic drop in price, a fairly full picture of why the VCR has become so popular emerges.

You might begin writing the paper with an introduction that establishes the magnitude of increased sales (information you can obtain through research), and then state your thesis: "The rapid increase in the popularity of VCR's can be attributed to their convenience, flexibility, and economy." At this stage it is important to choose the causes you will treat in depth, and those you will either just mention or omit. You should choose the causes that are the most significant and about which you have a substantial amount to say. The body of the paper will consist of your supporting each of the main causes with evidence: personal experience, testimony of others, logic, and possibly some research. For example, you can support reason number three above by calculating how much it cost the last time you and a friend went to a movie, and then comparing that to the cost of renting a film. You might have to concede that you cannot see a first-run film at home, but you can counter this point by explaining that the time between a film's initial theater showing and its being available on cassette is not very long, and many people feel that it is worth the wait. Evidence to confirm this point can come from your own experience and from the experiences of your friends.

Reason number four, that the VCR is especially useful to parents with young children, can be argued through a causal chain that looks like this:

REMOTE CAUSE	IMMEDIATE CAUSES	EFFECT
Rising number of baby-boom couples having children of their own (Document through research)	1. Few children's movies showing in theaters 2. High cost of taking entire family out to the movies 3. Parents want to control when and what children watch	Increased purchases of VCR's

You should use research and relevant personal experience to support each remote and immediate cause.

You can expect to write cause-and-effect papers and essay exams in almost every class you take in college. In physics, biology, chemistry, economics, political science, psychology, English, history, art, music, and education, you will be asked to analyze why something happens or happened, or what might be the effects of a certain phenomenon. Your purposes will be to inform, understand, or argue, and your audience will most often be your professors. In fact, cause-and-effect reasoning is at the heart of the educational process. Through the rigorous and objective study of causality we discover the complexity of human life, shedding uninformed stereotypes and shallow opinions as we explore our subjects more deeply. The student who mechanically responds to the question "What caused the Civil War?" with the rote answer "slavery," or to a question on Freud's effect on the twentieth century with a one word reply—"sex"—is only at the beginning of his or her higher education.

Outside the classroom, as well, we are each part of an intricate web of causes and effects that we only partially grasp. We might wonder why we chose the college we did, our job, our spouse. Bob Greene, a writer who specializes in reflective essays, recently wrote an essay called "Cut," in which he tries to explain the effects on his adult life of being cut from his junior high school basketball team:

> All these years later, I remember it as if I were still standing right there in the gym. . . . I don't know how the mind works in matters like this; I don't know what went on in my head following that day when I was cut. But I know that my ambition has been enormous ever since then; I know that for all of my life since that day, I have done more work than I had to be doing, taken more assignments than I had to be taking, put in more hours than I had to be spending. I don't know if all of that came from a determination never to allow myself to be cut again—never to allow someone to tell me that I'm not good enough again—but I know it's there. And apparently it's there in a lot of other men, too.

In his essay Greene isolates a seemingly minor event that would ultimately have a profound effect on his life. Through writing cause-and-effect essays, then, all of us can answer significant questions about our world and about ourselves.

Thomas McGuane
ME AND MY BIKE AND WHY
★ ★ ★

Thomas McGuane, who was raised in the Midwest, is a novelist, screenwriter, director, and rancher. As a result of his Irish heritage, McGuane was exposed early to a tradition of "fantastic storytellers," a tradition he has carried on in novels like The Sporting Club *(1969),* The Bushwacked Piano *(1971), and* Ninety-Two in the Shade *(1973), and in screenplays for* Rancho Deluxe *(1975),* The Missouri Breaks *(1976), and* Tom Horn *(1980).*

An avid sportsman, McGuane has been a frequent contributor to Sports Illustrated, *where many of the pieces collected in* An Outside Chance: Essays on Sport *(1980) first appeared. The collection is as close to autobiographical writing as McGuane has come, and in essays like "Me and My Bike and Why" the author examines the motives behind his obsession with various sports like motorcycling, calf-roping, and fishing. Surprisingly, for a writer who seems particularly aware of his masculinity, McGuane honestly reveals his fears and failures in this essay.*

───────

Like many who buy a motorcycle, there had been for me the problem of getting over the rather harrowing insurance statistics as to just what it is that is liable to happen to you. Two years in California—a familiar prelude to acts of excess—had made of me an active motorcycle spectator. I watched and identified, finally resorting to bikers' magazines; and evolved a series of foundationless prejudices.

Following the war, motorcycling left a peculiar image in the national consciousness: porcine individuals wearing a sort of yachting cap with a white vinyl bill, the decorative braid pulled up over the hat, their motorcycles plated monsters, white rubber mud flaps studded with ruby stars hung from both fenders. Where are those machines now? Surely Andy Warhol can't have bought them all. Not every one of them is a decorative planter in a Michigan truck garden. But wherever they are, it is certain that the ghosts of cretinism collect close around the strenuously baroque plumbing of those inefficient engines and speak to us of an America that has gone.

It was easy for me initially to deplore the big road bikes, the motorcycles of the police and Hell's Angels. But finally even these "hogs" and show bikes had their appeal, and sometimes I had dark fantasies of myself on El Camino Real, hands hung overhead from the big chopper bars, feet in front on weirdly automotive pedals, making all the decent people say: "There goes one."

I did it myself. Heading into San Francisco with my wife, our Land Rover blaring wide open at 52 miles per, holding up a quarter mile of good people behind us, people who didn't see why anybody needed four-wheel drive on the Bayshore Freeway, we ourselves would from time to time see a lonesome Angel or Coffin Cheater or Satan's Slave or Gypsy Joker on his big chopper and say (either my wife or myself, together sometimes): "There goes one."

Anyway, it was somewhere along in here that I saw I was not that type, and began to think of sporting machines, even racing machines, big ones, because I had no interest in starting small and working my way up as I had been urged to do. I remember that I told the writer Wallace Stegner what I intended, and he asked, "Why do you people do this when you come to California?"

"It's like skiing," I said, purely on speculation.

"Oh, yeah? What about the noise?"

But no one could stop me.

There was the dire question of money that ruled out many I saw. The English-built Triumph Metisse road racer was out of the question, for example. Some of the classics I found and admired—Ariel Square Fours, Vincent Black Shadows, BSA Gold Stars, Velocette Venoms or Phantom Clubmen, Norton Manxes—had to be eliminated on grounds of cost or outlandish maintenance problems.

Some of the stranger Japanese machinery, two-cycle, rotary-valved engines, I dismissed because they sounded funny. The Kawasaki Samurai actually seemed refined, but I refused to consider it. I had a corrupt Western ideal of a bike's exhaust rap, and the tuned megaphone exhausts of the Japanese motorcycles sounded like something out of the next century, weird loon cries of Oriental speed tuning.

There is a blurred moment in my head, a scenario of compulsion. I am in a motorcycle shop that is going out of business. I am writing a check that challenges the contents of my bank account. I am given ownership papers substantiated by the state of California, a crash helmet, and five gallons of fuel. Some minutes later I am standing beside my new motorcycle, sick all over. The man who sold it to me stares palely through the Thermopane window covered with the decals of the noble marques of "performance." He wonders why I have not moved.

I have not moved because I do not know what to do. I wish to advance upon the machine with authority but cannot. He would not believe I could have bought a motorcycle of this power without knowing so much as how to start its engine. Presently he loses interest and looks for another tormented creature in need of a motorcycle.

Unwatched, I can really examine the bike. Since I have no notion of how to operate it, it is purely an *objet*. I think of a friend with a road racer on a simple mahogany block in front of his fireplace, except that he rides his very well.

The bike was rather beautiful. I suppose it still is. The designation, which now seems too cryptic for my taste, was "Matchless 500," and it was the motorcycle I believed I had thought up myself. It is a trifle hard to describe the thing to the uninitiated, but, briefly, it had a 500-cc., one-cylinder engine—a "big single" in the patois of bike freaks—and an eloquently simple maroon teardrop-shaped tank that is as much the identifying mark on a Matchless, often otherwise unrecogniz-able through modification, as the chevron of a redwing blackbird. The front wheel, delicate as a bicycle's, carried a Dunlop K70 tire (said to "cling") and had no fender; a single cable led to the pale machined brake drum. Over the knobby rear wheel curved an extremely brief magnesium fender with, instead of the lush buddy-seat of the fat motorcycles, a minute pillion of leather. The impression was of performance and of complete disregard for comfort. The equivalent in automo-biles would be, perhaps, the Morgan, in sailboats the Finn.

I saw all these things at once (remember the magazines I had been reading, the Floyd Clymer books I had checked out of the library), and in that sense my apprehension of the motorcycle was perfectly literary. I still didn't know how to start it. Suddenly it looked big and mean and vicious and no fun at all.

I didn't want to experiment on El Camino Real, and moreover, it had begun to rain heavily. I had made up my mind to wheel it home, and there to peruse the operation manual, whose infuriating British locutions the Land Rover manual had prepared me for.

I was surprised at the sheer inertial weight of the thing; it leaned toward me and pressed against my hip insistently all the way to the house. I was disturbed that a machine whose place in history seemed so familiar should look utterly foreign at close range. The fact that the last number on the speedometer was 140 seemed irresponsible.

It was dark by the time I got home. I wheeled it through the back gate and down the sidewalk through a yard turned largely to mud. About halfway to the kitchen door, I somehow got the thing tilted away from myself, and it slowly but quite determinedly toppled over in the mud, with me, gnashing, on top of it.

My wife came to the door and peered into the darkness. "Tom?" I refused to vouchsafe an answer. I lay there in the mud, no longer struggling, as the spring rains of the San Francisco peninsula singled me out for special treatment. I was already composing the ad in the *Chronicle* that motorcycle people dream of finding: "Big savings on Matchless 500. Never started by present owner. A real cream puff." My wife threw on the porch light and perceived my discomfiture.

The contretemps had the effect of quickly getting us over the surprise that I had bought the motorcycle, questions of authorization, and so on. I headed for the showers. Scraped and muddy, I had excited a certain amount of pity. "I'll be all right."

No one told me to retard the spark. True enough, it was in the manual, but I had been unable to read that attentively. It had no plot, no characters. So my punishment was this: when I jumped on the kick starter, it backfired and more or less threw me off the bike. I was limping all through the first week from vicious blowbacks. I later learned it was a classic way to get a spiral fracture. I tried jumping lightly on the kick starter and, unfairly, it would blast back as viciously as with a sharp kick. Eventually it started, and sitting on it, I felt the torque tilt the bike under me. I was afraid to take my hands off the handlebars. My wife lowered the helmet onto my head; I compared it to the barber's basin Don Quixote had worn into battle, the Helmet of Mambrino.

I slipped my toe up under the gearshift lever, lifted it into first, released the clutch, and magically glided away and made all my shifts through fourth, at which time I was on Sand Hill Road and going 50, my shirt in a soft air bubble at my back, my Levi's wrapped tight to my shins, my knuckles whitening under the giddy surge of pure undetained motion as I climbed gently into the foothills toward Los Altos. The road got more and more winding as I ascended, briskly but conservatively. Nothing in the air was lost on me as I passed through zones of smell and temperature as palpable transitions, running through sudden warm spots on the road where a single redwood 100 feet away had fallen and let in a shaft of sunlight. The road seemed tremendously spacious. The sound was behind me, so that when I came spiraling down out of the mountains and saw some farm boy had walked out to the side of the road to watch me go by, I realized he had heard me coming for a long time. And I wondered a little about the racket.

These rides became habitual and presumably more competent. I often rode up past La Honda for a view of the sea at the far edge of a declining cascade of manzanita-covered hills, empty and foggy. The smell of ocean was so perfectly evocative in a landscape divided among ranches and truck gardens whose pumpkins in the foggy air seemed to have an uncanny brilliance. A Japanese nursery stood along the road in clouds of tended vines on silver redwood lattice. I went past it to the sea and before riding home took a long walk on the ribbed, immense beach.

A fascinating aspect of the pursuit, not in the least bucolic, was the bike shop where one went for mechanical service, and which was a meeting place for the bike people, whose machines were poised out front in carefully conceived rest positions. At first, of course, no one would talk to me, but my motorcycle ideas were theirs; I was not riding one of the silly mechanisms that purred down the highways in a parody of the equipment these people lived for.

One day an admired racing mechanic—"a good wrench"—came out front and gave my admittedly well-cared-for Matchless the once-over. He announced that it was "very sanitary." I was relieved. The fear, of course, is that he will tell you, "The bike is wrong."

"Thank you," I said modestly. He professed himself an admirer of the "Matchbox," saying it was "fairly rapid" and had enough torque to "pull stumps." Ultimately, I was taken in, treated kindly, and given the opportunity to ride some of the machinery that so excited me: the "truly potent" Triumph Metisse, an almost uncontrollable supercharged Norton Atlas from New Mexico, and a couple of road-racing machines with foot pegs way back by the rear sprocket and stubby six-inch handlebars—so that you lay out on the bike and divide a sea of wind with the point of your chin.

One day I "got off on the pavement," that is, crashed. It was not much of a crash. I went into a turn too fast and ran off the shoulder and got a little "road burn" requiring symbolic bandages at knees and elbows. I took the usual needling from the crew at the bike shop, and with secret pleasure accepted the temporary appellation, "Crash Cargo." I began taking dawn trips over the mountains to Santa Cruz, sometimes with others, sometimes alone, wearing a wool hunting shirt against the chill and often carrying binoculars and an Audubon field guide.

Then one day I was riding in my own neighborhood when a man made a U-turn in front of me and stopped, blocking the road. It was too late to brake and I had to put the bike down, riding it like a sled as it screeched across the pavement. It ran into the side of the car and I slid halfway under, the seat and knees torn out of my pants, scraped and bruised but without serious injury. I had heard the sharp clicking of my helmet against the pavement and later saw the depressions that might have been in my skull.

The man got out, accusing me of going 100 miles an hour, accusing me of laying for a chance to create an accident, accusing me of being a Hell's Angel, and finally admitting he had been daydreaming and had not looked up the street before making his illegal maneuver. The motorcycle was a mess. He pleaded with me not to have physical injuries. He said he had very little insurance. And a family. "Have a heart."

"You ask this of a Hell's Angel?"

At the motorcycle shop I was urged to develop nonspecific spinal trouble. A special doctor was named. But I had the motorcycle minimally repaired and sent the man the bill. When the settlement came, his name was at the top of the stationery. He was the owner of the insurance agency.

Perhaps it was the point-blank view from below of rocker panels and shock absorbers and the specious concern of the insurance man for my health that gave my mortality its little twinge. I suddenly did not want to get off on the pavement anymore or bring my road burn to the shop under secret bandages. I no longer cared if my bike was rapid and sanitary. I wanted to sell it, and I wanted to get out of California.

I did both those things, and in that order. But sometimes, in the midst of more tasteful activities, I miss the mournful howl of that big single engine as it came up on the cam, dropped revs, and started over on a new ratio; the long banking turns with the foot pegs sparking against the pavement and the great crocodile's tears the wind caused to trickle out from under my flying glasses. I'm behind a sensible windshield now, and the soaring curve of acceleration does not come up through the seat of my pants. I have an FM radio, and the car doesn't get bad mileage.

QUESTIONS

1. How do McGuane's initial experiences with the bike undercut his romantic image of biking? Cite specific instances.

2. How do McGuane's descriptions of his rides suggest the causes of his fascination with motorcycles? What other experiences add to their mystique?

3. Why does McGuane link selling the bike and leaving California? What does the final paragraph reveal about how his decision still affects him?

4. What does the "Why" in the title refer to? In what ways is this a cause-and-effect essay? What other rhetorical modes does McGuane employ?

5. Look closely at the paragraph that begins "The bike was rather beautiful." How does the author's language reveal his feelings about this machine? Does he convince you that a motorcycle can be beautiful?

6. Do you think McGuane tells enough about why he was attracted to motorcycles? Explain.

SUGGESTION FOR WRITING

Tell the story of a time you felt compelled to try a new sport or hobby. What factors led to your interest? Describe your initial attempts at mastery. How did the reality compare to the image you had of your abilities? How did it all turn out? (It would be exciting if your subject were something like skydiving, but even the desire to drive or to paint in oils would make fine topics.)

Gloria Steinem
THE IMPORTANCE OF WORK
★ ★ ★

Gloria Steinem, a well-known feminist, writer, and magazine editor, is an active and articulate advocate of women's causes. The granddaughter of an early feminist, Steinem, who was educated at Smith College, has been a freelance writer and publisher for most of her career. In 1972, she founded Ms. *magazine. Steinem and her magazine have chronicled the feminist movement, championing the long and ultimately unsuccessful attempt to persuade the nation to adopt an Equal Rights Amendment, as well as other causes like freedom of choice in abortions, freedom from sexual harassment, and equal pay for equal work. In the introduction to her recently published* Outrageous Acts and Everyday Rebellions, *a collection of essays written over the past twenty years, Steinem explains what attracts her to writing: "(1) When I'm doing it, I don't feel that I should be doing something else instead; (2) it produces a sense of accomplishment and, once in a while, pride; and (3), it's frightening."*

In "The Importance of Work," originally published in Ms. *in 1979, the author uses cause and effect to argue for a woman's right to employment, a right that Steinem feels is, and has always been, under attack.*

Toward the end of the 1970s, *The Wall Street Journal* devoted an eight-part, front-page series to "the working woman"—that is, the influx of women into the paid-labor force—as the greatest change in American life since the Industrial Revolution.

Many women readers greeted both the news and the definition with cynicism. After all, women have always worked. If all the productive work of human maintenance that women do in the home were valued at its replacement cost, the gross national product of the United States would go up by 26 percent. It's just that we are now more likely than ever before to leave our poorly rewarded, low-security, high-risk job of homemaking (though we're still trying to explain that it's a perfectly good one and that the problem is male society's refusal both to do it and to give it an economic value) for more secure, independent, and better-paid jobs outside the home.

Obviously, the real work revolution won't come until all productive work is rewarded—including child rearing and other jobs done in the home—and men are integrated into so-called women's work as well as vice versa. But the radical change being touted by the *Journal* and other media is one part of that long integration process: the unprecedented flood of women into salaried jobs, that is, into the labor force as it has been male-defined and previously occupied by men. We are already more than 41 percent of it—the highest proportion in history. Given the fact that women also make up a whopping 69 percent of the "discouraged labor force" (that is, people who need jobs but don't get counted in the unemployment statistics because they've given up looking), plus an official female unemployment rate that is substantially higher than men's, it's clear that we could expand to become fully half of the national work force by 1990.

Faced with this determination of women to find a little independence and to be paid and honored for our work, experts have rushed to ask: "Why?" It's a question rarely directed at male workers. Their basic motivations of survival and personal satisfaction are taken for granted. Indeed, men are regarded as "odd" and therefore subjects for sociological study and journalistic reports only when they *don't* have work, even if they are rich and don't need jobs or are poor and can't find them. Nonetheless, pollsters and sociologists have gone to great expense to prove that women work outside the home because of dire financial need, or if we persist despite the presence of a wage-earning male, out of some desire to buy "little extras" for our families, or even out of good old-fashioned penis envy.

Job interviewers and even our own families may still ask salaried women the big "Why?" If we have small children at home or are in some job regarded as "men's work," the incidence of such questions increases. Condescending or ac-cusatory versions of "What's a nice girl like you doing in a place like this?" have not disappeared from the workplace.

How do we answer these assumptions that we are "working" out of some pressing or peculiar need? Do we feel okay about arguing that it's as natural for us to have salaried jobs as for our husbands—whether or not we have young children at home? Can we enjoy strong career ambitions without worrying about being thought "unfeminine"? When we confront men's growing resentment of women competing in the work force (often in the form of such guilt-producing accusations as "You're taking men's jobs away" or "You're damaging your children"), do we simply state that a decent job is a basic human right for everybody?

I'm afraid the answer is often no. As individuals and as a movement, we tend to retreat into some version of a tactically questionable defense: "Womenwork-becausewehaveto." The phrase has become one word, one key on the typewriter— an economic form of the socially "feminine" stance of passivity and self-sacrifice. Under attack, we still tend to present ourselves as creatures of economic necessity and familial devotion. "Womenworkbecausewehaveto" has become the easiest thing to say.

Like most truisms, this one is easy to prove with statistics. Economic need *is* the most consistent work motive—for women as well as men. In 1976, for instance, 43 percent of all women in the paid-labor force were single, widowed, separated, or divorced, and working to support themselves and their dependents. An additional 21 percent were married to men who had earned less than ten thousand dollars in the previous year, the minimum then required to support a family of four. In fact, if you take men's pensions, stocks, real estate, and various forms of accumulated wealth into account, a good statistical case can be made that there are more women who "have" to work (that is, who have neither the accumulated wealth, nor husbands whose work or wealth can support them for the rest of their lives) than there are men with the same need. If we were going to ask one group "Do you really need this job?", we should ask men.

But the first weakness of the whole "have to work" defense is its deceptiveness. Anyone who has ever experienced dehumanized life on welfare or any other confidence-shaking dependency knows that a paid job may be preferable to the dole, even when the handout is coming from a family member. Yet the will and self-confidence to work on one's own can diminish as dependency and fear increase. That may explain why—contrary to the "have to" rationale—wives of men who earn less than three thousand dollars a year are actually *less* likely to be employed than wives whose husbands make ten thousand dollars a year or more.

Furthermore, the greatest proportion of employed wives is found among families with a total household income of twenty-five to fifty thousand dollars a year. This is the statistical underpinning used by some sociologists to prove that women's work is mainly important for boosting families into the middle or upper middle class. Thus, women's incomes are largely used for buying "luxuries" and "little extras": a neat double-whammy that renders us secondary within our families, and makes our jobs expendable in hard times. We may even go along with this interpretation (at least, up to the point of getting fired so a male can have our job). It preserves a husbandly ego-need to be seen as the primary breadwinner, and still allows us a safe "feminine" excuse for working.

But there are often rewards that we're not confessing. As noted in *The Two-Career Couple,* by Francine and Douglas Hall: "Women who hold jobs by choice, even blue-collar routine jobs, are more satisfied with their lives than are the full-time housewives."

In addition to personal satisfaction, there is also society's need for all its members' talents. Suppose that jobs were given out on only a "have to work" basis to both women and men—one job per household. It would be unthinkable to lose the unique abilities of, for instance, Eleanor Holmes Norton, the distinguished chair of the Equal Employment Opportunity Commission. But would we then be forced to question the important work of her husband, Edward Norton, who is also a distinguished lawyer? Since men earn more than twice as much as women on the average, the wife in most households would be more likely to give up her job. Does that mean the nation could do as well without millions of its nurses, teachers, and secretaries? Or that the rare man who earns less than his wife should give up his job?

It was this kind of waste of human talents on a society-wide scale that traumatized millions of unemployed or underemployed Americans during the Depression. Then, a one-job-per-household rule seemed somewhat justified, yet the concept was used to displace women workers only, create intolerable dependencies, and waste female talent that the country needed. That Depression experience, plus the energy and example of women who were finally allowed to work during the manpower shortage created by World War II, led Congress to reinterpret the meaning of the country's full-employment goal in its Economic Act of 1946. Full employment was officially defined as "the employment of those who want to work, without regard to whether their employment is, by some definition, necessary. This goal applies equally to men and to women." Since bad economic times are again creating a resentment of employed women—as well as creating more need for women to be employed—we need such a goal more than ever. Women are again being caught in a tragic double bind: We are required to be strong and then punished for our strength.

Clearly, anything less than government and popular commitment to this 1946 definition of full employment will leave the less powerful groups, whoever they may be, in danger. Almost as important as the financial penalty paid by the powerless is the suffering that comes from being shut out of paid and recognized work. Without it, we lose much of our self-respect and our ability to prove that we are alive by making some difference in the world. That's just as true for the suburban woman as it is for the unemployed steel worker.

But it won't be easy to give up the passive defense of "wework-becausewehaveto."

When a woman who is struggling to support her children and grandchildren on welfare sees her neighbor working as a waitress, even though that neighbor's husband has a job, she may feel resentful; and the waitress (of course, not the waitress's husband) may feel guilty. Yet unless we establish the obligation to provide a job for everyone who is willing and able to work, that welfare woman may herself be penalized by policies that give out only one public-service job per household. She and her daughter will have to make a painful and divisive decision about which of them gets that precious job, and the whole household will have to survive on only one salary.

A job as a human right is a principle that applies to men as well as women. But women have more cause to fight for it. The phenomenon of the "working woman" has been held responsible for everything from an increase in male impotence (which turned out, incidently, to be attributable to medication for high blood pressure) to the rising cost of steak (which was due to high energy costs and beef import restrictions, not women's refusal to prepare the cheaper, slower-cooking cuts). Unless we see a job as part of every citizen's right to autonomy and personal fulfillment, we will continue to be vulnerable to someone else's idea of what "need" is, and whose "need" counts the most.

In many ways, women who do not have to work for simple survival, but who choose to do so nonetheless, are on the frontier of asserting this right for all women. Those with well-to-do husbands are dangerously easy for us to resent and put down. It's easier still to resent women from families of inherited wealth, even though men generally control and benefit from that wealth. (There is no Rockefeller Sisters Fund, no J.P. Morgan & Daughters, and sons-in-law may be the ones who really sleep their way to power.) But to prevent a woman whose husband or father is wealthy from earning her own living, and from gaining the self-confidence that comes with that ability, is to keep her needful of that unearned power and less willing to disperse it. Moreover, it is to lose forever her unique talents.

Perhaps modern feminists have been guilty of a kind of reverse snobbism that keeps us from reaching out to the wives and daughters of wealthy men; yet it was exactly such women who refused the restrictions of class and financed the first wave of feminist revolution.

For most of us, however, "womenworkbecausewehaveto" is just true enough to be seductive as a personal defense.

If we use it without also staking out the larger human right to a job, however, we will never achieve that right. And we will always be subject to the false argument that independence for women is a luxury affordable only in good economic times. Alternatives to layoffs will not be explored, acceptable unemployment will always be used to frighten those with jobs into accepting low wages, and we will never remedy the real cost, both to families and to the country, of dependent women and a massive loss of talent.

Worst of all, we may never learn to find productive, honored work as a natural part of ourselves and as one of life's basic pleasures.

QUESTIONS

1. How does Steinem use statistics to show that economic considerations may not be the primary reason most women work? Evaluate these figures. Do you think they would still be valid today, nine years later? Are you aware of any lingering opposition to women's employment outside the home?

2. Analyze the effectiveness of Steinem's using questions as a form of statement in paragraph six.

3. How do Steinem's word choice and tone reveal her strong feelings about her subject? Cite examples.

4. Five of Steinem's paragraphs consist of one sentence. Since a paragraph that short is not developed, defend or criticize the author's stylistic choice here. Find the five paragraphs and comment on how each functions.

SUGESTION FOR WRITING

Find and interview several women who work outside the home. Ask them why they work, and what effect their working has on other aspects of their lives. Then write an essay supporting or contradicting Steinem's central points.

Pete Hamill
WINNING ISN'T EVERYTHING
★ ★ ★

Journalist, novelist, screenwriter, and contributor to numerous periodicals, Brooklyn-born Pete Hamill has been an observer and critic of American culture since the early sixties. Although he has traveled widely and lived for a time in Europe, Hamill is primarily an urban writer, with a specific interest in the political, social, and sporting lives of New Yorkers. In "Winning Isn't Everything," Hamill confronts what he sees as the American obsession with winning, analyzing its causes and warning us of its negative effects.

———

One of the more widely accepted maxims of modern American life was uttered on a frozen winter afternoon during the early Sixties. The late Vince Lombardi, who coached the Green Bay Packers when they were the greatest team in football, said it. "Winning isn't everything," he declared. "It's the only thing."

Vince Lombardi's notion was immediately appropriated by an extraordinary variety of American males: presidents and lesser politicians, generals, broadcasters, political columnists, Little League coaches, heads of corporations and probably millions of others. In fact, it sometimes seems that Lombardi's words have had greater impact than any sentence uttered by an American since Stephen Decatur's "our country, right or wrong."

That's surprising on many levels, beginning with the obvious: It's a deceptively simple premise. Winning *isn't* "the only thing." Such an idea muddles the idea of competition, not simply in sports, but in all aspects of our lives. We've learned the hard way in this century that the world is a complex place; it's certainly not the National Football League. Winning isn't the only thing in love, art, marriage, commerce, or politics; it's not even the only thing in sports.

In sports, as in so many other areas of our national life, we've always cherished gallant losers. I remember one afternoon in the fall of 1956 when Sal Maglie was pitching for the Brooklyn Dodgers against the hated Yankees. Maglie was an old man that year, as age is measured in sports. But this was the World Series, and he hauled his thirty-nine-year-old body to the mound, inning after inning, gave everything he had, held the Yankees to a few scattered hits and two runs—and lost. That day Don Larsen pitched his perfect game: no runs, no hits, no errors. Yet, to me, the afternoon belonged to Maglie—tough, gallant, and a loser.

There was an evening in Manila when Joe Frazier went up against Muhammad Ali for the third and final time. That night, Frazier brought his workman's skills into combat against the magic of the artist, called on his vast reservoir of courage and will, and came up empty at the end of fourteen rounds. Frazier was the loser, but that evening, nobody really lost. Because of that fight, Joe Frazier can always boast with honor that he made Muhammad Ali a great fighter. He was the test, the implacable force who made Ali summon all of his own considerable reserves of skill, heart, and endurance for a final effort. The contest consumed them both. Neither was ever again a good fighter. But during their violent confrontation, winning or losing was, in the end, a marginal concern; that all-consuming effort was everything.

There are hundreds of similar examples of losers who showed us how to be more human, and their performances make the wide acceptance of Lombardi's notions even more mystifying. Lombardi's thesis, in fact, represented something of a shift in the nation's popular thought. Americans had been the people who remembered the Alamo or Pearl Harbor; we blew taps over the graves of those who lost at the Battle of the Bulge or Anzio or the Yalu Basin. Those soldiers had all been defeated, but we honored them for their display of a critical human quality: courage.

Ernest Hemingway once defined courage as grace under pressure, and that's always struck me as an eminently useful definition. The best professional athletes not only possess that kind of courage but, more important, are willing to display it to strangers. Baseball's Reggie Jackson or Richard ("Goose") Gossage, for instance, function most completely as athletes and as men when appearing before gigantic crowds under pressure: bases loaded, late innings, a big game. They come to their tasks with gladness and absolute focus, neither whimpering, complaining nor shirking when doing their job; they just try their best to get that job done. And, of course, sometimes they fail. Gossage gives up a single and his team loses. Jackson strikes out. No matter. The important thing is that such men keep their appointments with confidence and grace. Courage has become so deep a part of their character that they don't even think about it. (They certainly *want* to win. Sometimes they absolutely lust for victory. But they know that winning isn't everything. All a man can do is his best.)

Competition isn't really a problem for Americans. All sports, in one way or another, are competitive. But an individual's primary competition is with himself and all his attendant weaknesses. That's obviously true of boxing, where fear must be dominated and made to work to the fighter's benefit. Yet it's also true for team sports, as well as such solitary endeavors as golf, where a player must learn control before anything else. The problem isn't competition, which is a part of life; it's in the notion of the necessity of triumph. A man can lose but still win. And the point of competition in sports is an old and not very fashionable one: It builds character.

That's especially true of prizefighters, the athletes I've known best. Outside the ring, almost all fighters are the gentlest of men. They carry themselves with the dignity of those who have little to prove, either to others or themselves. They're never bullies, rarely use their dangerous skills against ordinary citizens and avoid pointless confrontations. When a fighter hears that a colleague has been involved in a bar brawl or a swingout with a cop, he dismisses that fighter as a cowardly bum. Most of the boxers I know are honest, generous, funny. Yet they also know that as good as they are, there might be someone down the line who has their number. Again, they would prefer to be winners. But they're aware that losing, if a courageous effort is made, is never a disgrace. The highest compliment one fighter can pay another is to say that he has "heart."

There are lessons to be learned from such atheletes that can be applied to how we live our lives. In the long run, we'll all come up losers because there's no greater loss than death. And since primitive man first began to think, we humans have devised strategies to deal with dying. Religion is the most obvious one, usually demanding that we adhere to a moral code on earth in exchange for a serene existence after death. Ideologies offer secular versions of the same instinct, insisting that we sacrifice now, directing our lives toward the ideal of a better future, with each man becoming an architect of his own utopia. Patriotism and nationalism carry some of the same fearful baggage.

An athlete's goals are less cosmic, his field of struggle less grandiose and therefore more applicable to ordinary citizens. Great athletes teach us that life is a series of struggles, not one giant effort. Just when we appear to have triumphed, we must stop like Sisyphus and again begin rolling the boulder up that mountain. The true athlete teaches us that winning isn't everything, but struggle is—the struggle to simply get up in the morning or to see hope through the minefields of despair.

Viewed that way, a marriage, or any relationship with another human being, is an ongoing struggle. The mastering of a skill or craft doesn't end with the granting of a diploma; it goes on for life. The relationship between parents and children doesn't end when the children turn eighteen. The running of a corporation isn't a one-shot affair, measured by a single year's statements of profits and losses; it's a continuing process, accomplished by human beings who learn from mistakes, plunge fearlessly into the struggle, take risks and prepare for the future.

It's probably no accident that American capitalism, with its often permanently infantile male executives, experienced a decline that coincided with the period when Vince Lombardi's values received their widest acceptance. The results are visible everywhere. Sit on a plane with American businessmen and they'll be chattering about the Pittsburgh Steelers. Join a group of Japanese businessmen and they'll be discussing twenty-first-century technology. One group is trapped in a philosophy that demands winning as its goal; the other cares more about patient, long-term growth—and for the moment at least, the latter is winning.

Another great maxim of the years of America's triumphs also came from the sports pages via the writer Grantland Rice. "It matters not who won or lost," declared the esteemed chronicler of the prewar years, "but how they played the game." By the time Vince Lombardi came along, such sentiments were being sneered at. We had then become a superpower, capable of blowing up the world. The man of grace, courage, endurance, and compassion was replaced in the public imagination by the swaggering macho blowhard; Humphrey Bogart gave way to John Wayne. With such attitudes dominating the landscape, we were certain to get into trouble, and we did. Vietnam and Watergate underscored the idea of winning at all costs. Yet today we seem incapable of admitting that an obsession with winning often leads to the most squalid of defeats.

Solid marriages are often built upon the experience of disastrous ones. Politicians who lose elections become tempered for the contests that follow, sometimes going on to solid, useful careers. Painters, playwrights, novelists, and other artists often learn as much from their failures as they do from those rare moments when vision, craft and ambition come together to produce masterpieces. It's also that way in sports.

I remember a night when my friend José Torres, then a middleweight, was boxing Florentino Fernandez in Puerto Rico. I couldn't go to the fight, so I spent the night tuning in and out of the all-news radio stations, anxious about the result because Florentino was a great puncher. About three in the morning, Torres called.

"Oh, Pete," he said, close to tears. "I'm so sorry."

"What happened?"

"I got knocked out," Torres replied, his voice brimming with emotion, since he'd never lost as a professional. We started discussing what had happened. Emotions cooled; the talk became technical. Torres explained that he had learned some things about himself, about boxing. He now understood some of his flaws, and thought he could correct them. We talked for an hour. Then I asked what he was going to do next.

"Go to the gym," he said. "I'm going to be champion of the world."

Two years later, Torres *was* the world's light-heavyweight champion. He didn't quit after his first defeat. That night in San Juan he didn't say winning was the only thing, that it was time to pack it in. He had learned something from defeat, and knew that one violent night, somewhere down the line, he would show the world what he had learned. And that was precisely what he did. But he was aware of something else too: Sooner or later, someone might come along who was better than he was, for at least one evening. After all, even champions are human. Even champions eventually lose. That happened to José Torres as well. But then it didn't really matter. José Torres, like the rest of us, had learned that winning wasn't everything. Living was all, and in life, defeat and victory are inseparable brothers.

QUESTIONS

1. Hamill argues that Lombardi's "maxim" is a contributing cause of the decline of American capitalism. Does he adequately prove the connection? Discuss.

2. Why, according to Hamill, did our heroes change from "the man of grace, courage, endurance, and compassion" to "the swaggering macho blowhard," from Humphrey Bogart to John Wayne? What effect did this change have on our national life? Do you agree with Hamill's analysis?

3. Discuss the way Hamill uses examples to prove that "winning isn't everything."

4. Why is the José Torres anecdote an effective conclusion to the essay?

5. Determine Hamill's attitude toward the athletes he mentions by underlining and analyzing the adjectives he uses to describe them.

6. The nature of Hamill's argument forces him to treat disparate subjects (death and sports, marriage and boxing) side by side. What transitions does he use to move the reader from point to point?

7. Do you accept Hamill's analogies between sports and life? Explain.

SUGGESTION FOR WRITING

Take a familiar maxim, such as "All's fair in love and war," "It is better to give than receive," or "Might makes right," and analyze its validity. Is it applicable to our lives? Is it true? Include in your analysis the effects the maxim has on you, your acquaintances, and on the community at large.

Marie Winn
MAD MAGAZINE
★ ★ ★

Marie Winn's books all embody the search for causes and the analysis of effects. From her children's books, The Fisherman Who Needed a Knife: A Story About Why People Use Money *(1970) and* The Man Who Made Five Tops: A Story About Why People Do Different Kinds of Work *(1970) to* The Plug-In Drug: Television, Children, and the Family *(1977), Winn explores why things are done as they are in our culture, and what effects the culture has on each of us. Her concern with the effects modern life has on children led to her devastating attack on the influence of television. In* Children Without Childhood *(1983), she criticizes contemporary society as a whole—divorce, working parents, sex and violence in the media, and drugs—seeing it as a destroyer of childhood.*

In "Mad Magazine," Winn isolates one cause among many (such as Judy Blume's books, contemporary films, and the rebellion against authority characteristic of the 1960s) for the loss of childhood. Winn researched her book by interviewing parents and children in New York City, Denver, and a small community in upstate New York, to maintain geographical, if not socioeconomic, diversity. (Most of her interviewees were middle-class.) She believes she has tapped a "representative selection of average American parents and children," upon whose experiences she bases her conclusions.

There was once a time when children believed that adults were inevitably good, that all presidents were as honest as Abe Lincoln, that their parents' world was wiser and better than their own child world, a time when children were expected to give up their seats to adults in public conveyances, to reserve strong language for the company of their peers, and in every way to treat adults with "respect." Then along came *Mad* magazine. If there is a single cultural force in the last twenty-five years epitomizing the change that has overtaken childhood, it is that singular publication.

When *Mad* first appeared in the early fifties it was an offshoot of the principal medium of popular child culture of the day—comics. It had a comic-book format, with stories told by cartoon figures speaking via word-filled balloons above their heads. But while comic books of earlier years ran the gamut from "cute" Walt Disney types to the gruesome "Tale of the Crypt" variety of horror comics, nevertheless they all belonged to the category of fantasy, long an accepted adjunct of childhood. Then *Mad* introduced a new element: satire. Before *Mad,* satire traditionally entered young people's lives in late adolescence, often via college humor magazines. *Mad* was the first satirical magazine for children, a sort of Swift for Kids, dealing with children's own reality—their parents, school, and culture—in an irreverent and mocking way. Its readership has grown ever younger, from high-school-age kids in the sixties to nine- and ten-year-olds today.

In the first years, *Mad*'s sharp satirical lance was aimed at the cultural media children were exposed to—old classics, comics, radio, movies, and, with increasing frequency, television. Action comic strips of the *Superman* variety were ridiculed in a feature called "Superduper Man." "Prince Violent" mocked the pseudo-historical genre of comic strip. "Dragged Net" laughed at the "real-life" police dramas that were popular on the radio in the fifties. As television began to take up more of children's free time, a procession of parodies of TV programs and especially commercials began to appear. "From the gaudy grille of Ca-dil-lac to the fins of Che-vro-let. We will push GM's new mo-dels and make obso-les-cence pay!" ran a parody in the late fifties. By 1960 television's pre-eminent position in children's lives was noted by *Mad:* in "A Checklist for Baby-Sitters," the most important consideration for whether to take the job was the condition of the television set. Food, baby-sitting rates, and record player follow shortly. In the last position, as number 10, was the type and number of children to be cared for.

While writers for *Mad* in its first decade chose mainly cultural material to satirize, from the mid-sixties on the focus turned more and more to the child's social environment: parents and the family as an institution. Parents were appalled at the mocking, disrespectful attitude the magazine seemed to encourage towards adults; children adored it, soaked it up like sponges. A feature entitled "If Babies Could Take Parent Pictures," for instance, captions one of its illustrations: "Here's my idiot father trying to drive and take pictures at the same time. I was lucky to get home alive." The phrase "My idiot father" hardly has a jarring sound in the 1980s when much of what kids say to adults is unprintable, but in 1960 the words were shocking. At some point during those two decades a long-established convention came to an end, one that had compelled children to repress their anger and impatience, forcing them to mutter under their breath, perhaps, but rarely allowing them to be openly abusive towards adults. *Mad* magazine may have been more influential in the move towards free expression among children than has heretofore been acknowledged.

As Al Feldstein, editor-in-chief of *Mad* for the past twenty-five years (sometimes known as Chief Madman), describes the change:

"What we did was to take the absurdities of the adult world and show kids that adults are not omnipotent. That their parents were being two-faced in their standards—telling kids to be honest, not to lie, and yet themselves cheating on their income tax. We showed kids that the world out there is unfair, that a lot of people out there are lying to them, cheating them. We told them there's a lot of garbage out in the world and you've got to be aware of it. Everything you read in the papers is not necessarily true. What you see on television is mostly lies. You're going to have to learn to think for yourself."

A relentless parade of features exposing parental hypocrisies caused shock-waves of admiration to reverberate among *Mad*'s young readers (who were not unaware of their older siblings' embattled protests against the more profound hypocrisies of the Great Society as it engaged in the Vietnam "conflict"). For example, a regular feature of the mid-sixties entitled "What They Say and What It Really Means" portrays a mother and father addressing their teenage daughter and her seedy-looking boyfriend: "We have nothing against the boy, darling," is What They Say. "It's just that you're both so terribly young." Then the writers spell out What It Really Means: "Wait until you find a boy of your own religion who's got money"—parental bigotry and venality and hypocrisy knocked down in one fell swoop.

As the sixties wore on towards the seventies and adult culture grew increasingly sophisticated and sexually open, *Mad*'s parodies grew ever more adult themselves, dealing more and more often with adult sexuality, women's liberation, the drug and alcohol scene, and other unchildlike subjects. Movie satires abandoned Walt Disney and appeared with titles such as "Boob and Carnal and Alas and Alfred." A take-off on the song "Matchmaker" from the musical *Fiddler on the Roof* was called "Headshrinker" and included such lines as "I'm Sheila, a free-sex fanatic, I'm Nancy, a speed freak just now, I'm Joy, who makes bombs in the attic, and answers the phone with quotations from Mao," and ended prophetically, "Headshrinker, headshrinker, this is our fate, kids we can't stand, parents we hate."

Child readers of the mid-1970s were now swept along in adult society's increasing preoccupation with sex. "Mom and I are proud of you," says a parent to a teenage daughter in a feature of the 1970s. "We heard that you and Steve were the only students in the history of your college who didn't go to bed together on your first date." The daughter answers via a balloon above her head: "That's true, Dad. But we did make out on a couch, on the floor, etc."

As divorce began to reach epidemic proportions in the second half of the 1970s, *Mad* did not fail to comment on it. A 1975 parody called "Broken Homes and Gardens" had a mother and father who declared that they *weren't* going to get a divorce. "Because of the kids," they explained. "Neither of us wants them." In 1976 appeared "Unweddings of the Future," in which invitations were sent out by the parents of the soon-to-be-ex-bride.

Comparing an issue of *Mad* of the 1980s with one from the 1950s provides an almost shocking view of the change that childhood had undergone in those years. The magazine of December 1980, for example, features a parody of the movie *Little Darlings,* a film about two thirteen-year-old girls at summer camp who have a race to see which of them can lose her virginity first. The *Mad* version includes an outdoor salesman hawking a new kind of children's wares: "Get your training diaphragms here!" he cries. "She's starting foreplay now," a little girl observes as she spies on a pair of prospective mini-lovers. When one of the pubescent heroines gets cold feet during her final seduction scene, her gangly swain protests, "I'm getting frustrated! Y'know, there are NAMES for girls like you!" His partner asks, "Is Crazy Teenager one of them?" He replies, "No . . . but you got the INITIALS right!!!" Will *Mad*'s child readership "get" the allusion? An informal survey of several average seventh-graders suggests that the CT epithet is well known to that age group today.

An ironic footnote: *Little Darlings* received an R rating, officially barring admission to unaccompanied children under seventeen—that is, to almost all *Mad*'s readership. Nevertheless great numbers of pre-teenagers gained access to *Little Darlings,* as they do to many other R movies.

It is almost impossible to imagine children of 1955 openly reading about diaphragms and foreplay. But that was still the Golden Age of Innocence. One of the reasons it was so much easier to maintain children in that special state twenty-five years ago, and why it is impossible to bring it back today, is precisely because in those days movies like *Little Darlings* did not exist.

QUESTIONS

1. What is Winn's thesis? Where is it found in the essay?

2. Does Winn see *Mad* causing the loss of childhood innocence or merely as a reflection of changing attitudes? Explain.

3. How well does Winn's use of the quotation from *Mad*'s Editor-in-Chief support her case? She implies that Feldstein's position is wrong. What does this reveal about her underlying assumptions? Might a reader see something positive in Feldstein's words?

4. How effective are the quotations from the magazine Winn selects to support her case? Discuss several examples. Has she made a convincing case against *Mad?*

5. Is Winn making an indirect argument for censorship? Should certain magazines be kept out of children's hands? Is *Mad* one of them?

6. How does Winn's introduction create a context for her argument? Study the length and structure of the sentences in the introduction. How does Winn use style to reinforce content here?

7. Do you agree with Winn's assertion in paragraph four that "the phrase 'my idiot father' hardly has a jarring sound in the 1980s when much of what kids say to adults is unprintable . . ."? Examine your own language and that of your friends. Is Winn overstating to make a case, or is she being accurate?

SUGGESTION FOR WRITING

Imagine you are a 12 year old whose parents have forbidden your reading *Mad.* What would you say to them in defense of your reading it? What positive effects might reading it have? (If you prefer, choose another age and another magazine— at 17, for example, *Cosmopolitan;* at 18, *Playboy* or *Playgirl.*)

Stephen Jay Gould
LOSING THE EDGE

★ ★ ★

Stephen Jay Gould, one of the most respected science writers in the country today, has won the American Book Award in science (1981) and the National Book Critics Circle Award for general nonfiction (1981). In addition to teaching geology, comparative zoology, and the history of science at Harvard, he writes a monthly column, "This View of Life," for Natural History *magazine. Gould is an ardent opponent of the view that science is a coldly objective, value-free enterprise. Science, according to Gould, is a "creative human activity," carried on within a particular culture, and affected by that environment's biases and assumptions. Cause-and-effect reasoning, which is basic to science, is particularly vulnerable to these influences. In his book* The Mismeasure of Man, *for example, Gould argues that scientists who have tried to prove that certain races or nationalities are biologically inferior have been anything but objective in their practices. In his research he discovered that many eminent scientists had consciously and unconsciously used false data to show a supposed causal relationship between effects (lower scores on standardized IQ tests) and causes (genetic inferiority), because this was a connection their societies assumed existed. Gould believes that when people are aware enough to keep their biases out of the reasoning process, they can legitimately use cause and effect to solve almost any problem.*

In the essay "Losing the Edge," originally published in Vanity Fair, *Gould applies scientific techniques to a problem in a nonscientific field—baseball—with unexpected results.*

I wish to propose a new kind of explanation for the oldest chestnut of the hot stove league—the most widely discussed trend in the history of baseball statistics: the extinction of the .400 hitter. Baseball aficionados wallow in statistics, a sensible obsession that outsiders grasp with difficulty and ridicule often. The reasons are not hard to fathom. In baseball, each essential action is a contest between two individuals—batter and pitcher, or batter and fielder—thus creating an arena of truly individual achievement within a team sport.

The abstraction of individual achievement in other sports makes comparatively little sense. Goals scored in basketball or yards gained in football depend on the indissoluble intricacy of team play; a home run is you against him. Moreover, baseball has been played under a set of rules and conditions sufficiently constant during our century to make comparisons meaningful, yet sufficiently different in detail to provide endless grist for debate (the "dead ball" of 1900–20 versus the "lively ball" of later years, the introduction of night games and relief pitchers, the changing and irregular sizes of ball parks, nature's own versus Astroturf).

No subject has inspired more argument than the decline and disappearance of the .400 hitter—or, more generally, the drop in league-leading batting averages during our century. Since we wallow in nostalgia and have a lugubrious tendency to compare the present unfavorably with a past "golden era," this trend acquires all the more fascination because it carries moral implications linked metaphorically with junk foods, nuclear bombs, and eroding environments as signs of the decline of Western civilization.

Between 1901 and 1930, league-leading averages of .400 or better were common enough (nine out of thirty years) and achieved by several players (Lajoie, Cobb, Jackson, Sisler, Heilmann, Hornsby, and Terry), and averages over .380 scarcely merited extended commentary. Yet the bounty dried up abruptly thereafter. In 1930 Bill Terry hit .401 to become the last .400 hitter in the National League; and Ted Williams's .406 in 1941 marked the last pinnacle for the American League. Since Williams, the greatest hitter I ever saw, attained this goal—in the year of my birth—only three men have hit higher than .380 in a single season: Williams again in 1957 (.388, at age thirty-nine, with my vote for the greatest batting accomplishment of our era), Rod Carew (.388 in 1977), and George Brett (.390 in 1980). Where have all the hitters gone?

Two kinds of explanation have been offered. The first, naïve and moral, simply acknowledges with a sigh that there were giants in the earth in those days. Something in us needs to castigate the present in the light of an unrealistically rosy past. In researching the history of misconduct, I discovered that every generation (at least since the mid-nineteenth century) had imagined itself engulfed in a crime wave. Each age has also witnessed a shocking decline in sportsmanship. Similarly, senior citizens of the hot stove league, and younger fans as well (for nostalgia seems to have its greatest emotional impact on those too young to know a past reality directly), tend to argue that the .400 hitters of old simply cared more and tried harder. Well, Ty Cobb may have been a paragon of intensity and a bastard to boot, and Pete Rose may be a gentleman by comparison, but today's play is anything but lackadaisical. Say what you will, monetary rewards in the millions do inspire single-minded effort.

The second kind of explanation views people as much of a muchness over time and attributes the downward trend in league-leading batting to changes in the game and its styles of play. Most often cited are improvements in pitching and fielding, and more grueling schedules that shave off the edge of excellence.

Another explanation in this second category invokes the numerology of baseball. Every statistics maven knows that following the introduction of the lively ball in the early 1920s (and Babe Ruth's mayhem upon it), batting averages soared in general and remained high for twenty years. League averages for all players (averaged by decade) rose into the .280s in both leagues during the 1920s and remained in the .270s during the 1930s, but never topped .260 in any other decade of our century. Naturally, if league averages rose so substantially, we should not be surprised that the best hitters also improved their scores.

Still, this simple factor cannot explain the phenomenon entirely. No one hit .400 in either league during 1931–40, even though league averages stood twenty points above their values for the first two decades of our century, when fancy hitting remained in vogue. A comparison of these first two decades with recent times is especially revealing. Consider, for example, the American League during 1911–20 (league average of .259) and 1951–60 (league average of .257). Between 1911 and 1920, averages above .400 were recorded during three years, and the leading average dipped below .380 only twice (Cobb's .368 and .369 in 1914 and 1915). This pattern of high averages was not just Ty Cobb's personal show. In 1912 Cobb hit .410, while the ill-fated Shoeless Joe Jackson recorded .395, Tris Speaker .383, the thirty-seven-year-old Nap Lajoie .368, and Eddie Collins .348. By comparison, during 1951–60, only three league-leading averages exceeded Eddie Collins's fifth-place .348 (Mantle's .353 in 1956, Kuenn's .353 in 1959, and Williams's .388, already discussed, in 1957). And the 1950s was no decade of slouches, what with the likes of Mantle, Williams, Minoso, and Kaline. A general decline in league-leading averages throughout the century cannot be explained by an inflation of general averages during two middle decades. We are left with a puzzle. As with most persistent puzzles, what we probably need is a new *kind* of explanation, not merely a recycling and refinement of old arguments.

I am a paleontologist by trade. We students of life's history spend most of our time worrying about long-term trends. Has life gotten more complex through time? Do more species of animals live now than 200 million years ago? Several years ago, it occurred to me that we suffer from a subtle but powerful bias in our approach to the explanation of trends. Extremes fascinate us (the biggest, the smallest, the oldest), and we tend to concentrate on them alone, divorced from the systems that include them as unusual values. In explaining extremes, we abstract them from larger systems and assume that their trends have self-generated reasons: if the biggest become bigger through time, some powerful advantage must attach to increasing size.

But if we consider extremes as the limiting values of larger systems, a very different kind of explanation often applies. If the *amount of variation* within a system changes (for whatever reason), then extreme values may increase (if total variation grows) or decrease (if total variation declines) without any special reason rooted in the intrinsic character or meaning of the extreme value itself. In other words, *trends in extremes* may result from systematic changes in amounts of variation. Reasons for changes in variation are often rather different from proposed (and often spurious) reasons for changes in extremes considered as independent from their systems.

Let me illustrate this unfamiliar concept with an example from my own profession. A characteristic pattern in the history of most marine invertebrates is called "early experimentation and later standardization." When a new body plan first arises, evolution seems to try out all manner of twists, turns, and variations upon it. A few work well, but most don't. Eventually, only a few survive. Echinoderms now come in five basic varieties (two kinds of starfish, sea urchins, sea cucumbers, and crinoids—an unfamiliar group, loosely resembling many-armed starfish on a stalk). But when echinoderms first evolved, they burst forth in an astonishing array of more than twenty basic groups, including some coiled like a spiral and others so bilaterally symmetrical that a few paleontologists have mistaken them for the ancestors of fish. Likewise, mollusks now exist as snails, clams, cephalopods (octopuses and their kin), and two or three other rare and unfamiliar groups. But they sported ten to fifteen other fundamental variations early in their history.

This trend to a shaving and elimination of extremes is pervasive in nature. When systems first arise, they probe all the limits of possibility. Many variations don't work; the best solutions are found, and variation diminishes. As systems regularize, their variation decreases.

From this perspective, it occurred to me that we might be looking at the problem of .400 hitting the wrong way round. League-leading averages are extreme values within systems of variation. Perhaps their decrease through time simply records the standardization that affects so many systems as they stabilize. When baseball was young, styles of play had not become sufficiently regular to foil the antics of the very best. Wee Willie Keeler could "hit 'em where they ain't" (and compile a .432 average in 1897) because fielders didn't yet know where they should be. Slowly, players moved toward optimal methods of positioning, fielding, pitching, and batting—and variation inevitably declined. The best now met an opposition too finely honed to its own perfection to permit the extremes of achievement that characterized a more casual age. We cannot explain the decrease of high averages merely by arguing that managers invented relief pitching, while pitchers invented the slider—conventional explanations based on trends affecting high hitting considered as an independent phenomenon. Rather, the entire game sharpened its standards and narrowed its ranges of tolerance.

Thus I present my hypothesis: the disappearance of the .400 hitter is largely the result of a more general phenomenon—a decrease in the variation of batting averages as the game standardized its methods of play—and not an intrinsically driven trend warranting a special explanation in itself.

To test such a hypothesis, we need to examine changes through time in the difference between league-leading batting averages and the general average for all batters. This difference must decrease if I am right. But since my hypothesis concerns an entire system of variation, then, somewhat paradoxically, we must also examine differences between *lowest* batting averages and the general average. Variation must decrease at both ends—that is, within the entire system. Both highest and lowest batting averages must converge toward the general league average.

I therefore reached for my trusty *Baseball Encyclopedia,* that *vade mecum* for all serious fans (though, at more than 2,000 pages, you can scarcely tote it with you). The encyclopedia reports league averages for each year and lists the five highest averages for players with enough official times at bat. Since high extremes fascinate us while low values are merely embarrassing, no listing of the lowest averages appears, and you have to make your way laboriously through the entire roster of players. For lowest averages, I found (for each league in each year) the five bottom scores for players with at least 300 at bats. Then, for each year, I compared the league average with the average of the five highest and five lowest scores for regular players. Finally, I averaged these yearly values decade by decade.

In the accompanying chart, I present the results for both leagues combined—a clear confirmation of my hypothesis, since both highest and lowest averages approach the league average through time.

THE DECLINE IN EXTREMES

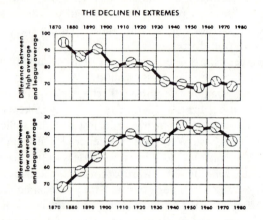

Our decrease toward the mean for high averages seems to occur as three plateaus, with only limited variation within each plateau. During the nineteenth century (National League only; the American League was founded in 1901), the mean difference between highest average and league average was 91 points (range of 87 to 95, by decade). From 1901 to 1930, it dipped to 81 (range of only 80 to 83), while for five decades since 1931, it has averaged 69 (with a range of only 67 to 70). These three plateaus correspond to three marked eras of high hitting. The first includes the runaway averages of the 1890s, when Hugh Duffy reached .438 (in 1894) and all five leading players topped .400 in the same year. The second plateau includes all the lower scores of .400 batters in our century, with the exception of Ted Williams (Hornsby was tops at .424 in 1924). The third plateau records the extinction of .400 hitting.

Lowest averages show the same pattern of decreasing difference from the league average, with a precipitous decline by decade from 71 to 54 points during the nineteenth century, and two plateaus thereafter (from the mid-40s early in the century to the mid-30s later on), followed by the one exception to my pattern—a fallback to the 40s during the 1970s.

Nineteenth-century values must be taken with a grain of salt, since rules of play were so different then. During the 1870s, for example, schedules varied from 65 to 85 games per season. With short seasons and fewer at bats, variation must increase, just as, in our own day, averages in June and July span a greater range than final-season averages, several hundred at bats later. (For these short seasons, I used two at bats per game as my criterion for inclusion in statistics for low averages.) Still, by the 1890s, schedules had lengthened to 130–150 games per season, and comparisons to our own century become more meaningful.

I was rather surprised—and I promise readers that I am not rationalizing after the fact but acting on a prediction I made before I started calculating—that the pattern of decrease did not yield more exceptions during our last two decades, because baseball has experienced a profound destabilization of the sort that calculations should reflect. After half a century of stable play with eight geographically stationary teams per league, the system finally broke in response to easier transportation and greater access to almighty dollars. Franchises began to move, and my beloved Dodgers and Giants abandoned New York in 1958. Then, in the early 1960s, both leagues expanded to ten teams, and in 1969 to twelve teams in two divisions.

These expansions should have caused a reversal in patterns of decrease between extreme batting averages and league averages. Many less than adequate players became regulars and pulled low averages down (Marvelous Marv Throneberry is still reaping the benefits in Lite beer ads). League averages also declined, partly as a result of the same influx, and bottomed out in 1968 at .230 in the American League. (This lamentable trend was reversed by fiat in 1969 when the pitching mound was lowered and the strike zone diminished to give batters a better chance.) This lowering of league averages should also have increased the distance between high hitters and the league average. Thus I was surprised that an increase in the distance between league and lowest averages during the 1970s was the only result I could detect of this major destabilization.

As a nonplaying nonprofessional, I cannot pinpoint the changes that have caused the game to stabilize and the range of batting averages to decrease over time. But I can suggest the sorts of factors that will be important. Traditional explanations that view the decline of high averages as an intrinsic trend must emphasize explicit inventions and innovations that discourage hitting—the introduction of relief pitching and more night games, for example. I do not deny that these factors have important effects, but if the decline has also been caused, as I propose, by a general decrease in variation of batting averages, then we must look to other kinds of influences.

We must concentrate on increasing precision, regularity and standardization of play—and we must search for the ways that managers and players have discovered to remove the edge that the truly excellent once enjoyed. Baseball has become a science (in the vernacular sense of repetitious precision in execution). Outfielders practice for hours to hit the cutoff man. Positioning of fielders changes by the inning and man. Double plays are executed like awesome clockwork. Every pitch and swing is charted, and elaborate books are kept on the habits and personal weaknesses of each hitter. The "play" in play is gone.

When the world's tall ships graced our bicentennial in 1976, many of us lamented their lost beauty and cited Masefield's sorrow that we would never "see such ships as those again." I harbor opposite feelings about the disappearance of .400 hitting. Giants have not ceded to mere mortals. I'll bet anything that Carew could match Keeler. Rather, the boundaries of baseball have been drawn in and its edges smoothed. The game has achieved a grace and precision of execution that has, as one effect, eliminated the extreme achievements of early years. A game unmatched for style and detail has simply become more balanced and beautiful.

QUESTIONS

1. How does Gould use the discoveries of paleontology to supply a new kind of explanation for the extinction of the .400 hitter? What hypothesis emerges?

2. How does Gould go about proving his hypothesis? Does he succeed? How does he explain the results? What historical information does he supply to further explain the statistics?

3. How do Gould's examples help clarify the general points he makes? Find specific instances.

4. Evaluate the essay's language (its level of difficulty, its use of sports jargon). At what audience is Gould aiming? How do you know?

5. Isolate the opening sentences of each of the essay's paragraphs, and study them as transitions. How do they move the reader through each stage of the argument?

6. How does Gould feel about baseball? Justify your response.

SUGGESTION FOR WRITING

Think of a similar "puzzle" in any field you are familiar with—sports, history, entertainment. Discuss the standard explanations, and then offer your own solution. For example, you might discuss the dramatic decrease in the racing time of female runners, the increasing number of people attending college in the past few years despite predictions of a decrease, the extremely high divorce rate in America. You will probably have to do some research, as Gould did.

STUDENT ESSAY

Andy Duncan
WAITING FOR BRUCE

★ ★ ★

Andy Duncan was born in Columbia, S.C., in 1964 and raised in the nearby town of Batesburg. Although his earliest goal was to be a cartoonist, his plans shifted in high school when he began writing parodies of the novels assigned in English class.

Much of his time at the University of South Carolina was spent in the office of the campus newspaper, The Gamecock. *His columns (most of them humorous) eventually earned him a university award for outstanding student journalism. In the following piece, Duncan considers the underlying causes of a recent mass phenomenon and offers some provocative insights on the pleasures of being "part of the crowd."*

Though committed to a career in journalism, Duncan hasn't entirely forsaken his childhood ambition, insisting that he would "still rather draw cartoons than write."

On a cold, drizzly day last fall—the kind of day most people like to park themselves in a warm living room and watch a football game, popcorn or chips near at hand—I watched hundreds of wet but happy customers stand in line outside the local record store, waiting to buy Bruce Springsteen's first live album. It had just gone on sale that day. A harried manager marveled, "I've never had this many people calling on the day an album came out. We're expecting massive sales." In fact, it was quite a sight. The line coming in marched by the line going out, all of it looking, except for the laughter and easy talking, like precision drilling.

I've never liked crowds much (who does?), associating them with department stores where I couldn't breathe, restaurants where I had to wait an hour for a table, stomach growling with hunger, and movie theaters where, after doing patient time in line, I was turned away anyhow because the seats were sold out. Yet here were people eager to be part of a crowd, and a wet, cold crowd at that. By late afternoon of that November 10th, almost every record store in town had sold out and restocked its shelves at least once. The same thing happened in every other city in North Carolina and every other state in the Union. And I wondered why. It made me start to think in a new way about crowds.

When I asked my friends for their opinions about the phenomenon, several eyed me with astonishment and cried, "How can you ask that? Haven't you listened to the record? It's a great album!" Now doubtless this is true, but since when is quality a guarantee of massive sales? When did the Brandenburg Concertos last top the charts? One of the best albums in my meager collection is Randy Newman's *Little Criminals,* released in 1977. It contains many great songs, but its only hit was a song called "Short People," which is not a great song. I bought the album for $2 at Papa Jazz's used record store. So much for greatness as a ticket to ride. Greatness is what my father would call a broke stick.

Another suggested reason for the record turnout was scarcity: Maybe the first-day buyers feared the album would sell out quickly and wanted to be sure they got a copy in time.

Did these customers really believe the world's supply of Springsteen albums was, like oil, a finite resource? That at 3 or 4 in the afternoon of November 10, the last truckload would roar away from the Columbia Records warehouse, leaving the company president dusting his hands on his overalls, mopping his brow with a dingy bandana and saying, "Well, that's all there is. There isn't any more"? Surely not. Everyone knows Columbia hasn't earned its contented capitalist sleep all these years by making music scarce.

The cynics credit the album's success to all the publicity it generated before it was released. "Springsteen must have one fine press agent," a friend of mine said. During the preceding week, radio stations constantly reminded me that Monday would be a Big Day. Magazine and newspaper coverage fed upon itself and begat more coverage. All this no doubt contributed to the crowds.

But if the ballyhoo alone caused people to march in lock-step automation to their neighborhood record stores, why doesn't similar publicity cause similar responses in other cases? How do you explain the utter failure, a few months before the Springsteen album, of a movie called *Howard the Duck?* It also was ballyhooed in *Rolling Stone.* It also was promoted heavily—on television and radio, in newspapers and theaters across the land. I was reminded constantly of its release date; I just didn't care, that's all. No one else in America cared either, except the movie executives who realized they'd spent a big pile of perfectly good money on the cinematic equivalent of the Hindenburg.

Other examples abound, from the new Coke to Pia Zadora. Each reminds us that Americans can make up their own minds without Madison Avenue, thank you very much. Publicity helped Springsteen, but help was all it did.

What really brought all those people to the record stores that day, I believe, is better described than defined, and best described by example.

Picture a fan at a Bruce Springsteen concert. He's in the uppermost rafters of a sold-out house, and down there on stage Bruce looks about as tall as a pencil eraser. But our fan is cheering himself hoarse with the 20,000 other voices in the hall, dancing in place and generally having a blast.

Now. Picture the same fan in the same distant seat, Springsteen and company still down there on that envelope-sized stage—and not a single other spectator in the place. A concert for an audience of one, sitting back in the umpteenth row, all alone in a vast, empty cavern. How much fun would our fan have then?

The difference between seeing a concert live and seeing a concert on television is the crowd. You aren't just watching a performance; you're watching a performance in the same room as thousands of other people who are watching the performance and enjoying it as much as you are. Their enthusiasm feeds your own. And that sharing is what brought you to the concert. The band gets the applause, but the crowd is why you came.

Why do we still attend the World Series in person, when a much better view, not to mention instant replay, is available from the comfort of our living rooms? To be part of the crowd. Why do we still pack movie theaters on weekends to see films that will air on cable television within the year? To be part of the crowd. Why do thousands of fans flock to science fiction conventions and Monopoly tournaments and fiddling exhibitions and fishing jamborees to do things they could as easily do by themselves? To do them as part of a crowd.

All those Springsteen fans headed for the record store on November 10 because they knew a Springsteen crowd would be there, and they wanted to be part of it. Sometimes we all need our fun reinforced by mob action.

A couple of weeks later, the new *Star Trek* movie opened. And there I was with a few hundred friends shoulder-to-shoulder in the movie theater, cheering and laughing and grinning at the screen and at each other. You think I'm going to miss out on a crowd like that? Beam me up, Scotty, in a pink Cadillac!

QUESTIONS

1. What is the question Duncan attempts to answer over the course of his essay? How does that question help him to organize "Waiting for Bruce"? Point to the place in the essay that signals to the reader that Duncan is ready to answer his question.

2. What is the thesis of Duncan's essay, and where is that thesis articulated? What effect would a different organizational scheme have (if, for example, Duncan's thesis were expressed at the beginning of the essay)?

3. Why would Duncan depict the president of Columbia Records as he does? How did you respond to this portrayal?

4. How does Duncan contrast his "old" with his "new" attitude towards crowds? If you have always disliked crowds, does Duncan's essay help you to view them differently?

SUGGESTIONS FOR WRITING

1. Choose a particularly popular rock singer or rock group and write an essay that accounts for the singer's or the group's popularity. If one of the things you argue is that the singer's or group's music is superior to that of other singers, quote some representative lyrics.

2. Describe an occasion in which you were part of a large crowd, a crowd that helped make the occasion more exciting, pleasurable, and memorable than it otherwise would have been. Alternatively, describe an experience made unpleasant or frightening because of the crowd you were part of.

3. Write an essay that explains why, in a democratic civilization that has always had a distrust of elites, Americans seem almost to worship their rock and movie stars. Why do we reward these people so extravagently for their contributions to our civilization?

Ben Brooks
A POSTAL CREED
★ ★ ★

Ben Brooks's unusual story, "A Postal Creed," won Third Prize in the prestigious O'Henry Prize Story competition in 1982. Difficult as it often is to classify literary works according to a rhetorical category (Definition, Comparison/Contrast), "A Postal Creed" is clearly organized around causes and effects. Unlike an essay, however, Brooks's story does not attempt a point-by-point analysis. We do see the effects of the mail carrier's strange behavior, but we are left at the end wondering about the causes. Ben Brooks, born in 1948, is currently a writer-in-residence in the Massachusetts public schools. His stories have been published in The Denver Quarterly, Confrontation, Epoch, *and* Story Quarterly.

He died and a raiding party, led by his wife, scrounged through the attic so there was nothing at all left in two days. He was not that old—still active when his foot ran through a rotten board and dirty splinters shot up the inside of his pants and cut into a muscle and tore it. In the hospital they bandaged him but he developed fever, and then breathing trouble, and then he died. The moment of death seemed to teeter between light and heavy, relief but at the same time a weight, a burden, clotting inside. They ran preservative into his veins and sent him home so the neighbors could see. His wife, looking for an old hat in the attic, came across his collection. Mildewed boxes in a corner, where the roof slanted down and a board underfoot sagged. She took one look and called the authorities, and in two days it was gone. With her old pink hat on she had a sudden panic. She needed to ward off suspicion, that she saw could lick up at her like wild flames, might shoot from angry neighbors, flames with black-tipped scars. One call and it was done.

He had welfare checks, birthday cards, magazines, personal letters, advertisements, packages. Some were not even opened. Some dated back 22 years. He'd been a mailman that long, U. S. Postal Service. He never cashed checks or answered letters, but sometimes he kept what he carried. In one box they found candy gone moldy, and in another two dead mice. Odor burst into the attic when they slit the cardboard. One check was for $400, made out to Randall Grant, from the First City Bank of Trenton.

"Epluribus Jones," the minister said one morning, "a good man." He had a black robe on that came nearly to his wrists, a chain about his neck, a hat in the fashion of Sir Isaac Newton. Epluribus was in an open coffin. His hands were folded over his belt. He lay below the pulpit. They'd left him in the blue-gray uniform of the Postal Service, but clipped the shiny visor of the hat away so the coffin could close. They buried him in the early afternoon. His postal patrons came to watch.

Word of what he'd done spread through the route like fire in a droughted forest. Public outrage, so cleanly focused, does that. Telephones burst with indignation, and windows dropped so neighbors could shout through. It was too late to hush it, the first box found. People want their mail. Lines formed at the Post Office before the flowers on his grave were trampled. People want their mail. They crammed into the waiting room and hovered about the windows, watching for unusual packets. The new widow locked herself in her home, and drew curtains and mourned.

Back mail is a serious thing. One man remembered a magazine he'd never received, though he'd written an angry letter to the publisher. They owed him

12 issues. A woman recalled a welfare check, and another the time she'd been in the hospital and certain people had not sent cards. Everyone wants to know what's what. "A defunct mail-carrier," the dead man's colleague said at the window. "We cannot help now what was done. There's no one here to blame." But he had to apologize. "We're doing the sorting as fast as we can." Households along the route were strung with wire. Information sizzled. What one guessed another dreaded.

The sorting was slow work. Some of the addresses no longer existed. Some patrons had moved, others died. People were angry. Everything was opened before it was handed away. They were looking for a reason. Patrons sat on the high tables in the back of the room, where they bolt the zip code books. Some had it in mind to sue. Others made noise, and tore thick handfuls of government numbers away.

The neighborhood changed quickly in the aftermath. The outrage of mail undelivered boiled over. Consider this: A man with money went to a self-service pump at a gas station on Fourth Street and started pumping gasoline into a huge nylon-skinned balloon. He had the balloon on a trailer hitched to the rear of his car. It was blimp-shape, limp as a dead whale. He filled the balloon tight. Its sides wobbled and gasoline sloshed inside. An iridescent drip salivated down the smooth skin below the mouth of the tank. This was a time of scarcity. Cars curled around the corner and down the street waiting for gas. "I'm going to burn it!" the man shouted. "Money buys!" People shut their engines off to conserve. They froze in their cars. "Money buys!" The man handed the hose to his son, and went from window to window. "I'm going to have an explosion in my backyard and burn the whole goddam thing. Money buys!"

The blimp took shape. The sides of the balloon stretched out. The man's son held the hose tight as a lifeline. "Sheer waste!" the man yelled. "You hear?" His cries spread like dirty vapor and settled into pores. He took the hose from his son when the blimp was full and sprayed gasoline over asphalt. Little rivers formed under cars. The man who owned the station kept his eyes on the meter. He notched on paper each time it turned over. The bill came to $512.72. The man paid fast with cash. People left their cars to throw gravel (and plastic spoons from gutters) at the gorged blimp. The street ran with gas as if the earth had shifted. But the man could afford it. And every Christmas he'd handed Epluribus five dollars, and he'd been shocked that there were three packages undelivered, and a horde of mail in a shoebox.

The owner of the station rushed the rest of his customers through. Why not? He stood by the pump keeping tally on his notepad. He had a greasy blue jacket and a square gray hat with a fur rim turned up on all four sides. "OK, OK," he said, "next one, come on, help yourself now." But every patron was dripping gasoline on the ground and paying for it. Even the poorest, at least one squirt. The owner stuffed money in his pockets. His station ran out of gas, sucked dry. Waiting cars drove off skidding into curbs. The owner left for home two hours early, fat with money. And a twice frustrated customer bought a mousetrap with a razor bar, which he set for the new mailman in the letter slot of his door.

The biggest upset was never mail that had been expected but not received. That already had a niche in the brain—mail always known, finally explained. The biggest upset became mail never even suspected. There were letters from long-lost lovers, scribbled invitations, notes telling of small inheritances or announcing deaths, learned six years late.

A man from Washington came to supervise the sorting. Some pieces were impossible to identify. Epluribus had shed their envelopes. The man did not dare hang them naked on the Post Office boards. Too many prowling cats. They would fight over each piece—every claim a bullet to fire later in court. They were waiting for the whole episode to come to an end. Then it would be clear what damages could be pulled. A few brought lawyers to sit with them in the rear of the Post Office, paying out by the hour and supplying coffee.

The minister, the wife, the man himself, the neighbors. Members of the congregation signed an official reprimand, a castigation, because the minister said, "good man." Some demanded his recall by higher church officials. The wife was harassed until she nailed shut her windows and silenced her phone, and the man himself was bombarded in his box by invective and acid, and hot earth turned mucousy liquid seeped into his space. Neighbors raged and howled but never felt justice. The Postal Inspector kept turning up at their doors with new pieces of mail. The thing could not seem to end. One was a letter from an old friend suggesting a reunion, long missed, and another gave news from a hometown of four years back. Anger did not seem to affect time, and information, delayed, turned rotten like fruit and spoiled and brought bugs and worms and fast-breeding germs.

Can it be part of a man, those aspects divulged in others' dreams and fantasies? Epluribus, melting down with spring, face still frozen in the stiff cloth hat, was here an agent of death, there nailed to a brick wall, pelted with small stones. In one dream he lay before stampeding horses, and they parted to run by, avoiding trampling him. He was little known out of uniform, and regarded only as a messenger. Is it then part of his being how he acts in another man's dream, or what role he takes in another's life? "People waiting to hear," postmen mutter. They watch the crowd nervously. The postal creed inches foolishly along the walls of the waiting room, repeated sarcastically by patrons. It is always Epluribus they picture. Tempers are short. His widow tucked his old mailbag under her mattress, out of sight. Along its cracks the leather is clean and golden. The brass buckles holding the straps are spotted. "Neither rain nor snow," they echo, as if an operator were tapping it out of them at intervals.

The coffin was shut tightly but the treated wood leaked, and Epluribus lay waiting for the ground around him to thaw. The graveyard was a new one where the grass was clipped as carefully as hair, but over Epluribus it was burned bare by chemicals. It employed two watchmen but already his headstone was knocked to the ground. The ropes that had laid him to rest had tangled so his feet were higher than his head. His widow did not dare to mourn him in public. People came by her house throwing pebbles at windows, and at night they shone flashlights, and rang the front door buzzer in calm hatred.

One piece of mail said:

Dear Sarah,
I love you like I never loved before. I would like to be your husband.

It was unsigned and out of envelope. The supervisor from Washington and the postal employees over his shoulder could only imagine consequences—the spurned lover, never answered; unaware Sarah, seeming cold. Was she married? Was he? Had they gotten together anyway? They tucked the little letter on crinkly blue paper into the corner of a blotter in the back of the Post Office, a reminder of duty's sacredness. Epluribus's box in the ground was mahogany, and lined with red velvet, but in the dark there were no longer colors, and his serious look, sewed on, was for none but himself. Some letters he'd burned on a wooden keg in the attic, careful with the ashes, and some he'd read in private, and others just stashed. Dead leaves from a nearby oak, brown and crisp, stuck to the bare earth above him like litter, but they were too light to be felt. The wind pulled at them, the sharp points of the leaves dancing and tickling the ground. When dogs outside the gate stopped to bark at the stillness, he could not hear, but when some of his old neighbors pissed on his grave, they slowly soaked through, and the ground, poisoned, tried to close off, pinching in on his coffin. No one would be buried near him. Former colleagues began to snicker at the letter to Sarah, malignantly glad, and they added comments around the edges of the page, obscenities penned unobserved. Is it Epluribus, really, whose spirit informs the woman her son's been killed in battle, or who withholds that information from another? Never opening the envelope he's slipped into his leather bag's side pocket, letting lies and impossible hopes bloom like deadly flowers in a mind, unwatered. Or is a messenger just a messenger—legs, a hand, a voice; blank eyes, no will?

Washington transferred the postmaster to another station, but brought no charges. He was bitter and became sloppy. He left a proud gray building deteriorating, its corners still clean and sharp, its door high, but marred with slogans in red. A window was broken, and early one morning a dozen rotten eggs were cracked over its steps. How far does a man's responsibility go? If he is unconscious of the results of his deeds, or sees them from his own perspective, can he still be blamed, or praised? If, careless, he causes an accident in his wake, and another is hurt—but he never even knows of the accident—is that guilt part of him? Behind Epluribus people grieved, and they raged, and a few laughed, looking to their day in court. And the postmaster too, the superior. The whole neighborhood changed because one simple operation, that was always taken for granted, caught on a hook and ripped, and showed the gray slimy veins of its underside. Was this Epluribus, a force of social change? Or was he just a man with a perverse delight, who took pleasure in vexing certainty, and disturbing the routine of his job?

New lawyers set up offices in the neighborhood, and unhappy people moved away. Postal patrons waited one behind the next, unsure which tack would work best: deprivation of mail, mental anguish, fraud and deceit, theft, trespassing. They multiplied damages, considered class action, tabulated fantastic figures. The rich man who'd explode a blimp in his yard felt an ulcer form in his bowels like a small planet, wondering what else he was missing—and with vengeance he set about teaching his son. The hose-bearer. His lesson was ruthlessness.

Epluribus Jones passed through seasons in his box, always rotting. His skin wrinkled and peeled back at his nails, his nose withered away, and his knee turned in the box to an almost impossible angle because its weight shifted when cartilage dropped off. His widow advertised the house for sale but no one would touch it. When the real estate woman brought out customers there was always a neighbor on hand to tell a bad story, a curse. They invented pasts more hideous than fact, and when she threatened to take them to court they laughed, saying, "try it." Neighborhood values fell daily. All about the widow Jones lots were sold. Signs stood on abandoned yards like flags, and developers and gangsters began competing for blocks, eager for control.

The whole neighborhood turned over except for the widow Jones. She took a second husband and kept her house. He was a new man in town. He yanked the nails from the windows. Values rose. Patrons relocated without suing, but remembered Epluribus and watched their new postmen with suspicion. In his grave Epluribus was down to bone and teeth. His box had rotted through and anything seeped in. The husband wanted to move but the widow Jones said no. It was their first test, a fight. Around them new apartment buildings swelled up, a storefront, a restaurant. He could have gotten a lot of money for the lot. Her own sign was still in the yard, rusting, but she rebuffed all callers.

It appeared the developers outbid the gangsters. Everything looked clean. Cold brown veneers dropped down over walls and floors, and workmen speckled red bricks with white. Men in suits came to the widow Jones, now Mrs. Martin, to talk to her about selling. They carried vinyl briefcases with polished clasps. They mentioned fantastic money, but she refused. Her new husband sat silently, listening.

Epluribus was eventually forgotten. The cemetery was plowed and developed, headstones turned under the earth with bodies. New postmen walked new routes, one after another. The new neighborhood sunk naturally into its site, as if the earth and the streets made a cradle for it. Children were born and went to school, couples fought, old men and women died. Brown walls faded gray. Floors, stepped across too often, cracked. The reputation of the neighborhood was solid. Bad citizens stood out like lights, and were watched and talked about until they moved away. Everything changed in cycles except Mrs. Martin—the old woman with a lot that stuck out like one bad debt. On real estate maps she was colored bright green. Her For Sale sign was pure rust, and its edges crumbled to the touch.

Time runs like a dump truck downhill. If the hill is long enough, and circles back, eventually everything is squashed. The mischief wrought by Epluribus mattered less and less, as the people whose mail he'd kept died, or forgot, or lost interest. A woman who might have married was now dead anyway. A book never read—so what? News, a few dollars here and there, hurt feelings, suspense. The ones left were all in their seventies and had more important things on their minds. Mrs. Martin was 82 herself. She still held on to the cracked mail pouch, which now hung on a nail on the wall. She fed old Mr. Martin, who'd had a stroke, by spoon, and listened to radio.

Epluribus's bones had been well used in cement. What was left behind fed grass. His eyes, his set face, his mind, the reasons he'd had for jettisoning expectations were as dead as he. Only the pouch remained—the old wife, the old house—to remember. But what was in her heart she never said. She pinched old Mr. Martin's chin to force open his lips, and slipped in the spoon. He'd never understood why she would not sell, and now that was too late too. He'd left his own life for hers. Even that did not matter—he was beyond caring or resenting. He waited for the spoon, eyes rolling downward: warm cereal dropped below his tongue and settled out in a pool; an occasional surprise of cold; something gristly to chew.

Then the neighborhood went to gangsters. They were a new kind, who did not worry about appearances. Pinball machines went up in lobbies, rents were raised, repairs were forgotten. Weapons became as common as shoes. Mrs. Martin added a new lock to each door, and tucked the old mailbag back under the mattress. She was old enough to remember Epluribus and wonder—not why he had stolen the mail he had been trusted to deliver, but why he'd never shared his secret with her, why he'd doubted her. Maybe he learned from himself not to trust. If you cheat, but seem not to, then others who seem innocent must be suspected as well. Epluribus must have been a suspicious man, she decided, not to have trusted her. He led her back to the past, where there were soft cushions for her mind. But she could not think what could have caused doubt, until she remembered her own secrets too.

She remembered a time she'd been unable to explain where some money he'd given her had gone. Weeks had passed, and she'd forgotten how she'd spent it. He'd shaken her shoulders with anger. Spats and fights, half-heard telephone conversations came back. Questions, denials, stone silence. The past became clear as television to her, and episodes were pictures, and voices were as they had always been. Mr. Martin had gotten worse, but she'd refused to let him leave the house for a hospital. If he needed anything he turned his wrist and a bell tinkled. It tinkled too when he died. She had her groceries delivered, her laundry taken out, and used the phone for the plumber and a cleaning woman.

Mr. Martin's funeral was in an urn. She knew there was no point in burial. They put him in a lot with sharp green grass, and gravel paths marked by flowers in spring. He had a eulogy but not much more. His body flamed nicely, nearly dried out when they lit it. His skin flaked earlier when he was on exhibit, but no one noticed. No one even walked by. In the new cemetery headstones were in rows a foot apart, nine inches between rows. Ceramic vessels were stoppered tightly to preserve ashes.

Mr. Martin had left home far away to marry the widow Jones. He had always thought he would take her back with him. She had always refused to come. In the years that passed he lost touch back home, but never laid new roots. He worked for a time as a dress designer, and for a while he ran a store. When all the new buildings went up he got a job in one, semi-retired as desk clerk and watchman. A few people nodded hello when he gave them their messages. The gangsters left him alone.

Epluribus Jones did one unexpected thing in his life. Perhaps that is why he did it—he did not want to be only what others thought he was. Then they imagined other things of him, outrageous things, things he never was except in their thoughts. His wife clung to his memory trying to explain. He stayed clear and pink when everything else was gray. Why he did what he did, why he kept it a secret, whether it made him a different man from the one she knew. When she married she held Mr. Martin as if by a chain to her need to remember—the house, the cracked bag on the wall—until his own past withered away. Epluribus died first, victim of a long sick splinter. Then Mr. Martin, then their wife. In the end the only thing that was there to mark change was the neighborhood, turned to trash. The people who wept and the people who raged, the rich man who poured gasoline into a nylon blimp and burned it, and the lawyers who wanted to sue—they all died too. Some left children, but few remembered to pass on the story. It was old in its time. And none knew all its meanings. Even the son who held the hose for his father died, worn out in the end by greed and hostility. But the tale exists—here it is—the facts, apart from their memory. And the feelings they engendered, and the consequences, and the people who watched from the periphery, and made it a small part of their own stories. And what they learned, what they all learned. Once it occurred its permanence was assured, until such time as everything is washed over. Even death to participants, broken links in the chain of memory, have not erased past. Turn it as you will. Epluribus kept the mail, and did not tell his wife. The neighborhood festered and changed. Someone remembered.

QUESTIONS

1. Describe the long-term effects of Jones's action on the community. Can you explain them?

2. What significance does the letter carrier's name have? Why does Brooks spend so much time describing him in the grave?

3. Respond to the Brooks's question: "Was this Epluribus a force of social change? Or was he just a man with a perverse delight, who took pleasure in vexing certainty, and disturbing the routine of his job?" Does the story provide an answer?

4. Images of deterioration occur throughout the story. Underline some and discuss their importance to the story's point.

5. Structurally, the narrative alternates between what is happening to Jones and what is happening to the neighborhood. Why has the author chosen this structure?

SUGGESTION FOR WRITING

Think of some habitual activity in your life that everyone expects you to do. Imagine yourself openly or secretly stopping it. Tell the story of why you stopped and of the effects your stopping had—on yourself and others.

Donald W. Baker
PROFESSOR

Donald W. Baker, Milligan Professor of English and poet-in-residence at Wabash College, has been teaching for over 35 years—a long time, as his poem confirms. Baker's poems and stories are cryptic yet accessible, full of closely observed detail and personal reflection. Many reveal his lifelong concern with how politics impinges on the individual life; his World War II experiences as a navigator on a bomber infused him with a strong antipathy for war, and he writes, in part, "out of anger and frustration and fear for my children and grandchildren." Like many poets, who often meditate on causes and effects, Baker frequently asks "why?" and "what if?" In "Professor" he looks back on a career of college teaching, weighing its effects and considering alternatives.

Baker's books of poetry are Twelve Hawks and Other Poems *(1974),* Formal Application: Selected Poems, 1960–1980 *(1982), and* Unposted Letters and Other Poems *(1984).*

You turn thousands, millions
of pages, one by one, under bulbs
twitching like eyelids. Then you
look up, and your life scuttles
under a bookshelf. There you sit,
framed: Statue With Necktie. When
the beak clacks, the brain splits,
spills out mistakes in a pulp.
I'm one of them, garrulous always,
everything dies into words,
ambition, love, laid out in long

phrases. I should dump my family,
go to Toronto. That's a silly
death, that wanting to be unborn.
Or shave my head, smoke my
way through Yucatán with dope
and machete. A friend of mine
did that, all the way into 590
AD or thereabouts, altar, dead
gods, the world's belly, he said,
scarlet and green with macaws.
Then he came back with a beard,
a feathered professor, Statue
With Beak, clacking away, sounding
like five thousand years. I should
try something rash, for God's sake,
hunt for umbilical truth. Jog
into Uganda. Swim the Zambesi. Why?
I'd climb out, tie my tie, reappear,
still shedding words, turning pages.

QUESTIONS

1. Explain the line "everything dies into words."

2. Deduce Baker's attitude about being a professor from specific words and images in the poem.

3. Why does Baker switch from the second person pronoun ("you") to the first person pronoun ("I") in the ninth line of his poem? What is the effect of this change?

SUGGESTION FOR WRITING

Try your hand at writing a poem, using Baker's as a model, on the effects on yourself or someone else of a profession or role you are familiar with ("mother," "father," "doctor," "student," "brother," "daughter," "waiter," "soccer player"). Whenever possible, find images to carry your meaning instead of abstract words—show instead of tell.

CHAPTER *Six*

SCIENCE AND TECHNOLOGY
Process Analysis

Process analysis—the technique of describing, in a strict, chronological sequence, precisely how something is (or was) done—is such a specialized type
of exposition that it might seem to be of limited use. There are, however,
countless occasions when writers find it indispensable. Indeed, a glance at
newsstand magazines and best-selling books suggests that, of all forms of nonfiction writing, process analysis may well be the most popular.

Perhaps because Americans are such an optimistic and practical-minded
people, who believe that there is no problem in life that can't be solved with
a little bit of "Yankee know-how," we seem to have an insatiable appetite for
works which assure us that, merely by following a simple, step-by-step plan, we
can achieve complete happiness: lose weight, win friends, get rich quick, overcome our fears and inhibitions. "Women's" magazines like *McCall's, Ladies
Home Journal,* and *Good Housekeeping* consist in large part of process articles,
offering explicit instructions on various activities, from makeup to child care,

sewing to sex. A single issue of *Family Circle* might run the recipe for the world's richest, seven-layer Devil's Food cake, followed immediately by directions for a foolproof, ten-day, "New You" diet. Meanwhile, "men's" magazines like *Popular Mechanics, Guns & Ammo,* and *Field & Stream* tell their readers how to build their own thirty-foot, backyard dish antennas, fine tune the scopes on their Winchesters, and improve their flycasting technique. And of the hundred or so sale books listed in a recent advertisement for Barnes & Noble, one of New York City's largest bookstores, nearly all were self-help, or "how to," manuals.

Even popular fiction often exploits the public's boundless interest in knowing how things work. Police procedural novels like Ed McBain's "87th Precinct" series, for example, give readers an insider's view of the criminal investigation process. The novels of Frederick Forsyth, best-selling author of *The Day of the Jackal, The Dogs of War,* and others, contain so much information on subjects like gun-running, passport forgery, and assassination techniques that they sometimes read like do-it-yourself guides for aspiring mercenaries.

Process writing is so common that you don't have to search through a bookshelf or magazine rack to find examples; all you have to do is open a kitchen cabinet and glance at a box of Jello, cake mix, "minute rice," instant soup, or any other convenience food that comes with printed directions. The sort of process writing found on such packages is usually described as *instructional* (its only purpose is to deliver straightforward instructions), and is so pervasive that is hard to imagine existing without it. Instructional process writing appears in the owner's manuals that tell us how to set up and operate our appliances. It allows us to pursue our hobbies and develop new skills—to teach ourselves how to paint, play the guitar, take better photographs, restore antiques. It makes it possible for the most unskilled homeowners to perform their own household repairs. Indeed—since cookbooks consist mainly of this type of process writing—it even has a daily impact on our diets.

Instructional process writing is meant, in effect, to simulate the voice of a teacher or guide, so it generally uses the present tense and imperative mood, as though the writer were delivering a direct command to the reader. This is the same way we speak when we give verbal directions ("Go three blocks south on Main Street, then make a left at the first traffic light") or instructions ("Don't grip the racket so tightly. Loosen up a bit. Now keep an eye on the ball . . ."). In his book *Entertaining Science Experiments with Everyday Objects,* for example, Martin Gardner instructs readers in the method of watermark writing, "a novel, little known way to write secret messages":

> Dip a sheet of blank paper in water, place it on a smooth, hard surface (such as a windowpane or mirror), and cover it with a dry sheet. Write on the dry sheet, using a hard lead pencil and firm pressure. Discard the dry sheet. You will find the writing clearly visible on the wet one. The writing will vanish without a trace when the paper dries, but will reappear when the sheet is dipped in water.

Occasionally, instructions are written in the second person ("you") and future tense ("Before proceeding with these instructions, you will need the following materials"). Both styles, of course, serve the same end—that of enabling readers to perform an unfamiliar procedure by following a sequence of clearly defined steps. To clarify his instructions even more, Gardner also provides a simple drawing of the set-up for his clever technique. In fact, written directions are often accompanied by drawings, particularly when they explain a complicated procedure. While instructional writing is vital to many areas of our lives, it is limited, for the most part, to practical uses. As a result, you will probably do less of it in the average composition course than in your day-to-day life. (For instance, having invited a new friend to your home for dinner, you might be asked to write out the directions to your house. Afterwards, the same person, having raved about a dessert you've concocted, might request a copy of the recipe.)

Like the selections reprinted in this chapter, most of your own essays will require a somewhat different, but related, approach. This type of writing—sometimes called *informational*—describes the stages of some interesting procedure to show how it is (or was) accomplished. Here, the writer's intention is to explain or analyze a process, not tell readers how to duplicate it. Popular books and magazines are full of informational process writing. There is not a single issue of *Time* or *Newsweek,* for instance, that does not contain at least one or two examples of it, features that analyze how a revolutionary invention (such as the artificial heart) works, how a daredevil commando raid on a hijacked jetliner was carried out, how a complicated bit of international diplomacy was negotiated. Best-sellers explain everything from the operation of the cosmos to the inner workings of the human body to the secrets behind the special effects in *Star Wars.* The world is full of invisible processes—biological, technological, geophysical—which, with our passion for practical knowledge (and impatience with unsolved mysteries), we love to have explained.

While the selections in this chapter analyze a wide range of processes, they share a similar style. Unlike instructional writing, which, in the manner of a cookbook recipe, breaks a procedure down into short (often numbered) directions, informational process writing generally takes the form of a continuous narrative. Sometimes it uses the first person (as in the pieces by D. Keith Mano and David Sudnow), while at other times it uses the third (as in the case of the Richard Selzer selection). This type of process analysis can also be written in either the present tense ("He folds her scarf into a triangle, places it across her forehead and ties two ends of it at the back of her head") or the past ("To give him the shorter and pudgier legs of youth, they lowered his pants line and covered up his spindly legs with a baggy outfit").

You can see how informational process writing differs stylistically from instructional process writing by comparing the two examples below, taken from Ernest Hemingway's famous short story "The Big Two-Hearted River," which concerns a young veteran of the First World War named Nick Adams, who has recently returned from overseas and is taking a restorative fishing trip in the Michigan woods. Here, the author describes, in meticulous detail, how Nick finds and clears a place to pitch his tent. The paragraph on the left is Hemingway's original prose; on the right is the same material, recast in the form of instructions:

PROCESS INFORMATION	PROCESS INSTRUCTION
The ground rose, wooded and sandy, to overlook the meadow, the stretch of river and the swamp. Nick dropped his pack and rod-case and looked for a level piece of ground. He was very hungry and wanted to make his camp before he cooked. Between two jack pines, the ground was quite level. He took the ax out of the pack and chopped out two projecting roots. That leveled a piece of ground large enough to sleep on. He smoothed out the sandy soil with his hand and pulled all the sweet fern bushes by their roots. His hands smelled good from the sweet fern. He smoothed the uprooted earth. He did not want anything making lumps under the blankets. When he had the ground smooth, he spread his three blankets. One he folded double, next to the ground. The other two he spread on top.	1. Look for a level piece of ground, preferably between two pine trees. Using your ax, chop out any projecting roots. 2. Smooth out the soil with your hands and remove all fern bushes by their roots. Smooth the uprooted earth. 3. To make a bed, fold one of your blankets double and lay it on the ground. Then, spread the remaining two blankets on top.

At times, an entire essay might be devoted to the analysis of a process. In your own classes you might be required to write a science paper explaining how the dinosaurs disappeared, a history essay tracing the chain of events that led to the outbreak of the Civil War, or an English exam analyzing the stages a fictional character passes through in his journey from childhood innocence to adult wisdom.

At other times, a process explanation might appear as only a small part of a larger piece of writing. The popular science writer Carl Sagan, for example, begins an essay on space exploration called "The Sun's Family" by tracing, in two paragraphs, the 4.6 billion year development of the Earth.

Depending on your purpose, process analysis can be used either to support an argument or simply to present information. Your thesis statement should, of course, express your intention. If your aim is to persuade, you will need a forceful thesis: "Anyone who has ever visited a meat packing plant and seen the slaughtering process firsthand can never feel comfortable about eating beef again" or "Because they can be such humiliating and, on occasion, even lethal procedures, fraternity hazings should be outlawed from American colleges." On the other hand, the thesis for an essay that intends to do nothing more than explain a process can be as simple as "Repairing a carburetor is much easier than most people think" or "There is a new device on the market that allows amateur photographers to develop color pictures at home in three easy steps."

Whether you are offering information or instructions, the rules for writing a process paper are always the same. (The following advice might be titled, "How to Write a How-to Paper.")

1. Before you begin writing your essay, review the entire process in your mind. Visualize all the steps in the order you would perform them and, if necessary, jot them down in a simple list. Occasionally, a newspaper prints a recipe that accidentally omits a crucial piece of information, and the angry letters subsequently sent in by readers who have dutifully followed the directions only to end up with a tasteless pot roast or an inedible apple pie attest to a fundamental precept of process writing: Never leave out any essential steps.

On the other hand, it is not necessary to spell out every trivial detail. If, for example, you were writing instructions on how to replace a faulty electrical outlet, it would be enough to say that the reader should start the procedure by shutting off the power. You would not have to write," First, walk over to the fuse box and, after opening the little metal door, unscrew the appropriate fuse, using either hand."

2. If the process you are analyzing is large and complex, begin by breaking it down into several main stages. Let us say that you are writing a paper on how Hollywood movies are made. One logical way of approaching this task would be to divide the process into three major parts and then describe the steps within each. Here is what the outline for such a paper might look like:

I. Preproduction
   A. Writing the screenplay
   B. Casting the film
   C. Scouting the locations

II. Production
   A. Direction
   B. Cinematography
   C. Special effects

III. Postproduction
   A. Editing the "final cut"
   B. Adding the soundtrack music
   C. Promotion and distribution

3. Remember that, while it is perfectly acceptable—indeed, unavoidable at times—to use technical language, you should (as in all of your writing) keep the amount of jargon you use to a minimum and make sure to define any terms that are likely to be unfamiliar to your readers. Notice how, in the following paragraph from an essay on the making of the original *King Kong,* the authors take care to define a key term, stop-motion animation:

> The main technique used to bring King Kong to life was stop-motion animation. This method exploits a type of magic that is uniquely cinematic: it can be performed solely by means of a motion picture camera. Essentially, stop-motion consists of taking a small model (generally of some awesome creature, either extinct or mythological), arranging it in a certain pose, shooting a frame of film, making a slight change in the position of the model, shooting another frame of film, and so on. On screen, the rapid progression of individually photographed frames creates an illusion of continuous movement, a kind of three-dimensional flipbook effect. Although rumors still persist that, for some scenes in the movie, the giant ape is played by a man in a monkey suit, the truth is that Kong was never anything but an animated model, eighteen-inches high, with a metal skeleton, sponge-rubber muscles, and skin made out of clipped rabbit fur.

The audience you are writing for will, of course, determine exactly which terms you need to define. The selection above is obviously addressed to the "general reader," someone with little or no specialized knowledge of cinematic technique. By contrast, the following excerpt, from an article that appeared in the trade journal *American Cinematographer,* is addressed to an audience of professionals and relies heavily on technical language in explaining how one of the effects in *Raiders of the Lost Ark* was created:

> Then we tackled the problem of creating the ghosts. . . . We had a girl who was featured in only one of the shots. We made her up and flew her around on a wire rig. I shot the plates of her in sharp focus and then rear-projected them through an inversion layer in a tank in order to achieve confusion and to break up the image. . . . Once I had her image, I shot a skeleton to match, lining it up by projection to get the effect of a "live" ghost turning into the face of Death. We then did a white-in optical and rear-projected that element through a tank. . . . This was done using our motion-control camera and high-speed track, with a rear-projector in synchronization.

4. Because a process is a chronological sequence of events, it is important to use transitions to clarify the precise order and timing of the steps. Words and phrases like "then," "as soon as," "afterwards," and "following this" show readers exactly how and when one stage leads to the next; when two or more steps occur simultaneously, terms like "meanwhile" and "at the same time" are required. Notice the use of such transitional "time-indicators," which are italicized, in the following excerpt from a printed recipe for a layer cake:

Measure 3 cups of the batter into each pan. Bake for 10 minutes. *Then* quickly reverse the pans top to bottom and front to back to insure even baking. Bake for 3 to 5 minutes more until the tops of the cakes spring back when lightly pressed with a fingertip. They will be a pale golden color when done. *While* the cakes are baking spread out two smooth linen or cotton towels. *As soon as* the layers are done, invert them onto the towels. Quickly remove the pans, peel off the paper linings, and cover each layer loosely with a second smooth linen or cotton towel. Let stand until cool.

Meanwhile, prepare the buttercream.

5. Process writing is always in danger of becoming monotonous, of lapsing into "First this happens, then this happens, then this happens, then this happens. . . ." The best way to avoid this flaw is to inject some variety into your sentence structure. In the following excerpt, karate expert Don Ethan Miller recounts an embarrassing attempt to shatter a brick with his bare hands during a demonstration before a Russian audience:

My Russian friends proudly produced a construction brick easily twice the size and three times the weight of the baked red bricks I was accustomed to splitting back home. Undaunted, I set it precisely to bridge the space between a pair of similar bricks laid parallel on the stage floor. I knelt, and held one end of the brick slightly off the base with my left hand. Rising slightly from my kneeling position, I inhaled, raised my right hand in a short arc up to shoulder level, and then, yelling sharply, brought my clenched fist down with the full force of my body behind it, tightening all my muscles just at the moment of impact to transmit the force into the stone. Nothing happened. I felt a dull pain in the base of my hand, and the shock wave of the blow traveled back up my arm and shoulder. No matter; this sometimes happens if the blow is not exactly right. I immediately reset the oversize brick and struck down again, quickly, absolutely as hard as I could. But again, it merely smacked into the base brick and stopped.

Notice how Miller avoids repetition by varying the length, complexity, and syntax of his sentences. In this way he is able to turn a potentially dull subject—a description of how he hit a brick several times—into a vivid, even dramatic, piece of process writing.

D. Keith Mano
PLASTIC SURGERY
★ ★ ★

If a prize were awarded to the Professional Writer With the Most Offbeat Resumé, the winner might well be D. Keith Mano, whose career highlights include acting with England's National Shakespeare company and serving as vice president of a New York City cement company called X-Pando. Novelist, essayist, and critic, Mano has published articles and reviews in various magazines (he is a frequent contributor to Playboy*) and writes a regular column, "The Gimlet Eye," for* National Review. *Among his novels are* Bishop's Progress *(1968),* Horn *(1969),* The Death and Life of Harry Goth *(1971), and* The Bridge *(1973).*

"Plastic Surgery" originally appeared in the November 13, 1981 issue of the National Review.

——————

Her right breast is cut: slit open like fresh tallow beneath: a two-inch incision under the hang of it. Dr. James Reardon has spread her wound for me. Red fat tissue, the meat of breasts, is glossy there: not good eating, I think: over-rich. With an electric scalpel-cautery, Reardon will slice and slice through this ragged human packing. The instrument snaps blue sparks out: cut, coagulate, cut. Occasionally some minute vessel will spray fine blood, then stanch.

After a minute the breast and underlying muscle are loose, up. Reardon starts to rummage in. With a retractor light I can see the super-nudity of rib cage and this hollow pouch he has made behind her small pap. We strip-search it: crimson, lit, shaggy-fibered inside: a weird vest pocket. As you stuff throw pillows, Reardon has begun to push the colorless silicone implant in. Her bosom is swelling with false pride now. The implant, more sinuous than gelatin, a good female impersonator, squeezes through that two-inch gash. No, not large enough yet: she'll want, Reardon guesses, to be built better than this. Next size up, please. Her snub and gnarled nipple lolls, orange with antiseptic, while Reardon is coaxing the glib implant out. And I am disconcerted. There's so little blood: so little *to* a female breast, which things have long been the business and quick speculation of my male eye.

I am, after all, in a strange protectorate: sterile mayhem is customary here. The kind assumptions we hold about flesh—personal nature, erotic value, tenderness—do not prevail in an operating room. I touch my scrub-suited arm. Skin plates us over: muscle can engage and disengage power: the breast is, well, an appendage not often of use. Dr. Reardon has practiced plastic surgery for 11 years: you, she may trust his deft bloodshed. Nothing I say is meant to judge or impugn him: I admire his frankness and generosity. Yet, being not native to the land, I find it all grotesque: that female breast stuff can be holed in such dispassion: the way, once, I slit calfskin with a child's leather-working kit. This woman will never, except before God, be so hugely undressed. She is lying now, unsutured still, phony-glamorous: alluring to all men but we four who know. From each flesh rip, as from a socket, I watch one glassy silicone eye blear out. It alienates me. She has begun to look mechanical: unalive inside. Flesh just a housing for some android gadgetry.

"That black bag," I ask the anaesthetist, "why d'you keep squeezing it?"

"Well, her diaphragm is paralyzed now. I have to breathe for her. See." He will clutch at the bag. Her servile ribs fan out: aaaah, she is inspired by him. A hobgoblin moment: I think what enormous surrogate forces are around me. But I don't experience outrage for her: she of the manipulated wind. By a Silastic voluptuousness this woman intends to paralyze and cause swelling in men. For that power, I find it all appropriate, she should trade some of her nature away.

Their patter—surgeon, assistant, anaesthetist—has the tick-whirr that fine clock escapements have. Unemphatic, even in tenor: low: a good beat to thread skin by. It is, I think, the way we talk among foreigners: expressionless, so that they cannot translate face or tone: this foreign body here, for one. And the irreverence, the *M*A*S*H* note, will disinvolve. "Let's stuff her with raisins and walnuts, huh?" "Has the guy from NATIONAL REVIEW fainted yet?" "Great, great: she can hire out as a ship's figurehead now." I like their irony: it settles me down. I trust them more, certainly, than I do the patient: who is torn and mindless: who would admonish my complacent flesh. This group-practiced chat is, anyhow, preferable to silence. Silence might announce tension. As when, later, we do a nose job.

"Rhinoplasts aren't my favorite," the anaesthetist has told me. "They're messy. The patient's fairly light at that point—we put them to sleep only actually for the injections. Then they're awake after the nose is all numbed. But they're groggy. They usually have no recall, but they're on spontaneous respiration. They're responsive if you talk to them. Where he breaks the bone a bit—that's the part where I usually whistle or sing or something. And usually—they tease me about it—I look the other way."

Live Cartilage comes out: a thick, red toenail paring of it. I see blood froth. Reardon is cutting within the nose tip: he carves a sort of human rind away. The woman has been moaning: her nostrils are flared almost inside out: she will hawk phlegm up. The surgical hardware seems, to me, almost burlesque: mallet, chisel, rasp: tools for sullen carpentry. They do not banter now. Forty-five minutes have gone by: longer, I judge, than Reardon might expect. A bump on her nose bridge won't shear off. Reardon points the chisel, and his assistant—it is grisly, gristly this procedure—will start to hit with a mallet: rap, rap, rap, rap, *rap*. My anaesthetist friend has looked some other way. The woman is guzzling spit: a hopeless knee has risen in half-conscious protest: nnnnn, she can just say. Reardon asks again for the largest metal rasp: I note one in his voice. He sticks it far up the nostril and, with full body weight down, begins to saw. I have never heard such a monstrous sound: bone or cartilage abrades, shreds. But it is done. Reardon asks for my approval. Yes, different: yes, if you will, better. And now, to form a cast, doughy gauze-plaster strips are laid down. As you would put wet cloth over sculpted clay.

I sit after. Not giddy: disorganized, rather, by what I have seen. I must withdraw from it and very soon: so that I can see a face as face. Or, some night, touch my wife's breast with naïve lust again.

QUESTIONS

1. Trace the subtle changes in Mano's attitude toward what he observes in the operating room. How are his reactions colored by the fact he is a male? For whom does he feel more sympathy: for the woman receiving a breast implant or the woman undergoing a "nose job"? Why? What does he mean when, at

the end of his essay, he says he is "disorganized" by the things he has witnessed?

2. What are the surgeons' attitudes toward the operations they are performing? How does the anaesthetist's response differ?

3. Mano's essay, although detailed, is unlike many process analyses because it does not give us a step-by-step outline of certain surgical procedures. What, then, is Mano's purpose in writing it?

4. How does Mano's choice of language help make his essay vivid and arresting? Many readers might find "Plastic Surgery" stomach-turning. Why? Is it simply the subject matter which is upsetting, or the way in which Mano describes it as well? Explore these questions.

5. Find analogies Mano draws between the plastic surgery he observes and other activities. Discuss how these analogies help to clarify Mano's and the surgeons' attitudes toward the surgery and the human body.

6. Medical jargon is almost entirely absent from this essay. Imagine it rewritten, replete with jargon, by a doctor. How would both the tone and the content be affected? Would the reader's response be different? Explain.

SUGGESTIONS FOR WRITING

1. After thinking of an activity that you have mastered (a sport, hobby, job), write an essay in which you describe the process as objectively as possible, so that the reader has no idea of your attitude toward your subject. Then write another process analysis in which your pleasure in (or dislike of) the same activity is revealed through a judicious choice of vocabulary, analogy, and metaphor.

2. In an essay, either defend or condemn the sort of plastic surgery that Mano depicts.

3. Write a causal analysis in which you try to account for the increasing popularity of cosmetic surgery in contemporary America.

Richard Selzer
TUBE FEEDING

Born in upstate New York in 1928, Richard Selzer received his M.D. from Albany Medical College and did postdoctoral work at Yale. He lives in Connecticut, where he has a practice as a general surgeon, serves on the faculty of the Yale Medical School, and somehow manages to find time to compose eloquent, often deeply affecting, stories and essays about his calling—the "high enterprise" (as he has described it) of medicine. His

work has appeared in such popular magazines as Harper's, Mademoiselle, *and* Esquire *and has been collected in a number of books, including* Rituals of Surgery *(1974),* Mortal Lessons *(1977),* Letters to a Young Doctor *(1982), and* Taking the World in for Repairs *(1986).*

The following piece, from his 1979 collection Confessions of a Knife, *is typical of Selzer's essays, which often have the shape and feel of fiction.*

A man enters a bedroom. He is carrying a lacquered tray upon which stands a glass pitcher of eggnog. There is also a napkin in a napkin ring, a white enamel funnel, and an emesis basin. In the bed a woman lies.

It is eight o'clock in the morning. Precisely as he turns the knob of the door, she hears the church bells. At the sound, a coziness comes over her. There is nothing more certain than that he will appear, when he is most needed, when everything is ready. She has been awake for two hours, considering the treason of her body. But now that is over. She feels privileged to have known ahead of time of his coming, as though it were an event that had been foretold to her. She smiles up at him.

"Lovely," he says, and smiles. He carries the tray to the nightstand near the bed and sets it down. He bends then to kiss her head which is almost bald from the chemotherapy.

"What's lovely?" she asks him.

His smile broadens.

"The morning. Breakfast. You."

"Just lovely," he says again as she knows he will.

He opens the drawer of the nightstand and, after a moment of hesitation, selects a silk scarf. He holds it up.

"This one?" he asks.

She nods. He folds the scarf into a triangle, places it across her forehead and ties two ends of it at the back of her head. He tucks the folds in at the sides with a small flourish. He has become adept at this. Even now, after so many weeks, he marvels at the smallness of her head. It is so tiny and finely veined, no more than a pale knob, really, or a lamp of milk glass etched by the suture lines of the skull.

Before the chemotherapy, she had had dark brown hair which she sometimes braided into pigtails. It had given her a girlish look that amused him until he read somewhere that people who were dying of a lingering illness often took on a childlike appearance. Thereafter he wondered whether a long dying was really a slow retracing of life until the instants of death and conception were the same.

Hours before, she had opened her eyes to see him stepping into the room to give her the dose of pain medication. The moonlight streamed where he stood, an arc of blackness carving the moon of his face in half, hiding the lower part from her view. She wondered what he was thinking then. She thought it might possibly be like what she felt as a child when she picked the crumbs out of her grandfather's beard as he slept.

That was several hours ago. There would still be time before the pain returned. He could always tell when the pain was beginning to come back. Almost before she could. Her eyes took on a glitter that was a presentiment of the pain. All along he had considered the pain to be a mistake on the part of her body. Something had gone awry, been derailed, and so she had the pain. It was the kind of mistake that was an honest piece of ignorance by a person he loved. Between the long prairies of pain, there were narrow strips of relief when the dream of health was still given to her. In these intervals she would lie as on hillocks of cool grass, having caught at last, among her fingertips, the butterfly for which she had such nostalgia.

The man sits, one buttock on the bed, his legs arranged for balance.

"Ready?" he asks.

She nods. He never seems to notice the great red beard of tumor that, having begun in her salivary gland, had grown until it fills, now, the space between her face and her chest. There, where once her neck had been, she is swollen to bursting. Like a mating grouse, she thinks, or one of those blowfish. It is as though there is a route which his mind obeys, carefully, so that he sees only her brow where the skin is still pale and smooth, nothing below her eyes. She was someone who had always counted appearance for so much. Her own looks had stood her in such good stead. After all, she would say to him, I caught *you,* didn't I? And then came the cancer which, if it had only remained internal, hidden, would have kept for her the outline of her self. But this tumor had burst forth, exuberant, studding her face, mounding upon her neck, twisting and pulling her features until she was nothing but a grimace trapped in a prow of flesh.

"I look like Popeye," she said once.

He had not smiled.

The man rises, then kneels playfully beside the bed. To the woman, he seems taller in this position than he had while standing. As though, in the act of folding, he had grown. Kneeling *is* the proper posture for prayer, she thinks.

Now the man stands again. He folds down the sheet to the level of the woman's hips. Her abdomen is scaphoid, like an old boat which had been pulled up onto the land long ago, its mast and appointments pirated. Still, in the bend of each rib, there was retained the hint of wind and bright water. From the left upper quadrant of her abdomen, from what looks like a stab wound, there hangs a thick tube of brown rubber. The end of the tube, some eighteen inches from the skin, is closed off by a metal clamp, a pinchcock. The number *34* is stamped in black on the tube, announcing its caliber. The man takes the stiff tube in his left hand, letting it ride across his fingers. He removes the white gauze pad that has been folded over the open end and secured there by a rubber band. Always at this point, she feels that the act is exploratory, as though they are children left alone in a house, and have discovered for the first time how to do something mysterious and adult, each needing the assurance of the other.

The man releases the pinchcock. A few drops of mucoid fluid drip into the emesis basin. Sometimes there is a little blood. He is relieved when there is none. He wipes the end of the tube with the napkin and inserts the nozzle of the calibrated funnel into the gastrostomy tube, setting it firmly lest it slip out during the feeding. They look at each other and smile. She knows what is coming. He holds the empty funnel upright in his hand as though it were a goblet of wine, raising it so that it dances between their faces.

"Bon appetit!" he toasts her.

There is a sound like the bleat of a goat, as gas escapes from her stomach through the tube. He is always touched by the melancholy little noise. The man tests the temperature of the eggnog with the tip of a finger, which he then licks clean.

"Just right," he says.

Now he pours from the pitcher until the topmost mark of the funnel is reached. He gives the funnel to her to hold, the way a parent will indulge a child, letting her participate. Together they watch the level in the funnel slowly fall. The woman gives a deep sigh as she feels the filling of her stomach.

"Is that good?" he asks her.

"Yes," she nods and smiles, then looks away from him, preoccupied with the feeling.

For him it is not unlike a surgical operation that has become fixed and unchanging in the hands of the man who performs it over and again. Each time there are the same instruments; the steps are followed logically; the expectation of success is high. Once it happened that the mouth of the woman suddenly filled with the eggnog. He had administered the feeding too quickly. Overdistention of the stomach had brought on reverse peristalsis, and a column of the white liquid was catapulted up toward the blocked throat with such force that the barricade of tumor was forced, and the mouth achieved. It was sudden, but he was prepared for it. With one hand, he held the curved emesis basin at her chin. With the other, he lowered the tubing to siphon the eggnog back into the funnel. In a minute the spasm was over, and the feeding was resumed. All the while that this was taking place, the man did not cease to murmur to her.

"There, there," he had said, and wiped the woman's chin with the linen napkin. Then he had waited while she struggled to control her coughing.

She had always taken pleasure in his manner toward her—a kind of gallantry that he assumed for occasions—nights when they would go to the theater, or evenings when she knew that later he would make love to her. Now, of course, she understood that his gallantry was a device. She listened to him say "lovely" and "there, there," and she tried to forget for a while what she knew too well, that at the bottom of each of these tube feedings was the sediment of despair.

It is halfway through the feeding. All at once the man is startled by the sight of something white in the bed. For a moment, he does not know what it is. In that moment of uncertainty, a line has been crossed. Then he knows that it is the eggnog running from the hole in her body, the hole from which the tube has slipped! This time, too, he understands what has happened. Just behind the inner tip of the tube, there is a little thin-walled balloon that holds just five cc. of water, enough to distend it to a size greater than that of the hole in her stomach, so that the tube will not slip out. The little balloon has broken; the tube has slipped out. Now the man gazes at the empty hole in his wife's abdomen. Despair seizes him, mounts into desperation. He knows that he must replace the old tube with a new one.

"You must do it immediately," the surgeon had warned, "or very soon, the hole will begin to shrink and heal in. Then you will not be able to insert it."

The man rises from where he has been sitting on the bed. He walks to the dresser, where the extra tube is kept. There is a hollowness in him; he hears echoes. He senses that a limit has been reached. But he clenches himself.

"It's all right," he says aloud. "Here's a new one. Don't you fret about it."

But he is sweating and his fingers tremble as he dips the end of the new tube into the pitcher of eggnog to lubricate it. Once again, he is sitting on the bed. He slides the nose of the tube into the hole. It does not go. It will not fit. So soon! Again he tries to advance the tube. It is no use. He cannot. He twists and turns it, pushing harder. The woman winces. He is hurting her! He looks up to see the knobbed purple growth bearding her face. The lopsided head she raises in her distress seems to him a strange tropical fruit, a mutant gourd that has misgrown from having been acted upon by radiation and chemicals. And so it had. It is as though he is seeing it for the first time. Once, long ago, he had gripped her neck in rage. Oh God! Did the cancer come from that? Then he remembers how he used to lap the declivities of that neck.

He pushes the tube harder. What will he do if he cannot get it in? She will starve. All at once there is a terrifying "give," and the tube slides in. He inflates the little balloon with the water he has drawn up into a syringe, injecting it into the tiny tract alongside the main channel of the thing. He pulls back on the tube until he feels it abutting against the wall of her stomach. It is done.

"There," he says.

The man rises from the bed and leaves the room. He hurries down the hall to the bathroom where he reels above the toilet and vomits with as much stealth as he can manage. In the bed, the woman hears his retching. The day before, he had brought her white peonies from the garden. He had thrust his face into the immaculate flowers and inhaled deeply. Then he had arranged them in a vase on the dresser. She gazes at them now. One of the peonies sleeps unopened, resting against the blazing wakefulness of its kin. It will not bloom, she thinks. It is a waste. For a while she had thought it might open, but not anymore. As she watches, a small breeze from the opening door sends the blind bud waving from side to side. No, she thinks. It will live asleep. To awaken would be to die.

The man returns to her bedside. He takes up the funnel to reinsert it in the tube, to resume the feeding. She reaches out and stays his hand.

"It is enough," she says. "No more."

The man flushes the tube through with a small amount of water to prevent clogging, then replaces the gauze square and the clamp.

He pulls the sheet up over her abdomen, then picks up the lacquered tray that holds the pitcher, the napkin ring, the emesis basin, and the white enamel funnel. At the door he turns and smiles.

"You take a nice little nap, now," he says.

Her eyes are already closed.

In the kitchen, the man washes the pitcher and the funnel, and, climbing on a chair, he puts them away on the top shelf of the cupboard. At the rear, where he won't be apt to see them again for a long time.

QUESTIONS

1. How important a role does process analysis play in Selzer's essay? What practical information is the reader given about feeding someone through a tube?

2. Discuss the various elements of narrative you encounter in this essay: setting, imagery, characterization, point of view. In your opinion, what emotional response is Selzer trying to elicit from his readers? What details of the narrative help him to do this?

3. Why does Selzer wait so long to show you how grossly disfigured by cancer the bedridden woman is? How would his essay be changed if Selzer had immediately revealed her disfigurement to the reader?

4. What has happened by the end of the essay and why has it happened? What role does the vase of peonies play?

5. Why does Selzer choose to write this in present tense? What effect does this choice of tense have?

6. Selzer uses a number of metaphors to suggest the physical and emotional effects of cancer on its victim and her husband. Find and discuss them.

7. In another writer's hands, this essay might have been maudlin—a sentimental "tearjerker." Discuss how Selzer's tone and the kind of dialogue he has written help him avoid this pitfall.

SUGGESTIONS FOR WRITING

1. Describe a task you have performed which you found to be emotionally trying, highly unpleasant or—because of its inherent delicacy and difficulty— extremely nerve-racking.

2. Doctors are often accused by their patients and other observers of lacking sensitivity when dealing with someone who is ill, even seriously ill—of failing, that is, to respond to the emotional needs of patients and their families. (This essay, written by a surgeon, suggests that Selzer is an exception.) Drawing on your own personal experience, as well as that of friends and family, write an essay arguing that doctors either do or do not deserve the charge of insensitivity that is often leveled against them.

Jeremy Bernstein
NUCLEAR RESEARCH: SHOOTING THE PUSSYCAT
★ ★ ★

Although Jeremy Bernstein's earliest ambition was to be a jazz trumpeter, he became a physicist instead, taking his M.A. and Ph.D. in physics at Harvard. After spending several years at the Institute for Advanced Study in Princeton and the National Science Foundation, he became a professor of physics, first at New York University, then at the Stevens Institute of Technology, where he has taught since 1967. Bernstein is also a staff writer for The New Yorker *magazine, where he contributes articles on computers, physics, and other scientific topics.*

A prolific author, Bernstein has published numerous books, including The Analytical Engine: Computers—Past, Present, and Future *(1964; rev. 1981),* A Comprehensible World: On Modern Science and Its Origins *(1967),* Einstein *(1973), and, most recently,* Science Observed: Essays Out of My Mind *(1982), from which the following selection is taken.*

———

I spent the summer months of 1958 and 1959 in La Jolla, California, as a consultant for the then newly founded General Atomic Company. La Jolla was, and I suppose still is, a pleasantly sybaritic beach community with excellent surfing, done mostly on the Wind'n'sea Beach celebrated in Tom Wolfe's *The Pump House Gang.* My connection with General Atomic came about because of my friendship with Freeman Dyson, who was, and still is, a professor at the Institute for Advanced Study in Princeton, where I spent two years from 1957 to 1959. Dyson was invited in 1956 to be a consultant for General Atomic by its then president, Frederic de Hoffmann; sometime later, Dyson asked me to join him. (He has written about these years in his fascinating autobiography, *Disturbing the Universe.*) He arrived that summer, along with the rest of the consultants, at what he describes in his book as a "little red schoolhouse." De Hoffmann had, in fact, rented a schoolhouse that had been abandoned by the San Diego Public School system—since General Atomic then had no buildings of its own. By the time of my appearance the company had acquired its own buildings. But, buildings or not, in 1956 de Hoffmann, who was a tremendous entrepreneur, had managed to attract to La Jolla a stellar group of physicists, including Dyson, with the idea of the company's entering the field of reactor design and construction. Dyson notes in his book that three groups of consultants were formed under the rubrics Safe Reactor, Test Reactor, and Ship Reactor. The latter two were, respectively, a design for a reactor with a very high neutron flux, to be used for materials testing, and a design for a reactor to be used to power merchant ships. Neither of these was ever built by the company.

I recall that Dyson told me he got into the business of designing a safe reactor because no one else (except Edward Teller) in the group wanted to do it. To most of them it did not seem like a very glamorous problem, but Dyson, who is acknowledged to be one of the best problem solvers in physics, took it on as a challenge. In due course—a few weeks' time—he invented the general concept of the TRIGA, an acronym invented by de Hoffmann to stand for "Training, Research, and Isotopes, General Atomic." This reactor was designed for use, primarily at universities and large medical centers, in training students and for the production of short-lived, medically useful isotopes. It sold, according to Dyson, for $144,000 and, at last count, about sixty had been sold. In fact, he notes in his book, "It is one of the very few reactors that made money for the company which built it."

Before getting on to why I am bringing all of this up at the present time I should like to describe briefly in what way the TRIGA is a safe reactor. To explain this in a schematic way, let me first review how a reactor works. Reactors are powered by nuclear fission. In particular the so-called fuel elements of the common reactors consist of long, thin rods containing pellets of uranium that have been "enriched" so as to contain more of the fissionable isotope U^{235} than is normally found in nature. In nature more than 99 percent of the uranium is found in the U^{238} isotope, which is not readily fissionable. In a TRIGA, for example, the fuel elements contain an enrichment of 20 percent of the U^{235} isotope. When a slow neutron encounters a U^{235} nucleus, it has a good chance of splitting it and releasing energy and additional neutrons which can then carry on the chain reaction that produces energy.

This brings me to the second point. If the neutrons are to be made effective, they must be slowed down. This is accomplished by putting the fuel rods in a so-called moderator. In the TRIGA, as in most of the common reactors, the moderator is ordinary water. The fuel elements are in a small swimming pool which glows a pleasant incandescent blue when the reactor is operating. The power generated by the TRIGA is so low that one can stand safely above the pool while the reactor is working. Reactors used by the power industry are at least ten thousand times more powerful, and one cannot approach them when they are in operation. The water in the pool serves the double function of slowing down the neutrons and cooling the fuel elements so they won't melt—the "melt-down." The fissions generate heat, and in a power reactor this heat produces steam, which drives electric turbines. In the power reactors the essential thing, from a safety point of view, is to make sure that under no circumstance does one lose cooling water and thus expose the heated fuel elements. We all know now, from what happened at Three Mile Island, how crucial this is. In power reactors the safety is "engineered." It consists of having many back-up cooling systems which the reactor engineers can bring to bear in an emergency. But, as we saw in the Three Mile Island incident, these safety measures are vulnerable to human error. There the reactor operators shut off the emergency cooling system at a crucial moment. The accident would have been prevented if they had done nothing and let the emergency system operate automatically.

What Teller's group—that is, Dyson—was up to was to create a reactor that was "intrinsically" safe: it would shut itself off no matter what anyone did during an emergency—simply as a law of nature. Dyson's brilliant idea was to design a reactor in such a way that half the moderator was in the water and half was in the fuel elements themselves. The element that slows the neutrons in the water moderator is the hydrogen. Hence Dyson, working with an Iranian metallurgist Massoud Simnad, and others found out how to bond uranium-hydride—a compound of uranium and hydrogen—to a metal compound of zirconium and hydrogen. In this way the fuel elements themselves contain hydrogen; when something goes wrong the hydrogen gets heated up and then, it turns out, it will no longer moderate the neutrons and the whole chain reaction will come to an abrupt stop. In fact, in a TRIGA the reactor shuts itself off in a *few thousandths of a second.* I have watched it do this myself in tests in which the control rods that usually keep the number of neutrons at a safe level were blown out of the reactor by compressed air. What one saw was a brief flash in the swimming pool and then nothing. (By the way, among the people who helped produce the final TRIGA design was Theodore B. Taylor, whose concern for nuclear safety was underscored in John McPhee's book *The Curve of Binding Energy.* Ted Taylor was our group leader at General Atomic when I joined Dyson there in 1958 to try to build an atom-bomb powered spaceship, the *Orion*—a project that was abandoned a few years later. But that is another story.)

Before I come to the point of *this* story I must make a few additional remarks about the safety of nuclear reactors. Prompt shutdown of the chain reaction that keeps a reactor going is unfortunately not the whole safety story. If it were, there would have been no serious incident at Three Mile Island since the operators there managed to shut the chain reaction off in about thirty seconds. Unlike other power sources a reactor continues to generate substantial heat even after the fuel stops "burning." The reason for this is that when the uranium nucleus splits in the fission process it splits into a variety of medium-weight nuclei that are radioactive. These radioactive fission products continue to decay and the motion of the decay products represents energy that manifests itself as heat. The amount of heat that is generated depends on the prior history of how the reactor has been used, but a rough formula is that about 10 percent of the power capacity of the reactor remains as heat when the chain reaction is shut down. To have a clearer idea about the numbers, we may recall that the power of a reactor is usually given in watts—a unit of energy per second—an energy rate. How big is a watt? To get a feeling for this, recall that normal household light bulbs are usually about a hundred watts, which, coincidentally, is the energy rate that is dissipated by the human body. A clothes dryer consumes energy at a rate of about four thousand watts. But a big power reactor at full operation generates about a *billion* watts so that 10 percent of this is about a hundred million watts. When the reactor is shut down, as it was at Three Mile Island, this enormous heat energy must be dissipated if the reactor is not to melt down. It is useful to keep the scale of these numbers in mind in what follows.

Now to the point. As early as 1952, physicists and engineers at Columbia University in Manhattan recognized the need for a safe training reactor that could be operated in a university located within a big city. In 1958 the TRIGA became operational, and by 1963 Columbia had received both government funds and a construction permit from the then Atomic Energy Commission to buy and build a facility for a relatively small TRIGA. The design called for a 250,000-watt reactor. It was to have been run, for training purposes, about eight hours a week at *ten* watts. A few hours a week it would have been run at full power to make isotopes. In the most extreme situation any emergency shutdown would have generated about fifteen thousand watts—the power equivalent of four clothes dryers. This heat would not have been difficult to dissipate. From 1963 until the present, however, Columbia's TRIGA has been tied up in an endless round of litigation between the university and various concerned citizen groups. Finally, in June 1974, the Supreme Court upheld the validity of the original construction permit. In fact the reactor has been built, but it has never been fueled. In 1979, William McGill, then the president of Columbia, announced that it would *never* be fueled as long as he was president. He retired in 1980.

It seems to me that McGill's decision and his reason for it—which, according to the *New York Times,* were "not because of doubts about safety but because of community fears" ("I am much more concerned with the psychological explosion than I am about a nuclear explosion," he stated)—are another illustration of the fact that the energy crisis has so far succeeded in bringing out the worst in nearly everybody. Did it not occur to then President McGill that the same reasoning he used to ban the TRIGA could be used to ban any controversial academic subject at Columbia? Did it not also occur to him that without training facilities, nuclear engineers—both here and abroad—will be even less well equipped to deal with emergencies than the Three Mile Island engineers seem to have been? It should also be noted that no one, no anti-nuclear group, has asked that any of the other sixty-odd TRIGAs be shut down. This in itself is some sort of testimonial to their safety. Columbia's administration has adopted a Luddite position that is unique. It can be compared to General MacArthur's decision to smash the Japanese cyclotrons just after the war on the grounds that these machines were somehow weapons of war. No one can be complacent about nuclear safety after Three Mile Island. But to keep a TRIGA from operating is, as a Columbia professor remarked, like being in an Indian village where a man-eating tiger has been discovered and to respond to this genuine and legitimate concern by shooting someone's pet cat.

QUESTIONS

1. Bernstein's essay analyzes several processes. What are they? Besides describing these processes, what else does he attempt to do? What is the point of his essay? How does Bernstein use process analysis to support his position on the TRIGA reactor and on nuclear energy?

2. How much knowledge of nuclear reactors does Bernstein assume that his readers have? Why isn't his discussion of reactors more complex? For what kind of audience is this essay written?

3. What went wrong, according to Bernstein, at Three Mile Island? How was the TRIGA reactor made foolproof against similar misfortune?

4. Two-thirds of the way through his essay, Bernstein discusses the energy produced, or consumed, by light bulbs, the human body, and clothes dryers. Why does he do this? Is the naming of these things an effective rhetorical strategy? Why?

5. Consult a good dictionary, or an encyclopedia, to find out who the Luddites were. Why does Bernstein compare them to the administrators of Columbia University?

6. What simile does Bernstein use to express his chagrin over the failure of Columbia University to fuel its TRIGA reactor? How does the simile clarify Bernstein's own attitude toward nuclear reactors?

SUGGESTIONS FOR WRITING

1. Most of us possess one skill—sometimes technical, sometimes artistic—that others cannot master. We might be able to sew a dress or knit a sweater, to fix a car engine or play a superior game of tennis, to surf or draw enviably. Choose something you do well and describe how you do it. Extend your analysis to include the benefits and pleasures your activity gives you.

2. Take some process associated with college that you are familiar with: registering for courses as a freshman, choosing and pledging a fraternity or sorority, applying for financial aid, preparing yourself for mid-terms or final exams, getting a high grade-point average. Analyze this process in a fresh and interesting fashion. You can, of course, choose to use any tone you like—humorous, satirical, or serious.

David Sudnow
INTERFACE
★ ★ ★

A former sociology professor at Berkeley, David Sudnow currently lives in New York City, where he has been performing and teaching jazz piano since 1983. He is the author of numerous articles and several books, including the critically acclaimed Ways of the Hand: The Organization of Improvised Conduct *(1978).*

"Interface" is the second chapter of Sudnow's 1983 book, Pilgrim in the Microworld, *which is both an entertaining account of his growing obsession with video games and a serious, often philosophical, reflection on the relationship between the self and the "luminous microworld" of the computer.*

The professor's house was one of those wraparound affairs perched on stilts high in the Berkeley Hills overlooking San Francisco Bay, and as soon as I arrived at the faculty party I spotted the grand piano in an elegant study with oriental rugs, floor-to-ceiling books, as much a look of scholarship as you'd see anywhere. That would make my evening.

In a half hour a gathering had formed around the piano. Then, in the midst of "The Man I Love," there was an explosion in the next room. "Maybe I will meet him someday, maybe . . . What the hell was that?" my lead singer cracked. "They're playing a video game Herb bought for Christmas," said the hostess with slight irritation. "He couldn't keep it wrapped up. The kids hardly get to it. I don't know if he'll finish the talk he's supposed to give in Frankfurt next month."

Well, we weren't about to give up Gershwin for Atari, about to sit in front of a TV with little plastic joysticks in our hands. So as several people found a polite way to back off and sneak out of the study, a dedicated threesome remained committed to singing. Then someone pretty good must have gotten to the joystick as we got into "I've Got a Crush on You." "All the day and nighttime . . . *wham . . . varoooooom . . . bam . . . crash . . . bam bam . . .* Hear me cry . . . *ooooooo . . . bam bam bam.*" I played at fitting the "Stars and Stripes Forever" to their action but the timing wouldn't mix. We had to stop. I needed a refill anyway, and the hostess would tell them at least to turn down the volume because they were ruining the party.

The party was in the next room, as many as thirty of them in there at times, never less than ten, and it was three in the morning when I finally left Herb to play by himself. Between drinks and nearly two straight hours one on one with him at Missile Command once everybody left and we didn't have to give up turns, I could barely see my way down the hill. Here's the screen frozen in the height of action:

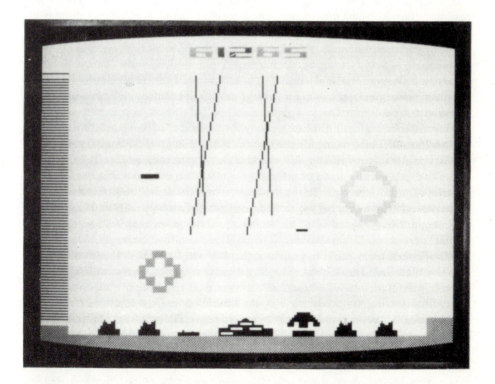

Intercontinental ballistic missiles descend from the sky toward six cities on earth, as the player employs a two-handed joystick-push-button device to intercept their trajectories. The stick controls a half inch long cursor line, a sight that can be moved and stopped anywhere within the visibly televised skyspace. And with one hand you try to place it beneath an incoming missile, at least if you're taking the game seriously and care about the welfare of Cleveland, New York, or any other city in the world. Atari will take your dollars, francs, or rubles. You then push the button with the other hand to launch an antiballistic missile from the "silo" in the center of the landscape to the designated cursor location. And if you've properly judged distance and time, your ABM meets their ICBM head-on and *wham,* the folks below are spared for the while. The overall object of the game, thank goodness, is to avoid the total destruction of all cities. Atari and Company play the bad guys, from any political standpoint you occupy, while you defend whatever counts for life, liberty, and the pursuit of happiness in a world of six towns. Which I suppose some calculate to be enough of a world.

Every so often the onslaught stops and there's a pause that defines a "round" of play. Rounds allow turn-taking competition against the enemy, with no logic except in a truly insane world, but still, a series of volleys is a reasonable enough way to run a war. You can reload ammo, attend the wounded, deal with first strike second strike problems, or run to the fridge for a beer. Between rounds the score is posted, and a siren then warns of a next incoming volley. The attack resumes. Should, heaven help you, all cities get hit, the world blows up and it's THE END. Unless of course you charmingly succeed in attaining a high enough score to win a replacement city. Points are earned for every successful shot, the destruction of more rapid, accurate "smart missiles" earning the most. These marvelous weapons make a screaming sound all their own, and gain their intelligence in being precisely guided to a city, never falling into the little countryside between towns. Were the cities near each other or far apart, and was their equidistant spacing intended literally or as an abstraction? The scale of things was obscure, and the microworld had a decidedly mathematical look about it. I guess the big one does too when you're thinking of trajectories.

For every ten thousand points a city is rebuilt, though not necessarily in the same spot, and depending on how you imagine the delay between rounds, the urban reconstruction occurs with instant Atari technology or over the course of generations. They don't say what happens to the people, even whether the cities are populated, and presumably considerations of taste have left out burning bodies. Should the score reach the city replacement figure of ten thousand before any town has been annihilated, your silo skills don't go unrewarded. For you now have a "city in memory," which doesn't mean you remember what it was like or even where it was. And when the first one actually does blow up, this remembered achievement makes for an automatic replacement. The memorized city just pops up out of the electric brain, instantaneously appearing somewhere else to strategically fill the gap. Early rounds involve slow enemy missiles—carryovers from a prior war?—but with each new round the speed, numerical density, and relative proportion of screeching smart missiles increases, making matters more contemporary and defense more and more tricky no matter how patriotically you behave.

Few temptations can drag me from a well-tuned Steinway on a Saturday night, not into a next room with lots of people anyhow, so the next day I went out and bought a color TV and a home Atari console that plugged into it. Now, I'm not big on war, wasn't even allowed a cap gun as a kid, and Missile Command models the calculated insanity of the worst imaginable twentieth-century scenario. How powerful and eerie that the computerized arena seduces us to transcend the nightmare it presents.

A whole party full of Berkeley intellectuals blasting their way through an evening of warfare, stoned on button pushing. Sure, everybody made fun of it all. There were the perfectly expectable disclaimers and expressions of horror, enough first-rate political satire to give Lenny Bruce a run for his money. Sure, the women came off with the most vociferous disdain. The world was coming to an end. It was a conspiracy to train our kids for the real thing. Not to mention the ultimate destruction of the evening. Most of them hung out in the kitchen, but every so often a new one stuck her nose in the game room, feigning utter disinterest. I thought I spotted some female fists clenched. And beneath all the joking, this guy after that wormed his way close to the controls to say, "Hey, let me try that for a while."

None of us was a warmonger. And neither were our kids. But the pace of things. The speed. The fast twists and turns. The fireworks. The luminescence. Take a Polaroid picture on a street corner in Bombay, a ten-second kind, and inside of three there'll be fifty people hovering around, with a depth of curiosity so heavily smacking of worship you can see the reverence and fear in their faces, whether it's a picture of a dead body or their own child held up for a smiling pose. That doesn't matter. It's the thing in its fully emblematic significance, token of a new world and way of being. Watch them watch your ten-second Polaroid come up, and you can see them looking across the Atlantic. We were looking out there. Way out.

Missiles come in from the top of the screen, the outer limits of one's radar, upper horizon of the new world landscape with its little curve to make your body feel a bit more at home. Several trickle on and then down screen at the same rate, three or four lines very slowly coming from the top. So you've got plenty of time. You learn to move your cursor beneath them, one by one, and without much practice, a half hour at most, you can judge how far below you need to be in relation to their speed when you push the button. And at the time the missile gets to the cursor the enemy has arrived there too.

You go from one missile to the next, aim, hold it, and fire. And that's fine till they start coming faster. Then you need a new technology for moving. You try machine gunning, pointing all over the place while rapping the button, a give-them-all-you've-got last round of the snowball fight. But the rules don't let you. Only three explosions are allowed on the screen at once, a seemingly absurd restriction in a kind of war where reloading ammo makes little sense. But Atari controls all microworld rules, the umpire is built right in, and the arbitrary restriction constrains and organizes the rest of play. While a three-shot limit is a slight defect in the game's authenticity, along with atonal melodies and replaced cities, its consequences for how you've got to attack are neat enough to make up for it, as with many such restrictions. Machine gunning won't work because you can't keep firing. The video air of memorized places must periodically clear, lightening the electric brain's burden, rearranging its memorized thoughts enough to give new considerations room and time to register and count off paces in the clearing. But it counts fast, thinks that way, and you've got to stay on your thumbs.

One little maneuver I came upon did seem like a move in the right direction. In a simple situation with three missiles coming slowly down together on the same horizontal plane,

I smoothly swept right beneath their paths without stopping the cursor, firing en passant. When my placement and rhythm were together, as my missiles got to where the cursor had been when I'd pushed the button, theirs were there too. It was a panning action with several little articulations along the way, the hands in synchrony, one wiping past while the other inserted punctuations. As you watch the cursor move, your look appreciates the sight with thumbs in mind, and the joystick-button box feels like a genuine implement of action. *Bam, bam, bam,* got you three right in your tracks, whatever the hell you are.

When doing well, I could pick off a few missiles with one continuously smooth gesture. Nothing to call the Pentagon about and hardly grounds for trading in the piano. Just a snazzy little skill. But as the game progresses, the sky blazes with missiles racing toward earth, keeping you awfully busy saving the world. So you'd have to have some such smooth way of improvising round the sky, continuously tracing through a sequence of places that wouldn't pile up to overload you, with quick analysis and good handicraft. Just look at the screen in advanced stages of play. All six cities can be annihilated in the first five seconds. The Department of Defense thinks they can handle that on their TVs, and Atari implies you can on yours, so what's wrong with a little advance preparation? Look at the barrage and you know it's got to involve some pretty fancy action. Touch Gershwin? That's another question.

Whether useful or not, my little movement was nice to watch and feel, and whenever Herb took a break I switched the reset control and started over again so I could practice joysticking back and forth, gliding past those slow missiles, connecting up with the lines, each explosion right on the button, each electric roar right where it belonged. I was just as content to watch the world blow up and start all over again whenever things got heavy, playing this little three-note melody to refine the accuracy of my video stroke.

Punctuate a moving picture? I'm no painter and don't dance in mirrors. But here I could watch a mysterious transformation of my movements taking place on the other side of the room, my own participation in the animated interface unfolding in an extraordinary spectacle of lights, colors, and sounds. Improvised painting, organized doodling, with somebody doodling against you to make sure you keep doing it.

The little silly panning shot was a trip. I thought of the arcade and the electro-umbilical hookup I'd seen. I'd stay in an arcade for more of that too, for the flashy lights of the little landscape whose warfulness I could at least pretend not to imagine, for that cursor of pure power you could swing where you wanted, for those wild changing color coordinations and even the little plastic controls that now felt like a way into a new world. If you couldn't take a microworld home with you, I could see standing in an arcade just to be able to put together anything well with the new crystal brain kit, to mount the first step of control over its affairs, its booms and bursts. And especially for action like this shot, with its touch of grace.

Most sedentary, you say, hardly an arena for vigorous action, awfully cold and calculating, the terrain for human involvement reduced from a several acre plot to the microworld of a TV tube and the calibrating motions of two or three digits. The farmer who once gazed and plowed toward an endless horizon now sits on his can in an office scanning a nine-inch video display of his inventory, seedling growth rates, soil composition, market prices, and PAC-MAN.

But what about finger work in a tightly voiced Bach fugue, or the little movements of writing, reading, and singing? What of Rembrandt's brush strokes? To be good for the embodied spirit certainly action needn't stimulate the pulmonary vascular system. For one thing, there's more time left for jogging when you log in hours at your "P.C.," and God knows tilling the soil is no great bargain. It all depends on who ends up with the dirty work they won't make robots do. No big software market for street cleaning programs these days.

Human history was cultivated through speech and the motions of fingers, one could say, the tiniest not biggest actions. After all, take away all the carved, painted, and inscribed meanings, the thoughts giving rise to its symbolic significance as a shape, and what's the Great Pyramid alongside Beethoven's Fifth, or something like this:

this:

$$E = mc^2$$

or even this:

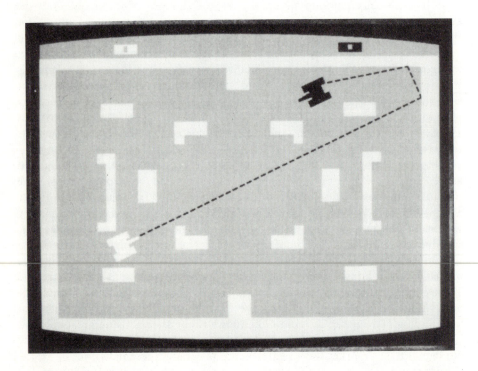

"Just" labor.

Now the computer. Our organically perfect tool. Seated upright on behinds just made for that, our hands dangle near the lap at their most relaxed point of balance, while these fingers, capable of such marvelous interdigitation, have a territory for action whose potentials and richness are electronically enhanced beyond the wildest dream. And the eyes are freed from hand guidance work, free to witness and participate in the spectacle from above.

Before, the piano was the quintessential human instrument. Of all things exterior to the body, in its every detail it most enables our digital capacities to sequence delicate actions. Pushing the hand to its anatomical limit, it forces the development of strength and independence of movement for fourth and fifth fingers, for no other tool or task so deeply needed. This piano invites hands to fully live up to the huge amount of brain matter with which they participate, more there for them than any other body part. At this genetically predestined instrument we thoroughly encircle ourselves within the finest capabilities of the organ.

Then a typewriter, speeding the process whereby speech becomes visible, the extraordinary keyboard for sequencing and articulating perhaps awaiting a still truer sounding board, strings, and tuning, a still more suited canvas for thought.

Then TV.

Then super-fast super-tiny electric switches to rapidly translate keyboard motions into an infinite variety of sights and sounds. Computers.

The three are united. We program the arrangement of circuits to indefinitely vary the effects each stroke and sequence of strokes can generate on screen, building codes and codings of codes, so now this key stands for that, that key for this, dozens of shorthands and shorthands for shorthands. Computer languages. Typewriter strokes get heftier. Sentences gain power.

Then to complement the ensemble further, we add a rapidly expanding assortment of hand tools for tuning, depressing, sequencing, switching, fine tuning, and more. The typewriter is best for linear movement, up and down and side to side, its keys laid out in banks with spaces in between. This word piano can't fill the visible spaces between its printed sounds, and greater fluidity of motion is wanted for more graphic finger drawing, violinlike brushes to glide and slide over the glass canvas. So there come knobs, joysticks, track balls, "mice," light pens, and more. The finest nuances and varieties of manual dexterity are interfaced with the televised display. Typewriter keys become infinitely multipurposed, the TV screen leaves behind the human drama it borrowed from our past to get into our homes, and biotechnical handicraft takes a giant step forward.

The full sequencing, calibrating, caressing potentials of human hands now create sights, sounds, and movements. And the eyes are free to watch, wonder, and direct from above, free to witness the spectacle and help the hands along without looking down. A keyboard for painters, a canvas for pianists. With lots of programs to choose from, lots of ways to instantaneously vary and organize the tunings and makeup of the palette. All the customary boundaries get blurred when you're painting paragraphs, performing etchings, sketching movies, and graphing music.

I was hooked.

QUESTIONS

1. Describe in detail how Missile Command is played.

2. Where in his essay does Sudnow anticipate various objections that the reader might raise to the spreading influence and presence of the computer in our lives? How does he respond to these objections? What does he mean when he says that the ancient pyramids are " 'just' labor"? According to Sudnow, why are they less significant than the game of Missile Command?

3. How, in general, would you characterize Sudnow's attitude toward technology? Does his statement that "the TV screen leaves behind the human drama it borrowed from our past to get into our homes" clarify his attitude?

4. A peculiarity of Sudnow's prose style is that he frequently writes sentence fragments. Find some of these. What effect do they have?

5. Why does Sudnow draw an analogy between the Atari game and the flash of the Polaroid camera in Bombay? How does this analogy help to clarify his and his friends' attitude toward the computer?

6. Explain Sudnow's use of the phrases "painting paragraphs, performing etchings, sketching movies, and graphing music" at the end of his essay.

SUGGESTIONS FOR WRITING

1. Write a process analysis describing how a computer game is played. Be sure to discuss its increasing difficulty as one masters the simpler levels of the game, and mention the various strategies you employ to score highly or to win.

2. Write about a particular product of modern technology that has altered your life in a positive or negative way. Alternatively, assess your attitude towards technological change in general.

Sherry Turkle
WHY THE COMPUTER DISTURBS

★ ★ ★

Born in Brooklyn and educated at Radcliffe, the University of Chicago, and Harvard (where she received a joint Ph.D. in sociology and personality psychology), Sherry Turkle—currently an associate professor at MIT— won renown for her 1984 book, The Second Self: Computers and the Human Spirit. *During six years of fieldwork, Turkle became a kind of high-tech anthropologist, immersing herself in the various subcultures of the computer world. She interviewed over four hundred people, from video game fanatics to artificial-intelligence theorists, in an effort to understand the psychological impact of computers on the individuals who use them, as well as on American society at large. Her resulting study was widely praised and established Turkle's reputation as an important social scientist. She has been described as both a "Piaget for the computer age" and "the Margaret Mead of silicon," and in* Esquire *magazine's 1985 survey of America's "leadership class," she is honored—along with such diverse individuals as Bruce Springsteen and Gary Trudeau—as one of the outstanding "men and women under forty who are changing the nation."*

"Why the Computer Disturbs" is excerpted from the first chapter of The Second Self.

Matthew, a good-natured and precocious child of five, was eagerly learning to write computer programs to make graphic designs on the screen. His mood changed abruptly and he left the computer in tears when he understood how to make a recursive program: a program whose action includes setting in motion an exactly similar program whose action includes setting in motion an exactly similar program, and so on. Once started, the program will (if it has no "stop rule") go on "forever," limited only by the hardware, the amount of "memory" of the machine.

It is not enough to say that Matthew was afraid. His experience was complex and confusing, one that many people have shared. When I was a little girl I had a book on the cover of which was a picture of a little girl looking at the cover of the same book, on which, ever so small, one could still discern a picture of a girl looking at the cover, and so on. I found the cover compelling, yet somehow it frightened me. Where did the little girls end? How small could they get? When my mother took me to a photographer for a portrait, I made him take a picture of me reading the book. That made matters even worse. Whenever I looked at the photograph or the book I couldn't stop thinking about them, yet could find no way to capture for myself or for anyone else exactly what it was that was so upsetting and so gripping for me.

Other children meet this experience in the form of questions about where the stars end or whether there is ever a final image when mirrors reflect mirrors. In all of these cases, what disturbs is closely tied to what fascinates and what fascinates is deeply rooted in what disturbs.

When I was in trouble with self-referential pictures I could get no help. The adults around me were no better able to handle the infinite series of ever smaller little girls than I was, except to assert their authority by telling me not to think about such things. Children's encounters with ideas like self-reference, infinity, and paradox are disturbing and exciting and are made all the more mysterious by the fact that appeals to parents about them are likely to provoke frustrating admonitions not to think about such slippery questions. Yet such questions become storm centers in the mind.

The computer touches on several of these slippery questions. The idea of infinity is one of them. What constitutes being alive is another.

Young children see almost everything in the world as alive in one way or another. This "animism" pervades the child's thinking until the development of concepts that help draw the line between the alive and the not-alive. Childhood animism has two faces: it makes the world friendly and understandable, but it can make it frightening as well. Emerging from animism is more than a chapter in the intellectual development of the child—it is a struggle against the insecurities that come from not knowing what objects can act independently and potentially antagonistically. Children spend a great deal of energy trying to get such matters under control, and thus it is not surprising that they are disturbed when a computer behaves halfway between a person and a thing.

For the child for whom little seems under total control, toys and simple machines are reassuring exceptions. Dolls, soldiers, windup toys—all of these "come alive," but only at the child's command. Computer toys that talk, cheat, and win are not so compliant. Yet they have a "holding power." In part it is the holding power of the feared. Children love roller coasters and horror movies, but much of the time on the ride and in the theater may be spent with closed eyes. We are drawn to what frightens us, we play with what disturbs us, in part to try to reassert our control over it.

Laura is six years old, a beautiful child from suburban Boston. Her family calls her "Princess." I have interviewed several other six-year-olds from her neighborhood. Most of them seem streetwise. Laura is an innocent. She watches very little television, some *Sesame Street,* and her favorite, *Mister Rogers' Neighborhood,* which she likes because "there is magic and Mr. Rogers is very kind." She has no mechanical toys, "nothing that winds up or has batteries," she tells me, "just dolls and storybooks." As we chat, sprawled on the floor of my office, she remarks that she has never played with a tape recorder or a typewriter, and she gingerly tries mine out. And yet, when she is presented with the computer toys—Simon, Merlin, and Speak and Spell—she has no reticence. "My mother has a microwave like this," is her first comment about the touch-sensitive controls on Merlin, the toy that plays tic-tac-toe.

Laura begins her play session calmly. She quickly checks out the toys and has definite opinions. The toys have "minds," says Laura, but they are not alive, because "they don't have a brain—they know how to do things with minds." Laura says this in a tone that suggests disbelief that anyone could think otherwise. Of all the things she has ever met before, she thinks that Merlin is most like "a machine, a clock." And the thing that Laura says is most special about clocks is that "they don't do anything by themselves." When I ask Laura if her alarm clock "remembers" when to wake her up, she is firm about the answer. "No, you set it. And then it does it. But not by itself."

As Laura plays she becomes less composed. Merlin's "tic-tac-toe mind" turns out to be a formidable opponent. "How does he win so much? It tries to make me lose." Laura is completely engrossed. She doesn't look up. My presence is forgotten. I ask her if she thinks Merlin could lose if it made a mistake. Her "Yes" is almost inaudible. She is not sure at all. Laura begins to turn Merlin off between games, a ritual whose intent seems to be to weaken the toy. Her efforts are in vain: Merlin continues to win. After five minutes of this frustration, she puts Merlin aside and picks up Speak and Spell, a toy that can talk. Laura spells out her name on its keyboard. The toy obediently calls out the letters and displays them on a small screen: "L-A-U-R-A." She seems satisfied and relaxes. This is going to be more reassuring than Merlin. Then Laura puts Speak and Spell into "Say it" mode.

Speak and Spell has a button that turns it on and another that turns it off. It also has buttons for choosing among different possible play modes. In "Spell" mode, the toy calls out a word and waits for the child to spell it by pressing out letters on its keyboard. After the child has made a guess, the game offers congratulations or a second chance before it provides the correct spelling. In the "Hangman" game mode, the toy offers blank spaces and clue letters on the screen and invites the child to complete the secret word. And then there is "Say it" mode, designed for younger children who, like Laura, may not be able to spell much more than their names. In "Say it" mode the machine calls out the phrase "SAY IT" followed by one of the words in its several-hundred-word vocabulary: "SAY IT . . . HAPPY." "SAY IT . . . LOSE." "SAY IT . . . HOUSE." And the child is given a few seconds to repeat the word before being offered another one.

Not surprisingly, since this is the way of electrical objects, Speak and Spell is designed so that you can turn it off at will. You can turn it off without finishing the "Hangman" guessing game or without completing the spelling of a word in progress. But the first version of Speak and Spell that came on the American market had a "bug," a programming mistake: you can't turn it off while it is in its "Say it" mode. This mode offers ten words, ten "Say it" commands, and it brooks no interruption until the presentation of the ten words is finished. You cannot change modes, and you cannot turn the toy off.

When Speak and Spell is in "Say it" mode its program doesn't check to see whether the user has pressed "Off" before completing its ten-word cycle. Although the programming error is trivial, it was discovered only after it had been "burned into" the computer chip manufactured for the toy. Correcting the mistake was deemed too costly. And, besides, the problem didn't seem very serious.

The uninterruptible "Say it" cycle takes long enough so that within their first few sessions with Speak and Spell most children try to turn it off while it is in "Say it" mode and discover they cannot. In a small way, they are meeting a situation that is at the heart of almost every science fiction movie ever made about a computer. It is the story of the machine out of control. As far as the child can tell, this machine has developed a mind of its own.

Halfway through the cycle, Laura wants to turn "Say it" off and get back to spelling her name. She presses the "Off" button. She persists, pressing it again and again, then trying several other buttons. "Why isn't this thing coming off?" She tries four or five buttons in a row, then all of them at once. Now Laura is panicked. She puts one of her hands on as many buttons as it will cover. She tries both of her hands. The machine goes on until it is done. Laura is quite upset.

The "Say it" bug contradicts our most basic expectation of a machine. When you turn the switch to "Off," machines stop. The cliché response to people's fears about computers "taking over" is that you can always "pull the plug." Laura's agitation is not unlike that of an adult who suddenly has reason to doubt the cliché.

Children can be frightened by the "Say it" bug, but at the same time they find it compelling. Once they discover the bug, they make it happen again and again. It gives them a chance to play with the machine as alive, out of control.

When Paul, seven, discovers the "Say it" bug, he is startled, but he doesn't say anything. His first reaction is to put Speak and Spell down on the ground. Then, kneeling above the toy but keeping some distance, he presses "Say it" again. This time, Paul presses all of its buttons in turn and then uses the palms of his hands, trying to press all of its buttons at the same time, trying to make it stop. The toy remains unobedient, but when its ten words have come to an end it stops unexpectedly. Paul puts the Speak and Spell in "Say it" mode again, but this time, just as it is demanding its fourth word, Paul turns it over, opens its back cover, and removes its batteries. Paul has found the way to "pull the plug." A group of children gather round. Most have run into the "Say it" bug, but no one had thought of batteries. There is much excitement. The children take turns doing Paul's trick. They put the toy in "Say it" mode and then take out the batteries, all the while shrieking their delight about "killing the Speak and Spell." The children allow the toy its most autonomous behavior, and then, when it is most like a living thing, they kill it.

The children are not only killing the Speak and Spell, they are also bringing it back to life. Somewhat older children play with more sophisticated computers in similar ways. As I have said, they delight in "crashing" the system, in overloading it or getting it into a state where it will not be able to function, and then they "bring it up" again.

In the first computer-rich elementary-school classroom I studied, there quickly grew up a community of experts at crashing and reviving the computer, skills that demanded considerable sophistication. This group of ten- and eleven-year-old experts didn't crash the system to inconvenience the teachers or the other students. They crashed the system in order to watch it go down and have an occasion to bring it up. After a few weeks of incessant crashes and virtuoso resuscitations, Peter and John, the two most skilled experts, developed a new variant on the crash/revive routine. They wrote a computer program that simulated a crash. This program made the computer appear ready for the "log in" command needed to "wake up" its operating system. But when someone went through the procedure of logging in, the screen would go blank, the system apparently dead. This would give the authors of the "pseudocrash" program an opportunity to do their "magic"—to type in a few characters and revive the machine.

At the time I was struck by the dramatic and witty flair of these fifth-grade "pseudocrashers." They seemed quite extraordinary. But in the years that followed, I saw that this episode was typical. Sooner or later, wherever there is a computer complex enough to make mastering its operating system a challenge, there develops the culture of the crash and the appearance of some variant of a pseudocrash program.

I ask a four-year-old named Ralph to draw a picture of something "not alive." He takes a large piece of paper and concentrates on weaving a small, dense mesh of lines in the middle of the sheet with a black crayon. And then he asks me to write out the name of the picture for him: Spider. Ralph looks up and announces, "Spiders are not alive." "Why?" I ask. He replies, "Because you can kill them."

Ralph has observed that spiders and ants can be stepped on, killed without hesitation, and to Ralph this makes them less alive to the point where he is willing to say they are not alive. But, of course, he contradicts himself, because you can't kill something that doesn't live. The tension in his answer shows him aware of the insect's marginal status as a living thing, a marginality that gives "permission" to experiment with the taboo on killing.

Speak and Spell in its "Say it" mode is also on the border. It is not alive, but seems to act willfully, of its own accord. Like the "marginal" insects, it can be an occasion for what seems an almost ritual exploration of life and death: pulling out the batteries and putting them back again. Appreciating the emotional charge of this ritual brings a more complicated and paradoxical picture of what is at stake when a child thinks about whether or not a computer is alive. Seeing the computer as alive adds to the emotion of killing it. But the relationship goes both ways: the excitement of killing the toy, of crashing the program, is itself an inducement to seeing the computational object as alive. It is exciting to play with the idea of life and death, and it is exciting to feel responded to by a "living" machine.

QUESTIONS

1. In the second paragraph of this selection, Turkle begins to discuss a "self-referential" picture that disturbed but "compelled" her when she was a child. Why does she describe this memory? How is it connected to her remarks about children and computers?

2. In the middle of this selection, Turkle describes how a computer toy, Speak and Spell, works. Discuss its operation. What is its "bug," and why is Laura upset by it? Describe the reaction of Paul, a slightly older child, to the same toy.

3. How does Turkle use narrative in her essay? What effect does it have? What difference would it make to "Why the Computer Disturbs" if all narrative were eliminated?

4. Discuss Turkle's use of analogies at various points in her essay to help her clarify the point she is making.

5. Point out specific words and phrases Turkle employs to help make her "subjects"—the children she has observed and is describing—come alive and be seen by the reader as individuals.

SUGGESTIONS FOR WRITING

1. Write an essay addressed to an alien creature visiting from elsewhere in the universe, telling it how to distinguish here on earth between what is alive and what is not.

2. Interview some young children of different ages about what they think is
    alive. You should observe striking variety in their responses. Write up the
    results of your interviews.

3. If you have a computer of your own, write a process analysis instructing a
    user how to do a simple task with it: to write and print a letter, for example,
    or to create and print a simple program. Assume that your audience is
    unfamiliar with your computer. Alternatively, address your instructions to
    a bright 6-year-old. (Hint: you will have to work harder to keep the interest
    of a 6-year-old.) Test your instructions on your computer.

STUDENT ESSAY

Steven Schneiderman
ARTIFICIAL STUPIDITY
★ ★ ★

*As an undergraduate at Queens College, the City University of New York,
Steven Schneiderman won several university literary awards for his poetry
and fiction. His work has appeared in "little magazines" across the country. Schneiderman is also a master magician, whose skills in both literature and legerdemain are brought together in his self-published magic
magazine,* Ruminations.

*It is easy to see how a young writer and sleight-of-hand specialist
might become infatuated with computers—machines whose power to perform seemingly impossible tasks appears nothing short of miraculous. A
computer cannot do everything, however, and in the following piece
Schneiderman describes his somewhat disillusioning discovery of the
capabilities—and ultimate limitations—of his word-processor.*

───

After spending many years typing term papers for college, I grew tired of using
Correct-type and White-out to conceal my typing inadequacies. Hunt and peck
is not an apt description of my skills at the keyboard; search and destroy comes
closer. Between the misspellings and the misplaced punctuation, I spent more
time retyping my papers than I did writing the first draft.

So in an attempt to receive higher grades and to end the drudgery of typing,
I succumbed to technology's quiet but persistent call, and I bought a micro-
computer, an Osborne 1, the world's first portable business computer. A friend
had shown me how he used his system for school work and a small business he
ran on the side. It looked simple enough. Insert a square thing called a floppy
disk into a slit called a floppy drive, and start typing away, for once without
worrying about three spelling mistakes in one word or about several words
running together. Finish typing, press a button, instant spelling checker. Press

another button, instant punctuation checker. Press a final button, instant error-free typing. What could be an easier way to earn an A+?

When I got my Osborne home, I was eager to start working on my next paper. I unpacked it from its styrofoam wrapping, and I carefully set it down in a place of honor on my desk, beside my beaten-up typewriter. The Smith-Corona stared at the new kid on the block and hummed angrily. "Sorry, old friend," I said to my typewriter, "but you're going into early retirement."

I switched my computer on and stared at the blinking lights with glee. This will get me that A+ without fail, I thought—once I figure out how to work the thing. Enter the Osborne User's Guide to Madness. It was over 800 pages thick, and each page was important. How was I ever going to get my paper completed on time when I had to first sit down and read this nonsense? My friend had made it sound so easy. Now I was back to square one. I had thought all I had to do was type in some words, and the machine would then edit all the awkwardness and errors out of my prose. I had thought, in fact, that the computer would be operated just as a typewriter is, except for the magic buttons I would press. Instead, I didn't even know where to start looking for them.

Spending the next few weeks before my paper was due reading the manual, rather than writing drafts, I discovered that the computer was not quite the Einstein I thought it was. On the contrary, it was actually no smarter than I. In essence, it was entirely dependent upon my input in order to work properly. The computer, for example, can't take my lumbering prose and make it dance and dazzle. In fact, since it doesn't understand a word you type into it, it doesn't know the difference between my writing and Shakespeare's or between *gobbledegook* and Shakespeare, let alone between a dangling modifier and a comma splice. It simply transfers the phrases—plain or ornamented, awkward or graceful—that are typed on its keyboard to a special internal area called the Random Access Memory, or RAM. A mechanical brain known as the CPU or Central Processing Unit studies all the words in the RAM and transforms the letters of the words into numbers. The CPU only thinks in binary terms: everything breaks down into two digits, zeros and ones. And these digits flip little circuits into on and off states. All my hard work thus becomes nothing more than tiny, unseen, electrical impulses. To substitute a more precise word for a vaguer one, to warn me that the analogy I've struggled to express isn't quite apt, is light years beyond its capacity.

This explains how the computer breaks down my thoughts, but how does it use programs in a seemingly intelligent manner? The manual stated that programs are stored on some form of magnetic media—floppy disks, for instance. When these are inserted into a slot in the computer called a disk drive, information on the disk can be loaded into the computer's RAM and processed by the CPU. Once the computer analyzes the program in its disk drive, it's still up to me to tell it what to do. After inserting the processing disk, I claimed some elbow room in the RAM to work in, calling the space by the safe but unoriginal title MY PAPER. Then I typed in the entire term paper. It had as many errors as my old Smith-Corona produced, of course—but this time I didn't worry about them.

What makes word processing so much more efficient than regular typing is the way in which you can use a program to manipulate and edit your text. All word processors have a variety of built-in commands which allow you to type over words, insert words between other words, delete entire sentences, move phrases from one end of a sentence to another, and much more. Thus they make it easy for you to take chances, to try a variety of things. What the computer can do for you is governed only by the type of word processor you are using and how well you can use it. I referred back to the manual constantly to see how many ways I could change the appearance of my work. A press of a key here and a tap of a key there brought about unusual and often surprising results. I discovered how much easier it was to proofread my own work while viewing it on a big screen. I also gained a new perspective on my writing abilities.

I permanently stored the file MY PAPER in the computer's memory, then replaced the word processing disk with a spelling checker disk. Once I had told it the name of the file to check, the computer started to whir and bleep. After the program showed me a list of all my careless misspellings, it made the corrections for me. And it never ridiculed me for getting some pretty simple words wrong.

I was beginning to enjoy myself. I could see long glimpses of the easy life my friend had told me about. I ejected the spelling checker and loaded the punctuation program. Once again, the machine beeped and blipped with satisfaction, unsplicing my comma splices, unfragmenting my fragments, and putting a halt to my run-ons. Meantime—having nothing to do—I watched MTV.

The final step was to print the paper on my printer. No more hours of mistyping and no more sloppy erasures, I gloated. With a gentle press of the key, the printer started to rat-a-tap-tap away. I strolled to the kitchen to make myself a roast beef on rye. Creating makes me hungry, but I'd avoided eating at my Smith-Corona since that night in high school when I'd smeared mayo on the third draft of a history paper and dumped my Coke on the typewriter's keys. Now I felt I could indulge myself. Old Os would do the work for me, and I didn't even have to stay in the same room to supervise. By the time I'd finished my 2 A.M. snack, the printing was completed, and my paper was in hand: perfectly written, spelled, punctuated, and typed. The professor was going to love it . . . .

A few weeks later, it was returned to me with a grade of B—, not quite what I had expected. "But why the low grade?" I asked the professor. "I worked so hard on this paper, and just look at how perfectly spelled, punctuated, and typed it is."

"Yes," he agreed, "you have done a very neat job, but the essay is weak—here and here it's illogical and, in general, your ideas need more development. You don't receive your grade for the good looks of your paper, you know; it's the thought that counts!"

Thought? I had never even thought about that. I had believed that the computer held the keys to my success, when all along it was really I who did. This taught me something important: the reason they call the "brain" of the computer Artificial Intelligence is because it can't do the thinking for you; that's left entirely to the user. And this time, I didn't take the time to think for myself.

QUESTIONS

1. Discuss the elements of humor in Schneiderman's essay. What do they add? What difference would it make to the essay if they were removed?

2. What misconceptions about computers and about writing did Schneiderman have before he wrote the essay he talks about in "Artificial Stupidity"?

3. Schneiderman's essay contains two process analyses. The first is his description of how a computer works. How complete is that process analysis? Does it help you to understand how a computer works? Can you think of ways Schneiderman might have extended his analysis?

4. What other kind of process analysis does the essay contain? How complete is it?

5. Why does Schneiderman call his essay "Artificial Stupidity"?

SUGGESTIONS FOR WRITING

1. Write a detailed process analysis explaining how to get an A+ on a paper written for freshman composition. Then, compare your version to those of your fellow students. How much agreement do you find? Read, or show, your version to your instructor. What is his or her response? Then rewrite your analysis, incorporating what you have learned from your classmates and instructor.

2. In a process analysis, describe the difficulties or disasters you have had with a mechanical process—putting together furniture that required assembly, for instance, or using a new and complex computer or VCR, or fixing a car engine or other machine.

Woody Allen
A GIANT STEP FOR MANKIND
★ ★ ★

Over the course of his long and highly successful career, Woody Allen has evolved from a gag writer for other comedians into one of America's most celebrated humorists and filmmakers. Born in Brooklyn in 1935, Allen went to work in 1953 for NBC-TV, where he wrote material for such personalities as Sid Caesar, Art Carney, Buddy Hackett, and Jack Parr.
   Allen first achieved celebrity as a stand-up comedian in the early

1960s. In 1964, a film producer who had seen Allen's nightclub act offered him a chance to write a script. Allen's first two movies were big moneymakers, which enabled him to obtain the financing to direct, star in, and write the screenplays for his subsequent films, including Take the Money and Run *(1969),* Bananas *(1970),* Sleeper *(1973),* Annie Hall *(1977),* Manhattan *(1979),* Zelig *(1983),* The Purple Rose of Cairo *(1984),* Hannah and Her Sisters *(1986), and his latest,* Radio Days *(1987). Beginning as an heir to such classic comedians as W.C. Fields and the Marx Brothers, Allen has developed, in the view of many critics, into one of America's most important directors and screen artists.*

He has also written two successful Broadway plays (Play It Again, Sam *and* Don't Drink the Water), *released several hit comedy albums, and published a number of best-selling books, which consist mainly of humorous pieces that appeared first in* The New Yorker. *The following story is reprinted from Allen's 1980 collection,* Side Effects.

Lunching yesterday on chicken in ichor—a house specialty at my favorite midtown restaurant—I was forced to listen to a playwright acquaintance defend his latest opus against a set of notices that read like a Tibetan Book of the Dead. Drawing tenuous connections between Sophocles' dialogue and his own, Moses Goldworm wolfed down his vegetable cutlet and raged like Carry Nation against the New York theatre critics. I, of course, could do nothing more than offer a sympathetic ear and assure him that the phrase "a dramatist of zero promise" might be interpreted in several ways. Then, in the split second it takes to go from calm to bedlam, the Pinero manqué half rose from his seat, suddenly unable to speak. Frantically waving his arms and clutching his throat, the poor fellow turned a shade of blue invariably associated with Thomas Gainsborough.

"My God, what is it?" someone screamed, as silverware clattered to the floor and heads turned from every table.

"He's having a coronary!" a waiter yelled.

"No, no, it's a fit," said a man at the booth next to me.

Goldworm continued to struggle and wave his arms, but with ever-diminishing style. Then, as various mutually exclusive remedies were advanced in anxious falsettos by sundry well-meaning hysterics in the room, the playwright confirmed the waiter's diagnosis by collapsing to the floor like a sack of rivets. Crumpled in a forlorn heap, Goldworm seemed destined to slip away before an ambulance could arrive, when a six-foot stranger possessing the cool aplomb of an astronaut strode to stage center and said in dramatic tones, "Leave everything to me, folks. We don't need a doctor—this is not a cardiac problem. By clutching his throat, this fellow has made the universal sign, known in every corner of the world, to indicate that he is choking. The symptoms may appear to be the same as those of a man suffering from a heart attack, but this man, I assure you, can be saved by the Heimlich Maneuver!"

With that, the hero of the moment wrapped his arms around my companion from behind and lifted him to an upright position. Placing his fist just under

Goldworm's sternum, he hugged sharply, causing a side order of bean curd to rocket out of the victim's trachea and carom off the hat rack. Goldworm came to apace and thanked his savior, who then directed our attention to a printed notice, supplied by the Board of Health, affixed to the wall. The poster described the aforementioned drama with perfect fidelity. What we had witnessed was indeed "the universal choking signal," conveying the victim's tripartite plight: (1) Cannot speak or breathe, (2) Turns blue, (3) Collapses. The diagnostic signs on the notice were followed by clear directions on the administration of the lifesaving procedure: the selfsame abrupt hug and resulting airborne protein we had witnessed, which had relieved Goldworm of the awkward formalities of the Long Goodbye.

A few minutes later, strolling home on Fifth Avenue, I wondered if Dr. Heimlich, whose name is now so firmly placed in the national consciousness as the discoverer of the marvelous maneuver I had just seen performed, had any idea of how close he had once come to being scooped by three still utterly anonymous scientists who had worked for months on end in search of a cure for the same perilous mealtime trauma. I also wondered if he knew of the existence of a certain diary kept by an unnamed member of the pioneer trio—a diary that came into my possession at auction quite by mistake, because of its similarity in heft and color to an illustrated work entitled "Harem Slaves," for which I had bid a trifling eight weeks' salary. Following are some excerpts from the diary, which I set down here purely in the interest of science:

January 3. Met my two colleagues today for the first time and found them both enchanting, although Wolfsheim is not at all as I had imagined. For one thing, he is heavier than in his photo (I think he uses an old one). His beard is of a medium length but seems to grow with the irrational abandon of crabgrass. Add to this thick, bushy brows and beady eyes the size of microbes, which dart about suspiciously behind spectacles the thickness of bulletproof glass. And then there are the twitches. The man has accumulated a repertoire of facial tics and blinks that demand nothing less than a complete musical score by Stravinsky. And yet Abel Wolfsheim is a brilliant scientist whose work on dinner-table choking has made him a legend the world over. He was quite flattered that I was familiar with his paper on Random Gagging, and he confided to me that my once skeptically regarded theory, that hiccupping is innate, is now commonly accepted at M.I.T.

If Wolfsheim is eccentric-looking, however, the other member of our triumvirate is exactly what I had expected from reading her work. Shulamith Arnolfini, whose experiments with recombinant DNA led to the creation of a gerbil that could sing "Let My People Go," is British in the extreme—predictably tweedy, with her hair skun in a bun, and with horn-rimmed glasses resting halfway down a beak nose. Furthermore, she possesses a speech impediment so audibly juicy that to be near her when she pronounces a word like "sequestered" is equivalent to standing at the center of a monsoon. I like them both and I predict great discoveries.

January 5. Things did not get under way as smoothly as I had hoped, for

Wolfsheim and I have had a mild disagreement over procedure. I suggested doing our initial experiments on mice, but he regards this as unnecessarily timid. His idea is to use convicts, feeding them large chunks of meat at five-second intervals, with instructions not to chew before swallowing. Only then, he claims, can we observe the dimensions of the problem in its true perspective. I took issue on moral grounds, and Wolfsheim became defensive. I asked him if he felt science was above morality, and took issue with his equating humans and hamsters. Nor did I agree with his somewhat emotional assessment of me as a "unique moron." Fortunately, Shulamith took my side.

January 7. Today was a productive one for Shulamith and me. Working around the clock, we induced strangulation in a mouse. This was accomplished by coaxing the rodent to ingest healthy portions of Gouda cheese and then making it laugh. Predictably, the food went down the wrong pipe, and choking occurred. Grasping the mouse firmly by the tail, I snapped it like a small whip, and the morsel of cheese came loose. Shulamith and I made voluminous notes on the experiment. If we can transfer the tail-snap procedure to humans, we may have something. Too early to tell.

February 15. Wolfsheim has developed a theory that he insists on testing, although I find it simplistic. He is convinced that a person choking on food can be saved by (his words) "giving the victim a drink of water." At first I thought he was joking, but his intense manner and wild eyes indicated a definite commitment to the concept. Clearly, he has been up for days toying with this notion, and in his laboratory glasses of water filled to various levels were everywhere. When I responded skeptically, he accused me of being negative, and began twitching like a disco dancer. You can tell he hates me.

February 27. Today was a day off, and Shulamith and I decided to motor to the countryside. Once we were out in nature, the whole concept of choking seemed so far away. Shulamith told me that she had been married before, to a scientist who had pioneered a study of radioactive isotopes, and whose entire body vanished in mid-conversation while he was testifying before a Senate committee. We talked about our personal preferences and tastes and discovered that we were both fond of the same bacteria. I asked Shulamith how she would feel if I kissed her. She said, "Swell," giving me the full moist spray peculiar to her speech problem. I have come to the conclusion that she is quite a beautiful woman, particularly when viewed through an X-ray-proof lead screen.

March 1. I now believe Wolfsheim is a madman. He tested his "glass of water" theory a dozen times, and in no case did it prove effective. When I told him to stop wasting valuable time and money, he bounced a petri dish off the bridge of my nose, and I was forced to hold him at bay with the Bunsen burner. As always, when work becomes more difficult frustrations mount.

March 3. Unable to obtain subjects for our dangerous experiments, we have been forced to cruise restaurants and cafeterias, hoping to work rapidly should we be lucky enough to find someone in distress. At the Sans Souci Deli, I tried lifting a Mrs. Rose Moscowitz by her ankles and shaking her, and although I managed to dislodge a monstrous chunk of kasha, she seemed ungrateful. Wolfsheim suggested that we might try slapping choke victims on the back, and pointed out that important back-slapping concepts had been suggested to him by Fermi at a symposium on digestion in Zurich thirty-two years ago. A grant to explore this was refused, however, when the government decided in favor of nuclear priorities. Wolfsheim, incidentally, has turned out to be a rival in my affair with Shulamith, and confessed affection for her yesterday in the biology lab. When he tried to kiss her, she hit him with a frozen monkey. He is a very complex and sad man.

March 18. At Marcello's Villa today we chanced upon a Mrs. Guido Bertoni in the act of choking on what was later identified as either cannelloni or a Ping-Pong ball. As I had foreseen, slapping her on the back did not help. Wolfsheim, unable to part with the old theories, tried administering a glass of water, but unfortunately seized it from the table of a gentleman well placed in the cement and contracting community, and all three of us were escorted out of the service entrance and up against a lamppost, over and over.

April 2. Today Shulamith raised the notion of a pincers—that is, some form of long tweezers or forceps to extract food that falls into the windpipe. Each citizen would carry one such instrument on his person and be educated in its use and handling by the Red Cross. In eager anticipation, we drove to Belknap's Salt of the Sea to remove a badly wedged crabcake from the esophagus of a Mrs. Shana Mendel. Unfortunately, the gasping woman became agitated when I produced the formidable tweezers, and sank her teeth into my wrist, causing me to drop the instrument down her throat. Only the quick action of her husband, Nathan, who held her above the ground by her hair and raised and lowered her like a yo-yo, prevented a fatality.

April 11. Our project is coming to a close—unsuccessfully, I am sorry to say. Funding has been cut off, our foundation board having decided that the remaining money might be more profitably spent on some joy-buzzers. After I received the news of our termination, I had to have fresh air to clear my head, and as I walked alone at night by the Charles River I couldn't help reflecting on the limits of science. Perhaps people are *meant* to choke now and then when they eat. Perhaps it is all part of some unfathomable cosmic design. Are we so conceited as to think research and science can control everything? A man swallows too large a bite of steak, and gags. What could be simpler? What more proof is needed of the exquisite harmony of the universe? We will never know all the answers.

April 20. Yesterday afternoon was our last day, and I chanced upon Shulamith in the Commissary, where she was glancing over a monograph on the new herpes vaccine and gobbling a matjes herring to tide her over till dinnertime. I approached stealthily from the rear and, seeking to surprise her, quietly placed my arms around her, experiencing at that moment the bliss that only a lover feels. Instantly she began choking, a portion of herring having lodged suddenly in her gullet. My arms were still around her, and, as fate would have it, my hands were clasped just under her sternum. Something—call it blind instinct, call it scientific luck—made me form a fist and snap it back against her chest. In a trice, the herring became disengaged, and a moment later the lovely woman was as good as new. When I told Wolfsheim about this, he said, "Yes, of course. It works with herring, but will it work with ferrous metals?"

I don't know what he meant and I don't care. The project is ended, and while it is perhaps true that we have failed, others will follow in our footsteps and, building upon our crude preliminary work, will at last succeed. Indeed, all of us here can foresee the day when our children, or certainly our grandchildren, will live in a world where no individual, regardless of race, creed, or color, will ever be fatally overcome by his own main course. To end on a personal note, Shulamith and I are going to marry, and until the economy begins to brighten a little she and Wolfsheim and I have decided to provide a much-needed service and open up a really first-class tattoo parlor.

QUESTIONS

1. What qualities of the scientist's mind and aspects of the scientific mode of inquiry are ridiculed by Allen in "A Giant Step for Mankind"? What other details of the story contribute to the satirical effect?

2. The diary describes a process of scientific inquiry that leads to a discovery, although the discovery is abandoned. (Why is it abandoned?) Analyze this process. Do you find the connections between the steps of the process you usually see in such analysis? Do you think some scientific breakthroughs are achieved in the same way that the writer of the diary has achieved his?

3. Point out metaphors and similes in Allen's story, and discuss how they help him make what he is describing clearer or more vivid.

4. As the diary writer strolls alongside the Charles River in Boston after his grant money has been cut off, he reflects on the nature of the universe. How would you characterize the language of that reflection? What does the sentence "A man swallows too large a piece of steak, and gags" do to the tone of the rest of the passage? How do you think Allen means for us to react to his character's musings?

5. Although nearly all of us possess a sense of humor, the ability to write humorously is far less common, and Woody Allen is brilliant at it. Study his story carefully, drawing up lists of things—words, phrases, incidents, descriptive details—that you think are funny. Then discuss what *makes* these things funny.

SUGGESTION FOR WRITING

Choose a scientific discovery you are familiar with (perhaps from having learned about it in a biology, chemistry, or physics class) and, in a serious essay, describe the process that led to it. Imagine that your audience is intelligent, but not familiar with scientific jargon or with the specific problem the scientist was addressing. You may need to consult some reference source to write this paper. If so, be sure to paraphrase the information you use instead of copying it verbatim. In addition, make sure to attribute any information you use to your source.

Tom Clark
SONNET
★ ★ ★

Tom Clark's poems have been collected in numerous volumes, including Airplanes *(1966),* Green *(1971),* Smack *(1972),* Suite *(1974),* Chicago *(1975),* When Things Get Tough on Easy Street *(1978), and, most recently,* Paradise Resisted *(1984). In addition to poetry, he has also written books on a variety of subjects, including a biography,* Jack Kerouac *(1986), and several works on professional baseball. Clark sees no contradiction between his aesthetic and athletic interests. On the contrary, when an interviewer asked him how he came to be both a poet and an author of sports books, Clark replied, "These are two fields that I think have a natural relationship. The best poems and the best baseball games share a dramatic tension you can't find in many other places."*
The following poem is from Clark's 1969 volume, Stones.

The orgasm completely
Takes the woman out of her
Self in a wave of ecstasy
That spreads through all of her body.
Her nervous, vascular and muscular
Systems participate in the act.
The muscles of the pelvis contract
And discharge a plug of mucus from the cervix
While the muscular sucking motions of the cervix
Facilitate the incoming of the semen.
At the same time the constriction of the pelvic
Muscles prevent the loss of the semen. The discharge
Makes the acid vaginal lubricant
Alkaline, so as not to destroy the spermatozoa.

QUESTIONS

1. A sonnet, which is a lyric poem of fourteen lines, has long been the poetic form associated with the expression of romantic love. Not only is Clark's poem an unconventional sonnet, then, but some students may feel that "Son-

net" is not even a poem. Discuss this idea. What is a poem? How is a poem different from prose? Are there "appropriate" and "inappropriate" subjects for poetry? Should a subject be "poetic"? (And if so, what is a "poetic" subject?)

2. "Sonnet" is a process analysis. Can a process analysis be happily "wedded" to a poem? Why or why not?

3. Characterize the diction of this poem—the *kind* of words Clark uses. Does this choice of diction seem unusual for a poem? For a description of sexual love? Why would Clark, who could use any kind of language he pleased, choose this particular kind? How does Clark's diction help you to determine his attitude toward his subject?

4. Poems generally contain ample figurative language—metaphors and similes, for example—as well as ample concrete images. How would you characterize the images that are contained in the last eight lines of "Sonnet"? Do they make sex seem appealing? Why is "Sonnet" so bereft of the images and metaphors that help to make other poems memorable?

SUGGESTIONS FOR WRITING

1. Argue that "Sonnet" either would or would not be a useful addition to a junior high school or high school sex education course. If you decide it should be included, indicate how you would use it.

2. Write an essay (or a poem) in which you copy Clark's technique to describe, in the barest and most scientific terms, the steps of an activity you have hitherto regarded as highly pleasurable: kissing someone, eating a hot fudge sundae, shooting the perfect basket, enjoying a swim on a 99-degree summer day. Describe as objectively and technically as possible the changes your body goes through during any of these activities. (You may need to do some research to write this.) Ignore your emotional and spiritual gratification. After you finish writing, read your essay or poem aloud. How would you have to change your piece so that it would capture the pleasurable aspects of your experience?

CHAPTER
Seven

POPULAR ART
Classification

Classification is not just a method writers use to organize essays; it is a basic act that we perform all the time. When we separate a pile of laundry into individual stacks (shirts, socks, underwear), each to be stored in its own drawer; when we pigeonhole people in terms of their behavior, values, or appearance (introvert-extravert, Preppie-Yuppie, hunk-nerd); when we rank movies according to a personal rating system ("Must-See," "So-So," "Turkey")—in all of these cases we are engaged in essentially the same process, namely, that of sorting things into distinct categories, arranging them according to type. Moreover, in each of these instances we are employing this process for the same reason—for classification. Whether we use it to accomplish a routine chore (such as putting away our laundry) or, at the opposite extreme, to organize a complex body of knowledge (in the way a paleontologist might assign a newly discovered fossil to a particular class of prehistoric mollusk), it always serves the same purpose. Classification allows us to give structure to our experience, to take an unwieldy mass of material and put it into a logical and comprehensible order.

It is conventional to distinguish between the methods of *classification,* in which a large number of things are sorted into a few, clearly labeled categories, and *division,* in which a single, many-faceted subject is broken down into a convenient number of individual parts. For example, in a popular New York City guidebook called *The Underground Gourmet,* which lists places in the city where a couple can eat a decent meal for less than twenty-five dollars, the authors, Milton Glaser and Jerome Snyder, first divide Manhattan into discrete geographical areas (East Side below 14th Street, East Side 14th–34th Streets, Greenwich Village, etc.); then, within each area, they classify the restaurants according to national cuisine (Chinese, French, Spanish, German, etc.). Although division and classification would seem to be the opposite of each other, they are (as Glaser and Snyder's guidebook shows) complementary, and in practice so closely interrelated that there is no real advantage in treating them separately. We will use one term, classification, to describe an organizing method that consists of dividing your main topic (television shows, for example) into logical and consistent categories (situation comedies, police dramas, soaps) and then grouping your supporting examples within these categories.

While the general rationale for using classification is always to impose order and coherence on a large, sprawling subject—to turn a jumble of facts into a tightly organized piece of writing—there are as many specific uses for the method as there are writing topics. The intention of Glaser and Snyder, for instance, is simply to make it possible for readers to locate cheap neighborhood restaurants serving specific cuisines in New York City. New York City is, of course, not merely large and sprawling; it is an intimidatingly vast metropolis containing countless obscure ethnic restaurants. By using classification, however, the authors create a neatly arranged system as easy to use as a phone book, so that a reader who lives, for instance, on the west side of Manhattan between 59th and 86th Streets and who is suddenly overcome with an urge for a dish of Norwegian *lapskaus* can satisfy his or her craving with no trouble.

At other times, writers use classification to help prove a point, clarify an issue, or explore a theme. While satiric in tone, Mel Marcus's piece, "The ABC's of TV" uses classification to argue that American TV, which elitist critics tend to regard as a kind of cultural garbage heap, offers programs that, in fact, vary widely in both content and quality and that ought to be taken as seriously as "le cinema." Stephen King's *thematic* classification of American horror films allows him to examine, in a very systematic way, the various anxieties and fears that underlie this popular motion picture genre.

The simplest form of classification—sometimes called *binary* classification—consists of dividing your subject into two main, opposing categories: workers and bosses, givers and takers, winners and losers, heroes and villains, ascetics and gluttons, smokers and nonsmokers, vegetarians and meat-eaters. The binary method does, of course, have its serious uses; like other forms of classification, it can help us uncover patterns of structure and meaning in subjects that, at a glance, seem largely devoid of both. But because this method lends itself to the kind of whimsical overstatement favored by professional humorists, it is often found in comic writing. Ogden Nash's poem, "I Have It on Good Authority," for instance, contains an example of binary classification in the lines:

There are two kinds of people who
    blow through life like a breeze,
And one kind is gossipers and the
    other kind is gossipees.

In a similar way, Fran Lebowitz begins a witty essay called "Things" by declaring, "All of the things in the world can be divided into two basic categories:
natural things and artificial things. Or, as they are more familiarly known, nature
and art. Now, nature, as I am only too well aware, has her enthusiasts, but on
the whole, I am not to be counted among them. To put it rather bluntly, I am
not the type who wants to go back to the land—I am the type who wants to
go back to the hotel." Using her two, all-inclusive categories, Lebowitz then
provides a simple chart to "graphically illustrate the vast superiority of that
which is manufactured over that which is not":

NATURE	ART
The sun	The toaster oven
Your own two feet	Your own two Bentleys
Windfall apples	Windfall profits
Roots and berries	Linguini with clam sauce, etc.

Classifying something, then, requires that it be separated into a minimum of
two categories. There is, however, no fixed maximum; the number of divisions
depends entirely on the size and complexity of the subject. The system used by
zoologists to classify the members of the animal kingdom, for instance, consists
of a hierarchy of groups that moves from phylla down through classes, orders,
families, genera, and species, with provision for additional ranks such as sub-
phylla, superorders, and subfamilies, where needed. Indeed, as the eminent
folklorist Stith Thompson has pointed out, the serious study of any branch of
knowledge requires, as a first step, the creation of a coherent classification
system.

Needless to say, the kind of classification papers you will be writing for class
will not involve anything as elaborate as the zoologist's scheme. For the most
part, the selections in this chapter divide their subjects into fewer than six
categories; a number of them use no more than three—Mel Marcus's ranking
of television programs into three levels of quality, A, B, and C; Michael Malone's
division of TV sitcoms into *tribal* comedies, *family* comedies, and *couple* comedies. Even a very diverse body of material can generally be organized into a
manageable number of categories.

Seeing a large, varied, and apparently amorphous topic reduced to a handful
of neatly labeled categories can be deeply satisfying to readers. For this reason,
slick magazines and best-selling books (especially of the "pop-psych" variety)
commonly rely on the technique of breaking down a complex subject into a
small number of easy-to-grasp subdivisions. Eric Berne's enormously successful

book, *Games People Play*, for example, argues that all social interactions are actually highly ritualized (if unconscious) "games," which he classifies under six sociological headings (Life Games, Marital Games, Party Games, Sexual Games, Underworld Games, Consulting Room Games) and identifies with catchy names ("If It Weren't for You," "Let's You and Him Fight," "See What You Made Me Do"). As Berne's book indicates, a great advantage of classification is that it allows writers a simple, clear-cut way of organizing and presenting a great deal of complicated information. (Indeed, one shortcoming of articles and books on popular psychology is their fondness for inventing classifications that are *too* simplistic, that pigeonhole people in tidy, predetermined categories that fail to recognize the infinite variations in human behavior.)

Classification can serve another, equally important function. It can not only provide a structure for your paper but also help you clarify your ideas—enable you, that is, to make meaningful connections you might not otherwise perceive. If you had never seen playing cards before and someone dropped a thoroughly shuffled deck on a table in front of you, you would probably stare at it in bewilderment until, in examining the faces of the fifty-two cards, you noticed that they were distinguished by two different colors and four separate emblems: two red shapes (a heart and a diamond) and two distinctive black symbols (spade and club, though of course you wouldn't be familiar with these designations). By sorting them into four stacks according to suit, you would soon realize that, within each group, the cards progressed from one through ten and then moved, in ascending order of royalty, up to the king. You still wouldn't know how to play gin rummy, but you would have discovered an orderly and coherent relationship among objects that had formerly seemed thoroughly random and confusing.

Similarly, the very act of taking raw data and sorting them into categories can help you discover significant patterns in the subject you are dealing with. There will be times, of course, when you won't have to search very hard for such patterns; often they will be predetermined by the nature of your topic. Let us say that you are asked to write a research paper which examines the reading habits of the American public by analyzing the kinds of books that were most popular in a given year. The wording of this topic suggests three obvious ways of breaking it down into categories. First, you might use the classification method common to best-seller lists and divide books into four categories (hardcover fiction, hardcover nonfiction, paperback fiction, and paperback nonfiction). Second, you could arrange titles according to genre (for example, mystery and suspense, science fiction and fantasy, western and combat, and so on). Finally, you might group titles in terms of sales figures (100,000+ copies, 250,000+ copies, etc.).

Which of these three you should choose depends on the specific purpose of your essay. Because it deals with statistics, the third method of classification would probably be most useful for a paper on the economics of publishing (for example, one that shows how sales and marketing considerations determine which books make it into print). The second method, on the other hand—

because it focuses on content—would be best for a paper examining our cultural tastes.

Let us assume, however, that, instead of presenting you with a very specific, narrowly defined topic, your composition teacher assigns you a paper on the general subject of best-sellers. After spending some time doing library research and gathering data from sources like *The New York Times Book Review* and *Publishers Weekly,* you decide to concentrate on nonfiction paperbacks. You collect the titles of recent best-sellers and come up with a list that looks something like this:

1. Wendy Stehling. *Thin Thighs in Thirty Days*

2. Carole Jackson. *Color Me Beautiful*

3. John T. Molloy. *Molloy's Live for Success*

4. Dan Kiley. *The Wendy Dilemma: When Women Stop Mothering Their Men*

5. Kenneth Blanchard and Spencer Johnson. *The One Minute Manager*

6. Ellington Darden. *The Nautilus Bodybuilding Book*

7. Jane Fonda. *Jane Fonda's Workout Book*

8. Martha Friedman. *Overcoming the Fear of Success*

9. Harold H. Broomfield. *Making Peace with Your Parents*

10. Durk Pearson and Sandy Shaw. *Life Extension*

11. Leo Buscaglia. *Living, Loving, and Learning*

12. Douglas Casey. *Crisis Investing*

13. Norman King. *The Money Market Book*

14. Lonnie Barback and Linda Levine. *Shared Intimacies*

15. Mark McCormack. *What They Don't Teach You at Harvard Business School*

16. Henrie Weisinger and Norman Lorenz. *Nobody's Perfect: How to Give Criticism and Get Results*

Your next logical step is to group together those titles that share a significant characteristic. Studying your list, you arrive at the following categories:

I.   Fitness and Beauty (titles 1, 2, 6, 7, 10)

II.   Money and Success (titles 3, 5, 8, 12, 13, 15)

III. Personal Relationships (titles 4, 9, 11, 14, 16)

The resulting outline not only provides you with a clear, logical structure for your paper; it also suggests an interesting thesis: namely, that, based on the evidence of recent nonfiction best-sellers, it seems clear that the old-fashioned American belief in the possibility of improving (even perfecting) our lives through hard work, determination, and "know-how" remains as strong as ever.

When writing a classification paper, you should watch out for certain pitfalls. First, you must make sure that your categories don't overlap. Adding a section on "self-help" to the above outline would only confuse matters, since each of the existing categories can be considered a form of self-help. Second, you must be sure to treat your groupings in equal detail. It would make your paper lopsided to write two lengthy sections on fitness and success, for example, and then devote only a sentence or two to personal relationships. Finally, while you should not, of course, overlook any major aspect of a particular subject, keep in mind that it is not always necessary to include every conceivable subcategory. In his essay on horror films, for instance, Stephen King examines several types of anxiety—economic, political, and primal—to illustrate his point that these movies serve an important psychological function by giving shape and expression to our unconscious fears. Theoretically, King could have included other categories, too: spiritual, marital, or parental anxieties, to name just a few. In this case (as in others), however, a small number of representative categories makes the point quite effectively; a more extensive treatment might easily have become repetitive. With these few rules in mind—and a bit of practice—you will find that classification can serve as one of the handiest organizational tools at a writer's disposal.

Edith Efron
THE SOAPS—ANYTHING BUT 99–44/100 PERCENT PURE
★ ★ ★

Soap operas, which began as radio serials in the early 1930s, have been an enormously popular form of daytime entertainment for half a century. How much have these domestic melodramas changed over the years? According to critic Madeleine Edmondson, coauthor of From Mary Noble to Mary Hartman: The Complete Soap Opera Book, *the answer is: Very little. "The men and women of soapland," she writes, "may look very modern, wearing the latest fashions, using current jargon, playing the guitar, or even lallygagging about in their waterbeds—but they have hardly changed at all in the fifty years of soap opera."*

In the following essay, however, Edith Efron—a staff writer for TV Guide—*takes issue with this assertion. According to Efron, today's soaps have undergone a radical transformation. Their traditional "source of drama" is no longer the trials and tribulations of a noble housewife, who, "with husband in wheelchair, struggled helplessly against adversity." Rather it is what one commentator euphemistically calls "the male-female relationship"—in a word, sex.*

Before coming to TV Guide, *Efron worked as reporter and editor on a number of magazines, including* Time, Look, *and* Life. *She is also the author of two books:* The News Twisters *(1971) and* How CBS Tried to Kill a Book *(1972).*

———

Some months ago, the sleepy, Victorian world of daytime drama made news. The news was that it had ceased to be sleepy and Victorian. In fact, said the reports, the soap operas were doing something no one could quite believe: "peddling sex."

Announced one astounded critic: "Folks squawking about cheap nighttime sex should harken to the sickly sexuality of daytime soap opera. *Love of Life* details frank affairs between married women and men; *Search for Tomorrow* has a single girl in an affair with a married man, result: pregnancy; *The Secret Storm* has another single girl expecting a married man's child."

And, under the headlines "Era of Souped-Up Soapers" and "Torrid Days on TV Serial Front," *Variety,* the weekly newspaper of the entertainment industry, reported that there was a daytime "race to dredge up the most lurid incidents in sex-based human wretchedness," and cited "a torrid couch scene involving a housewife with gown cleaved to the navel who was sloshed to the gills on martinis, working her wiles on a husband (not hers). The fade to detergent blurb left little doubt as to the ensuing action."

Even a superficial investigation of events in the soap-opera world confirms that these reports are true.

To understand this phenomenon, one must enter the total universe of the soap operas. And if one does, one soon discovers that the central source of drama is not what it used to be in the old days, when the brave housewife, with husband in wheel chair, struggled helplessly against adversity. The soaps have shifted drastically on their axes; the fundamental theme today is, as Roy Winsor, producer of *Secret Storm,* puts it: "the male-female relationship."

More specifically, the theme of nine of the 10 daytime shows on the air when this study was launched is the mating-marital-reproductive cycle set against a domestic background. The outer world is certainly present—one catches glimpses of hospitals, offices, courtrooms, business establishments—but the external events tend to be a foil for the more fundamental drama, which is rooted in the biological life cycle. Almost all dramatic tension and moral conflict emerge from three basic sources: mating, marriage and babies.

The mating process is the cornerstone of this trivalue system. The act of searching for a partner goes on constantly in the world of soap opera. Vacuous teen-age girls have no thought whatever in their heads except hunting for a man. Older women wander about, projecting their intense longing to link themselves to unattached males. Heavily made-up villainous "career women" prowl, relentlessly seeking and nabbing their prey: the married man. Sad, lonely divorcèes hunt for new mates.

This all-consuming, single-minded search for a mate is an absolute good in the soap-opera syndrome. Morality—and dramatic conflict—emerge from how the search is conducted. Accordingly, there is sex as approached by "good" people, and sex as it is approached by villains.

"Good" people's sex is a somewhat extraordinary phenomenon, which can best be described as "icky." In *The Doctors,* Dr. Maggie confides, coyly, to her sister: "He kissed me." Her sister asks, even more coyly: "Did you want him to kiss you?" Maggie wriggles, and says: "He says I did." Then archly adds: "You know? I did." Maggie has already been married; her sister has had at least one lover. Coyness, not chastity, is the sign of their virtue.

"Good" people's sex is also passive, diffident and apologetic. In *The Doctors,* Sam, after an unendurably long buildup, finally takes Dr. Althea, a troubled divorcée, in his arms, and kisses her once, gently, on the lips. He then looks rueful, says, "I'm sorry," and moves to look mournfully out the window. "I'm not," murmurs Althea softly, and floats out of the room.

The "good" people act like saddened goldfish; the villains, on the other hand, are merely grotesque. One gets the impression that villains, both male and female, have read a lot of Ian Fleming, through several layers of cheesecloth.

To wit: a dinner between villainess Valerie Shaw and Dr. Matt in *The Doctors* in which Valerie leers, ogles and hints ("A smart woman judges a man by his mouth. . . . Yours is strong and sensual. I'm glad I came to dinner"), announces she will be his "playmate" and boasts throatily, "I play hard and seriously—but not necessarily for keeps."

And in *Love of Life* a sinister chap named Ace drinks in a bar with a teen-age girl who used to be his mistress. "We used to ignite," he breathes insinuatingly. They exchange a kiss—presumably so inflammable that the camera nervously cuts the picture off beneath their chins. "Not bad, baby," he gasps heavily.

This endless mating game, of course, has a purpose: It leads to marriage, the second arch-value in the soap-opera universe. And the dominant view of marriage in the soaps is also worthy of mention. According to the "good" women, it consists of two ingredients: "love" and homemaking.

"Love," in the soaps, tends to be a kind of hospitalization insurance, usually provided by females to male emotional cripples. In these plays, a woman rarely pledges herself to "honor and obey" her husband. She pledges to cure him of his alcoholism, to forgive his criminal record, paranoia, pathological lying, premarital affairs—and, generally, to give him a shoulder to cry on.

An expression of love, or a marriage proposal, in the daytime shows, often sounds like a sobbing confession to a psychiatrist. In *Search for Tomorrow* Patti's father, a reformed drinker, took time out from brooding over his daughter's illegitimate pregnancy to express his "love" for his wife. It consisted of a thorough—and convincing—rehash of his general worthlessness and former drinking habits. "I need you," he moaned. "That's all I want," she said.

In *General Hospital* Connie's neurotic helplessness proved irresistible some weeks ago; Dr. Doug declared his love. They engaged in a weird verbal competition as to who was more helpless than whom, who was more scared than whom, who "needed" whom more than whom. Doug won. Connie would be his pillar of strength.

Homemaking, the second ingredient of a "good" woman's marriage, is actually a symbolic expression of "love." There is a fantastic amount of discussion of food on these shows, and it is all strangely full of marital meaning. On *The Guiding Light* the audience sat through a detailed preview of the plans for roasting a turkey (the stuffing has raisins in it), which somehow would help get separated Julie and Michael together again. On *The Doctors* one ham was cooked, eaten and remorselessly discussed for three days; it played a critical role in the romance of Sam and Dr. Althea.

If domesticity is a marital "good," aversion to it is a serious evil. On *Secret Storm* a husband's arrival from work was greeted by a violent outburst by his wife, who handed him a list of jobs he had not done around the house. His neglect of the curtain rod was a sure sign that he was in love with a temptress who works in his office. Conversely, if a wife neglects her house, the marriage is rocky.

After mating and marriage, the third crucial value in the soap-opera universe is reproduction. The perpetuation of the species is the ultimate goal toward which almost all "good" people strive. And "The Baby" is the household god.

"Good" people discuss pregnancy endlessly. Young wives are either longing to be pregnant, worried because they are not pregnant, getting pregnant or fighting heroically "not to lose the baby." And at whatever stage of this process they happen to be, it justifies their being inept, irritable, hysterical and irrational.

"Good" men, needless to say, are unfailingly sympathetic to the reproductive process and are apparently fascinated by every detail of it. In *The Doctors* you knew one chap was a "good" husband because he referred to himself as "an expectant father" and earnestly discussed his wife's "whoopsing" with his friends.

The superlative value of "The Baby" is best revealed when he makes his appearance without benefit of a marriage license. He is usually brought into the world by a blank-faced little girl who has been taught to believe that the only valid goal in life is to mate, marry and reproduce, and who has jumped the gun. The social problem caused by this error in timing is solved in different ways. The girl has an abortion (Patricia, *Another World*); she loses the baby in an accident (Patti, *Search for Tomorrow*); she gives the baby up for adoption (Ellen, *As the World Turns*); she has the baby and marries its father (Julie, *Guiding Light*); she has the baby and marries someone else (Amy, *Secret Storm*).

The attitude of the baby-worshipping "good" people to this omnipresent social catastrophe is strangely mixed. The girl is viewed as a helpless victim of male villainy: "She loved the fellow too much," said Angie's father sadly in *General Hospital*. Of course, she has acquired the baby "the wrong way" and must—and does—suffer endlessly because of it. Nonetheless, she is having "The Baby." Thus she receives an enormous amount of sympathy, guidance and help from "good" people.

It seems almost unnecessary to say that only "bad" people in soap operas are anti-baby. The fastest bit of characterization ever accomplished in the history of drama was achieved on *Secret Storm,* when Kip's father recently arrived on the scene. He said: "I can't stand all this talk about babies." This instantly established him as a black-hearted villain.

The worst people of all, in the soaps, however, are the "career women," unnatural creatures who actually enjoy some activity other than reproducing the species. With the single exception of *The Doctors,* which features two "good" career women, Drs. Maggie and Althea, even the feeblest flicker of a desire for a career is a symptom of villainy in a woman who has a man to support her. Some weeks ago, we could predict that Ann Reynolds, in *The Young Marrieds,* was heading for dire trouble. She was miserable over her lost career, she had no babies, and she said those most evil of words: "I want a purpose in life."

It is hardly surprising to discover that even when the female characters achieve their stated ideal, they are almost invariably miserable. A man to support them, an empty house to sit in, no mentally demanding work to do and an endless vista of future pregnancies do not seem to satisfy the younger soap-opera ladies. They are chronically bored and hysterical.

They also live in dread of the ever-present threat of adultery, because their husbands go outside every day and meet wicked career women. They also agonize frequently over the clash between their "needs as a woman" and their "needs as a mother."

The male denizens of this universe are equally miserable for parallel reasons. They suffer quite a bit from unrequited love. They are often sick with jealousy, tortured by their wives' jealousy of their careers and outer-world existence. They, too, have a remarkable amount of trouble reconciling their "needs as men" with their "needs as fathers."

So we find, amid all the gloom in Sudsville, a lot of drinking, epidemic infidelity, and countless cases of acute neurosis, criminality, psychotic break-downs and post-maternal psychosis.

And this, dear reader, is the "sex" that the soap operas are "peddling" these days. It is a soggy, dreary spectacle of human misery, and is unworthy of all those "torrid" headlines. In fact, if one wants to be soured forever on the male-female relationship, the fastest way to achieve this state is to watch daytime drama.

The real question is not "where did all the sex come from?" but where did this depressing view of the male-female relationship come from? Hardened observers of TV's manners and mores have claimed that sex is being stressed in the soaps because it "sells." But the producers of soaps retort hotly that this has nothing to do with it. Their story lines, they insist, simply reflect social reality.

Says Frank Dodge, producer of *Search for Tomorrow:* "We always try to do shows that are identifiable to the public. These shows are a recognition of existing emotions and problems. It's not collusion, but a logical coincidence that adultery, illegitimate children and abortions are appearing on many shows. If you read the papers about what's going on in the suburbs—well, it's more startling than what's shown on the air."

"The moral fiber has been shattered in this Nation, and nothing has replaced it," says Roy Winsor, producer of *Secret Storm.* "There's a clammy cynicism about life in general. It deeply infects the young. It leads to a generation that sits, passively, and watches the world go by. The major interest is the male-female relationship. That's the direction the daytime shows are going in. Some of the contemporary sickness has rubbed off onto TV."

A consultation with some authorities on feminine and family psychology seems to support these gentlemen's contentions about the soap operas. "They're realistic," says Dr. Harold Greenwald, training analyst of the National Psychological Association for Psychoanalysis and supervising psychologist of the Community Guidance Service in New York. "I think they're more realistic than many of the evening shows. They're reflecting the changes taking place in our society. There are fewer taboos. The age of sexual activity in the middle classes had dropped and it has increased in frequency. There is more infidelity. These plays reflect these problems."

Dr. William Menaker, professor of clinical psychology at New York University, says: "The theater, the novel, and the film have always reflected people's concern with the sexual life; and in this sense, what's on the air reflects these realities of life. Increasing frankness in dealing with these problems isn't a symptom of moral decay but rather reflects the confused values of a transitional period of sociosexual change.

"Unfortunately, the vision of sex that seems to emerge on these shows is mechanical and adolescent, immature. The 'love' seems equally childish; it is interacting dependency, rather than a mutual relating between two autonomous adults. As for anti-intellectualism of these shows, it is actually antifeminine. It shows the resistance of both writers and audience to the development of the total feminine personality. There is no doubt that these shows are a partial reflection of some existing trends in our society; it is not a healthy picture."

Finally, Betty Friedan, author of *The Feminine Mystique,* says: "The image of woman that emerges in these soap operas is precisely what I've called 'The Feminine Mystique.' The women are childish and dependent; the men are degraded because they relate to women who are childish and dependent; and the view of sex that emerges is sick. These plays reflect an image built up out of the sickest, most dependent, most immature women in our society. They do not reflect all women. In reality there are many who are independent, mature, and who possess identity. The soaps are reflecting the sickest aspect of women."

On the basis of these comments, one can certainly conclude that all this "sex-based human wretchedness" is on the air because it exists in society. And the producers' claims that this is dramatic "realism" appear to have some validity.

But does the fact that a phenomenon exists justify its incessant exploration by the daytime dramas? Two of the three experts consulted actively refrain from making moral judgments. Betty Friedan, however, does not hesitate to condemn the soap operas. "The fact that immature, sick, dependent women exist in our society is no justification for these plays," she says. "The soap operas are playing to this sickness. They are feeding it. They are helping to keep women in this helpless, dependent state."

QUESTIONS

1. In what way do soap operas, according to the experts Efron cites, reflect social realities? Look again at Efron's description of the content of these programs. Do you think these experts are right?

2. Given Efron's description of soap operas, why is it natural that a feminist like Betty Friedan would find these shows so reprehensible? Do you think that Efron shares Friedan's opinion of the soaps? Why or why not?

3. How does Efron seem to feel about the soaps' extreme preoccupation with "the mating process"? How does her language—her choice of words and phrases—convey her attitude to the reader?

4. How would you characterize Efron's attitudes towards soap operas in general? Point to places where her attitude comes across most clearly. How does the *dialogue* she quotes give us a sense, not only of the content of these shows, but of her own feelings about them?

5. This essay has a very logical structure. How does Efron use the "trivalue system" of mating, marriage, and babies to organize her examination of the soaps? How does she subdivide each of these topics into categories? What categories does she use? As an exercise, outline the organizational scheme of this essay.

SUGGESTION FOR WRITING

According to the authorities Efron quotes, the world of soap operas is a reflection of real life, of contemporary social realities. To a large extent, this observation can be made about most television shows. Even programs that seem completely nonrealistic—"Star Trek," "The A-Team," "Fantasy Island"—reveal a great deal about the prevailing values, beliefs, and aspirations of our society. Using classification as your organizing principle, write a detailed essay in which you show how contemporary TV shows reflect the current state of American society.

Mel Marcus
THE ABC'S OF TV
★ ★ ★

Of all forms of pop-culture study, film criticism is certainly the most respectable. Since the late 1960s, film-study courses have been proliferating in colleges, and the bibliography of scholarly works on directors like Alfred Hitchcock, John Ford, and Howard Hawks seems to grow bigger by the day. By comparison, criticism which looks closely at the thematic and artistic content of commercial TV is virtually nonexistent. As Michael

Malone points out in his essay, "And Gracie Begat Lucy Who Begat Laverne" (p. 307), renowned film critic Pauline Kael recently "urged budding movie analysts to take up television study instead"—not only because the field is so important but also because so little significant work has been done in it.

While there is clearly a large element of satire in the following essay, it makes an interesting attempt to define some simple aesthetic standards for three of the most popular types of television series. The article originally appeared in the July 9, 1983 issue of TV Guide *and is the work of critic Andy Meisler, writing under his pen name, Mel Marcus.*

Poor television, the Hypocrite Film Lover's Friend. Do you ever wonder, at one of those boring cocktail parties, why innocent set-owners are subject to such abuse?

"A vast wasteland. A veritable shot of Novocain to the frontal lobes," say the magic box's detractors. *Le cinema,* they insist, is the medium of art and culture.

Pure balderdash, and I've just figured out why. Not long ago I passed a local "art" theater flaunting a deathless double bill: "Kiss Me Deadly" and "The Killing." Lines of shivering doctoral-dissertation types snaked their way down the block. A nasal voice, dripping with 80-proof smugness, rose above the general foot-stamping. "Two . . . *exquisite* egg-zamples of the B-movie john-ruh," said this cretin. I forgot all about him until several weeks later. It was Tuesday night, time for *Remington Steele,* and my favorite semi-feminist detective was in rare form.

"Blam! Blam!" went a tightly clutched automatic, neatly winging a bad guy. "Pop! Pop!" went the obligatory champagne bottles, as Brosnan, Zimbalist & Co. wrapped up their moth-eaten plot. And then, like a bolt out of the video, an Insight. "An exquisite example," said I, "of the B-television genre."

B *television?* Yes. For years, cinema snobs have been trashing television unfairly. True, several movies each year—the "Tootsies," the "Gandhis," the "Citizen Kanes"—are truly A pictures; significant, intelligent works. The vast majority, though—the "Cannonball Runs," "Texas Chainsaw Massacres," "Reefer Madnesses"—are actually killer B's, low-budget balance sheets masquerading as entertainment. By some trick of film critics' logic, though, these dogs are *never* compared with their A-rated counterparts.

Well, OK: two can play at this game. Why should *Masterpiece Theatre,* for instance, be lumped into the same category as *Bare Essence?* A simple rating system of A, B, and C (going the cinephiles one better) will keep things in proper perspective. Consider, if you will, these proposed rating guidelines.

I. Cop Shows. Type-A crime busters, the cream of the crop, will in large part reflect the awful realities of crime. Shooting victims bleed, occasional mysteries go unsolved, police revolvers contain only six shots. No psychic detectives, canine mascots or helicopter chases allowed. EXAMPLES: *Hill Street Blues, The Rockford Files,* PBS's *Mystery!* series.

Type-B whodunits, while nodding in the A's general direction, depend more on sure-fire plot devices. Anonymous tips, unauthorized phone taps and tearful confessions are OK. Villainy can be explained by unhappy childhoods, but said villains must pay the price—a Cautionary flesh wound and a pledge to Never Do It Again. Short car chases (maximum length: four blocks or one screen minute) and gun battles (a regrettable last resort) are allowed. Everything ties up neatly at the end. But *no* hang-gliding, dirt-biking or computer-controlled good or bad guys. EXAMPLES: *Quincy, Kojak, Matt Houston, Hart to Hart,* etc., etc.

Type-C shows are virtually unrestricted in their use of mind-numbing short-cuts. Helicopters are mandatory, as are car crashes, crackling radio calls and terrorized fashion models and/or aerobic-dancing instructors. Guns should preferably be shot out of malefactors' hands. No hint of paperwork, plea-bargaining or parole boards will be allowed. EXAMPLES: *S.W.A.T., Knight Rider, CHiPs.*

II. Hospital Shows. Type A's will make the startling admission that most patients suffer discomfort in your average hospital ward. Doctors are overworked, though not underpaid, and talk about tax shelters a lot. No "miracle drugs," impromptu heart transplants or visits by sports stars to young leukemia sufferers. EXAMPLE: *St. Elsewhere,* on a good day.

Type B's will "strive" for authenticity. Diseases will be researched and explained conscientiously. Little beads of sweat will pop out on surgeons' masked faces. Medical errors will be made only by secondary characters or guest stars. New serums can be flown in by Lear jet, but just in time. Families can—indeed, must—be reconciled at their loved ones' deathbeds. EXAMPLES: *Trapper John, M.D., Medical Center, Ryan's Four.*

Type-C medicos will be godlike creatures, either movie-star handsome or silver-haired and distinguished. Diseases here are vague, nasty inconveniences that curl up and die when the correct superdrug is found. Patients often are churlish when told they have a terminal illness, but cheer up nicely after some pithy advice from their doctor/father figures. EXAMPLES: *Marcus Welby, M.D., Emergency!, General Hospital.*

III. Sitcoms. The rules are simple. An A comedy will be both (a) funny and (b) reflective of life as lived on the Planet Earth. No funny Martians, funny witches, funny werewolves, funny Nazis, etc., etc. You already know most of the EXAMPLES: *The Mary Tyler Moore Show, M*A*S*H, Cheers, Taxi, All in the Family.*

Type B's will satisfy one requirement, but not both. EXAMPLES: *Mork & Mindy, One Day at a Time, Three's Company, The New Odd Couple.*

Type C's—by far the most numerous—will both confuse an eavesdropping extra-terrestrial and allow Neil Simon to sleep soundly. Need we even mention *Hogan's Heroes, Gomer Pyle, USMC, The Brady Bunch, Diff'rent Strokes....????*

What's that you say? You don't agree with these categories? Good! Constant debate keeps the film buffs' little world afloat; and so it will be for us *videastes.*

There'll be whole magazine articles—whole *magazines*—devoted to the relative merits of, say, *The Mod Squad* versus *Adam-12*. There'll be festivals and retrospectives ("*The Jeffersons:* The Early Years").

Who knows? The film zealots might even shut up, throw away their stale popcorn and admit to watching *M*A*S*H* reruns all along.

QUESTIONS

1. Would you describe this piece as primarily humorous—or does it make a serious, valid point? Explain.

2. Do the distinctions Marcus draws between the different types of shows within each category—between Type A and Type B cop shows, for example—make sense? Why or why not?

3. Marcus writes in a snappy, "pop" style, well-suited to his subject (as well as to the publication in which this article originally appeared, *TV Guide*). What are some of the specific characteristics of this style? Point to particular words and phrases that give this essay its distinctive flavor.

4. Marcus uses both categories and subcategories to organize the material in this article. Describe his organizational strategy.

SUGGESTIONS FOR WRITING

1. Marcus applies his rating system to three kinds of TV shows—cop shows, hospital shows, and sitcoms. Using the same system, classify the programs in any other TV genres you can think of (soap operas, game shows, etc.).

2. Marcus clearly feels that the snobbery of film buffs is unjustified—that movies are not inherently superior to TV. Citing examples of movies and television shows that you are familiar with, write an essay in which you either support or take issue with Marcus's position.

Michael Malone
AND GRACIE BEGAT LUCY WHO BEGAT LAVERNE
★ ★ ★ ★

Michael Malone, a writer and college instructor, has contributed articles and reviews to various publications, including The Nation, Harper's, *and* The New York Times Book Review. *He is also the author of a number of novels and nonfiction books, including* Painting the Roses Red *(1975),* The Delectable Mountains *(1977),* Psychetypes *(1977),* Star Sex: Men

in the Movies *(1978), and* Dingley Falls *(1980). His most recent novel
is* Handling Sin *(1986).*

*The following essay originally appeared in the October 1981 issue of
the television magazine,* Channels of Communication.

———————

By changing fashions to fit the times, by loosening their themes and tightening
their T-shirts, a few daytime television epics of domestic calamity have somehow
managed to defy age and to live on all the days of our lives; indeed, of our parents'
lives and perhaps our children's as well. No prime-time series, however, has ever
proved so impervious to shifting seasons. Even the most successful appear to have
a natural life span, to grow old and lose their ratings, to be left for younger rivals.

But inevitably, when this love affair between the American public and some
popular television series comes to an end, its absence leaves behind, unsatisfied,
whatever fantasy or emotional need that particular departed show had been
managing to fulfill in our culture. Inevitably, a new program is born to replace
the old: We lose Lucy and Ethel but we gain their daughters, Laverne and Shirley.
Ozzie and Harriet may have departed but, safe in the "Happy Days" of the fifties,
Richie's family is as good and wise as Ricky Nelson's once was. And if Ricky's
singing could transform a family show into a vehicle for a teenage idol, so twenty
years later, in a program planned around Richie's family, could Henry Winkler's
Fonz skyrocket into a preteen merchandising industry. In some ways, Archie
Bunker's father is Ralph Kramden and his grandfather Chester A. Riley. "All
in the Family" belongs to a family.

These parental predecessors can be traced back along the branches of television's family tree. And it is in this genealogy of popular series that the heart of
the medium can be found: The most persistent (and therefore presumably the
most meaningful) themes and relationships of our favorite shows—the situation
comedies—tell us who we think we are, or want to be. (In a talk on film criticism
Pauline Kael gave at Harvard in the early seventies, she earnestly urged budding
movie analysts to take up television study instead, because of its incomprehensibly
vast and almost entirely unexplored influence, more pervasive than any force
since the medieval church.) Again and again, the same essential features appear,
not merely because producers are consciously trying to reassemble the ingredients
of earlier successes, but because they are unconsciously resupplying those collective myths and types of characters intrinsic to the genre and important to our
culture.

The show ubiquitously known as the "sitcom" has outlasted or outdrawn our
fifties craze for thirty-nine cowboy shows a week, our sixties craze for doctors and
lawyers, and even our perennial infatuation with idiosyncratic detectives like
blind Longstreet, crippled Ironside, bumbling Columbo, obese Cannon, and bald,
dapper Kojak. The sitcom has trounced in ratings and durability satiric comedy
styles of the British "Monty Python" sort, or of the "spoof" series—"Get Smart"
and "Batman"—and every other type of television show. Today, situation come-

dies regularly number three out of the four top-rated prime-time programs. They are thirty-minute shows with descendants going back thirty years.

That this is the favorite format should not surprise us; it is preeminently suited to the medium of television entertainment, for technical as well as social reasons. A television screen is a small opening in a box, very like the little proscenium of a puppet theater. Seated in the familiar surroundings of our homes, we are watching four-inch-high people scurrying across this opening. In sitcoms they are usually getting themselves caught up in mistakes, misunderstandings, or mishaps; their actions get faster and broadly physical, they shout and pout and then kiss and patch up. It is all very much like a Punch-and-Judy show. Television cannot sustain the epic or the tragic stance, which asks for very different aesthetic and psychological responses: For one thing, such drama demands that we see characters as greater than ourselves, which is difficult to do when they are only four inches high and in our own ordinary living rooms. Nor can television evoke, as films can, the awed wonder of romance. The mythic stature accorded deified images like Gable or Garbo on a *literally* larger-than-life screen, viewed in the vast dark communal space of a movie theater, is laughably incongruous if transferred to television.

By its nature, television lends itself not to tragedy and myth but to comedy and domesticity, the foundation of situation comedy. (They are also the foundation of commercials, a form indigenous to television and a close relative of the sitcom.) All comedy is domestic in the sense that its harmonizing function moves it toward marriage, family, and community, and away from the great solitude of heroics and grand romance. But the particular kind of domesticity celebrated in situation comedies is the significant result of television having come into its own during the early fifties, when family values reigned supreme in America. Then the virtues of the self-contained and happy suburban home governed our culture in ways that had not been true before and are unlikely to recur in our own cynical times. The early comedies like "Ozzie and Harriet" symbolized domestic utopia: every family in its own private home, every home with a television set for each member. The medium, like the suburban mode of life, fostered uniformity but not community. From their middle-class living rooms, monogamous couples and their happy, wholesome children stared into the middle-class living rooms of the Nelsons or the Erwins ("The Trouble with Father") or the Andersons ("Father Knows Best") or the Williamses ("Make Room for Daddy") or the Ricardos ("I Love Lucy"), and saw themselves affably mirrored there. Of course, the pushing problem of "making it" never got its foot in the door of early sitcoms. What did Ozzie Nelson do for a living, anyhow?

As commonly used, "situation comedy" means any continuing series of half-hour comic episodes in which members of a regular cast get involved in an amusingly troublesome incident; quick complications entangle them, and an even quicker resolution unravels everything.

Among the many reasons for the sitcom's becoming television's typical programming style was that its half-hour length was perfect for a continuing series.

Not only were audiences comfortable with this format from radio days, but back in the time when a show was fully sponsored by a single company, most advertisers were reluctant to double their expenses—and their risk of failure—by taking on an hour-long program.

Some critics, among them Horace Newcomb in *TV: The Most Popular Art,* want to separate *situation* comedies like "I Love Lucy" (with its physical farce, fixed characters, and emphasis on plot rather than interaction), from *domestic* comedies like "My Three Sons" (with its gentler humor, developing characters, and emphasis on human relationships). And it is true that only the loosest definition of sitcom could cover at once the slapstick cartoon buffoonery of "The Misadventures of Sheriff Lobo," the social satire of "M*A*S*H," and the warm-hearted sermonizing of "The Brady Bunch." In fact, new labels such as "dramedy" and "com-dram" have recently been dreamed up for such programs as "Eight Is Enough," which are only comedies in the sense that they espouse the "happy ending," not in the sense that they have the "witty" dialogue, incongruities, and absurd coincidences of laugh-producing plots. Brandy French, manager of program development for Columbia Pictures Television Syndication, describes such Garry Marshall series as "Happy Days" and "Laverne & Shirley" as "dramalettes," a hybrid of the orthodox sitcom and the instructional moral fable popular in the fifties. Significantly, both these shows are *set* in the fifties, and in both we can see how the distinctions between sitcom and domestic comedy blur.

Both "Laverne & Shirley" and its parent "Lucy" have fixed characters (two women, two men), fixed realistic sets, and a weekly problem that builds to some slap-stick climax. One incident (the famous mayhem in a production-line skit) offers a typical example: Working in a candy factory, Lucy and Ethel fall hopelessly behind when the conveyor belt speeds up. Physical chaos is the result. Opening a restaurant by themselves, Laverne and Shirley fall hopelessly behind, as cook and waitress, when the orders speed up. Physical chaos is the comic result. Lucy and Ethel try to break into show business. Laverne and Shirley try to break into modeling. But unlike the absolutely ritualized chicaneries, calamities, and ultimate remorse into which Lucy fell—her tearful bawling was always laughable—Laverne's and Shirley's hurts and humiliations are more apt to be treated "seriously," so that we are asked to respond first with sympathetic sentiment; then comes the joke, and we're released into laughter.

Television comedy's family tree has three major branches coming from the actual root of all drama—human relationships. They might be called *tribal* comedy, *family* comedy, and *couple* comedy. Beginning with its parent series, "You'll Never Get Rich" ("The Phil Silvers Show"), tribal comedy brings together, often around a central star, a diverse assortment of characters whose separate lives are connected by some external situation—usually the workplace (as in "The Mary Tyler Moore Show," "Alice," "Barney Miller," "Taxi," or "WKRP in Cincinnati"), but sometimes war (as in Sergeant Bilko's offspring, "McHale's Navy," or "Hogan's Heroes," or "M*A*S*H"). The student tribes beleaguering our Miss

Brooks and Mr. Kotter provide a variation on the work-colleague show. Surviving a shipwreck—the excuse for "Gilligan's Island"—is, like war, an extraordinary circumstance forcing together strange bedfellows.

Initially the casts of these tribal series are apt to be ensembles of stock characters: an egghead, a dreamer, a Don Juan, a cynic, an innocent. Many series include some version of (or parodic inversion of) the sexpot/dumb-blonde female, one of our most venerable comic types, with an ancestral line reaching back through the likes of Suzanne Somers to Goldie Hawn to Marilyn Monroe to Jean Harlow. Tina Louise in "Gilligan's Island" was pretty much the pure stereotype. "WKRP in Cincinnati" turns the cliché around. There, Jennifer, played by Loni Anderson, looks like a classic dumb-blonde bombshell but proves to be an intelligent woman with a strong sense of irony. In "M*A*S*H," Loretta Swit's character is neither a ding-bat nor a sexual joke, despite her name, "Hot Lips." "The Mary Tyler Moore Show" gave us, in Georgette and Phyllis, two different portraits of a dumb blonde (sans sex), each inimitable. Indeed, if a series has good writers and good actors, and the luck of longevity, all its characters will grow in substance until we can no longer even remember the form in which we first knew them.

The group is ostensibly a random collection of adult strangers, but is subliminally an extended family ("the 'Taxi' family") with authoritative or permissive parent surrogates and older or younger siblings. Barney Miller is a good "father." Ted Baxter was the bad baby of "The Mary Tyler Moore Show." And as in real families, members may grow up and move away; this rite of passage is called the spinoff. From the Moore show alone came "Rhoda," "Phyllis," and "Lou Grant." But it is rare for a spinoff to do as well as a parent show. Brandy French suggests that the spinoff dilutes the very *community* developed by the original ensemble, the "family" togetherness that brought success.

A few shows, like the Dick Van Dyke and Bob Newhart series, bridge the tribal and familial formats, intermixing home and work life, though true *family* comedies spend more time where the bread is baked than where it is won. In the beginning, family comedies generally came equipped with both parents, and the male got star billing. All children were highly visible (not merely title characters like "Leave It to Beaver" or "Dennis the Menace"); their troubles or troublemaking frequently provided the story line. After all, in the fifties, successfully raising children in the upwardly mobile family was supposed to be the goal.

The first family series can be divided into two types: There was the "wise dad" style of "Father Knows Best," in which father, with a little help from loyal, practical mom, quietly guided the family from one *right* solution to another. "Make Room for Daddy," "The Jimmy Stewart Show," "The Brady Bunch," and "Eight Is Enough" are all, in different ways, sage sons of "Father Knows Best." At the same time we had the "dumb dad" style—the inversion of this fifties ideal. There was "The Trouble with Father," in which Stu Erwin needed a lot of help from his loving, wise wife and tolerant daughters. Chester A. Riley of "The Life of Riley" was even more a blundering victim of endless mishaps; in fact, old Rile was an idiot—like his relatives, Ralph Kramden, Fred Flintstone, and Archie Bunker—without even a modicum of internal awareness.

As the fifties glided into the sixties, family sitcoms began to reflect the cracks in the mirror of our domestic bliss. As if designed to show the dream to be a nightmare, "The Addams Family" and "The Munsters" gave us comedies about two perfectly nice, happy, harmonious middle-class families, who are completely unaware that they *horrify* because they are inhuman monsters. Urbanites go to "Green Acres," where they are ridiculously out of place. "The Beverly Hillbillies" naively insist on their old-time mountain ways in the midst of modern Los Angeles, where the Clampetts (all very nice people) make no sense to anyone.

In one new series after another, the family unit was broken and one parent disappeared. It was usually the mother, as if the wives of the fifties had already heard the distant trumpet of the women's movement and had charged away, leaving the bread in the toaster. Wise dad (or wise uncle or wise guardian) was left to carry on alone. He did just fine without a wife; in fact, without the distractions of a spouse he made a marvelously attentive parent. Who could ask for more words of wisdom than Fred MacMurray gave his boys on "My Three Sons"? Though not necessary, a surrogate mother was nice, like Aunt Bea on "The Andy Griffith Show" or Mrs. Livingston on "The Courtship of Eddie's Father." But it didn't need to be a female; for example, Mr. French the butler played the role in "Family Affair," as did Uncle Charley in "My Three Sons."

While single-father series continue to be made ("Diff'rent Strokes"), they have been superceded in popularity since the late emancipating sixties by the single-mother series, one of the first of which dealt with the trials and triumphs of a black widow with a small son. "Julia" had to work as a nurse; the mother of "The Partridge Family" smartly turned her large brood into a well-paying rock group. Other mothers sought help where they could find it: Mrs. Muir found a father-figure for her children (albeit an insubstantial one) in a virile, seafaring ghost. In current comedies like "Alice" and "One Day at a Time," single female parents tend to have deeper problems, stronger needs, and more realistic lives. Mel's bustling diner is worlds away from the quiet tree-shady house where father knew best. Alice doesn't live there anymore.

The third kind of situation comedy, structured around a *couple,* is the most popular of all. Ever since Lucy Ricardo first sent Ricky into a Spanish sputter, and crafty Kingfish first outfoxed gullible Andy, the odd-couple relationship has lain at the core of successful television comedies, as indeed it lies at the core of many great comic novels. Don Quixote and Candide tumble unscathed and unaware through the threatening chaos they have wandered into, or helped create, as their more sensible partners try to save them. In sitcoms the kooks are often the wives, and the pragmatic straightmen their exasperated husbands—as in "I Love Lucy," "I Married Joan," Burns and Allen (with the unforgettable Gracie's inspired non sequiturs), and "All in the Family." But the duo may be daughter and father ("My Little Margie"), or son and father ("Sanford and Son").

By personality traits or living habits, these two people are profoundly incompatible; one is compulsive, the other a slob; one is an ideologue, the other apolitical. The comedy in "The Odd Couple," "Maude," and "Angie" stems from such mismatches. A few sitcoms have taken the eccentricity of the zany partner to its logical extreme by creating a character who is literally fantastical. In "Bewitched" and "I Dream of Jeannie," we meet two stereotypes of the middle-class male, each with an all-American career—one's an advertising executive, the other an astronaut. Both have the comic misfortune to love and be loved by a gorgeous woman with supernatural powers. Samantha of "Bewitched" is a witch; Jeannie is a genie. Their magic is so vast that they could give these men whatever their hearts desired. The comedy erupts when the men try forcing the women to be ordinary middle-class wives, and not to use their scary powers even for so much as defrosting ground chuck.

"Mork & Mindy" charmingly turns this stereotype on its head by making the male the kooky extraterrestrial and Mindy his down-to-earth straight-human. In fact, compared to the Orkan Mork, Lucy is no sillier than Eric Sevareid. Also in "Mork & Mindy," we recover a little bit of the sexual and romantic love that has been intrinsic to comedy since its classical origins (boy gets girl) but has never been much in evidence in sitcoms—again because of their birth in the fifties. Mork's oddness makes it possible for him to live with Mindy while keeping their relationship safe in that suspended eroticism that heightens romance and honors the censors at the same time. For all its risqué double-entendres, "Three's Company" (reflecting the new "swinging life styles"—two women and a man) depends on the same "will they or won't they?" formula that kept Doris Day out of Rock Hudson's clutches until the knot was tied.

It is common practice to double the sitcom couple into a foursome. As on "Maude" and "The Ropers," the lead married couple becomes friendly with another couple: the Kramdens with the Nortons, the Rileys with the Gillises, the Ricardos with the Mertzes. On "All in the Family," Gloria and Mike stood in for the other couple, though the Bunkers also had a few sets of neighbors—like the Jeffersons—designed to trigger Archie's Pavlovian prejudices. The two couples can form strong friendships, male to male (Ralph Kramden and Ed Norton) and female to female. Thus, "I Love Lucy" founded two sitcom traditions. From the Lucy/Ricky relationship came all the "I married a dingbat but I love her" series. From the wonderful friendship of Lucy and Ethel Mertz come all the "My Friend Irma," "Rhoda," "Mork," and "Laverne" shows in which loyalty and love prove stronger than reason, and more fun.

Like Lucy and Ethel before them, Laverne and Shirley have charged into one scheme after another. The difference is that Laverne and Shirley are trying to get *ahead,* to make it. Their men are not supporting husbands, only friends. In a way Laverne and Shirley, factory workers, want what Lucy and Ethel have—a married, middle-class life. Their series represents a significant economic shift in sitcoms towards working-class characters; as comedies about lawyers ("Adam's Rib," "The Associates") have become less popular, comedies about blue-collar workers, about waitresses and cab drivers, succeed by taking us back to that most unsuburban world of "The Honeymooners," where the common themes are coping with poverty and working on an American dream to escape it.

But there is also a way in which Lucy and Ethel, happily-married middle-class women of the fifties, wanted what Laverne and Shirley have—the knowledge that they can support themselves, the freedom to define themselves. That Lucy went sneaking behind Ricky's patriarchal back to earn money to replace "his" money, or to try breaking into his show business world; that she dragged Ethel with her (and with Ethel each of us)—all this secret rebellion tells us something about why "I Love Lucy" was America's favorite situation comedy from the very beginning, and why the character Lucy has given birth to so many zany children. "My name is Morky Ricardo," Mork tells the psychiatrist at his sanity hearing. "My best friends are Fred and Ethel Mertz."

QUESTIONS

1. How does Malone account for the durability, the perennial appeal, of the sitcom? In what way is the sitcom "preeminently suited to the medium of television"? How does Malone support his statement that television lends itself "not to tragedy and myth but to comedy and domesticity"?

2. What are the "three major branches" on the "family tree" of television comedy? What are the distinguishing characteristics of each branch?

3. In what way were the earliest sitcoms a reflection of their time—the early 1950s? How did sitcoms change in response to the social upheavals of the 1960s?

4. How does Malone use metaphor to make his introductory paragraph interesting? How does he extend his metaphor into the second paragraph?

5. Malone is always careful to strengthen his generalizations with examples drawn from particular shows. Locate several paragraphs which consist of a general topic sentence followed by a number of specific, supporting examples.

SUGGESTIONS FOR WRITING

1. Write an essay in which you try to account for the long-lasting appeal of television sitcoms. Base your essay on your own familiarity with these shows.

2. Write an essay in which you classify current sitcoms according to Malone's categories (tribal comedies, family comedies, couple comedies).

3. Malone suggests that sitcoms accurately reflect the values, beliefs, and conditions that are prevalent at a particular time in our society. In an essay, analyze some current situation comedies (programs like "The Cosby Show,"

"Kate and Allie," etc.), showing what they reveal about life in present-day America. Alternatively, take issue with Malone's assertion and state, referring to specific programs, what you think sitcoms reflect. Then prove your case.

Stephen King
WHY WE CRAVE HORROR MOVIES
★ ★ ★

Stephen King generally does not fare well with literary critics, who are fond of dismissing his books as puerile and poorly written chillers. King himself is unassuming about his novels, describing them as "the literary equivalent of a Big Mac and a large fries from McDonald's." Certainly his readers gobble them up as fast as he turns them out, which is fast, indeed. Since his first novel, Carrie, *appeared in 1974, King has published fifteen bestselling books, including* Salem's Lot, The Shining, The Dead Zone, Firestarter, Cujo, Christine, *and* Pet Sematary.

Today there are more than fifty million copies of King's books in print, and ten of his horror tales have been made into movies. One critic, writing in Newsweek *magazine, attributes King's success to the simple fact that "a lot of people have appallingly bad taste." Certainly, King is not an elegant stylist, but like many popular writers, he is a highly gifted storyteller. Moreover, he seems closely in touch with those deep-seated anxieties and dreads which it is the business of the horror writer to express (and thereby relieve).*

Though King has taught college courses with titles like "Themes in Supernatural Literature" and "Fantasy and Science Fiction," he seems uncomfortable with his intellectual side. Still, King is a serious theoretician of horror, and the following selection is one of the shrewdest analyses of the horror genre ever written. Originally printed in Playboy *magazine, it was later incorporated into his nonfiction book,* Danse Macabre *(1981).*

If you're a genuine fan of horror films, you develop the same sort of sophistication that a follower of the ballet develops; you get a feeling for the depth and the texture of the genre. Your ear develops with your eye, and the sound of quality always comes through to the keen ear. There is fine Waterford crystal that rings delicately when struck, no matter how thick and chunky it may look; and then there are Flintstone jelly glasses. You can drink your Dom Perignon out of either one, but, friends, there is a difference.

The difference here is between horror for horror's sake and art. There is art in a horror film when the audience gets more than it gives. Not when our fears are milked just to drive us crazy but when an actual liaison is found between our fantasy fears and our real fears. Few horror movies are conceived with art in mind; most are conceived for profit. The art is not consciously created but, rather, is thrown off, as an atomic pile throws off radiation. There are films that skate right up to the border where art ceases to be thrown off and exploitation begins, and those films are often the field's most striking successes. *The Texas Chainsaw Massacre* is one of those. I would happily testify to its redeeming social merit in any court in the country. I would not do so for *The Gory Ones,* a 1972 film in which we are treated to the charming sight of a woman being cut open with a two-handed bucksaw; the camera lingers as her intestines spew out onto the floor. The difference is more than the difference between a chain saw and a bucksaw; it is something like 70,000,000 light-years. The *Chainsaw Massacre* is done with taste and conscience. *The Gory Ones* is the work of morons with cameras.

If horror movies have redeeming social merit, it is because of that ability to form liaisons between the real and the unreal. In many cases—particularly in the Fifties and then again in the early Seventies—the fears expressed are sociopolitical in nature, a fact that gives such disparate pictures as Don Siegel's *Invasion of the Body Snatchers* and William Friedkin's *The Exorcist* a crazily convincing documentary feel. When the horror movies wear their various sociopolitical hats—the B picture as tabloid editorial—they often serve as an extraordinarily accurate barometer of those things that trouble the night thoughts of a whole society.

But horror movies don't always wear a hat that identifies them as disguised comments on the social or political scene (as David Cronenberg's *The Brood* comments on the disintegration of the generational family). More often the horror movie points farther inward, looking for those deep-seated personal fears, those pressure points we all must cope with. This adds an element of universality to the proceedings and may produce an even truer sort of art.

This second kind of horror film has more in common with the Brothers Grimm than with the op-ed pages of tabloid newspapers. It is the B picture as fairy tale. It doesn't want to score political points but, rather, to scare the hell out of us by crossing certain taboo lines. So if my idea about art is correct (it giveth more than it receiveth), this sort of film is of value to the audience by helping it better understand what those taboos and fears are, and why it feels so uneasy about them.

I think we'd all agree that one of the great fears with which all of us must deal on a purely personal level is the fear of dying; without good old death to fall back on, the horror movies would be in bad shape. A corollary to this is that there are "good" deaths and "bad" deaths; most of us would like to die peacefully in our beds at the age of 80 (preferably after a good meal, a bottle of really fine vino and a really super lay), but very few of us are interested in finding out how it might feel to get slowly crushed under an automobile lift while crankcase oil drips slowly onto our foreheads.

Lots of horror films derive their best effects from this fear of the bad death (as in *The Abominable Dr. Phibes,* in which Phibes dispatches his victims one at a time using the 12 plagues of Egypt, slightly updated, a gimmick worthy of the *Batman* comics during their palmiest days). Who can forget the lethal binoculars in *The Black Zoo,* for instance? They came equipped with spring-loaded six-inch prongs, so that when the victim put them to her eyes and then attempted to adjust the field of focus. . . .

Others derive their horror simply from the fact of death itself and the decay that follows death. In a society in which such a great store is placed in the fragile commodities of youth, health and beauty, death and decay become inevitably horrible—and inevitably taboo. If you don't think so, ask yourself why the second grade doesn't get to tour the local mortuary along with the police department, the fire department and the nearest McDonald's. One can imagine—or I can in my more morbid moments—the mortuary and McDonald's combined; the highlight of the tour, of course, would be a viewing of the McCorpse.

No, the funeral parlor is taboo. Morticians are modern priests, working their arcane magic of cosmetics and preservation in rooms that are clearly marked off limits. Who washes the corpse's hair? Are the fingernails and toenails of the dear departed clipped one final time? Is it true that the dead are encoffined sans shoes? Who dresses them for their final star turn in the mortuary viewing room? How is a bullet hole plugged and concealed? How are strangulation bruises hidden?

The answers to all those questions are available, but they are not common knowledge. And if you try to make the answers part of your store of knowledge, people are going to think you a bit peculiar. I know: In the process of researching a forthcoming novel about a father who tries to bring his son back from the dead, I collected a stack of funeral literature a foot high—and any number of peculiar glances from folks who wondered why I was reading *The Funeral: Vestige or Value?*

But this is not to say that people don't have a certain occasional interest in what lies behind the locked door in the basement of the mortuary, or what may transpire in the local graveyard after the mourners have left . . . or at the dark of the moon. *The Body Snatcher* is not really a tale of the supernatural, nor was it pitched that way to its audience; it was pitched as a film (as was that notorious Sixties documentary *Mondo Cane*) that would take us beyond the pale, over that line that marks the edge of taboo ground:

CEMETERIES RAIDED, CHILDREN SLAIN FOR BODIES TO DISSECT! the movie poster drooled. UNTHINKABLE REALITIES AND UNBELIEVABLE *FACTS* OF THE DARK DAYS OF EARLY SURGICAL RESEARCH *EXPOSED* IN *THE MOST DARING SHRIEK-AND-SHUDDER SHOCK SENSATION EVER BROUGHT TO THE SCREEN!* (All of this printed on a leaning tombstone.)

But the poster does not stop there; it goes on specifically to mark out the exact location of the taboo line and to suggest that not everyone may be adventurous enough to transgress that forbidden ground: IF YOU CAN TAKE IT, SEE GRAVES RAIDED! COFFINS ROBBED! CORPSES CARVED! MIDNIGHT MURDER! BODY BLACK-MAIL! STALKING GHOULS! MAD REVENGE! MACABRE MYSTERY! AND DON'T SAY WE DIDN'T WARN YOU!

All of it has sort of a pleasant, alliterative ring, doesn't it?

These areas of unease—the political-social-cultural and those of the more mythic, fairy-tale variety—have a tendency to overlap, of course; a good horror picture will put the pressure on at as many points as it can. *They Came from*

Within, for instance, is about sexual promiscuity on one level; on another level, it's asking you how you'd like to have a leech jump out of a letter slot and fasten itself onto your face. These are not the same areas of unease at all.

But since we're on the subject of death and decay (a very grave matter, heh-heh-heh), we might look at a couple of films in which this particular area of unease has been used well. The prime example, of course, is *Night of the Living Dead,* in which our horror of these final states is exploited to a point where many audiences found the film well-nigh unbearable. Other taboos are also broken by the film; at one point, a little girl kills her mother with a garden trowel . . . and then begins to eat her. How's that for taboo breaking? Yet the film circles around to its starting point again and again, and the key word in the film's title is not living but dead.

At an early point, the film's female lead, who has barely escaped being killed by a zombie in a graveyard where she and her brother have come to put flowers on their dead father's grave (the brother is not so lucky), stumbles into a lonely farmhouse. As she explores, she hears something dripping . . . dripping . . . dripping. She goes upstairs, sees something, screams . . . and the camera zooms in on the rotting, weeks-old head of a corpse. It is a shocking, memorable moment. Later, a government official tells the watching, beleaguered populace that, although they may not like it (i.e., they will have to cross that taboo line to do it), they must burn their dead; simply soak them with gasoline and light them up. Later still, a local sheriff expresses our own uneasy shock at having come so far over the taboo line. He answers a reporter's question by saying, "Ah, they're dead . . . they're all messed up."

The good horror director must have a clear sense of where the taboo line lies if he is not to lapse into unconscious absurdity, and a gut understanding of what the countryside is like on the far side of it. In *Night of the Living Dead,* George Romero plays a number of instruments, and he plays them like a virtuoso. A lot has been made of this film's graphic violence, but one of the film's most frightening moments comes near the climax, when the heroine's brother makes his reappearance—still wearing his driving gloves and clutching for his sister with the idiotic, implacable single-mindedness of the hungry dead. The film is violent—as its sequel, *Dawn of the Dead*—but the violence has its own logic, and in the horror genre, logic goes a long way toward proving morality.

The crowning horror in Alfred Hitchcock's *Psycho* comes when Vera Miles touches that chair in the cellar and it spins lazily around to reveal Norman's mother at last—a wizened, shriveled corpse from which hollow eye sockets stare up blankly. She is not only dead; she has been stuffed like one of the birds that decorate Norman's office. Norman's subsequent entrance in dress and make-up is almost an anticlimax.

In A.I.P.'s *The Pit and the Pendulum,* we see another facet of the bad death—perhaps the absolute worst. Vincent Price and his cohorts break into a tomb through its brickwork, using pick and shovel. They discover that the lady, his wife, has, indeed, been entombed alive; for just a moment, the camera shows us her tortured face, frozen in a rictus of terror, her bulging eyes, her clawlike fingers, the skin stretched tight and gray. This is, I think, the most important moment in the post-1960 horror film, signaling a return to an all-out effort to terrify the audience . . . and a willingness to use any means at hand to do it.

Fiction is full of *economic* horror stories, though very few of them are supernatural; *The Crash of '79* comes to mind, as well as *The Money Wolves, The Big Company Look* and the wonderful Frank Norris novel *McTeague.* I want to discuss only one movie in this context, *The Amityville Horror.* There may be others, but this one example will serve, I think, to illustrate another idea: that the horror genre is extremely limber, extremely adaptable, extremely useful; the author or film maker can use it as a crowbar to lever open locked doors . . . or as a small, slim pick to tease the tumblers into giving. The genre can thus be used to open almost any lock on the fears that lie behind the door, and *The Amityville Horror* is a dollars-and-cents case in point.

It is simple and straightforward, as most horror tales are. The Lutzes, a young married couple with two or three kids (Kathleen Lutz's by a previous marriage), buy a house in Amityville. Previous to their tenancy, a young man has murdered his whole family at the direction of "voices." For this reason, the Lutzes get the house cheaply.

But they soon discover that it wouldn't have been cheap at half the price, because it's haunted. Manifestations include black goop that comes bubbling out of the toilets (and before the festivities are over, it comes oozing out of the walls and the stairs as well), a roomful of flies, a rocking chair that rocks by itself and something in the cellar that causes the dog to dig everlastingly at the wall. A window crashes down on the little boy's fingers. The little girl develops an "invisible friend" who is apparently really there. Eyes glow outside the window at three in the morning. And so on.

Worst of all, from the audience's standpoint, Lutz himself (James Brolin) apparently falls out of love with his wife (Margot Kidder) and begins to develop a meaningful relationship with his ax. Before things are done, we are drawn to the inescapable conclusion that he is tuning up for something more than splitting wood.

Stripped of its distracting elements (a puking nun, Rod Steiger shamelessly overacting as a priest who is just discovering the Devil after 40 years or so as a man of the cloth, and Margot Kidder doing calisthenics in a pair of bikini panties and one white stocking), *The Amityville Horror* is a perfect example of the tale to be told around the campfire. All the teller really has to do is to keep the catalog of inexplicable events in the correct order, so that unease escalates into outright fear.

All of which brings us around to the real watchspring of *Amityville* and the reason it works as well as it does: The picture's subtext is one of economic unease, and that is a theme that director Stuart Rosenberg plays on constantly. In terms of the times—18 percent inflation, mortgage rates out of sight, gasoline selling at a cool $1.40 a gallon—*The Amityville Horror,* like *The Exorcist,* could not have come along at a more opportune moment.

This breaks through most clearly in a scene that is the film's only moment of true and honest drama, a brief vignette that parts the clouds of hokum like a sunray on a drizzly afternoon. The Lutz family is preparing to go to the wedding of Kathleen Lutz's younger brother (who looks as if he might be all of 17). They are, of course, in the Bad House when the scene takes place. The younger brother has lost the $1500 that is due the caterer and is in an understandable agony of panic and embarrassment.

Brolin says he'll write the caterer a check, which he does, and later he stands off the angry caterer, who has specified cash only in a half-whispered washroom argument while the wedding party whoops it up outside. After the wedding, Lutz turns the living room of the Bad House upside down looking for the lost money, which has now become *his* money, and the only way of backing up the bank paper he has issued the caterer. Brolin's check may not have been 100 percent Goodyear rubber, but in his sunken, purple-pouched eyes, we see a man who doesn't really have the money any more than his hapless brother-in-law does. Here is a man tottering on the brink of his own financial crash.

He finds the only trace under the couch: a bank money band with the numerals $500 stamped on it. The band lies there on the rug, tauntingly empty. *"Where is it?"* Brolin screams, his voice vibrating with anger, frustration and fear. At that one moment, we hear the ring of Waterford, clear and true—or, if you like, we hear that one quiet phrase of pure music in a film that is otherwise all crash and bash.

Everything that *The Amityville Horror* does well is summed up in that scene. Its implications touch on everything about the house's most obvious and insidious effect—and also the only one that seems empirically undeniable: Little by little, it is ruining the Lutz family financially. The movie might as well have been subtitled "The Horror of the Shrinking Bank Account." It's the more prosaic fallout of the place where so many haunted-house stories start. "It's on the market for a song," the realtor says with a big egg-sucking grin. "It's supposed to be haunted."

Well, the house that the Lutzes buy is, indeed, on the market for a song (and there's another good moment—all too short—when Kathleen tells her husband that she will be the first person in her large Catholic family to actually own her own home; "We've always been renters," she says), but it ends up costing them dearly. At the conclusion, the house seems to literally tear itself apart. Windows crash in, black goop comes dribbling out of the walls, the cellar stairs cave in . . . and I found myself wondering not if the Lutz clan would get out alive but if they had adequate homeowner's insurance.

This is a movie for every woman who ever wept over a plugged-up toilet or a spreading water stain on the ceiling from the upstairs shower; for every man who ever did a slow burn when the weight of the snow caused his gutters to give way; for every child who ever jammed his fingers and felt that the door or window that did the jamming was out to get him. As horror goes, *Amityville* is pretty pedestrian. So's beer, but you can get drunk on it.

"Think of the bills," a woman sitting behind me in the theater moaned at one point. I suspect it was her own bills she was thinking about. It was impossible to make a silk purse out of this particular sow's ear, but Rosenberg at least manages to give us Qiana, and the main reason that people went to see it, I think, is that *The Amityville Horror,* beneath its ghost-story exterior, is really a financial demolition derby.

Think of the bills, indeed.

If movies are the dreams of the mass culture—one film critic, in fact, has called watching a movie "dreaming with one's eyes open"—and if horror movies are the nightmares of the mass culture, then many horror movies of recent times express America's coming to terms with the possibility of nuclear annihilation over political differences.

The contemporary political horror films begin, I think, with *The Thing* (1951), directed by Christian Nyby and produced by Howard Hawks (who also had a hand in the direction, one suspects). It stars Margaret Sheridan, Kenneth Tobey and James Arness as the blood-drinking human carrot from Planet X.

A polar encampment of soldiers and scientists discovers a strong magnetic field emanating from an area where there has been a recent meteor fall; the field is strong enough to throw all the electronic gadgets and gizmos off whack. Further, a camera designed to start shooting pictures when and if the normal background-radiation count suddenly goes up has taken photos of an object that dips, swoops and turns at high speeds—strange behavior for a meteor.

An expedition is dispatched to the spot, and it discovers a flying saucer buried in the ice. The saucer, superhot on touchdown, melted its way into the ice, which then refroze, leaving only the tail fin sticking out (thus relieving the special-effects corps of a potentially big-budget item). The Army guys, who demonstrate frost-bite of the brain throughout most of the film, promptly destroy the extraterrestrial ship while trying to burn it out of the ice with thermite.

The occupant (Arness) is saved, however, and carted back to the experimental station in a block of ice. He/it is placed in a storage shed, under guard. One of the guards is so freaked out by the thing that he throws a blanket over it. Unlucky man! Quite obviously, all his good stars are in retrograde, his biorhythms low and his mental magnetic poles temporarily reversed. The blanket he's used is of the electric variety, and it miraculously melts the ice without shorting out. The Thing escapes and the fun begins.

The fun ends about 60 minutes later with the creature being roasted medium rare on an electric-sidewalk sort of thing that the scientists have set up. A reporter on the scene sends back the news of humankind's first victory over invaders from space, and the film fades out, not with a THE END title card but with a question mark.

The Thing is a small movie done on a low budget. Like *Alien,* which would come more than a quarter century later, it achieves its best effects from feelings of claustrophobia and xenophobia. But, as I said before, the best horror movies will try to get at you on many different levels, and *The Thing* is also operating on a political level. It has grim things to say about eggheads (and knee-jerk liberals—in the early Fifties, you could have put an equal-sign between the two) who would indulge in the crime of appeasement.

The Thing is the first movie of the Fifties to offer us the scientist in the role of The Appeaser, that creature who for reasons either craven or misguided would open the gates to the Garden of Eden and let all the evils fly in (as opposed, say, to those mad labs proprietors of the Thirties, who were more than willing to open Pandora's box and let all the evils fly out—a major distinction, though the results are the same). That scientists should be so constantly vilified in the technohorror films of the Fifties—a decade that was apparently dedicated to the idea of turning out a whole marching corps of men and women in white lab coats—is perhaps not so surprising when we remember that it was science that opened those same gates so that the atomic bomb could be brought into Eden: first by itself and then trundled on missiles.

The average Jane or Joe during those spooky eight or nine years that followed the surrender of Japan had extremely schizoid feelings about science and scientists—recognizing the need for them and, at the same time, loathing the things they had let in forever. On the one hand, the average Jane or Joe had found a new pal, that neat little all-round guy, Reddy Kilowatt; on the other hand, before getting into the first reel of *The Thing,* they had to watch newsreel footage as an Army mock-up of a town *just like theirs* was vaporized in a nuclear furnace.

Robert Cornthwaite plays the appeasing scientist in *The Thing,* and we hear from his lips the first verse of a psalm that any filmgoer who grew up in the Fifties and Sixties became familiar with very quickly: "We must preserve this creature for science." The second verse goes: "If it comes from a society more advanced than ours, it must come in peace. If we can only establish communications with it, and find out what it wants—"

Twice, near the film's conclusion, Cornthwaite is hauled away by soldiers; at the climax, he breaks free of his guards and faces the creature with his hands open and empty. He begs it to communicate with him and to see that he means it no harm. The creature stares at him for a long, pregnant moment . . . and then bats him casually aside, as you or I might swat a mosquito. The medium-rare roasting on the electric sidewalk follows.

Now, I'm only a journeyman writer and I will not presume to teach history here. I will point out that the Americans of that time were perhaps more paranoid about the idea of appeasement than at any other time before or since. The dreadful humiliation of Neville Chamberlain and England's resulting close squeak at the beginning of Hitler's war was still very much with those Americans, and why not? It had all happened only 12 years prior to *The Thing*'s release, and even Americans who were just turning 21 in 1951 could remember it all very clearly. The moral was simple—such appeasement doesn't work; you gotta cut 'em if they stand and shoot 'em if they run. Otherwise, they'll take you over a bite at a time (and in the case of the Thing, you could take that literally).

If all this seems much too heavy a cargo for a modest little fright flick like *The Thing* to bear, remember that a man's point of view is shaped by the events he experiences and that his politics is shaped by his point of view. I am only suggesting that, given the political temper of the times and the cataclysmic world events that had occurred only a few years before, the viewpoint of this movie is almost preordained. What do you do with a blood-drinking carrot from outer space? Simple. Cut him if he stands and shoot him if he runs. And if you're an appeasing scientist like Cornthwaite (with a yellow streak up your back as wide as the no-passing line on a highway), you simply get bulldozed under.

By contrast, consider the other end of this telescope. The children of World War Two produced *The Thing;* 26 years later, a child of Vietnam and the self-proclaimed Love Generation, Steven Spielberg, gives us a fitting balance weight to *The Thing* in *Close Encounters of the Third Kind.* In 1951, the soldier standing sentry duty (the one who has foolishly covered the block of ice with an electric blanket) empties his automatic into the alien when he hears it coming; in 1977, a young guy with a happy, spaced-out smile holds up a sign reading STOP AND BE FRIENDLY. Somewhere between the two, John Foster Dulles evolved into Henry Kissinger and the pugnacious politics of confrontation became *détente.*

In *The Thing,* Tobey occupies himself with building an electric boardwalk to kill the creature; in *Close Encounters,* Richard Dreyfuss occupies himself with building a mock-up of Devil's Butte, the creatures' landing place, in his living room. The Thing is a big, hulking brute who grunts; the creatures from the stars in Spielberg's film are small, delicate, childlike. They do not speak, but their mother ship plays lovely harmonic tones—the music of the spheres, we assume. And Dreyfuss, far from wanting to murder these emissaries from space, goes with them.

I'm not saying that Spielberg is or would think of himself as a member of the Love Generation simply because he came to his majority while students were putting daisies in the muzzles of M-1s and Jimi Hendrix and Janis Joplin were playing at Fillmore West. Neither am I saying that Hawks, Nyby, Charles Lederer (who wrote the screenplay for *The Thing*) and John W. Campbell (whose *novella Who Goes There?* formed the basis for the film) fought their way up the beaches of Anzio or helped raise the Stars and Stripes on Iwo Jima. But events determine point of view and point of view determines politics, and *CE3K* seems to me every bit as preordained as *The Thing.* We can understand that the latter's "Let the military handle this" thesis was a perfectly acceptable one in 1951, because the military had handled the Japs and the Nazis perfectly well in Duke Wayne's Big One, and we can also understand that the former's attitude of "Don't let the military handle this" was a perfectly acceptable one in 1977, following the military's less-than-startling record in Vietnam.

The movies I have been discussing are those that try to link real (if sometimes free-floating) anxieties to the nightmare fears of the horror film. But now, let me put out even this dim light of rationality and discuss a few of those films whose effects go considerably deeper, past the rational and into those fears that seem universal.

Here is where we cross into the taboo lands for sure, and it's best to be frank up front. I think that we're all mentally ill; those of us outside the asylums only hide it a little better—and maybe not all that much better, after all. We've all known people who talk to themselves, people who sometimes squinch their faces into horrible grimaces when they believe no one is watching, people who have some hysterical fear—of snakes, the dark, the tight place, the long drop . . . and, of course, those final worms and grubs that are waiting so patiently underground.

When we pay our four or five bucks and seat ourselves at tenth-row center in a theater showing a horror movie, we are daring the nightmare.

Why? Some of the reasons are simple and obvious. To show that we can, that we are not afraid, that we can ride this roller coaster. Which is not to say that a really good horror movie may not surprise a scream out of us at some point, the way we may scream when the roller coaster twists through a complete 360 or plows through a lake at the bottom of the drop. And horror movies, like roller coasters, have always been the special province of the young; by the time one turns 40 or 50, one's appetite for double twists or 360-degree loops may be considerably depleted.

We also go to re-establish our feeling of essential normality; the horror movie is innately conservative, even reactionary. Freda Jackson as the horrible melting woman in *Die, Monster, Die!* confirms for us that no matter how far we may be removed from the beauty of a Robert Redford or a Diana Ross, we are still light-years from true ugliness.

And we go to have fun.

Ah, but this is where the ground starts to slope away, isn't it? Because this is a very peculiar sort of fun, indeed. The fun comes from seeing others menaced—sometimes killed. One critic has suggested that if pro football has become the voyeur's version of combat, then the horror film has become the modern version of the public lynching.

It is true that the mythic, "fairy-tale" horror film intends to take away the shades of gray (which is one reason *When a Stranger Calls* doesn't work; the psycho, well and honestly played by Tony Beckley, is a poor schmuck beset by the miseries of his own psychosis; our unwilling sympathy for him dilutes the film's success as surely as water dilutes Scotch); it urges us to put away our more civilized and adult penchant for analysis and to become children again, seeing things in pure blacks and whites. It may be that horror movies provide psychic relief on this level because this invitation to lapse into simplicity, irrationality and even outright madness is extended so rarely. We are told we may allow our emotions a free rein . . . or no rein at all.

If we are all insane, then sanity becomes a matter of degree. If your insanity leads you to carve up women like Jack the Ripper or the Cleveland Torso Murderer, we clap you away in the funny farm (but neither of those two amateur-night surgeons was ever caught, heh-heh-heh); if, on the other hand, your insanity leads you only to talk to yourself when you're under stress or to pick your nose on your morning bus, then you are left alone to go about your business . . . though it is doubtful that you will ever be invited to the best parties.

The potential lyncher is in almost all of us (excluding saints, past and present; but then, most saints have been crazy in their own ways), and every now and then, he has to be let loose to scream and roll around in the grass. Our emotions and our fears form their own body, and we recognize that it demands its own exercise to maintain proper muscle tone. Certain of these emotional muscles are accepted—even exalted—in civilized society; they are, of course, the emotions that tend to maintain the status quo of civilization itself. Love, friendship, loyalty, kindness—these are all the emotions that we applaud, emotions that have been immortalized in the couplets of Hallmark cards and in the verses (I don't dare call it poetry) of Leonard Nimoy.

When we exhibit these emotions, society showers us with positive reinforcement; we learn this even before we get out of diapers. When, as children, we hug our rotten little puke of a sister and give her a kiss, all the aunts and uncles smile and twit and cry, "Isn't he the sweetest little thing?" Such coveted treats as chocolate-covered graham crackers often follow. But if we deliberately slam the rotten little puke of a sister's fingers in the door, sanctions follow—angry remonstrance from parents, aunts and uncles; instead of a chocolate-covered graham cracker, a spanking.

But anticivilization emotions don't go away, and they demand periodic exercise. We have such "sick" jokes as, "What's the difference between a truckload of bowling balls and a truckload of dead babies?" (You can't unload a truckload of bowling balls with a pitchfork . . . a joke, by the way, that I heard originally from a ten-year-old). Such a joke may surprise a laugh or a grin out of us even as we recoil, a possibility that confirms the thesis: If we share a brotherhood of man, then we also share an insanity of man. None of which is intended as a defense of either the sick joke or insanity but merely as an explanation of why the best horror films, like the best fairy tales, manage to be reactionary, anarchistic and revolutionary all at the same time.

The mythic horror movie, like the sick joke, has a dirty job to do. It deliberately appeals to all that is worst in us. It is morbidity unchained, our most base instincts let free, our nastiest fantasies realized . . . and it all happens, fittingly enough, in the dark. For those reasons, good liberals often shy away from horror films. For myself, I like to see the most aggressive of them—*Dawn of the Dead,* for instance—as lifting a trap door in the civilized forebrain and throwing a basket of raw meat to the hungry alligators swimming around in that subterranean river beneath.

Why bother? Because it keeps them from getting out, man. It keeps them down there and me up here. It was Lennon and McCartney who said that all you need is love, and I would agree with that.

As long as you keep the gators fed.

QUESTIONS

1. How many different *kinds* of horror movie does King identify in this piece? What are they? What labels does he attach to the various categories? What examples of films does he provide in his discussion of each category?

2. On what grounds does King defend horror movies? Why does he claim that such movies have "redeeming social merit"? Is his argument persuasive?

3. Explain the meaning of King's concluding analogy—his comparison between horror films and alligator-feeding.

4. King's prose is often criticized by book reviewers for its loose, conversational quality—what one critic has called King's "let's go have a beer and talk" style. Locate the passages which, in your opinion, best exemplify that style. How do you respond to it? Is the criticism legitimate? Discuss.

5. How would you describe King's tone in this piece? Does it seem appropriate to the subject of horror? Does the humor in this selection *work?* Why or why not?

SUGGESTIONS FOR WRITING

1. Do you, like King, feel that horror movies are not simply entertaining but socially and psychologically valuable? Or do you, like many other people, regard them as so much worthless trash? Write an essay in which you either defend or condemn horror movies. Be sure to give reasons for your opinion, and include as many specific examples of horror films as possible.

2. As King points out, horror movies give expression to a wide range of common fears. Nuclear bomb anxieties underlie many 1950s horror films *(Them!, The Incredible Shrinking Man, The Amazing Colossal Man).* The fear of being punished for illicit sexual activity seems to be at the root of the modern-day "slasher" movies *(Halloween, Friday the 13th, Slumber Party Massacre),* in which young couples are butchered by knife- (or axe- or chainsaw-) wielding psychopaths. Other films play on the primal fear of the dead *(I Walked with a Zombie, White Zombie, Night of the Living Dead).* Make a list of all the horror films you've seen, then write an essay in which you classify those films according to the kinds of fears and anxieties they deal with.

Molly Haskell
THE WOMAN'S FILM
★ ★ ★

A writer whose main focus is on the portrayal of women in the movies, Molly Haskell grew up in Virginia and graduated from Sweet Briar College. Her first New York job was in the French Film Office, where she wrote and edited a bulletin and newsletter on French cinema. Since that time, she has gained recognition as a sharp, witty analyst of film. Her essays have appeared in a wide range of publications, including Ms., Esquire, Glamour, Psychology Today, Saturday Review, Vogue, Film Comment, *and* The New York Times. *A member of both the National*

Society of Film Critics and the New York Film Critics Circle, she has served as a movie reviewer on National Public Radio, and has produced several television documentaries on women artists.

The following selection is excerpted from Haskell's provocative and influential book, From Reverence to Rape *(1974), a study of how American movies have reflected—and shaped—our attitudes toward women.*

What more damning comment on the relations between men and women in America than the very notion of something called the "woman's film"? And what more telling sign of critical and sexual priorities than the low caste it has among the highbrows? Held at arm's length, it is, indeed, the untouchable of film genres. The concept of a "woman's film" and "women's fiction" as a separate category of art (and/or kitsch), implying a generically shared world of misery and masochism the individual work is designed to indulge, does not exist in Europe. There, affairs of the heart are of importance to both men and women and are the stuff of literature. In England, the woman's film occupies a place somewhere between its positions in France and in America; *Brief Encounter* and *The Seventh Veil* are not without soap opera elements, but they are on a slightly higher plane than their American counterparts.

Among the Anglo-American critical brotherhood (and a few of their sisters as well), the term "woman's film" is used disparagingly to conjure up the image of the pinched-virgin or little-old-lady writer, spilling out her secret longings in wish fulfillment or glorious martyrdom, and transmitting these fantasies to the frustrated housewife. The final image is one of wet, wasted afternoons. And if strong men have also cried their share of tears over the weepies, that is all the more reason (goes the argument) we should be suspicious, be on our guard against the flood of "unearned" feelings released by these assaults, unerringly accurate, on our emotional soft spots.

As a term of critical opprobrium, "woman's film" carries the implication that women, and therefore women's emotional problems, are of minor significance. A film that focuses on male relationships is not pejoratively dubbed a "man's film" (indeed, this term, when it is used, confers—like "a man's man"—an image of brute strength), but a "psychological drama." European films, too, are automatically exempted from the "woman's film" caste; thus, the critical status of *Mayerling* over *Love Affair*, *Le Carnet du Bal* over *Angel*, *Jules and Jim* over *Design for Living*, *My Night at Maud's* over *Petulia*, and *The Passion of Anna* over Bergman's English-language *The Touch*. Also exempted are films with literary prestige, like *Carrie* or *Sunday, Bloody Sunday*.

In the thirties and forties, the heyday of the "woman's film," it was as regular an item in studio production as the crime melodrama or the Western. Like any routine genre, it was subject to its highs and lows, and ranged from films that adhered safely to the formulae of escapist fantasy, films that were subversive only "between the lines" and in retrospect, and the rare few that used the conventions to undermine them. At the lowest level, as soap opera, the "woman's film" fills a masturbatory need, it is soft-core emotional porn for the frustrated housewife. The weepies are founded on a mock-Aristotelian and politically conservative aesthetic whereby women spectators are moved, not by pity and fear but by self-pity and tears, to accept, rather than reject, their lot. That there should be a need and an audience for such an opiate suggests an unholy amount of real misery. And that a term like "woman's film" can be summarily used to dismiss certain films, with no further need on the part of the critic to make distinctions and explore the genre, suggests some of the reasons for this misery.

In the woman's film, the woman—*a* woman—is at the center of the universe. Best friends and suitors, like Bette Davis' satellites (Geraldine Fitzgerald and George Brent) in *Dark Victory,* live only for her pleasure, talk about her constantly, and cease to exist when she dies. In the rare case where a man's point of view creeps in, as screenwriter Howard Koch's did in *No Sad Songs for Me,* it is generally reconciled with the woman's point of view. Thus, after Margaret Sullavan dies, the husband (Wendell Corey) will marry the woman (Viveca Lindfors) he almost had an affair with. But it is with the dead wife's blessing (she has actually chosen the woman who will replace her as wife and mother), and with the knowledge that when the chips were down, he preferred the wife to the "other woman." The result is the same as that of *Dark Victory:* The two loved ones—the remainders—may unite out of loneliness, but always with the shadow and memory of the "great woman" (vivid and in her prime) between them. If woman hogs this universe unrelentingly, it is perhaps her compensation for all the male-dominated universes from which she has been excluded: the gangster film, the Western, the war film, the *policier,* the rodeo film, the adventure film. Basically, the woman's film is no more maudlin and self-pitying than the male adventure film (what British critic Raymond Durgnat calls the "male weepies"), particularly in the male film's recent mood of bronco-busting buddies and bleary-eyed nostalgia. The well of self-pity in both types of films, though only hinted at, is bottomless, and in their sublimation or evasion of adult reality, they reveal, almost by accident, real attitudes toward marriage—disillusionment, frustration, and contempt—beneath the sunny-side-up philosophy congealed in the happy ending.

The underlying mystique of the man's film is that these are (or were) the best of times, roaming the plains, or prowling the city, in old clothes and unshaven, the days before settling down or going home, days spent battling nature or the enemy. In such films, the woman becomes a kind of urban or frontier Xantippe with rather limited options. She can be a meddling moralist who wants the hero to leave off his wandering; or a last resort for him, after his buddies have died or departed; or an uptight socialite to whom the hero can never confess his criminal, or even just shadowy, past; or a nagging nice-girl wife, who pesters the hero to spend more time with her, instead of always working, working, working or killing, killing, killing. The most common pattern is probably the wife competing with her husband's other life—business, crime, or crime detection; and since these activities are the dramatic focus and lifeblood of the film, the wife becomes a killjoy, distracting not only the hero but the audience from the fun and danger.

Marriage becomes the heavy. The implication is clear: All the excitement of life—the passion, the risk—occurs outside marriage rather than within it. Marriage is a deadly bore, made to play the role of the spoilsport, the ugly cousin one has to dance with at the ball. An excruciating example, and they abound, occurs in *The Big Clock,* in the husband-wife relationship of Ray Milland and Maureen O'Sullivan. Milland, an advertising executive, has been framed for murder; he is in life-or-death danger as he tries to track down the real culprit. Meanwhile O'Sullivan—naturally, as the wife, the last to be informed—keeps complaining of Milland's long hours at the office and his failure to take her on a promised wedding trip. Indeed, the murderer (Charles Laughton) is by far a more sympathetic character than the wife. By intruding on and sometimes interfering with the melodrama, such women become harpies even when they aren't meant to— *The Big Clock,* after all, was directed by Maureen O'Sullivan's husband, John Farrow.

That love is woman's stuff is a hoary Anglo-Saxon idea, devolving from the (American) tough guy and (British) public school etiquette that to show emotion is bad form, a sign of effeminacy, and that being tender in love is the equivalent of doing the dishes or darning socks. The association takes. For the housewife, betrayed by her romantic ideals, the path of love leads to, becomes, the dead end of household drudgery. The domestic and the romantic are entwined, one redeeming the other, in the theme of self-sacrifice, which is the mainstay and oceanic force, high tide and low ebb, of the woman's film. The equation of time and Tide is not so risible as it seems, just as the emphasis in the women's movement on domestic arrangements is not a trivializing of "larger issues." Rather, it is an intuitive recognition that the essence of salvation is not in the single leap of the soul, but in the day-to-day struggle to keep the best of oneself afloat—the discovery that perdition is not the moment of Faustian sellout, but the gradual dribbling of self-esteem, and self, down the drain of meaningless activity.

To the view that women's concerns, and the films that depict them, are of minor significance in the drama of life and art, women themselves have acquiesced, and critics have led the way. James Agee was almost alone among critics in not dismissing the woman's film summarily. In a favorable review of *Brief Encounter,* he wrote that when he associated the film with the best of women's magazine fiction, he did not intend a backhand compliment. "For it seems to me that few writers of supposedly more serious talent even undertake themes as simple and important any more: so that, relatively dinky and sentimental as it is—a sort of vanity-sized *Anna Karenina—Brief Encounter* is to be thoroughly respected."

But for every Agee, there have been critics whose voices dripped sarcasm and whose pens went lax when they came to review a woman's film. In his 1946 book *On Documentary,* the late John Grierson, the father of the "serious subject" critics, interrupted his anti-Hollywood and prosocial-realism diatribe to deplore Anthony Asquith's waste of time and talent on *Dance, Pretty Lady.* Grierson, admitting the film was "a delight to the eye," nonetheless deplored its subject: "This is it, bless you. Claptrap about a virginity. Why the entire sentiment that makes a plot like that possible went into discard with the good, prosperous, complacent Victoria. It was, relatively, an important matter then. But it is mere infant fodder now when you consider the new problems we carry in our bellies, and think of the new emphases we must in mercy to ourselves create out of our different world." Apparently the way to a socially conscious critic's heart is through his stomach. A woman's virginity (infant fodder, indeed!), and where and how she lost it, is at least as important as the high and mighty manly themes of the films Grierson approved of.

The depreciation of women's films takes a different form among critics who are not socially conscious—the aesthetically open, "movie-movie critics" represented, in the thirties and forties, by Agee, Otis Ferguson, Robert Warshow, and Manny Farber. There, the prejudice is more subtle: It is not that they love women less, but that they admire men more. Even Ferguson and Agee, who were enraptured with certain female presences on the screen, reserved their highest accolades for the films that showed men doing things and that captured the look and feel of down-at-heel losers, criminals, or soldiers, men battling nature or big-city odds. Agee never avoided the emotional or sentimental side of film (in the forties, who could?), but like the others, he had a slight case of Hemingwayitis. This infatuation with the masculine mystique was the pale-face New York intellectual's compensation for life in a cubicle, a *nostalgie de la boue* for the real grit and grime, as opposed to synthetic smudge—the kind that rubs off on your hands from typewriter erasures or newspapers.

There has been a corollary blindness on the part of most film critics to the achievements of the "woman's director," to the mixture of seriousness and high style that Europeans like Max Ophuls, Douglas Sirk, Otto Preminger, and Lubitsch bring to women's subjects, not just enhancing but transforming them; or to the commitment of a John Stahl or Edmund Goulding to material from which other directors withdraw in tasteful disdain (as did Wyler and Stevens, "graduating" as soon as they got the opportunity from the woman's film subjects of their early and best work to the bloated seriousness of their later work); or to the complete identification of a director like George Cukor with the woman's point of view, so that the attitude expressed is not his so much as hers.

Central to the woman's film is the notion of middle-classness, not just as an economic status, but as a state of mind and a relatively rigid moral code. The circumscribed world of the housewife corresponds to the state of woman in general, confronted by a range of options so limited she might as well inhabit a cell. The persistent irony is that she is dependent for her well-being and "fulfillment" on institutions—marriage, motherhood—that by translating the word "woman" into "wife" and "mother," end her independent identity. She then feels bound to adhere to a morality which demands that she stifle her own "illicit" creative or sexual urges in support of a social code that tolerates considerably more deviation on the part of her husband. She is encouraged to follow the lead of her romantic dreams, but when they expire she is stuck.

Beyond this common plight of a generic nature, there are as many kinds of woman's film as there are kinds of women. One division, providing the greatest tension with conventions of the genre, is between the upper-middle-class elite and the rest of the world, between women as models and women as victims. There are the "extraordinary" women—actresses like Marlene Dietrich, Katharine Hepburn, Rosalind Russell, Bette Davis, and characters like Scarlett O'Hara and Jezebel—who are the exceptions to the rule, the aristocrats of their sex. Their point of view is singular, and in calling the shots they transcend the limitations of their sexual identities. But their status as emancipated women, based as it is on the very quality of being exceptional, weakens their political value as demonstration-model victims and makes them, in their independence, unpopular with a majority of men and women.

Then there are the "ordinary" women—women whose options have been foreclosed by marriage or income, by children or age, who are, properly speaking, the subject of women's films at their lowest and largest common denominator. As audience surrogates, their heroines are defined negatively and collectively by their mutual limitations rather than by their talents or aspirations. Their point of view is not singular but plural, political rather than personal. They embrace the audience as victims, through the common myths of rejection and self-sacrifice and martyrdom as purveyed by the mass media. These—the media—have changed over the years, from magazines like *Good Housekeeping, Cosmopolitan, The Saturday Evening Post,* and from novels like those of Fannie Hurst, Edna Ferber, and Kathleen Norris, through the movies of the twenties, thirties, and forties, to television soap opera today. But the myths have not changed, nor has the underlying assumption: that these women are stuck, and would rather be stuck than sorry. The purpose of these fables is not to encourage "woman" to rebel or question her role, but to reconcile her to it, and thus preserve the status quo. The fictions are her defense not only against "man," but against the "extraordinary woman." For the average housewife, who has not quite gotten around to sex therapy or sensitivity training or group grope, prostitution, drugs, or even drink, these matinee myths are her alcoholic afternoons.

Between these two, there is a third category, one to which the better women's films aspire: It is the fiction of the "ordinary woman who becomes extraordinary," the woman who begins as a victim of discriminatory circumstances and rises, through pain, obsession, or defiance, to become mistress of her fate. Between the suds of soap opera we watch her scale the heights of Stendhalian romance. Her ascent is given stature and conviction not through a discreet contempt for the female sensibility, but through an all-out belief in it, through the faith, expressed in directorial sympathy and style, that the swirling river of a woman's emotions is as important as anything on earth. The difference between the soap opera palliative and the great woman's film *(Angel, Letter from an Unknown Woman)* is like the difference between masturbatory relief and mutually demanding love.

QUESTIONS

1. In what sense does the "very notion" of the woman's film as a separate cinematic category serve as a "damning comment on the relations between men and women in America"?

2. How does the man's film differ from the woman's film? How are the two types
    of film similar? Why is the man's film taken more seriously by movie critics
    than the woman's film? How does Haskell account for the "infatuation with
    the masculine mystique" among so many movie critics?

3. What are the three main categories of the woman's film? How do they differ
    from one another?

4. What is the main point of Haskell's essay? How does her point emerge from
    the categories referred to in the previous question?

5. What does Haskell mean by calling the woman's film the "untouchable of
    film genres"? How is that statement metaphorical? How does it relate to the
    sentence that precedes it?

6. Haskell writes that, whenever male movie critics of the "serious subject"
    school had to review a woman's film, their "voices dripped sarcasm." In
    describing these critics, Haskell becomes fairly sarcastic herself. Point to
    places in this selection where Haskell's own voice "drips sarcasm"—places
    where her tone is particularly biting and derisive.

SUGGESTIONS FOR WRITING

1. Most of the films Haskell discusses in this selection are from the 1930s and
    1940s. Write an essay in which you classify the different types of women most
    commonly found in *contemporary* movies (or television programs). You may
    use Haskell's categories if you think they still apply.

2. Haskell suggests that the reason male critics do not take women's films
    seriously is that men regard women's real-life problems as relatively trivial.
    How do you feel about this issue? Do you believe that the problems women
    face in life are less significant than those with which men must contend?
    Write an essay explaining your point of view.

STUDENT ESSAY

Stephen Pool
EDUCATION REDISCOVERED: THE NEW AMERICAN UNIVERSITY

*Though the following essay describes the cinema as the "new American
university" and proceeds to catalogue some of the "course offerings" available to the modern moviegoer, the author, Stephen Pool, clearly believes
in the importance of more traditional forms of learning. A native of
Michigan, Pool produced this essay when a student at Detroit's Wayne
State University, where he specialized in literature and classical languages.*

Pool's contention that blockbusters like Top Gun *and* Raiders of the Lost Ark *create standards of style and behavior for contemporary audiences is unquestionably valid. It is worth noting, however, that in describing the influences on his own thinking and writing, Pool cites Homer, Thomas Merton, and F. Scott Fitzgerald as his major intellectual and stylistic models.*

What is college for? So asked a recent title of an article in *Time*. "I'm taking accounting so I'll have a secure, good-paying job when I finish," a junior told me last autumn. "It's a raging four-year party that slows down during vacation." This from a disaffected Ohio State student who dispelled any notions in my mind that real learning goes on at college these days. And the *Time* article seemed correct in saying that the modern university is mainly vocationally oriented. It provides, to a greater or lesser degree, four years of job training and skill development for the majority of the nation's student body. One education researcher has bemoaned the fact that "the great commonalities of learning" have been lost.

That the traditional commonalities of the university have been lost is perhaps true. To say that the commonalities of learning have been lost, however, is to miss entirely the real means of education in the contemporary world, as a trip to the local movie theater will prove. Like a college, the cinema has separate departments and many courses of study, offering instruction in areas ranging from outerwear to ideology. In a society where life for most people takes place strictly on a superficial level, what better place to learn than at the movies?

One especially prevalent and influential kind of knowledge film transmits comes in the area of fashion. With winter breaking into a lope last November, a visit to Henry the Hatter seemed in order. I was greeted at the door of this outpost in Detroit's desolate downtown by Henry's son himself. "And what are we looking for today, sir?" I was in for a wool beret. Preferably in black. Henry Jr. directed me to a series of shelves containing my size and retired behind the counter. A middle-aged man impeccably dressed in a conservative grey suit stood at the end of the counter admiring his mirror image wearing a brown fedora. "How much?" He turned to get a side view. "Forty-five dollars, and I can't keep them in at that price. It's the only genuine Indiana Jones fedora available." Henry noticed my stare. "Like to try one on?" I declined, and, feeling a bit stuffy, moved back outside. As I walked home, I realized how powerfully film exists as a fashion educator. *Raiders of the Lost Ark* and its offspring *Indiana Jones and the Temple of Doom* had apparently provided the impetus for the would be archeologist in the store. What was truly important about these films was not the forgettable story line, not the characters, but the clothing Indiana wore. The movies were a course in dressing for success. "God, I'd love an old flight jacket like that," one of my friends had thought aloud as we drove home after *Temple*. At the time it was difficult to obtain this newly essential cultural equipment unless you could cajole grandpa into passing his on. But it wasn't long before the opportunistic, and ironically named, Banana Republic sprang to life. Here you could get that flight jacket, and with what relief—you wouldn't have to beat it for days with an old stick: it was already aged! Not only that, but you could buy the whole outfit; you could literally *be* Indiana Jones. Now no large retail store is without its section of khakis and battered brown jackets.

The cinema also contains a category of instruction in behavior. Perhaps the most important film (educationally, that is) for my generation is *Animal House*. As a course in modern hedonism, it is unsurpassed. Whereas after a classic Bogart film one might leave the theater talking in a clipped, demanding accent, or stride out of a Clint Eastwood film with a new and improved squint, viewers left *Animal House* with the behavioral essentials of a successful undergraduate experience. Seeing the Animal House characters get sloppy drunk and pursue cheap sex was a college education in the truest sense—the movie theater was the place to learn what to do once you got to the university. The long-term effect of this is still apparent on campus, where toga parties thrown by fraternities across the nation are among the year's highlights for many students. One undergraduate at Duke told me of a campus fraternity that held a toga party every semester. Several beer trucks would park on the street outside, and the event my acquaintance described was usually attended by nearly 3,000 revelers. "It's kind of hard to meet people in that sort of situation, or even to find someone you know," he admitted. "So what happens?" I asked. "Well, during the one last semester I pretty much hung around the beer truck with some buddies until I passed out. I woke up in a strange apartment with only my pants on. No one was home, and since I wasn't sure how I got there or where the rest of my clothes were, I left before anyone came back." This student, only one among many, had fully applied what he had learned— something any professor could be proud of.

At times, film combines several categories to transmit a more general range of vital information. On a hot night in mid-July last summer, the phone rang. "Want to go see *Top Gun?*" Sure, why not. I was surprised to walk into a nearly full theater on a Wednesday at the very non-cool hour of 7:00 (the 9:45 showing is "fashionably late" around here). It quickly became clear that this was a broad, interdisciplinary sort of class, which was teaching proper fashion, the key to personal success, and even a correct political view. Tom Cruise's getup of 501 jeans and aviator sunglasses had spawned an overwhelming mass of lookalikes on the beach, on the streets, everywhere. Until I saw the movie, I couldn't compre- hend the pleasure gained from sunbathing and playing beach games in jeans. The keys to success, as enumerated by the film, were a certain brashness coupled with glamorous, muscular good looks. While the skinny and (God forbid!) married Goose gets to die in the plane crash scene, the attractive Cruise goes on to beat the Russians, win the dream life and carry off the dream girl, Kelly McGillis. The Cruise character loses little except perhaps a sense that he is human. And the teaching even extends to politics, where an onscreen cheer goes up (one in the theater as well) when the inscrutable Russians are vaporized. There are nothing but tears onscreen (and muffled sobs in the theater) when the bloodied face of Goose disappears for the last time. This promotion of a radically pro-U.S., pro-Reagan, macho political stance even inspired some moviegoers to apply their new knowledge by signing up for the Navy immediately after seeing the film.

Indeed, moviegoers tend to be ideal "students," who not only crave an education but respond to their lessons with a kind of involvement and enthusiasm rarely encountered in the college classroom. As I watched *Top Gun,* the eerie movie light illuminated a couple seated several rows ahead. As the onscreen jets engaged in mock dogfights, they became visibly excited and spoke rapidly to each other. During the obligatory lovemaking scene, the pair cuddled. When the Cruise character's partner died, they both visibly sagged. When the Russians appeared, they sat up alert, poised for the unrestrained cheer and applause that they, and the rest of the audience, burst into minutes later when the same Russians were blown up.

As an educational center, the cinema is inherently attractive. The air-conditioned theater is a Mecca when it gets hot, and summer school, as it were, is often overenrolled. The university of the motion picture has no entrance requirements, the courses are not mentally taxing, and tuition is relatively low. And now, with the advent of the ten-screen suburban theater, a virtual schedule of classes, constantly changing and covering all possible topics of study, is posted outside, for ease of reference. As a thoughtful student of the cinema must concede, however, this university is a failed vision. The learning that takes place exists only within the magical space of the theater, and cannot successfully be carried outside for long. Reality simply does not operate in the same manner as the "real life" portrayed in the movies. But I didn't tell that to the couple I had seen sitting in front of me who now walked ahead, pausing to clasp hands before emerging, transformed, into the floodlit warmth of the parking lot.

QUESTIONS

1. A satire is an artistic work that ridicules the vices or follies of a person, a group of people, an institution, or an entire society. It also advocates (usually implicitly) a higher standard of conduct. Is Pool's essay a satire? Discuss.

2. What is Pool's thesis? Analyze how he develops this thesis.

3. Discuss Pool's use of students' remarks in his essay. What do these conversations, particularly the one Pool has with the Duke undergraduate, add to the essay? Can you tell what the writer's attitude is toward his fellow students?

4. How important, according to Pool, is the "instruction" we get from movies?

5. Look at the end of the essay. Why does Pool conclude with the image of the hand-clasping couple walking into the floodlit parking lot? What is he trying to achieve here? Does he succeed?

SUGGESTIONS FOR WRITING

1. Classify some of the movies that you have seen according to type or genre (e.g., adventure films, horror movies, science fiction/fantasy films, westerns,

love films) and then write about the elements of plot, character, and so on that films in each category have in common. Refer to specific films and details of those films frequently.

2. As Pool's essay implies, Hollywood has more influence over the way we think about things and behave than we are perhaps aware of. Choose a few significant subjects (e.g., sex, marriage, love, war, crime, cities, adolescence) and write an essay about the way Hollywood shapes our attitudes toward them.

3. In his essay, Pool claims that America is a country in which "life for most people takes place strictly on a superficial level." What does he mean by this? In an essay, take issue with or support this idea.

Donald Barthelme
HOW I WRITE MY SONGS BY BILL B. WHITE
★ ★ ★

The term "anti-story" is often applied to contemporary works of experimental fiction. " 'Anti-stories,' " according to critics Jerome Klinkowitz and John Somer, are "exercises as if in parody against the traditional elements of plot, subject, development, and meaning." One of the most acclaimed practitioners of this innovative form of writing is Donald Barthelme.

Born in Philadelphia in 1931 and raised in Texas, Barthelme worked as a newspaper reporter and museum curator (in Houston) before moving to New York City in 1962. After serving as the editor of a short-lived art and literature journal, he became a full-time writer and frequent contributor to The New Yorker *magazine. Barthelme's stories tend to be language experiments, composed of strange juxtapositions, surreal situations, and collage effects. In spite of their fragmentary, frequently absurd nature, however, his fictions do not refuse to offer meaning. On the contrary, as critic Morris Dickstein has written, Barthelme "juxtaposes strange forms and fragments in a way that creates new forms and new meanings."*

Throughout the years Barthelme has received numerous prizes and honors, from a Guggenheim Fellowship to the National Book Award. His books include: Snow White *(1967),* Unspeakable Practices, Unnatural Acts *(1968),* City Life *(1970),* The Dead Father *(1975), and* Amateurs *(1976). This essay originally appeared in* The New Yorker *(1978).*

Some of the methods I use to write my songs will be found in the following examples. Everyone has a song in him or her. Writing songs is a basic human trait. I am not saying that it is easy; like everything else worthwhile in this world it requires concentration and hard work. The methods I will outline are a good way to begin and have worked for me but they are by no means the only methods that can be used. There is no one set way of writing your songs, every way is just as good as the other as Kipling said. (I am talking now about the lyrics; we will talk about the melodies in a little bit.) The important thing is to put true life into your songs, things that people know and can recognize and truly feel. You have to be open to experience, to what is going on around you, the things of daily life. Often little things that you don't even think about at the time can be the basis of a song.

A knowledge of all the different types of songs that are commonly accepted is helpful. To give you an idea of the various types of songs there are I am going to tell you how I wrote various of my own, including "Rudelle," "Last Night," "Sad Dog Blues," and others—how I came to write these songs and where I got the idea and what the circumstances were, more or less, so that you will be able to do the same thing. Just remember, *there is no substitute for sticking to it* and listening to the work of others who have been down this road before you and have mastered their craft over many years.

In the case of "Rudelle" I was sitting at my desk one day with my pencil and yellow legal pad and I had two things that were irritating me. One was a letter from the electric company that said "The check for $75.60 sent us in payment of your bill has been returned to us by the bank unhonored etc. etc." Most of you who have received this type of letter from time to time know how irritating this kind of communication can be as well as embarrassing. The other thing that was irritating me was that I had a piece of white thread tied tight around my middle at navel height as a reminder to keep my stomach pulled in to strengthen the abdominals while sitting—this is the price you pay for slopping down too much beer when your occupation is essentially a sit-down one! Anyhow I had these two things itching me, so I decided to write a lost-my-mind song.

I wrote down on my legal pad the words:

When I lost my baby
I almost lost my mine

This is more or less a traditional opening for this type of song. Maybe it was written by somebody originally way long ago and who wrote it is forgotten. It often helps to begin with a traditional or well-known line or lines to set a pattern for yourself. You can then write the rest of the song and, if you wish, cut off the top part, giving you an original song. *Songs are always composed of both traditional and new elements.* This means that you can rely on the tradition to give your song "legs" while also putting in your own experience or particular way of looking at things for the new.

Incidentally the lines I have quoted may look pretty bare to you but remember you are looking at just one element, the words, and there is also the melody and the special way various artists will have of singing it which gives flavor and freshness. For example, an artist who is primarily a blues singer would probably give the "when" a lot of squeeze, that is to say, draw it out, and he might also sing "baby" as three notes, "bay-ee-bee," although it is only two syllables. Various artists have their own unique ways of doing a song and what may appear to be rather plain or dull on paper becomes quite different when it is a song.

I then wrote:

When I lost my baby
I almost lost my mine
When I lost my baby
I almost lost my mine
When I found my baby
The sun began to shine.

You will notice I retained the traditional opening because it was so traditional I did not see any need to delete it. With the addition of various material about Rudelle and what kind of woman she was, it became gold in 1976.

Incidentally while we are talking about use of traditional materials here is a little tip: you can often make good use of colorful expressions in common use such as "If the good Lord's willin' and the creek don't rise" (to give you just one example) which I used in "Goin' to Get Together" as follows:

Goin' to get to-geth-er
Goin' to get to-geth-er
If the good Lord's willin' and the creek don't rise.

These common expressions are expressive of the pungent ways in which most people often think—they are the salt of your song, so to say. Try it!

It is also possible to give a song a funny or humorous "twist":

Show'd my soul to the woman at the bank
She said put that thing away boy, put that thing away
Show'd my soul to the woman at the liquor store
She said put that thing away boy, 'fore it turns the wine
Show'd my soul to the woman at the 7-Eleven
She said: Is that all?

You will notice that the meter here is various and the artist is given great liberties.

Another type of song which is a dear favorite of almost everyone is the song that has a message, some kind of thought that people can carry away with them and think about. Many songs of this type are written and gain great acceptance every day. Here is one of my own that I put to a melody which has a kind of martial flavor:

How do you spell truth? L-o-v-e is how you spell truth
How do you spell love? T-r-u-t-h is how you spell love
Where were you last night?
Where were you last night?

When "Last Night" was first recorded, the engineer said "That's a keeper" on the first take and it was subsequently covered by sixteen artists including Walls.

The I-ain't-nothin'-but-a-man song is a good one to write when you are having a dry spell. These occur in songwriting as in any other profession and if you are in one it is often helpful to try your hand at this type of song which is particularly good with a heavy rhythm emphasis in the following pattern

Da da da da *da*
Whomp, whomp

where some of your instruments are playing da da da da *da,* hitting that last note hard, and the others answer whomp, whomp. Here is one of my own:

I'm just an ordinary mane
Da da da da *da*
Whomp, whomp
Just an ordinary mane
Da da da da *da*
Whomp, whomp
Ain't nothin' but a mane
Da da da da *da*
Whomp, whomp
I'm a grizzly mane
Da da da da *da*
Whomp, whomp
I'm a hello-goodbye mane
Da da da da *da*
Whomp, whomp
I'm a ramblin'-gamblin' mane
Da da da da *da*
Whomp, whomp
I'm a *mane's* mane
I'm a woeman's mane
Da da da da *da*
Whomp, whomp
I'm an upstairs mane
Da da da da *da*
Whomp, whomp
I'm a today-and-tomorrow mane

Da da da da *da*
Whomp, whomp
I'm a Freeway mane
Da da da da *da*
Whomp, whomp

Copyright © 1977 by French Music, Inc.

Well, you see how it is done. It is my hope that these few words will get you started. Remember that although this business may seem closed and standoffish to you, looking at it from the outside, inside it has some very warm people in it, some of the finest people I have run into in the course of a varied life. The main thing is to persevere and to believe in yourself, no matter what the attitude of others may be or appear to be. I could never have written my songs had I failed to believe in Bill B. White, not as a matter of conceit or false pride but as a human being. I will continue to write my songs, for the nation as a whole and for the world.

QUESTIONS

1. What makes this story different from other, more conventional short stories you are familiar with? What is it about? Does it have an identifiable theme?

2. White advises aspiring songwriters to "put true life into their songs." Judging from the quoted song lyrics, does he seem to practice what he preaches? Why or why not?

3. In what way is this story satirical? What are some of the things Barthelme is satirizing in it? Do you find this story funny? Why or why not?

4. How would you characterize Bill B. White's tone in this story? Judging from his language and his ideas, what sort of person does he seem to be?

5. Go through the story, locating all the clichés you can find. Why is the story so full of stale, hackneyed expressions?

6. White urges beginning songwriters to use "pungent" expressions in their lyrics. How "pungent" is White's own language? Is there a difference between the language of his songs and the language he uses to address his readers?

SUGGESTION FOR WRITING

In providing examples of his songwriting technique, White cites three different types of "commonly accepted" songs: the "lost-my-mind" song, the message song, and the "I-ain't nothin'-but-a-man" song. How many other types of songs can you think of? Write an essay in which you classify today's popular music according to its most common themes (broken love affairs, sexual longing, teen rebellion, lost innocence). Provide specific examples of each type of song.

Frank O'Hara
TO THE FILM INDUSTRY IN CRISIS
★ ★ ★

Frank O'Hara was born in Baltimore in 1926 and raised in Worcester, Massachusetts. After serving in the Navy during World War II and then attending Harvard University and the University of Michigan, he moved to Manhattan in 1951. There he became deeply involved in the New York art scene and a leading member of the so-called "New York School" of poets, a group of young writers who associated with—and drew much of their inspiration from—the abstract expressionist painters of the day (Jackson Pollock, Willem De Kooning, Franz Kline, and others). He was also on the staff of the Museum of Modern Art. About to be promoted to full curator, he was killed in an accident at the age of 40.

O'Hara's high-spirited poetry often blends dreamlike, surrealistic imagery with a distinctively casual voice. His poems have a spontaneous quality to them; indeed, some of his best poems were dashed off in spare moments. This offhanded approach is an accurate indication, not only of O'Hara's natural powers as a writer, but also of his unpretentious attitude toward poetry. In an essay called "Personism: A Manifesto," O'Hara writes, "Too many poets act like a middle-aged mother trying to get her kids to eat too much cooked meat and potatoes with drippings (tears). I don't give a damn whether they eat or not. . . . Nobody should experience anything they don't need to, if they don't need poetry bully for them. I like the movies too. . . ."

Not you, lean quarterlies and swarthy periodicals
with your studious incursions toward the pomposity of ants,
nor you, experimental theatre in which Emotive Fruition
is wedding Poetic Insight perpetually, nor you,
promenading Grand Opera, obvious as an ear (though you
are close to my heart), but you, Motion Picture Industry,
it's you I love!

In times of crisis, we must all decide again and again whom we love.
And give credit where it's due: not to my starched nurse, who taught me
how to be bad and not bad rather than good (and has lately availed
herself of this information), not to the Catholic Church
which is at best an oversolemn introduction to cosmic entertainment,
not to the American Legion, which hates everybody, but to you,
glorious Silver Screen, tragic Technicolor, amorous Cinemascope,
stretching Vistavision and startling Stereophonic Sound, with all
your heavenly dimensions and reverberations and iconoclasms! To

Richard Barthelmess as the "tol'able" boy barefoot and in pants,
Jeanette MacDonald of the flaming hair and lips and long, long neck,
Sue Carroll as she sits for eternity on the damaged fender of a car
and smiles, Ginger Rogers with her pageboy bob like a sausage
on her shuffling shoulders, peach-melba-voiced Fred Astaire of the feet,
Eric von Stroheim, the seducer of mountain-climbers' gasping spouses,
the Tarzans, each and every one of you (I cannot bring myself to prefer
Johnny Weissmuller to Lex Barker, I cannot!), Mae West in a furry sled,
her bordello radiance and bland remarks, Rudolph Valentino of the moon,
its crushing passions, and moonlike, too, the gentle Norma Shearer,
Miriam Hopkins dropping her champagne glass off Joel McCrea's yacht
and crying into the dappled sea, Clark Gable rescuing Gene Tierney
from Russia and Allan Jones rescuing Kitty Carlisle from Harpo Marx,
Cornel Wilde coughing blood on the piano keys while Merle Oberon berates,
Marilyn Monroe in her little spike heels reeling through Niagara Falls,
Joseph Cotten puzzling and Orson Welles puzzled and Dolores del Rio
eating orchids for lunch and breaking mirrors, Gloria Swanson reclining,
and Jean Harlow reclining and wiggling, and Alice Faye reclining
and wiggling and singing, Myrna Loy being calm and wise, William Powell
in his stunning urbanity, Elizabeth Taylor blossoming, yes, to you

and to all you others, the great, the near-great, the featured, the extras
who pass quickly and return in dreams saying your one or two lines,
my love!
Long may you illumine space with your marvellous appearances, delays
and enunciations, and may the money of the world glitteringly cover you
as you rest after a long day under the kleig lights with your faces
in packs for our edification, the way the clouds come often at night
but the heavens operate on the star system. It is a divine precedent
you perpetuate! Roll on, reels of celluloid, as the great earth rolls on!

QUESTIONS

1. What, precisely, is O'Hara celebrating in this poem? What is it about the movies that inspires his love?

2. How would you describe O'Hara's tone in this poem?

3. The central part of this poem consists of a catalogue of famous actors and actresses in representative roles or poses. Is this list effective? Why or why not?

4. *Hyperbole* (or overstatement) is the use of deliberately exaggerated or extravagant language to achieve a particular effect. Point to examples of hyperbolic language in this poem and explain why O'Hara uses it and what effect he achieves with it.

SUGGESTION FOR WRITING

Write an essay in which you try to explain what it is you love best about the movies (or any other form of popular art, such as television, comic books, or rock music). Be as precise and descriptive as you can. Include detailed examples, as O'Hara does, of your favorite movie actors (TV stars, comic book heroes, rock groups).

CHAPTER Eight

LANGUAGE
Definition

Definition, like classification discussed in the previous chapter, is a method of organizing by labeling. But whereas classification is a system of sorting out numbers of things into groups ("E.T.," "Star Wars," and "Alien" are all labeled *science fiction* films), definition examines the essential nature of what lies behind the label (Science fiction is . . .). According to Peggy Rosenthal, whose essay "The Power of a Positive *Self*" is included in this chapter, "A definition is (by definition) a boundary, an assumption of finiteness. A tightly defined word has definite boundaries and therefore limited room for concepts to fit into it. But a loosely defined word like "self" is flexible, stretchy; its sides can move out easily to accommodate all the concepts that come into it from the various places where it operates." "Table," "carrot," "car," "restaurant," "pizza" are all examples of what Rosenthal calls "tightly defined" words. Another label for such words is *concrete,* words that name things we can experience directly with our senses. Yet even these relatively stable words, on whose definitions we all agree, can be "loose" if we are not sure of the context in which they are being used. "Table," for example, may be referring to the wooden, glass, or metal object we sit at, to a row or column of data, or, as a verb, to the parliamentary act "to table" a motion (to postpone consideration). Generally, we do not puzzle over the definitions of such words; the context will make them obvious. But the other category of words, those Rosenthal calls "loosely defined," can be confusing. She argues that "self," a word we probably all use every day, means so many different things to different people that it actually has no stable definition. Words like "self," "freedom," "anxiety," "love," and "genius" are also called *abstract* words.

In college writing you will be primarily concerned with this second category of words, although you will, of course, be expected to also use tightly defined words appropriately. In papers, on essay exams, and in oral reports you will often be asked to write an *extended* definition (a definition of a paragraph or longer) of a concept, a phenomenon, or an institution. All of the essays in this chapter are extended definitions; two of the writers in this anthology, in fact, have even written book-length definitions—Susan Brownmiller's *Femininity* and Joseph Epstein's *Ambition.*

Writers employ various techniques to define their subjects. In "Pure Lust," for example, Mary Daly begins with the standard dictionary definition of "lust." Although this method tends to be overused, especially by inexperienced writers, Daly's purpose is to change our current preoccupation with only one of the dictionary definitions. Thus she has a good reason for starting in this way. Daly also uses the *etymological* approach, seeking new, more positive meanings for the word "lust" in its original Latin root. Writers also use *synonyms* and *antonyms,* defining a word or concept according to what it is similar to or different from. Marcelle Clements in "Terminal Cool" comes up with "agitated," "insecure," "romantic," and "goony" as antonyms for the word she is trying to define, "cool." A related technique is the use of metaphor. Joseph Epstein's invoking the image of garlic as a symbol for vulgarity is an example. He uses a concrete image to bring an abstraction more firmly into the reader's consciousness.

Definition can be found in essays organized according to several of the other rhetorical modes included in this book, while definition essays also make use of these other modes of narration, description, process, comparison/contrast, and argument. For example, Epstein employs narration and description to create the memorable sketch of his Uncle Jake, which helps us to see what vulgarity is—and is not. Often, writers use argument to redefine a particularly troublesome word or controversial concept. Daly in "Pure Lust" argues that special uses of language can be damaging. William Safire, in his weekly columns in *The New York Times,* frequently uses argument to expose imprecise diction. In a recent article called "Geezer Power" he criticizes *euphemism,* the substitution of an inoffensive word or phrase for a more direct but disturbing one:

> Anybody who is so sensitive about the word *old* that he insists on being called a "golden ager" or "senior citizen" is too old to cut the mustard of controversy. I am *middle-aged;* I wish I were young again, but I don't get any

surge of youthful energy out of calling any crises in my middle-agedness "midlife." "Old" is something nobody likes to be (except considering the alternative), but if you are old, then old is what you are, and calling yourself "venerable" or "in the sunset years" isn't going to make you any younger.

All of us use definition for many purposes. As the Safire excerpt implies, there is a close relationship between the words we use and the way we perceive ourselves and the world. The Biblical Adam, a toddler, and an immigrant to a new country begin to feel at home in their respective environments when they can name things. In addition, only then can they begin to talk to others, since people cannot communicate at all unless they agree on a common language based on mutually understood definitions. Therefore the primary purpose for employing definition in a talk or an essay is to facilitate communication.

But to communicate, we must know our audience. Questions you should ask yourself when you begin to write a definition are "How much do my readers know about this word or this subject?" "Should I define basic terms or only more advanced or abstract ones?" and "Am I using familiar words in a special, unfamiliar way?" (If you are, you are writing a *stipulative* definition.) Usually the audience will consist of your instructor, who will often know more than you do about your subject. But because you may be asked in composition classes to write about a subject you know more about than your instructor—rock music or computer software, for example—be sure to define all of the *jargon* or specialized language you may use. You might even consider adding a glossary (an alphabetized key to terms) at the end of your essay so that the reader is not interrupted while reading.

Another purpose of the definition essay is to make distinctions. We distinguish between things constantly. Whether we are an infant who begins to define herself by first realizing that she is distinct from her parents or whether we are a teenager choosing a Bruce Springsteen rather than a Phil Collins album, we are making discriminations and, as a result, discovering our likes, dislikes, and limitations. In this way, we define ourselves in relation to our world, and define the world, as well. A recent *New York Times* article, "Yuppie Is Dead, Long Live the 'New Collar' Voter," is an example of a definition essay whose purpose is to make distinctions. The article reports on a Professor Ralph Whitehead, Jr., of the University of Massachusetts, who argues that "Yuppies" (an acronym for Young Urban Professionals) is a label that may be culturally important but has no political value. He defines a new group, which he calls the "New Collar Voter," as middle Americans under the age of 45 whose annual income is $20,000–40,000 and who work primarily in the service economy. After doing extensive research, Whitehead notes, among other things, that the New Collar voters are mostly children of blue-collar parents and are "politically independent and ideologically fickle." Whitehead uses an anecdote to distinguish further between the two groups: "You tell a New Collar voter about a $600 toilet seat at the Defense Department and he'll want to fire the people involved. You tell a Yuppie about one and he'll want to know what colors it comes in." Whitehead asserts that this newly defined group has much more political impact than the Yuppies have.

A third purpose of the definition essay, related to making distinctions, is establishing standards. People often have a need to choose what is the best in any given category: the ten best films of 1985, the best pizza in Cincinnati, the best college in the United States, the ten best- (and worst-) dressed Americans. But fairness demands that, in order to make these choices, we need to define our standards. Before choosing her "bests" from the 187 pizzas she tried, Gael Greene, writing for *New York* magazine, defines excellence in a pizza: "Quality ingredients are important: fresh homemade mozzarella, preferably in slices, not grated; a distinguished tomato sauce, not just a timid tinting of diluted tomato paste; serious sausage and sauteed mushrooms; pedigreed parmigiana. But the hand of the pizza-maker counts, too. And the heat of the oven. Nothing quite rivals the flavor," she concludes, of a pizza cooked in a "coal-burning oven." Because Greene is a well-known food critic, we tend to accept her definition of "the best." If we happen not to like sausage, however, we can make personal adjustments. By defining her standards clearly, Greene permits us to develop our own.

Definition essays are also used to inform. Defining something for readers, we introduce them to what may be new to them, or to what they may have overlooked. Richard Rodriguez in "Pocho," excerpted from his autobiography, defines a word many people do not know. In doing so, he admits his readers into what may be the unfamiliar world of the Chicano family. As readers, we can sometimes put the information we get to practical use. After reading a definition of the work a corporate lawyer performs, for example, a student might decide to specialize in some other branch of the law instead.

Finally, definition essays can be used to persuade. By defining or redefining a term, concept, practice, or institution, writers can lead readers to change their views. The "Yuppie" essay discussed above was both informational and persuasive: Whitehead convinced one Senate candidate in 1984 to aim his campaign at the New Collar, rather than the Yuppie, voter. (The Senator did, and he won.) Mary Daly's essay, "Pure Lust," is persuasive as well. Like other feminist writers, Daly believes we are imprisoned by the way we define certain words. "Masculine" and "feminine," for example, are associated by most of us with certain characteristics: strength, hardness, and rationality, on the one hand, and weakness, softness, and emotionalism on the other. Any woman who shows strength may be categorized as "masculine," while any man who shows his emotions may be labeled "feminine." The effect of this labeling, feminists and others argue, may be to keep each of us from developing into complete human beings.

Writers like Daly and Susan Brownmiller (whose essay "Emotion" appears in Chapter Four), then, define in order to change their readers' understanding of and response to certain highly charged words. A student in one of our classes, using the word "terrorism," recently tried to do the same. Because we are bombarded by the word in the media, the student maintained that we cannot even think about the causes the "terrorists" are fighting for. He noted that terrorists do not label themselves with this word. Rather they call themselves revolutionaries, freedom fighters, liberators, or armies—as in the Irish Republican Army—partly because of the more positive *connotations* (the meanings we associate with a word beyond its *denotative,* or dictionary, definition) of these words. He pointed out that he was not supporting terrorism as a tactic. Yet when he penetrated the externally imposed label to explore the issues behind it, the writer was able to understand and even to sympathize with certain groups he had previously condemned wholesale, and without much thought. Definition, then, can free us from restrictive ways of thinking, helping us to see the world anew.

Over the course of your college career, you may be asked to define many words, processes, or phenomena—in a history class, the *Enlightenment;* in physics, *entropy;* in psychology, *phobia;* and in philosophy, *existentialism.* Let us imagine that your composition instructor has asked you to write a paper defining the "Ideal Teacher." Although it is likely that you have had opinions about all of your teachers and have shared these with classmates, probably you have never expressed your opinions in writing.

How should you begin? You might follow the practice of Joseph Epstein, author of "What Is Vulgar?," who prepares to write his regularly published essays by stocking a folder with apt quotations, anecdotes, titles of relevant books and articles, random thoughts—anything connected to his chosen subject. The advantage of using this method is that, when you sit down to write, you bring to the blank page a collection of material from which to select. Free-writing and brainstorming with the phrases "my best teacher" and "my worst teacher" in mind should also generate examples, anecdotes, and ideas. Decide precisely what you liked about your favorite teachers; determine what you disliked about teachers for whom you had no affection or respect. Surprises may await you. On reflection, you may discover that certain practices of an elementary school teacher you did not appreciate when you were 8 (being made to recite in front of the class or do extra work in math, though you had no aptitude or liking for it) seem to make more sense to you now as a college student. You also might keep a notebook in which you closely observe current teachers. Make notes of their classroom techniques and behavior, of their personalities, of the knowledge they seem to possess of their field, of their attitudes toward students, of the number and type of assignments they require, and of their grading standards.

If you use several of the above prewriting techniques, you will not only have ample material to work with, but you will also have the raw data needed to formulate your definition. Just as Gael Greene had to explain her criteria for the "Best Pizza," based no doubt on a lifetime of eating it, you need to analyze all of your varied classroom experiences, positive and negative, to create your definition of the ideal teacher. You might arrive at a list of traits similar to the following:

Continues to learn about her field

Feels and projects excitement about her field

Manages to explain difficult concepts to students

Establishes a lively classroom presence

Cares about what students have to say and about
their individual progress

Assigns a challenging but reasonable amount of work

Grades fairly

These, then, would constitute your definition of the ideal teacher. The body of your essay would be an extended definition employing other rhetorical modes for illustration and support. For example, you may have had one model teacher in mind all along, in which case you could include a character sketch and description that would show how she fulfilled your criteria. If your ideal teacher is a composite of various teachers you have known, then selecting appropriate anecdotes about them to illuminate several of the above qualities would be a useful strategy. ("I could never understand logarithms when Mr. G. taught them, but in summer school Ms. L made them clear to me in an afternoon.") Comparing and contrasting two teachers—one you admired, one you did not—will very likely bring out the traits you are advocating. Somewhere in the essay you might also include a narrower definition of "teacher" to clarify your personal view. Before you suggest an ideal, however, you will need to list the minimal criteria expected of every teacher. Even if your readers do not agree with your list, they will at least know the assumptions upon which your argument rests. And ultimately, this extended definition essay should be persuasive. It is not enough to say these are your criteria for the ideal teacher. You must convince readers through logic, experience, and research that they should accept, or at least seriously consider, your definition.

Richard Rodriguez
POCHO

★ ★ ★

In his memoir, Hunger of Memory: The Education of Richard Rodriguez *(1982), from which "Pocho" is taken, Rodriguez tells the story of how learning English made him a "victim to a disabling confusion" in his life. Born in 1944 in San Francisco to Mexican parents, the author spoke only Spanish in his early childhood years. As a consequence, his first school experiences were disorienting and unhappy. When his parents, responding to a request from the school, began to speak English exclusively at home, Rodriguez learned the language rapidly, but at the expense, he felt, of family closeness. Something precious had been lost. He went on to great success in school, ultimately earning a B.A. from Stanford, an M.A. from Columbia, and a Fulbright Fellowship to study Renaissance literature in London. Yet his treatment as a "minority" plagued Rodriguez until he abandoned his academic career, with several job offers in hand, to spend six years writing this book. An opponent of affirmative action, he felt that it was unfair for him to receive preferential treatment, qualified as he obviously was, merely because he was a Chicano. Rodriguez's arguments against affirmative action and bilingual education play a prominent, and controversial, role in* Hunger of Memory.

"Pocho," excerpted from an early section of the book called "Aria," defines the author's precarious position as a child caught between two worlds, one English, the other Spanish.

I grew up victim to a disabling confusion. As I grew fluent in English, I no longer could speak Spanish with confidence. I continued to understand spoken Spanish. And in high school, I learned how to read and write Spanish. But for many years I could not pronounce it. A powerful guilt blocked my spoken words; an essential glue was missing whenever I'd try to connect words to form sentences. I would be unable to break a barrier of sound, to speak freely. I would speak, or try to speak, Spanish, and I would manage to utter halting, hiccuping sounds that betrayed my unease.

When relatives and Spanish-speaking friends of my parents came to the house, my brother and sisters seemed reticent to use Spanish, but at least they managed to say a few necessary words before being excused. I never managed so gracefully. I was cursed with guilt. Each time I'd hear myself addressed in Spanish, I would be unable to respond with any success. I'd know the words I wanted to say, but I couldn't manage to say them. I would try to speak, but everything I said seemed to me horribly anglicized. My mouth would not form the words right. My jaw would tremble. After a phrase or two, I'd cough up a warm, silvery sound. And stop.

It surprised my listeners to hear me. They'd lower their heads, better to grasp what I was trying to say. They would repeat their questions in gentle, affectionate voices. But by then I would answer in English. No, no, they would say, we want you to speak to us in Spanish. ('*. . . en español.*') But I couldn't do it. *Pocho* then they called me. Sometimes playfully, teasingly, using the tender diminutive—*mi pochito.* Sometimes not so playfully, mockingly, *Pocho.* (A Spanish dictionary defines that word as an adjective meaning 'colorless' or 'bland.' But I heard it as a noun, naming the Mexican-American who, in becoming an American, forgets his native society.) '¡ *Pocho*!' the lady in the Mexican food store muttered, shaking her head. I looked up to the counter where red and green peppers were strung like Christmas tree lights and saw the frowning face of the stranger. My mother laughed somewhere behind me. (She said that her children didn't want to practice 'our Spanish' after they started going to school.) My mother's smiling voice made me suspect that the lady who faced me was not really angry at me. But, searching her face, I couldn't find the hint of a smile.

Embarrassed, my parents would regularly need to explain their children's inability to speak flowing Spanish during those years. My mother met the wrath of her brother, her only brother, when he came up from Mexico one summer with his family. He saw his nieces and nephews for the very first time. After listening to me, he looked away and said what a disgrace it was that I couldn't speak Spanish, *'su proprio idioma.'* He made that remark to my mother; I noticed, however, that he stared at my father.

I clearly remember one other visitor from those years. A long-time friend of my father from San Francisco would come to stay with us for several days in late August. He took great interest in me after he realized that I couldn't answer his questions in Spanish. He would grab me as I started to leave the kitchen. He would ask me something. Usually he wouldn't bother to wait for my mumbled response. Knowingly, he'd murmur: *'¿Ay Pocho, Pocho, adónde vas?'* And he would press his thumbs into the upper part of my arms, making me squirm with currents of pain. Dumbly, I'd stand there, waiting for his wife to notice us, for her to call him off with a benign smile. I'd giggle, hoping to deflate the tension between us, pretending that I hadn't seen the glittering scorn in his glance.

I remember that man now, but seek no revenge in this telling. I recount such incidents only because they suggest the fierce power Spanish had for many people I met at home; the way Spanish was associated with closeness. Most of those people who called me a *pocho* could have spoken English to me. But they would not. They seemed to think that Spanish was the only language we could use, that Spanish alone permitted our close association. (Such persons are vulnerable always to the ghetto merchant and the politician who have learned the value of speaking their clients' family language to gain immediate trust.) For my part, I felt that I had somehow committed a sin of betrayal by learning English. But betrayal against whom? Not against visitors to the house exactly. No, I felt that I had betrayed my immediate family. I *knew* that my parents had encouraged me to learn English. I *knew* that I had turned to English only with angry reluctance. But once I spoke English with ease, I came to *feel* guilty. (This guilt defied logic.) I felt that I had shattered the intimate bond that had once held the family close. This original sin against my family told whenever anyone addressed me in Spanish and I responded, confounded.

But even during those years of guilt, I was coming to sense certain consoling truths about language and intimacy. I remember playing with a friend in the backyard one day, when my grandmother appeared at the window. Her face was stern with suspicion when she saw the boy (the *gringo*) I was with. In Spanish she called out to me, sounding the whistle of her ancient breath. My companion looked up and watched her intently as she lowered the window and moved, still visible, behind the light curtain, watching us both. He wanted to know what she had said. I started to tell him, to say—to translate her Spanish words into English. The problem was, however, that though I knew how to translate exactly *what* she had told me, I realized that any translation would distort the deepest meaning of her message: It had been directed only to me. This message of intimacy could never be translated because it was not *in* the words she had used but passed *through* them. So any translation would have seemed wrong; her words would have been stripped of an essential meaning. Finally, I decided not to tell my friend anything. I told him that I didn't hear all she had said.

This insight unfolded in time. Making more and more friends outside my house, I began to distinguish intimate voices speaking through *English.* I'd listen at times to a close friend's confidential tone or secretive whisper. Even more remarkable were those instances when, for no special reason apparently, I'd become conscious of the fact that my companion was speaking only to me. I'd marvel just hearing his voice. It was a stunning event: to be able to break through his words, to be able to hear this voice of the other, to realize that it was directed only to me. After such moments of intimacy outside the house, I began to trust hearing intimacy conveyed through my family's English. Voices at home at last punctured sad confusion. I'd hear myself addressed as an intimate at home once again. Such moments were never as raucous with sound as past times had been when we had had 'private' Spanish to use. (Our English-sounding house was never to be as noisy as our Spanish-speaking house had been.) Intimate moments were usually soft moments of sound. My mother was in the dining room while I did my homework nearby. And she looked over at me. Smiled. Said something—her words said nothing very important. But her voice sounded to tell me *(We are together)* I was her son.

(Richard!)

Intimacy thus continued at home; intimacy was not stilled by English. It is true that I would never forget the great change of my life, the diminished occasions of intimacy. But there would also be times when I sensed the deepest truth about language and intimacy: *Intimacy is not created by a particular language; it is created by intimates.* The great change in my life was not linguistic but social. If, after becoming a successful student, I no longer heard intimate voices as often as I had earlier, it was not because I spoke English rather than Spanish. It was because I used public language for most of the day. I moved easily at last, a citizen in a crowded city of words.

QUESTIONS

1. What are the two meanings of *Pocho* presented in the essay? Are they mutually exclusive?

2. What connotations were attached to the word *Pocho?*

3. Why did people in the Spanish community refuse to speak English? How did this make them more vulnerable?

4. What rhetorical mode does Rodriguez primarily employ in this essay? How do the anecdotes he tells help him express his insights?

5. Comment on the author's use of Spanish words and phrases in the essay. Are the meanings clear from the context or does the reader need to know Spanish?

SUGGESTION FOR WRITING

We all have words that only have significance to a small number of intimates—friends, family, fellow students or workers. Choose one of those words and define it in an essay, using an extended narrative or a series of shorter anecdotes. (You may use other modes as well, as Rodriguez does).

Mary Daly
PURE LUST
★ ★ ★

The idiosyncratic style of the following essay, taken from Mary Daly's book Pure Lust: Elemental Feminist Philosophy *(1984), reflects an unconventional sensibility. And indeed Daly, an Associate Professor of Theology at Boston College, is no ordinary teacher of religion. Ever since the publication of her book* The Church and the Second Sex *in 1968, during the initial stages of the women's movement, the author has been a radical voice for women's equality within the traditional Roman Catholic Church. In her subsequent books,* Beyond God the Father: Toward a Philosophy of Women's Liberation *(1973) and* Gyn/Ecology; The Metaethics of Radical Feminism *(1978), Daly has gone even further in challenging what she sees as the "patriarchal" structure of religion. "My fundamental interest is the women's revolution," she states in* Contemporary Authors, *"which I see as the radical source of possibility for other forms of liberation from oppressive structures. I am interested precisely in the spiritual dimension of women's liberation, in its transforming potential in relation to religious consciousness and the forms in which this consciousness expresses itself." Clearly, the major form in which consciousness expresses itself is language. In the following excerpt, Daly attempts to change the way women perceive themselves and their possibilities by redefining the word "lust."*

The Title of This Book

The title *Pure Lust* is double-sided. On one side, it Names the deadly dis-passion that prevails in patriarchy—the life-hating lechery that rapes and kills the objects of its obsession/aggression. Indeed, the usual meaning of *lust* within the Lecherous State of patriarchy is well known. It means "sexual desire, especially of a violent self-indulgent character: LECHERY, LASCIVIOUSNESS."* Phallic lust, violent and self-indulgent, levels all life, dismembering spirit/matter, attempting annihilation. Its refined cultural products, from the sadistic pornography of the

---

*Except when otherwise indicated, all definitions given in this work are from *Webster's Third New International Dictionary of the English Language.*

Marquis de Sade to the sadomasochistic theology of Karl Barth, are on a continuum: they are essentially the same. This lust is *pure* in the sense that it is characterized by unmitigated malevolence. It is *pure* in the sense that it is ontologically evil, having as its end the braking/breaking of female be-ing.* Its goal is the obliteration of natural knowing and willing, of the deep purposefulness which philosophers have called *final causality*—our innately ordained Self-direction toward Happiness.†

The word *Lust* has utterly Other meanings than this, however. It means "VIGOR, FERTILITY (the increasing lust of the earth or of the plant—Francis Bacon)." It means "an intense longing: CRAVING." It means "EAGERNESS, ENTHUSIASM." The word, then, derived from the Latin *lascivus,* meaning wanton, playful, is double-edged. Wise women wield our wits, making this word our wand, our Labrys. For it Names not only the "thrust of the argument" that assails women and nature on all levels (mythic, ideological, institutional, behavioral) but also the way out—the vigor, eagerness, and intense longing that launches Wild women on Journeys beyond the State of Lechery.

Primarily, then, *Pure Lust* Names the high humor, hope, and cosmic accord/harmony of those women who choose to escape, to follow our hearts' deepest desire and bound out of the State of Bondage, Wanderlusting and Wonderlusting with the elements, connecting with auras of animals and plants, moving in planetary communion with the farthest stars. This Lust is in its essence astral. It is pure Passion: unadulterated, absolute, simple sheer striving for abundance of be-ing. It is unlimited, unlimiting desire/fire. One moved by its magic is Musing/Remembering. Choosing to leave the dismembered state, she casts her lot, life, with the trees and the winds, the sands and the tides, the mountains and moors. She is Outcast, casting her Self outward, inward, breaking out of the casts/castes of phallocracy's fabrications/fictions, moving out of the maze of mediated experience. As she lurches/leaps into starlight her tears become tidal, her cackles cosmic, her laughter Lusty.

The struggle Named by the Labrys of this title is between reality and unreality, between the natural Wild, which is be-ing, and man-made fabrications that fracture her substance, simulate her soul. It is between the desire, eagerness, vigor, enthusiasm of/for expanding be-ing, which philosophers have called final

---

*I use *be-ing* in this hyphenated form to signify that this is intended not as a noun but as a verb, meaning participation in the Ultimate/Intimate Reality: *Be-ing,* the Verb.

†The *final cause,* according to an old scholastic philosophical axiom, is the "cause of causes, because it is the cause of the causality of all the other causes." According to Aristotelian and scholastic philosophy, it is one of the four causes. As I explained in *Beyond God the Father* (Boston: Beacon Press, 1973), pp. 180–81: "When Aristotle wrote of the 'final cause,' he intended 'cause' to mean that which brings about an effect. Scholastic philosophers followed the Aristotelian theory of the 'four causes' to explain change. . . . The final cause is the purpose which starts the whole process in motion. . . . The final cause is the first cause, since it moves the agent to act upon the matter, bringing forth a new form." Thus the efficient cause (agent), the material cause (matter), and the formal cause (form) are all actualized by the final cause. Deep ontological purposefulness, or telic centering, is the target of phallic lust. Final causality, in this profound sense, is the object of attack within phallocratic society.

causality, and blockage/blockers of this reaching of be-ing. Such blockage *is* the
State of Lechery, in which longing for participation in transcendent Be-ing is
reified, displaced, plasticized, rehabilitated.

Elemental female Lust is intense longing/craving for the cosmic concres-
cence that is creation. It is charged, tense, in tension with the tenses of fabricated
"father time." Incensed, it burns through the shallow impressions of insipid
senses, sensing the Sources, Astral Forces, Angels and Graces that call from the
Deep. This Lusting is divining: foreseeing, foretelling, forecasting. Unlike the dim
divines and divinities, the deadheads of dead-land whose ill-luminations blind us,
Lusty women portend with luster, our radiance from within that radiates from
and toward Original Powers of creation.

The word *luster* is itself a double-edged word, a Labrys, having quite opposite
definitions. It means, on the one hand, "a glow of reflected light: GLOSS, SHEEN,"
and "a coating or substance that gives luster to a surface." On the other hand,
it means "a glow of light from within: LUMINOSITY, SHINE: (luster of the stars)"
and "an inner beauty: RADIANCE." These opposed definitions give clues concerning the condition of women and of words.

When reflecting the artificial lights of patriarchal prisons, words help us
recognize the superficial coatings, the flashy phoniness of the fathers' foreground
falsifications. Thus, for example, the word *woman* Names the alienating arche-
type that freezes female be-ing, locking us into prisons of "forever feminine" roles.
But when we wield words to dis-close the inner beauty, the radiance of the Race
of Lusty Women, we/they blaze open pathways to our Background/homeland.
Thus *woman,* wisely wielded, Names a Wild and Lusty Female claiming wisdom,
joy, and power as her own.

In their double-edged dimensions, then, words wield/yield messages about
the tragedy of women and all Wild be-ing confined within imprisoning patriarchal
parameters. Besides/beyond this, they radiate knowledge of an ancient age, and
they let us know that they, the words themselves, are treasures trying to be freed,
vibrations whose auras await awakening ears.

Breaking the bonds/bars of phallocracy requires breaking through to radiant
powers of words, so that by releasing words, we can release our Selves. Lusty
women long for radiant words, to free their flow, their currents, which like our
own be-ing have been blocked and severed from ancestral Memory. The Race of
Lusty Women, then, has deep connections with the Race of Radiant Words.

QUESTIONS

1. How is "lust" defined in the first paragraph? What alternative definition of
   "lust" ("Pure Lust") does Daly offer in the second paragraph? Why does she
   characterize this new view of lust as "pure Passion" and male lust as "deadly
   dis-passion"? How is the new definition a "way out" for oppressed women?

2. How does she *extend* the definition of "lust" in the following paragraphs?

3. What purpose for writing this extended definition emerges in the final two paragraphs?

4. Why does Daly use the homonyms "braking/breaking of female be-ing" in paragraph one?

5. Look for other examples of Daly playing with words—homonyms, puns, alliteration, rhyme. How does she use such play to further her argument?

6. What is the purpose of Daly's unconventional punctuation—her habit of breaking up words with hyphens and combining them with slashes?

7. How does Daly's use of language reflect her theme?

SUGGESTION FOR WRITING

Choose a word that has negative connotations and write an extended definition essay in which you argue that the word can be seen positively. Examples might be "selfish," "boredom," "communism," and "divorce." (You also could approach the exercise from the opposite direction, starting with a word with a positive connotation and defining it negatively, e.g., "ambition," "freedom," "romantic.") Try to use some of Daly's techniques in your essay.

Marcelle Clements
TERMINAL COOL

Born in Paris, France, in 1948, Marcelle Clements emigrated to America in 1958, where she attended the High School of Music and Art in New York City and then Bard College. Since the late seventies, she has been a freelance writer in New York; Viking Press is publishing a collection of her pieces, The Dog Is Us. *When asked how she prepares to write a piece like "Terminal Cool," Clements responded: "I spend anywhere from several weeks to several months thinking and researching, that is, accumulating much too much data and much too many ideas. Then, I descend into a period of extended depression and exasperation while I try to come up with an organizing principle and a structure that will encompass all my seemingly incompatible bits."*

"Terminal Cool" originally appeared in Esquire *magazine in March 1984.*

In certain adolescent milieus of the 1960s, there reigned an aesthetic of silence concerning some topics. Certain phrases were never uttered except under monstrous duress. For example: "I need you." Like "I want you," "Reach out, I'll be there," "You keep me hangin' on," or "Please, please, please," they were reserved strictly for rock'n'roll songs. "I love you" was too hokey for words. In fact, when seventeen-year-old girls exchanged confidences in their dormitories, "He's serious about me" was a putdown. And how a boy behaved in a breakup scene was a respected indicator of the degree to which he was cool or uncool, a paramount consideration at the time, because the concept of cool combined the two virtues that adolescents most ardently desired: integrity and sex appeal.

"Saying 'Don't leave me' was totally out of the question when we were in school," I recently observed to an old friend.

"Hey, I said it once," he answered. "In my sophomore year. Just before I fell apart and had to leave school for three months."

Right.

For Sixties adolescents, there were many types of cool to choose from: biker cool, street-corner cool, Zen cool, Jewish-comic cool, antiwar-movement cool, John Kennedy button-down cool, coffeehouse-intellectual cool—not to be confused with folk-song cool, largely enacted in coffeehouses but which also had contingents in city parks, in people's living rooms, and in subway stations. By the mid-Sixties cool types were too numerous to name, and I'm thinking about just the relatively sedate East Coast. In the West, they had surfer cool, prankster cool, and God knows what else.

So, around that time, thousands of intellectually befuddled, morally perplexed, acne-ridden adolescents became incredibly cool, by sheer will. It might have seemed important at the time to be naturally cool, but in fact it wasn't. Almost no one is naturally cool anyway: the genetic odds are against that bizarre combination of intelligence, wit, alienation, and low metabolism. But if you were too agitated, insecure, romantic, or goony to come by cool naturally, you could still look cool and act cool, if you wanted it badly enough. Eventually, with practice, you could actually organize your psyche according to cool principles with surprising success. Soon enough, it became second nature to ride enigmatically off into the sunset or stay behind in Casablanca. In its final phase, cool was not a posture, but an attitude. Yet it was accessible to the most callow aspirant. In a way, just wanting to be cool (even if you didn't think of it that way but, instead, more vaguely, as having a certain relationship to your environment) took you halfway there, because the very nurturing of the desire meant that you had already gotten rid of untold amounts of uncool baggage.

It would require a ridiculously convoluted history of the morals and moods of postwar America to untangle the web of cultural threads that led to the mass juvenile depression of the late Fifties and early Sixties. But, by the mid-Sixties, this collective depression was molded into a style of deportment that conferred status upon those who could elaborate it with elegance. As soon as we went away to college, no longer putting up with irritating adults exhorting us to be cheerful and mocking us for our predilections for bohemian values, we could be as despondent as we pleased. It was kind of fun doing it as a group. Of course, no one then admitted that it was fun. (*Happiness* was a word never mentioned, like *marriage* or *business.*) Fun was too mundane, like parents' cocktail parties. Thrills were all right, though, and the more extreme the better. Thrill seeking, after all, was a classic tactic of the disenfranchised and a historically correct balm for clinical ennui.

Anything to avoid being square—an ethical imperative at the time. But that was twenty years ago. These days nobody seems to be afraid of being square anymore. At least, it's a topic that's never brought up at the dinner parties where women in angel shag hairdos and men in Armani jackets exchange professional gossip. And *cool* is now a word never mentioned without derision.

Yet one woman I know recently confided: "I miss it. There's a thing I used to tell myself that ran 'Every day, in every way, I'm getting cooler and cooler.' And that kind of comforted me. I don't have any religion or any organized ideals or anything. So I used thinking about cool to keep me from getting subhuman."

Naturally, only a woman could have made that remark. After all, guys were always much too cool to ever talk about it. . . . And they were right, of course: to acknowledge the attitude was to expose its authenticity to question.

Cool had a lot to do with sex, sex appeal, and sex roles. Girls have never received enough credit for the fantastic leap of the mind they took in the Sixties when they decided to take the cool aesthetic seriously. In these post-women's lib days, we've come to take a lot for granted. But when the seventeen-year-old girl from the comfortable home started adopting some of the attitudes of the black jazz musician, the lessons of centuries of class and gender indoctrination were dumped in the trash along with the pink plastic curlers. And gladly, too.

Yet, boys were always cooler. Cool boys were much more feminine than their sloshed and rowdy frat-house counterparts, but basically all the characteristics of the cool personality were male traits. All of the cool prototypes were males: saxophone players, cowboys, hoods, male homosexual poets, basketball players, bass guitarists, Bogarts and Brandos.

It wasn't something we thought about, but looking back to college days, I'd have to admit that my girlfriends and I imitated boys a lot. We dressed like them, we talked like them, we tried to imitate their attitudes: at first when we were in their company, later with each other, and finally, even to ourselves. And why shouldn't we have? What else was there to imitate? The so-called offbeat prototypes from old films, the Katharine Hepburns and the Gloria Grahames, were basically only putting up a good front in reaction to men. Some antiestablishment types appealed: the Supremes, say, or Anna Magnani, or Susan Sontag. One could admire these women, but it was difficult to identify with them.

No, the boys we went to school with were onto much more sophisticated material. We had more in common with them than with any women of the past or present. And besides, they were clearly having fun—in a grim, alienated way, of course—so we weren't about to be left behind. At my old school, the girls became champion thrill-seekers and aces in the I-can-take-it department; they were thought of as pals by their male friends and as wild (or worse) by everyone else (especially their mothers). It's a mistake to ignore the obvious.

The first thing girls did was to imitate male sexual behavior. And it turned out that as soon as the label *fast* became obsolete—at least in the view of the subgroup—all of feminine behavior could be altered, because most of the circumscriptions had existed only to achieve the *demure* model. Once the sexually demure barrier had been shattered, the other constraints became irrelevant as well, and ever so much easier to dismiss. So girls stepped out of their skirts and put on jeans, talked less, went hitchhiking around the country, took the most mind-bending drugs available, loved and left, had adventures, courted danger, and occasionally went to sleep drunk with their boots on . . . just like boys.

I distinctly remember a guy at school who made my heart leap in a fierce way saying to me: "Lesbians are so cool." The funny thing is, I think that was probably his way of making an advance. It worked, too; I knew he was right, and it made me feel real jealous.

Yet, if you were still attracted to boys, you wound up retaining a good deal of your feminine emotional equipment, and in fact all the time you were evolving in the male-oriented context you were also growing as a woman. My God, were we confused, continually adding one more illogically acquired trait to an already hopelessly ambiguous personality. We were like guests with a serendipitous appetite at a buffet dinner, piling an incongruous assortment of foods onto our plates. No wonder personalities were indecipherable. One of my college friends recalls: "To be cool was either total affectation or total lack of affectation. With the coolest girls, you could never tell which they were."

If boys couldn't understand us, it was because we really weren't like them, notwithstanding all our efforts. And it wasn't only biochemical, either. There were too many concepts in the terminal-cool mentality that we could grasp but not absorb. For example, girls might have been enticed by black music and style, but few could match their male friends' crucial and rich ambivalence—infatuation poisoned by envy—toward black culture. After all, most girls had only the crash course. And in matters of style, even though they had traveled a longer road, they could never really be as cool as boys: the voice was still too inflected; the eyes too expressive; the hand gestures, the tilt of the head never successfully stifled—the style of the powerless, of the participant observed by the infinitely cooler outsider. In the end, in timeless fashion, the best way females could conquer power was to seduce it.

Like the courtship patterns of all inhibited cultures, the cool seduction was, of course, tremendously titillating. In addition to normal human nostalgia for Sex of the Past, I'd bet almost every woman who has experienced them still harbors wistful affection for these seductions. They were so well suited to feminine erotic-emotional predilections: drawn out, restrained, indirect, subtle, with exquisite attention paid to detail. Never mind if this was due as much to adolescent fear as to flair for sensual drama. The combination somehow made for wonderfully complex and preoccupying social activity.

For one thing, these attractions were so meandering. *Does he want to? Do I want to?* At my old campus, which was nestled in an idyllic Hudson River valley landscape, kids used to go down to the riverbank and lie down together for hours on the pine needles, drive each other crazy, not doing or saying anything, just watching the sun glimmer on the waterfall. Then they'd walk back to their classes and maybe not speak to each other again for weeks.

The languid pace of these seductions was compounded by the fact that, as of 1965 or so, the girls I knew still did not overtly initiate sexual encounters—though whether this was because of leftover sexual mores or the new girl-cool code is beyond the scope of my memory. The trouble was that in 1965 boys didn't want to overtly initiate sexual encounters either. Pushy, you know. Aggressive. Risky. Uncool.

The coolest boys, the real heartbreakers, seemed inaccessible to the point of cruelty. Unless a girl happened to be good friends with him, the most attention one of these guys would show her would be to maybe say, "What are you up to?" when he put his tray down at the table where she was sitting in dining commons. And that was if he really liked her. And when he left, he'd say "See you later." So after lunch, she'd go back to her room and brood and try to talk herself out of caring about it.

Even if this guy was her friend, he was so enigmatic that she'd develop a helpless compulsion to climb into his brain. She somehow knew he liked her, but she couldn't be sure whether he felt *that way* for months (or at least weeks, which seemed like an eternity at the time). But then one night, when a bunch of people had gone down to the local bar together, she'd catch him watching her dance with someone else. And if she smiled at him, then later, when they all left, he would stay next to her on the walk back to campus and he'd wait for the group to assume a propitious formation so that he could speak to her in a conversational tone but not be overheard and say, probably, "Do you want to get high?" in the most casual way.

When the group reached main campus and disbanded, none of the others would say anything when she walked away with him toward his dorm, and the two of them wouldn't say anything to each other either. Once upstairs in his room, they'd both sit on his bed, leaning against the wall, but he wouldn't touch her, except to pass a joint. He'd put on a record and perhaps he'd tell her something funny about one of his teachers, or show her some object in his possession, a book of Francis Bacon paintings maybe. Hours would go by like that in the little dimly lit room, and she didn't know anymore what to expect. He'd stop putting records on, and now they'd become silent; they would just hear faint music coming from other people's rooms. And then if she stayed very still, he'd slide away from her so he could put her foot on his lap, and he'd slip off her boot.

When he finally leaned over to kiss her (maybe not until afterward), his eyes would be closed and his mouth very open and his teeth somewhat in the way. But her eyes would be open, and she'd see that he had an expression that was kind of like pain on his face, which made her feel a queer mixture of joy and malaise. Why malaise? It wasn't until years later, if she remembered it, that she'd realize that the expression was simply tenderness, and that she had known it even then but hadn't believed it.

These boys always seemed to have a secret. It should have been easy to see that the secret was loneliness, but it was so effectively encapsulated by irony and nonchalance that we were fooled every time. Boys were so mysterious that we could idealize them to an absurd degree. And so we did, not understanding that to do so was also a form of cruelty. A really cool guy seemed like an irresistible challenge, but ultimately the challenge was to get him to be uncool, or to make him tender. It's only now, all these years later, that it's become clear that a lot of what seemed so cool was probably simply shyness and fear. Only a few years earlier these boys had engaged in the standard century-old teenage fumblings, awkward gropings with the age-old clammy hands and excess saliva. Suddenly they found themselves in this absolutely amazing sexual funhouse, with all the girls they liked apparently available, and these poor boys were stuck with having to act cool when they were, well, scared. *Is she really willing?* Is that what they were thinking while we racked our brains to figure out why they tormented us? And we were as thickheaded as they were to deny the evidence that they were as willing to give us tenderness as we were willing to be seduced.

But then, there's all the more reason to ask, Why malaise? Well, perhaps it wasn't only thickheadedness, perhaps we didn't want to process the evidence, because it would have meant wrecking our fantasies.

Time passed. And with experience, these sad but sweet scenes degenerated, as inhibited tenderness hardened into cynicism—a far more dangerous form of fear. Eventually, it began to seem that the coolest sexuality was vicarious, remembered, imagined, removed. "After sex you could be cool," a friend says. "During wasn't cool at all, of course. And before, it could be pretty cool, but it was really too tense. But afterward, you could feel terrifically cool."

As a reaction to the uptight standards of society, sex was cool, but how could you be cool while you were having sex? According to the cool subgroup standard, then, the coolest form of sexuality became sexual tension: the sex you didn't consummate, the nights you spent with someone on LSD when you never took off your clothes; the look you once exchanged, by accident, with your best friend's lover. The coolest relationships were ambiguous friendships, often with someone you'd slept with once, but it seemed so long ago that it only mattered in the sense that it was something already taken care of.

Of course, there was an unprecedented amount of sexual activity. But if you were actually going to engage in sex, at least it could be kind of somber (thereby preserving distance). Despite the fact that so-called sexual liberation is always situated in the Sixties, it wasn't until the next decade that the whole "joyful" sex syndrome materialized—*The Joy of Sex* wasn't published until 1972; the manuals of the mid-Sixties conveyed the solemn and controlled sensuality of Eastern cultures, *The Perfumed Garden* and *The Kama Sutra.*

And precisely because there were so many casual affairs, the approach was rather . . . minimalist. Eventually not even making love was exempt from those outward signs of cool behavior that were also the symptoms of depression. For example, it was quite silent. It was silently requested, with a single gesture, only a touch perhaps, and silently acquiesced to, with a glance. Except for the record player in the room, the act itself was silent, too. Between cuts, there wasn't a sound. In the mid-to-late Sixties, kids must have reached millions of orgasms without a word or a moan, and afterward lain next to one another soundlessly. At the time, even "Did you come?" would have been considered an irremediably uncool invasion of privacy.

So many lonely children. So cool.

I think that's what finally wrecked the cool aesthetic: it was simply too lonely. People started wanting to have long-term relationships, and after they'd failed at them a number of times because they were so damn cool, they decided to bail out of cool. As horrendously difficult and humiliating as it might have been to turn toward someone you loved and say, "I need you," it wasn't as hard and as painful as that terrifying solitude you felt in a stranger's bed if you'd succeeded in becoming detached enough to make all your lovers into strangers, or the uneasy solitude you felt with even your closest friends if you'd become cynical enough to make all your friends mere cohabitants of a sad planet, or the devastating spiritual solitude you felt if you had taken enough lysergic acid so that even the original joke—that everything was a joke—became a joke and *that* was really too sad to laugh at anymore.

Curiously, the final deathblow to the terminal-cool mentality came not from the outside but from its own entropy. Because of the nature of their interactions with each other—or lack of them—within just a few years many of these kids had become almost intolerably isolated. And that isolation was compounded by the psychological effects of the drugs they took. Marijuana comes immediately to mind: it was the coolest drug, of course, because it generated the most ironic states of consciousness. But the *uncool* expansion of consciousness produced by psychedelics offered possibilities for the most extreme applications of cool—and were therefore ultimately the instrument of its demise just because the ego, at least as it's currently constituted, is simply not designed to withstand such battering on a sustained basis and still remain intact. Most of the people I knew then became unwilling to pay the price of psychedelic solitude for the psychedelic thrill and by that time, for many, it was no longer a thrill. "It got to be so the best part was reentry," one of my friends recalls. "I'd realize I was finally coming down and I'd think *Thank God, back to the world.*"

That's what happened: suddenly the soiled, messy, ridiculous, completely uncool real world started to seem more alluring than the endless mazes of the pure but cold territory of the perpetual outsider. So one by one, and eventually by the thousands, they defected from the terminal-cool ethos. There's been a good deal of smug commentary about the return of this group to straight America. But I think it's unfair to mock these people for acquiring the three-piece suits and the mortgages and the lawn furniture, and for starting to use words like *business* and *marriage.* Essentially, they just came in from the cold.

All these years later, the cool concept seems laden with contradictions. But the ultimate conundrum, it seems to me, is that many of the people who were adherents to that code in the Sixties and then willfully abandoned it in the next decade, when they opted to be part of the world, really haven't succeeded in completely ridding themselves of its constructs, even now that it's become so uncool to be cool.

Actually, it's only recently that I've noticed this—maybe it has something to do with the times, or perhaps with the stage my particular age group is in. "I'm going right from an adolescent identity crisis to a mid-life crisis without so much as a two-week vacation," a friend of mine mused recently. I laughed after he said that, and so did he. If we ever needed to use the cosmic bulldozer sense of humor we developed in the mid-Sixties, it's now, now that we have to deal with the insufferably cool final issues. You know, the futility and/or necessity of love, procreation, planning the architecture of one's life, and—we'll take all the help we can get on this one—mortality.

But cool's gone underground, in a way, just where it was before the Sixties. Of course, old sensibility types haven't remained intact, but you can still locate them if you're in an archaeological frame of mind. The signifiers are subtle now that the really dramatic differences have been settled and people go to the same hairdressers and see the same movies and have the same politics or lack of them and have similar marriages, or lack of them. But, for many people, cool is still part of an attitude toward one's environment, and, in personal relations, a type of discretion and an element of seduction.

Naturally, I'm not talking about the pathetic Sixties casualties who still brandish the flag for a long-defeated cause: they were always uncool anyway. Too overt. The people I'm talking about look and act like almost everybody else. But soon after you meet them you hear them make a slightly incongruous remark— ah, you remark to yourself, *dissociation.* Upon examination the logistics of their lives don't seem to quite hang together—*nonchalance.* They may be successful in their careers but even if they exhibit the kind of maniacal ambition that's become a pro forma requisite for just hanging in there these days, they don't appear to support the system they've become a part of—*disaffection.* And then you catch them with a carefully neutral expression on their face at a strange moment, and that's the conclusive tip-off—*inappropriate irony.*

To spot these people is like looking for markers on a road where no one travels anymore. Many of them are still silent, although some now hide their silence under a wall of words. Often, they're well hidden under the angel shag haircuts and the Armani jackets. But that only makes them seem . . . uh . . . cooler. . . . No?

In its defunct, or "terminal," manifestation, cool turned out to be a failure as a way of containing one's emotions or as a methodology for relations between the sexes. And the type of integrity that it embodied became irrelevant in the rush to satisfy more-pressing needs. Other modes have been used in the last decade, just to survive. And, besides, terminal cool was an aspect of the sensibility of a subgroup that has apparently been dispersed. These days, when isolation has become a norm, everyone has his or her own version of what cool is.

But perhaps cool as part of an ethos is only dormant. If the aesthetic of the old cool depended on silence, it was also a powerful statement about conventional mores, love, war, and social inequity. Maybe there will come a time when we will choose to collectively stand back once more to question our conventions. Maybe the need for cool is cyclical, and there will be other, better forms of cool to be found in the future fashions for the mind.

QUESTIONS

1. What methods does Clements use to define "cool" in the first paragraph? What rhetorical modes does she employ to extend the definition throughout the essay?

2. What is (was?) "square"? Are people square today? In what ways? Is there another word we use to mean the same thing now?

3. After reading the essay, how would you define "cool"? Why does Clements call her essay *"Terminal* Cool"? Discuss whether "coolness," in your opinion, is adequately defined.

4. What is Clements's final attitude toward "cool"? Is it positive, negative, or both? Explain.

5. At what audience is Clements aiming? Write a profile of her intended reader based on the language and content of the essay.

6. Write an outline of the essay by writing a one-sentence summary of each paragraph. Then discuss the essay's organizational strategy.

SUGGESTIONS FOR WRITING

1. For the 2005 issue of *Esquire* magazine, you are writing about the dominant concept, the "ethos," of the eighties. How would you label and define it? Was it positive or negative? What long-term effects will it have?

2. Now that you have a definition of "cool" in mind, write an essay defining a type of "cool" you are knowledgeable about: Clint Eastwood Cool, Prep School Cool, Chicago Cool, Bowling Cool, Shopping Mall Cool. Naturally, you may use a different label than "cool" if you wish.

Peggy Rosenthal
THE POWER OF A POSITIVE *SELF*
★ ★ ★

In her book, Words and Values: Some Leading Words and Where They Lead Us *(1984), Peggy Rosenthal disputes the general assumption that we control our own language. By examining the power certain words have over how we act and define ourselves, Rosenthal proves that it is words that manipulate us, not the other way around. A graduate of Brown University, who earned a Ph.D. in English from Rutgers University in 1971, Rosenthal has been studying language for most of her life. Currently, she is working on a book about clichés as cultural artifacts. A long-term project is to extend her thesis that words control us to a study of the language of nuclear war. To what extent, she asks, are we trapped by language into narrow, and potentially fatal, ways of looking at war and peace?*

During the 1970s and 1980s, it has been impossible to avoid the word "self"—it pops up everywhere in the media. (There is even a magazine called Self!*) In "The Power of a Positive* Self" *Rosenthal traces the sources of the word's very positive contemporary connotations and warns us of "self's" potential dangers.*

Our Best-Selling and God-Given Self

Have we accepted this *self* that psychology offers us? How much of our sense of *self,* as we ordinarily use the word, comes from psychology? All, we might be tempted to say—especially when we notice how many of our best-sellers (those prime providers of terms for public, and private, discourse) either are written by psychologists or are, like *Passages,* popularizations of psychology. *Passages,* in fact, has itself become a passage: a conduit through which the terms of self-oriented psychology have poured into the main stream of general discourse.

While *self* is not a frequent term in *Passages,* the self as conceived by psychology is the book's subject, and all the familiar *self* associations of psychology are there. The "inner realm" is for Sheehy where the action is; her study—like Freud's, Jung's, Maslow's, Gaylin's—is of our "internal life system." And her proudly positive *inner* is, in the best Rogersian fashion, set against an *outer* conceived as restrictive and artificial: when you move into midlife, "you are moving out of roles and into the self." This inner self—like May's, Maslow's, Rogers's—is the source (the only "authentic" source) of values: the move into the self is a move "away from external validations and accreditations, in search of an inner validation"; and "one of the great rewards of moving through the disassembling period to renewal [another positively loaded term] is coming to approve of oneself ethically and morally and quite independent of other people's standards and agenda."

"Coming to approve of oneself ethically and morally" turns out, in the book—as in Gaylin and Rogers—to be inseparable from feeling good about oneself. Sheehy, as we would expect from our familiarity with *self's* associates in psychology, makes much of *feeling,* both as a main subject and as a main term in her vocabulary. "How do we *feel* about our way of living in the world at any given time?" she asks as one of the book's central questions, letting her italics show where her emphasis lies.

But, of course, this emphasis on feelings is not only Sheehy's. It has become—through *Passages* and all the other mass media productions through which psychology's terms come to us—the emphasis almost everywhere we go. When, for example, we go to meetings on the job, we find that once-objective business (a company's marketing changes, a college's curriculum changes) has been sucked inside and comes out of speakers' mouths as "how I feel about these changes." If we go to church, we're likely to hear sermons on the importance of feeling good about ourselves and having a "positive self-image." And if we happen to go to medical school, we're likely to find the anatomy professor concentrating on how to "help the students deal with possible emotional tensions arising from the experience of the dissecting lab." The dissecting lab is no longer a classroom but an "experience"; an experience must be "felt"; and Sheehy's question "How do we *feel* about our way of living in the world at any given time?" seems to be asked now at every given time.

While we're asked constantly about our feelings, we're assured constantly about our individual uniqueness. From Mister Rogers's assurance, to the four-year-old in each of us, that "you're a very special person" to Dr. Wayne Dyer's best-selling line that "you are unique in all the world" to Dr. Joyce Brothers's sales pitch that each of us should have "a unique and personal program" for success, psychology's line about the value of the individual seems to have spread everywhere. Or, more accurately (since the line isn't only psychology's), what has spread is psychology's version of a general humanist line: as *The Humanist* magazine reminds us, "the preciousness and dignity of the individual person is a central humanist value."

As pop psychology spreads the positive *unique-individual* line through our culture, it necessarily spreads also the confusions and ambiguity that we saw running through psychology's use of the line. When, for example, Sheehy offers "each of us . . . the opportunity to emerge reborn, authentically unique, with an enlarged capacity to love ourselves and embrace others," she's offering us, along with that uniqueness, the ambiguity between given and goal that psychology leaves unresolved in *unique.* For if we have to "emerge" unique, we're presumably not unique already; yet our given uniqueness is one of the working assumptions that Sheehy takes over from developmental-personality psychology. To qualify the aimed-for uniqueness with *authentically* (and thus apparently to distinguish it from ordinary or inauthentic uniqueness) is to make no real qualification at all. *Authentic* is what we could call an "empty plus": it carries positive value but is void of content ("says nothing," as we often put it).

All my talk about the "spread" of psychology's *self,* via the popular media into our common language, makes psychology sound like a creeping vine or like a virus spreading through the population or like a guerrilla force acting underground to take us over town by town (or term by term). These implications of my metaphor are, of course, inaccurate and unfair to psychology: psychology has no conspiracy against us, and it's not an alien force. It's part of us, part of our culture: the part, we could say, that studies for us what we want (even long) to know about our individual selves. If psychology gives us its *self,* this is because we ask for it.

So while we can truly say that we get psychology's *self* through the mass media, we can't say that we get it against our will. Nor can we say, despite the dominant impression given by popular literature and by this analysis of it so far, that the *self* we get is entirely psychology's. Obviously, to a large extent it is—so obviously, maybe, that this examination of how the mass media repeat psychology's lines has been, for many readers, simply repetitive. But if we now look more closely into these best-selling lines, we can see something more in them than what psychology alone has put there. In, for example, that promise of Sheehy's of "the opportunity to emerge reborn" there's a touch of evangelicalism that we can't say comes from psychology. Or, if it does—and there is, certainly, something of the promise of a new life in Maslow's and Rogers's goal of a new or renewed or higher self—it comes into both professional and pop psychology from elsewhere: from, originally, Christianity. There are other places, too, where Christianity enters into our sense of *self;* and we should look briefly at one of them in order to correct the impression that the *self* we get through the mass media, and hence our common sense of *self,* is entirely and simply psychology's.

In our common (both widespread and frequent) assertion of the value of each individual, we're indeed expressing what *The Humanist* called a "central humanist value." But before "the preciousness and dignity of the individual person" was a central humanist value, it was a central Christian value. By moving the locus of spiritual activity from external rites and laws into the individual, Christianity brought God's infinite value into each person. *Individual* and *internal* have thus always carried pluses for Christianity: the plus signs of God's presence in the individual. "Are you not aware that you are the temple of God, and that the Spirit of God dwells in you?" St. Paul asks rhetorically. One way of looking at what has happened to the positive term *individual* over the past two thousand years is to see the plus sign remaining over *individual* while the source of the word's plus, the Spirit of God, is gradually removed by the secular Renaissance-Romantic-psychology tradition. To St. Paul's question, psychology (speaking for secular humanism generally) answers no. And yet this answer doesn't decrease the value placed by us on the individual. In fact, it reinforces it.

This reinforcement works because we hear or see words but not the concepts behind them. Behind (or in) the Christian *individual* is the concept of God; behind (or in) the secular humanist *individual* is the concept of man alone. But while these concepts are far (infinitely far) apart, the words expressing them can be identical. Assertions of "our individual uniqueness" or "the preciousness of the individual" can sound exactly the same no matter who makes them. When Billy Graham asserts, for example, that "the central theme of the universe is the purpose and destiny of every individual," he sounds just like *The Humanist* (even though he means something different). And because Christian and secular voices can sound the same, each "sounds better" because we've heard the same line from the other; each, that is, lends its particular authority to the line. When Graham, then, tells us that each conversion process is "very personal" ("God looks at each of us differently, because each of us is different"), this sounds right because we've heard Mister Rogers telling us, since we were four, that each of us is special and different; and when Dr. Wayne Dyer assures each of us that "you are unique in all the world," we tend to believe it even more because we've heard it in church.

We've heard it even if we don't go to church—heard, that is, the Christian lines asserting the value of the individual. We tend to pride ourselves on living in a secular culture; yet a culture in which a major television network considers it profitable to broadcast Billy Graham during prime time, and in which the *New*

York Times regularly (religiously!) prints the Pope's addresses, is hardly simply secular. Even those of us who grow up without opening the Bible cannot have avoided contact with Christian lines. Where those lines contradict the lines of a secular authority like psychology, of course we have to choose which to follow. But where the lines overlap, as in assertions of the worth of the individual, we can easily nod our approval to both. The fact that Christianity places positive value on the individual just reinforces our sense of that value, and thus adds to the positive sense of *self* that we get from secular sources.

What Good Is the Self?

If we return now to the original question of this chapter—the question of how much of our sense of *self* comes from psychology—we find that the answer has to be a bit complicated. In the area of *self* covered by *individual,* our sense of positive value seems to come at least as much from Christianity as from psychology, though the amount is hard to measure since in most praise of the individual we can't tell where that praise is coming from. As for the rest of the extensive area covered by *self* and its associated terms, we've seen that while our common *self* is to a large extent psychology's, psychology's *self* is to a large extent not its own but that of four hundred years of Western culture. The Renaissance's positive valuing of subjectivity, individuality, and creativity; seventeenth-century philosophy's positive valuing of self-consciousness and identity; Romanticism's positive valuing of all these along with internalness, freedom, and feelings—all this is carried on in psychology's *self.*

This is quite a lot of good (or goods) to be carried by a single word! And yet there's still more. Because besides Christianity and psychology (and through it the Renaissance-Romantic tradition), other powerful traditions and ideologies come into play in *self* and add their weight to the word.

We've seen, for example, that *freedom* is one of the plus terms associated with *self* in the Romantic tradition carried on by psychology; but *freedom,* along with terms like *independence* and *self-determination,* has also been a plus word in every expression of democratic political ideals since the French Revolution. Furthermore, terms like *self-sufficiency* and *control,* which operate in close connection with the *freedom* set in both psychology and democratic political discourse, are plus terms also in the ideology of modern technology. These terms, of course, have different applications in each of these places. For technology, *self-sufficiency* and *control* are terms applied primarily to machines and ideal mechanical functioning; for democracy, these terms apply to governments and to people as political units; for psychology, they apply to individual personality. Yet the application in each case is to something valued positively by the ideology or discipline concerned.

These terms then carry along with them, in all of their uses, the positive values of all the ideologies and disciplines and activities and traditions of thought in which they operate. I don't mean that they necessarily carry along the particular applications from these various places; nor do I mean that we're aware of all these sources adding their weight to a word we use. What I mean is that our sense of a word's positive value is increased, usually without our awareness, when that word carries positive value in ideologies and activities and so on other than the one we're consciously using it in—especially when those other sources of its value are themselves highly prized by our culture.

Take, for example, the call for independence in "Your Declaration of Independence," a 1977 *Harper's Bazaar* article: "Independence, simply, is the freedom to choose what is pertinent to your needs at any given time. It is a feeling of freedom that comes from within." Because of the neat overlap of political and psychological terms here, the positive political values of *independence* and *freedom* are brought to bear on the positive psychological values of *independence, needs, feeling,* and *within.* For the authors of this "Declaration," as well as for readers who respond positively to it, *independence* is attractive because it carries some of our most cherished political and psychological values; and it has this double attraction whether or not the authors and readers are aware of the sources of this attraction. Similarly, in the calls we've heard so often in recent years to "pull our own strings"—whether in ads like *Ms* magazine's picture of a female marionette with text urging women to cut the strings that control them from outside, or in best-sellers like *Pulling Your Own Strings*—what is being appealed to is our generally and overwhelmingly positive sense of *self-sufficiency* and *control of our lives,* a sense which derives from the combined positive appeal of these terms in psychology, democracy, and technology. Because of the multiple strength of this appeal, then, we tend to go along unquestioningly with our sense that *self-sufficiency* is a good thing—pulled less by our own strings than by those of the powerful networks of meaning and value operating on the word from behind the scenes.

It's odd, maybe, to think of words working like this, apart from our awareness or our conscious intentions: we're so used to assuming our control of everything (we're so attracted by the idea of pulling our own strings) that we assume that, where our language is concerned, we can simply "say what we mean" as long as we just take a minute to choose our words carefully. That words can mean things apart from what we intend for them, that words say what *they* mean more than what *we* mean, is indeed disconcerting. Yet when we look at how our common language actually operates—when we look, for example, at why certain words attract us—we have to admit that it operates to a large extent outside of our conscious intentions. We can indeed increase the extent of our consciousness of its operations, as we're doing here, and thereby give ourselves more control over our language than we usually have. But unless we make this deliberate effort to watch how our words are working, we'll be worked on by them and manipulated by their meanings unawares.

One thing we've seen so far about the way words operate is that they act as receptacles into which different disciplines and ideologies and traditions of thought pour their particular meanings, their favorite value-laden concepts. The word *self,* we can now say, is the container of heavily weighted meaning from some of our culture's most influential sources; it's a loaded term. This is the case even though *self* has no precise definition, either in any of the places where its value comes from or in our everyday use. If you ask someone who speaks in terms of his self—who talks about fulfilling himself or having a negative self-image or knowing his true self—what exactly he means by his *self,* he's unlikely to be able to tell you. How could he have a precise definition when the sources of his sense of *self* don't give him one? What they give him instead of a definition is, as we've seen, a complex of positively valued concepts—an overwhelmingly good (yes) feeling. And it might be that if *self* had a tighter definition, it couldn't carry such a variety of concepts. A definition is (by definition) a boundary, an assumption of finiteness. A tightly defined word has definite boundaries and therefore limited room for concepts to fit into it. But a loosely defined word like *self* is flexible, stretchy; its sides can move out easily to accommodate all the concepts that come into it from the various places where it operates. And the more concepts it has room for, the more it then tends to draw in other terms associated with these concepts—and thus the more likely it is to operate, by itself or through its associates, in our everyday thought.

Our practically undefined *self,* then, brings with it an array of concepts: mainly from the Renaissance, Romanticism, and psychology, but also from Christianity, democracy, and technology (and from evolutionary theory too, as we'll see in Part Two). And these concepts carry almost unanimously positive value. No wonder we're so filled with self: because *self* is filled with the prize concerns of centuries of our culture.

All the positive concepts converging in the word *self* are enough to explain its great attraction for us. Yet there's another sort of attraction, too, that I think self has: what we might call a natural attraction. In a study like this one, which focuses intensively on words, it's easy to lose sight of other forces that operate in our lives besides (or, probably, along with) language. We have to step back occasionally, therefore, so as to keep our study of language in proper perspective. And if we step back from the word *self* and from the intellectual constructs that are our concepts of self, we can see still another force pulling us toward self, the force of what appears to be natural self-interest or self-concern. I use the word "natural" uneasily, since the debate on what constitutes our true human nature is far from settled. Yet from what we can observe, and from what people have observed throughout history, self-concern does seem to be a fact, a given of our natures. That is, we tend naturally to look out for our own interest (however that interest is perceived).

If self-concern is clearly a given, how to take it is not so clear. The given may be a fact. But the taking is a question of values. During the course of Western culture, our self-concern has been taken, valued, in a variety of ways ranging from Rousseau's embracing of self-love as the prime natural good to Jesus's command that we utterly deny our natural self and follow him instead. Usually, though, at any one time there have been voices on either side, such as we heard in the sixteenth-century battle between Renaissance positive *self-interest* and Christian negative *self-interest.* Sometimes voices on either side can even come from a single source: the meaning of self-love for both Rousseau and Jesus, for example, was extremely complex and included valuings of self-concern opposite to those of their main injunctions.

What has happened today is that *self,* the word, has added its voice to the positive side. And its voice is a loud one, swelled by the praise attached to *self* in all the many places in which the word is heard. Our current language, then, is pulling us in the same direction that we naturally tend to go in anyway. With our language—our words and the concepts behind them—adding its considerable force to an already natural attraction, we're entirely sucked into self. (Or almost entirely. What few forces remain to pull us away will be examined in the final chapters of the book.) As for the sort of behavior our *self-*absorption leads us into, that can best be seen in conjunction with a look at another set of terms with which *self* is often joined: the *growth and development* set.

QUESTIONS

1. What historical and cultural forces have merged to form the current positive view of "self"? What other words often linked with "self" also have positive connotations?

2. Do you agree or disagree that "self" is "practically undefined"? Explain. Does Rosenthal define it? What similes does she use to characterize the spread of "psychology's *self*" through our culture? How do these similes help express Rosenthal's point?

3. What is "natural" about our positive view of "self"? Why is Rosenthal uncomfortable about using the word "natural" at all?

4. Why does Rosenthal see the current positive view of the *unique-individual* as a confusing and ambiguous "line" (paragraph six)? What does her use of the word "line" imply about her attitude?

5. What is Rosenthal trying to warn us about in her discussion of words like "self," "self-sufficiency," "independence," and "freedom"? Discuss whether her warning is made explicit in her essay. Are her fears justified?

6. Most readers will find this essay difficult. Analyze the reasons for its difficulty. Then try rewriting sentences or paragraphs in such a way that their meaning is, in your opinion, clearer. (Be careful, however, not to distort Rosenthal's ideas.)

SUGGESTIONS FOR WRITING

1. Go through *People* magazine—or *Life, Esquire, Seventeen,* or any other magazine that is popular—and look for a frequently used word that has the same power as *self.* Then write an extended definition of that word, using

Rosenthal's essay as a model. You may need to do some background research on the word in the *Oxford English Dictionary* and compare how the word is used in different contexts. In addition, you may want to interview friends.

2.   Think of a word or phrase that you feel people accept and use uncritically—a word or phrase that people automatically associate with "the good," for instance, or that leads them to undertake an action or embrace a philosophy they have failed to assess adequately—and write an extended definition and analysis.

Joseph Epstein
WHAT IS VULGAR?
★ ★ ★

In a recent interview with Publisher's Weekly, *Joseph Epstein said that the most important object of his writing is "to get my ideas—or, more exactly, what I* care *about—across with as much clarity as possible." A concern for "clarity," the precise use and understanding of language, lies behind Epstein's essay "What Is Vulgar?," originally published in the* American Scholar, *a magazine Epstein edits. Every three months Epstein writes an essay for the magazine on any subject that interests him, in the tradition of such "familiar" essayists as Addison and Steele, Montaigne, Hazlitt, E.B. White, and Joan Didion. "The familiar essayist," as Epstein defines him, "lives, and takes his professional sustenance, in the everyday flow of things."*

In the following piece, Epstein sharpens his and the reader's under-standing of a rather loosely defined word, "vulgar." The author's second-ary purpose, one which becomes apparent by the essay's conclusion, is to persuade the reader to share his *point of view,* his *taste in things. "If I do* have *a mission," Epstein asserts, "it is to intrude, with authority, and set things right." Like Daly, LeGuin, and Rodriguez, then, Epstein is not only interested in defining the world, he wishes to* redefine *it as well.*

Currently at work on a book-length definition of "snobbery," Epstein teaches at Northwestern University and has published Divorced in Amer-ica *(1975),* Ambition *(1981), and three collections of essays—*Familiar Territory *(1980),* The Middle of My Tether *(1983), and* Plausible Preju-dices *(1985).*

What's vulgar? Some people might say that the contraction of the words *what* and *is* itself is vulgar. On the other hand, I remember being called a stuffed shirt by a reviewer of a book of mine because I used almost no contractions. I have forgotten the reviewer's name but I have remembered the criticism. Not being of that category of writers who never forget a compliment, I also remember being called a racist by another reviewer for observing that failure to insist on table manners in children was to risk dining with Apaches. The larger criticisms I forget, but, oddly, these goofy little criticisms stick in the teeth like sesame seeds. Yet that last trope—is it, too, vulgar? Ought I really to be picking my teeth in public, even metaphorically?

What, to return to the question in uncontractioned form, is vulgar? Illustrations, obviously, are wanted. Consider a relative of mine, long deceased, my father's Uncle Jake and hence my grand-uncle. I don't wish to brag about bloodlines, but my Uncle Jake was a bootlegger during Prohibition who afterward went into the scrap-iron—that is to say, the junk—business. Think of the archetypal sensitive Jewish intellectual faces: of Spinoza, of Freud, of Einstein, of Oppenheimer. In my uncle's face you would not have found the least trace of any of them. He was completely bald, weighed in at around two hundred fifty pounds, and had a complexion of clear vermilion. I loved him, yet even as a child I knew there was about him something a bit—how shall I put it?—outsized, and I refer not merely to his personal tonnage. When he visited our home he generally greeted me by pressing a ten- or twenty-dollar bill into my hand—an amount of money quite impossible, of course, for a boy of nine or ten, when what was wanted was a quarter or fifty-cent piece. A widower, he would usually bring a lady-friend along; here his tastes ran to Hungarian women in their fifties with operatic bosoms. These women wore large diamond rings, possibly the same rings, which my uncle may have passed from woman to woman. A big spender and a high roller, my uncle was an immigrant version of the sport, a kind of Diamond Chaim Brodsky.

But to see Uncle Jake in action you had to see him at table. He drank whiskey with his meal, the bottle before him on the table along with another of seltzer water, both of which he supplied himself. He ate and drank like a character out of Rabelais. My mother served him his soup course, not in a regular bowl, but in a vessel more on the order of a tureen. He would eat hot soup and drink whiskey and sweat—my Uncle Jake did not, decidedly, do anything so delicate as perspire—and sometimes it seemed that the sweat rolled from his face right into his soup dish, so that, toward the end, he may well have been engaged in an act of liquid auto-cannibalism, consuming his own body fluids with a whiskey chaser.

He was crude, certainly, my Uncle Jake; he was coarse, of course; gross, it goes without saying; uncouth, beyond question. But was he vulgar? I don't think he was. For one thing, he was good-hearted, and it somehow seems wrong to call anyone vulgar who is good-hearted. But more to the point, I don't think that if you had accused him of being vulgar, he would have known what the devil you were talking about. To be vulgar requires at least a modicum of pretension, and this Uncle Jake sorely lacked. "Wulgar," he might have responded to the accusation that he was vulgar, "so vat's dis wulgar?"

To go from persons to things, and from lack of pretension to a mountain of it, let me tell you about a house I passed one night, in a neighborhood not far from my own, that so filled me with disbelief that I took a hard right turn at the next corner and drove round the block to make certain I had actually seen what I thought I had. I had, but it was no house—it was a bloody edifice!

The edifice in question totally fills its rather modest lot, leaving no backyard at all. It is constructed of a white stone, sanded and perhaps even painted, with so much gray-colored mortar that, even though it may be real, the stone looks fake. The roof is red. It has two chimneys, neither of which, I would wager, functions. My confidence here derives from the fact that nothing much else in the structure of the house seems to function. There is, for example, a balcony over a portico—a portico held up by columns—onto which the only possible mode of entry is by pole vault. There is, similarly, over the attached garage, a sun deck whose only access appears to be through a bathroom window. The house seems to have been built on the aesthetic formula of functionlessness follows formlessness.

But it is in its details that the true spirit of the house emerges. These details are not minuscule, and neither are they subtle. For starters, outside the house under the portico, there is a chandelier. There are also two torch-shaped lamps on either side of the front door, which is carved in a scallop pattern, giving it the effect of seeming the back door to a much larger house. Along the short walk leading up to this front door stand, on short pillars, two plaster of paris lions—gilded. On each pillar, in gold and black, appears the owner's name. A white chain fence, strung along poles whose tops are painted gold, spans the front of the property; it is the kind of fence that would be more appropriate around, say, the tomb of Lenin. At the curb are two large cars, sheets of plastic covering their grills; there is also a trailer; and, in the summer months, a boat sits in the short driveway leading up to the garage. The lawn disappoints by being not Astro-Turf but, alas, real grass. However, closer inspection reveals two animals, a skunk and a rabbit, both of plastic, in petrified play upon the lawn—a nice, you might almost say a finishing, touch. Sometimes, on long drives or when unable to sleep at night, I have pondered upon the possible decor of this extraordinary house's den and upon the ways of man, which are various beyond imagining.

You want vulgar, I am inclined to exclaim, I'll show you vulgar: the house I have just described is vulgar, patently, palpably, pluperfectly vulgar. Forced to live in it for more than three hours, certain figures of refined sensibility—Edith Wharton or Harold Acton or Wallace Stevens—might have ended as suicides. Yet as I described that house, I noted two contradictory feelings in myself: how pleasant it is to point out someone else's vulgarity, and yet the fear that calling someone else vulgar may itself be slightly vulgar. After all, the family that lives in this house no doubt loves it; most probably they feel that they have a real showplace. Their house, I assume, gives them a large measure of happiness. Yet why does my calling their home vulgar also give me such a measure of happiness? I suppose it is because vulgarity can be so amusing—other people's vulgarity, that is.

Here I must insert that I have invariably thought that the people who have called me vulgar were themselves rather vulgar. So far as I know I have been called vulgar three times, once directly, once behind my back, and once by association. In each instance the charge was intellectual vulgarity: on one occasion a contributor to a collection of essays on contemporary writing that I once reviewed called me vulgar because I didn't find anything good to say about this book of some six hundred pages; once an old friend, an editor with whom I had had a falling out over politics, told another friend of mine that an article I had written seemed to him vulgar; and, finally, having patched things up with this friend and having begun to write for his magazine again, yet a third friend asked me why I allowed my writing to appear in that particular magazine, when it was so patently—you guessed her, Chester—vulgar.

None of these accusations stung in the least. In intellectual and academic life, vulgar is something one calls people with whom one disagrees. Like having one's ideas called reductionist, it is nothing to get worked up about—certainly nothing to take personally. What would wound me, though, is if word got back to me that someone had said that my manners at table were so vulgar that it sickened him to eat with me, or that my clothes were laughable, or that taste in general wasn't exactly my strong point. In a novel whose author or title I can no longer remember, I recall a female character who was described as having vulgar thumbs. I am not sure I have a clear picture of vulgar thumbs, but if it is all the same, I would just as soon not have them.

I prefer not to be thought vulgar in any wise. When not long ago a salesman offered to show me a winter coat that, as he put it, "has been very popular," I told him to stow it—if it has been popular, it is not for me. I comb my speech, as best I am able, of popular phrases: you will not hear an unfundamental "basically" or a flying "whatever" from these chaste lips. I do not utter "bottom line"; I do not mutter "trade-off." I am keen to cut myself out from the herd, at least when I can. In recent years this has not been difficult. Distinction has lain in plain speech, plain dress, clean cheeks. The simple has become rococo, the rococo simple. But now I see that television anchormen, hairdressers, and other leaders in our society have adopted this plainer look. This is discomfiting news. Vulgar is, after all, as vulgar does.

Which returns us yet again to the question: What is vulgar? *The Oxford English Dictionary,* which provides more than two pages on the word, is rather better at telling us what vulgar was than what it is. Its definitions run from "I. The common or usual language of a country; the vernacular. *Obs.*" to "13. Having a common and offensively mean character; coarsely commonplace; lacking in refinement or good taste; uncultured, ill-bred." Historically, the word vulgar was used in fairly neutral description up to the last quarter of the seventeenth century to mean and describe the common people. Vulgar was common but not yet contemned. I noted such a neutral usage as late as a William Hazlitt essay of 1818, "On the Ignorance of the Learned," in which Hazlitt writes: "The vulgar are in the right when they judge for themselves; they are wrong when they trust to their blind guides." Yet, according to the *OED,* in 1797 the *Monthly Magazine* remarked: "So the word *vulgar* now implies something base and groveling in actions."

From the early nineteenth century on, then, vulgar has been purely pejorative, a key term in the lexicon of insult and invective. Its currency as a term of abuse rose with the rise of the middle class; its spread was tied to the spread of capitalism and democracy. Until the rise of the middle class, until the spread of capitalism and democracy, people perhaps hadn't the occasion or the need to call one another vulgar. The rise of the middle class, the spread of capitalism and democracy, opened all sorts of social doors; social classes commingled as never before; plutocracy made possible almost daily strides from stratum to stratum. Still, some people had to be placed outside the pale, some doors had to be locked—and the cry of vulgarity, properly intoned, became a most effective Close Sesame.

Such seems to me roughly the social history of the word vulgar. But the history of vulgarity, the thing itself even before it had a name, is much longer. According to the French art historian Albert Dasnoy, aesthetic vulgarity taints Greek art of the fourth and third centuries B.C. "An exhibition of Roman portraits," Dasnoy writes, "shows that, between the Etruscan style of the earliest and the Byzantine style of the latest, vulgarity made its first full-blooded appearance in the academic realism of imperial Rome." Vulgarity, in Dasnoy's view, comes of the shock of philosophic rationalism, when humankind divests itself of belief in the sacred. "Vulgarity seems to be the price of man's liberation," he writes, "one might even say, of his evolution. It is unquestionably the price of the freeing of the individual personality." Certainly it is true that one would never think to call a savage vulgar; a respectable level of civilization has to have been reached to qualify for the dubious distinction of being called vulgar.

"You have surely noticed the curious fact," writes Valéry, "that a certain *word,* which is perfectly clear when you hear or use it in *everyday* speech, and which presents no difficulty when caught up in the rapidity of an ordinary sentence, becomes mysteriously cumbersome, offers a strange resistance, defeats all efforts at definition, the moment you withdraw it from circulation for separate study and try to find its meaning after taking away its temporary function." Vulgar presents special difficulties, though: while vulgarity has been often enough on display—may even be a part of the human soul that only the fortunate and the saintly are able to root out—every age has its own notion of what constitutes the vulgar. Riding a bicycle at Oxford in the 1890s, Max Beerbohm reports, "was the earmark of vulgarity." Working further backward, we find that Matthew Arnold frequently links the word vulgar with the word hideous and hopes that culture "saves the future, as one may hope, from being vulgarized, even if it cannot save the present." "In Jane Austen's novels," Lionel Trilling writes, "vulgarity has these elements: smallness of mind, insufficiency of awareness, assertive self-esteem, the wish to devalue, especially to devalue the human worth of other people." Hazlitt found vulgarity in false feeling among "the herd of pretenders to what they do not feel and to what is not natural to them, whether in high or low life."

Vulgarity, it begins to appear, is often in the eye of the beholder. What is more, it comes in so many forms. It is so multiple and so complex—so multiplex. There are vulgarities of taste, of manner, of mind, of spirit. There are whole vulgar ages—the Gilded Age in the United States, for one, at least to hear Mark Twain and Henry Adams tell it. (Is our own age another?) To compound the complication there is even likeable vulgarity. This is vulgarity of the kind that Cyril Connolly must have had in mind when he wrote, "Vulgarity is the garlic in the salad of life." In the realm of winning vulgarity are the novels of Balzac, the paintings of Frans Hals, some of the music of Tchaikovsky (excluding the cannon fire in the 1812 Overture, which is vulgarity of the unwinning kind).

Rightly used, profanity, normally deemed the epitome of vulgar manners, can be charming. I recently moved to a new apartment, and the person I dealt with at the moving company we employed, a woman whose voice had an almost strident matter-of-factness, instructed me to call back with an inventory of our furniture. When I did, our conversation, starting with my inventory of our living room, began:

"One couch."

"One couch."

"Two lamp tables, a coffee table, a small gateleg table."

"Four tables."

"Two wing chairs and an occasional chair."

"Three chairs."

"One box of bric-a-brac."

"One box of shit."

Heavy garlic of course is not to every taste; but then again some people do not much care for endive. I attended city schools, where garlic was never in short supply and where profanity, in proper hands, could be a useful craft turned up to the power of fine art. I have since met people so well-mannered, so icily, elegantly correct, that with a mere glance across the table or a word to a waiter they could put a chill on the wine and indeed on the entire evening. Some people have more, some less, in the way of polish, but polish doesn't necessarily cover vulgarity. As there can be diamonds in the rough, so can there be sludge in the smooth.

It would be helpful in drawing a definitional bead on the word vulgar if one could determine its antonym. But I am not sure that it has an antonym. Refined? I think not. Sophisticated? Not really. Elegant? Nope. Charming? Close, but I can think of charming vulgarians—M. Rabelais, please come forth and take a bow. Besides, charm is nearly as difficult to define as vulgarity. Perhaps the only safe thing to be said about charm is that if you think you have it, you can be fairly certain that you don't.

If vulgarity cannot be defined by its antonym, from the rear so to say, examples may be more to the point. I once heard a friend describe a woman thus: "Next to Sam Jensen's prose, she's the vulgarest thing in New York." From this description, I had a fairly firm sense of what the woman was like. Sam Jensen is a writer for one of the newsmagazines; each week on schedule he makes a fresh cultural discovery, writing as if every sentence will be his last, every little movie or play he reviews will change our lives—an exhibitionist with not a great deal to exhibit. Sam Jensen is a fictitious name—made up to protect the guilty—but here are a few sentences that he, not I, made up:

The great Victorian William Morris combined a practical socialism with a love for the spirit of the King Arthur legends. What these films show is the paradox democracy has forgotten—that the dream of Camelot is the ultimate dream of freedom and order in a difficult but necessary balance.

The screenplay by Michael Wilson and Richard Maibaum is not from an Ian Fleming novel; it's really a cookbook that throws Roger Moore as Bond into these action recipes like a cucumber tossed into an Osterizer. Osterization is becoming more and more necessary for Moore; he's beginning to look a bit puckered, as if he's been bottled in Bond.

From these sentences—with their false paradoxes, muffed metaphors, obvious puns, and general bloat—I think I can extrapolate the woman who, next to this prose, is the vulgarest thing in New York. I see teeth, I see elaborate hairdo, much jewelry, flamboyant dress, a woman requiring a great deal of attention, who sucks up most of the mental oxygen in any room she is in—a woman, in sum, vastly overdone.

Coming at things from a different angle, I imagine myself in session with a psychologist, playing the word association game. "Vulgar," he says, "quick, name ten items you associate with the word vulgar." "Okay," I say, "here goes:

1. Publicity

2. The Oscar awards

3. The Aspen Institute for Humanistic Studies

4. Talk shows

5. Pulitzer Prizes

6. Barbara Walters

7. Interviews with writers

8. Lauren Bacall

9. Dialogue as an ideal

10. Psychology."

This would not, I suspect, be everyone's list. Looking it over, I see that, of the ten items, several are linked with one another. But let me inquire into what made me choose the items I did.

Ladies first. Barbara Walters seems to me vulgar because for a great many years now she has been paid to ask all the vulgar questions, and she seems to do it with such cheerfulness, such competence, such amiable insincerity. "What did you think when you first heard your husband had been killed?" she will ask, just the right hush in her voice. "What went on in your mind when you learned that you had cancer, now for the third time?" The questions that people with imagination do not need to ask, the questions that people with good hearts know they have no right to ask, these questions and others Barbara Walters can be depended upon to ask. "Tell me, Holy Father, have you never regretted not having children of your own?"

Lauren Bacall has only recently graduated to vulgarity, or at least she has only in the past few years revealed herself vulgar. Hers is a double vulgarity: the vulgarity of false candor—the woman who, presumably, tells it straight—and the vulgarity provided by someone who has decided to cash in her chips. In her autobiography, Miss Bacall has supposedly told all her secrets; when interviewed on television—by, for example, Barbara Walters—the tack she takes is that of the ringwise babe over whose eyes no one, kiddo, is going to pull the cashmere. Yet turn the channel or page, and there is Miss Bacall in a commercial or advertisement doing her best to pull the cashmere over ours. Vulgar stuff.

Talk shows are vulgar for the same reason that Pulitzer Prizes and the Aspen Institute for Humanistic Studies are vulgar. All three fail to live up to their pretensions, which are extravagant: talk shows to being serious, Pulitzer Prizes to rewarding true merit, the Aspen Institute to promoting "dialogue" (see item 9), "the bridging of cultures," "the interdisciplinary approach," and nearly every other phony shibboleth that has cropped up in American intellectual life over the past three decades.

Publicity is vulgar because those who seek it—and even those who are sought by it—tend almost without exception to be divested of their dignity. You have to sell yourself, the sales manuals used to advise, in order to sell your product. With publicity, though, one is selling only oneself, which is different. Which is a bit vulgar, really.

The Oscar awards ceremony is the single item on my list least in need of explanation, for it seems vulgar prima facie. It is the air of self-congratulation—of, a step beyond, self-adulation—that is so splendidly vulgar about the Oscar awards ceremony. Self-congratulation, even on good grounds, is best concealed; on no grounds whatever, it is embarrassing. But then, for vulgarity, there's no business like show business.

Unless it be literary business. The only thing worse than false modesty is no modesty at all, and no modesty at all is what interviews with writers generally bring out. "That most vulgar of all crowds the literary," wrote Keats presciently—that is, before the incontestable evidence came in with the advent and subsequent popularity of what is by now that staple of the book review and little magazine and talk show, the interview with the great author. What these interviews generally come down to is an invitation to writers to pontificate upon things for which it is either unseemly for them to speak (the quality of their own work) or upon which they are unfit to judge (the state of the cosmos). Roughly a decade ago I watched Isaac Bashevis Singer, when asked on a television talk show what he thought of the Vietnam War, answer, "I am a writer, and that doesn't mean I have to have an opinion on everything. I'd rather discuss literature." Still, how tempting it is, with an interviewer chirping away at your feet, handing you your own horn and your own drum, to blow it and beat it. As someone who has been interviewed a time or two, I can attest that never have I shifted spiritual gears so quickly from self-importance to self-loathing as during and after an interview. What I felt was, well, vulgar.

Psychology seems to me vulgar because it is too often over-bearing in its confidence. Instead of saying, "I don't know," it readily says, "unresolved Oedipus complex" or "manic-depressive syndrome" or "identity crisis." As with other intellectual discoveries before (Marxism) and since (structuralism), psychology acts as if it is holding all the theoretical keys, but then in practice reveals that it doesn't even know where the doors are. As an old *Punch* cartoon once put it, "It's worse than wicked, my dear, it's vulgar."

Reviewing my list and attempting to account for the reasons why I have chosen the items on it, I feel I have a firmer sense of what I think vulgar. Exhibitionism, obviousness, pretentiousness, self-congratulation, self-importance, hypocrisy, overconfidence—these seem to me qualities at the heart of vulgarity in our day. It does, though, leave out common sense, a quality which, like clarity, one might have thought one could never have in overabundance. (On the philosophy table in my local bookstore, a book appeared with the title *Clarity Is Not Enough;* I could never pass it without thinking, "Ah, but it's a start.") Yet too great reliance on common sense can narrow the mind, make meager the imagination. Strict common sense abhors mystery, seldom allows for the attraction of tradition, is intolerant of questions that haven't any answers. The problem that common sense presents is knowing the limits of common sense. The too commonsensical man or woman grows angry at anything that falls outside his or her common sense, and this anger seems to me vulgar.

Vulgarity is not necessarily stupid but it is always insensitive. Its insensitivity invariably extends to itself: the vulgar person seldom knows that he is vulgar, as in the old joke about the young woman whose fiancé reports to her that his parents found her vulgar, and who, enraged, responds, "What's this vulgar crap?" Such obvious vulgarity can be comical, like a nouveau riche man bringing opera glasses to a porno film, or the Chicago politician who, while escorting the then ruling British monarch through City Hall, supposedly introduced him to the assembled aldermen by saying, "King, meet the boys." But such things are contretemps merely, not vulgarity of the insidious kind.

In our age vulgarity does not consist in failing to recognize the fish knife or to know the wine list but in the inability to make distinctions. Not long ago I heard a lecture by a Harvard philosophy professor on a Howard Hawks movie, and thought, as one high reference after another was made in connection with this low subject, "Oh, Santayana, 'tis better you are not alive to see this." A vulgar performance, clearly, yet few people in the audience of professors and graduate students seemed to notice.

A great many people did notice, however, when, in an act of singular moral vulgarity, a publisher, an editor, and a novelist recently sponsored a convicted murderer for parole, and the man, not long after being paroled, murdered again. The reason for these men speaking out on behalf of the convict's parole, they said, was his ability as a writer: his work appeared in the editor's journal; he was to have a book published by the publisher's firm; the novelist had encouraged him from the outset. Distinctions—crucial distinctions—were not made: first, that the man was not a very good writer, but a crudely Marxist one, whose work was filled with hatreds and half-truths; second, and more important, that, having killed before, he might kill again—might just be a pathological killer. Not to have made these distinctions is vulgarity at its most vile. But to adopt a distinction new to our day, the publisher, the editor, and the novelist took responsibility for what they had done—responsibility but no real blame.

Can an entire culture grow vulgar? Matthew Arnold feared such might happen in "the mechanical and material civilisation" of the England of his day. Vladimir Nabokov felt it already had happened in the Soviet Union, a country, as he described it, "of moral imbeciles, of smiling slaves and poker-faced bullies," without, as in the old days, "a Gogol, a Tolstoy, a Chekhov in quest of that simplicity of truth [who] easily distinguished the vulgar side of things as well as the trashy systems of pseudo-thought." Moral imbeciles, smiling slaves, poker-faced bullies—the curl of a sneer in those Nabokovian phrases is a sharp reminder of the force that the charge of "vulgar" can have as an insult—as well as a reminder of how deep and pervasive vulgarity can become.

But American vulgarity, if I may put it so, is rather more refined. It is also more piecemeal than pervasive, and more insidious. Creeping vulgarity is how I think of it, the way Taft Republicans used to think of creeping socialism. The insertion of a science fiction course in a major university curriculum, a television commercial by a once-serious actor for a cheap wine, an increased interest in gossip and trivia that is placed under the rubric Style in our most important newspapers: so the vulgar creeps along, while everywhere the third- and fourth-rate—in art, in literature, in intellectual life—is considered good enough, or at any rate highly interesting.

Yet being refined—or at least sophisticated—American vulgarity is vulnerable to the charge of being called vulgar. "As long as war is regarded as wicked," said Oscar Wilde, "it will always have its fascination. When it is looked upon as vulgar, it will cease to be popular." There may be something to this, if not for war then at least for designer jeans, French literary criticism, and other fashions. The one thing the vulgar of our day do not like to be called is vulgar. So crook your little finger, purse your lips, distend your nostrils slightly as you lift your nose in the air the better to look down it, and repeat after me: *Vulgar! Vulgar! Vulgar!* The word might save us all.

QUESTIONS

1. How does Epstein use the anecdote and description of Uncle Jake to define "vulgar"? Why, according to Epstein, is Uncle Jake, ultimately, *not* vulgar?

2. How does the example of the house illustrate vulgarity? What self-discovery does the author make while describing the house?

3. Analyze Epstein's word association list and his reasons for choosing each word. How do they help us to define "vulgar"? What alternate list would you make?

4. What qualities does Epstein list, finally, as being vulgar?

5. How does this definition essay turn into an argument? What is Epstein defending?

6. How does Epstein's use of "garlic" as a metaphor for "vulgar" help us to understand the word better? Find other examples of metaphors in the essay and evaluate their effectiveness.

7. Epstein, aware of what a definition essay should be, is consciously writing a model one. Applying the criteria set forth in this chapter's introduction, evaluate his success in terms of structure and technique.

SUGGESTIONS FOR WRITING

1. At one point, Epstein writes "Vulgarity is in the eye of the beholder." Write your own extended definition of the word "vulgar," using illustrations from your experience.

2. Epstein maintains that "in our age vulgarity" consists of "the inability to make distinctions," and he gives two illustrations of what he means. Later he suggests that vulgarity may be "creeping" across America, even that our entire culture may be growing vulgar. Attack this view or defend it in an essay of your own.

STUDENT ESSAY

Gregory A. Castanias
HAZING: THE IMPLICATIONS OF A NAME
★ ★ ★

A 1987 graduate of Wabash College, Greg Castanias was a philosophy and English major. His latest projects include convincing his alma mater to admit women and, as he says, "to finish that damn Rod McKuen book." He lists as his hobbies "very amateur sports, reading, and publicly humiliating insincere people." He is a poet who subscribes to Valery's axiom that "a poem is never finished, only abandoned," and he hopes to abandon enough poems to publish a book someday. Castanias spent one year as president of his fraternity, Lambda Chi Alpha. His plans for the future include law school.

Possibly the worst thing that has happened to the image of the American college fraternity system in the past twenty years was the release of National Lampoon's *Animal House.* This movie, a parody of Vietnam-era college life, introduced American filmgoers (many of them unfamiliar with fraternities) to terms like "hazing" and "pledge." Recently, though, the National Interfraternity Council (NIC) passed legislation which essentially outlawed the ages-old practice of fraternity hazing. This was a step to ensure both the physical and psychological safety of all fraternity members as well as the legal safety of the fraternal organizations which belong to the NIC. Alas, this legislation became something of an activity in finger-pointing. While it was reasonably easy to call certain activities "hazing," it seemed to be hard if not impossible to establish a firm definition.

Remember the pledgeship ritual of the Omega Theta Pi fraternity from *Animal House?* The class of *pledges* (students who wish to become members of a fraternity or sorority, but first undergo a "trial" period to see if they would be worthwhile members) are lined up in a candlelit room, wearing only underwear, and hit with paddles by *actives* (students who have successfully endured the pledgeship period and have been "initiated" by means of a secret ceremony). After each spanking, the pledge is forced to say "Thank you sir—may I have another?" Only when the actives decide that the pledges had enough do they stop. This was, it is generally agreed, a cinematic portrayal of hazing.

What about Pinto? Pinto was a pledge at the Animal House (the Delta Tau Chi house), a hilarious but pathetic individual who longed to be one of the guys. To be one of the guys in *this* fraternity required not paddlings but, simply, that Pinto pick up some food at the grocery, which for the Deltas was a rather different activity than we are accustomed to. An active tucks Pinto's sweater into the front of his pants, and proceeds to fill his sweater with wrapped steaks from the meat counter. As Pinto walks out of the store, the young lady at the cash register questions his recent weight gain. Pinto tells her, "It's okay—I'm pledging a fraternity." Not only does Pinto gain freedom with this statement, he gets a date with the cashier as well.

"It's okay—I'm pledging a fraternity." This line was so funny in the theaters because it *isn't* okay to steal twenty pounds of meat. But was this prank hazing? Maybe it was, if the pledge was in peril of getting into serious trouble. Certainly the NIC would include this negative outcome under their definition. But maybe it wasn't, since it could have been a positive activity. Perhaps Pinto learned an object lesson about doing whatever tasks, pleasant or unpleasant, asked of him by his fraternity. Yet "maybe" isn't the kind of word that helps the NIC with its task of defining hazing.

So far, I have resisted giving "hazing" a firm definition, but from the film we can generally define hazing as something done *to* pledges, *by* actives, which will have some negative outcome. That said, why am I so concerned with hazing in the movies?

Animal House was only a movie. Believe it or not, though, activities comparable to these *still* go on, in spite of NIC rulings, in spite of individual fraternity rulings, in spite of college administrations which forbid the practice on their campuses. On my campus, for example, I know of one fraternity which has a demerit system for its pledges. When a pledge accumulates enough demerits, the pledge gets the punishment of the Scarlet Letter. Hester Prynne never knew how easy she had it—*this* Scarlet Letter "P" is four feet high, made of a heavy metal, and must be carried on campus, to classes, for a day. Anyone who asks the pledge what the "P" is for must be answered with "I'm a p—s poor pledge, sir (or ma'am)!"

In their view, this fraternity is not spitting in the face of the NIC, nor would they consider this activity to be "hazing," since (1) it has as its goal to teach responsibility to the pledges, and (2) it sounds like fun. In this sense, the activity is good, because it teaches a positive lesson; hence, it could not be hazing.

Yet the means which are used to achieve these ends have some serious flaws. I said earlier that hazing is done *to* pledges, *by* actives. The "P" is an outward sign of a pledge's screw-up to the entire campus; yet I would venture to guess that many active members frequently screw up something that they are charged to do. And they don't carry any letter at all. Thus a wedge is driven between actives and pledges which may be impossible to eliminate, and which certainly violates the fraternal values these groups are supposed to uphold.

Eileen Stevens probably wishes that her son had been able to carry a "P" around his campus. Unfortunately for him, the actives at the fraternity which he pledged had a different version of the active/pledge relationship. One Friday night, some actives took her son out into the country where he was locked in a car trunk with a case of beer, a bottle of whiskey, and a bottle of wine. He was ordered to consume all of the alcohol before he would be allowed to leave the car trunk. The men who in a few weeks would have been his "brother," his equal, had killed him. Eileen Stevens' son had shown his willingness to do whatever task befell him; alas, he died trying.

Eileen Stevens founded CHUCK (the Coalition to Halt Useless College Killings) in his memory, because she believed that any lesson her son might have learned from his ordeal was not as valuable as his life. She believes, as a few national fraternities do, that the most dangerous lessons are taught when actives *do* things *to* pledges; and furthermore, the most *valuable* lessons are learned when actives do the same things *with* pledges.

The actives who caused Eileen Stevens' son to die and the actives who impose the scarlet "P" on their pledges have a lot in common: they both consider it fun, and for some reason necessary, to watch the pledges learn their lesson in these ways. Perhaps, though, these same lessons could be learned not in a master/servant relationship between active and pledge, but in a mentor/student relationship. In such a relationship, the active would be at the side of the pledge, participating in all learning activities *with* him. Thus the need for "hazing," as I have defined it, will be eliminated. At the very least, pledgeship would become safer and less psychologically destructive, for if actives are doing the same things as the pledges, there aren't going to be any dangerous or potentially destructive activities involved. At best, if fraternities hold as their goal the creation of a bond of brotherhood, useful in college and in life afterward, and a positive environment in which the individual might flourish, they will be living according to their highest ideals.

QUESTIONS

1. Why does the writer believe "hazing" requires a firmer definition? Do you agree that it does?

2. How do the illustrations from *Animal House* help him better define the term? Do you see the Pinto episode as "hazing"? Explain.

3. Evaluate the writer's transition between the film discussion and real life. How does he justify using the film?

4. Do you agree or disagree with labeling the "Scarlet Letter 'P' " as "hazing"? Explain.

5. Why does the writer follow the example of the Scarlet Letter "P" with the story about the death of Eileen Stevens's son? Do you agree that they have "a lot in common"?

6. Describe the strategy the writer employs in the final paragraph. What is he trying to do? Does he succeed?

7. How would you summarize the writer's purpose in this essay? Has he achieved his purpose? Discuss.

SUGGESTIONS FOR WRITING

1. After evaluating the audience to which the writer is trying to appeal, re-write the essay's opening and closing paragraphs with a *different* audience in mind.

2. Think of a controversial term that is the center of a debate on your campus, and write an essay presenting your preferred definition. "Student athlete," "plagiarism," and "date rape" are three possible terms you might define.

Ursula K. Le Guin
THE AUTHOR OF THE ACACIA SEEDS AND OTHER EXTRACTS FROM THE *JOURNAL OF THE ASSOCIATION OF THEROLINGUISTICS*

★ ★ ★

As the foremost writer of science fiction in America today Ursula K. Le Guin is, and has always been, vitally interested in language. Brought up in an intensely intellectual environment in Berkeley, California (her father is a well-known anthropologist and her mother a writer), Le Guin is wary of conventional categories. " 'Science fiction' is a label, very much like 'Yankee' or 'Middle Westerner,' " she notes in a Publishers Weekly *interview, "useful in pointing to a region and hinting at certain probable qualities; useless when used as a definition; and tiresome when used as a put-down." Le Guin would prefer, if labels are needed, being called a fiction writer. Her most celebrated work is* The Earthsea Trilogy, *the last volume of which,* The Farthest Shore *(1972), won the National Book Award.*

In her numerous novels, short stories, and poems, Le Guin has created strange new worlds with invented objects, words, and modes of perception. Men and women in The Left Hand of Darkness *(1969) can freely change gender, thus liberating them from sexual stereotypes. "The Author of the Acacia Seeds . . .," taken from Le Guin's short story collection* The Compass Rose *(1982), raises basic questions about language on earth. Is our definition of language, the story implicitly asks, too narrow? Does our species own exclusive rights to language?*

Ms. Found in an Anthill

The messages were found written in touch-gland exudation on degerminated acacia seeds laid in rows at the end of a narrow, erratic tunnel leading off from one of the deeper levels of the colony. It was the orderly arrangement of the seeds that first drew the investigator's attention.

The messages are fragmentary, and the translation approximate and highly interpretative; but the text seems worthy of interest if only for its striking lack of resemblance to any other Ant texts known to us.

Seeds 1–13

[I will] not touch feelers [I will] not stroke. [I will] spend on dry seeds [my] soul's sweetness. It may be found when [I am] dead. Touch this dry wood! [I] call! [I am] here!

Alternatively, this passage may be read:

[Do] not touch feelers. [Do] not stroke. Spend on dry seeds [your] soul's sweetness. [Others] may find it when [you are] dead. Touch this dry wood! Call: [I am] here!

No known dialect of Ant employs any verbal person except the third person singular and plural and the first person plural. In this text, only the root forms of the verbs are used; so there is no way to decide whether the passage was intended to be an autobiography or a manifesto.

Seeds 14–22

Long are the tunnels. Longer is the untunneled. No tunnel reaches the end of the untunneled. The untunneled goes on farther than we can go in ten days [*i.e.*, forever). Praise!

The mark translated "Praise!" is half of the customary salutation "Praise the Queen!" or "Long live the Queen!" or "Huzza for the Queen!"—but the word/mark signifying "Queen" has been omitted.

Seeds 23–29

As the ant among foreign-enemy ants is killed, so the ant without ants dies, but being without ants is as sweet as honeydew.

An ant intruding in a colony not its own is usually killed. Isolated from other ants, it invariably dies within a day or so. The difficulty in this passage is the word/mark "without ants," which we take to mean "alone"—a concept for which no word/mark exists in Ant.

Seeds 30–31

Eat the eggs! Up with the Queen!

There has already been considerable dispute over the interpretation of the phrase on Seed 31. It is an important question, since all the preceding seeds can be fully understood only in the light cast by this ultimate exhortation. Dr. Rosbone ingeniously argues that the author, a wingless neuter-female worker, yearns hopelessly to be a winged male, and to found a new colony, flying upward in the nuptial flight with a new Queen. Though the text certainly permits such a reading, our conviction is that nothing in the text *supports* it—least of all the text of the immediately preceding seed, No. 30: "Eat the eggs!" This reading, though shocking, is beyond disputation.

We venture to suggest that the confusion over Seed 31 may result from an ethnocentric interpretation of the word "up." To us, "up" is a "good" direction. Not so, or not necessarily so, to an ant. "Up" is where the food comes from, to be sure; but "down" is where security, peace, and home are to be found. "Up" is the scorching sun; the freezing night; no shelter in the beloved tunnels; exile; death. Therefore we suggest that this strange author, in the solitude of her lonely tunnel, sought with what means she had to express the ultimate blasphemy conceivable to an ant, and that the correct reading of Seeds 30–31, in human terms, is:

Eat the eggs! Down with the Queen!

The desiccated body of a small worker was found beside Seed 31 when the manuscript was discovered. The head had been severed from the thorax, probably by the jaws of a soldier of the colony. The seeds, carefully arranged in a pattern resembling a musical stave, had not been disturbed. (Ants of the soldier caste are illiterate; thus the soldier was presumably not interested in the collection of useless seeds from which the edible germs had been removed.) No living ants were left in the colony, which was destroyed in a war with a neighboring anthill at some time subsequent to the death of the Author of the Acacia Seeds.

—G. D'Arbay, T. R. Bardol

Announcement of an Expedition

The extreme difficulty of reading Penguin has been very much lessened by the use of the underwater motion-picture camera. On film it is at least possible to repeat, and to slow down, the fluid sequences of the script, to the point where, by constant repetition and patient study, many elements of this most elegant and lively literature may be grasped, though the nuances, and perhaps the essence, must forever elude us.

It was Professor Duby who, by pointing out the remote affiliation of the script with Low Greylag, made possible the first tentative glossary of Penguin. The analogies with Dolphin which had been employed up to that time never proved very useful, and were often quite misleading.

Indeed it seemed strange that a script written almost entirely in wings, neck, and air should prove the key to the poetry of short-necked, flipper-winged water-writers. But we should not have found it so strange if we had kept in mind the fact that penguins are, despite all evidence to the contrary, birds.

Because their script resembles Dolphin in *form,* we should never have assumed that it must resemble Dolphin in *content.* And indeed it does not. There is, of course, the same extraordinary wit, the flashes of crazy humor, the inventiveness, and the inimitable grace. In all the thousands of literatures of the Fish stock, only a few show any humor at all, and that usually of a rather simple, primitive sort; and the superb gracefulness of Shark or Tarpon is utterly different from the joyous vigor of all Cetacean scripts. The joy, the vigor, and the humor are all shared by Penguin authors; and, indeed, by many of the finer Seal *auteurs.* The temperature of the blood is a bond. But the construction of the brain, and of the womb, makes a barrier! Dolphins do not lay eggs. A world of difference lies in that simple fact.

Only when Professor Duby reminded us that penguins are birds, that they do not swim but *fly in water,* only then could the therolinguist begin to approach the sea literature of the penguin with understanding; only then could the miles of recordings already on film be restudied and, finally, appreciated.

But the difficulty of translation is still with us.

A satisfying degree of promise has already been made in Adélie. The difficulties of recording a group kinetic performance in a stormy ocean as thick as pea soup with plankton at a temperature of 31° Fahrenheit are considerable; but the perseverance of the Ross Ice Barrier Literary Circle has been fully rewarded with such passages as "Under the Iceberg," from the *Autumn Song*—a passage now world famous in the rendition by Anna Serebryakova of the Leningrad Ballet. No verbal rendering can approach the felicity of Miss Serebryakova's version. For, quite simply, there is no way to reproduce in writing the all-important *multiplicity* of the original text, so beautifully rendered by the full chorus of the Leningrad Ballet company.

Indeed, what we call "translations" from the Adélie—or from any group kinetic text—are, to put it bluntly, mere notes—libretto without the opera. The ballet version is the true translation. Nothing in words can be complete.

I therefore suggest, though the suggestion may well be greeted with frowns of anger or with hoots of laughter, that *for the therolinguist*—as opposed to the artist and the amateur—the kinetic sea writings of Penguin are the *least* promising field of study: and, further, that Adélie, for all its charm and relative simplicity, is a less promising field of study than is Emperor.

Emperor!—I anticipate my colleagues' response to this suggestion. Emperor! The most difficult, the most remote, of all the dialects of Penguin! The language of which Professor Duby himself remarked, "The literature of the emperor penguin is as forbidding, as inaccessible, as the frozen heart of Antarctica itself. Its beauties may be unearthly, but they are not for us."

Maybe. I do not underestimate the difficulties: not least of which is the imperial temperament, so much more reserved and aloof than that of any other penguin. But, paradoxically, it is just in this reserve that I place my hope. The emperor is not a solitary, but a social bird, and while on land for the breeding season dwells in colonies, as does the adélie; but these colonies are very much smaller and very much quieter than those of the adélie. The bonds between the members of an emperor colony are rather personal than social. The emperor is an individualist. Therefore I think it almost certain that the literature of the emperor will prove to be composed by single authors, instead of chorally; and therefore it will be translatable into human speech. It will be a kinetic literature, but how different from the spatially extensive, rapid, multiplex choruses of sea writing! Close analysis, and genuine transcription, will at last be possible.

What! say my critics—Should we pack up and go to Cape Crozier, to the dark, to the blizzards, to the −60° cold, in the mere hope of recording the problematic poetry of a few strange birds who sit there, in the mid-winter dark, in the blizzards, in the −60° cold, on the eternal ice, with an egg on their feet?

And my reply is, Yes. For, like Professor Duby, my instinct tells me that the beauty of that poetry is as unearthly as anything we shall ever find on earth.

To those of my colleagues in whom the spirit of scientific curiosity and aesthetic risk is strong, I say, Imagine it: the ice, the scouring snow, the darkness, the ceaseless whine and scream of wind. In that black desolation a little band of poets crouches. They are starving; they will not eat for weeks. On the feet of each one, under the warm belly feathers, rests one large egg, thus preserved from the mortal touch of the ice. The poets cannot hear each other; they cannot see each other. They can only feel the other's *warmth*. That is their poetry, that is their art. Like all kinetic literatures, it is silent; unlike other kinetic literatures, it is all but immobile, ineffably subtle. The ruffling of a feather; the shifting of a wing; the touch, the slight, faint, warm touch of the one beside you. In unutterable, miserable, black solitude, the affirmation. In absence, presence. In death, life.

I have obtained a sizable grant from UNESCO and have stocked an expedition. There are still four places open. We leave for Antarctica on Thursday. If anyone wants to come along, welcome!

—D. Petri

Editorial. By the President of the Therolinguistics Association

What is Language?

This question, central to the science of therolinguistics, has been answered—heuristically—by the very existence of the science. Language is communication. That is the axiom on which all our theory and research rest, and from which all our discoveries derive; and the success of the discoveries testifies to the validity of the axiom. But to the related, yet not identical question, What is Art? we have not yet given a satisfactory answer.

Tolstoy, in the book whose title is that very question, answered it firmly and clearly: Art, too, is communication. This answer has, I believe, been accepted without examination or criticism by therolinguistics. For example: Why do therolinguists study only animals?

Why, because plants do not communicate.

Plants do not communicate; that is a fact. Therefore plants have no language; very well; that follows from our basic axiom. Therefore, also, plants have no art. But stay! That does *not* follow from the basic axiom, but only from the unexamined Tolstoyan corollary.

What if art is not communicative?

Or, what if some art is communicative, and some art is not?

Ourselves animals, active, predators, we look (naturally enough) for an active, predatory, communicative art; and when we find it, we recognise it. The development of this power of recognition and the skills of appreciation is a recent and glorious achievement.

But I submit that, for all the tremendous advances made by therolinguistics during the last decades, we are only at the beginning of our age of discovery. We must not become slaves to our own axioms. We have not yet lifted our eyes to the vaster horizons before us. We have not faced the almost terrifying challenge of the Plant.

If a non-communicative, vegetative art exists, we must rethink the very elements of our science, and learn a whole new set of techniques.

For it is simply not possible to bring the critical and technical skills appropriate to the study of Weasel murder mysteries, or Batrachian erotica, or the tunnel sagas of the earthworm, to bear on the art of the redwood or the zucchini.

This is proved conclusively by the failure—a noble failure—of the efforts of Dr. Srivas, in Calcutta, using time-lapse photography, to produce a lexicon of Sunflower. His attempt was daring, but doomed to failure. For his approach was kinetic—a method appropriate to the *communicative* arts of the tortoise, the oyster, and the sloth. He saw the extreme slowness of the kinesis of plants, and only that, as the problem to be solved.

But the problem was far greater. The art he sought, if it exists, is a non-communicative art: and probably a non-kinetic one. It is possible that Time, the essential element, matrix, and measure of all known animal art, does not enter into vegetable art at all. The plants may use the meter of eternity. We do not know.

We do not know. All we can guess is that the putative Art of the Plant is *entirely different* from the Art of the Animal. What it is, we cannot say; we have not yet discovered it. Yet I predict with some certainty that it exists, and that when it is found it will prove to be, not an action, but a reaction: not a communication, but a reception. It will be exactly the opposite of the art we know and recognise. It will be the first *passive* art known to us.

Can we in fact know it? Can we ever understand it?

It will be immensely difficult. That is clear. But we should not despair. Remember that so late as the mid-twentieth century, most scientists, and many artists, did not believe that even Dolphin would ever be comprehensible to the human brain—or worth comprehending! Let another century pass, and we may seem equally laughable. "Do you realise," the phytolinguist will say to the aesthetic critic, "that they couldn't even read Eggplant?" And they will smile at our ignorance, as they pick up their rucksacks and hike on up to read the newly deciphered lyrics of the lichen on the north face of Pike's Peak.

And with them, or after them, may there not come that even bolder adventurer—the first geolinguist, who, ignoring the delicate, transient lyrics of the lichen, will read beneath it the still less communicative, still more passive, wholly atemporal, cold, volcanic poetry of the rocks: each one a word spoken, how long ago, by the earth itself, in the immense solitude, the immenser community, of space.

QUESTIONS

1. How do the language and structure of Le Guin's story indicate it is a parody of scientific or academic writing? Use specific examples to support your answer.

2. What scientific sounding facts and allusions maintain the parody's effect?

3. What is Le Guin's purpose in writing this science fiction fantasy? Is her story intended to be more than an entertaining parody? Explain.

4. Why does Le Guin break the story into three sections, supposedly written by three different people? What function does each of the three sections have?

5. What connotation does the word "up" have for ants? What does this detail of the story suggest about language in general?

6. Does this story change your definition of *language?* If so, in what way?

SUGGESTION FOR WRITING

Using Le Guin's technique as a model, if you like, define the language system of anything that would not be expected to have one—cars and trucks ("vehilinguistics"), houses ("domolinguistics"), food in a market ("nutrilinguistics"). Use free-writing and brainstorming techniques to get started. Adopt the role of an authority on the subject who is writing an article for a scientific journal.

Roy Blount, Jr.
YOU MAKE ME FEEL LIKE A NATURAL PERSON TO TRY AND COME UP WITH A TERM BY WHICH A PARTICULAR WOMAN MAY BE REFERRED TO FAVORABLY AND WITH FEELING IN TIMES SUCH AS THESE

★ ★ ★

Roy Blount, Jr., is one of the funniest people writing in America today. Several critics have compared him to Mark Twain, and certainly the wide range of subjects he attacks, his wit, intelligence, and Southern regional approach all make the comparison valid. Born in Indianapolis in 1941 but raised primarily in the South, Blount attended Vanderbilt and Harvard. He has worked as a teacher, journalist, and freelance magazine writer. The following poem, reprinted from his collection One Fell Soup; or, I'm Just a Bug on the Windshield of Life *(1982), is typical of Blount in that it combines humor, sensitivity to language, and a concern for social issues.*

Blount has also written About Three Bricks Shy of a Load *(1974),* Crackers *(1980), which is about Jimmy Carter and his family, and, most recently,* What Men Don't Tell Women *(1984).*

Woman *is either political or merely generic;*
A doll *or a* dame *is a dullard.*
Femme *and* lass *are crass or esoteric;*
Lady, *I guess, is like* colored.

Girl, *it is argued, is too much like* boy.
Broad *is just used for effect.*
A bird, chick *or* frail's *like a pet or a toy;*
Tomato *connotes disrespect.*

Eve the Eternal *is too rich and fruity;*
Damsel's *as loaded as* wench.
For you: add a touch of patootie
To a cross between siren *and* mensch.

QUESTIONS

1. What does Blount mean by the phrase "in times such as these" in his title? And why is the title almost as long as his poem?

2. What is wrong with each choice Blount makes? (Look up any words you do not know.)

3. Why does he finally select the terms in the last two lines "patootie," "siren," and "mensch"? What do they mean?

4. Characterize Blount's tone in this poem.

SUGGESTIONS FOR WRITING

You are working for an ad agency and the client company wants you to come up with exactly the right words to describe its product for a new ad campaign. Write an ad for any product, real or imaginary, and include these words. (For example, "Coke is *it*" or "Sony, *no baloney.*") Then write a paragraph justifying your choice of words.

CHAPTER *Nine*

CONTROVERSIES
Argument and Persuasion

Whether we realize it or not, we have been engaged in argument and persuasion since our earliest years. From our first howlings in the crib, designed to induce a parent's immediate presence, to our attempts to wangle just one more piece of cake or one more half hour's play before bed, we have been sharpening the strategies we use to make others give us what we want. These early efforts would be labeled *persuasion,* because the basic appeals have been emotional or nonrational. The crying or begging are appeals to pity or an attempt to annoy the hearer into action. As we mature, we tend to move toward more rational means of persuasion, or toward *argument.* When teenagers want permission to drive the family car, they may employ arguments like "I have a license issued by the state. They obviously think I can drive. Why don't you?" "How will I ever get the practice I need if I never get the car?" "If you don't let me drive, I may have to get a ride home from a party sometime with an irresponsible person." With the exception of the last point, which contains the emotional tone of a threat, each of these arguments appeals solely to the listener's reason.

In an ideal situation, it might be possible to distinguish neatly between persuasion and argument. In addition to persuasion's reliance on emotional appeals and argument's on rational, persuasion involves getting people to take a desired action, while argument is intended to convince them of the validity of an idea. In real life, however, argument and persuasion are often inextricably connected. Lawyers arguing cases in court are expected to be more rational in their approach than advertising copywriters trying to sell a product. But lawyers, in trying to convince people, will use emotional techniques (subtly biased language, special tones of voice, facial expressions, and physical gestures) if they are permitted to by the judge. (In addition, they may appeal to a jury's sense of pity or capacity to empathize with the defendant.) Similarly, an advertising copywriter, in addition to using provocative images and evocative language to persuade an audience that a product is superior, will use facts, figures, and expert testimony, because human beings respond to the rational approach as well as to the emotional.

The following two examples will show both the differences between persuasive and argumentative writing, and how they may overlap. The first is a car advertisement from a national newsmagazine:

Some Outdated Impressions of
Volvo Are About to Go Up in Smoke

For more than 58 years, Volvo has relentlessly pursued the challenge of producing automobiles of unparalleled comfort, safety and durability. All of which has resulted in enormously powerful and positive impressions of our automobiles.

We are, however, about to generate some new perceptions of Volvo. Perceptions based upon performance.

Enter the new Volvo 700 Series with its most awesome member being the 760 Intercooled Turbo. The latter being capable of launching you to 55 mph in a time that could prove more than a little embarrassing to most Autobahn hardware. What's more, this staggering performance is being presented along with an even greater commitment to our more traditional virtues of safety, luxury, comfort and durability.

The new Volvo 700 Series.

It's caused more than a few outdated impressions of Volvo to vanish in a cloud of smoke.

With considerable haste we might add.

A large color photograph of the new Volvo, poised on a starting line before a race, its back wheels spinning and smoking as it strains to lurch forward, dominates the two-page advertisement.

The copy is printed in a strip beneath the picture, and is obviously intended to mirror, in language, the excitement of the image. The phrases "enormously powerful," "awesome," "launching," "staggering," and the reference to embarrassing other cars on the highway are appeals to the emotional thrills of speed and winning in competition. If we buy this car, the ad implies, we will become powerful—we will become winners. Other car ads in the same magazine, with three times as much copy, try to convince the reader, using facts, figures, and charts, that their car's "thermal efficiency" and 3.07 inches long piston stroke make it a superior piece of engineering. The Volvo ad writers, wanting to change the car's safe, family-oriented image, decided they needed a stronger emotional appeal to create a new perception. Yet they cleverly begin and end the ad by reiterating the "old" values the car still possesses—comfort, safety, and durability. The car, then, becomes all things to all people; in the Volvo one will be able to drive at exciting speeds (or at least get to the speed limit as quickly as Mario Andretti), but also travel comfortably and safely.

The Volvo ad's appeal to emotion makes it a classic example of persuasion. In contrast, Captain Vere, one of the central characters in Herman Melville's *Billy Budd,* appeals to reason, not to the emotions, in arguing a case before a military court. Billy Budd, a young man serving aboard a man-of-war in the British navy, has accidentally killed his superior officer. Vere insists to his fellow officers that Budd must be executed for his act:

> "To steady us a bit, let us recur to the facts.—In wartime at sea a man-of-war's man strikes his superior in grade, and the blow kills. Apart from its effect the blow itself is, according to the Articles of War, a capital crime. Furthermore—"
>
> "Ay, sir," emotionally broke in the officer of marines, "in one sense it was. But surely Budd purposed neither mutiny nor homicide."
>
> "Surely not, my good man. And before a court less arbitrary and more merciful than a martial one, that plea would largely extenuate. . . . But how here? We proceed under the law of the Mutiny Act. In feature no child can resemble the father more than that Act resembles in spirit the thing from which it derives—War. In His Majesty's service—in this ship, indeed—there are Englishmen forced to fight for the King against their will. Against their conscience, for aught we know. Though as their fellow creatures some of us appreciate their position, yet as navy officers what reck [care] we of it? Still less recks the enemy. Our impressed men he would fain cut down in the same swath with our volunteers. . . . War looks but to the frontage, the appearance. And the Mutiny Act, War's child, takes after the father. Budd's intent or non-intent is nothing to the purpose."

In this excerpt, Vere's facts, laws, language, and analogies totally dominate the emotional argument of the marine. After conceding that in a different situation the officer would certainly be right (*concession* is, itself, an important argumentative strategy), Vere goes on to show how in a military situation governed by the Mutiny Act he is not. He uses analogy to argue that the Mutiny Act is like war, and since in war the soldiers' values and reservations about fighting are irrelevant, so in this case Budd's intentions are not germane, and the court must not consider them. Vere goes on to win the case by striking down every subsequent opposing argument suggested by the other officers. Thus, he achieves his purpose—convincing others that his view is the the correct one.

Purpose is obviously a critical consideration in argument and persuasion.

The Volvo ad's purpose is to persuade the reader to buy the car; Vere's purpose, as we have said, is to convince the court that his view is correct, so that it will hang Billy Budd. Sometimes, as in Harry Edwards's essay "Educating Black Athletes" (p. 419), there may be more than one purpose. Edwards is arguing for a controversial rule that will prevent student athletes with combined SAT's below 700 from competing; he also wishes to persuade educators to change priorities in the country. One purpose is quite specific (accept the new rule), the other, more general (change our way of thinking). And Edwards uses different evidence to argue each purpose. When we keep purpose in sight, we can select more appropriate and effective strategies.

While in college, you will have the opportunity to write argumentative and persuasive essays about many different issues, both in and out of the classroom. Any college newspaper is generally filled with debatable issues: students arguing for longer library hours, more parking space, more student spirit; faculty calling for greater student attendance at cultural events, an end to University support for defense projects, and more parking space; administrators asking for curbs on the consumption of alcohol at campus parties, for limits on fraternity hazing, for a commitment to the liberal arts as opposed to vocationalism, and for students and faculty to keep out of administrators' parking spaces. In the classroom, you will be asked to develop and defend an interpretation of a particular text, argue for the superiority of one theory over another, persuade your classmates and instructor that a line of reasoning is flawed. Almost every paper you write for class should defend a position; and all essay exams are essentially nothing more than attempts to persuade the instructor that you have mastered the subject. The issues you write and speak about in class will not all seem as arguable as those in the campus newspaper or those covered by the writers collected in this chapter (capital punishment, using animals in research, bilingual education), but it is important to find a defensible point in almost any writing assignment. (We will talk more about this below, when we look at thesis statements).

After we define our purpose, we must define our readers. In fact, an awareness of audience is more critical to argumentative and persuasive writing than to any other form of writing we have discussed in this book. When our purpose is to convince or persuade, clearly we must have some sense of whom we are trying to reach so we can adjust the nature of our arguments, the amount of information we include, and our tone to fit the reader. Before you write an argument or persuasion essay, you should carefully analyze your audience in relation to your subject and purpose by asking questions like: Does the age of my readers matter, given what I am trying to prove? Is the sex of my readers relevant? How well-educated are they? How much information do my readers already have about the subject? Do they have any vested interest in the subject? Do they already have an opinion? The more clearly you can define your readers, the easier the process of writing will be and the more effective the finished product.

Let's look at how one might go about writing an argument/persuasion paper for a composition class to see how matters of logic, emotion, purpose, and audience come together in practice. Imagine that your composition instructor assigns an argument paper with an open topic, asking that you write about a subject you are interested in and know something about. The usual controversial subjects come to mind—capital punishment, abortion, raising or lowering the drinking age—but all of them seem like predictable choices. What can you do? In addition to trying free-writing and brainstorming, techniques for getting started introduced in Chapter One, you might try writing a letter of complaint to some-one who has angered you. The object is not to send the letter, but to discover an issue you care about and to translate some of your angry feelings into words. If you eventually choose to write about that issue, it will have your emotional commitment, a vital feature of argumentative writing, as the professional pieces collected in this chapter reveal. Each of the essays has a core of emotion, ranging from the bitterness Wendy Rose expresses in her poem "I Expected My Skin and My Blood to Ripen" to David Bruck's controlled outrage at the unfairness of capital punishment to John Simon's haughty distaste for teaching nonstandard English. Although writers of argumentative essays must use logic and facts, emotion gives their writing greater persuasiveness because their personal com-mitment increases reader interest and, sometimes, identification.

Imagine, then, that the object of your letter of complaint is your composition instructor who, unfairly and harshly, you think, gave you a D on your last paper. In your letter, you accuse her of nit-picking over spelling and punctuation errors and of ignoring the substance of what you wanted to say. For a while, you say, you were so discouraged that you considered dropping the class, or even dropping out of school. As you continue to write the letter, you begin to get angry at the whole idea of grades. What good are they anyway, especially in the hands of coldhearted professors? After finishing the letter, examine it to see whether it contains a subject for an essay. Perhaps you will discover that more general and hence more useful concerns emerge from the letter—that is, broader issues than your having received a D—for an argument paper should be about an issue that is of interest to more than one person. Questions like "Which are important aspects of writing and which are trivial?" and "Shouldn't professors be more encouraging?" come to your mind. Finally, you focus on grades as a subject: "What good are they?"

This last is a provocative query, but a question is too open-ended to serve as a *thesis* for your essay. A reader could easily respond in a way you do not intend. A thesis should be a statement that expresses your opinion, such as "Grades are useless." Here you have chosen a controversial subject and ex-pressed an opinion that can be defended. Yet it is not clear enough, for your audience might complain, "What grades?" and "What does 'useless' mean?" A different version could be, "All grades in college should be abolished." This sounds like a good thesis at first, but as you think about it you begin to wonder whether you are making too large a claim ("*All* grades?"), one you would have trouble defending. You hear the objections in your mind: "Graduate and profes-sional schools could not distinguish between applicants!" and "Pass-fail classes lead to mediocrity!" Because you discover that you agree with these views, you decide that this is not a thesis you want to defend. Finally, you narrow your thesis to the following: "Essays written in composition classes should be returned to students with the teacher's comments on them, but not a grade." This is a workable thesis because it is debatable (opposing arguments immediately come to mind), narrow enough to defend, and a reasonable claim. The thesis also implies an action a reader could take if convinced by your argument.

Finding an appropriate thesis may seem a long, involved, and frustrating chore, but discovering what you want to defend is the most important part of the writing process. As you write you may modify your thesis, but having a clear statement of purpose provides a starting point, and helps you decide what to write each step of the way.

The next step in writing the argument essay is to think of arguments that support your thesis. After brainstorming for a while you come up with the following:

1.   Composition, unlike most classes, primarily teaches a skill, not mastery of a body of knowledge, so grading of individual papers is inappropriate.

2.   Grades often distract students from attending to their instructor's written comments.

3.   Grades make the instructor the only audience that counts. Peers should also have a say.

4.   Grades emphasize the "product," instead of the "process," of writing.

5.   Students write better when they know papers will not be graded.

While you are thinking of arguments that support your thesis, opposing arguments will probably come to mind. Because their audience is likely to think of opposing ideas, effective debaters anticipate them, and either *refute* them, by showing they are contrary to fact or *fallacious* (illogical), or *concede* them (that is, accept their validity). In your essay, state the opposing arguments fairly. (Setting up a *straw man,* a weak and possibly distorted argument that you can easily knock down, will undermine reader confidence in you and your case.) For example, someone might argue against eliminating grades on composition papers by saying that students need to know where they stand, and that teacher comments alone do not tell them. This is a reasonable point, and you might concede it early in your essay, but explain that this anxiety could be alleviated during teacher/student conferences. Another criticism of your thesis might be that, since students must receive a final mark for the course, doing away with grades on individual papers is just an escape from reality for students, who are only postponing the inevitable poor mark, and for teachers, who can avoid having to deal with angry students unhappy over the grades on their papers. This argument can be refuted on two grounds. First, it is an example of *circular reasoning,* a form of *begging the question,* because it does not argue the merits of grading or not grading individual papers, but assumes that all students will be given poor grades. Second, it is an example of an *ad hominem* (to the man) argument, which attacks the motives of the opposition. The implication here is that people who argue that individual compositions ought not be graded have no rational support for their position and, furthermore, that they are irresponsible, immature, and eager to avoid conflict and adversity.

After choosing the main arguments that will defend and develop your thesis, you need to support those arguments with some combination of the following: logic, either *inductive* (drawing general conclusions from specific examples) or *deductive* (reasoning from the general premises to specific instances); facts and statistics taken from many sources (magazines, newspapers, books, television, interviews); the opinions of experts; personal experience (so long as you avoid overgeneralizing from a single case); and analogies. (Remember, however, that while analogy can illustrate a point or suggest the truth, it cannot serve as conclusive proof.) For instance, you might support your assertion that grades on individual papers in composition courses are inappropriate through a combination of deductive reasoning, called a *syllogism,* and analogy. In a syllogism, if a major premise is true and a minor premise is true also, then the conclusion following from those premises is true. An example is: "All children lose their first teeth" (major premise); "Betty is a child" (minor premise); "Betty will lose her teeth" (conclusion). For our paper, then, we might create the following syllogism: "Only in those courses that periodically assess students' mastery of the subject matter through exams are grades appropriate; composition is not one of them." Each of these premises requires some explanation, but if they are explained adequately, a reader would have to accept your conclusion.

Using analogy, you could go on to argue that composition is more like driver's education than like American history. We learn to drive by driving, through making mistakes and being praised for successes. It would be as pointless, and potentially damaging, to grade the early efforts of a composition student as it would be to give a letter grade to a beginning driving student. Employ analogy carefully, however, for a reader may notice differences between the things you are comparing that you did not notice, and this might lead to questions on other aspects of your argument. To support your assertion that grades overemphasize the "product" instead of the "process" in writing, you can utilize common sense, personal experience, and a reference to the authority of your textbook, where the "process" idea may be extolled. Finally, the argument that students write better when they know papers will not be graded requires the support of research. Such an assertion simply cannot be proved without an organized study. Although you cannot undertake such a study yourself, in the past ten years much research has been carried out in the field of composition, and by referring to standard research tools like indexes, bibliographies, and data bases, you will be able to find several relevant studies. Remember to quote sources accurately and succinctly.

In organizing your essay, you will want to place your strongest arguments in the most effective positions—immediately after your introductory paragraph or right before your concluding paragraph. Reserve some striking anecdote or quotation for the opening or closing paragraphs where you can allow your language to become more emotional and metaphorical. Consider the following opening from Eric Zorn's *Newsweek* essay, reprinted in this chapter, on rock videos: "Something terrible has happened to popular music in this country. Over the last few years it has touched its finger to the Tar Baby of television and now finds itself unable to pull away. Consider the following depressing news." Zorn goes on to list some startling facts about music videos. His opening sentence makes a surprising statement that is likely to grab the attention of most readers— "What could be so terrible?" a reader will wonder. The Tar Baby image appeals to the reader's visual sense and prods his or her mind to figure out the metaphor. The facts that follow continue to rouse the reader's curiosity. Zorn's concluding paragraph, "I wonder how many of us are really ready for that?," takes a chance because the question could be answered positively (a response Zorn does not want). But if, like Zorn, you feel confident you have made a persuasive case, a rhetorical question can be an effective way to conclude the essay.

Throughout the argumentative/persuasive essay, especially one written for a college assignment, you should strive for a reasonable, calm tone. Strong feelings are necessarily present at the birth of your paper, but writing several drafts will help you control those emotions. You do not want to alienate your reader with unsupported or irrational generalizations written in prose that keeps slipping into tears, sentimentality, or fury. For the most part, the professional writers collected here have kept their language under control while retaining an emotional commitment to their subjects. You will, no doubt, find some of their essays more convincing than others; this is understandable since they were written for a variety of purposes and audiences. Each writer, however (with the exception of the authors of the poem and short story), follows the general strategy of argumentation outlined above by taking a clear position on one side of an issue and arguing it effectively, using appeals both to reason and to emotion, by taking opposing arguments into consideration, by being aware of audience, and, finally, by controlling tone. Ultimately, all writers of argumentative essays have a common overall purpose—to persuade us that their opinion on a controversial issue should become our own.

Frederick A. King
ANIMALS IN RESEARCH: THE CASE FOR EXPERIMENTATION

★ ★ ★

As the introduction to this chapter suggests, in evaluating arguments we must be aware of a writer's expertise and biases. Frederick A. King is undoubtedly an expert in the field of animal research. After earning his B.A. at Stanford, King earned an M.A. and Ph.D. in psychology from Johns Hopkins. He has taught psychiatry, neurosurgery, and physiology at Ohio State, the University of Florida, and at Emory University in Atlanta, where he is currently director of the Yerkes Primate Center, professor of anatomy, and associate dean of the medical school. Thus King has had a lifelong involvement with animal research and experimentation. As informed and critical readers, we must keep that fact in mind when reading his argument.

In "Animals in Research: The Case for Experimentation," first published in Psychology Today *(September 1984), King uses research findings and facts to support his assertions. As in all ethical debates, however, whether we agree or disagree comes down to personal values. Should animals have the same rights as humans? Do the human benefits outweigh an animal's possible pain or death?*

The Mobilization for Animals Coalition (MFA) is an international network of more than 400 animal-protectionist organizations that address themselves to a variety of issues, including hunting, trapping, livestock protection, vegetarianism and pets. Their primary concern, however, is an adamant opposition to animal research. Some groups within the movement want to severely curtail research with animals, but the most visible and outspoken faction wants to eliminate it.

The astonishing growth of this activist movement during the past three years has culminated this year in an intense attack on the use of animals in psychological research. This past spring, John McArdle of the Humane Society of the United States charged that torture is the founding principle and fundamental characteristic of experimental psychology, and that psychological experimentation on animals among all the scientific disciplines is "the ideal candidate for elimination. No major scientific endeavor would suffer by such an act." A recent pamphlet published by the MFA stated, "Of all these experiments, those conducted in psychology are the most painful, pointless and repulsive."

The following specific allegations have been made by the MFA: Animals are given intense, repeated electric shocks until they lose the ability even to scream in pain; animals are deprived of food and water and allowed to suffer and die from hunger and thirst; animals are put in isolation until they are driven insane or die from despair and terror; animals are subjected to crushing forces that smash their bones and rupture their internal organs; the limbs of animals are mutilated or amputated to produce behavioral changes; animals are the victims of extreme pain and stress, inflicted out of idle curiosity, in nightmarish experiments designed to make healthy animals psychotic.

Such irresponsible accusations of research cruelty have consistently characterized the publications of the MFA. However, a recent study by psychologists D. Caroline Coile and Neal E. Miller of Rockefeller University counters these charges. Coile and Miller looked at every article (a total of 608) appearing in the past five years in journals of the American Psychological Association that report animal research. They concluded that none of the extreme allegations made by the MFA could be supported.

Coile and Miller admit that charges of cruelty may have gone unreported or been reported elsewhere but, they say, if such studies did occur, "they certainly were infrequent, and it is extremely misleading to imply that they are typical of experimental psychology."

Furthermore, there are standards and mechanisms to ensure that research animals are treated in a humane and scientifically sensible way. These mechanisms include the Federal Animal Welfare Act of 1966 (amended in Congress in 1970, 1976 and 1979); periodic inspection of all animal-research facilities by the Department of Agriculture; visits by federal agencies that fund animal research and are increasingly attentive to the conditions of animal care and experimental procedures that could cause pain or distress; and a comprehensive document, "Guide for the Care and Use of Laboratory Animals," prepared by the National Academy of Sciences. In addition, virtually every major scientific society whose members conduct animal research distributes guidelines for such research. Above and beyond all of this, most universities and research institutes have animal-care committees that monitor animal research and care.

The United States Public Health Service is revising its guidelines to require institutions that do research with animals to designate even clearer lines of authority and responsibility for animal care. This will include detailed information about how each institution complies with the new regulations as well as a requirement that animal-research committees include not only the supervising laboratory veterinarian and scientists but also a nonscientist and a person not affiliated with the institution. These committees will review programs for animal care, inspect all animal facilities and review and monitor all research proposals before they are submitted to agencies of the United States Public Health Service. The committees will also have the power to disapprove or terminate any research proposal.

This is not to say that research scientists are perfect. There will be occasional errors, cases of neglect and instances of abuse—as is the case with any human endeavor, whether it be the rearing of children, the practicing of a trade or profession or the governing of a nation. But a high standard of humane treatment is maintained.

The choice of psychological research for special attack almost certainly stems from the fact that such research is viewed as more vulnerable than are studies of anatomy, physiology or microbiology. In the minds of many, psychology is a less well-developed science than the biological sciences and the benefits that have accrued from psychological research with animals are less well known. Hence, it is more difficult to grasp the necessity for animal research in behavioral studies than it is in biomedical studies.

Anyone who has looked into the matter can scarcely deny that major advances in medicine have been achieved through basic research with animals. Among these are the development of virtually all modern vaccines against infectious diseases, the invention of surgical approaches to eye disorders, bone and joint injuries and heart disease, the discovery of insulin and other hormones and the testing of all new drugs and antibiotics.

The benefits to humans of psychological research with animals may be less well known than those of medical research but are just as real. Historically, the application of psychological research to human problems has lagged considerably behind the applied use of medical research. Mental events and overt behavior, although controlled by the nervous system and biology of an organism, are much more difficult to describe and study than are the actions of tissues or organ systems. To describe the complex interplay of perceptions, memories, cognitive and emotional processes with a physical and social environment that changes from moment to moment, elaborate research designs had to be developed. Since even a single type of behavior, such as vocalization, has so many different forms, a wide variety of ways of measuring the differences had to be developed. Finally, because much psychological research makes inferences from behavioral observations about internal states of an organism, methods were needed to insure that the interpretations were valid. Such complexities do not make the study of animal or human behavior less scientific or important than other kinds of research, but they do make it more difficult and slow its readiness for clinical applications.

Basic psychological research with animals has led to important achievements in the interest of human welfare. Examples include the use of biofeedback, which had its origin in studies of behavioral conditioning of neuromuscular activities in rats and other animals. Today, biofeedback can be used to control blood pressure and hypertension and help prevent heart attacks. In the case of paralyzed patients, it can be used to elevate blood pressure, enabling those who would otherwise have to spend their lives lying down to sit upright. Biofeedback techniques also are used in the reduction and control of severe pain and as a method of neuromuscular control to help reverse the process of scoliosis, a disabling and disfiguring curvature of the spine. Biofeedback can also be a cost-effective alternative to certain medical treatments and can help avoid many of the complications associated with long-term drug use.

Language studies with apes have led to practical methods of teaching language skills to severely retarded children who, prior to this work, had little or no language ability. Patients who have undergone radiation therapy for cancer can now take an interest in nutritious foods and avoid foods that have little nutritional value, thanks to studies of conditioned taste aversion done with animals. Neural and behavioral studies of early development of vision in cats and primates—studies that could not have been carried out with children—have led to advances in pediatric ophthalmology that can prevent irreversible brain damage and loss of vision in children who have cataracts and various other serious eye problems.

Behavioral modification and behavioral therapy, widely accepted techniques for treating alcohol, drug and tobacco addiction, have a long history of animal studies investigating learning theory and reward systems. Programmed instruction, the application of learning principles to educational tasks, is based on an array of learning studies in animals. These are but a few examples of the effectiveness and usefulness for humans of psychological research with animals.

Those opposed to animal research have proposed that alternatives to animal research, such as mathematical and computer models and tissue cultures, be used. In some cases, these alternatives are both feasible and valuable. Tissue cultures, for example, have been very effective in certain toxicological studies that formerly required live animals. For psychological studies, however, it is often necessary to study the whole animal and its relationship to the environment. Visual problems, abnormal sexual behavior, depression and aggression, for example, are not seen in tissue cultures and do not lend themselves to computer models. When human subjects cannot be used for such studies, animals are necessary if the research is to be done at all.

Extremists within the animal-rights movement take the position that animals have rights equal to or greater than those of humans. It follows from this that even if humans might benefit from animal research, the cost to animals is too high. It is ironic that despite this moral position, the same organizations condone—and indeed sponsor—activities that appear to violate the basic rights of animals to live and reproduce. Each year 10,000,000 dogs are destroyed by public pounds, animal shelters and humane societies. Many of these programs are supported and even operated by animal-protectionist groups. Surely there is a strong contradiction when those who profess to believe in animal rights deny animals their right to life. A similar situation exists with regard to programs of pet sterilization, programs that deny animals the right to breed and to bear offspring and are sponsored in many cases by antivivisectionists and animal-rights groups. Evidently, animal-rights advocates sometimes recognize and subscribe to the position that animals do not have the same rights as humans. However, their public posture leaves little room for examining these subtleties or applying similar standards to animal research.

Within the animal-protectionist movement there are moderates who have confidence in scientists as compassionate human beings and in the value of research. Their primary aims are to insure that animals are treated humanely and that discomfort in animal experimentation is kept to a minimum. It is to this group that scientists and scientific organizations have the responsibility to explain what they do, why and how they do it and what benefits occur.

I believe that the values guiding contemporary animal research represent prevailing sentiment within the scientific community and, indeed, within society at large. And I believe that these values are congruent with those of the moderates within the animal-protectionist movement. As articulated by ethicist Arthur Caplan, rights, in the most realistic sense, are granted by one group to another based on perceived similarities between the groups. Plainly, animals lack those characteristics that would allow them to share in the rights we grant to humans. We do not grant domestic animals the right to go where they wish or do what they want because they are obviously unable to comprehend the responsibilities and demands of human society. In fact, we do not as a society even grant all domestic animals and pets the right to live.

This does not mean, however, that we do not have a moral responsibility to animals. I believe, along with Caplan and the scientific research community at large, that we hold a moral stewardship for animals and that we are obliged to treat them with humane compassion and concern for their sentience. Many animal forms can and do feel pain and are highly aware of their environment. This awareness makes them worthy of our respect and serious concern. Caplan is certainly correct when he says that this moral obligation ought to be part of what it means to be a scientist today.

Science must proceed. The objective quest for knowledge is a treasured enterprise of our heritage and culture. Scientific inquiry into the nature of our living world has freed us from ignorance and superstition. Scientific understanding is an expression of our highest capacities—those of objective observation, interpretive reasoning, imagination and creativity. Founded on the results of basic research, often conducted with no goal other than that of increased understanding, the eventual practical use of this knowledge has led to a vastly improved well-being for humankind.

Extremists in the animal-rights movement probably will never accept such justifications for research or assurances of humane treatment. They may reject any actions, no matter how conscientious, that scientists take in realistically and morally reconciling the advance of human welfare with the use of animals. But, fortunately, there are many who, while deeply and appropriately concerned for the compassionate treatment of animals, recognize that human welfare is and should be our primary concern.

QUESTIONS

1. What is King's reaction to the opposition's accusations? How does he begin to refute them? Later in the essay, how does King counter the attack on his field?

2. What safeguards does King argue are taken in animal research? Does this line of defense imply that there have been abuses? Explain. What concession does King make in paragraph eight?

3. How does King defend the use of animals in research? Do you find his case persuasive? Why, according to him, are the alternatives to animal research inadequate?

4. Why doesn't King begin arguing for animal experimentation at the beginning of his essay? Is he using the "straw man" technique? Does it work?

5. What appeals to emotion does this scientist use in his argument?

6. What tone does King try to achieve throughout the essay? How does he want the reader to view him? What picture of King, and of scientists in general, do we get from the final two paragraphs, and from the essay as a whole?

SUGGESTION FOR WRITING

After doing some research, write a rebuttal to King's essay. Use any of the above questions to suggest areas of vulnerability in King's argument. You should use his essay to help you structure your response.

Art Buchwald
YOU'LL LOVE THIS BOMB
★ ★ ★

Syndicated in over 500 newspapers throughout the world, Art Buchwald's columns satirize many aspects of American life, but his special target is politicians. Buchwald left high school and then college without graduating from either, and went to Europe, where in fourteen years of writing for the Paris edition of the New York Herald Tribune *he mastered the form which would make him so popular: the short, humorous, yet barbed exposé. His writing evokes the satires of Jonathan Swift and Mark Twain, the populist simplicity of Will Rogers, and the Jewish humor and political wit of Sam Levinson and Mort Sahl. The titles of some of Buchwald's books published since he moved to Washington, D.C. in 1962 reveal his range of subjects and his irreverent sense of humor:* Son of the Great Society *(1966),* Getting High in Government Circles *(1971),* I Am Not a Crook *(1974),* The Buchwald Stops Here *(1978), and, most recently,* While Reagan Slept *(1983), which includes "You'll Love This Bomb." In this piece, reminiscent of Swift's eighteenth-century essay "A Modest Proposal," which "modestly" suggests solving Ireland's food and overpopulation problems by using Irish babies as food, Buchwald argues* for *the neutron bomb. Or is that* against?

Despite constant assurances of people very high in the government, there are still some skeptics in this country and Western Europe who are not sold on the argument that we need to build a neutron bomb. The fact of the matter is that the United States not only *needs* it—but it is inconceivable that we could ever have lived without it.

The neutron bomb is the greatest thing to come along since sliced bread. When set off it produces high levels of radiation, cooking people, but leaving structures and buildings standing. Unlike present atomic weapons where blast and heat do most of the damage, the neutron bomb actually penetrates its target, frying anyone inside.

The same people who are always standing in the way of progress are asking, "Why do we need a neutron bomb?"

The question doesn't deserve a response, but I'll give one anyway. We need one if we hope to fight an integrated war on foreign soil.

The United States military's new strategy is to prepare itself for conventional nuclear and chemical war battles. Because the Soviets outnumber the NATO forces, the neutron bomb will give us the parity we need to deter the Russians from attacking the West.

You would think the Europeans would be overjoyed that we were going ahead with an enhanced bomb which might kill them but preserve all their beautiful palaces and churches.

The reaction has been just the opposite. Instead of saying, "Thank you, Uncle Sam," they have told us to stuff our neutron bombs in the ground.

I say if that's the way they feel about it, we should keep our bombs in Utah and see what kind of conventional nuclear war they can fight without them. If they want to use the second-rate, low-yield atomic weapons they now have at their disposal, good luck to them.

But when they start crying for the high-yield mini-nukes that can really do a man's job, we'll remind them of the fuss they made when we offered to place the neutron weapon on their soil.

The point that opponents keep missing is that we are not building a bomb to start a war, but to stop one. If the Soviets know we have a neutron bomb ready, they're not going to attack the West, unless, of course, they have a neutron bomb of their own.

By this time, we should have our laser death beam weapon in production, which will deter the Soviets from starting anything with their enhanced weapons.

In the arms war, the trick is always to stay one step ahead of the other guy.

I don't want anyone to get the idea that the neutron bomb is our ultimate weapon, and that we can relax after we get enough stockpiled. The bomb, for all its publicity, is just a nice little option a field commander has at his disposal when the going gets tough. It's not the end-all for killing large segments of the population, but if we can save pieces of valuable real estate from being destroyed, it will pay for itself in no time at all.

QUESTIONS

1. Is Buchwald a supporter or an opponent of the neutron bomb? How do you know?

2. Find examples of military or defense department jargon. How does Buchwald use this language for his own purposes?

3. How would you characterize Buchwald's tone in this essay?

SUGGESTION FOR WRITING

Think of a fairly serious issue about which you have strong feelings (you might look at a newspaper or listen to the news to get ideas for subjects if necessary.) Censorship of rock lyrics, prayer in the public schools, budget cuts affecting student loans, nuclear weapons, and abortion are all possibilities. Decide what your position is on one of these issues and then write a short essay arguing in support of your point of view by *pretending* to support the other side, as Buchwald has done. Make the position of the other side seem ridiculous, unjust, petty, inhumane, or un-American through the arguments you advance in its favor. (You need not worry about "playing fair" here; your purpose is to convince readers to adopt beliefs opposed to what you ostensibly are advocating.) For this essay, brainstorming would be an especially effective prewriting technique.

Eric Zorn
MEMORIES AREN'T MADE OF THIS
★ ★ ★

Currently a writer on the metropolitan desk of the Chicago Tribune, *Eric Zorn was born in 1958 in New Haven, Connecticut. He came to the paper after graduating from the University of Michigan in 1980. Zorn's provocative essay attacking rock videos, "Memories Aren't Made of This"* reflects his own love of music; he plays the violin, banjo, and guitar. "One of the truly great but least understood components of music," he writes, "is the way it can tap long-forgotten emotions and unlock unconscious memories." Rock videos, he argues, short-circuit that connection. If you are a member of the MTV generation, you can measure Zorn's arguments against your own experiences.*

Something terrible has happened to popular music in this country. Over the last few years it has touched its finger to the Tar Baby of television and now finds itself unable to pull away. Consider the following depressing news:

★   There are 200 regular television programs in America that feature nothing but the combination of film clips and rock songs.

★   Warner Amex's Music Television (MTV), the cable network based solely on these music videos, hits nearly 20 million homes and is the hottest basic cable operation in history.

★   The marriage of music and television has proved to be so popular that it is credited with almost singlehandedly snapping the recording industry out of a four-year slump in 1983 and changing the face of popular music by introducing the new bands and new sounds radio wouldn't touch.

★ Today's pop-music groups find that they must produce video versions of their songs if they wish to survive. Many are making video-cassette albums that customers buy instead of records.

★ Really cool people now speak of "seeing" the latest songs as opposed to hearing them. More than a majority of MTV viewers recently sampled say they "play back" the video in their minds when they hear a song on the radio.

This all indicates strongly that music videos are no passing fad. They're here to stay, just like TV itself when it first came along in the late 1940s to add pictures to the old radio dramas.

I find this all terribly sad. The proliferation of music videos threatens to produce an entire generation of people who will all but miss out on the sublime, extremely personal element of music.

What nobody has bothered to point out in the course of all this hoopla attendant upon rock video is that music has always had a visual element of a sort: the images, people and places that the listener sees in his mind's eye when a favorite song or symphony comes on.

One of the truly great but least understood components of music is the way it can tap long-forgotten emotions and unlock unconscious memories. Many feelings and old visual impressions are so deeply hidden in the recesses of the mind that sometimes only the sudden surprise of a melody can lead the way to them.

Special songs can act for us like the tea and madeleine cake in Marcel Proust's huge novel, "A Remembrance of Things Past," as a simple spark that sets off a blaze of recollections.

"Mr. Tambourine Man" by Bob Dylan brings back the long walks my best buddy and I used to take on the beach near his mom's cottage on Cape Cod; "Mrs. Robinson" by Simon and Garfunkel conjures up the kitchen in the first house my parents ever owned; "Amie" by Pure Prairie League reminds me of springtime in the old college dormitory and my first train trip to Chicago.

When I hear someone fiddle "Lamplighter's Hornpipe," I think of a particular section of Altgeld Street near DePaul University where I first heard that tune on tape; and "Seasons in the Sun" by Terry Jacks, a terrible song, brings on the delightful memory of a young woman named Martine for whom I yearned so tragically in 11th grade I could scarcely move myself to speak to her.

For Martine, wherever she is, it is safe to say "Seasons in the Sun" has entirely different associations. That's the great thing about music. No matter how many millions of people bought that record or heard it on the radio, there will always be something about its smarmy lyrics that will be special only to me.

Not every song still has this power, however. I've already had a few of them ruined when, in idle moments, I have lingered too long in front of a TV set showing music videos. When, for example, I hear Michael Jackson's "Billie Jean," the first, overwhelming image I get in my mind is of the lithe little Mr. Jackson capering around and pointing his lithe little finger every which way. No good memories. No bad memories. Nothing but the exact same memories that everyone else will have of this song for decades to come.

Who can hear "Suicide Is Painless," the theme song from "M*A*S*H," and think of anything else but helicopters? Who can hear "Yellow Submarine" by the Beatles and not be flooded with thoughts of the brightly colored Peter Max cartoons that splashed through the movie of the same name?

Antiseptic Music: What we're really talking about here is the wholesale substitution of common, shared memories for individual memories; a substitution that ends up robbing us of pieces of our own lives. The personal side of music is steadily being replaced by the corporate side, so that the associations and mental pictures that go along with songs for the MTV generation don't relate to *their* lives, but to the lives of the people who conceived the videos.

We're left with popular music that has the same distant, antiseptic feel as network television: you may enjoy it, but you must admit that it doesn't, in any meaningful way, feel as though it *belongs* to you. The combination of sight and sound not only promotes passive viewing, but serves to depersonalize the entertainment offered.

Young lovers today, I suspect, do not elbow each other excitedly when an old Duran Duran clip comes on the TV screen and coo, "Look, darling, they're showing our video."

And that's depressing news: future generations will be locked into the prefabricated memories of a false musical experience, restricted by monolithic visual interpretations of songs that pre-empt and defy the exercise of individual experience, motion and memory.

Videos will not be the death of pop music, radio or the old rock groups that never thought to film themselves moving their lips to the words. But ultimately the insidious combination of film and song will sap away some of the great power of music and change how we feel about it in a very fundamental way.

I wonder how many of us are really ready for that?

QUESTIONS

1. What does Zorn accomplish by introducing so many facts about music videos early in his essay?

2. Zorn argues that music can "tap long-forgotten emotions and unlock unconscious memories." What anecdotes and examples does he use to support this point? Are they convincing?

3. This essay raises questions about the value of "common, shared memories," when those memories, instead of arising out of personal experience, are manufactured for a mass audience. Does he convince you that such memories are destructive?

4. To what audience is Zorn appealing? You might find clues in his choice of song titles and in language such as "young lovers today."

5. How is language used to persuade? Do the words "terrible" and "depressing," for example, which appear in the first paragraph, predispose the reader to accept Zorn's judgment?

6. Does Zorn use any of the classic argument/persuasion strategies described in the introduction? Which ones?

SUGGESTION FOR WRITING

Use prewriting techniques such as free-association, listing, and free-writing to help you think of something that is different now from what it was when you were growing up. Following Zorn's model, explain what the loss means—to you individually and/or to America generally—and persuade someone younger than you that he/she will be missing something significant.

John Simon
PLAYING TENNIS WITHOUT A NET
★ ★ ★

Born in Yugoslavia in 1925 and educated at Harvard (B.A. 1946, M.A. 1948, Ph.D. in English, 1959), John Simon has built a reputation as one of America's foremost cultural critics. After a brief career teaching literature and humanities at Harvard, MIT, and Bard College, Simon turned to writing theater and film criticism for publications like the Hudson Review, Commonweal, Esquire, *and* New York. *He is widely known as a learned, witty, and occasionally merciless critic who can, in a review, sink a Broadway show or a fledgling career with one torpedo-like phrase. "He is as absolute and arrogant in his judgments as any dictator of culture," as one critic describes him, possessing "a rigidity that is his great strength and weakness." Simon is particularly sensitive to lapses in standard English usage, and as "Playing Tennis Without a Net" reveals, he becomes angry when our language is tampered with, especially when the tamperers are English teachers.*

This essay was included in Paradigm's Lost: Reflections on Literacy and Its Decline *(1980), a collection of Simon's work.*

The National Council of Teachers of English is about to debate once again at its 1979 annual meeting in New York a resolution passed in a 1974 business meeting of the Conference on College Composition and Communication that accepted as valid "all the regional, ethnic, and social dialects of American English." The C.C.C.C. voted, in other words, to make acceptable in schools and colleges any kind of English that until recently was called substandard, although the N.C.T.E. then added an equivocal codicil stating that there was "a distinction between spoken and written English." The document justifying this resolution is a special issue of the journal *College Composition and Communication* entitled "Students' Right to Their Own Language."

The first and most obvious flaw in all this is the N.C.T.E.'s jesuitical assumption that one can differentiate between spoken and written English—that one can tell students that "I be baaad" (meaning "I am good") is acceptable when spoken but inadequate when written. There is enough schizophrenia on the rampage in the world without nurturing further forms of it in the classroom. But the very ideas behind the resolution and the brochure that is meant to proselytize for them strike me as not a little absurd and, ultimately, pernicious.

The committee to which we owe the C.C.C.C. language statement consists of a baker's dozen of academics, apparently carefully chosen to represent both renowned and obscure institutions and to include women, blacks, Hispanics, and teachers at community colleges. Nothing could be more democratic. In the introduction to the eighteen-page double-column statement, the committee permits itself a rare irony: "Lack of reliable information . . . seldom prevents people from discussing language questions with an air of absolute authority." To prove their own authoritativeness, the committee members helped one of their number, Jenefer Giannasi (whose Christian name reads rather as if she didn't know how to spell it), compile a thirteen-page single-column bibliography, containing mostly items on sociolinguistics, descriptive linguistics, and such—my favorite being "Davis, Philip W.: *Modern Theories of Language,*" which deals with "the theories of Saussure, Hjelmslev, Bloomfield, the Post-Bloomfieldians, and the Prague School; tagmemics; Firthian linguistics; stratificational grammar; transformational generative grammar." Nevertheless, Miss Giannasi and her colleagues write things like "a controversy which must be faced before staff can react to students' needs," which is rather like what you hear from medical receptionists: "Doctor will see you now." Clearly, there are cases where neither Bloomfield nor the Post-Bloomfieldians, to say nothing of tagmemics, prove to be of much help.

But right at the beginning, our committee commits an error in logic that is considerable for such valiant structural linguists. The committee bemoans the fact that all kinds of people—"businessmen, politicians, parents, and the students themselves"—insist "that the values taught by the schools must reflect the prejudices held by the public." It soon becomes apparent that what these people want and agitate for through their representatives on various boards is nothing more or less than what has generally been called Standard English, which the committee prefers to call edited written English or edited American English (E.A.E.). In its democratic, pluralistic zeal, the committee obviously reprehends what I am still quite happy to call Standard English for being "Anglo" and ignoring, indeed affronting, the customs and needs of "the people," many of whom belong to black, Latin-American, or other ethnic groups. Yet, clearly, businessmen, politicians, parents, and students themselves (not to mention the historians, mathematicians, and nurses adduced earlier in the pamphlet) include a lot of people, probably at least as many as there are members of various ethnic groups. Why then should *their* traditions and demands be ignored?

The point, of course, is that everyone has a right to his ignorance and no one is compelled to become educated. But everyone is then also entitled to suffer the consequences of choosing not to become educated. This is very different, needless to say, from having been discouraged from becoming educated or from, worse yet, having been deliberately prevented from so becoming. But when I read our supposed educators' statement that "we need to discover whether our attitudes toward 'educated English' are based on some inherent superiority of the dialect itself or on the social prestige of those who use it," I begin to despair. Could anything be sadder than the fact that those quotation marks around educated English come from the pen of an educator—someone who ought to be proud of the fact that generations of educators have labored to evolve and codify that English? Yet now the C.C.C.C.'ers act as if there were something fishy and indecent about all this, something to condescend to with quotation marks, because, as they later put it, it is merely the dialect of the middle class. The poor old middle class, by the way, gets it coming and going. After centuries of kicks from above, it can now look forward to centuries of kicks from below.

And we read on: "We need to ask ourselves whether our rejection of students who do not adopt the dialect most familiar to us is based on any real merit in our dialect or whether we are actually rejecting the students themselves, rejecting them because of their racial, social, and cultural origins." Not only is ignorance going to be defended on the sacred ground of the right to nonconformity, but also it will be upheld on the still more sacred grounds of antiracism and antielitism. Under the circumstances, it is not surprising to find our committee arguing forthwith that "Mary daddy home" is just as comprehensible and good as "Mary's daddy is at home" and that "the grammar of one American dialect may require 'he is' in the third person singular present tense; the grammar of another dialect may require 'he be' in that slot."

Of course, what is the use of arguing with English teachers who pronounce "Mary daddy home" equally clear as "Mary's daddy is at home"? The former concatenation of words (it would be preposterous to call it a construction) could just as easily mean "the home of Mary's daddy" or "Mary's daddy has gone home" or "Mary and daddy are at home" or God only knows what else. (Or perhaps I should write "Don't nobody but God know that," which our authors find "just as clear" and "in certain circumstances [unspecified] more emphatic.") It may be true that we can gradually figure out from the context what was meant, but why should we have to make such an effort? And suppose the speaker were trying to discuss more complicated matters with that kind of grammar. Where would *that* conversation lead?

As for "I be," "you be," "he be," etc., which should give us all the heebie-jeebies, these may indeed be comprehensible, but they go against all accepted classical and modern grammars and are the product not of a language with roots in history but of ignorance of how language works. It may be a regrettable ignorance, innocent and touching, one that unjust past social conditions cruelly imposed on people. But it *is* ignorance, and bowing down to it, accepting it as correct and perhaps even better than established usage, is not going to help matters. On the contrary, that way lies chaos. The point is that if you allow this or that departure from traditional grammar, everything becomes permissible—as, indeed, it has become, which is why we are in the present pickle.

Here is what our C.C.C.C.'ers have to say about this: "Once a teacher understands the arbitrary nature of the oral and written forms, the pronunciation or spelling of a word becomes less important than whether it communicates what the student wants to say. In speech. *PO*lice communicates as well as po*LICE,* and in writing, 'pollice' is no insurmountable barrier to communication, although all three variations might momentarily distract a person unfamiliar with the variant." One difficulty with addressing oneself thoroughly to the absurdity of this pamphlet is that where every sentence, like the above, pullulates with logical and moral errors, one doesn't know where to begin with a rebuttal.

To start with, what does the crucial but glided-over term "less important" mean to the committee? Should pronunciation and spelling mistakes be ignored entirely? Almost entirely? On alternate Tuesdays only? Should they be punished with merely one stroke of the ferule, as opposed to two for physical assault on the teacher? Furthermore, why should people have to be distracted even momentarily by having to figure out what other people are saying? There are situations in which these could cause serious damage. But, above all, language is not just a matter of communication. It is a way of expressing one's fastidiousness, elegance, and imaginativeness; it is also a way of displaying one's control over a medium, just as a fine horseman displays his horsemanship by the way he sits in the saddle and handles his horse. Even a person who desperately hangs on to the mane of his mount might make it from point A to point B, but that doesn't make him an equestrian.

The basic contradiction in which the committee wallows is this: on the one hand, we are told that blacks and Chicanos and other minorities cannot be expected to know and speak the "dialect" of the established "Anglo" middle class and that we must have sympathy and respect for their dialects; on the other hand, we are told that these youngsters are just as bright as anybody else and can learn correct E.A.E. as easily as anyone. I am willing to give credence to either of these assertions, but I find it difficult to accept *both.* Thus we find our C.C.C.C.'ers declaring on page 7 that "dialect itself is not an impediment to reading" and "cannot be posited as a reason for a student's failure to be able to read E.A.E." But on page 12 we read: "Standardized tests depend on verbal fluency, both in reading the directions and in giving the answers, so even slight variations in dialect may penalize students by slowing them down." Well now, which will it be?

Again, we are told on page 6 that "dialect switching . . . becomes progressively more difficult as the speaker grows older." But on page 16 we read that "it is unreasonable for teachers to insist that students make phonemic shifts, which we as adults have difficulty in making." Well, if it's so much easier for young people to learn, why can't their elders expect them to do so? It is, however, useless to expect anything resembling logic from people who could write the following: "All languages are the product of the same instrument, namely, the human brain. It follows, then, that all languages and all dialects are essentially the same in their deep structure, regardless of how varied the surface structure might be. [This is equal to saying that the human brain is the human brain.]" And with this, the committee thinks that it has proved that all dialects are equally good.

But they are not—just as all human brains are not equally good, a simple fact that in their democratic, egalitarian frenzy the C.C.C.C.'ers cannot admit. Indeed, they will go so far as to assert that "if speakers of a great variety of American dialects do master E.A.E.—from Senator Sam Ervin to Senator Edward Kennedy, from Ernest Hemingway to William Faulkner—there is no reason to assume that dialects such as urban black and Chicano impede the child's ability to learn to write E.A.E. while countless others do not." Notice the choice of people of outstanding intellectual gifts or at least of privileged background from earliest childhood: these are not typical cases and so prove nothing. And just as individual situations vary, so do the circumstances behind dialects. For instance, the kinds of English that blacks and Chicanos speak are based on underlying thought structures that are not native and idiomatic but derived from African languages and from Spanish—and not the best Spanish at that—and so are not germane to the English language at all.

The disingenuousness of the committee is downright insidious. It argues that "just as most Americans added 'sputnik' to their vocabularies a decade or more ago, so speakers of other dialects can add such words as 'periostitis' or 'interosculate' whenever their interests demand it." Consider: "Sputnik" was at that time in every headline, in every news broadcast everywhere. The other two terms will always be abstruse for the average citizen, and "interosculate" is almost ridiculous—no doubt deliberately chosen for that reason.

With similar dishonesty, the committee perceives an analogy between fighting "he be" and "he don't" and the alleged efforts of yesteryear's teachers to prevent accreditation of "jazz," "lariat," and "kosher." But, clearly, there are no more proper ways of saying "lariat" or "jazz" or "kosher," whereas there are such things as "he is" and "he doesn't." In fact, one wonders why people who believe so fanatically in the rights, if not indeed the superiority, of other dialects chose to cast their tract in E.A.E., especially since they are not particularly good at it. They write "alternate approaches" for "alternative approaches"; "because 'Johnny can't read' doesn't mean that Johnny is immature" for "that 'Johnny can't read,' " etc.; "different than" for "different from"; "equally as willing" for "equally willing"; and are capable of writing sentences like "Classroom reading materials can be employed to further our students' reading ability and, at the same time, can familiarize them with other varieties of English." Who would want to familiarize reading materials ("them") with varieties of English? Or take this alleged sentence: "For example, an unfamiliar speech rhythm and resulting pronunciation while ignoring the content of the message." And in the very next sentence (page 4) there is a "they" for which there is no antecedent.

"E.A.E. allows much less variety than the spoken forms," the C.C.C.C.'ers pronounce. But that is just the point: to speak correctly yet with individualism and variety is, to adapt Frost's old trope, to play a good game of tennis with the net up; without a net, anyone can perform all kinds of meaningless prodigies. In any case, the point of language is not simply to communicate but to communicate with originality and imaginativeness—within the bounds of propriety. Otherwise, as Stéphane Mallarmé so wisely observed, "it might suffice by way of exchanging human thought to take or put into another's hand silently a coin." When language becomes a mere convenience, like the mute passing of money from hand to hand, it ceases to have any aesthetic or, indeed, humanistic value. And when accepted language begins to model itself on what a culturally underprivileged group or individual says, it becomes a parochialism. This is the very opposite of an ecumenical language, which is perhaps difficult to master, but which, once mastered, unites all its initiates in a common pursuit and a shared beauty.

QUESTIONS

1. Can you determine what Simon is attacking in the third paragraph? To what extent is this an *ad hominem* (an attack on the person, and not the case) argument?

2. Discuss the committee's "error in logic" that Simon notes in paragraph four. To what point is Simon leading?

3. Using examples from the essay, characterize Simon's attitude toward correct grammar and usage. What is the view of the committee on matters of correctness? With which position do you most agree?

4. What is Simon's final point about language? What does he mean by contrasting "parochialism" and "ecumenical"?

5. In what ways is Simon's own language use—grammar and vocabulary—a model of standard English? Make a list of words you may not know ("jesuitical," "reprehends," "pullulates") and look them up.

6. Is it a useful strategy on Simon's part to criticize the correctness of the committee's written English? Does he go too far in his contempt for the opposition, or does his obvious emotion help his case?

7. Simon structures his essay and bases his arguments on a reading of the committee's pamphlet. Does he quote enough to be convincing, or would you rather read the entire pamphlet before judging the issue?

SUGGESTIONS FOR WRITING

1. Find a copy of the pamphlet Simon refers to (the special issue of *College Composition and Communication* will probably be in your college library), and write a brief essay evaluating the fairness of Simon's representation.

2. Find a piece of writing (an essay, a letter to the editor, an editorial, a movie or book review) with which you strongly disagree and write a critique of it, much as Simon has done. Write at least two drafts. In the first, let your negative feelings flow freely. In the second, try for a more balanced critique.

Harry Edwards
EDUCATING BLACK ATHLETES
★ ★ ★

Considered the founder of the academic field of sports sociology, Harry Edwards was born in St. Louis in 1942. According to his autobiography, The Struggle That Must Be *(1981), his ghetto upbringing initiated a lifelong commitment to making America a better place to live for all its citizens. After earning his B.A. at San Jose State University, Edwards was courted intensely by several professional football teams. He chose, instead, to attend Cornell University as a Woodrow Wilson Fellow, where he earned his M.A. (1966) and Ph.D. (1972) in sociology. He has written six books, including* Sociology of Sport *(1973) and* Playing to Win: A Short Guide to Sensible Black Sports Participation *(1982), and over a hundred articles and reviews.*

Edwards, a teacher at the University of California at Berkeley and a social activist, takes an extremely controversial stand in his article "Educating Black Athletes," first published in The Atlantic Monthly *in 1983. His support of the NCAA Rule 48, which would set a minimum Scholastic Aptitude Test score for college athletes, places him in opposition to most other black leaders and educators.*

For decades, student athletes, usually seventeen-to-nineteen-year-old freshmen, have informally agreed to a contract with the universities they attend: athletic performance in exchange for an education. The athletes have kept their part of the bargain; the universities have not. Universities and athletic departments have gained huge gate receipts, television revenues, national visibility, donors to university programs, and more, as a result of the performances of gifted basketball and football players, of whom a disproportionate number of the most gifted and most exploited have been black.

While blacks are not the only student athletes exploited, the abuses usually happen to them first and worst. To understand why, we must understand sports' impact upon black society: how popular beliefs that blacks are innately superior athletes, and that sports are "inherently" beneficial, combine with the life circumstances of young blacks, and with the aspirations of black student athletes, to make those students especially vulnerable to victimization.

Sports at all levels are widely believed to have achieved extraordinary, if not exemplary, advances in the realm of interracial relations since the time when Jackie Robinson became the first black to play major-league baseball. To some extent, this reputation has been deliberately fostered by skilled sports propagandists eager to project "patriotic" views consistent with America's professed ideals of racial justice and equality of opportunity. To a much greater extent, however, this view of sports has been encouraged by observers of the sporting scene who have simply been naive about the dynamics of sports as an institution, about their relationship to society generally, and about the race-related realities of American sports in particular.

Many misconceptions about race and sports can be traced to developments in sports that would appear on the surface to represent significant racial progress. For instance, though blacks constitute only 11.7 percent of the U.S. population, in 1982 more than 55 percent of the players in the National Football League were black, and, in 1981, twenty-four of the twenty-eight first-round NFL draft choices were black. As for the two other major professional team sports, 70 percent of the players making National Basketball Association rosters during the 1982–1983 season, and 80 percent of the starters that same season, were black, while 19 percent of America's major-league baseball players at the beginning of the 1982 season were black.

Black representation on sports honor rolls has been even more disproportionate. For example, the past nine Heisman trophies, awarded each year to the "best" collegiate football player in the land, have gone to blacks. In the final rushing statistics of the 1982 NFL season, thirty-six of the top forty running backs were black. In 1982, not a single white athlete was named to the first team of a major Division I All-American basketball roster. Similarly, twenty-one of the twenty-four athletes selected for the 1982 NBA All-Star game were black. Since 1955, whites have won the NBA's "most valuable player" award only five times, as opposed to twenty-three times for blacks. And, of course, boxing championships in the heavier weight divisions have been dominated by black athletes since the 1960s. But a judicious interpretation of these and related figures points toward conclusions quite different from what one might expect.

Patterns of opportunity for blacks in American sports, like those in the society at large, are shaped by racial discrimination, a phenomenon that explains the disproportionately high number of talented black athletes in certain sports and the utter exclusion of blacks from most other American sports, as well as from decision-making and authority positions in virtually all sports.

Most educated people today accept the idea that the level of black representation and the quality of black performance in sports have no demonstrable relationship to race-linked genetic characteristics. Every study purporting to demonstrate such a relationship has exhibited critical deficiencies in methodological, theoretical, or conceptual design. Moreover, the factors determining the caliber of sports performances are so complex and disparate as to render ludicrous any attempt to trace athletic excellence to a single biological feature.

Thus, despite a popular view that blacks are "natural" athletes, physically superior to athletes from other groups, the evidence tends to support cultural and social—rather than biological—explanations of their athletic success.

Briefly:

—Thanks to the mass media and to long-standing traditions of racial discrimination limiting blacks' access to many high-prestige occupational opportunities, the black athlete is much more visible to black youths than, say, black doctors or black lawyers. Therefore, unlike white children, who see many different potential role models in the media, black children tend to model themselves after, or to admire as symbolically masculine, the black athlete—the one prevalent and positive black success figure they are exposed to regularly, year in and year out, in America's white-dominated mass media.

—The black family and the black community tend to reward athletic achievement much more and earlier than any other activity. This also lures more young blacks into sports-career aspirations than the actual opportunities for sports success would warrant.

—Because most American sports activities are still devoid of any significant black presence, the overwhelming majority of aspiring black athletes emulate established black role models and seek careers in only four or five sports—basketball, football, baseball, boxing, and track. The brutally competitive selection process that ensues eliminates all but the most skilled black athletes by the time they reach the collegiate and advanced-amateur ranks. The competition is made all the more intense because even in these sports, some positions (such as quarterback, center, and middle linebacker in football, and catcher in baseball) are relatively closed to blacks.

—Finally, sports are seen by many black male youths as a means of proving their manhood. This tends to be extraordinarily important to blacks, because the black male in American society has been systematically cut off from mainstream routes of masculine expression, such as economic success, authority positions, and so forth.

Despite the great pool of athletic talent generated in black society, black athletes still get fewer than one in ten of the athletic scholarships given out in the United States. And, at least partially as a result of the emphasis placed upon developing their athletic talents from early childhood, an estimated 25 to 35 percent of male black high school athletes qualifying for athletic scholarships cannot accept those scholarships because of accumulated academic deficiencies. Many of these young men eventually end up in what is called, appropriately enough, the "slave trade"—a nationwide phenomenon involving independent scouts who, for a fee (usually paid by a four-year college), search out talented but academically "high-risk" black athletes and place them in accommodating junior colleges, where their athletic skills are further honed while they earn the grades they need to transfer to the sponsoring four-year schools.

Of those who are eventually awarded collegiate athletic scholarships, studies indicate, as many as 65 to 75 percent may never graduate from college. Of the 25 to 35 percent who do eventually graduate from the schools they play for, an estimated 75 percent graduate either with physical-education degrees or in majors created specifically for athletes and generally held in low repute. The problem with these "jock majors," and increasingly with the physical-education major as well, is that they make poor credentials in the job market. One might assume that ample occupational opportunities would be available to outstanding black former athletes, at least within the sports world. But the reality is quite different. To begin with, the overwhelming majority of black athletes, whether scholarship-holders or professionals, have *no* post-career occupational plans or formal preparation for any type of post-career employment either inside or outside sports. These blacks are unemployed more often, and earn less when they do have jobs, than their non-athletic college peers; they are also likely to switch jobs more often, to hold a wider variety of jobs, and to be less satisfied with the jobs they hold—primarily because the jobs tend to be dull, dead-end, or minimally rewarding.

Few Americans appreciate the extent to which the overwhelming majority of young males seeking affluence and stardom through sports are foredoomed to fail. The three major team sports provide approximately 2,663 jobs for professional athletes, regardless of color, in a nation of 226 million people, roughly half of whom are male. This means that only one American male in about 42,000 is a professional football, basketball, or baseball player.

While the proportion of blacks in professional basketball is 70 percent, in professional football 55 percent, and in professional baseball 19 percent, only about 1,400 black people (up from about 1,100 since the establishment of the United States Football League) are making a living as professional athletes in these three major sports today. And if one adds to this number all the black professional athletes in all other American sports, all the blacks in minor and semi-professional sports leagues, and all the black trainers, coaches, and doctors in professional sports, one sees that fewer than 2,400 black Americans can be said to be making a living in professional athletics today.

This situation, considered in combination with the black athlete's educational underdevelopment, helps explain why so many black athletes not only fail to achieve their expectations of life-long affluence but also frequently fall far short of the levels achieved by their non-athletic peers.

Despite the fact, then, that American basketball, boxing, football, and baseball competitions have come more and more to look like Ghana playing Nigeria, sport continues to loom like a fog-shrouded minefield for the overwhelming majority of black athletes. It has been a treadmill to oblivion rather than the escalator to wealth and glory it was believed to be. The black athlete who blindly sets out today to fill the shoes of Dr. J., Reggie J., Magic J., Kareem Abdul-J., or O.J. may well end up with "No J."—no job that he is qualified to do in our modern, technologically sophisticated society. At the end of his sports career, the black athlete is not likely to be running or flying through airports like O.J. He is much more likely to be sweeping up airports—if he has the good fortune to land even that job.

These are the tragic circumstances that prompted Joe Paterno, 1982 Division I football "Coach of the Year" of the New York Football Writers' Association, to exclaim in January from the floor of the 1983 NCAA convention in San Diego: "For fifteen years we have had a race problem. We have raped a generation and a half of young black athletes. We have taken kids and sold them on bouncing a ball and running with a football and that being able to do certain things athletically was going to be an end in itself. We cannot afford to do that to another generation." With that statement, Coach Paterno gave impetus to the passage of the NCAA's "Rule 48," which set off what is probably the most heated race-related controversy within the NCAA since the onset of widespread racial integration in major-college sports programs during the 1950s and 1960s.

Put most simply, Rule 48 stipulates that, beginning in 1986, freshman athletes who want to participate in sports in any of the nation's 277 Division I colleges and universities must have attained a minimum score of 700 (out of a possible 1,600) on the Scholastic Aptitude Test (SAT) or a score of 15 (out of a possible 36) on the American College Test (ACT), and must have achieved a C average in eleven designated high school courses, including English, mathematics, social sciences, and physical sciences. Further, as *The N.C.A.A. News* reported, Rule 48

> does not interfere with the admissions policies of any Division I institution. Nonqualifiers under this legislation may be admitted and attend class. Such a student could compete as a sophomore if he or she satisfies the satisfactory-progress rules and would have four varsity seasons starting as a sophomore if he or she continues to make satisfactory progress.
>
> Further, under related Proposal No. 49-B, any student who achieves at least 2.0 in all high school courses but does not meet the new terms of No. 48 can receive athletically related financial aid in his or her first year, but cannot practice or compete in intercollegiate athletics. This student would have three varsity years of participation remaining.

The outcry in response to the passage of Rule 48 was immediate. Ironically, the most heated opposition to the rule came from black civil-rights leaders and black college presidents and educators—the very groups one might have expected to be most supportive of the action. Their concern was over those provisions of Rule 48 specifying minimum test scores as a condition for sports participation, particularly the 700 score on the SAT. Leading the black criticism of the NCAA's new academic standards were the National Association For Equal Opportunity in Higher Education (NAFEO), representing 114 traditionally black colleges and universities; the National Alliance of Black School Educators (NABSE); Rev.

Jesse Jackson, president of People United to Serve Humanity (Operation PUSH); Rev. Benjamin Hooks, executive director of the National Association for the Advancement of Colored People (NAACP); and Rev. Joseph Lowery, president of the Southern Christian Leadership Conference (SCLC). They argued, first, that blacks were not consulted in the formulation of Rule 48; second, that the minimum SAT score requirement was arbitrary; and, finally, that the SAT and the ACT are racist diagnostic tests, which reflect a cultural bias favoring whites. They believed that the 700 SAT and 15 ACT score requirements would unfairly penalize black student athletes, given that 55 percent of black students generally score lower than 700 on the SAT and 69 percent score lower than 15 on the ACT. And why would the majority of NCAA Division I institutions vote to support a rule that would reduce participation opportunities for black athletes? For NAFEO and its supporters, the answer was clear. The most outspoken among the critics of Rule 48 was Dr. Jesse N. Stone, Jr., the president of the Southern University System of Louisiana, who said:

> The end result of all this is the black athlete has been too good. If it [Rule 48] is followed to its logical conclusion, we say to our youngsters, "Let the white boy win once in a while." This has set the black athlete back twenty-five or thirty years. The message is that white schools no longer want black athletes.

Members of the American Council on Education (ACE) committee charged with developing Rule 48 vehemently denied claims that no blacks were involved in the process. Whatever the truth of the matter, the majority of black NCAA delegates felt that their interests and views had not been represented.

I could not agree more with NAFEO, Jackson, Hooks, Lowery, *et al.* on their contention that the minimum SAT and ACT test scores are arbitrary. Neither the ACE nor the NCAA has yet provided any reasoned or logical basis for setting the minimum scores. But whereas NAFEO and others say that the scores are arbitrary and too high, I contend that they are arbitrary and so *low* as to constitute virtually no standards at all. I have other, more fundamental disagreements with the NAFEO position.

One need not survey very much literature on the racist abuse of diagnostic testing in this country to appreciate the historical basis of NAFEO's concerns about rigidly applied test standards. But the demand that Rule 48 be repealed on the grounds that its test-score requirements are racist and will unfairly affect blacks is both factually contestable and strategically regrettable. The evidence is overwhelming that the SAT and the ACT discriminate principally on the basis of class, rather than race. The greater discrepancy between black and white scores occurs on the math section of the SAT, where cultural differences between the races logically would have the least impact. Even on the verbal sections of these diagnostic tests, differences in black and white scores are at least partially explained as class-related phenomena. As Dr. Mary Frances Berry, a NAFEO supporter, asserts:

> A major differential [among test scores] was *not* between black and white students, but between students from well-off families and students from poor families. The better-off the family, the higher the score—for whites *and* blacks.

Dr. Norman C. Francis, president of the traditionally black Xavier University of Louisiana and immediate past chairman of the College Board, agrees:

> The SAT is not merely a measure of potential aptitude, as many believe, but is also an achievement test which accurately measures what students have learned to that point. Most students do poorly on the test simply because they have never been taught the concepts that will help them to understand what testing and test-taking is all about. It is an educational disadvantage, not an inability to learn. . . . The plain truth is that students in poorer schools are never taught to deal with word problems and . . . critical analysis. The problem therefore is not with the students, nor with the test, but rather with an educational system which fails to teach youngsters what they need to know.

Rule 48, therefore, involves far more than a simple black-white controversy, as 1981 SAT test statistics bear out. While 49 percent of black male students in 1981 failed to achieve at least a 700 on the combined SAT, as compared with 14 percent of the whites and 27 percent of other minorities, far more whites (31,140) and other minorities (27,145) than blacks (15,330) would have been affected under Rule 48.

Furthermore, between 1981 and 1982, blacks' verbal scores rose nine points and mathematics scores rose four points, compared with a two-point gain in verbal and a one-point gain in math for the white majority.

NAFEO claims that black athletes would have less access to traditionally white Division I institutions in the wake of Rule 48. But even though proportionately more blacks score below Rule 48's minimum-score requirements, it is unlikely that significant numbers of blacks would be deprived of opportunities to attend traditionally white schools on athletic scholarships. Indeed, if the enrollment of black athletes falls off at any Division I schools for this reason, I submit that the schools most likely to suffer will be the traditionally black colleges. NCAA disciplinary records show that traditionally white institutions have led the way in amateur-athletic rules infractions and in exploiting black athletes. Why? Because they have the largest financial investment in their athletic programs, and because they and their athletic personnel stand to reap the greatest rewards from athletic success. With so much at stake, why would schools that for so long have stretched, bent, and broken rules to enroll black athletes no longer want them?

The loopholes in Rule 48 are sufficient to allow any school to recruit any athlete it really wants. Junior colleges are not covered under the rule, so schools could still secure and develop athletes not eligible for freshman sports participation at four-year Division I colleges. Further, Rule 48 allows Division I schools to recruit freshman athletes who are academically ineligible to participate, and even to provide them with financial support. After several meetings with NAFEO representatives, Rev. Jesse Jackson, and others, I am strongly convinced that for many within the ranks of Rule 48's detractors, fiscal rather than educational issues are the priority concern. The overwhelming majority of athletes recruited by traditionally black Division I schools are black, score below Rule 48 minimum-test-score requirements, and tend to need financial support in order to attend college. However, because they have far more modest athletic budgets than traditionally white schools, traditionally black schools are not nearly so able to provide financial support for both a roster of active athletes and a long roster of newly recruited athletes ineligible for athletic participation under Rule 48. Traditionally black Division I schools, already at a recruiting disadvantage owing to smaller budgets and less access to lucrative TV exposure, would be placed at an even more critical recruiting disadvantage, since they would not be able to afford even those athletes they would ordinarily be able to get.

Thus, the core issue in the Rule 48 controversy is not racist academic standards, or alleged efforts by whites to resegregate major-college sports, so much as parity between black and white institutions in the collegiate athletic arms race.

Strategically, the position of NAFEO, the NABSE, and the black civil-rights leaders vis-à-vis Rule 48 poses two problems. First, they have missed the greatest opportunity since the *Brown* v. *Board of Education of Topeka* case thirty years ago to make an impressive statement about quality and equality in education. And, since they had the attention of the nation, they also squandered a rare opportunity to direct a national dialogue on restructuring the role and stipulating the rights of athletes in the academy. Second, with no real evidence to support their claims of racist motives on the part of Rule 48's white supporters, or of simple race bias in the rule's stipulations, these black educators and civil-rights leaders left the unfortunate and unintended impression that they were against *all* academic standards because they believed that black students are unable to achieve even the moderate standards established under Rule 48.

Notwithstanding the transparent criticisms leveled by Rule 48's detractors, the measure does contain some real flaws relative to its proposed goal of shoring up the academic integrity of Division I athletic programs. First, the standards stipulated in Rule 48 are *too low*. A score of 700 on the SAT, for example, projects less than a fifty-fifty chance of graduating from most Division I schools.

Second, Rule 48 does not address in any way the educational problems of students once they have matriculated, which is where the real educational rip-off of collegiate student athletes has occurred. Rather, it establishes standards of high school preparation and scholastic achievement necessary for students who wish to participate in college sports as freshmen.

Nonetheless, the NCAA action is worthy of support, not as a satisfactory solution to the educational problems of big-time collegiate sports but as a step—a very small and perhaps even inept step—toward dealing with these problems. Rule 48 communicates to young athletes, beginning with those who are sophomores in high school, that we expect them to develop academically as well as athletically. In California, 320,000 students each year participate in California Interscholastic Federation athletic programs and most undoubtedly aspire to win athletic scholarships to Division I institutions. However, only 5 percent of these students will ever participate in college sports at any level (including junior college), and the overwhelming majority will never even enroll at a four-year school. If Rule 48 does indeed encourage greater academic seriousness among high school athletes, the vast majority of high school student athletes who are *not* going on to college may benefit most from the NCAA's action—since they face the realities of life after sports immediately upon graduation from high school.

Further, were I not to support Rule 48, I would risk communicating to black youth in particular that I, a nationally known black educator, do not believe that they have the capacity to achieve a 700 score on the SAT, with three years to prepare for the test, when they are given a total of 400 points simply for answering a single question in each of the two sections of the test, and when they have a significant chance of scoring 460 by a purely random marking of the test. Finally, I support the NCAA's action because I believe that black parents, black educators, and the black community must insist that black children be taught and that they learn whatever subject matter is necessary to excel on diagnostic and all other skills tests.

Outcries of "racism," and calls for black boycotts of or exemptions from such tests, seem to me neither rational nor constructive long-term responses to the problem of black students' low test scores. Culture can be learned and taught. Class-specific values and perspectives can be learned and taught. And this is what we should be about as black educators—preparing our young people to meet the challenges they face on these tests, and, by extension, in this society.

I believe that (1) student athletes and non-athletes alike should be given diagnostic tests on a recurrent basis to assure skills achievement; (2) test-score standards should and must be raised, based upon the skill demands and challenges of our contemporary world; and (3) the test standards set should be established as post-enrollment goals and not pre-enrollment obstacles.

In the case of scholarship athletes, every institution should have the right to set its own academic enrollment standards. But those same institutions *must* acknowledge a binding corollary obligation and responsibility to develop and implement support programs sufficiently effective to fulfill their implied contracts with the athletes recruited.

For all of its divisive impact, the debate over Rule 48 has illuminated a much larger crisis involving the failure of this nation to educate its young, athletes and non-athletes, properly. In 1967, the national average on the SAT was 958; by 1982, it had dropped to 893. Furthermore, even students who score well on diagnostic tests frequently require remedial work to handle college-level course work. From 1975 to 1980, the number of remedial math courses in public four-year colleges increased by 72 percent; they now constitute a quarter of all math courses offered by those institutions. At two-year colleges, 42 percent of math courses are below the level of college algebra.

In high school transcripts, according to a study done for the National Commission on Excellence in Education, credit value for American history has declined by 11 percent over the past fifteen years, for chemistry by 6 percent, for algebra by 7 percent, and for French by 9 percent. In the same period, credit value for remedial English has risen by 39 percent and for driver education by 75 percent. Only 31 percent of recent high school graduates took intermediate algebra, only 16 percent took geography, and only 13 percent took French. High school students have abandoned college-preparatory and vocational-education "tracks" in droves, so that between 1964 and 1979 the number who chose the "general" track rose from 12 to 42 percent. About 25 percent of all credits earned by general-track graduates were in physical and health education, driver education, home management, food and cooking, training for adulthood and marriage, remedial courses, and for work experience outside school.

Part of the problem is with our teachers: the way they are recruited, their low status, and their even lower rewards. According to a recent article in *U.S. News & World Report,* "A study conducted for the National Institute of Education, which looked at college graduates who entered teaching in the late '70s, found that those with the highest academic ability were much more likely to leave their jobs than those who were lower achievers. Among high-achieving students, only 26 percent intended to teach at age thirty, as compared with approximately 60 percent of those with the lowest academic ability." In yet another study, one third of the nearly 7,000 prospective teachers who took the California minimum-competency test failed to meet the most basic skills requirements. And in 1982, the average SAT score of students indicating teaching as their intended field of study ranked twenty-sixth among average scores achieved by students declaring twenty-nine different fields of interest.

Black colleges are not blameless with respect to inadequate teacher preparation. Currently, at least twenty states require teacher candidates to pass a state qualifying exam. In Florida, 79 percent of white teacher-college graduates achieved a passing rate, compared with 35 percent for black test-takers. The two black schools that produce the largest number of black teacher candidates in that same state had the worst passing rates—37 percent and 16 percent.

That state's Association of Black Psychologists held a press conference and denounced the tests as "instruments of European cultural imperialism," and urged the black community—as a front—to resist the tests. But there is really only one legitimate concern relative to such tests: Do they measure what should be taught in schools of education if teachers are to be competent?

The majority of black students today come from schools in which blacks either predominate or make up the entire student body. And much—if not most—of the failure to educate black youths has occurred under black educators. In the 1960s, from Ocean Hill-Brownsville, in New York, to Watts, in California, blacks quite rightly criticized inner-city schools where white teachers and white superintendents were indifferent to the learning abilities of black students. Many of these school systems now have a majority of black teachers and black superintendents, and many black students still do not learn. Can we afford to be any less critical when white incompetence is replaced by black incompetence? Given what is at stake, the answer must be an emphatic and resounding No. We must let all of our educators know that if they are not competent to do their jobs, they have no business in our schools.

But pointing out teachers' inadequacies is not enough. For all of its modernity, education still advances on "four legs." Though formal instruction takes place in the classroom, education is the result of coordinated effort on the part of parents, the school, the community, and the larger society. Parents who do not participate in school activities, who do not attend parent-teacher conferences to review their children's academic progress, who generally show little or no interest in school-related issues—indeed, who do not know, and have never even asked, the name of the teacher charged with instructing their children—over the years communicate to those children the idea that education doesn't matter. The community that undercuts the solvency of its libraries and schools communicates the idea that education doesn't matter. The school that emphasizes and revels in the glories of sports, while fighting efforts to set academic standards for sports participation, communicates the idea that education doesn't matter.

Current national policy, which calls for severe cuts in educational funding, and defense expenditures of $1.6 trillion over the next four years, is both contradictory and shortsighted. Education *is* a national-defense issue. As Jefferson pointed out at this nation's birth, an educated, informed populace is necessary to the operation of a viable democracy. As the world's leading democracy, we simply cannot afford the current burden of 26 million adults who are functionally illiterate and 46 million who are only marginally literate. Since the late 1970s, the U.S. military has found that it must print comic-book versions of some of its manuals in order to accommodate the educational deficiencies of troops charged with operating and maintaining some of the most sophisticated weapons in history. Along with greater emphasis upon parental involvement in schools, insistence upon teacher competence, and greater academic expectations of our students, we must put more, not less, money into education.

The National Center for Education Statistics estimates that the average 1980-1981 salary for classroom teachers was $17,602—up from $9,269 in 1971. However, in constant 1981 dollars, teachers have lost money, because their 1971 average salary translates to roughly $20,212. The outlook for the future is equally bleak. Education cannot attract and hold the best-trained and most competent people without offering competitive salaries. Particularly in the more technologically applicable disciplines, education is suffering a severe "brain-drain." Thus, in 1981, nationwide, half the teachers hired to teach high school math and science were not certified to teach those subjects, while more than forty states reported shortages of qualified teachers in those areas.

Compared with other national school systems, American education comes up short. The American school year is 180 days, and the average student misses roughly eighteen of those, but Japan, Germany, and most other industrial nations require at least 220 days a year. In the Soviet Union, students from the first grade on attend school six days a week. About 35 percent of their classwork is in science. They take five years of arithmetic, then are introduced to algebra and geometry, followed by calculus. The national minimum curriculum also calls for one year each of astronomy and mechanical drawing, four years of chemistry, five years of physics, and six years of biology.

In sum, education must be put at the very top of the U.S. domestic agenda. Clearly, we must demonstrate greater concern for and commitment to educational quality for all American youths—athletes as well as non-athletes. I am confident that with adequate support and proper encouragement, they can achieve whatever levels of performance are necessitated by the challenges they face. In today's world, neither they nor we have any other choice.

QUESTIONS

1. Defend or oppose the proposition that Edward's article is about something larger than Rule 48.

2. Why are many black leaders opposed to Rule 48? How does Edwards answer each point? Does he convince you?

3. Are there reasons Edwards himself does not like Rule 48? What is the effect of his mentioning them? Does it damage his argument?

4. Does Edwards propose solutions to any of the problems he addresses? If so, what are they?

5. Edwards is very careful to present points of view different from his own. Find some examples of this in the essay, and then discuss whether this is an effective persuasive device.

6. Edwards refers to himself as a "black educator." Why does he feel it is necessary to inform the reader of this fact? Is it also a persuasive device?

7. Look carefully at Edwards's language. Then try to determine to whom he is writing—to the minimally prepared black or white athlete? The black leaders opposed to Rule 48? College coaches? Whom? Discuss.

8. Edwards relies on statistics and authority to provide his essay with an "objective," informative tone. What else contributes to that tone? Do you think he feels very deeply about any of the issues he writes about? What makes you think so?

SUGGESTIONS FOR WRITING

1. To sharpen your awareness of the way audience, purpose, and language are interrelated, rewrite Edwards's essay for a different group. You might choose to be giving a talk to a group of high school athletes (male and/or female, black and/or white), the Association of Black College Presidents, the parents

of prospective college athletes, some of the black leaders mentioned in the article, or any other audience to whom the issue would be relevant and which is different from that of the essay as it stands.

2.   There are many controversies surrounding collegiate and professional sports: equal facilities for male and female college athletes, the offer of money or "no-show" jobs to athletes as an incentive to play for a given school, point-shaving, "tampering" with undergraduates by professional teams, violence in professional hockey, the designated hitter rule in baseball. Choose an issue that interests you, do some background research, and decide who might be on the "pro" side of the issue, who on the "con." After writing a debate between representatives of the sides, indicate in a conclusion which side deserves to win the debate, justifying your choice.

David Bruck
DECISIONS OF DEATH
★ ★ ★

The death penalty continues to be one of the most controversial issues in American life today. Many states currently have people on death row, and news reports of executions air with increasing frequency. David Bruck, a defense attorney in Columbia, South Carolina, specializing in capital cases, is involved with the issue professionally and personally. Although clearly opposed to the death penalty, Bruck, born in 1949 in Montreal, Canada, and educated at Harvard and the University of South Carolina, sees little hope that his position will be accepted, given the country's current mood. His essay, however, like most successful arguments, does not reflect a defeatist attitude or take a defensive stance; Bruck defends his position aggressively. In a periodical like the New Republic, *where "Decisions of Death" was published (December 13, 1983), a writer is given enough space to argue at length, unlike on Op-Ed pages, in newspaper columns, or in letters to the editor. Bruck, taking advantage of this extended format, employs many of the argumentative strategies discussed in this chapter's introduction—facts, logic, personal experience, experts' testimony, and various emotional appeals—to their fullest extent. Despite the general public's opposition to his view, Bruck's purpose is, no doubt, to persuade the relatively small but influential* New Republic *readership to become vocal opponents of capital punishment.*

There are 1,150 men and 13 women awaiting execution in the United States. It's not easy to imagine how many people 1,163 is. If death row were really a row, it would stretch for 1.3 miles, cell after six-foot-wide cell. In each cell, one person, sitting, pacing, watching TV, sleeping, writing letters. Locked in their cells nearly twenty-four hours a day, the condemned communicate with each other by shouts, notes, and hand-held mirrors, all with a casual dexterity that handicapped people acquire over time. Occasionally there is a break in the din of shouted conversations—a silent cell, its inhabitant withdrawn into a cocoon of madness. That's what death row would look like. That's what, divided up among the prisons of thirty-four states, it does look like.

This concentration of condemned people is unique among the democratic countries of the world. It is also nearly double the number of prisoners who were on death row in 1972 when the Supreme Court, in *Furman* v. *Georgia,* averted a massive surge of executions by striking down all the nation's capital punishment laws.

But in another sense, death row is very small. If every one of these 1,163 inmates were to be taken out of his or her cell tomorrow and gassed, electrocuted, hanged, shot, or injected, the total of convicted murderers imprisoned in this country would decline from some 33,526 (at last count) to 32,363—a reduction of a little over 3 percent. Huge as this country's death row population has become, it does not include—and has never included—more than a tiny fraction of those who are convicted of murder.

It falls to the judicial system of each of the thirty-eight states that retain capital punishment to cull the few who are to die from the many who are convicted of murder. This selection begins with the crime itself, as the community and the press react with outrage or with indifference, depending on the nature of the murder and the identity of the victim. With the arrest of a suspect, police and prosecutors must decide what charges to file, whether to seek the death penalty, and whether the defendant should be allowed to plea-bargain for his life. Most of these decisions can later be changed, so that at any point from arrest to trial the defendant's chances of slipping through the death penalty net depend on chance: the inclinations and ambitions of the local prosecutor, the legal and political pressures which impel him to one course of action or another, and the skill or incompetence of the court-appointed defense counsel.

In the courtroom, the defendant may be spared or condemned by the countless vagaries of the trial by jury. There are counties in each state where the juries almost always impose death, and counties where they almost never do. There are hanging judges and lenient judges, and judges who go one way or the other depending on who the victim's family happens to be, or the defendant's family, or who is prosecuting the case, or who is defending it.

Thus at each stage between arrest and sentence, more and more defendants are winnowed out from the ranks of those facing possible execution: in 1979, a year which saw more than eighteen thousand arrests for intentional homicides and nearly four thousand murder convictions throughout the United States, only 159 defendants were added to death row. And even for those few who are condemned to die, there lies ahead a series of appeals which whittle down the number of condemned still further, sparing some and consigning others to death on the basis of appellate courts' judgments of the nuances of a trial judge's instructions to the jury, of whether the court-appointed defense lawyer had made the proper objections at the proper moments during the trial, and so on. By the time the appeals process has run its course, almost every murder defendant who faced the possibility of execution when he was first arrested has by luck, justice, or favor evaded execution, and a mere handful are left to die.

This process of selection is the least understood feature of capital punishment. Because the media focus on the cases where death has been imposed and where the executions seem imminent, the public sees capital punishment not as the maze-like system that it is, but only in terms of this or that individual criminal, about to suffer just retribution for a particular crime. What we don't see in any of this now-familiar drama are hundreds of others whose crimes were as repugnant, but who are jailed for life or less instead of condemned to death. So the issues appear simple. The prisoner's guilt is certain. His crime is horrendous. Little knots of "supporters" light candles and hold vigils. His lawyers rush from court to court raising arcane new appeals.

The condemned man himself remembers the many points of his procession through the judicial system at which he might have been spared, but was not. He knows, too, from his years of waiting in prison, that most of those who committed crimes like his have evaded the execution that awaits him. So do the prosecutors who have pursued him through the court system, and the judges who have upheld his sentence. And so do the defense lawyers, the ones glimpsed on the TV news in the last hours, exhausted and overwrought for reasons that, given their client's crimes, must be hard for most people to fathom.

I am one of those lawyers, and I know the sense of horror that propels those last-minute appeals. It is closely related to that horror that violent crime awakens in all of us—the random kind of crime, the sniper in the tower or the gunman in the grocery store. The horror derives not from death, which comes to us all, but from death that is inflicted *at random,* for no reason, for being on the wrong subway platform or the wrong side of the street. Up close, that is what capital punishment is like. And that is what makes the state's inexorable, stalking pursuit of this or that particular person's life so chilling.

The lawyers who bring those eleventh-hour appeals know from their work how many murderers are spared, how few are sentenced to die, and how chance and race decide which will be which. In South Carolina, where I practice law, murders committed during robberies may be punished by death. According to police reports, there were 286 defendants arrested for such murders from the time that South Carolina's death penalty law went into effect in 1977 until the end of 1981. (About a third of those arrests were of blacks charged with killing whites.) Out of all of those 286 defendants, the prosecution had sought the death penalty and obtained final convictions by the end of 1981 against 37. And of those 37 defendants, death sentences were imposed and affirmed on only 4; the rest received prison sentences. What distinguished those 4 defendants' cases was this: 3 were black, had killed white storeowners, and were tried by all-white juries; the fourth, a white, was represented at his trial by a lawyer who had never read the state's murder statute, had no case file and no office, and had refused to talk to his client for the last two months prior to the trial because he'd been insulted by the client's unsuccessful attempt to fire him.

If these four men are ultimately executed, the newspapers will report and the law will record that they went to their deaths because they committed murder and robbery. But when so many others who committed the same crime were spared, it can truthfully be said only that these four men were *convicted* because they committed murder: they were *executed* because of race, or bad luck, or both.

If one believes, as many do, that murderers deserve whatever punishment they get, then none of this should matter. But if the 1,163 now on death row throughout the United States had actually been selected by means of a lottery from the roughly 33,500 inmates now serving sentences for murder, most Americans, whatever their views on capital punishment as an abstract matter, would surely be appalled. This revulsion would be all the stronger if we limited the pool of those murderers facing execution by restricting it to blacks. Or if we sentenced people to die on the basis of the race of the *victim,* consigning to death only those—whatever their race—who have killed whites, and sparing all those who have killed blacks.

The reason why our sense of justice rebels at such ideas is not hard to identify. Violent crime undermines the sense of order and shared moral values without which no society could exist. We punish people who commit such crimes in order to reaffirm our standards of right and wrong, and our belief that life in society can be orderly and trusting rather than fearful and chaotic. But if the punishment itself is administered chaotically or arbitrarily, it fails in its purpose and becomes, like the crime which triggered it, just another spectacle of the random infliction of suffering—all the more terrifying and demoralizing because this time the random killer is organized society itself, the same society on which we depend for stability and security in our daily lives. No matter how much the individual criminal thus selected for death may "deserve" his punishment, the manner of its imposition robs it of any possible value, and leaves us ashamed instead of reassured.

It was on precisely this basis, just eleven years ago, that the Supreme Court in *Furman* v. *Georgia* struck down every death penalty law in the United States, and set aside the death sentences of more than six hundred death row inmates. *Furman* was decided by a single vote (all four Nixon appointees voting to uphold the death penalty laws), and though the five majority justices varied in their rationales, the dominant theme of their opinions was that the Constitution did not permit the execution of a capriciously selected handful out of all those convicted of capital crimes. For Justice Byron White and the rest of the *Furman* majority, years of reading the petitions of the condemned had simply revealed "no meaningful basis for distinguishing the few cases in which [death] is imposed from the many in which it is not." Justice Potter Stewart compared the country's capital sentencing methods to being struck by lightning, adding that "if any basis can be discerned for the selection of these few to be sentenced to die, it is on the constitutionally impermissible basis of race." Justice William O. Douglas summarized the issue by observing that the Constitution would never permit any law which stated that anyone making more than $50,000 would be exempt from the death penalty . . . [nor] a law that in terms said that blacks, those that never went beyond the fifth grade in school, those who made less than $3,000 a year, or those who were unpopular or unstable would be the only people executed. *A law which in the overall view reaches that result in practice has no more sanctity than a law which in terms provides the same.* [Emphasis added.]

On the basis of these views, the Supreme Court in *Furman* set aside every death sentence before it, and effectively cleared off death row. Though *Furman* v. *Georgia* did not outlaw the death penalty as such, the Court's action came at a time when America appeared to have turned against capital punishment, and *Furman* seemed to climax a long and inexorable progression toward abolition. After *Furman,* Chief Justice Warren E. Burger, who had dissented from the Court's decision, predicted privately that there would never be another execution in the United States.

What happened instead was that the majority of state legislatures passed new death sentencing laws designed to satisfy the Supreme Court. By this year, eleven years after *Furman,* there are roughly as many states with capital punishment laws on the books as there were in 1972.

In theory the capital sentencing statutes under which the 1,163 prisoners now on death row were condemned are very different from the death penalty laws in effect prior to 1972. Under the pre-*Furman* laws, the process of selection was simple: the jury decided whether the accused was guilty of murder, and if so, whether he should live or die. In most states, no separate sentencing hearing was held: jurors were supposed to determine both guilt and punishment at the same time, often without benefit of any information about the background or circumstances of the defendant whose life was in their hands. Jurors were also given no guidelines or standards with which to assess the relative gravity of the case before them, but were free to base their life-or-death decision on whatever attitudes or biases they happened to have carried with them into the jury room. These statutes provided few grounds for appeal and worked fast: as late as the 1950s, many prisoners were executed within a few weeks of their trials, and delays of more than a year or two were rare.

In contrast, the current crop of capital statutes have created complex, multi-tiered sentencing schemes based on lists of specified "aggravating" and "mitigating" factors which the jury is to consider in passing sentence. Sentencing now occurs at a separate hearing after guilt has been determined. The new statutes also provide for automatic appeal to the state supreme courts, usually with a requirement that the court determine whether each death sentence is excessive considering the defendant and the crime.

The first of these new statutes—from Georgia, Florida, and Texas—came before the Supreme Court for review in 1976. The new laws were different from one another in several respects—only Georgia's provided for case-by-case review of the appropriateness of each death sentence by the state supreme court; Florida's permitted the judge to sentence a defendant to death even where the jury had recommended a life sentence; and the Texas statute determined who was to be executed on the basis of the jury's answer to the semantically perplexing question of whether the evidence established "beyond a reasonable doubt" a "probability" that the defendant would commit acts of violence in the future. What these statutes all had in common, however, was some sort of criteria, however vague, to guide juries and judges in their life-or-death decisions, while permitting capital defendants a chance to present evidence to show why they should be spared. Henceforth—or so went the theory behind these new laws—death sentences could not be imposed randomly or on the basis of the race or social status of the defendant and the victim, but only on the basis of specific facts about the crime, such as whether the murder had been committed during a rape or a robbery, or whether it had been "especially heinous, atrocious and cruel" (in Florida), or "outrageously or wantonly vile, horrible or inhuman" (in Georgia).

After considering these statutes during the spring of 1976, the Supreme Court announced in *Gregg* v. *Georgia* and two other cases that the new laws satisfied its concern, expressed in *Furman,* about the randomness and unfairness of the previous death sentencing systems. Of course, the Court had no actual evidence that these new laws were being applied any more equally or consistently than the ones struck down in *Furman.* But for that matter, the Court had not relied on factual evidence in *Furman,* either. Although social science research over the previous thirty years had consistently found the nation's use of capital punishment to be characterized by arbitrariness and racial discrimination, the decisive opinions of Justices White and Stewart in *Furman* cited none of this statistical evidence, but relied instead on the justices' own conclusions derived from years of experience with the appeals of the condemned. The *Furman* decision left the Court free to declare the problem solved later on. And four years later, in *Gregg* v. *Georgia,* that is what it did.

It may be, of course, that the Court's prediction in *Gregg* of a new era of fairness in capital sentencing was a sham, window dressing for what was in reality nothing more than a capitulation to the mounting public clamor for a resumption of executions. But if the justices sincerely believed that new legal guidelines and jury instructions would really solve the problems of arbitrariness and racial discrimination in death penalty cases, they were wrong.

Before John Spenkelink—a white murderer of a white victim—was executed by the state of Florida in May 1979, his lawyers tried to present to the state and federal courts a study which showed that the "new" Florida death penalty laws, much like the ones which they had replaced, were being applied far more frequently against persons who killed whites than against those who killed blacks. The appeals courts responded that the Supreme Court had settled all of these arguments in 1976 when it upheld the new sentencing statutes: the laws were fair because the Supreme Court had said they were fair; mere evidence to the contrary was irrelevant.

After Spenkelink was electrocuted, the evidence continued to mount. In 1980 two Northeastern University criminologists, William Bowers and Glenn Pierce, published a study of homicide sentencing in Georgia, Florida, and Texas, the three states whose new death penalty statutes were the first to be approved by the Supreme Court after *Furman*. Bowers and Pierce tested the Supreme Court's prediction that these new statutes would achieve consistent and even-handed sentencing by comparing the lists of which convicted murderers had been condemned and which spared with the facts of their crimes as reported by the police. What they found was that in cases where white victims had been killed, black defendants in all three states were from four to six times more likely to be sentenced to death than were white defendants. Both whites and blacks, moreover, faced a much greater danger of being executed where the murder victims were white than where the victims were black. A black defendant in Florida was thirty-seven times more likely to be sentenced to death if his victim was white than if his victim was black; in Georgia, black-on-white killings were punished by death thirty-three times more often than were black-on-black killings; and in Texas, the ratio climbed to an astounding 84 to 1. Even when Bowers and Pierce examined only those cases which the police had reported as "felony-circumstance" murders (i.e., cases involving kidnapping or rape, and thus excluding mere domestic and barroom homicides), they found that both the race of the defendant and the race of the victim appeared to produce enormous disparities in death sentences in each state.

A more detailed analysis of charging decisions in several Florida counties even suggested that prosecutors tended to "upgrade" murders of white victims by alleging that they were more legally aggravated than had been apparent to the police who had written up the initial report, while "downgrading" murders of black victims in a corresponding manner, apparently to avoid the expensive and time-consuming process of trying such murders of blacks as capital cases. Their overall findings, Bowers and Pierce concluded,

> are consistent with a single underlying racist tenet: that white lives are worth more than black lives. From this tenet it follows that death as punishment is more appropriate for the killers of whites than for the killers of blacks and more appropriate for black than for white killers.

Such stark evidence of discrimination by race of offender and by race of victim, they wrote, is "a direct challenge to the constitutionality of the post-*Furman* capital statutes . . . [and] may represent a two-edged sword of racism in capital punishment which is beyond statutory control."

This new data was presented to the federal courts by attorneys for a Georgia death row inmate named John Eldon Smith in 1981. The court of appeals replied that the studies were too crude to have any legal significance, since they did not look at all the dozens of circumstances of each case, other than race, that might have accounted for the unequal sentencing patterns that Bowers and Pierce had detected.

The matter might have ended there, since the court's criticism implied that only a gargantuan (and extremely expensive) research project encompassing the most minute details of many hundreds of homicide cases would be worthy of its consideration. But as it happened, such a study was already under way, supported by a foundation grant and directed by University of Iowa law professor David Baldus. Using a staff of law students and relying primarily on official Georgia state records, Baldus gathered and coded more than 230 factual circumstances surrounding each of more than a thousand homicides, including 253 death penalty sentencing proceedings conducted under Georgia's current death penalty law. Baldus's results, presented in an Atlanta federal court hearing late last summer, confirmed that among defendants convicted of murdering whites, blacks are substantially more likely to go to death row than are whites. Although blacks account for some 60 percent of Georgia homicide victims, Baldus found that killers of black victims are punished by death less than one-tenth as often as are killers of white victims. With the scientific precision of an epidemiologist seeking to pinpoint the cause of a new disease, Baldus analyzed and reanalyzed his mountain of data on Georgia homicides, controlling for the hundreds of factual variables in each case, in search of any explanation other than race which might account for the stark inequalities in the operation of Georgia's capital sentencing system. He could find none. And when the state of Georgia's turn came to defend its capital sentencing record at the Atlanta federal court hearing, it soon emerged that the statisticians hired by the state to help it refute Baldus's research had had no better success in *their* search for an alternative explanation. (In a telephone interview after the Atlanta hearing, the attorney general of Georgia, Michael Bowers, assured me that "the bottom line is that Georgia does not discriminate on the basis of race," but referred all specific questions to his assistant, who declined to answer on the grounds that the court proceeding was pending.)

The findings of research efforts like Baldus's document what anyone who has worked in the death-sentencing system will have sensed all along: the Supreme Court notwithstanding, there is no set of courtroom procedures set out in lawbooks which can change the prosecution practices of local district attorneys. Nor will even the most elaborate jury instructions ever ensure that an all-white jury will weigh a black life as heavily as a white life.

At bottom, the determination of whether or not a particular defendant should die for his crime is simply not a rational decision. Requiring that the jury first determine whether his murder was "outrageously or wantonly vile, horrible, or inhuman," as Georgia juries are invited to do, provides little assurance that death will be imposed fairly and consistently. Indeed, Baldus's research revealed that Georgia juries are more likely to find that a given murder was "outrageously or wantonly vile, horrible, or inhuman" when the victim was white, and likelier still when the murderer is black—hardly a vindication of the Supreme Court's confidence in *Gregg* v. *Georgia* that such guidelines would serve to eliminate racial discrimination in sentencing.

At present, 51 percent of the inhabitants of death row across the country are white, as were seven of the eight men executed since the Supreme Court's *Gregg* decision. Five percent of the condemned are Hispanic, and almost all of the remaining 44 percent are black. Since roughly half the people arrested and charged with intentional homicide each year in the United States are white, it would appear at first glance that the proportions of blacks and whites now on Death Row are about those that would be expected from a fair system of capital sentencing. But what studies like Baldus's now reveal is how such seemingly equitable racial distribution can actually be the product of racial discrimination, rather than proof that discrimination has been overcome.

The explanation for this seeming paradox is that the judicial system discriminates on the basis of the race of the *victim* as well as the race of the defendant. Each year, according to the F.B.I.'s crime report, about the same numbers of blacks as whites are arrested for murder throughout the United States, and the totals of black and white murder victims are also roughly equal. But like many other aspects of American life, our murders are segregated: white murderers almost always kill whites, and the large majority of black killers kill blacks. While blacks who kill whites tend to be singled out for harsher treatment—and more death sentences—than other murderers, there are relatively few of them, and so the absolute effect on the numbers of blacks sent to death row is limited. On the other hand, the far more numerous black murderers whose victims were also black are treated relatively leniently in the courts, and are only rarely sent to death row. Because these dual systems of discrimination operate simultaneously, they have the overall effect of keeping the numbers of blacks on death row roughly proportionate to the numbers of blacks convicted of murder—even while individual defendants are being condemned, and others spared, on the basis of race. In short, like the man who, with one foot in ice and the other in boiling water, describes his situation as "comfortable on average," the death sentencing system has created an illusion of fairness.

In theory, law being based on precedent, the Supreme Court might be expected to apply the principles of the *Furman* decision as it did in 1972 and strike down death penalty laws which have produced results as seemingly racist as these. But that's not going to happen. *Furman* was a product of its time: in 1972 public support for the death penalty had been dropping fairly steadily over several decades, and capital punishment appeared to be going the way of the stocks, the whipping post, and White and Colored drinking fountains. The resurgence of support for capital punishment in the country over the last decade has changed that, at least for now. Last summer the Supreme Court upheld every one of the four death sentences it had taken under consideration during its 1982–83 session, and in November the Court heard arguments by California in support of its claim that the states should not be required to compare murder sentences on a statewide basis in order to assure fairness in capital sentencing. The justices may have given an indication of their eventual decision on California's appeal when, just three hours before they heard that case, they lifted a stay of execution in a Louisiana case where a condemned prisoner named Robert Wayne Williams had been attempting to challenge the very limited method of comparison used by the Louisiana courts: as a result, Williams may well be dead by the time the California decision is handed down this spring. When in 1972 the Supreme Court was faced with a choice between fairness and the death penalty, it chose fairness. This time the odds are all with the death penalty.

Even with the Court's increasingly hard-line stance on capital appeals, there will probably not be any sudden surge of executions in the next year or two. One of the unreckoned costs of the death penalty is the strain it places on the state and federal judicial systems. Any large number of imminent executions would overload those systems to the point of breakdown. A great deal is being said nowadays about the need to speed up capital appeals: Justice Lewis Powell even added his voice to the chorus last spring at the very moment that the Supreme Court had the question of stays of execution under consideration in a pending case. But this attitude tends to moderate the closer one gets to a specific case. No judge wants to discover after it's too late that he permitted someone to be executed on the basis of factual or legal error, and for that reason alone the backlog of death row prisoners can be expected to persist.

Still, the pace of executions is going to pick up to a more or less steady trickle: possibly one a month, possibly two, maybe more. In September Mississippi's William Winter became the first governor since Ronald Reagan to permit an execution by lethal gas: Jimmy Lee Gray died banging his head against a steel pole in the gas chamber while the reporters counted his moans (eleven, according to the Associated Press). A month later, J. A. Autry came within minutes of dying by lethal injection in Texas, only to have Supreme Court Justice Byron White reverse his decision of the day before and stay the execution. Now Autry is reprieved until the Supreme Court decides whether California (and by implication Texas) must compare capital sentences to ensure some measure of fairness: if the Court rules that they don't have to, Autry will in all likelihood be executed next year.

So far, the power of the death penalty as a social symbol has shielded from scrutiny the huge demands in money and resources which the death sentencing process makes on the criminal justice system as a whole. Whatever the abstract merits of capital punishment, there is no denying that a successful death penalty prosecution costs a fortune. A 1982 study in New York state concluded that just the trial and first stage of appeal in a death penalty case under that state's proposed death penalty bill would cost the taxpayers of New York over $1.8 million—more than twice as much as imprisoning the defendant for life. And even that estimate does not include the social costs of diverting an already overburdened criminal justice system from its job of handling large numbers of criminal cases to a preoccupation with the relative handful of capital ones. But the question of just how many laid-off police officers one execution is worth won't come up so long as the death penalty remains for most Americans a way of expressing feelings rather than a practical response to the problem of violent crime.

It is impossible to predict how long the executions will continue. The rise in violent crime in this country has already begun to abate somewhat, probably as a result of demographic changes as the baby boom generation matures beyond its crime-prone teenage and early adult years. But it may well turn out that even a marked reduction in the crime rate won't produce any sharp decrease in public pressure for capital punishment: the shift in public opinion on the death penalty seems to have far deeper roots than that. The death penalty has become a potent social symbol of national resolve, another way of saying that we're not going to be pushed around anymore, that we've got the willpower and self-confidence to stand up to anyone, whether muggers or Cubans or Islamic fanatics, that we're not the flaccid weaklings that "they" have been taking us for. The death penalty can only be understood as one of the so-called "social issues" of the Reagan era: it bears no more relationship to the problem of crime than school prayer bears to the improvement of public education. Over the past half-century, executions were at their peak during the Depression of the 1930s, and almost disappeared during the boom years of the 1950s and early 1960s. The re-emergence of the death penalty in the 1970s coincided with the advent of chronic inflation and recession, and with military defeat abroad and the decline of the civil rights movement at home. Given this historical record, it's a safe bet that whether the crime rates go up or down over the next several years, public support for executions will start to wane only as the country finds more substantial foundations for a renewal of confidence in its future.

In the meantime we will be the only country among all the Western industrial democracies which still executes its own citizens. Canada abolished capital punishment in 1976, as did France in 1981: England declined to bring back hanging just this summer. By contrast, our leading companions in the use of the death penalty as a judicial punishment for crime will be the governments of the Soviet Union, South Africa, Saudi Arabia, and Iran—a rogues' gallery of the most repressive and backward-looking regimes in the world. Just last week Christopher Wren reported in *The New York Times* that the total number of executions in the People's Republic of China may reach five thousand or more this year alone.

It's no accident that democracies tend to abolish the death penalty while autocracies and totalitarian regimes tend to retain it. In his new book, *The Death Penalty: A Debate,* John Conrad credits Tocqueville with the explanation for this, quoting from *Democracy in America:*

> When all the ranks of a community are nearly equal, as all men think and feel in nearly the same manner, each of them may judge in a moment the sensations of all the others; he casts a rapid glance upon himself, and that is enough. There is no wretchedness into which he cannot readily enter, and a secret instinct reveals to him its extent. . . . In democratic ages, men rarely sacrifice themselves

for one another, but they display general compassion for the members of the human race. They inflict no useless ills, and they are happy to relieve the griefs of others when they can do so without much hurting themselves; they are not disinterested, but they are humane . . .

Tocqueville went on to explain that his identification of America's democratic political culture as the root of the "singular mildness" of American penal practices was susceptible of an ironic proof: the cruelty with which Americans treated their black slaves. Restraint in punishment, he wrote, extends as far as our sense of social equality, and no further: "the same man who is full of humanity toward his fellow creatures when they are at the same time his equals becomes insensible to their affliction as soon as that equality ceases."

In that passage, written 150 years ago, Tocqueville reveals to us why it is that the death penalty—the practice of slowly bringing a fully conscious human face to face with the prospect of his own extinction and then killing him—should characterize the judicial systems of the least democratic and most repressive nations of the world. And it reveals too why the vestiges of this institution in America should be so inextricably entangled with the question of race. The gradual disappearance of the death penalty throughout most of the democratic world certainly suggests that Tocqueville was right. The day when Americans stop condemning people to death on the basis of race and inequality will be the day when we stop condemning anyone to death at all.

QUESTIONS

1. Bruck uses several persuasive techniques to convince the reader to adopt his opinions. He appeals to our emotions, he uses statistics, and he uses the testimony of authorities. Find examples of these techniques and discuss their placement and effectiveness.

2. Would you say this essay was written primarily to inform or to persuade? Justify your opinion by citing the essay.

3. Why does Bruck go into detail about *Furman* v. *Georgia?* Did he need to provide as much information about it as he does? Try to create a more concise account—what is the effect?

4. The final paragraph contains a striking definition of the death penalty. What other definitions does Bruck provide? Why is it appropriate to call them persuasive devices?

5. The controlling metaphor of "Decisions of Death" is that of a lottery. Is it effective? Think of the connotations of the word "lottery" to help you decide.

6. Compare and contrast the introduction and the conclusion of "Decisions of Death." Do they clearly belong to the same essay? What makes each work?

SUGGESTION FOR WRITING

One of the reasons "Decisions of Death" is persuasive is that Bruck argues against the death penalty on grounds most of us have no knowledge of and haven't considered. Take a current "controversial" issue (abortion rights, school prayer, divorce, gun control, use of nuclear energy) about which you are concerned but about which you think "everything" has been said, and write a short essay exploring it from a new angle. You will need to let your imagination go in the prewriting stages of this essay, so you don't prematurely discount an idea. A trip to the library to do research may be necessary as well.

STUDENT ESSAY

Ken Ogorek
BOTH GENDERS WIN: THE BENEFITS OF ALL-MALE COLLEGES

★ ★ ★

Ken Ogorek, a South Bend, Indiana native, graduated with honors in 1983 from La Salle High School. At Wabash College in Crawfordsville, Indiana (one of two remaining all-male liberal arts colleges in the country), he studied psychology, religion, and English. He also tutored in the Writing Center, served as his fraternity's president, and formed the "friendly supper club," to promote understanding between people in the community from different backgrounds. Ogorek will pursue a career in human services. His argument paper on the benefits of an all-male college culminates four years of experience, reflection, and debate in a unique educational environment, and was a commencement address in 1986.

Most universities in the United States admit both men and women students. Many single gender colleges live on, though, and only two of these are all-male. I go to one of them, and the co-education issue is a hot one here. Even after more than seven semesters at an all-male college, though, I feel that these schools can be good for both men and women.

Advocates of co-education at this school generally accuse single gender colleges of breeding homosexuals, social cripples and/or incompetent business people. These, they say, are the results of living in an environment where male-female interaction of any kind is inhibited or maybe even avoided. And although I choose not to deal directly with these arguments in this essay, my objections to them should be obvious.

Some traditional single gender arguments have long been popular on my campus. One is tradition, and another is "Fewer distractions during the week."

Also, pajama tops are always suitable for class, and shaving is optional. On the whole, though, I'd have to say that these arguments are pretty weak. So I'm going to enter a different realm in making my case for all-male colleges.

Basically, most of the pro-co-ed rhetoric can be summed up by a statement something like this: "Guys from all-male colleges don't understand women." This of course implies that men are different from women. And I won't dispute this fact. But how and why are men and women different? These questions have fueled much scientific research, the results of which can be summarized as follows: Yes, to some extent, men and women are born different. Men on the whole seem predisposed to be more aggressive and differ from women in both verbal and quantitative capacities. But far more influential than biology in emphasizing and even creating these types of differences is the dynamic process of gender role socialization, which involves a lot of male-female interaction. Carry this idea far enough and, if men and women could live in (relatively) complete isolation from each other, then they might turn out to be pretty much alike.

Pro-co-ed retort: "But they aren't. Men need a woman's point of view." Fine. And certainly one way for college men to hear such a point of view is to go to college with women. But co-ed classrooms also involve pressure to play traditional gender roles. For example, at a co-ed college, the brilliantly insightful Susan might decide not to offer her highly pertinent opinion during class discussion because she's somewhat attracted to Nose Tackle Bud, who isn't renowned for going out with Nobel Prize winners. Because of possible situations like this one, all-female colleges are said to be good for women since students there can excel in the classroom without being afraid of scaring off potential dates. The woman who goes to an all-female college, then, is said to be more whole. She can achieve intellectually as well as being "allowed" to express emotion and be nurturant. Susan can date Bud and, who knows, maybe even enlighten him?

Well, if the complete person is one who fully develops both intellectual and emotional capacities, and if pressure to fulfill traditional socialized gender roles inhibits intellectual achievement in women, then these same roles muffle nurturance and emotional expressiveness in men. Again, at the co-ed school, Bud might choke down his tears while "Old Yeller" is being shown for his *Studies in Disney* class because he's afraid of exposing his sensitivity and vulnerability to Susan. Granted, he might do the same in an all-male classroom, but at least one possible motivation to do so is eliminated there. If today's man is to be whole by the former definition, then he must be allowed to show his feelings in ways that tradition has denied him. Bud must be allowed to cry. Arguments like the above for all-female schools are good ones—and they work in favor of all-male colleges, too—maybe even more so since male gender role flexibility lags behind that of females.

Even on "neutral" intellectual ground, single gender colleges can help to enrich their students' development. Consider the co-ed classroom where each gender might collectively wait for the other to generate "its" outlook. This process is relatively passive when compared to the more active thought and subsequent discussion that can happen when people must consider for themselves how others might approach an issue (since no "others" are around to spoonfeed a perspective). The graduate of an all-male college may be well-prepared to understand a woman since he may have already spent a lot of time attempting to think like one.

Men who graduate from all-male colleges, then, can be in good ways more like women, better equipped to empathize with their points of view, closer to them in every sense of the word, perfectly prepared to interact with them in all arenas. These men from single gender schools, without co-ed classrooms or even necessarily daily "chumming around" between genders, can in fact be good for women. Thus our old friends Bud and Susan can enjoy a good cry. Together.

All-male colleges can be good for men (and, hence, for women) in another way, too. I'll illustrate this point with a personal speculation. I'm a Psychology major, and if ever I was to perform an experiment, I would compare friendships between men here with those at a similar but co-ed school. My guess is that in terms of healthy nurturance and emotionally expressive support, we rely more on each other for those aspects of relationships that other men normally turn for to women. So even without routine interaction with women, we are becoming well-rounded, well-adjusted people. From personal experience I can say that my friendships here have always been pretty deep in this sense—more so, I think, than they would be if I went to a co-ed school.

I know that all-male colleges aren't places where optimal adjustment necessarily happens. (Where is such a place, anyway?!) And I certainly don't expect you, man or woman, to pack up and transfer to a single gender school (if you're not already at one, that is). My point is that the extinction of all-male colleges in favor of environments that cannot guarantee a fuller education (both intellectually and emotionally) would eliminate the potential benefits of these single gender schools, and would therefore be unfortunate.

QUESTIONS

1. What is the purpose of Ogorek's second paragraph? Do you agree after reading the essay that the writer's objections are obvious? Explain.

2. What is Ogorek's strategy in the third paragraph? Does it work? Explain.

3. Outline the logic of Ogorek's argument in the fourth paragraph. Do you accept each link in the chain of reasoning? Does his conclusion follow?

4. Evaluate Ogorek's claim that co-ed classrooms "involve pressure to play traditional gender roles" which can inhibit achievement. How do your experiences support or contradict this argument?

5. If Ogorek has convinced us that single-sex education can be better for women, then should we be convinced that it may be better for men too? Discuss.

6. Think about the argument made in the paragraph beginning "even on neutral intellectual grounds. . . ." How convincing is Ogorek here? What are the implications of having no "others" around in a classroom?

7. How important is the daily "chumming around" between sexes on your campus? Do you think same-sex friendships at your school would be different if the school were single-sex or co-ed? Has Ogorek proved his point about friendships?

8. After reading Ogorek's essay, are you convinced there is still a place for all-male colleges in today's world? Which of his arguments did you find most convincing? Which least? Why?

9. Describe Ogorek's style. Is it typical or atypical of an undergraduate? Choose specific words and phrases to support your description.

SUGGESTIONS FOR WRITING

1. Imagine yourself debating Ogorek before an audience of students and faculty at his all-male college. Assuming that most of the audience agrees with him, write a rebuttal, including opening and closing remarks.

2. Choose any assertion made by the writer you think is debatable, and write an essay arguing your side of the issue. Possible debatable assertions might be: "Men are more aggressive than women," or the statement that socialization is more important than biology in creating differences between the sexes.

Jayne Anne Phillips
SOMETHING THAT HAPPENED
★ ★ ★

Born in 1952 in West Virginia, Jayne Anne Phillips has published three collections of short stories, the last being the critically acclaimed Black Tickets *(1979), and a novel,* Machine Dreams *(1984). Michiko Kakutani in* The New York Times *labeled her one of the "most gifted writers" of her generation, able to illuminate "the secret core of ordinary lives with clear-sighted unsentimentality." The story "Something That Happened" does unsentimentally expose the realities of middle-class family life, through the eyes of its incisively witty, middle-aged protagonist. Phillips's story, while not conforming to the traditional form of the argument essay, treats one controversial issue, divorce, and dramatizes the debate over appropriate female roles through the arguments between the sisters. In "Something That Happened," then, we see how short story writers differ from essayists in their mode of presenting controversial issues—characters replace the author's voice, and dialogue and dramatic conflict substitute for the logical presentation of a case.*

I am in the basement sorting clothes, whites with whites, colors with colors, delicates with delicates—it's a segregated world—when my youngest child yells down the steps. She yells when I'm in the basement, always, angrily, as if I've slipped below the surface and though she's twenty-one years old she can't believe it.

"Do you know what day it is? I mean do you know what day it is, Kay?" It's this new thing of calling me by my first name. She stands groggy eyed, surveying her mother.

I say, "No, Angela, so what does that make me?" Now my daughter shifts into second, narrows those baby blues I once surveyed in such wonder and prayed *Lord, lord, This is the last.*

"Well never mind," she says. "I've made you breakfast." And she had, eggs and toast and juice and flowers on the porch. Then she sat and watched me eat it, twirling her fine gold hair.

Halfway through the eggs it dawns on me, my ex-wedding anniversary. Angela, under the eye-liner and blue jeans you're a haunted and ancient presence. When most children can't remember an anniversary, Angela can't forget it. Every year for five years she has pushed me to the brink of remembrance.

"The trouble with you," she finally speaks, "is that you don't care enough about yourself to remember what's been important in your life."

"Angela," I say, "in the first place I haven't been married for five years, so I no longer have a wedding anniversary to remember."

"That doesn't matter" [twirling her hair, not scowling]. "It's still something that happened."

Two years ago I had part of an ulcerated stomach removed and I said to the kids, "Look, I can't worry for you anymore. If you get into trouble, don't call me. If you want someone to take care of you, take care of each other." So the three older girls packed Angela off to college and her brother drove her there. Since then I've gradually reassumed my duties. Except that I was inconspicuously absent from my daughters' weddings. I say inconspicuously because, thank God, all of them are hippies who got married in fields without benefit of aunts and uncles. Or mothers. But Angela reads *Glamour,* and she'll ask me to her wedding. Though Mr. Charm has yet to appear in any permanent guise, she's already gearing up to it. Pleadings. Remonstrations. Perhaps a few tears near the end. But I shall hold firm, I hate sacrificial offerings of my own flesh. "I can't help it," I'll joke, "I have a weak stomach, only half of it is there."

Angela sighs, perhaps foreseeing it all. The phone is ringing. And slowly, there she goes. By the time she picks it up, cradles the receiver to her brown neck, her voice is normal. Penny bright, and she spends it fast. I look out the screened porch on the alley and the clean garbage cans. It seems to me that I remembered everything before the kids were born. I say kids as though they appeared collectively in a giant egg, my stomach. When actually there were two years, then one year, then two, then three between them. The Child Bearing Years, as though you stand there like a blossomed pear tree and the fruit plops off. Eaten or rotted to seed to start the whole thing all over again.

Angela has fixed too much food for me. She often does. I don't digest large amounts so I eat small portions six times a day. The dog drags his basset ears to my feet, waits for the plate. And I give it to him, urging him on so he'll gobble it fast and silent before Angela comes back.

Dear children, I always confused my stomach with my womb. Lulled into confusion by nearly four pregnant years I heard them say, "Oh, you're eating for two," as if the two organs were directly connected by a small tube. In the hospital I was convinced they had removed my uterus along with half of my stomach. The doctors, at an end of patience, labeled my decision an anxiety reaction. And I reacted anxiously by demanding an X-ray so I could see that my womb was still there.

Angela returns, looks at the plate which I have forgotten to pick up, looks at the dog, puts her hand on my shoulder.

"I'm sorry," she says.

"Well," I say.

Angela twists her long fingers, her fine thin fingers with their smooth knuckles, twists the diamond ring her father gave her when she was sixteen.

"Richard," I'd said to my husband, "she's your daughter, not your fiancée."

"Kay," intoned the husband, the insurance agent, the successful adjuster of claims, "she's only sixteen once. This ring is a gift, our love for Angela. She's beautiful, she's blossoming."

"Richard," I said, shuffling Maalox bottles and planning my bland lunch, "Diamonds are not for blossoms. They're for those who need a piece of the rock." At which Richard laughed heartily, always amused at my cynicism regarding the business which principally buttered my bread. Buttered his bread, because by then I couldn't eat butter.

"What is it you're afraid to face?" asked Richard. "What is it in your life you can't control; you're eating yourself alive. You're dissolving your own stomach."

"Richard," I said, "it's a tired old story. I have this husband who wants to marry his daughter."

"I want you to see a psychiatrist," said Richard, tightening his expertly knotted tie. "That's what you need, Kay, a chance to talk it over with someone who's objective."

"I'm not interested in objectives," I said. "I'm interested in shrimp and butter sauce, Tabasco, hot chiles and an end of pain."

"Pain never ends," said Richard.

"Oh, Richard," I said, "no wonder you're the King of the Southeast Division."

"Look," he said, "I'm trying to put four kids through college and one wife through graduate school. I'm starting five investment plans now so when our kids get married no one has to wait twenty-five years to finish a dissertation on George Eliot like you did. Really, am I such a bad guy? I don't remember forcing you into any of this. And your goddamn stomach has to quit digesting itself. I want you to see a psychiatrist."

"Richard," I said, "if our daughters have five children in eight years [which most of them won't, being members of Zero Population Growth who quote the foreword of *Diet for a Small Planet* every Thanksgiving] they may still be slow with Ph.D.'s despite your investment plans."

Richard untied his tie and tied it again. "Listen," he said. "Plenty of women with five children have Ph.D.'s."

"Really," I said. "I'd like to see those statistics."

"I suppose you resent your children's births," he said, straightening his collar. "Well, just remember, the last one was your miscalculation."

"And the first one was yours," I said.

It's true. We got pregnant, as Richard affectionately referred to it, in a borrowed bunk bed at Myrtle Beach. It was the eighth time we'd slept together. Richard gasped that of course he'd take care of things, had he ever failed me? But I had my first orgasm and no one remembered anything.

After the fourth pregnancy and first son, Richard was satisfied. Angela, you were born in a bad year. You were expensive, your father was starting in insurance after five years as a high school principal. He wanted the rock, all of it. I had a rock in my belly we thought three times was dead. So he swore his love to you, with that ring he thee guiltily wed. Sweet Sixteen, does she remember? She never forgets.

Angela pasted sugar cubes to pink ribbons for a week, Sweet Sixteen party favors she read about in *Seventeen,* while the older girls shook their sad heads. Home from colleges in Ann Arbor, Boston, Berkeley, they stared aghast at their golden-haired baby sister, her Villager suits, the ladybug stickpin in her blouses. Angela owned no blue jeans; her boyfriend opened the car door for her and carried her books home. They weren't heavy, he was a halfback. Older sister no. 3: "Don't you have arms?" Older sister no. 2: "He'll take it out of your hide, wait and see." Older sister no. 1: "The nuclear family lives in women's guts. Your mother has ulcers, Angela, she can't eat gravy with your daddy."

At which point Richard slapped oldest sister, his miscalculation, and she flew back to Berkeley, having cried in my hands and begged me to come with her. She missed the Sweet Sixteen party. She missed Thanksgiving and Christmas for the next two years.

Angela's jaw set hard. I saw her reject politics, feminism, and everyone's miscalculations. I hung sugar cubes from the ceiling for her party until the room looked like the picture in the magazine. I ironed sixteen pink satin ribbons she twisted in her hair. I applauded with everyone else, including the smiling halfback, when her father slipped the diamond on her finger. Then I filed for divorce.

The day Richard moved out of the house, my son switched his major to premed at the state university. He said it was the only way to get out of selling insurance. The last sound of the marriage was Richard being nervously sick in the kitchen sink. Angela gave him a cold wash cloth and took me out to dinner at Senor Miguel's while he stacked up his boxes and drove them away. I ate chiles rellenos, guacamole chips in sour cream, cheese enchiladas, Mexican fried bread and three green chile burritos. Then I ate tranquilizers and bouillon for two weeks.

Angela was frightened.

"Mother," she said, "I wish you could be happy."

"Angela," I answered, "I'm glad you married your father, I couldn't do it any more."

Angela finished high school that year and twelve copies each of *Ingenue, Cosmopolitan, Mademoiselle.* She also read the Bible alone at night in her room.

"Because I'm nervous," she said, "and it helps me sleep. All the trees and fruit, the figs, begat and begat going down like the multiplication tables."

"Angela," I said, "are you thinking of making love to someone?"

"No Mother," she said, "I think I'll wait. I think I'll wait a long time."

Angela quit eating meat and blinked her mascaraed eyes at the glistening fried liver I slid onto her plate.

"It's so brown," she said. "It's just something's guts."

"You've always loved it," I said, and she tried to eat it, glancing at my midriff, glancing at my milk and cottage cheese.

When her father took over the Midwest and married a widow, Angela declined to go with him. When I went to the hospital to have my stomach reduced by half, Angela declined my invitations to visit and went on a fast. She grew wan and romantic, said she wished I taught at her college instead of City, she'd read about Sylvia Plath in *Mademoiselle.* We talked on the telephone while I watched the hospital grounds go dark in my square window. It was summer and the trees were so heavy.

I thought about Angela, I thought about my miscalculations. I thought about milk products and white mucous coatings. About Richard's face the night of the first baby, skinny in his turned-up coat. About his mother sending roses every birth, American Beauties. And babies slipping in the wash basin, tiny wriggling arms, the blue veins in their translucent heads. And starting oranges for ten years, piercing thick skins with a fingernail so the kids could peel them. After a while, I didn't want to watch the skin give way to the white ragged coat beneath.

Angela comes home in the summers, halfway through business, elementary education or home ec. She doesn't want to climb the Rockies or go to India. She wants to show houses to wives, real estate, and feed me mashed potatoes, cherry pie, avocados and artichokes. Today she not only fixes breakfast for my ex-anniversary, she fixes lunch and dinner. She wants to pile up my plate and see me eat everything. If I eat, surely something good will happen. She won't remember what's been important enough in my life to make me forget everything. She is spooning breaded clams, french fries, nuts and anchovy salad onto my plate.

"Angela, it's too much."

"That's OK, we'll save what you don't want."

"Angela, save it for who?"

She puts down her fork. "For anyone," she says. "For any time they want it."

In a moment, she slides my plate onto her empty one and begins to eat.

QUESTIONS

1. What is the "something that happened"?

2. Angela is the only child who is a major character in the story. Do her personality and/or actions make a stronger or weaker case for Kay?

3. At the end of the story, Kay refers to "what's been important enough in my life to make me forget everything." To what is she referring? Does this make her more sympathetic?

4. "Something That Happened" does not follow a straight chronological order. What does Phillips accomplish by "framing" the story with the present and dealing with the past in the middle?

SUGGESTION FOR WRITING

Sometimes the important events in our lives are more effectively presented indirectly than directly. Think of something that happened in your life which deeply affected the way you thought, acted, or felt—a difficult move to a new neighborhood when you were a child, for example. Using as many of Phillips's fictional techniques as you wish (flashback, "framing," first-person narration, conflict, dialogue), recreate the event so your reader will get the point or theme of your story without your spelling it out.

Wendy Rose
I EXPECTED MY SKIN AND MY BLOOD TO RIPEN
★★★

Wendy Rose, born in California, is a native American poet, artist, and anthropologist, who studied and now teaches at the University of California at Berkeley. Among her books of poetry are Hopi Roadrunner Dancing *(1973),* Long Division: A Tribal History *(1976),* Academic Squaw *(1977),* Lost Copper *(1979), and* What Happened When the Hopi Hit New York *(1980). Her works have also been widely anthologized. Rose has an intense commitment to keeping her Hopi heritage alive, yet she resists being classified as a native American first, and poet second. Art, to Rose, is universal. "Writing is just something that always has been and just is,"she said in a* Contemporary Authors *interview. "For everything in this universe there is a song to accompany its existence; writing is another way of singing those songs. Everyone knows the words and tune; it's just that not everyone feels the confidence in themselves to keep their ears open and their senses feeling. Writing just comes from those less afraid of themselves (although possibly more afraid of other-than-themselves)." In her poem "I Expected My Skin and My Blood to Ripen," Rose uses powerful images and other poetic techniques to make an implicit point about the way native Americans have been treated in their own country.*

"When the blizzard subsided four days later (after the massacre), a burial party was sent to Wounded Knee. A long trench was dug. Many of the bodies were stripped by whites who went out in order to get the ghost shirts and other accoutrements the Indians wore . . . the frozen bodies were thrown into the trench stiff and naked . . . only a handful of items remain in private hands . . . exposure to snow has stiffened the leggings and moccasins, and all the objects show the effects of age and long use. . . ." There follows: moccasins at $140, hide scraper at $350, buckskin shirt at $1200, woman's leggings at $275, bone breastplate at $1000.
Plains Indian Art: Sales Catalog by Kenneth Canfield, 1977

I expected my skin and my blood
to ripen
not be ripped from my bones;
like green fruit I am peeled
tasted, discarded; my seeds are stepped on
and crushed
as if there were no future. Now
there has been
no past.   My own body gave up the beads
my own arms handed the babies away
to be strung on bayonets, to be counted
one by one like rosary stones and then
to be tossed to each side of life
as if the pain of their borning
had never been.
My feet were frozen to the leather,
pried apart, left behind—bits of flesh
on the moccasins, bits of papery deerhide
on the bones. My back was stripped
of its cover, its quilling intact; was torn,
was taken away, was restored.
My leggings were taken like in a rape
and shriveled to the size of stick figures
like they had never felt

the push of my strong woman's body
walking in the hills.
It was my own baby whose cradleboard I held.
would've put her in my mouth
like a snake
if I could, would've turned her
into a bush or old rock
if there'd been enough magic
to work such changes. Not enough magic
even to stop the bullets.
Not enough magic
to stop the scientists.
Not enough magic
to stop the collectors.

QUESTIONS

1. Why does Rose begin her poem with the long prose passage?

2. Analyze the central image in the poem, "ripening." Is it carried through the poem? Are there related images?

3. What is the poem's effect on you as reader? Why does it have the effect it does? (In addition to imagery, you might consider the way the lines are arranged on the page.)

4. In what ways could the poem be classified as an example of argument and persuasion? What is Rose's thesis?

SUGGESTION FOR WRITING

Using prewriting techniques we have discussed (for example, brainstorming and free-writing), discover something that makes you very angry. Write down the images that come to mind as you think of your subject. Then organize and shape these into a poem.

Appendix

James Baldwin
THE DISCOVERY OF WHAT IT MEANS TO
BE AN AMERICAN

★ ★ ★

James Baldwin—whom many critics regard as one of the finest essayists in contemporary American literature, as well as one of the foremost black writers of our time—was born in Harlem in 1924. The son of a fiercely religious, even fanatical minister, Baldwin himself preached for several years during his adolescence, an experience clearly reflected in his impassioned, eloquent prose style. Baldwin began writing during his childhood, and by the time he graduated from high school in 1942, he was determined to become a professional writer.

The next decade-and-a-half of Baldwin's life conform to a familiar, almost classic, pattern. For a number of years, he was a struggling young writer in Greenwich Village, learning his craft while supporting himself by a succession of odd jobs. Then, in 1948, he left the United States and became an expatriate in Paris. During his stay in Europe, his first books began to appear, including two that are generally regarded as among his best—the novel Go Tell It on the Mountain *(1953) and a collection of essays,* Notes of a Native Son *(1955).*

Since his return to America in 1957, Baldwin has produced a substan-

tial, if somewhat uneven, body of work: novels, short stories, and plays. Most critics, however, regard his essays—collected in Nobody Knows My Name *(1961),* More Notes of a Native Son *(1961),* The Fire Next Time *(1963), among others—as his major achievement. All of Baldwin's nonfiction since 1948 has recently been published in a single, omnibus volume,* The Price of a Ticket *(1985). Baldwin's work is dominated by his passionate concern with large social issues, particularly with the bitter antagonism between the races in our country.*

———

"It is a complex fate to be an American," Henry James observed, and the principal discovery an American writer makes in Europe is just how complex this fate is. America's history, her aspirations, her peculiar triumphs, her even more peculiar defeats, and her position in the world—yesterday and today—are all so profoundly and stubbornly unique that the very word "America" remains a new, almost completely undefined and extremely controversial proper noun. No one in the world seems to know exactly what it describes, not even we motley millions who call ourselves Americans.

I left America because I doubted my ability to survive the fury of the color problem here. (Sometimes I still do.) I wanted to prevent myself from becoming *merely* a Negro; or, even, merely a Negro writer. I wanted to find out in what way the *specialness* of my experience could be made to connect me with other people instead of dividing me from them. (I was as isolated from Negroes as I was from whites, which is what happens when a Negro begins, at bottom, to believe what white people say about him.)

In my necessity to find the terms on which my experience could be related to that of others, Negroes and whites, writers and non-writers, I proved, to my astonishment, to be as American as any Texas G.I. And I found my experience was shared by every American writer I knew in Paris. Like me, they had been divorced from their origins, and it turned out to make very little difference that the origins of white Americans were European and mine were African—they were no more at home in Europe than I was.

The fact that I was the son of a slave and they were the sons of free men meant less, by the time we confronted each other on European soil, than the fact that we were both searching for our separate identities. When we had found these, we seemed to be saying, why, then, we would no longer need to cling to the shame and bitterness which had divided us so long.

It became terribly clear in Europe, as it never had been here, that we knew more about each other than any European ever could. And it also became clear that, no matter where our fathers had been born, or what they had endured, the fact of Europe had formed us both was part of our identity and part of our inheritance.

I had been in Paris a couple of years before any of this became clear to me. When it did, I, like many a writer before me upon the discovery that his props have all been knocked out from under him, suffered a species of breakdown and was carried off to the mountains of Switzerland. There, in that absolutely alabaster landscape, armed with two Bessie Smith records and a typewriter, I began to try to re-create the life that I had first known as a child and from which I had spent so many years in flight.

It was Bessie Smith, through her tone and her cadence, who helped me to dig back to the way I myself must have spoken when I was a pickaninny, and to remember the things I had heard and seen and felt. I had buried them very deep. I had never listened to Bessie Smith in America (in the same way that, for years, I would not touch watermelon), but in Europe she helped to reconcile me to being a "nigger."

I do not think that I could have made this reconciliation here. Once I was able to accept my role—as distinguished, I must say, from my "place"—in the extraordinary drama which is America, I was released from the illusion that I hated America.

The story of what can happen to an American Negro writer in Europe simply illustrates, in some relief, what can happen to any American writer there. It is not meant, of course, to imply that it happens to them all, for Europe can be very crippling, too; and, anyway, a writer, when he has made his first breakthrough, has simply won a crucial skirmish in a dangerous, unending and unpredictable battle. Still, the breakthrough is important, and the point is that an American writer, in order to achieve it, very often has to leave this country.

The American writer, in Europe, is released, first of all, from the necessity of apologizing for himself. It is not until he *is* released from the habit of flexing his muscles and proving that he is just a "regular guy" that he realizes how crippling this habit has been. It is not necessary for him, there, to pretend to be something he is not, for the artist does not encounter in Europe the same suspicion he encounters here. Whatever the Europeans may actually think of artists, they have killed enough of them off by now to know that they are as real—and as persistent—as rain, snow, taxes or businessmen.

Of course, the reason for Europe's comparative clarity concerning the different functions of men in society is that European society has always been divided into classes in a way that American society never has been. A European writer considers himself to be part of an old and honorable tradition—of intellectual activity, of letters—and his choice of a vocation does not cause him any uneasy wonder as to whether or not it will cost him all his friends. But this tradition does not exist in America.

On the contrary, we have a very deep-seated distrust of real intellectual effort (probably because we suspect that it will destroy, as I hope it does, that myth of America to which we cling so desperately). An American writer fights his way to one of the lowest rungs on the American social ladder by means of pure bull-headedness and an indescribable series of odd jobs. He probably *has* been a "regular fellow" for much of his adult life, and it is not easy for him to step out of that lukewarm bath.

We must, however, consider a rather serious paradox: though American society is more mobile than Europe's, it is easier to cut across social and occupational lines there than it is here. This has something to do, I think, with the problem of status in American life. Where everyone has status, it is also perfectly possible, after all, that no one has. It seems inevitable, in any case, that a man may become uneasy as to just what his status is.

But Europeans have lived with the idea of status for a long time. A man can be as proud of being a good waiter as of being a good actor, and, in neither case, feel threatened. And this means that the actor and the waiter can have a freer and more genuinely friendly relationship in Europe than they are likely to have here. The waiter does not feel, with obscure resentment, that the actor has "made it," and the actor is not tormented by the fear that he may find himself, tomorrow, once again a waiter.

This lack of what may roughly be called social paranoia causes the American writer in Europe to feel—almost certainly for the first time in his life—that he can reach out to everyone, that he is accessible to everyone and open to everything. This is an extraordinary feeling. He feels, so to speak, his own weight, his own value.

It is as though he suddenly came out of a dark tunnel and found himself beneath the open sky. And, in fact, in Paris, I began to see the sky for what seemed to be the first time. It was borne in on me—and it did not make me feel melancholy—that this sky had been there before I was born and would be there when I was dead. And it was up to me, therefore, to make of my brief opportunity the most that could be made.

I was born in New York, but have lived only in pockets of it. In Paris, I lived in all parts of the city—on the Right Bank and the Left, among the bourgeoisie and among *les misérables,* and knew all kinds of people, from pimps and prostitutes in Pigalle to Egyptian bankers in Neuilly. This may sound extremely unprincipled or even obscurely immoral: I found it healthy. I love to talk to people, all kinds of people, and almost everyone, as I hope we still know, loves a man who loves to listen.

This perpetual dealing with people very different from myself caused a shattering in me of preconceptions I scarcely knew I held. The writer is meeting in Europe people who are not American, whose sense of reality is entirely different from his own. They may love or hate or admire or fear or envy this country—they see it, in any case, from another point of view, and this forces the writer to reconsider many things he had always taken for granted. This reassessment, which can be very painful, is also very valuable.

This freedom, like all freedom, has its dangers and its responsibilities. One day it begins to be borne in on the writer, and with great force, that he is living in Europe as an American. If he were living there as a European, he would be living on a different and far less attractive continent.

This crucial day may be the day on which an Algerian taxi-driver tells him how it feels to be an Algerian in Paris. It may be the day on which he passes a café terrace and catches a glimpse of the tense, intelligent and troubled face of Albert Camus. Or it may be the day on which someone asks him to explain Little Rock and he begins to feel that it would be simpler—and, corny as the words may sound, more honorable—to *go* to Little Rock than sit in Europe, on an American passport, trying to explain it.

This is a personal day, a terrible day, the day to which his entire sojourn has been tending. It is the day he realizes that there are no untroubled countries in this fearfully troubled world; that if he has been preparing himself for anything in Europe, he has been preparing himself—for America. In short, the freedom that the American writer finds in Europe brings him, full circle, back to himself, with the responsibility for his development where it always was: in his own hands.

Even the most incorrigible maverick has to be born somewhere. He may leave the group that produced him—he may be forced to—but nothing will efface his origins, the marks of which he carries with him everywhere. I think it is important to know this and even find it a matter for rejoicing, as the strongest people do, regardless of their station. On this acceptance, literally, the life of a writer depends.

The charge has often been made against American writers that they do not describe society, and have no interest in it. They only describe individuals in opposition to it, or isolated from it. Of course, what the American writer is describing is his own situation. But what is *Anna Karenina* describing if not the tragic fate of the isolated individual, at odds with her time and place?

The real difference is that Tolstoy was describing an old and dense society in which everything seemed—to the people in it, though not to Tolstoy—to be fixed forever. And the book is a masterpiece because Tolstoy was able to fathom, and make us see, the hidden laws which really governed this society and made Anna's doom inevitable.

American writers do not have a fixed society to describe. The only society they know is one in which nothing is fixed and in which the individual must fight for his identity. This is a rich confusion, indeed, and it creates for the American writer unprecedented opportunities.

That the tensions of American life, as well as the possibilities, are tremendous is certainly not even a question. But these are dealt with in contemporary literature mainly compulsively; that is, the book is more likely to be a symptom of our tension than an examination of it. The time has come, God knows, for us to examine ourselves, but we can only do this if we are willing to free ourselves of the myth of America and try to find out what is really happening here.

Every society is really governed by hidden laws, by unspoken but profound assumptions on the part of the people, and ours is no exception. It is up to the American writer to find out what these laws and assumptions are. In a society much given to smashing taboos without thereby managing to be liberated from them, it will be no easy matter.

It is no wonder, in the meantime, that the American writer keeps running off to Europe. He needs sustenance for his journey and the best models he can find. Europe has what we do not have yet, a sense of the mysterious and inexorable limits of life, a sense, in a word, of tragedy. And we have what they sorely need: a new sense of life's possibilities.

In this endeavor to wed the vision of the Old World with that of the New, it is the writer, not the statesman, who is our strongest arm. Though we do not wholly believe it yet, the interior life is a real life, and the intangible dreams of people have a tangible effect on the world.

Joan Didion
ON SELF-RESPECT
★ ★ ★

A fifth-generation descendant of California pioneers, Joan Didion was born in Sacramento in 1934 and did her undergraduate work at Berkeley. Having won Vogue *magazine's* Prix de Paris *during her senior year, she moved to New York City in 1956, and served as an associate feature editor of* Vogue *until 1963, when her first novel,* River Run, *was published. The following year, she and her husband, writer John Gregory Dunne (with whom she has collaborated on a number of projects, including several screenplays), settled in Los Angeles. Between 1963 and 1969, Didion wrote essays and feature articles for various popular magazines, including* Harper's, *the* National Review, *and the* Saturday Evening Post. *Her 1969 collection,* Slouching Towards Bethlehem, *was enthusiastically received by critics, who praised her as a brilliant reporter of the contemporary scene. Other novels, essay collections, and nonfiction books followed, including* Play It As It Lays *(1970),* A Book of Common Prayer *(1977),* The White Album *(1979),* Salvador *(1983), and* Democracy *(1984).*

The following essay is reprinted from Slouching Towards Bethlehem, *whose title alludes to a famous poem by W.B. Yeats, "The Second Coming." The opening stanza of that poem contains these lines: "Things fall apart; the centre cannot hold; / Mere anarchy is loosed upon the world." The sense of widespread cultural malaise conveyed in this passage—of contemporary society as a moral and spiritual wasteland—pervades Didion's work, which records, with determinedly unsentimental, "nononsense" clarity, the emptiness and fragmentation of modern life. But Didion is more than a detached observer. Central to her writing is the deeply felt effort to discover order and meaning in a world deprived of traditional values.*

Once, in a dry season, I wrote in large letters across two pages of a notebook that innocence ends when one is stripped of the delusion that one likes oneself. Although now, some years later, I marvel that a mind on the outs with itself should have nonetheless made painstaking record of its every tremor, I recall with embarrassing clarity the flavor of those particular ashes. It was a matter of misplaced self-respect.

I had not been elected to Phi Beta Kappa. This failure could scarcely have been more predictable or less ambiguous (I simply did not have the grades), but I was unnerved by it; I had somehow thought myself a kind of academic Raskolnikov, curiously exempt from the cause-effect relationships which hampered others. Although even the humorless nineteen-year-old that I was must have recognized that the situation lacked real tragic stature, the day that I did not make Phi Beta Kappa nonetheless marked the end of something, and innocence may well be the word for it. I lost the conviction that lights would always turn green for me, the pleasant certainty that those rather passive virtues which had won me approval as a child automatically guaranteed me not only Phi Beta Kappa keys but happiness, honor, and the love of a good man; lost a certain touching faith in the totem power of good manners, clean hair, and proven competence on the Stanford-Binet scale. To such doubtful amulets had my self-respect been pinned, and I faced myself that day with the nonplused apprehension of someone who has come across a vampire and has no crucifix at hand.

Although to be driven back upon oneself is an uneasy affair at best, rather like trying to cross a border with borrowed credentials, it seems to me now the one condition necessary to the beginnings of real self-respect. Most of our platitudes notwithstanding, self-deception remains the most difficult deception. The tricks that work on others count for nothing in that very well-lit back alley where one keeps assignations with oneself: no winning smiles will do here, no prettily drawn lists of good intentions. One shuffles flashily but in vain through one's marked cards—the kindness done for the wrong reason, the apparent triumph which involved no real effort, the seemingly heroic act into which one had been shamed. The dismal fact is that self-respect has nothing to do with the approval of others—who are, after all, deceived easily enough; has nothing to do with reputation, which, as Rhett Butler told Scarlett O'Hara, is something people with courage can do without.

To do without self-respect, on the other hand, is to be an unwilling audience of one to an interminable documentary that details one's failings, both real and imagined, with fresh footage spliced in for every screening. *There's the glass you broke in anger, there's the hurt on X's face; watch now, this next scene, the night Y came back from Houston, see how you muff this one.* To live without self-respect is to lie awake some night, beyond the reach of warm milk, phenobarbital, and the sleeping hand on the coverlet, counting up the sins of commission and omission, the trusts betrayed, the promises subtly broken, the gifts irrevocably wasted through sloth or cowardice or carelessness. However long we postpone it, we eventually lie down alone in that notoriously uncomfortable bed, the one we make ourselves. Whether or not we sleep in it depends, of course, on whether or not we respect ourselves.

To protest that some fairly improbable people, some people who *could not possibly respect themselves,* seem to sleep easily enough is to miss the point entirely, as surely as those people miss it who think that self-respect has necessarily to do with not having safety pins in one's underwear. There is a common superstition that "self-respect" is a kind of charm against snakes, something that keeps those who have it locked in some unblighted Eden, out of strange beds, ambivalent conversations, and trouble in general. It does not at all. It has nothing to do with the face of things, but concerns instead a separate peace, a private reconciliation. Although the careless, suicidal Julian English in *Appointment in Samarra* and the careless, incurably dishonest Jordan Baker in *The Great Gatsby* seem equally improbable candidates for self-respect, Jordan Baker had it, Julian English did not. With that genius for accommodation more often seen in women than in men, Jordan took her own measure, made her own peace, avoided threats to that peace: "I hate careless people," she told Nick Carraway. "It takes two to make an accident."

Like Jordan Baker, people with self-respect have the courage of their mistakes. They know the price of things. If they choose to commit adultery, they do not then go running, in an access of bad conscience, to receive absolution from the wronged parties; nor do they complain unduly of the unfairness, the undeserved embarrassment, of being named co-respondent. In brief, people with self-respect exhibit a certain toughness, a kind of moral nerve; they display what was once called *character,* a quality which, although approved in the abstract, sometimes loses ground to other, more instantly negotiable virtues. The measure of its slipping prestige is that one tends to think of it only in connection with homely children and United States senators who have been defeated, preferably in the primary, for reelection. Nonetheless, character—the willingness to accept responsibility for one's own life—is the source from which self-respect springs.

Self-respect is something that our grandparents, whether or not they had it, knew all about. They had instilled in them, young, a certain discipline, the sense that one lives by doing things one does not particularly want to do, by putting fears and doubts to one side, by weighing immediate comforts against the possibility of larger, even intangible, comforts. It seemed to the nineteenth century admirable, but not remarkable, that Chinese Gordon put on a clean white suit and held Khartoum against the Mahdi; it did not seem unjust that the way to free land in California involved death and difficulty and dirt. In a diary kept during the winter of 1846, an emigrating twelve-year-old named Narcissa Cornwall noted coolly: "Father was busy reading and did not notice that the house was being filled with strange Indians until Mother spoke about it." Even lacking any clue as to what Mother said, one can scarcely fail to be impressed by the entire incident: the father reading, the Indians filing in, the mother choosing the words that would not alarm, the child duly recording the event and noting further that those particular Indians were not, "fortunately for us," hostile. Indians were simply part of the *donnée*.

In one guise or another, Indians always are. Again, it is a question of recognizing that anything worth having has its price. People who respect themselves are willing to accept the risk that the Indians will be hostile, that the venture will go bankrupt, that the liaison may not turn out to be one in which *every day is a holiday because you're married to me.* They are willing to invest something of themselves; they may not play at all, but when they do play, they know the odds.

That kind of self-respect is a discipline, a habit of mind that can never be faked but can be developed, trained, coaxed forth. It was once suggested to me that, as an antidote to crying, I put my head in a paper bag. As it happens, there is a sound physiological reason, something to do with oxygen, for doing exactly that, but the psychological effect alone is incalculable: it is difficult in the extreme to continue fancying oneself Cathy in *Wuthering Heights* with one's head in a Food Fair bag. There is a similar case for all the small disciplines, unimportant in themselves; imagine maintaining any kind of swoon, commiserative or carnal, in a cold shower.

But those small disciplines are valuable only insofar as they represent larger ones. To say that Waterloo was won on the playing fields of Eton is not to say that Napoleon might have been saved by a crash program in cricket; to give formal dinners in the rain forest would be pointless did not the candlelight flickering on the liana call forth deeper, stronger disciplines, values instilled long before. It is a kind of ritual, helping us to remember who and what we are. In order to remember it, one must have known it.

To have that sense of one's intrinsic worth which constitutes self-respect is potentially to have everything: the ability to discriminate, to love and to remain indifferent. To lack it is to be locked within oneself, paradoxically incapable of either love or indifference. If we do not respect ourselves, we are on the one hand forced to despise those who have so few resources as to consort with us, so little perception as to remain blind to our fatal-weaknesses. On the other, we are peculiarly in thrall to everyone we see, curiously determined to live out—since our self-image is untenable—their false notions of us. We flatter ourselves by thinking this compulsion to please others an attractive trait: a gist for imaginative empathy, evidence of our willingness to give. *Of course* I will play Francesca to your Paolo, Helen Keller to anyone's Annie Sullivan: no expectation is too misplaced, no role too ludicrous. At the mercy of those we cannot but hold in contempt, we play roles doomed to failure before they are begun, each defeat generating fresh despair at the urgency of divining and meeting the next demand made upon us.

It is the phenomenon sometimes called "alienation from self." In its advanced stages, we no longer answer the telephone, because someone might want something; that we could say *no* without drowning in self-reproach is an idea alien to this game. Every encounter demands too much, tears the nerves, drains the will, and the specter of something as small as an unanswered letter arouses such disproportionate guilt that answering it becomes out of the question. To assign unanswered letters their proper weight, to free us from the expectations of others, to give us back to ourselves—there lies the great, the singular power of self-respect. Without it, one eventually discovers the final turn of the screw: one runs away to find oneself, and finds no one at home.

Annie Dillard
LIVING LIKE WEASELS
★ ★ ★

Like the great nineteenth-century author, Henry David Thoreau (to whom she is often compared), Annie Dillard combines the qualities of both the naturalist and the mystic. A self-described "stalker" of the higher meanings that inhere in nature, she is a writer who studies the minute details of the physical world—from the capillaries in a goldfish's tail to the muscles on the head of a caterpillar—in an impassioned effort to put herself in touch with God. As a reviewer for Commentary *magazine has written, Dillard is a "true transcendentalist," who "understands her task to be that of full alertness, of making herself a conscious receptacle of all impressions. She is a connoisseur of spirit, who knows that seeing, if intense enough, becomes vision."*

Born in Pittsburgh in 1945, Dillard received both her B.A. and M.A. from Hollins College in Roanoke, Virginia. In 1972, she lived for a year on Tinker Creek in the Roanoke Valley, a time she spent reading, taking notes, walking, and meditating on the mysteries of nature. Having assembled over 1000 index cards, she worked seven days a week for more than eight months, painstakingly recasting her observations and insights into a richly poetic account of her life amid the ponds, creeks, woods, and fields surrounding her home. The resulting book, Pilgrim at Tinker's Creek *(1974), became a national best-seller and won Dillard—then only 29—the Pulitzer Prize for a nonfiction work. Dillard has since published a number of other, highly praised books, including* Holy the Firm *(1977),* Living By Fiction *(1982), and* Teaching a Stone to Talk *(1982).*

"Living Like Weasels" is excerpted from the last of these volumes. In its blend of precise, naturalistic observation and visionary fervor, this selection is typical of the writing that has made Dillard one of America's most celebrated essayists.

A weasel is wild. Who knows what he thinks? He sleeps in his underground den, his tail draped over his nose. Sometimes he lives in his den for two days without leaving. Outside, he stalks rabbits, mice, muskrats, and birds, killing more bodies than he can eat warm, and often dragging the carcasses home. Obedient to instinct, he bites his prey at the neck, either splitting the jugular vein at the throat or crunching the brain at the base of the skull, and he does not let go. One naturalist refused to kill a weasel who was socketed into his hand deeply as a rattlesnake. The man could in no way pry the tiny weasel off, and he had to walk half a mile to water, the weasel dangling from his palm, and soak him off like a stubborn label.

And once, says Ernest Thompson Seton—once, a man shot an eagle out of the sky. He examined the eagle and found the dry skull of a weasel fixed by the jaws to his throat. The supposition is that the eagle had pounced on the weasel and the weasel swiveled and bit as instinct taught him, tooth to neck, and nearly won. I would like to have seen that eagle from the air a few weeks or months before he was shot: was the whole weasel still attached to his feathered throat, a fur pendant? Or did the eagle eat what he could reach, gutting the living weasel with his talons before his breast, bending his beak, cleaning the beautiful airborne bones?

I have been reading about weasels because I saw one last week. I startled a weasel who startled me, and we exchanged a long glance.

Twenty minutes from my house, through the woods by the quarry and across the highway, is Hollins Pond, a remarkable piece of shallowness, where I like to go at sunset and sit on a tree trunk. Hollins Pond is also called Murray's Pond; it covers two acres of bottomland near Tinker Creek with six inches of water and six thousand lily pads. In winter, brown-and-white steers stand in the middle of it, merely dampening their hooves; from the distant shore they look like miracle itself, complete with miracle's nonchalance. Now, in summer, the steers are gone. The water lilies have blossomed and spread to a green horizontal plane that is terra firma to plodding blackbirds, and tremulous ceiling to black leeches, crayfish, and carp.

This is, mind you, suburbia. It is a five-minute walk in three directions to rows of houses, though none is visible here. There's a 55 mph highway at one end of the pond, and a nesting pair of wood ducks at the other. Under every bush is a muskrat hole or a beer can. The far end is an alternating series of fields and woods, fields and woods, threaded everywhere with motorcycle tracks—in whose bare clay wild turtles lay eggs.

So. I had crossed the highway, stepped over two low barbed-wire fences, and traced the motorcycle path in all gratitude through the wild rose and poison ivy of the pond's shoreline up into high grassy fields. Then I cut down through the woods to the mossy fallen tree where I sit. This tree is excellent. It makes a dry, upholstered bench at the upper, marshy end of the pond, a plush jetty raised from the thorny shore between a shallow blue body of water and a deep blue body of sky.

The sun had just set. I was relaxed on the tree trunk, ensconced in the lap of lichen, watching the lily pads at my feet tremble and part dreamily over the thrusting path of a carp. A yellow bird appeared to my right and flew behind me. It caught my eye; I swiveled around—and the next instant, inexplicably, I was looking down at a weasel, who was looking up at me.

Weasel! I'd never seen one wild before. He was ten inches long, thin as a curve, a muscled ribbon, brown as fruitwood, soft-furred, alert. His face was fierce, small and pointed as a lizard's; he would have made a good arrowhead. There was just a dot of chin, maybe two brown hairs' worth, and then the pure white fur began that spread down his underside. He had two black eyes I didn't see, any more than you see a window.

The weasel was stunned into stillness as he was emerging from beneath an enormous shaggy wild rose bush four feet away. I was stunned into stillness twisted backward on the tree trunk. Our eyes locked, and someone threw away the key.

Our look was as if two lovers, or deadly enemies, met unexpectedly on an overgrown path when each had been thinking of something else: a clearing blow to the gut. It was also a bright blow to the brain, or a sudden beating of brains, with all the charge and intimate grate of rubbed balloons. It emptied our lungs. It felled the forest, moved the fields, and drained the pond; the world dismantled and tumbled into that black hole of eyes. If you and I looked at each other that way, our skulls would split and drop to our shoulders. But we don't. We keep our skulls. So.

He disappeared. This was only last week, and already I don't remember what shattered the enchantment. I think I blinked, I think I retrieved my brain from the weasel's brain, and tried to memorize what I was seeing, and the weasel felt the yank of separation, the careening splash-down into real life and the urgent current of instinct. He vanished under the wild rose. I waited motionless, my mind suddenly full of data and my spirit with pleadings, but he didn't return.

Please do not tell me about "approach-avoidance conflicts." I tell you I've been in that weasel's brain for sixty seconds, and he was in mine. Brains are private places, muttering through unique and secret tapes—but the weasel and I both plugged into another tape simultaneously, for a sweet and shocking time. Can I help it if it was a blank?

What goes on in his brain the rest of the time? What does a weasel think about? He won't say. His journal is tracks in clay, a spray of feathers, mouse blood and bone: uncollected, unconnected, loose-leaf, and blown.

I would like to learn, or remember, how to live. I come to Hollins Pond not so much to learn how to live as, frankly, to forget about it. That is, I don't think I can learn from a wild animal how to live in particular—shall I suck warm blood, hold my tail high, walk with my footprints precisely over the prints of my hands?—but I might learn something of mindlessness, something of the purity of living in the physical senses and the dignity of living without bias or motive. The weasel lives in necessity and we live in choice, hating necessity and dying at the last ignobly in its talons. I would like to live as I should, as the weasel lives as he should. And I suspect that for me the way is like the weasel's: open to time and death painlessly, noticing everything, remembering nothing, choosing the given with a fierce and pointed will.

I missed my chance. I should have gone for the throat. I should have lunged for that streak of white under the weasel's chin and held on, held on through mud and into the wild rose, held on for a dearer life. We could live under the wild rose wild as weasels, mute and uncomprehending. I could very calmly go wild. I could live two days in the den, curled, leaning on mouse fur, sniffing bird bones, blinking, licking, breathing musk, my hair tangled in the roots of grasses. Down is a good place to go, where the mind is single. Down is out, out of your ever-loving mind and back to your careless senses. I remember muteness as a prolonged and giddy fast, where every moment is a feast of utterance received. Time and events are merely poured, unremarked, and ingested directly, like blood pulsed into my gut through a jugular vein. Could two live that way? Could two live under the wild rose, and explore by the pond, so that the smooth mind of each is as everywhere present to the other, and as received and as unchallenged, as falling snow?

We could, you know. We can live any way we want. People take vows of poverty, chastity, and obedience—even of silence—by choice. The thing is to stalk your calling in a certain skilled and supple way, to locate the most tender and live spot and plug into that pulse. This is yielding, not fighting. A weasel doesn't "attack" anything; a weasel lives as he's meant to, yielding at every moment to the perfect freedom of single necessity.

I think it would be well, and proper, and obedient, and pure, to grasp your one necessity and not let it go, to dangle from it limp wherever it takes you. Then even death, where you're going no matter how you live, cannot you part. Seize it and let it seize you up aloft even, till your eyes burn out and drop; let your musky flesh fall off in shreds, and let your very bones unhinge and scatter, loosened over fields, over fields and woods, lightly, thoughtless, from any height at all, from as high as eagles.

Norman Mailer
CITIES HIGHER THAN MOUNTAINS
★ ★ ★

Norman Mailer has been a powerful force in American culture since his first novel, The Naked and the Dead, *appeared in 1948. The Harvard-educated writer has produced fiction, poetry, three films, and was instrumental, along with Tom Wolfe, in developing "new journalism." In books like* The Armies of the Night: History as a Novel, the Novel as History *(1968),* Miami and the Siege of Chicago *(1968),* The Fight *(1975), and* The Executioner's Song *(1979), Mailer filters real events—a Pentagon rally, political conventions, a boxing championship, and the execution of a murderer by the State of Utah—through his radical consciousness, and recreates what he has seen in a richly metaphoric prose style.*

Mailer is a socially conscious writer, obsessed by American culture and his personal relation to it. In "Cities Higher Than Mountains," from Cannibals and Christians *(1966), Mailer is offended and distressed by*

what he calls the vulgarity of American architecture, and by the empty
lives he thinks such architecture reflects. In this piece we see Mailer's talent
for precise observation and daring metaphor, his brilliant use of form, his
romanticism, and his prophetic desire to save the future through the power
of imagination.

In Lyndon Johnson's book, *My Hope for America,* the fifth chapter is titled
"Toward the Great Society." It contains this paragraph:

> . . . fifty years from now, . . . there will be four hundred million Americans,
> four-fifths of them in urban areas. In the remainder of this century, . . . we will
> have to build homes, highways, and facilities equal to all those built since this
> country was first settled. In the next forty years we must rebuild the entire urban
> United States.

It is a staggering sentence. The city we inhabit at this moment is already close
to a total reconstruction of the world our parents knew in their childhood. If there
is no nuclear war, if we shift from cold war to some kind of peace, and there is
a worldwide rise in the standard of living, then indeed we will build a huge new
country. It is possible that not one in a thousand of the buildings put up by 1899
will still be standing in the year 2000.

But what will America look like? How will its architecture appear? Will it
be the architecture of a Great Society, or continue to be the architecture of an
empty promiscuous panorama where no one can distinguish between hospitals
and housing projects, factories and colleges, concert halls, civic centers, and
airport terminals? The mind recoils from the thought of an America rebuilt
completely in the shape of those blank skyscrapers forty stories high, their walls
dead as an empty television screen, their form as interesting as a box of cleansing
tissue propped on end. They are buildings which reveal nothing so much as the
deterioration in real value of the dollar bill. They are denuded of ornament (which
costs money) their windows are not subtly recessed into the wall but are laid flush
with the surface like a patch of collodion on the skin, there is no instant where
a roof with a tower, a gable, a spire, a mansard, a ridge or even a mooring mast
for a dirigible intrudes itself into the sky, reminding us that every previous culture
of man attempted to engage the heavens.

No, our modern buildings go flat, flat at the top, flat as eternal monotony,
flat as the last penny in a dollar. There is so much corruption in the building
codes, overinflation in the value of land, featherbedding built into union rules, so
much graft, so much waste, so much public relations, and so much emptiness
inflated upon so much emptiness that no one tries to do more with the roof than
leave it flat.

As one travels through the arbitrary new neighborhoods of the present, those high
squat dormitories which imprison the rich as well as the poor, one is not surprised

that the violence is greater than it used to be in the old slum, up are the statistics for juvenile delinquency and for dope addiction. To live in the old slum jungle left many half crippled, and others part savage, but it was at least an environment which asked for wit. In the prison vistas of urban renewal, the violence travels from without to within, there is no wit—one travels down a long empty corridor to reach one's door, long as the corridors in the public schools, long as the corridors in the hospitals at the end of the road; the landscape of modern man takes on a sense of endless empty communications.

Sterile as an operating table is the future vista of suburban spread, invigorating as a whiff of deodorant is the sight of new office buildings. Small elation sits upon us as we contemplate the future, for the picturesque will be uprooted with the ugly, our populations will double, and in a city like New York, the brownstone will be replaced by a cube sixteen stories high with a huge park for parking cars and a little grass. The city will go up a little and it will go out, it will spread. We will live with glass walls in a cold climate. The entire world will come to look like Queens Boulevard. We will have been uprooted so many times that future man will come to bear the same relation to the past that a hydroponic plant bears to soil.

Yet some part of us is aware that to uproot the past too completely is a danger without measure. It must at the least produce a profound psychic discomfort. For we do not know how much our perception of the present and our estimate of the future depend upon our sense of what has gone before. To return to an old neighborhood and discover it has disappeared is a minor woe for some; it is close to a psychological catastrophe for others, an amputation where the lost nerves still feel pain. This century must appear at times like a great beast which has lost its tail, but who could argue that the amputation was not self-inflicted?

There seems at loose an impulse to uproot every vestige of the past, an urge so powerful one wonders if it is not with purpose, if it is not in the nature of twentieth-century man to uproot himself not only from his past, but from his planet. Perhaps we live on the edge of a great divide in history and so are divided ourselves between the desire for a gracious, intimate, detailed and highly particular landscape and an urge less articulate to voyage out on explorations not yet made. Perhaps the blank faceless abstract quality of our modern architecture is a reflection of the anxiety we feel before the void, a kind of visual static which emanates from the psyche of us all, as if we do not know which way to go.

If we are to spare the countryside, if we are to protect the style of the small town and of the exclusive suburb, keep the organic center of the metropolis and the old neighborhoods, maintain those few remaining streets where the tradition of the nineteenth century and the muse of the eighteenth century still linger on the mood in the summer cool of an evening, if we are to avoid a megalopolis five hundred miles long, a city without shape or exit, a nightmare of ranch houses, highways, suburbs and industrial sludge, if we are to save the dramatic edge of a city—that precise moment when we leave the outskirts and race into the country, the open country—if we are to have a keen acute sense of concentration and a breath of release, then there is only one solution: the cities must climb, they must not spread, they must build up, not by increments, but by leaps, up and up, up to the heavens.

We must be able to live in houses one hundred stories high, two hundred stories high, far above the height of buildings as we know them now. New cities with great towers must rise in the plain, cities higher than mountains, cities with room for 400,000,000 to live, or that part of 400,000,000 who wish to live high in a landscape of peaks and spires, cliffs and precipices. For the others, for those who wish to live on the ground and with the ground, there will then be new room to live—the traditional small town will be able to survive, as will the old neighborhoods in the cities. But first a way must be found to build upward, to triple and triple again the height of all buildings as we know them now.

Picture, if you please, an open space where twenty acrobats stand, each locking hands with two different partners. Conceive then of ten acrobats standing on the shoulders of these twenty, and five upon the ten acrobats, and three more in turn above them, then two, then one. We have a pyramid of figures: six thousand to eight thousand pounds is supported upon a base of twenty pairs of shoes.

It enables one to think of structures more complex, of pyramids of steel which rise to become towers. Imagine a tower half a mile high and stressed to bear a vast load. Think of six or eight such towers and of bridges built between them, even as huge vines tie the branches of one high tree to another; think of groups of apartments built above these bridges (like the shops on the Ponte Vecchio in Florence) and apartments suspended beneath each bridge, and smaller bridges running from one complex of apartments to another, and of apartments suspended from cables, apartments kept in harmonious stress to one another by cables between them.

One can now begin to conceive of a city, or a separate part of a city, which is as high as it is wide, a city which bends ever so subtly in a high wind with the most delicate flexing of its near-to-numberless parts even as the smallest strut in a great bridge reflects the passing of an automobile with some fine-tuned quiver. In the subtlety of its swayings the vertical city might seem to be ready to live itself. It might be agreeable to live there.

The real question, however, has not yet been posed. It is whether a large fraction of the population would find it reasonable to live one hundred or two hundred stories in the air. There is the dread of heights. Would that tiny pit of suicide, planted like the small seed of murder in civilized man, flower prematurely into breakdown, terror and dread? Would it demand too much of a tenant to stare down each morning on a flight of 2,000 feet? Or would it prove a deliverance for some? Would the juvenile delinquent festering in the violence of his monotonous corridors diminish in his desire for brutality if he lived high in the air and found the intensity of his inexpressible vision matched by the intensity of the space through a fall?

That question returns us to the perspective of twentieth-century man. Caught between our desire to cling to the earth and to explore the stars, it is not impossible that a new life lived half a mile in the air, with streets in the clouds and chasms beyond each railing could prove nonetheless more intimate and more personal to us than the present congestions of the housing-project city. For that future man would be returned some individuality from his habitation. His apartment in the sky would be not so very different in its internal details from the apartments of his neighbors, no more than one apartment is varied from another in Washington Square Village. But his situation would now be different from any other. His windows would look out on a view of massive constructions and airy bridges, of huge vaults and fine intricacies. The complexity of our culture could be captured again by the imagination of the architect: our buildings could begin to look a little less like armored tanks and more like clipper ships. Would we also then feel the dignity of sailors on a four-master at sea? Living so high, thrust into space, might we be returned to that mixture of awe and elation, of dignity and self-respect and a hint of dread, that sense of zest which a man must have known working his way out along a yardarm in a stiff breeze at sea? Would the fatal monotony of mass culture dissolve a hint before the quiet swaying of a great and vertical city?

John McPhee
THE PINBALL PHILOSOPHY
★ ★ ★

Born in 1931 in New Jersey, John McPhee received his bachelor's degree from Princeton University in 1953 and did graduate study at Cambridge University in England. He worked briefly as a television writer before taking a job at Time *magazine, where he spent seven years as an associate editor. Since 1964, he has been a staff writer for* The New Yorker.

Acclaimed as "the most versatile and literate journalist in America," McPhee is famous for his diverse, even eccentric, choice of subjects—one of his books, for example, is a "historical, geographical, botanical, and anecdotal study" of oranges—as well as his masterly prose style. Commenting on McPhee's offbeat interests, critic Richard Horwich has written, "Sometimes it seems that McPhee deliberately chooses unpromising subjects, just to show what he can do with them." Whatever the subject, however, McPhee's books are characterized by meticulous research and craftsmanship, and graceful, vigorous prose. "McPhee's powers of description are such," says Horwich, "that we often feel the shock of recognition even when what is being described is totally outside our experience. . . . McPhee penetrates the surface of things and makes his way toward what is essential and unchanging."

"The Pinball Philosophy" is excerpted from McPhee's 1979 collection, Giving Good Weight. *His other books include* Oranges *(1967),* The

Pine Barrens *(1968),* Levels of the Game *(1970),* The Curve of Binding
Energy *(1974),* The Survival of the Bark Canoe *(1975),* Coming into the
Country *(1977),* Basin and Range *(1981),* In Suspect Terrain *(1983), and*
Table of Contents *(1985).*

New York City, March 1975

J. Anthony Lukas is a world-class pinball player who, between tilts, does some
free-lance writing. In our city, he is No. ½. That is to say, he is one of two players
who share pinball preeminence—two players whose special skills within the sport
are so multiple and varied that they defy comparative analysis. The other star is
Tom Buckley, of the *Times.* Pinball people tend to gravitate toward Lukas or
Buckley. Lukas is a Lukasite. He respects Buckley, but he sees himself as the
whole figure, the number "1." His machine is a Bally. Public pinball has been
illegal in New York for many decades, but private ownership is permitted, and
Lukas plays, for the most part, at home.

Lukas lives in an old mansion, a city landmark, on West Seventy-sixth Street.
The machine is in his living room, under a high, elegant ceiling, near an archway
to rooms beyond. Bally is the Rolls-Royce of pinball, he explains as he snaps a
ball into action. It rockets into the ellipse at the top of the playfield. It ricochets
four times before beginning its descent. Lukas likes a four-bounce hold in the
ellipse—to set things up for a long ball. There is something faintly, and perhaps
consciously, nefarious about Lukas, who is an aristocratic, olive-skinned, Andalu-
sian sort of man, with deep eyes in dark wells. As the butts of his hands pound
the corners of his machine, one can imagine him cheating at polo. "It's a wrist
game," he says, tremoring the Bally, helping the steel ball to bounce six times off
the top thumper-bumper and, each time, go back up a slot to the ellipse—an
awesome economy of fresh beginnings. "Strong wrists are really all you want to
use. The term for what I am doing is 'reinforcing.' " His voice, rich and dense,
pours out like cigarette smoke filtered through a New England prep school.
"There are certain basics to remember," he says. "Above all, don't flail with the
flipper. You *carry* the ball in the direction you want it to go. You can almost
cradle the ball on the flipper. And always hit the slingshot hard. That's the
slingshot there—where the rubber is stretched between bumpers. Reinforce it
hard. And never—never—drift toward the free-ball gate." Lukas reinforces the
machine just as the ball hits the slingshot. The rebound comes off with blurring
speed, striking bumpers, causing gongs to ring and lights to flash. Under his
hands, the chrome on the frame has long since worn away.

Lukas points out that one of the beauties of his Bally is that it is asymmetri-
cal. Early pinball machines had symmetrical playfields—symmetrical thumper-
bumpers—but in time they became free-form, such as this one, with its field laid
out not just for structure but also for surprise. Lukas works in this room—stacks
of manuscript on shelves and tables. He has been working for many months on
a book that will weigh five pounds. It will be called *Nightmare: The Dark Side
of the Nixon Years*—a congenially chosen title, implying that there was a bright

side.* The pinball machine is Lukas's collaborator. "When a paragraph just won't go," he says, "and I begin to say to myself, 'I can't make this work,' I get up and play the machine. I score in a high range. Then I go back to the typewriter a new man. I have beat the machine. Therefore I can beat the paragraph." He once won a Pulitzer Prize.

The steel ball rolls into the "death channel"—Lukas's term for a long alley down the left side—and drops out of sight off the low end of the playfield, finished.

"I have thought of analogies between Watergate and pinball. Everything is connected. Bumpers. Rebounds. You light lights and score. Chuck Colson is involved in almost every aspect of the Watergate story: the dirty tricks, the coverup, the laundered money—all connected. How hard you hit off the thumper-bumper depends on how hard you hit off the sling-shot depends on how well you work the corners. In a sense, pinball is a reflection of the complexity of the subject I am writing about. Bear in mind, I take this with considerable tongue-in-cheek."

With another ball, he ignites an aurora on the scoreboard. During the ball's complex, prolonged descent, he continues to set forth the pinball philosophy. "More seriously, the game does give you a sense of controlling things in a way that in life you can't do. And there is risk in it, too. The ball flies into the ellipse, into the playfield—full of opportunities. But there's always the death channel—the run-out slot. There are rewards, prizes, coming off the thumper-bumper. The ball crazily bounces from danger to opportunity and back to danger. You need reassurance in life that in taking risks you will triumph, and pinball gives you that reaffirmation. Life is a risky game, but you can beat it."

Unfortunately, Lukas has a sick flipper. At the low end of the playfield, two flippers guard the run-out slot, but one waggles like a broken wing, pathetic, unable to function, to fling the ball uphill for renewed rewards. The ball, instead, slides by the crippled flipper and drops from view.

Lukas opens the machine. He lifts the entire playfield, which is hinged at the back, and props it up on a steel arm, like the lid of a grand piano. Revealed below is a neat, arresting world that includes spring-loaded hole kickers, contact switches, target switches, slingshot assemblies, the score-motor unit, the electric anti-cheat, three thumper-bumper relays, the top rebound relay, the key-gate assembly ("the key gate will keep you out of the death channel"), the free-ball-gate assembly, and—not least—the one-and-a-quarter-amp slo-blo. To one side, something that resembles a plumb bob hangs suspended within a metal ring. If the bob moves too far out of plumb, it touches the ring. Tilt. The game is dead.

Lukas is not an electrician. All he can do is massage the flipper's switch assembly, which does not respond—not even with a shock. He has about had it with this machine. One cannot collaborate with a sick flipper. The queasy truth comes over him: no pinball, no paragraphs. So he hurries downstairs and into a taxi, telling the driver to go to Tenth Avenue in the low Forties—a pocket of the city known as Coin Row.

———

*Lukas ultimately decided to be less congenial, and changed the title to *Nightmare: The Underside of the Nixon Years* (Viking Press, 1976).

En route, Lukas reflects on his long history in the game—New York, Cambridge, Paris—and his relationships with specific machines ("they're like wives"). When he was the *Times'* man in the Congo, in the early sixties, the post was considered a position of hardship, so he was periodically sent to Paris for rest and rehabilitation, which he got playing pinball in a Left Bank brasserie. He had perfected his style as an undergraduate at Harvard, sharing a machine at the *Crimson* with David Halberstam ("Halberstam is aggressive at everything he does, and he was very good"). Lukas's father was a Manhattan attorney. Lukas's mother died when he was eight. He grew up, for the most part, in a New England community—Putney, Vermont—where he went to pre-prep and prep school. Putney was "straitlaced," "very high-minded," "a life away from the maelstrom"—potters' wheels, no pinball. Lukas craved "liberation," and developed a yearning for what he imagined as low life, and so did his schoolmate Christopher Lehmann-Haupt. Together, one weekend, they dipped as low as they knew how. They went to New York. And they went to two movies! They went to shooting galleries! They went to a flea circus! They played every coin-operated machine they could find—and they stayed up until after dawn! All this was pretty low, but not low enough, for that was the spring of 1951, and still beyond reach—out there past the fingertips of Tantalus—was pinball, the ban on which had been emphatically reinforced a few years earlier by Fiorello H. LaGuardia, who saw pinball as a gambling device corruptive of the city's youth. To Lukas, pinball symbolized all the time-wasting and ne'er-do-welling that puritan Putney did not. In result, he mastered the game. He says, "It puts me in touch with a world in which I never lived. I am attracted to pinball for its seediness, its slightly disreputable reputation."

On Coin Row, Lukas knows just where he is going, and without a sidewise glance passes storefronts bearing names like The World of Pinball Amusement ("SALES—REPAIR") and Manhattan Coin Machine ("PARTS—SUPPLIES"). He heads directly for the Mike Munves Corporation, 577 Tenth Avenue, the New York pinball exchange, oldest house (1912) on the row. Inside is Ralph Hotkins, in double-breasted blazer—broker in pinball machines. The place is more warehouse than store, and around Hotkins, and upstairs above him, are rank upon rank of Gottliebs, Williamses, Ballys, Playmatics—every name in the game, including forty-year-old antique completely mechanical machines, ten balls for a nickel, the type that Mayor LaGuardia himself destroyed with an axe. Hotkins—a prosperous man, touched with humor, not hurting for girth—got his start in cigarette machines in the thirties, moved up to jukeboxes, and then, in 1945, while LaGuardia was still mayor, to game machines. He had two daughters, and he brought them up on pinball. They were in the shop almost every afternoon after school, and all day Saturday. One daughter now has a Ph.D. in English literature and the other a Ph.D. in political science. So much for the Little Flower. In this era of open massage and off-track betting, Hotkins has expected the ban to lift, but the courts, strangely, continue to uphold it.* Meanwhile, his customers—most of whom are technically "private"—include Wall Street brokerage houses

---

*And they did so until 1976, when pinball at last became legal.

where investors shoot free pinball under the ticker, Seventh Avenue dress houses that wish to keep their buyers amused, the Circus Circus peepshow emporium on West Forty-second Street, many salesrooms, many showrooms, and J. Anthony Lukas.

"Yes, Mr. Lukas. What can we do for you?"

Lukas greets Hotkins and then runs balls through a few selected machines. Lukas attempts to deal with Hotkins, but Hotkins wants Lukas's machine and a hundred and fifty dollars. Lukas would rather fix his flipper. He asks for George Cedeño, master technician, who makes house calls and often travels as far as Massachusetts to fix a pinball machine. Cedeño—blue work smock, white shoes, burgundy trousers, silver hair—makes a date with Lukas.

Lukas starts for home but, crossing Forty-second Street, decides on pure whim to have a look at Circus Circus, where he has never been. Circus Circus is, after all, just four blocks away. The stroll is pleasant in the afternoon sunlight, to and through Times Square, under the marquees of pornographic movies—*Valley of the Nymphs, The Danish Sandwich, The Organ Trail.* Circus Circus ("GIRLS! GIRLS! GIRLS! LIVE EXOTIC MODELS") is close to Sixth Avenue and consists, principally, of a front room and a back room. Prices are a quarter a peep in the back room and a quarter to play (two games) in the front. The game room is dim, and Lukas, entering, sees little at first but the flashing scoreboards of five machines. Four of them—a Bally, a Williams, two Gottliebs—flash slowly, reporting inexperienced play, but the fifth, the one in the middle, is exploding with light and sound. The player causing all this is hunched over, concentrating—in his arms and his hands a choreography of talent. Lukas's eyes adjust to the light. Then he reaches for his holster. The man on the hot machine, busy keeping statistics of his practice, is Tom Buckley.

"Tom."

"Tone."

"How is the machine?"

"Better than yours, Tone. You don't realize what a lemon you have."

"I love my Bally."

"The Bally is the Corvair of pinball machines. I don't even care for the art on the back-glass. Williams and Gottlieb are the best. Bally is nowhere."

Buckley, slightly older than Lukas, has a spectacled and professorial look. He wears a double-breasted blazer, a buff turtleneck. He lives on York Avenue now. He came out of Beechhurst, Queens, and learned his pinball in the Army—in Wrightstown, New Jersey; in Kansas City. He was stationed in an office building in Kansas City, and he moved up through the pinball ranks from beginner to virtuoso on a machine in a Katz drugstore.

Lukas and Buckley begin to play. Best of five games. Five balls a game. Alternate shots. The machine is a Williams FunFest, and Buckley points out that it is "classic," because it is symmetrical. Each kick-out well and thumper-bumper is a mirror of another. The slingshots are dual. On this machine, a level of forty thousand points is where the sun sets and the stars come out. Buckley, describing his own style as "guts pinball," has a first-game score of forty-four thousand three hundred and ten. While Lukas plays his fifth ball, Buckley becomes avuncular. "Careful, Tony. You might think you're in an up-post position, but if you let it slide a little you're in a down-post position and you're finished." Buckley's advice is generous indeed. Lukas—forty-eight thousand eight hundred and seventy— wins the first game.

It is Buckley's manner to lean into the machine from three feet out. His whole body, steeply inclined, tics as he reinforces. In the second game, he scores fifty thousand one hundred and sixty. Lukas's address is like a fencer's *en garde*. He stands close to the machine, with one foot projecting under it. His chin is high. Buckley tells him, "You're playing nice, average pinball, Tony." And Lukas's response is fifty-seven thousand nine hundred and fifty points. He leads Buckley, two games to none.

"I'm ashamed," Buckley confesses. And as he leans—palms pounding—into the third game, he reminds himself, "Concentration, Tom. Concentration is everything."

Lukas notes aloud that Buckley is "full of empty rhetoric." But Lukas, in Game 3, fires one ball straight into the death channel and can deliver only thirty-five thousand points. Buckley wins with forty. Perhaps Lukas feels rushed. He prefers to play a more deliberate, cogitative game. At home, between shots, in the middle of a game, he will go to the kitchen for a beer and return to study the situation. Buckley, for his part, seems anxious, and with good reason: one mistake now and it's all over. In the fourth game, Lukas lights up forty-three thousand and fifty points; but Buckley's fifth ball, just before it dies, hits forty-four thousand two hundred and sixty. Games are two all, with one to go. Buckley takes a deep breath, and says, "You're a competitor, Tony. Your flipper action is bad, but you're a real competitor."

Game 5 under way. They are pummelling the machine. They are heavy on the corners but light on the flippers, and the scoreboard is reacting like a storm at sea. With three balls down, both are in the thirty-thousand range. Buckley, going unorthodox, plays his fourth ball with one foot off the floor, and raises his score to forty-five thousand points—more than he scored in winning the two previous games. He smiles. He is on his way in, flaring, with still another ball to play. Now Lukas snaps his fourth ball into the ellipse. It moves down and around the board, hitting slingshots and flippers and rising again and again to high ground to begin additional scoring runs. It hits sunburst caps and hole kickers, swinging targets and bonus gates. Minute upon minute, it stays in play. It will not die.

When the ball finally slips between flippers and off the playfield, Lukas has registered eighty-three thousand two hundred points. And he still has one ball to go.

Buckley turns into a Lukasite. As Lukas plays his fifth ball, Buckley cheers. "Atta way! Atta way, babes!" He goes on cheering until Lukas peaks out at ninety-four thousand one hundred and seventy.

"That was superb. And there's no luck in it," Buckley says. "It's as good a score as I've seen."

Lukas takes a cool final look around Circus Circus. "Buckley has a way of tracking down the secret joys of the city," he says, and then he is gone.

Still shaking his head in wonder, Buckley starts a last, solo game. His arms move mechanically, groovedly, reinforcing. His flipper timing is offhandedly flawless. He scores a hundred thousand two hundred points. But Lukas is out of sight.

Alice Walker
BEAUTY: WHEN THE OTHER DANCER IS THE SELF
★ ★ ★

Alice Walker writes novels, poems, essays, and short stories. Her 1982 novel, The Color Purple, *the story of a poor, oppressed black woman struggling to improve her lot in a sexist and racist world, won an American Book Award and the Pulitzer Prize for fiction. The novel is not, strictly speaking, autobiographical, but Walker's own rise from obscurity and disadvantage (she was the youngest of eight children born to a Georgia sharecropper and a maid) to celebrity and high literary esteem parallels her hero's development.*

Walker's writing is characterized by personal honesty, a poetic style, and intense political commitment. Her first published essay was on the civil rights movement (and in 1976 she published a novel, Meridian, *centered on the movement), and she has been a contributing editor of* Ms. *magazine since 1974. Some critics have even called her work "too partisan." But as a "Womanist" (a label she created for "black feminist or feminist of color"), Walker is committed to writing from an ideological perspective. In her best work, her strong beliefs and powerful literary expressiveness reinforce each other. The autobiographical narrative reprinted here, from* In Search of Our Mothers' Gardens: Womanist Prose *(1983), is an example of such a successful union.*

It is a bright summer day in 1947. My father, a fat, funny man with beautiful eyes and a subversive wit, is trying to decide which of his eight children he will take with him to the county fair. My mother, of course, will not go. She is knocked out from getting most of us ready: I hold my neck stiff against the pressure of her knuckles as she hastily completes the braiding and then beribboning of my hair.

My father is the driver for the rich old white lady up the road. Her name is Miss Mey. She owns all the land for miles around, as well as the house in which we live. All I remember about her is that she once offered to pay my mother thirty-five cents for cleaning her house, raking up piles of her magnolia leaves, and washing her family's clothes, and that my mother—she of no money, eight children, and a chronic earache—refused it. But I do not think of this in 1947. I am two and a half years old. I want to go everywhere my daddy goes. I am excited at the prospect of riding in a car. Someone has told me fairs are fun. That there is room in the car for only three of us doesn't faze me at all. Whirling happily in my starchy frock, showing off my biscuit-polished patent-leather shoes and lavender socks, tossing my head in a way that makes my ribbons bounce, I stand, hands on hips, before my father. "Take me, Daddy," I say with assurance; "I'm the prettiest!"

Later, it does not surprise me to find myself in Miss Mey's shiny black car, sharing the back seat with the other lucky ones. Does not surprise me that I thoroughly enjoy the fair. At home that night I tell the unlucky ones all I can remember about the merry-go-round, the man who eats live chickens, and the teddy bears, until they say: that's enough, baby Alice. Shut up now, and go to sleep.

It is Easter Sunday, 1950. I am dressed in a green, flocked, scalloped-hem dress (handmade by my adoring sister, Ruth) that has its own smooth satin petticoat and tiny hot-pink roses tucked into each scallop. My shoes, new T-strap patent leather, again highly biscuit-polished. I am six years old and have learned one of the longest Easter speeches to be heard that day, totally unlike the speech I said when I was two: "Easter lilies / pure and white / blossom in / the morning light." When I rise to give my speech I do so on a great wave of love and pride and expectation. People in the church stop rustling their new crinolines. They seem to hold their breath. I can tell they admire my dress, but it is my spirit, bordering on sassiness (womanishness), they secretly applaud.

"That girl's a little *mess,*" they whisper to each other, pleased.

Naturally I say my speech without stammer or pause, unlike those who stutter, stammer, or, worst of all, forget. This is before the word "beautiful" exists in people's vocabulary, but "Oh, isn't she the *cutest* thing!" frequently floats my way, "And got so much sense!" they gratefully add . . . for which thoughtful addition I thank them to this day.

It was great fun being cute. But then, one day, it ended.

I am eight years old and a tomboy. I have a cowboy hat, cowboy boots, checkered shirt and pants, all red. My playmates are my brothers, two and four years older than I. Their colors are black and green, the only difference in the way we are dressed. On Saturday nights we all go to the picture show, even my mother; Westerns are her favorite kind of movie. Back home, "on the ranch," we pretend we are Tom Mix, Hopalong Cassidy, Lash LaRue (we've even named one of our dogs Lash LaRue); we chase each other for hours rustling cattle, being outlaws, delivering damsels from distress. Then my parents decide to buy my brothers guns. These are not "real" guns. They shoot "BBs," copper pellets my brothers say will kill birds. Because I am a girl, I do not get a gun. Instantly I am relegated to the position of Indian. Now there appears a great distance between us. They shoot and shoot at everything with their new guns. I try to keep up with my bow and arrows.

One day while I am standing on top of our makeshift "garage"—pieces of tin nailed across some poles—holding my bow and arrow and looking out toward the fields, I feel an incredible blow in my right eye. I look down just in time to see my brother lower his gun.

Both brothers rush to my side. My eye stings, and I cover it with my hand. "If you tell," they say, "we will get a whipping. You don't want that to happen, do you?" I do not. "Here is a piece of wire," says the older brother, picking it up from the roof; "say you stepped on one end of it and the other flew up and hit you." The pain is beginning to start. "Yes," I say. "Yes. I will say that is what happened." If I do not say this is what happened, I know my brothers will find ways to make me wish I had. But now I will say anything that gets me to my mother.

Confronted by our parents we stick to the lie agreed upon. They place me on a bench on the porch and I close my left eye while they examine the right. There is a tree growing from underneath the porch that climbs past the railing to the roof. It is the last thing my right eye sees. I watch as its trunk, its branches, and then its leaves are blotted out by the rising blood.

I am in shock. First there is intense fever, which my father tries to break using lily leaves bound around my head. Then there are chills: my mother tries to get me to eat soup. Eventually, I do not know how, my parents learn what has happened. A week after the "accident" they take me to see a doctor. "Why did you wait so long to come?" he asks, looking into my eye and shaking his head. "Eyes are sympathetic," he says. "If one is blind, the other will likely become blind too."

This comment of the doctor's terrifies me. But it is really how I look that bothers me most. Where the BB pellet struck there is a glob of whitish scar tissue, a hideous cataract, on my eye. Now when I stare at people—a favorite pastime, up to now—they will stare back. Not at the "cute" little girl, but at her scar. For six years I do not stare at anyone, because I do not raise my head.

Years later, in the throes of a mid-life crisis, I ask my mother and sister whether I changed after the "accident." "No," they say, puzzled. "What do you mean?"

What do I mean?

I am eight, and, for the first time, doing poorly in school, where I have been something of a whiz since I was four. We have just moved to the place where the "accident" occurred. We do not know any of the people around us because this is a different county. The only time I see the friends I knew is when we go back to our old church. The new school is the former state penitentiary. It is a large stone building, cold and drafty, crammed to overflowing with boisterous, ill-disciplined children. On the third floor there is a huge circular imprint of some partition that has been torn out.

"What used to be here?" I ask a sullen girl next to me on our way past it to lunch.

"The electric chair," says she.

At night I have nightmares about the electric chair, and about all the people reputedly "fried" in it. I am afraid of the school, where all the students seem to be budding criminals.

"What's the matter with your eye?" they ask, critically.

When I don't answer (I cannot decide whether it was an "accident" or not), they shove me, insist on a fight.

My brother, the one who created the story about the wire, comes to my rescue. But then brags so much about "protecting" me, I become sick.

After months of torture at the school, my parents decide to send me back to our old community, to my old school. I live with my grandparents and the teacher they board. But there is no room for Phoebe, my cat. By the time my grandparents decide there *is* room, and I ask for my cat, she cannot be found. Miss Yarborough, the boarding teacher, takes me under her wing, and begins to teach me to play the piano. But soon she marries an African—a "prince," she says—and is whisked away to his continent.

At my old school there is at least one teacher who loves me. She is the teacher who "knew me before I was born" and bought my first baby clothes. It is she who makes life bearable. It is her presence that finally helps me turn on the one child at the school who continually calls me "one-eyed bitch." One day I simply grab him by his coat and beat him until I am satisfied. It is my teacher who tells me my mother is ill.

My mother is lying in bed in the middle of the day, something I have never seen. She is in too much pain to speak. She has an abscess in her ear. I stand looking down on her, knowing that if she dies, I cannot live. She is being treated with warm oils and hot bricks held against her cheek. Finally a doctor comes. But I must go back to my grandparents' house. The weeks pass but I am hardly aware of it. All I know is that my mother might die, my father is not so jolly, my brothers still have their guns, and I am the one sent away from home.

"You did not change," they say.

Did I imagine the anguish of never looking up?

I am twelve. When relatives come to visit I hide in my room. My cousin Brenda, just my age, whose father works in the post office and whose mother is a nurse, comes to find me. "Hello," she says. And then she asks, looking at my recent school picture, which I did not want taken, and on which the "glob," as I think of it, is clearly visible. "You still can't see out of that eye?"

"No," I say, and flop back on the bed over my book.

That night, as I do almost every night, I abuse my eye. I rant and rave at it, in front of the mirror. I plead with it to clear up before morning. I tell it I hate and despise it. I do not pray for sight. I pray for beauty.

"You did not change," they say.

I am fourteen and baby-sitting for my brother Bill, who lives in Boston. He is my favorite brother and there is a strong bond between us. Understanding my feelings of shame and ugliness he and his wife take me to a local hospital, where the "glob" is removed by a doctor named O. Henry. There is still a small bluish crater where the scar tissue was, but the ugly white stuff is gone. Almost immediately I become a different person from the girl who does not raise her head. Or so I think. Now that I've raised my head I win the boyfriend of my dreams. Now that I've raised my head I have plenty of friends. Now that I've raised my head classwork comes from my lips as faultlessly as Easter speeches did, and I leave high school as valedictorian, most popular student, and *queen,* hardly believing my luck. Ironically, the girl who was voted most beautiful in our class (and was) was later shot twice through the chest by a male companion, using a "real" gun, while she was pregnant. But that's another story in itself. Or is it?

"You did not change," they say.

It is now thirty years since the "accident." A beautiful journalist comes to visit and to interview me. She is going to write a cover story for her magazine that focuses on my latest book. "Decide how you want to look on the cover," she says. "Glamorous, or whatever."

Never mind "glamorous," it is the "whatever" that I hear. Suddenly all I can think of is whether I will get enough sleep the night before the photography session: if I don't, my eye will be tired and wander, as blind eyes will.

At night in bed with my lover I think up reasons why I should not appear on the cover of a magazine. "My meanest critics will say I've sold out," I say. "My family will now realize I write scandalous books."

"But what's the real reason you don't want to do this?" he asks.

"Because in all probability," I say in a rush, "my eye won't be straight."

"It will be straight enough," he says. Then, "Besides, I thought you'd made your peace with that."

And I suddenly remember that I have.

I remember:

I am talking to my brother Jimmy, asking if he remembers anything unusual about the day I was shot. He does not know I consider that day the last time my father, with his sweet home remedy of cool lily leaves, chose me, and that I suffered and raged inside because of this. "Well," he says, "all I remember is standing by the side of the highway with Daddy, trying to flag down a car. A white man stopped, but when Daddy said he needed somebody to take his little girl to the doctor, he drove off."

I remember:

I am in the desert for the first time. I fall totally in love with it. I am so overwhelmed by its beauty, I confront for the first time, consciously, the meaning of the doctor's words years ago: "Eyes are sympathetic. If one is blind, the other will likely become blind too." I realize I have dashed about the world madly, looking at this, looking at that, storing up images against the fading of the light. *But I might have missed seeing the desert!* The shock of that possibility—and gratitude for over twenty-five years of sight—sends me literally to my knees. Poem after poem comes—which is perhaps how poets pray.

ON SIGHT

I am so thankful I have seen
The Desert
And the creatures in the desert
And the desert Itself.

The desert has its own moon
Which I have seen
With my own eye.
There is no flag on it.

Trees of the desert have arms
All of which are always up
That is because the moon is up
The sun is up
Also the sky
The stars
Clouds
None with flags.

If there *were* flags, I doubt
the trees would point.
Would you?

But mostly, I remember this:
I am twenty-seven, and my baby daughter is almost three. Since her birth I have worried about her discovery that her mother's eyes are different from other people's. Will she be embarrassed? I think. What will she say? Every day she watches a television program called "Big Blue Marble." It begins with a picture of the earth as it appears from the moon. It is bluish, a little battered-looking, but full of light, with whitish clouds swirling around it. Every time I see it I weep with love, as if it is a picture of Grandma's house. One day when I am putting Rebecca down for her nap, she suddenly focuses on my eye. Something inside me cringes, gets ready to try to protect myself. All children are cruel about physical differences, I know from experience, and that they don't always mean to be is another matter. I assume Rebecca will be the same.

But no-o-o-o. She studies my face intently as we stand, her inside and me outside her crib. She even holds my face maternally between her dimpled little hands. Then, looking every bit as serious and lawyerlike as her father, she says, as if it may just possibly have slipped my attention: "Mommy, there's a *world* in your eye." (As in, "Don't be alarmed, or do anything crazy.") And then, gently, but with great interest: "Mommy, where did you *get* that world in your eye?"

For the most part, the pain left then. (So what, if my brothers grew up to buy even more powerful pellet guns for their sons and to carry real guns themselves. So what, if a young "Morehouse man" once nearly fell off the steps of Trevor Arnett Library because he thought my eyes were blue.) Crying and laughing I ran to the bathroom, while Rebecca mumbled and sang herself off to sleep. Yes indeed, I realized, looking into the mirror. There *was* a world in my eye. And I saw that it was possible to love it: that in fact, for all it had taught me of shame and anger and inner vision, I *did* love it. Even to see it drifting out of orbit in boredom, or rolling up out of fatigue, not to mention floating back at attention in excitement (bearing witness, a friend has called it), deeply suitable to my personality, and even characteristic of me.

That night I dream I am dancing to Stevie Wonder's song "Always" (the name of the song is really "As," but I hear it as "Always"). As I dance, whirling and joyous, happier than I've ever been in my life, another bright-faced dancer joins me. We dance and kiss each other and hold each other through the night. The other dancer has obviously come through all right, as I have done. She is beautiful, whole and free. And she is also me.

Tom Wolfe
THE RIGHT STUFF
★ ★ ★

If one writer can be called the quintessential chronicler of his time, Tom Wolfe would be that writer for the sixties. His The Kandy-Kolored Tangerine-Flake Streamline Baby *(1965),* The Electric Kool-Aid Acid Test *(1968), and* Radical Chic and Mau Mauing the Flak Catchers *(1970) were controversial masterpieces of the "new journalism," works that combined novelistic techniques, solid reporting, and flamboyantly personal styles to tell the stories behind the headlines. But the mark of Wolfe's genius as a writer is his versatility; as he himself has said, there is "no set Tom Wolfe style."*

In The Right Stuff *(1980), an American Book Award and National Book Critics Circle Award winner, which tells the story of the original Mercury astronauts, Wolfe abandons the stream-of-consciousness, super-hip, manic sixties style, for more direct reporting. Yet the book has been acclaimed because Wolfe's original gifts are still in evidence—his desire to discover and report overlooked details, his attention to what is human in historical events, his keen ear for the way people speak, and his ability to see the larger meaning in what he is reporting.* The Right Stuff, *then, is literature in every sense.*

A young man might go into military flight training believing that he was entering some sort of technical school in which he was simply going to acquire a certain set of skills. Instead, he found himself all at once enclosed in a fraternity. And in this fraternity, even though it was military, men were not rated by their outward rank as ensigns, lieutenants, commanders, or whatever. No, herein the world was divided into those who had it and those who did not. This quality, this *it*, was never named, however, nor was it talked about in any way.

As to just what this ineffable quality was . . . well, it obviously involved bravery. But it was not bravery in the simple sense of being willing to risk your life. The idea seemed to be that any fool could do that, if that was all that was required, just as any fool could throw away his life in the process. No, the idea here (in the all-enclosing fraternity) seemed to be that a man should have the ability to go up in a hurtling piece of machinery and put his hide on the line and then have the moxie, the reflexes, the experience, the coolness, to pull it back in the last yawning moment—and then to go up again *the next day,* and the next day, and every next day, even if the series should prove infinite—and, ultimately, in its best expression, do so in a cause that means something to thousands, to a people, a nation, to humanity, to God. Nor was there *a test* to show whether or not a pilot had this righteous quality. There was, instead, a seemingly infinite series of tests. A career in flying was like climbing one of those ancient Babylonian pyramids made up of a dizzy progression of steps and ledges, a ziggurat, a pyramid extraordinarily high and steep; and the idea was to prove at every foot of the way up that pyramid that you were one of the elected and anointed ones who had *the right stuff* and could move higher and higher and even—ultimately, God willing, one day—that you might be able to join that special few at the very top, that elite who had the capacity to bring tears to men's eyes, the very Brotherhood of the Right Stuff itself.

None of this was to be mentioned, and yet it was acted out in a way that a young man could not fail to understand. When a new flight (i.e., a class) of trainees arrived at Pensacola, they were brought into an auditorium for a little lecture. An officer would tell them: "Take a look at the man on either side of you." Quite a few actually swiveled their heads this way and that, in the interest of appearing diligent. Then the officer would say: "One of the three of you is not going to make it!"—meaning, not get his wings. That was the opening theme, the *motif* of primary training. We already know that one-third of you do not have the right stuff—it only remains to find out who.

Furthermore, that was the way it turned out. At every level in one's progress up that staggeringly high pyramid, the world was once more divided into those men who had the right stuff to continue the climb and those who had to be *left behind* in the most obvious way. Some were eliminated in the course of the opening classroom work, as either not smart enough or not hardworking enough, and were left behind. Then came the basic flight instruction, in single-engine, propeller-driven trainers, and a few more—even though the military tried to make this stage easy—were washed out and left behind. Then came more demanding levels, one after the other, formation flying, instrument flying, jet training, all-weather flying, gunnery, and at each level more were washed out and left behind. By this point easily a third of the original candidates had been, indeed, eliminated . . . from the ranks of those who might prove to have the right stuff.

In the Navy, in addition to the stages that Air Force trainees went through, the neophyte always had waiting for him, out in the ocean, a certain grim gray slab; namely, the deck of an aircraft carrier; and with it perhaps the most difficult routine in military flying, carrier landings. He was shown films about it, he heard lectures about it, and he knew that carrier landings were hazardous. He first practiced touching down on the shape of a flight deck painted on an airfield. He was instructed to touch down and gun right off. This was safe enough—the shape didn't move, at least—but it could do terrible things to, let us say, the gyroscope of the soul. *That shape!—it's so damned small!* And more candidates were washed out and left behind. Then came the day, without warning, when those who remained were sent out over the ocean for the first of many days of reckoning with the slab. The first day was always a clear day with little wind and a calm sea. The carrier was so steady that it seemed, from up there in the air, to be resting on pilings, and the candidate usually made his first carrier landing successfully, with relief and even *élan.* Many young candidates looked like terrific aviators up to that very point—and it was not until they were actually standing on the carrier deck that they first began to wonder if they had the proper stuff, after all. In the training film the flight deck was a grand piece of gray geometry, perilous, to be sure, but an amazing abstract shape as one looks down upon it on the screen. And yet once the newcomer's two feet were on it . . . *Geometry*—my God, man, this is a . . . skillet! It *heaved,* it moved up and down underneath his feet, it pitched up, it pitched down, it rolled to port (this great beast *rolled!*) and it rolled to starboard, as the ship moved into the wind and, therefore, into the waves, and the wind kept sweeping across, sixty feet up in the air out in the open sea, and there were no railings whatsoever. This was a *skillet!*—a frying pan!—a short-order grill!—not gray but black, smeared with skid marks from one end to the other and glistening with pools of hydraulic fluid and the occasional jet-fuel slick, all of it still hot, sticky, greasy, runny, virulent from God knows what traumas—still ablaze!—consumed in detonations, explosions, flames, combustion, roars, shrieks, whines, blasts, horrible shudders, fracturing impacts, as little men in screaming red and yellow and purple and green shirts with black Mickey Mouse helmets over their ears skittered about on the surface as if for their very lives (you've said it now!), hooking fighter planes onto the catapult shuttles so that they can explode their afterburners and be slung off the deck in a red-mad fury with a *kaboom!* that pounds through the entire deck—a procedure that seems absolutely controlled, orderly, sublime, however, compared to what he is about to watch as aircraft return to the ship for what is known in the engineering stoicisms of the military as "recovery and arrest." To say that an F-4 was coming back onto this heaving barbecue from out of the sky at a speed of 135 knots . . . that might have been the truth in the training lecture, but it did not begin to get across the idea of what the newcomer saw from the deck itself, because it created the notion that perhaps the plane was gliding in. On the deck one knew differently! As the aircraft came closer and the carrier heaved on into the waves and the plane's speed did not diminish and the deck did not grow steady—indeed, it pitched up and down five or ten feet per greasy heave—one experienced a neural alarm that no lecture could have prepared him for: This is not an *airplane* coming toward me, it is a brick with some poor sonofabitch riding it *(someone much like myself!),* and it is not *gliding,* it is *falling,* a fifty-thousand-pound brick, headed not for a stripe on the deck but for *me*—and with a horrible *smash!* it hits the skillet, and with a blur of momentum as big as a freight train's it hurtles toward the far end of the deck—another blinding storm!—another roar as the pilot pushes the throttle up to full military power and another smear of rubber screams out over the skillet—and this is nominal!—quite okay!—for a wire stretched across the deck has grabbed the hook on the end of the plane as it hit the deck tail down, and the smash was the rest of the fifteen-ton brute slamming onto the deck, as it tripped up, so that it is now straining against the wire at full throttle, in case it hadn't held and the plane had "boltered" off the end of the deck and had to struggle up into the air again. And already the Mickey Mouse helmets are running toward the fiery monster . . .

And the candidate, looking on, begins to *feel* that great heaving sun-blazing deathboard of a deck wallowing in his own vestibular system—and suddenly he finds himself backed up against his own limits. He ends up going to the flight surgeon with so-called conversion symptoms. Overnight he develops blurred vision or numbness in his hands and feet or sinusitis so severe that he cannot tolerate changes in altitude. On one level the symptom is real. He really cannot see too well or use his fingers or stand the pain. But somewhere in his sub-conscious he knows it is a plea and a beg-off; he shows not the slightest concern (the flight surgeon notes) that the condition might be permanent and affect him in whatever life awaits him outside the arena of the right stuff.

Those who remained, those who qualified for carrier duty—and even more so those who later on qualified for *night* carrier duty—began to feel a bit like Gideon's warriors. *So many have been left behind!* The young warriors were now treated to a deathly sweet and quiet unmentionable sight. They could gaze at length upon the crushed and wilted pariahs who had washed out. They could inspect those who did not have that righteous stuff.

The military did not have very merciful instincts. Rather than packing up these poor souls and sending them home, the Navy, like the Air Force and the Marines, would try to make use of them in some other role, such as flight controller. So the washout has to keep taking classes with the rest of his group, even though he can no longer touch an airplane. He sits there in the classes staring at sheets of paper with cataracts of sheer human mortification over his eyes while the rest steal looks at him . . . this man reduced to an ant, this untouchable, this poor sonofabitch. And in what test had he been found wanting? Why, it seemed to be nothing less than *manhood* itself. Naturally, this was never mentioned, either. Yet there it was. *Manliness, manhood, manly courage . . .* there was something ancient, primordial, irresistible about the challenge of this stuff, no matter what a sophisticated and rational age one might think he lived in.

Perhaps because it could not be talked about, the subject began to take on superstitious and even mystical outlines. A man either had it or he didn't! There was no such thing as having *most* of it. Moreover, it could blow at any seam. One day a man would be ascending the pyramid at a terrific clip, and the next—

bingo!—he would reach his own limits in the most unexpected way. Conrad and Schirra met an Air Force pilot who had had a great pal at Tyndall Air Force Base in Florida. This man had been the budding ace of the training class; he had flown the hottest fighter-style trainer, the T-38, like a dream; and then he began the routine step of being checked out in the T-33. The T-33 was not nearly as hot an aircraft as the T-38; it was essentially the old P-80 jet fighter. It had an exceedingly small cockpit. The pilot could barely move his shoulders. It was the sort of airplane of which everybody said, "You don't get into it, you *wear* it." Once inside a T-33 cockpit this man, this budding ace, developed claustrophobia of the most paralyzing sort. He tried everything to overcome it. He even went to a psychiatrist, which was a serious mistake for a military officer if his superiors learned of it. But nothing worked. He was shifted over to flying jet transports, such as the C-135. Very demanding and necessary aircraft they were, too, and he was still spoken of as an excellent pilot. But as everyone knew—and, again, it was never explained in so many words—only those who were assigned to fighter squadrons, the "fighter jocks," as they called each other with a self-satisfied irony, remained in the true fraternity. Those assigned to transports were not humiliated like washouts—*somebody* had to fly those planes—nevertheless, they, too, had been *left behind* for lack of the right stuff.

Or a man could go for a routine physical one fine day, feeling like a million dollars, and be grounded for *fallen arches*. It happened!—just like that! (And try raising them.) Or for breaking his wrist and losing only *part* of its mobility. Or for a minor deterioration of eyesight, or for any of hundreds of reasons that would make no difference to a man in an ordinary occupation. As a result all fighter jocks began looking upon doctors as their natural enemies. Going to see a flight surgeon was a no-gain proposition; a pilot could only hold his own or lose in the doctor's office. To be grounded for a medical reason was no humiliation, looked at objectively. But it was a humiliation, nonetheless!—for it meant you no longer had that indefinable, unutterable, integral stuff. (It could blow at *any* seam.)

All the hot young fighter jocks began trying to test the limits themselves in a superstitious way. They were like believing Presbyterians of a century before who used to probe their own experience to see if they were truly among *the elect*. When a fighter pilot was in training, whether in the Navy or the Air Force, his superiors were continually spelling out strict rules for him, about the use of the aircraft and conduct in the sky. They repeatedly forbade so-called hotdog stunts, such as outside loops, buzzing, flat-hatting, hedgehopping and flying under bridges. But somehow one got the message that the man who truly *had* it could ignore those rules—not that he should make a point of it, but that he *could*—and that after all there was only one way to find out—and that in some strange unofficial way, peeking through his fingers, his instructor halfway expected him to challenge all the limits. They would give a lecture about how a pilot should never fly without a good solid breakfast—eggs, bacon, toast, and so forth— because if he tried to fly with his blood-sugar level too low, it could impair his alertness. Naturally, the next day every hot dog in the unit would get up and have a breakfast consisting of one cup of black coffee and take off and go up into a vertical climb until the weight of the ship exactly canceled out the upward pull of the engine and his air speed was zero, and he would hang there for one thick adrenal instant—and then fall like a rock, until one of three things happened: he keeled over nose first and regained his aerodynamics and all was well, he went into a spin and fought his way out of it, or he went into a spin and had to eject or crunch it, which was always supremely possible.

Likewise, "hassling"—mock dogfighting—was strictly forbidden, and so naturally young fighter jocks could hardly wait to go up in, say, a pair of F-100s and start the duel by making a pass at each other at 800 miles an hour, the winner being the pilot who could slip in behind the other one and get locked in on his tail ("wax his tail"), and it was not uncommon for some eager jock to try too tight an outside turn and have his engine flame out, whereupon, unable to restart it, he has to eject . . . and he shakes his fist at the victor as he floats down by parachute and his half-a-million-dollar aircraft goes *kaboom!* on the palmetto grass or the desert floor, and he starts thinking about how he can get together with the other guy back at the base in time for the two of them to get their stories straight before the investigation: "I don't know what happened, sir. I was pulling up after a target run, and it just flamed out on me." Hassling was forbidden, and hassling that led to the destruction of an aircraft was a serious court-martial offense, and the man's superiors knew that the engine hadn't *just flamed out,* but every unofficial impulse on the base seemed to be saying: "Hell, we wouldn't give you a nickel for a pilot who hasn't done some crazy rat-racing like that. It's all part of the right stuff."

The other side of this impulse showed up in the reluctance of the young jocks to admit it when they had maneuvered themselves into a bad corner they couldn't get out of. There were two reasons why a fighter pilot hated to declare an emergency. First, it triggered a complex and very public chain of events at the field: all other incoming flights were held up, including many of one's comrades who were probably low on fuel; the fire trucks came trundling out to the runway like yellow toys (as seen from way up there), the better to illustrate one's hapless state; and the bureaucracy began to crank up the paper monster for the investigation that always followed. And second, to declare an emergency, one first had to reach that conclusion in his own mind, which to the young pilot was the same as saying: "A minute ago I still *had* it—now I need your help!" To have a bunch of young fighter pilots up in the air thinking this way used to drive flight controllers crazy. They would see a ship beginning to drift off the radar, and they couldn't rouse the pilot on the microphone for anything other than a few meaningless mumbles, and they would know he was probably out there with engine failure at a low altitude, trying to reignite by lowering his auxiliary generator rig, which had a little propeller that was supposed to spin in the slipstream like a child's pinwheel.

"Whiskey Kilo Two Eight, do you want to declare an emergency?"

This would rouse him!—to say: "Negative, negative, Whiskey Kilo Two Eight is not declaring an emergency."

Kaboom. Believers in the right stuff would rather crash and burn.

Acknowledgments

Elizabeth Bishop: "Primer Class" from *The Collected Prose.* Reprinted by permission of Farrar, Straus and Giroux, Inc. Copyright © 1984 by Alice Methfessel.

Roy Blount, Jr.: "You Make Me Feel Like a Natural Person . . ." from *One Fell Soup, or I'm Just a Bug on the Windshield of Life.* Copyright © 1977 by Roy Blount, Jr. First appeared in *Esquire.*

Philip Booth: "Hard Country" from *Margins.* Copyright © 1967 by Philip Booth. Reprinted by permission of Viking Penguin Inc.

Ben Brooks: "A Postal Creed." Reprinted by permission of *Chicago Review,* copyright © 1980 by *Chicago Review.*

Susan Brownmiller: "Emotion" from *Femininity.* Copyright © 1983 by Susan Brownmiller. Reprinted by permission of Linden Press, a division of Simon & Schuster, Inc.

David Bruck: "Decisions of Death." Reprinted by permission of *The New Republic,* copyright © 1983, The New Republic, Inc.

Art Buchwald: "You'll Love This Bomb." Reprinted by permission of the Putnam Publishing Group from *While Reagan Slept.* Copyright © 1984 by Art Buchwald.

Tom Clark: "Sonnet" from *Stones.* Reprinted by permission of the author.

Marcelle Clements: "Terminal Cool." Copyright © 1984 by Marcelle Clements. First appeared in *Esquire.* Reprinted with permission of the author.

Harry Crews: "The Scalding" from *A Childhood: The Biography of a Place.* Copyright © 1978 by Harry Crews. Reprinted by permission of Harper & Row, Publishers, Inc.

Mary Daly: "Pure Lust" from *Pure Lust.* Copyright © 1984 by Mary Daly. Reprinted by permission of Mary Daly and Beacon Press.

Joan Didion: "On Self-Respect" from *Slouching Towards Bethlehem.* Reprinted by permission of Farrar, Straus and Giroux, Inc. Copyright © 1961, 1968 by Joan Didion.

Annie Dillard: "Living Like Weasels" from *Teaching a Stone to Talk: Expeditions and Encounters.* Copyright © 1982 by Annie Dillard. Reprinted by permission of Harper & Row, Publishers, Inc.

Harry Edwards: "Educating Black Athletes." Copyright © 1983. First appeared in *The Atlantic Monthly.* Reprinted with permission.

Edith Efron: "The Soaps—Anything But 99-44/100 Percent Pure." Reprinted with permission from *TV Guide*® Magazine. Copyright © 1965 by Triangle Publications, Inc., Radnor, PA.

Nora Ephron: "Baking Off." Copyright © 1976 by Nora Ephron. Reprinted from *Crazy Salad: Some Things About Women,* by permission of Alfred A. Knopf, Inc.

Joseph Epstein: "What Is Vulgar?" reprinted from *The Middle of My Tether, Familiar Essays,* by permission of W.W. Norton & Company, Inc. Copyright © 1983 by Joseph Epstein.

Martin Filler: "Graceland." Courtesy *House & Garden.* Copyright © 1984 by The Condé Nast Publications Inc.

Bruce Jay Friedman: "Living Together." Reprinted by permission of Candida Donadio & Assoc., Inc. Copyright © 1981 by Bruce Jay Friedman. First appeared in *Esquire.*

Gary Gildner: "First Practice" reprinted from *First Practice,* by permission of the University of Pittsburgh Press. Copyright © 1969 by the University of Pittsburgh Press.

Carol Gilligan: "Images of Relationships" reprinted by permission of the publishers from *In a Different Voice: Psychological Theory and Women's Development,* Cambridge, Mass.: Harvard University Press, Copyright © 1982 by Carol Gilligan.

John Glusman: "Righteousness." Copyright © 1984. Reprinted by permission of the author. First appeared in *Ms.*

Albert Goldman: "Graceland" from *Elvis.* Copyright © 1981. Reprinted by permission of McGraw-Hill Book Company.

Stephen Jay Gould: "Losing the Edge." Courtesy *Vanity Fair.* Copyright © 1983 by The Condé Nast Publications Inc.

Pete Hamill: "Winning Isn't Everything." Reprinted by permission of International Creative Management. Copyright © 1983 by Pete Hamill. Originally appeared in *GQ.*

Marvin Harris: "Why Nothing Works" from *America Now.* Copyright © 1981 by Marvin Harris. Reprinted by permission of Simon & Schuster, Inc.

Molly Haskell: "The Woman's Film" from *Reverence to Rape.* Copyright © 1973, 1974 by Molly Haskell. Reprinted by permission of Holt, Rinehart and Winston, Publishers.

Edward Hoagland: "Two Clowns." Copyright © 1971 by Edward Hoagland. Reprinted from *Walking the Dead Diamond River,* by permission of Random House, Inc.

Frederick A. King: "Animals in Research: The Case for Experimentation." Reprinted from *Psychology Today* Magazine. Copyright © 1984 American Psychological Association.

Stephen King: "Why We Crave Horror Movies." Copyright © 1980 by Playboy. First appeared in *Playboy* Magazine. Reprinted by permission of the author's agent Kirby McCauley Ltd.

Maxine Hong Kingston: "The Quiet Girl" from *The Woman Warrior: Memoirs of a Girlhood Among Ghosts.* Copyright © 1975, 1976 by Maxine Hong Kingston. Reprinted by permission of Alfred A. Knopf, Inc.

Michael Korda: "Symbols of Success" from *Success! How Every Man and Woman Can Achieve It.* Copyright © 1977 by Success Research Corporation. Reprinted by permission of Random House, Inc.

William Least Heat Moon: "Oil City Bar" from *Blue Highways: A Journey into America.* Copyright © 1982 by William Least Heat Moon. Reprinted by permission of Little, Brown and Company in association with the Atlantic Monthly Press.

Ursula K. Le Guin: "The Author of the Acacia Seeds and Other Extracts from the *Journal of the Association of Therolinguistics*" from *The Compass Rose.*

Copyright © 1982 by Ursula K. Le Guin. Reprinted by permission of Harper & Row, Publishers, Inc.

Alison Lurie: "Fashion and Status" from *The Language of Clothes.* Copyright © 1981 by Alison Lurie. Reprinted by permission of Random House, Inc.

Thomas McGuane: "Me and My Bike and Why" from *An Outside Chance: Essays on Sport.* Reprinted by permission of Farrar, Straus and Giroux, Inc. Copyright © 1972, 1980 by Thomas McGuane.

John McPhee: "The Pinball Philosophy" from *Giving Good Weight.* Reprinted by permission of Farrar, Straus and Giroux, Inc. Copyright © 1975, 1979 by John McPhee. This piece first appeared in *The New Yorker.*

Norman Mailer: "Cities Higher Than Mountains" from *Cannibals and Christians.* Reprinted by permission of the author and the author's agents, Scott Meredith Literary Agency, Inc., 845 Third Avenue, New York, NY 10022.

Michael Malone: "And Gracie Begat Lucy Who Begat Laverne" from *Fast Forward.* Copyright © 1983, Channels of Communication. Reprinted with permission of Andrews McMeel & Parker. All rights reserved.

D. Keith Mano: "Plastic Surgery." Copyright © 1981 by National Review, Inc. 150 E. 35 St., New York, NY 10016. Reprinted with permission.

Mel Marcus: "The ABC's of TV." Reprinted with permission from *TV Guide*® Magazine. Copyright © 1984 by Triangle Publications, Inc., Radnor, PA.

Howard Nemerov: "Boom!" from *The Collected Poems of Howard Nemerov,* The University of Chicago Press, 1977. Reprinted by permission of the author.

Joyce Carol Oates: "Stalking" from *Marriages and Infidelities.* Reprinted by permission of the publisher, Vanguard Press, Inc. Copyright © 1968, 1969, 1970, 1972 by Joyce Carol Oates.

Frank O'Hara: "To the Film Industry in Crisis" from *Meditations in an Emergency.* Reprinted by permission of Grove Press, Inc. Copyright © 1971.

Jayne Anne Phillips: "Something That Happened." Copyright © 1979 by Jayne Anne Phillips.

Adrienne Rich: "Living in Sin" from *Poems: Selected and New, 1950–1974.* Reprinted by permission of W.W. Norton & Company, Inc. Copyright © 1975, 1973, 1971, 1969, 1966 by W.W. Norton & Company, Inc. Copyright © 1955 by Adrienne Rich.

Richard Rodriguez: "Pocho" from *Hunger of Memory.* Copyright © 1981 by Richard Rodriguez. Reprinted by permission of David R. Godine, Publisher, Boston.

Andrew A. Rooney: "Wrappings" from *And More by Andy Rooney.* Copyright © 1982 by Essay Productions, Inc. Reprinted with permission of Atheneum Publishers.

Phyllis Rose: "Shopping and Other Spiritual Adventures in America Today." Reprinted by permission of Georges Borchadt, Inc. and the author. Copyright © 1984 by Phyllis Rose.

Wendy Rose: "I Expected My Skin and My Blood to Ripen." Published in *Lost Copper,* Malki Museum Press, 1980; *Academic Squaw: Reports to the World from the Ivory Tower,* Blue Cloud Press, 1977; *The Third Woman,* edited by

Dexter Fisher, Houghton-Mifflin, 1980; *Woman Poets of the World,* edited by Lashgari et al, Macmillan, 1983; *That's What She Said,* edited by Rayna Green, Indiana University Press. Reprinted by permission of Malki Museum Press and the author.

Peggy Rosenthal: "The Power of a Positive *Self*" from *Words and Values: Some Leading Words and Where They Lead Us.* Copyright © 1984 by Peggy Rosenthal. Reprinted by permission of Oxford University Press, Inc.

Phyllis Schlafly: "Understanding the Difference" from *The Power of the Positive Woman.* Copyright © 1977 by Phyllis Schlafly. Used by permission of Arlington House, Inc.

Richard Selzer: "Tube Feeding" from *Confessions of a Knife.* Copyright © 1979 by David Goodman and Janet Selzer, trustees. Reprinted by permission of Simon & Schuster, Inc.

John Simon: "Playing Tennis Without a Net" from *Paradigms Lost.* Copyright © 1976, 1977, 1978, 1979, 1980 by John Simon. Used by permission of Clarkson N. Potter, Inc.

Gloria Steinem: "The Importance of Work" from *Outrageous Acts and Everyday Rebellions.* Copyright © 1983 by East Toledo Productions, Inc. Reprinted by permission of Holt, Rinehart and Winston, Publishers.

David Sudnow: "Interface" from *Pilgrim in the Microworld.* Copyright © by David Sudnow. Published by Warner Books, Inc.

Time Magazine: "Male and Female: Differences Between Them." Copyright © 1972 Time Inc. All rights reserved. Reprinted by permission from *Time.*

Susan Allen Toth: "Christmas Vacation" from *Ivy Days: Making My Way Out East.* Copyright © 1984 by Susan Allen Toth. Reprinted by permission of Little, Brown and Company.

Sherry Turkle: "Why the Computer Disturbs" from *The Second Self.* Copyright © 1984 by Sherry Turkle. Reprinted by permission of Simon & Schuster, Inc.

John Updike: "Still of Some Use" in *The New Yorker;* Copyright © 1980. Reprinted by permission.

Alice Walker: "Beauty: When the Other Dancer Is the Self" from *In Search of Our Mothers' Gardens.* Copyright © 1983 by Alice Walker. Reprinted by permission of Harcourt Brace Jovanovich, Inc.

Eudora Welty: "Rodney's Landing." Copyright © 1944 by Eudora Welty. Reprinted from *The Eye of the Story: Selected Essays and Reviews,* by permission of Random House, Inc.

Edmund White: "Sexual Culture." Copyright © 1983 by Edmund White. Reprinted with permission of the author. First appeared in *Vanity Fair.*

Marie Winn: "Mad Magazine" from *Children Without Childhood.* Copyright © 1981, 1983 by Marie Winn. Reprinted by permission of Pantheon Books, a division of Random House, Inc.

Tom Wolfe: "The Right Stuff." Excerpt from *The Right Stuff.* Copyright © 1979 by Tom Wolfe. Reprinted by permission of Farrar, Straus and Giroux, Inc.

Eric Zorn: "Memories Aren't Made of This." Copyright © 1984 by Newsweek, Inc. All Rights Reserved. Reprinted by permission.